DATA STRUCTURES, ALGORITHMS, AND OBJECT-ORIENTED PROGRAMMING

McGRAW-HILL SERIES IN COMPUTER SCIENCE

Senior Consulting Editor

C. L. Liu, University of Illinois at Urbana-Champaign

Consulting Editor

Allen B. Tucker, Bowdoin College

Fundamentals of Computing and Programming
Computer Organization and Architecture
Computers in Society/Ethics
Systems and Languages
Theoretical Foundations
Software Engineering and Database
Artificial Intelligence
Networks, Parallel and Distributed Computing
Graphics and Visualization
The MIT Electrical and Computer Science Series

FUNDAMENTALS OF COMPUTING AND PROGRAMMING

*Abelson and Sussman: *Structure and Intrerpretation of Computer Programs*
Bergin: *Data Abstraction: The Object-Oriented Approach Using C++*
Heileman: *Data Structures, Algorithms, and Object-Oriented Programming*
Kamin and Reingold: *Programming with Class: A C++ Introduction to Computer Science*
Kernighan and Plauger: *The Elements of Programming Style*
Smith and Frank: *Introduction to Programming Concepts and Methods with Ada*
*Springer and Friedman: *Scheme and the Art of Programming*
Tremblay and Bunt: *Introduction to Computer Science: An Algorithmic Approach*
Tucker, Bernat, Bradley, Cupper, and Scragg: *Fundamentals of Computing I: Logic, Problem Solving, Programs, and Computers*
Tucker, Cupper, Bradley, Epstein, and Kelemen: *Fundamentals of Computing II: Abstraction, Data Structures, and Large Software Systems*

*Co-published by the MIT Press and McGraw-Hill, Inc.

DATA STRUCTURES, ALGORITHMS, AND OBJECT-ORIENTED PROGRAMMING

Gregory L. Heileman

The University of New Mexico

The McGraw-Hill Companies, Inc.

New York   St. Louis   San Francisco   Auckland   Bogotá   Caracas
Lisbon   London   Madrid   Mexico City   Milan   Montreal   New Delhi
San Juan   Singapore   Sydney   Tokyo   Toronto

McGraw-Hill
A Division of The **McGraw·Hill** *Companies*

DATA STRUCTURES, ALGORITHMS, AND OBJECT-ORIENTED PROGRAMMING

Copyright ©1996 by The McGraw-Hill Companies, Inc. All rights reserved. Printed in the United States of America. Except as permitted under the United States Copyright Act of 1976, no part of this publication may be reproduced or distributed in any form or by any means, or stored in a data base or retrieval system, without the prior written permission of the publisher.

This book is printed on acid-free paper.

1 2 3 4 5 6 7 8 9 0 DOC DOC 9 0 9 8 7 6

ISBN 0-07-027893-8

This book was set in Times Roman by ETP/Harrison.
The editor was Eric M. Munson;
the production supervisor was Leroy A. Young.
The cover was designed by Karen Quigley.
Project supervision was done by ETP/Harrison (Portland, Oregon).
R.R. Donnelley & Sons Company was printer and binder.
Cover Photo: Jennifer Baumann/Graphistock

Library of Congress Catalog Card Number: 95–82432

To Jeri, Kelsey and Grant

CONTENTS

The best way to understand an algorithm is to program it yourself.
—Gregory Chaitin

PREFACE

Computing is an art form. Some programs are elegant,
some are exquisite, some are sparkling.
My claim is it is possible to write grand programs,
noble programs, truly magnificent programs.

—Donald E. Knuth

This book provides a modern treatment of data structures and algorithms, and considers their implementation using techniques available in object-oriented programming languages. It is an outgrowth of my experience in teaching Data Structures courses from this perspective at both the University of New Mexico, and the University of Central Florida since 1988. The advantage offered by object-oriented programming is that it provides a good framework for implementing programs. This allows software design to become a more natural part of the programming process. The ability to utilize these techniques greatly simplifies the design and implementation of complex software systems by allowing software developers to work at a higher conceptual level.

A data structures course offers an excellent opportunity to introduce the concepts associated with object-oriented programming. The mechanisms provided by an object-oriented language allow one to realize, in a straightforward manner, many of the goals sought in designing and implementing data types. For example, the concept of abstract data types pervades much of the theory of data structures, and also forms the central concept of the class in object-oriented programming. This leads to the natural expression of abstract data types as classes.

Although the material that relates to object-oriented programming in this book could be presented devoid of any particular programming language, C++ was chosen for a number of reasons. First, it is a major language gaining in popularity. Second, the student gets to see concrete examples of object-oriented programming in use, along with listings of working code. This code is not intended to be "production quality"—the error handling is minimal, with emphasis placed on clarity rather than efficiency when the two conflict. Programmers wishing to rectify these shortcomings can easily do so. The main goal is to demonstrate the proper use of C++ in the layout of classes that implement many of the data structures and algorithms presented in this text. In doing so, the gap between pseudocode descriptions of algorithms, or high-level descriptions of problems, and actual implementations in an object-oriented language is bridged. This gap between description and implementation is often nontrivial (larger than many authors care to admit), involving technical details that can fill countless hours of a programmer's time.

ORGANIZATION OF THE BOOK

This book consists of three parts. The first part treats the background necessary for the study of data structures and their associated algorithms. This includes a consideration of how data structures are used, within the framework of object-oriented programming languages, to implement abstract data types. The first part also includes chapters that consider algorithmic analysis, the fundamentals of object-oriented programming, and the use of C/C++ in the implementation of abstract data types. Although C and C++ are treated in separate chapters in this part, the separation is somewhat arbitrary. The fact that C++ is a superset of C makes both chapters relevant. The mathematical tools necessary for the analyses performed in this part (and the remainder of the book) are presented in two appendices, which are intended to be self-contained.

The second part of the text is concerned with the study of basic data structures used to implement abstract data types. It begins by defining the dynamic set, an abstract data type that is used in a wide range of computer applications. In many applications, however, only a specific group of operations defined on the dynamic set abstract data type are required. In the chapters that compose this part, a number of data structures that are used to implement various groups of dynamic set operations are considered. When analyzing these data structures, the focus is primarily on how efficiently they support specific dynamic set operations. Emphasis is also placed on the construction of software classes that can be easily incorporated into applications that require the services they provide. This is an area in which the object-oriented approach offers particular advantages.

The final part of this book considers advanced data structures and analysis techniques. Programming is not stressed in this portion of the text; rather, the emphasis is on analysis. Amortized complexity analysis is the first topic considered. In certain situations, this technique can give a more accurate measure of the cost associated with a data type implementation than can the worst-case analysis used throughout the previous two parts. Many of the data structures presented in this part of the book are analyzed using this technique. The final chapter, covering graphs algorithms, allows us to demonstrate, in important application areas, the use of a variety of the data structures considered in this text.

Each chapter culminates with an extended example that demonstrates how the concepts considered in the chapter can be applied. Chapter notes that discuss historical background and point the reader to appropriate references are also provided at the conclusion of every chapter and appendix. I take full credit for any inaccuracies contained in these notes, and in any future editions will consider the inclusion of specific oversights brought to my attention. An errata list is maintained at `http://www.eece.unm.edu/faculty/heileman/oop`, along with a collection of additional material supporting this book.

TEACHING

All of the material in this book cannot be covered in a single semester. My colleagues and I have used this book in a one-semester undergraduate course dealing with data structures and algorithmic analysis. The students came to this course after having a year of programming (preferably in C or C++), and a course in discrete mathematics. A typical course covered all of the material in Parts I and II of this book, and selected material from Part III. The specific material selected from Part III depended upon the preferences of the instructor. In general, however, amortized analysis was only briefly discussed, and the material in Part III that is not heavily dependent on amortized analysis was emphasized. In particular, Sections 11.1–11.3, 12.1, 12.2, 13.1, 13.2, and nearly all of Chapter 14 can be taught without first covering amortized analysis in Chapter 10. Furthermore, the extended examples in Chapters 11–14 do not require a knowledge of amortized analysis. Alternatively, by treating amortized analysis in detail, a deeper investigation of some of the advanced data structures in Part III can be conducted. This, of course, will limit the breadth of coverage of Part III.

This book could also serve as the basis for a two-semester course in data structures and algorithms. This allows a more thorough coverage of the material in Part III during the second semester. In addition, more extensive programming assignments as well as investigations through term projects are allowed by this two-semester format.

Depending upon the background of the students, instructors may also need to cover selected material from the two appendices. Students should have encountered most of this material in a previous discrete mathematics course. Even if this is the case, they may wish to review these appendices in order to become refamiliarized with the notation.

The topic coverage in the appendices is as follows. Appendix A presents a number of mathematical functions that are frequently encountered in the study of data structures and algorithms. In addition, recurrence relations are reviewed, along with a demonstration of how simple recurrence relations can be solved using the concept of mathematical induction. Appendix B reviews basic set theory, along with counting rules that are used to determine the number of different ways to choose elements from various sets. This appendix also considers the important mathematical concept of graphs, with particular emphasis on trees.

This text should also prove useful to practicing programmers who wish to apply object-oriented programming to their applications. The presentation in Chapters 3 and 4 can serve those practitioners wishing to transition from C to C++. In addition, the first half of Chapter 4 offers a tutorial on the features associated with any object-oriented programming language, as well as a discussion on the object-oriented design philosophy. The real value of object-oriented programming comes from its ability to support software reuse. The code provided throughout Part II of the text forms a foundation of classes that should prove useful in a wide variety of applications. Furthermore, in addition to analyzing the efficiency of algorithms in traditional asymptotic terms, an effort has been made throughout the text to consider implementation issues, ease of use, and other details that are useful when trying to implement an algorithm.

ACKNOWLEDGMENTS

First and foremost I would like to acknowledge my students, who are too numerous to thank individually. They more than anyone have served to emphasize the need for this book, and to shape its contents. I would also like to thank Don Hush and John Rasure who taught courses from notes that eventually became this book, and offered a number of suggestions that were particularly helpful.

I am indebted to the many faculty colleagues who provided valuable suggestions through reviews. These include H. E. Dunsmore at Purdue University, Sharad Garg at the University of Delaware, Douglas Fisher and Stephen Schach at Vanderbilt University, Kye S. Hedlund at the University of North Carolina–Chapel Hill, Roy B. Levow at Florida Atlantic University, Ralph Morelli at Trinity College, Jeffrey F. Naughton at the University of Wisconsin–Madison, Michiel Noordewier at Rutgers University, Atul Prakash at the University of Michigan, Allen Tucker at Bowdoin College, and Robert Walker at Rensselaer Polytechnic Institute.

Other friends and colleagues who have graciously reviewed various portions of this material include Chaouki Abdallah, Michael Georgiopoulos, Bill Horne, and Edl Schamiloglu. Their helpful suggestions and criticisms were welcome contributions. A special thanks is given to Bernard Moret for the knowledge (and textbooks) he freely imparted over the years. I would also like to express my appreciation for the support and encouragement offered by ISTEC, as well as the BSP Groups at the University of New Mexico and the Universidade de Vigo.

For assistance in producing this text, I would like to acknowledge the ETP/Harrison company for their typesetting work, and Martha Balshem for the excellent job she did copyediting. Of the many fine people associated with McGraw-Hill, I would particularly like to thank my editor Eric Munson for his guidance and patience.

Finally I would like to thank my wife, Jeri, and our children, Kelsey and Grant, who have been a constant source of moral support throughout this incredibly difficult project. Without them this book could have been finished sooner, but with them my life is immeasurably more enjoyable.

Albuquerque, New Mexico   Gregory L. Heileman
January 1996

DATA STRUCTURES, ALGORITHMS, AND OBJECT-ORIENTED PROGRAMMING

PART

I

FUNDAMENTALS

INTRODUCTION TO PART I

The material contained in this part of the book provides the necessary foundation for the study of the data structures and algorithms presented in subsequent chapters. Specifically, Chapter 1 introduces the concept of abstract data types, and discusses the distinction between abstract data types, data types, and data structures. This chapter also introduces the pseudocode that will be used throughout the book to specify the steps taken in an algorithm. Finally, a model of computer memory is presented and subsequently used to explain the manner in which recursive procedures are implemented.

Chapter 2 demonstrates how to mathematically determine (using the tools reviewed in Appendices A and B) the computational resources required by specific algorithms. General classes of algorithmic techniques are discussed, along with the properties that make them appropriate for solving specific problems.

Chapter 3 contains a brief overview of the C programming language, and a discussion of some of the more important features of this language that are used in constructing user-defined data types. This chapter concludes with an example that demonstrates how the C programming language can be used to implement the MATRIX ADT discussed in Chapter 1. The reason for discussing the C programming language is that it provides the scaffolding upon which the C++ programming language is built. That is, C++ is a superset of the C language. Therefore, the better you understand C, the better you will understand C++. In addition, those already familiar with the C programming language will benefit from the separate presentation of C and C++. The features added to C to create C++ will be clearly evident when they are discussed in Chapter 4.

Finally, Chapter 4 discusses object-oriented programming and the C++ programming language. The first half of the chapter considers the requisite features of any object-oriented programming language, while the second half of the chapter considers how each of these features is implemented in the C++ programming language. The matrix example from the previous chapter is then reworked using the new features found in C++. This example is intended to demonstrate the power and flexibility offered by object-oriented languages such as C++.

CHAPTER
1

BACKGROUND

One of the most crucial issues associated with the design of a new system involves managing the complexity of the design process. Good designers typically use some form of abstraction as a tool for dealing with this complexity. Our use of the term *abstraction* here refers to the intellectual capability of considering an entity apart from any specific instance of that entity. For example, hardware designers attempting to design a computer typically concern themselves with the functionality of the integrated circuits they plan to use—not with the operation of the transistors found in these integrated circuits.

The development of a software system is also greatly simplified by the use of abstraction in the design process. In software design, this involves specifying the functionality of a software system in general "high-level" terms. Once it can be shown that this abstract specification of the system is correct, it is possible to add more detail, eventually leading to a detailed "low-level" description of the software system in terms that are directly implementable using the syntax of a given programming language. At each step in this process, the designer must verify that the additional detail added to the system design is correct. The advantage of this approach is that it limits the amount of complexity that must be dealt with at any step in the design process. This allows the designer to concentrate on the overall design of the system without getting mired down in implementation details.

During the progress of the design process discussed above, the various types of data necessary, as well as the operations that must be performed on this data, become evident. At that point, a special type of abstraction known as *data abstraction* can be

3

employed. This involves an abstract or *logical* description of both the data required by the software system, and the operations that can be performed on this data. The use of data abstraction during software development allows the software designer to concentrate on how the data in the system is used to solve the problem at hand, without having to be concerned with how the data is represented and manipulated in computer memory.

1.1 ABSTRACT DATA TYPES

In order to demonstrate how the development of computer programs is simplified by using abstract representations of data types (i.e., representations that are devoid of any implementation considerations) during the design phase, let us consider the alternative. Utilizing concrete representations of data types (i.e., representations that specify the physical storage of the data in computer memory) during design introduces unnecessary complication by forcing us to consider all of the issues involved in implementing a data type too early in the software development process.

In addition, utilizing a concrete data representation during design may yield a program that is dependent upon a particular data type implementation. If the implementation of the data type is later changed to yield a more efficient representation, then the program itself may become invalid—it was designed while considering the original data type implementation. This type of problem can be avoided by using abstract data types in the design process.

An *abstract data type* (*ADT*) is defined as a mathematical model of the data objects that make up a data type, as well as the functions that operate on these objects. It is important to recognize that the operations that manipulate the data objects are included in the specification of an ADT. For example, the SET ADT can be defined as a collection of data items that are accessed by operations such as union, intersection, and set difference.

Notice that the specification of an ADT does not imply any implementation considerations. The implementation of an ADT involves a translation of the ADT's specifications into the syntax of a particular programming language. This translation consists of the appropriate variable declarations necessary to define the data elements, and a procedure or *accessing routine* that implements each of the operations required by the ADT.

At this point it is useful to distinguish between ADTs, data types, and data structures. The term *data type* refers to the *implementation* of the mathematical model specified by an ADT. That is, a data type is a computer representation of an ADT. The term *data structure* refers to a collection of computer variables that are connected in some specific manner. This text is concerned with using data structures to implement various data types in the most efficient manner possible.

A programming language typically provides a number of *built-in data types*. For example, the int data type available in the C programming language provides an implementation of the mathematical concept of an integer number. That is, the INTEGER ADT defines the set of numbers given by the union of the set $\{-1, -2, \ldots, -\infty\}$

and the set of whole numbers, {0, 1, ..., +∞}. The INTEGER ADT also specifies the operations that can be performed on integer numbers. These operations include integer addition, subtraction, multiplication, and division, along with a number of other operations. The specification of the INTEGER ADT does not include any indication of how the data type should be implemented. For example, it is impossible to represent the full range of integer numbers in computer memory; however, the range of numbers that will be represented must be determined in the data type implementation.

In addition, a format for storing the integer numbers in computer memory must be selected when implementing the INTEGER ADT. The format chosen might be one's complement, two's complement, sign-magnitude, binary coded decimal (BCD), or some other format. These are just a few of the issues that must be considered when implementing the INTEGER ADT. Note, however, that they are ignored in the specification of the ADT. Furthermore, programmers generally do not have to concern themselves with these implementation considerations when they use the data type in a program.

In many cases the design of a computer program will call for data types that are not available in the programming language used to implement the program. In these cases, we must be able to construct the necessary data types by using built-in data types. As we shall see, this will often involve the construction of quite complicated data structures. The data types constructed in this manner are called ***user-defined data types***. Our study of data types will focus on user-defined data types. With this in mind, we will consider the development of a new data type from two different viewpoints: a logical view and an implementation view.

The ***logical view*** of a data type should be used during program design. This is simply the model provided by the ADT specification. The ***implementation view*** of a data type considers the manner in which the data elements are represented in memory, and how the accessing functions are implemented. From this viewpoint, we will mainly be concerned with how alternative data structures and accessing routine implementations affect the efficiency of the operations performed by the data type. There should only be one logical view of a data type; however, there may be many different approaches to implementing it.

An application program should manipulate a data type with regard to its logical representation rather than its physical storage. That is, communication between the application program and the data type implementation should only occur through the interface provided by the accessing routines specified in the ADT. This means that, as long as the interface provided by the data type remains unchanged, the implementation of the data type could be completely changed without affecting the application program using the data type.

Think of this as a wall separating the application program from the data type implementation. The only communication into the data type is through the parameters of the accessing routines. The only output back to the application program is through the return of information from the accessing routines. Unless the proper accessing routines are used, it should be impossible to penetrate the wall surrounding a data type implementation. This situation is depicted in Figure 1.1.

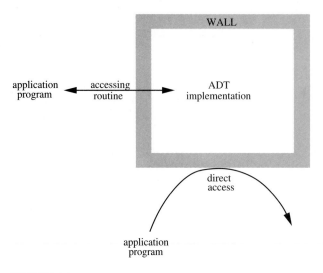

FIGURE 1.1
Ideally a "wall" is constructed around an ADT implementation so that an application program is only able to manipulate data through the use of accessing routines. In this case, direct manipulation of the data stored in the ADT implementation is not allowed.

The separation or "hiding" of the representation of a data type from applications that use the data type is known as ***data encapsulation***. In the terminology of software engineers, data encapsulation is said to be a form of ***information hiding***.[†] One advantage gained by the encapsulation of data types involves ease of modification. As mentioned previously, a properly encapsulated data type can be modified without affecting the application programs that use the data type. This might be necessary if, for example, a more efficient implementation were required. If an application program were allowed to directly access the data type, thereby circumventing the accessing routines, then modification of the data structures used to implement the data type might invalidate the application program entirely. This makes the application program extremely difficult to maintain because the data type implementation must be considered whenever the application program is modified.

Another advantage offered by data encapsulation involves ***reusability***. A properly encapsulated data type can be easily reused in other application programs that require the functionality provided by the data type, without knowledge of how the data type was implemented. In Chapter 4, a discussion of how object-oriented programming languages allow us to effectively realize the goals of data abstraction and data encapsulation is presented.

[†]Another form of information hiding involves the placement of machine-specific details within a given software module—this allows an application program to be more readily ported to other machines because only the module that contains the machine specific details needs to be modified.

1.1.1 ADT Specification

Let us now consider the two parts of an ADT specification, which are: a mathematical description of a collection of data objects, and a set of operations defined on elements from this collection of data objects. A rigorous approach to specifying the later part involves supplying a set of axioms that completely describe the behavior of the ADT operations. These axioms can then be used to formally verify the correctness of an ADT implementation. Unfortunately, determining a complete set of axioms is extremely difficult for nontrivial ADTs. For this reason we will only concern ourselves with informal descriptions of ADT operations.

An example of a MATRIX ADT specification is given below. The format used in this example will be followed throughout the book. That is, we will specify an ADT by first describing its data objects, and then listing the operations that can be performed on these data objects.

THE MATRIX ADT. The abstract data type MATRIX is used to represent matrices, as well as the operations defined on matrices. A *matrix* is defined as a rectangular array of elements arranged by rows and columns. A matrix with n rows and m columns is said to have *row dimension* n, *column dimension* m, and *order* $n \times m$. A matrix M of order $n \times m$ can be written as follows:

$$M = \begin{bmatrix} a_{11} & a_{12} & \cdots & a_{1m} \\ a_{21} & a_{22} & \cdots & a_{2m} \\ \vdots & & & \\ a_{n1} & a_{n2} & \cdots & a_{nm} \end{bmatrix}$$

where a_{ij} represents the element at row i and column j. Numerous operations are defined on matrices. A few of these are:

1. *RetrieveElement(i, j, M)*. Returns the element at row i and column j of matrix M.
2. *AssignElement(i, j, x, M)*. Assigns the value x to the element at row i and column j of matrix M.
3. *Assignment(M_1, M_2)*. Assigns the elements of matrix M_1 to those of matrix M_2. Matrices M_1 and M_2 must have the same order.
4. *Addition(M_1, M_2)*. Returns the matrix that results when matrix M_1 is added to matrix M_2. Matrices M_1 and M_2 must have the same order.
5. *Negation(M)*. Returns the matrix that results when matrix M is negated.
6. *Subtraction(M_1, M_2)*. Returns the matrix that results when matrix M_1 is subtracted from matrix M_2. Matrices M_1 and M_2 must have the same order.
7. *Scalar Multiplication(s, M)*. Returns the matrix that results when matrix M is multiplied by scalar s.
8. *Multiplication(M_1, M_2)*. Returns the matrix that results when matrix M_1 is multiplied by matrix M_2. The column dimension of M_1 must be the same as the row

dimension of M_2. The resultant matrix has the same row dimension as M_1, and the same column dimension as M_2.

9. *Transpose*(M). Returns the transpose of matrix M.

10. *Determinant*(M). Returns the determinant of matrix M.

11. *Inverse*(M). Returns the inverse of matrix M.

An implementation of this ADT must provide a means for representing matrix elements, and for implementing the operations described above. Typically, we will describe the implementation of an ADT operation using an ***algorithm***, which is a finite sequence of instructions that specifies precisely how the operation will be performed. Detailed discussions of MATRIX ADT implementations are presented in Sections 3.5 and 4.3.

Quite often in subsequent chapters we will be interested in analyzing the algorithms that implement specific ADT operations. In order to facilitate our discussions, we will express many of these algorithms using pseudocode. The notation we will follow when using pseudocode is presented in the following section.

1.2 PSEUDOCODE

Pseudocode is used to express algorithms in a manner that is independent of a particular programming language. The prefix *pseudo* is used to emphasize that this code is not meant to be compiled and executed on a computer. The reason for using pseudocode is that it allows one to convey basic ideas about an algorithm in general terms. Once programmers understand the algorithm being expressed by pseudocode, they can implement the algorithm in the programming language of their choice. This, in essence, is the difference between pseudocode and a computer program. A pseudocode program simply states the steps necessary to perform some computation, while the corresponding computer program is the translation of these steps into the syntax of a particular programming language.

We will find pseudocode useful when we wish to express an algorithm without worrying about how the algorithm will be implemented. This ability to ignore implementation details when using pseudocode will facilitate analysis by allowing us to focus solely on the computational aspects of an algorithm.

Pseudocode basically consists of keywords and English-like phrases that are indented to indicate flow of control. We will write keywords using boldface lower case letters, and the names of ADTs using uppercase letters. We will also use the following conventions:

1. The symbol ▷ is used to indicate that the remainder of a line should be treated as a comment. If more than one statement appears on a single line, a semicolon will be used to separate them.

2. Assignments statements have the form $x \leftarrow e$, which assigns the value of expression e to variable x. Multiple assignments can be performed in one statement; for example, $x \leftarrow y \leftarrow e$ assigns the value of expression e to variables x and y.

3. Loop constructs can be specified using one of three forms:

> **for** *assignment statement* **to** *terminal value* **do in steps of** *increment.*
> *loop statements*

> **while** *conditional expression* **do**
> *loop statements*

> **do**
> *loop statements*
> **while** *conditional expression*

To avoid the proliferation of **begin** and **end** statements, we will use indention to indicate the range of these constructs.

In the first two loop forms the conditional expressions are evaluated before deciding if the loops statements should be executed; while in the third loop form one iteration is performed before its conditional expression is evaluated.

For the first loop form, it is assumed that a loop variable is specified in the assignment statement. If the step by which the loop variable is to be incremented on each pass is not specified, it is assumed to be 1. We will also encounter loops in which the loop variable is decremented on each pass through the loop—this is accomplished by specifying a negative value for the loop increment.

Below we use a loop to calculate the sum of the even integer numbers between 2 and 20:

> *sum* $\leftarrow$ 0
> **for** $i \leftarrow 2$ **to** 20 **do in steps of** 2
>   *sum* $\leftarrow$ *sum* $+ i$

In this example, the loop variable i is incremented by 2 and added to the variable *sum* on each pass through the loop.

4. Conditional constructs will use the keywords **if–then–else**. Once again, indention will be used to indicate the range of a conditional statement.

5. A *pointer* is a data object that stores the memory address of (i.e., points to) another data object. The address of a data object is obtained by placing a "↑" in front of it. Thus, if p is a pointer variable, and x is some other data object, p is made to point to x using

> $p \leftarrow (\uparrow x)$

If we wish to modify x through p, then p must be *dereferenced* using "↓". For example, given the previous pointer assignment, the value 2 can be assigned to x using either

> $x \leftarrow 2$ or $(\downarrow p) \leftarrow 2$

A pointer variable that stores the value 0 is referred to as a *null pointer*. It is assumed that 0 is not a valid memory address.

6. Arrays are declared by appending one set of square brackets to a variable name for each dimension of the array. Specific array elements are accessed by enclosing an integer value in these square brackets. For example, $A[i]$ is used to access the i-th element of the one-dimensional array A, and $B[i][j]$ is used to access the j-th element in row i of the two-dimensional array B. A range of values within an array is accessed using the ".." notation. For instance, $A[i..j]$ indicates the subarray of A containing elements $A[i]$, $A[i+1]$, ..., $A[j]$.

7. A *composite data type* is composed of fields, each of which can be either a simple or composite data type. The value stored in a particular field is accessed by enclosing its name in square brackets. For example, if x is the name of a composite data object, and f is one of the fields in x, then the value of f is obtained using $x[f]$. Furthermore, the name of a composite data object alone represents a pointer to that object. That is, if x and y are composite data objects of the same type, the statement $x \leftarrow y$ makes x a pointer to y. This means that $x[f] = y[f]$ for any field f in these composite objects. In addition, any modification to $x[f]$ will be reflected in $y[f]$, and vice versa.

Note that an array is a special case of a composite data type in which each field has the same type. A specific attribute of a composite data object can be obtained by naming the desired attribute, and enclosing the name of the composite data object in square brackets. For example, the number of elements in array A is given by length$[A]$.

Quite often we will encapsulate either parts of an algorithm, or an entire algorithm, as a procedure. A pseudocode *procedure* is specified by giving its name, followed by a parameter list, and then the sequence of steps in the procedure. The motivation for including parameter lists in procedures is that they allow more generic procedures to be developed. That is, the data that a procedure will work on does not have to be specified beforehand, but instead can be varied from one procedure call to the next. Thus, a procedure is written so that it operates on the "dummy variables" supplied in the parameter list. These dummy variables are referred to as *formal parameters*, while the data supplied when the procedure is actually called are referred to as *actual parameters*.

As an example, a procedure that implements the matrix multiplication operation discussed in the previous section is given in Figure 1.2. We will follow the convention that the first letter in the name of a pseudocode procedure is given in uppercase. The parameter list for this procedure states that it will operate on two matrices, a and b—these are the formal parameters. Line 1 of the procedure is called an *assertion*. Assertions are used to verify relationships among specific variables in a procedure. Specifically, the assertion on line 1 states that the number of columns in matrix a must equal the number of rows in matrix b in order for this procedure to yield a correct result.

There are a number of mechanisms that can be used to pass the actual parameters to a procedure; two of these are discussed next. When parameters are passed using *pass-by-value*, a copy of the actual parameters (i.e., their values) is supplied to the formal parameters. Thus, any modification of these parameters is not reflected outside

```
Multiply(MATRIX a, MATRIX b)
1  assert number-of-columns[a] = number-of-rows[b]
2  for i ← 1 to number-of-rows[a] do
3     for j ← 1 to number-of-columns[b] do
4        c_ij ← 0
5        for k ← 1 to number-of-columns[a] do
6           c_ij ← (c_ij + a_ik · b_kj)
7  return c
```

FIGURE 1.2
A pseudocode procedure for performing matrix multiplication.

of the procedure. That is, a change in value of one of the parameters inside the procedure is local to that procedure. On the other hand, when parameters are passed using ***pass-by-reference***, the formal parameters are bound to the reference values of the actual parameters. This means that a change in the value of a parameter inside the procedure will actually change the value contained in the variable to which that parameter refers. Thus, a change in the value of a parameter inside the procedure is *not* local to that procedure.

For example, consider the following procedure, which simply increments the value of its integer input parameter:

```
Increment(integer a)
1  a ← (a + 1)
```

The actual parameter supplied by the calling routine will only be incremented if it is passed by reference to this procedure. If the actual parameter is passed by value, then the formal parameter a will be incremented, but this change will not be reflected in the actual parameter supplied by the calling routine.

By default, the parameters in our pseudocode procedures are passed by value. If we wish to indicate that a parameter is being passed by reference, we will indicate this by placing a "&" in front of the formal parameter name. For instance the previous procedure for incrementing a variable should be written as:

```
Increment(integer &a)
1  a ← (a + 1)
```

Exercise 1.3 considers another way in which this operation can be performed.

1.3 A MODEL OF COMPUTER MEMORY

In order to understand many programming issues, it is essential to have an understanding of how computer memory is organized. Computer memory is typically divided into two parts: ***main memory*** and ***secondary storage*** (e.g., disk and tape drives). Main memory is assumed to be ***random access***. That is, an access to any location in main memory takes a fixed amount of time, independent of the past history of memory accesses. Furthermore, the access time for main memory is typically orders of magnitude faster than the access time for secondary storage. For this reason, it is preferable to implement data structures in main memory—we will refer to these as *internal data structures*. In general, secondary storage will be used only if a data structure is too large to fit in main memory. We will refer to data structures that reside in secondary storage as *external data structures*. Throughout this text, unless stated otherwise, when the term data structure is used, we will be referring to an internal data structure.

Next, we consider a simple model of main memory that is useful in explaining how memory is allocated whenever a data structure is created, and reclaimed whenever a data structure is no longer needed. This model of computer memory will also be useful when we discuss recursion in the next section.

First, let us make a distinction between static and dynamic data structures. A data structure is said to be static if a *fixed* amount of memory is allocated for that data structure *before* program execution (i.e., at compile time). That is, the amount of memory allocated to a *static data structure* does not change during program execution. If we do not know in advance how much memory will be required by a data structure during program execution, then a dynamic data structure can be used to allocate memory as it is needed *during* program execution—this is referred to as *dynamic memory allocation*. Thus, with a *dynamic data structure*, the amount of memory that can be used by the data structure is not fixed at compile time.

With the previous discussion in mind, we may now refer to the model shown in Figure 1.3 as we discuss the allocation of memory. It is useful to view this model as a one-dimensional array of storage locations (or bytes) that is divided into three parts. Variables that will persist in memory throughout the execution of the program are allocated in *static memory*. The amount of storage allocated to static memory is determined at compile time, and this amount does not change during program execution.

A *run-time stack* is maintained by the computer system in low memory. The amount of storage that the run-time stack uses will vary during program execution.

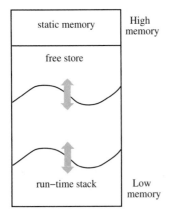

FIGURE 1.3

A logical model of main memory. In this model, memory is viewed as a one-dimensional array of bytes that is divided into three parts—static memory, free store, and run-time stack.

The arrows emanating from the run-time stack in Figure 1.3 indicate that the run-time stack "grows" toward high memory and "shrinks" toward low memory. Each time a procedure is called in a program, an ***activation record*** is created and stored in computer memory on the run-time stack. This activation record contains storage for all variables declared in the procedure, as well as either a copy of, or a reference to, the parameters that are being passed to the procedure. In addition, an activation record must contain some information that specifies where program execution will resume when the procedure is completed. At the completion of the procedure, the associated activation record will be removed from the run-time stack, and program control will return to the point specified in the activation record.

Finally, the logical model of main memory shown in Figure 1.3 shows a ***free store*** that "grows" toward low memory and "shrinks" toward high memory.[†] Memory that is allocated at run time (i.e., dynamically allocated memory) is stored on the free store. Note that the run-time stack and the free store "grow" toward each other in this model. Thus, an obvious error situation occurs if either too much memory is dynamically allocated without reclaiming it, or too many activation records are created.

While memory allocation and deallocation on the run-time stack are controlled by the computer system itself, such may not be the case for the free store. In many programming languages, the responsibility of reclaiming dynamically allocated memory is the programmer's. If the memory is not reclaimed by the programmer, then it will remain on the free store. This approach to reclaiming dynamically allocated memory is referred to as the ***explicit*** approach. On the other hand, in an ***implicit*** approach to the deallocation of dynamic memory, memory management functions provided by the system are responsible for reclaiming memory as it is no longer needed. The implicit approach is usually called ***garbage collection***.

1.4 RECURSIVE PROCEDURES

The model of computer memory presented in the previous section can be used to explain how a computer system implements ***recursive procedures***. A procedure is recursive if it can call itself. Recursive procedures generally solve a problem by reducing the problem to an instance of the same problem with smaller input. Often times a recursive solution to a problem is the most natural, and therefore yields the simplest procedure. We shall see many examples of this in subsequent chapters.

As an example, let us consider a procedure that computes the factorial function $f(n) = n! = n \cdot (n - 1) \cdots 1$, where n is assumed to be a natural number. This function may be rewritten as a recurrence relation:[‡]

$$f(n) = \begin{cases} 1, & \text{if } n = 0 \\ n \cdot f(n - 1), & \text{if } n > 0 \end{cases}$$

[†]The free store is often referred to as the ***heap***; however, this term is rather confusing due to the existence of a heap data structure (discussed in Chapter 9) which has nothing to do with the storage of dynamically allocated memory. For this reason, we will use the term *free store* instead.

[‡]Solution techniques for recurrence relations are reviewed in detail in Appendix A.4.

```
Factorial(natural n)
1   if  n = 0  then
2       return  1
3   else
4       return  n · Factorial(n − 1)    ▷ recursive call
```

FIGURE 1.4
A recursive procedure for computing the factorial function $f(n) = n! = n \cdot (n − 1) \cdots 1$, where n is a natural number.

This relation states that if $n = 0$, then the value of the function is 1, and if $n > 0$, then the value of the function is computed using the same function at a smaller value of n. A simple recursive procedure based on this recurrence relation is given in Figure 1.4. Line 4 of this procedure involves a recursive procedure call.

In order to gain a better understanding of how recursive procedures work, let us verify that Factorial() computes the correct result when it is passed the value 4. The steps taken by this procedure to compute 4! are shown in Figure 1.5. The columns to the left in this figure show the activation record and line number that the statement to the right corresponds to in the Factorial() procedure given in Figure 1.4. The first activation record is invoked by the initial call to Factorial() with $n = 4$. Inside this activation record, the procedure first checks to see if $n \leq 1$. Since it does not, control proceeds to line 4 where Factorial() invokes itself recursively with $n = 3$. This produces the second activation record, and so on, until the base case ($n = 1$) is finally reached. At this point, appropriate values are returned, and activation frames

activation record	line	
		Factorial(4)
1	4	**return** 4 · Factorial(3)
2	4	**return** 3 · Factorial(2)
3	4	**return** 2 · Factorial(1)
4	2	**return** 1
3	4	**return** 2 · 1
2	4	**return** 3 · 2
1	4	**return** 4 · 6

FIGURE 1.5
The recursive procedure calls that result when Factorial() is called with $n = 4$. Indentation is used to indicate the "depth" of the recursive procedure calls. At the maximum depth, four activation records will reside on the run-time stack. Note also that on the last line, the correct value of 24 is returned to the procedure that initially called Factorial().

are destroyed in the opposite order in which they were created, until the final result is returned to the procedure that initially called Factorial().

Implicit in the previous analysis was the assumption that parameters were passed to the Factorial() procedure by value. Indeed, this must be the case if the procedure is to work correctly. Consider what would happen if instead, parameters were passed by reference. In this case, the parameter value passed to each recursive call of the Factorial() procedure would be the same, and the procedure as a whole would never reach the base case. The procedure would not terminate, and thus could not compute the correct value. For this reason, pass-by-value must be used with recursive procedures.

In the Factorial() procedure presented in Figure 1.4, a single activation of the procedure can only initiate one recursive call (on line 4). This makes it fairly easy to "unfold" the recursive procedure, as was done in Figure 1.5, in order to study its behavior. On the other hand, if a single activation of a procedure body can initiate more than one recursive call, it is more difficult to visualize the recursion. An example of this is considered next.

1.4.1 The Tower of Hanoi Puzzle

A classic example used to demonstrate the power of recursion in problem solving is the Tower of Hanoi puzzle. In this puzzle, we are given three pegs labeled A, B, and C. Initially a tower of eight disks of different sizes are stacked on peg A in order of decreasing size. That is, the largest disk is on the bottom, and the smallest disk is on the top of the tower as shown in Figure 1.6. The objective is to transfer the entire tower to one of the other pegs, moving only one disk at a time, and never moving a larger disk on top of a smaller disk.

In order to solve this puzzle, let us consider a more general situation in which there are initially n disks on peg A. For the case of $n = 2$, we can solve this puzzle by first moving the top disk on peg A to peg B, then moving the lone remaining disk on peg A to peg C, and finally moving the disk on peg B to peg C. The entire tower has now been moved from peg A to peg C, without violating any of the constraints set forth in the puzzle. Can we apply this technique to larger towers? It appears that in general, the way to solve this puzzle is to somehow transfer the top $n - 1$ disks from peg A to peg B, then move the remaining disk on peg A (this is the largest disk) to peg C, and finally transfer the $n - 1$ disks on peg B to peg C. This sequence of moves is depicted in Figure 1.7.

Note that for $n = 2$, the sequence of moves discussed above yields a solution. For the more general case of n disks, though, the problem now becomes one of

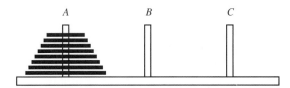

FIGURE 1.6
The initial setup for the Tower of Hanoi puzzle.

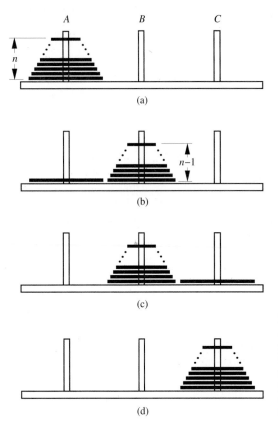

FIGURE 1.7

A general solution to the Tower of Hanoi puzzle. **(a)** Initially, n disks are on peg A. **(b)** The top $n-1$ disks on peg A are moved to peg B. **(c)** The lone remaining disk on peg A is moved to peg C. **(d)** The $n-1$ disks on peg B are moved to peg C, and the puzzle is completed.

moving $n-1$ disks from peg A to peg B without violating any of the problem constraints. Once again, we can think about solving this "subproblem" by first moving the top $n-2$ disks from peg A to peg C. Then the second largest disk (the top disk on peg A) would be moved to peg B, and finally the $n-2$ disks on peg C would be moved to peg B. Here again we have uncovered another subproblem—that of moving $n-2$ disks from peg A to peg C without violating any of the problem constraints.

Notice that each of the subproblems we have discussed is of the same form as the original problem, except for the number of disks being moved. This suggests the use of a single recursive procedure for solving all of the subproblems that make up the problem as a whole. A recursive procedure that accomplishes this task is shown in Figure 1.8. The algorithm in this procedure moves the top n disks on the peg denoted by i to the peg denoted by k. Thus, to move n disks from peg A to peg C, we would call this procedure using Tower(n, A, B, C).

Notice that any activation of Tower() when $n > 1$ will involve the initiation of two recursive calls, one on line 4 and one on line 6. Therefore, tracing through the recursive calls in the manner of Figure 1.5 does not seem practical in this case;

Tower(positive integer n, peg i, peg j, peg k)
    ▷ move the top n disks on peg i to peg k using peg j
1 **if** $n = 1$ **then**
2   move top disk on peg i to peg k
3 **else**
4   Tower($n - 1$, i, k, j)
5   move top disk on peg i to peg k
6   Tower($n - 1$, j, i, k)

FIGURE 1.8

A recursive procedure that implements the general solution to the Tower of Hanoi puzzle depicted in Figure 1.7.

however, a convenient structure called a ***recursion tree*** can often be used to visualize what happens in more complicated recurrences. An example of a recursion tree that shows the recursive procedure calls used by Tower() when $n = 4$ is given in Figure 1.9.

Consider the first activation record created as a result of the initial invocation of the procedure using Tower(4, A, B, C). The left half of Figure 1.9 (i.e., the first seven moves) results from the recursive call on line 4 of this first activation record. These moves cause the top three disks on peg A to be moved to peg B. Next, line 5 of the first activation record is executed moving the lone remaining disk on peg A to peg C. Finally, the right half of Figure 1.9 (i.e., the last seven moves) results from the recursive call on line 6 of the first activation frame. These moves cause the three disks on peg B to be moved on top of the disk on peg C. This completes the puzzle. You should verify for yourself that the sequence of moves given in Figure 1.9, when read from left to right, solves the Tower of Hanoi puzzle for $n = 4$.

If we let $T(n)$ represent the number of moves needed to solve the Tower of Hanoi puzzle when there are n disks, then it is easy to see that for the pseudocode procedure in Figure 1.8,

$$T(n) = \begin{cases} 1, & \text{if } n = 1 \\ 2T(n - 1) + 1, & \text{if } n > 1 \end{cases} \tag{1.1}$$

Specifically, if $n > 1$ our solution requires the moving of two stacks of $n - 1$ disks (lines 4 and 6), each requiring $T(n - 1)$ moves, plus one additional disk (line 5).

In Appendix A.4 we show that the closed form of recurrence (1.1) is given by $T(n) = 2^n - 1$. In our study of data structures and algorithms, we are generally not so much concerned with finding the *exact* closed form for a recurrence—determining the rate of growth of the recurrence (as a function of n) will generally suffice. The reason for this is given in the next chapter, but first we must discuss the method we will use for expressing the growth rate of a function.

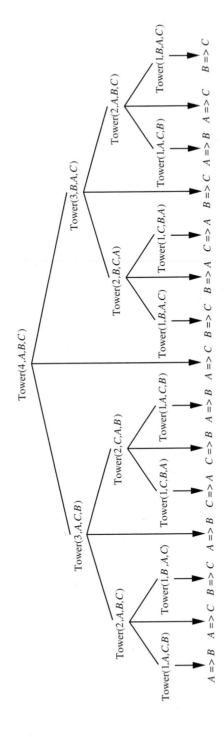

FIGURE 1.9
The recursion tree that results when the Tower of Hanoi procedure in Figure 1.8 is invoked with Tower(4, A, B, C). The notation (A => B) means move the top disk on peg A to peg B.

18

1.5   ASYMPTOTIC NOTATION

Asymptotic analysis is used to explore the behavior of a function, or a relationship between functions, as some parameter of the function tends toward an asymptotic value. This type of analysis can be used to show that two functions are roughly equal to each other, or that the value of some function grows asymptotically at a greater rate than some other function.

A notational convention used extensively in asymptotic analysis is O-notation. By using O-notation we will have a means of expressing an **asymptotic upper bound** on a function. If we let $\mathbb{Z}^+$ represent the set of nonnegative integers (i.e., natural numbers), and $\mathbb{R}^+$ the set of nonnegative real numbers, then this notation is defined as follows.

> **Definition 1.1. O-notation.**   Assume there are two arbitrary functions $f(n)$ and $g(n)$ such that $\{f(n), g(n) : \mathbb{Z}^+ \to \mathbb{R}^+\}$. It is said that $f(n)$ is "big-oh" of $g(n)$, written as
>
> $$f(n) = O(g(n))$$
>
> if there exist positive constants c and n_0 such that $f(n) \leq cg(n)$ for all $n \geq n_0$.

Let us consider Definition 1.1 in more detail. The statement $\{f(n), g(n) : \mathbb{Z}^+ \to \mathbb{R}^+\}$ means that $f(n)$ and $g(n)$ are functions that perform a mapping from the set of natural numbers to the set of nonnegative real numbers. Furthermore, in order to say that $f(n) = O(g(n))$, we must show that $f(n)$ is less than or equal to some constant multiple of $g(n)$, and that this inequality holds for all n greater than or equal to some constant n_0. If these constants do not exist, then $f(n) \neq O(g(n))$.

For example if $f(n) = n^3 + 20n^2 + 100n$, we may state that $f(n) = O(n^3)$ since for $n \geq 0$,

$$n^3 + 20n^2 + 100n \ \leq \ n^3 + 20n^3 + 100n^3 \ = \ 121n^3$$

Choosing $c = 121$ and $n_0 = 0$ we see that the inequality in Definition 1.1 is satisfied. This example demonstrates that for equations involving simple powers of n, we may safely ignore all but the highest order term when specifying big-oh bounds. This is due to the fact that as n grows large, the term involving the largest power of n will dominate all other terms in such an equation.

As a further demonstration of the use of O-notation, consider the functions $f(n) = \lg n$ and $g(n) = (n/4)^2$ shown in Figure 1.10.[†] Notice that for $a < n < b$, $f(n) > g(n)$. However, $g(n) \neq O(f(n))$ because the inequality $g(n) \leq cf(n)$ does not hold for all n greater than or equal to some constant n_0—no matter how large we choose c. Recall that we are dealing with asymptotic limits. Even if we choose $c = 10^{100}$, at some point, when n becomes very large, the value of $g(n)$ will exceed that of $10^{100} f(n)$. We can, however, write $f(n) = O(g(n))$ since for $n_0 = b$ and $c = 1$, the value of $cg(n)$ will be greater than or equal to that of $f(n)$ for all $n \geq n_0$.

[†]Throughout this text, we use $\lg n$ to denote $\log_2 n$.

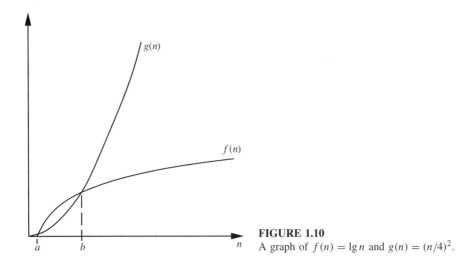

FIGURE 1.10
A graph of $f(n) = \lg n$ and $g(n) = (n/4)^2$.

These are not the only values of n_0 and c for which $f(n) \leq g(n)$. In fact, there are an infinite number of constants c and n_0 that satisfy the inequality.

The analysis performed in the previous example was really not necessary since it can be shown (see Appendix A.1.1) that any power function dominates any logarithmic function. This implies that for sufficiently large n, power functions upper bound logarithmic functions. Therefore, in future examples, if we already know that $g(n)$ dominates $f(n)$, we will not find it necessary to specify the constants c and n_0 that satisfy the inequality in Definition 1.1 in order to state that $f(n) = O(g(n))$.

It is also important to recognize that the equality in the statement $f(n) = O(g(n))$ is "one-way." Since the term $O(g(n))$ really specifies an infinite set of functions, this statement is saying that $f(n)$ belongs to the set of functions that can be bounded from above by a fixed multiple of $g(n)$, when n is sufficiently large. However, for mainly historical reasons, this relationship is usually represented by an equality. With this discussion in mind, it should be clear that the notation $O(g(n)) = f(n)$ should never be used.

We now derive some additional properties of the O-notation that result from Definition 1.1. Recall that we are dealing with asymptotic upper bounds. Thus, if $f(n) = O(g(n))$, and $h(n)$ is a function that is larger in value than $g(n)$ when n is sufficiently large, then $f(n) = O(h(n))$. This means that it is perfectly correct to write that for $f(n) = n^2$, $f(n) = O(n^3)$. However, in this case the upper bound is not tight.

Since logarithms to the base b of n are related to logarithms to the base a of n by a constant (see Appendix A.1.1 and note that $\log_b a$ is a constant in equation (A.4)), we may write $\log_b n = O(\log_a n)$. Furthermore, because the O-notation ignores multiplicative constants, we see that there is no difference between the expressions $O(\lg n)$, $O(\log_e n)$, or $O(\log_{10} n)$. Thus, we will simply use $O(\log n)$ to refer to any of these. The absence of the base of the logarithm in this notation is meant to emphasize this equivalence.

Finally, let us show that $O(f(n)^2) = O(f(n))^2$. It is not difficult to show that $O(f(n) \cdot g(n)) = f(n) \cdot O(g(n))$, which allows us to write $O(f(n)^2) = f(n) \cdot O(f(n))$. Since $f(n) = O(f(n))$ we have that $f(n) \cdot O(f(n)) = O(f(n)) \cdot O(f(n)) = O(f(n))^2$. This property will help us avoid parentheses, since we may rewrite expressions of the form $O((\log n)^2)$ as $O(\log n)^2$.

Next we consider Ω-notation, which is used to express an ***asymptotic lower bound*** on a function.

> **Definition 1.2.** Ω**-notation.** Assume there are two arbitrary functions $f(n)$ and $g(n)$ such that $\{f(n), g(n) : \mathbb{Z}^+ \to \mathbb{R}^+\}$. It is said that $f(n)$ is "big-omega" of $g(n)$, written as
>
> $$f(n) = \Omega(g(n))$$
>
> if there exist positive constants c and n_0 such that $f(n) \geq cg(n)$ for all $n \geq n_0$.

If we consider Figure 1.10, where $f(n) = \lg n$ and $g(n) = (n/4)^2$, then by choosing $n_0 = b$ and $c = 1$, we may write $g(n) = \Omega(f(n))$. However, $f(n) \neq \Omega(g(n))$ because values for c and n_0 cannot be found that satisfy $f(n) \geq cg(n)$ for all $n \geq n_0$. Recall from our previous discussion that the functions in Figure 1.10 are also related according to $f(n) = O(g(n))$. This exhibits a relationship between O-notation and Ω-notation. For any functions $f(n)$ and $g(n)$ defined as in Definitions 1.1 and 1.2,

$$f(n) = \Omega(g(n)) \quad \text{if and only if} \quad g(n) = O(f(n)) \tag{1.2}$$

The symmetry in the previous equation implies that the properties derived for O-notation will also hold for Ω-notation.

Finally we present Θ-notation, which is used to express an ***asymptotically tight*** bound on a function.

> **Definition 1.3.** Θ**-notation.** Assume there are two arbitrary functions $f(n)$ and $g(n)$ such that $\{f(n), g(n) : \mathbb{Z}^+ \to \mathbb{R}^+\}$. It is said that $f(n)$ is "big-theta" of $g(n)$, written as
>
> $$f(n) = \Theta(g(n))$$
>
> if there exist positive constants c_1, c_2, and n_0 such that $c_1 g(n) \leq f(n) \leq c_2 g(n)$ for all $n \geq n_0$.

This definition implies that $f(n) = \Theta(g(n))$ if and only if $f(n) = O(g(n))$ and $f(n) = \Omega(g(n))$. Thus, if we again consider the functions in Figure 1.10, we have $f(n) \neq \Theta(g(n))$ because $f(n) \neq \Omega(g(n))$. In other words, $g(n)$ does not provide an asymptotically tight bound on $f(n)$.

A useful approximation of $n!$ makes use of Θ-notation:

$$n! \approx \sqrt{2\pi n} \left(\frac{n}{e}\right)^n \left(1 + \Theta\left(\frac{1}{n}\right)\right) \tag{1.3}$$

where e is the base of the natural logarithm. This is known as ***Stirling's approximation***.

1.6 AN EXTENDED EXAMPLE: EXPONENTIATION

Consider the problem of computing the exponential function x^n, when n is a positive integer. The function x^n is defined as the product of n copies of x,

$$\underbrace{x \cdot x \cdot x \cdots x}_{n \text{ times}} \tag{1.4}$$

BRUTE-FORCE EXPONENTIATION ALGORITHM. One approach that can be used to compute x^n is to directly implement its definition given in equation (1.4). An algorithm that computes x^n in this manner is given below:

Power1(real x, positive integer n)
1   *result* $\leftarrow x$
2   **for** $i \leftarrow 1$ **to** $n - 1$ **do**
3   *result* $\leftarrow$ *result* $\cdot x$
4   **return** *result*

Let us now define $f_1(n)$ to be the number of multiplications required by Power1() to compute x^n as a function of n. Since this procedure is a direct implementation of equation (1.4), it follows that

$$f_1(n) = n - 1 \tag{1.5}$$

Furthermore, Power1() will always execute $n - 1$ multiplies—no more, and no less. This means that $f_1(n) = \Theta(n)$.

RECURSIVE EXPONENTIATION ALGORITHM. An alternate approach can be developed by first noting that x^n can be computed by squaring $x^{\lfloor n/2 \rfloor}$, and then multiplying the result by x if n is odd. That is,

$$x^n = \begin{cases} x^{\lfloor n/2 \rfloor} \cdot x^{\lfloor n/2 \rfloor} \cdot x, & \text{if } n \text{ is odd} \\ x^{n/2} \cdot x^{n/2}, & \text{if } n \text{ is even} \end{cases} \tag{1.6}$$

If Power1() is used to compute $x^{\lfloor n/2 \rfloor}$, then we have from equation (1.5) that $\lfloor n/2 \rfloor - 1$ multiplications are performed. To complete the computation of x^n, either one or two additional multiplications would be required, depending upon whether n is odd or even. Thus, by simply computing $\lfloor n/2 \rfloor$, and using this result to compute x^n, we have a means of effectively reducing the number of multiplications required to compute x^n by approximately one-half. Instead of being content with this result, observe that this same "trick" can be used to compute $x^{\lfloor n/2 \rfloor}$. Specifically, Power1() can be used to compute $x^{\lfloor \lfloor n/2 \rfloor / 2 \rfloor}$, and this result is squared (and multiplied by x if $\lfloor n/2 \rfloor$ is odd) to produce $x^{\lfloor n/2 \rfloor}$. This discussion suggests a recursive approach to the computation

activation record	line	
		Power2(2,5)
1	3	y ← Power2(2,2)
2	3	y ← Power2(2,1)
3	2	**return** 2
2	7	**return** $2 \cdot 2$
1	5	**return** $2 \cdot 4 \cdot 4$

FIGURE 1.11
The recursive function calls that result when Power2() is called with $x = 2$ and $n = 5$.

of x^n. The following recursive algorithm accomplishes this feat:

```
Power2(real x, positive integer n)
1   if n = 1 then
2       return x
3   y ← Power2(x,⌊n/2⌋)
4   if  n is odd then
5       return y · y · x
6   else
7       return  y · y
```

In Figure 1.11 we verify that Power2() computes the correct result when passed the values $x = 2$ and $n = 5$. The first activation record is invoked by the initial call Power2(2,5). Inside this activation record, the procedure first checks to see if $n = 1$, and since it does not, control proceeds to line 3 where the procedure invokes itself recursively using Power2(2,2). This produces the second activation record, and so on, until the base case ($n = 1$) is finally reached. At this point, appropriate values are returned, and activation records are destroyed in the opposite order in which they were created, until the final result is returned.

We now define $f_2(n)$ to be the number of multiplications required of Power2() to recursively compute x^n as a function of n. Since this is not a direct implementation of equation (1.4), $f_2(n)$ cannot be determined in the straightforward manner that $f_1(n)$ was. We can, however, note two distinct cases. If n is even on every procedure call to Power2(), then the minimum number of multiplications will be performed; however, if n is odd on every procedure call, then the maximum number of multiplications will be performed. If n is to be even on every recursive procedure call, then n must be exactly divisible by 2 on each of these procedure calls. Thus, if $n = 2^k$, where k is a positive integer, then every recursive function call will yield an even value for $⌊n/2⌋$. Conversely, $⌊n/2⌋$ will be odd on every recursive procedure call if n is initially $2^k - 1$. And since $2^k - 1$ is itself odd, the maximum number of multiplications will be performed.

Let us now derive expressions for $f_2(n)$ considering both of the situations discussed above. First, if $n = 2^k$, then the following recurrence relation may be derived directly from the Power2() algorithm:

$$f_2(2^k) = \begin{cases} 0, & \text{if } k = 0 \\ f_2(2^{k-1}) + 1, & \text{if } k > 0 \end{cases} \qquad (1.7)$$

This recurrence relation simply states that the number of multiplications required to compute x^{2^k} is one more than the number of multiplications required to compute $x^{2^{k-1}}$. This is due to the fact that $x^{2^k} = (x^{2^{k-1}}) \cdot (x^{2^{k-1}})$.

The case where $n = 2^k - 1$ can also be determined by looking at Power2()

$$f_2(2^k - 1) = \begin{cases} 0, & \text{if } k = 1 \\ f_2(2^{k-1} - 1) + 2, & \text{if } k > 1 \end{cases} \qquad (1.8)$$

The second line of this recurrence relation follows from the fact that

$$\lfloor (2^k - 1)/2 \rfloor = (2^k - 2)/2 = 2^{k-1} - 1$$

Equation (1.8) states that the number of multiplications required to compute x^{2^k-1} is two more than the number of multiplications required to compute $x^{2^{k-1}-1}$.

We now seek the closed forms for recurrence relations (1.7) and (1.8). From equation (1.7) we have that for

$$
\begin{array}{ll}
k = 0, & f_2(1) = 0 \\
k = 1, & f_2(2) = 1 \\
k = 2, & f_2(4) = 2 \\
k = 3, & f_2(8) = 3
\end{array}
$$

Thus, it appears that if $n = 2^k$, the number of multiplications required is k. Therefore, our initial guess (i.e., induction hypothesis) is that

$$f_2(2^\alpha) = \alpha \quad \text{for } 0 \le \alpha \le k - 1 \qquad (1.9)$$

The validity of this hypothesis is now proven using induction.[†] Substituting the induction hypothesis into recurrence relation (1.7) yields

$$
\begin{aligned}
f_2(2^k) &= f_2(2^{k-1}) + 1 \\
&= k - 1 + 1 = k
\end{aligned}
$$

Thus, equation (1.9) is the correct closed form of the recurrence relation given in (1.7).

Next, let us consider the case where n is odd on every recursive call to Power2()—i.e., $n = 2^k - 1$. Again we start by writing down the results of computing recurrence relation (1.8) for small values of k:

$$
\begin{array}{ll}
k = 1, & f_2(1) = 0 \\
k = 2, & f_2(3) = 2 \\
k = 3, & f_2(7) = 4 \\
k = 4, & f_2(15) = 6 \\
k = 5, & f_2(31) = 8 \\
k = 6, & f_2(63) = 10
\end{array}
$$

[†]See Appendix A.4 for a discussion of proof by induction.

In this case it appears that the value of $f(n)$ can be obtained by moving to the previous line, taking its value for k, and doubling it. That is, our induction hypothesis is

$$f_2(2^\alpha - 1) = 2(\alpha - 1) \quad \text{for } 1 \le \alpha \le k - 1 \tag{1.10}$$

Let us see if this guess holds for all values of α. Substituting the induction hypothesis into equation (1.8) gives us

$$\begin{aligned} f_2(2^k - 1) &= f_2(2^{k-1} - 1) + 2 \\ &= 2(k - 1 - 1) + 2 = 2(k - 1) \end{aligned}$$

Thus, we have proven that equation (1.10) is the closed form of recurrence relation (1.8).

What can we now say about the number of multiplications required by algorithm Power2() in general? We know that in the best-case situation, where $n = 2^k$, Power2() will perform k multiplications. Noting that in this case $\lg n = \lg 2^k = k$, we may rewrite

$$f_2(2^k) = k \quad \text{for } k \ge 0$$

as

$$f_2(n) = \lg n \quad \text{for } n = 2^k \text{ and } k \ge 0$$

Since we know that Power2() will require at least this number of multiplications to compute its result, we may write

$$f_2(n) = \Omega(\log n) \tag{1.11}$$

In the worst case situation, where $n = 2^k - 1$, Power2() will perform $2(k - 1)$ multiplications. Noting in this case that $\lg(n + 1) = \lg 2^k = k$, we may rewrite

$$f_2(2^k - 1) = 2(k - 1) \quad \text{for } k \ge 1$$

as

$$f_2(n) = 2[\lg(n + 1) - 1] \quad \text{for } n = 2^k - 1 \text{ and } k \ge 1$$

Using this result, it is not difficult to show (see Exercise 1.12) that

$$f_2(n) = O(\log n) \tag{1.12}$$

Taken together, equations (1.11) and (1.12) imply that

$$f_2(n) = \Theta(\log n)$$

In Chapter 2 we discuss how the running times of Power1() and Power2() are related to the number of multiplications they perform.

EXERCISES

1.1. What advantages does the use of data encapsulation offer in both software design and development?

1.2. Write pseudocode procedures for the following MATRIX ADT operations:
(*a*) Addition
(*b*) Transpose
(*c*) Determinant
(*d*) Inverse

1.3. The Increment() procedure given in Section 1.2 can be modified so that it accepts a pointer to an integer variable as an input parameter:

   NewIncrement(integer ($\uparrow a$))
   1   ($\downarrow a$) $\leftarrow$ (($\downarrow a$) + 1)

In order to use this procedure, the address of an integer variable must be passed by the calling routine to NewIncrement(). Will the integer variable in the calling routine be incremented as a result of this call?

1.4. Write a pseudocode procedure that computes the following recurrence relation:

$$T(n) = \begin{cases} 1, & \text{if } n = 1 \\ 2T(n-1) + n, & \text{if } n > 1 \end{cases}$$

1.5. What is the maximum number of activation records that will reside on the run-time stack at any given time during the computation of Tower(4, A, B, C)?

1.6. Consider the famous recurrence relation that defines the **_Fibonacci sequence_** on natural numbers:

$$F(n) = \begin{cases} 0, & \text{if } n = 0 \\ 1, & \text{if } n = 1 \\ F(n-1) + F(n-2), & \text{if } n > 1 \end{cases}$$

(*a*) Write a pseudocode procedure that computes $F(n)$ directly using this recurrence relation.
(*b*) Draw the recursion tree that results when your procedure is used to compute $F(4)$.
(*c*) Use induction to prove that the closed form for the Fibonacci numbers is given by $F(n) = \frac{1}{\sqrt{5}}(\phi^n - \hat{\phi}^n)$, where $\phi = (1 + \sqrt{5})/2$ is called the **_golden ratio_**, and $\hat{\phi} = -1/\phi$. Next, argue that $F(n) = \Theta(\phi^n)$.

1.7. How many recursive procedure calls are executed when computing
(*a*) Fibonacci(5), where Fibonacci() was developed in Exercise 1.6 (a).
(*b*) Fibonacci(10).
(*c*) Tower(5,A,B,C).
(*d*) Tower(10,A,B,C).

1.8. Professor Enit O'Help believes that there is a solution to the n-disk Tower of Hanoi puzzle that requires far fewer than $2^n - 1$ moves. The professor proposes first moving the top disk on peg A to peg B, then moving the remaining $n - 1$ disks on peg A to peg C, and finally moving the one disk on peg B to peg C. This sequence of moves is illustrated below:

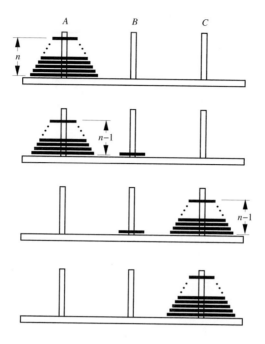

(a) The esteemed professor has provided the following recurrence relation that describes the number of moves required using the new solution

$$T(n) = \begin{cases} 1, & \text{if } n = 1 \\ T(n-1) + 2, & \text{if } n > 1 \end{cases}$$

What is the closed form of $T(n)$?

(b) Describe what is wrong with the professor's solution.

1.9. The following is a famous recurrence relation known as **_Ackermann's function_**:

$$A(m, n) = \begin{cases} n + 1, & \text{if } m = 0 \text{ and } n \geq 0 \\ A(m-1, 1), & \text{if } m \geq 1 \text{ and } n = 0 \\ A(m-1, A(m, n-1)), & \text{if } m, n \geq 1 \end{cases}$$

Note that one of the parameters of this recurrence relation is itself recursive. Calculate the values of $A(2, 2)$, $A(3, 3)$, and $A(2, 4)$.

1.10. Use the $\prec$ relation (defined in the footnote on page 406) to rank the following functions:

$$\lg n, \ \lg(\lg n), \ n \lg n, \ n^b, \ n^a, \ \frac{1}{n}, \ \frac{1}{\lg n}, \ n^n, \ b^n, \ 1, \ n^{\lg n}, \ b^{b^n}, \ \frac{1}{b^n}$$

Assume a and b are arbitrary constants, and $0 < a < 1 < b$. Write the relationship between all of these functions on one line. For example, if $f(n) \prec g(n)$ and $g(n) \prec h(n)$, write $f(n) \prec g(n) \prec h(n)$.

1.11. Compare the following pairs of functions using asymptotic notation. In each case, state whether $f(n) = O(g(n))$, $f(n) = \Omega(g(n))$, or $f(n) = \Theta(g(n))$.

$f(n)$	$g(n)$
$10^{-3}n^4$	$10^3 n^3$
n^2	$n \lg n$
$\lg n$	$\lg(\lg n)$
2^{n^2}	2^{2^n}
$100n + \log_{10} n$	$n + (\lg n)^2$
$\lg n$	$\lg n^2$
$n^{\lg n}$	n

1.12. Show that $\lg(n + 1) = O(\log n)$.

1.13. Use Stirling's approximation to show that $\lg(n!) = \Theta(n \log n)$.

1.14. The asymptotic notation discussed in Section 1.5 can be extended to the case of two parameters n and m. For example, given two arbitrary functions $f(n, m)$ and $g(n, m)$, we may write $f(n, m) = O(g(n, m))$ if there exist positive constants c, n_0, and m_0 such that $f(n, m) \leq c \cdot g(n, m)$ for all $n > n_0$ and $m > m_0$. Give the corresponding definitions for $\Omega(g(n, m))$ and $\Theta(g(n, m))$.

1.15. Professor Imin A. Phog was able to obtain amazing results using $\Theta(g(n)) - \Theta(g(n)) = 0$. What is wrong with Professor Phog's logic? What should the right-hand side of the professor's formula be?

1.16. Use the definition of O-notation to answer the following questions:
(a) Is $2^{n+1} = O(2^n)$?
(b) Is $2^{2n} = O(2^n)$?
(c) Given that $f(n) = O(g(n))$, does it follow that $2^{f(n)} = O(2^{g(n)})$?

CHAPTER NOTES

Dijkstra [45] discusses how the process of abstraction can be used to reduce the amount of complexity or detail that must be considered at any one time during the design and implementation of large software systems. There are a large number of textbooks devoted to the design process itself, and software design in particular. Fairley [53] provides a good treatment of the traditional software life cycle, which includes software cost estimation, requirements definition, design, verification, and maintenance.

An introduction to the algebraic technique for specifying abstract data types is provided by Guttag [72]. Goguen, Thatcher, and Wagner [64] presents a more theoretical treatment of this subject. A textbook that treats the study of data structures from this perspective is Martin [98].

Press et al. [123] present numerical algorithms for performing many matrix operations, such as the calculation of the determinant and inverse of a matrix. In addition, introductory numerical methods textbooks, such as [30] and [99], cover this topic.

Parameter passing mechanisms are described in many books on programming languages, such as Tennent [150] and Pratt [121].

An early work on recursion is Barron [12]. Burge [26] provides a more rigorous treatment. The text by Rohl [130] presents recursion in the context of the Pascal programming language.

The Fibonacci numbers were introduced by Leonardo Fibonacci in 1202. An excellent discussion of the Fibonacci numbers can be found in Graham, Knuth, and Patashnik [69]. An interesting article that discusses the uses of the golden ratio in art and science is Gardner [62]. The Tower of Hanoi puzzle was created by the French mathematician Édouard Lucas in 1883 [49]. Ackermann's function was originally presented by Ackermann in 1928 [2].

CHAPTER
2

ALGORITHMICS

In this chapter a number of methods used to evaluate the relative merits of an algorithm are discussed. These techniques will be quite useful in our analysis of the accessing routines associated with ADT implementations presented in subsequent chapters. In Section 1.1.1 we described an algorithm as a finite sequence of instructions that specify how a problem is to be solved. In this chapter we expand this definition as follows: An *algorithm* is any well-defined computational procedure, along with a specified set of allowable inputs, that produces some value or set of values as output. Here we are emphasizing that an algorithm must produce a valid output for all allowable inputs.

Some problems do not even possess algorithmic solutions. A classic example is the *halting problem*, in which an algorithm must be developed to determine if a given computer program will ever terminate (i.e., will the program complete its execution and halt). The inputs to this algorithm will be any computer program as well as the potential input to the program, while the output is simply a yes or no answer. A yes answer indicates that the input program will halt, while a no answer indicates that it will not. It can be shown that this problem is *noncomputable*, which means that it does not admit an algorithmic solution. That is, it is impossible to develop an algorithm that will determine, in a finite amount of time, whether an arbitrary computer program will terminate on a given input. Although we will not consider such problems in this text, it is useful to recognize their existence.

2.1 EFFICIENCY OF ALGORITHMS

Typically we are interested in analyzing the *efficiency* of a given algorithm. This involves determining the quantity of computer resources consumed by the algorithm. The resources that are usually measured include the amount of memory and the amount of computational time required by the algorithm. Determining the efficiency of an algorithm is by no means the only figure of merit that can be used to judge an algorithm. Of utmost importance is the *correctness* of the algorithm itself—that is, does the algorithm always produce the correct result for all possible input values. Suffice it to say that rigorously proving the correctness of a nontrivial algorithm can be an extremely difficult task, and is beyond the scope of this book. However, it is usually not too difficult to convince ourselves in a nonrigorous fashion that the algorithms presented in this book are correct. For pedagogical purposes, this will suffice.

A more qualitative figure of merit involves the *program complexity* of an algorithm, which considers both the difficulty of implementing an algorithm along with the efficiency of the algorithm itself. A measure for program complexity requires a consideration of the context in which the algorithm will be used. In many instances, it is more advantageous to implement a simple algorithm that solves a given problem, than to implement a more complex algorithm that solves the same problem using fewer resources. For example, consider the two algorithms for computing the exponential function described in Section 1.6. The first algorithm, Power1(), used a straightforward approach to compute this function using $n - 1$ multiplications; while the second algorithm, Power2(), used a more complicated recursive approach to compute the function using approximately $\lg n$ multiplications. If a user only needs to compute exponentials to small integer powers, then the number of multiplications saved by using Power2(), as opposed to Power1(), will be quite small. Furthermore, it may require a significant amount of time for the programmer to understand, implement, and debug the recursive exponentiation procedure. Because a programmer's time is valuable, it might be wise in this case to implement the straightforward exponentiation procedure. On the other hand, if exponentials to large integer powers must be computed, then a tremendous number of multiplications can be saved by using the recursive procedure. Consider the case where $n = 65,536$. To compute x^n, the Power1() procedure will execute 65,535 multiplications, while the Power2() procedure only executes 16 multiplications.

2.1.1 Running Time and Memory Usage

Our analysis of algorithms and data structures will mainly focus on efficiency considerations. This analysis is performed by considering the amount of resources an algorithm consumes as a function of the size of the input to the algorithm. For example, the efficiency of an algorithm might be determined by the amount of memory required, and/or by the amount of computational time required, as the size of the input to the algorithm grows.

We will use the term *memory space* (or simply *space*) to refer to the amount of memory required by an algorithm, and the term *running time* (or simply *time*) to refer to the computational time required by an algorithm. The space occupied by an algorithm is determined by the number and sizes of the variables and data structures used by the algorithm. The time required by an algorithm is determined by the number of elementary operations that must be performed during the algorithm's execution.

In many cases, the space and time required by an algorithm are inversely related. That is, we may be able to reduce space requirements by increasing the running time, or conversely, reduce time requirements by increasing memory space. This situation is referred to as the ***space-time tradeoff***. As an example consider again the exponentiation problem discussed in Section 1.6. Recall that every recursive procedure call produces an activation record that is stored in computer memory on the run-time stack. We will subsequently show that the running times of Power1() and Power2() are related to the number of multiplications they perform. Thus, for large exponents, the running time of Power2() is much less than that of Power1(); however, in this case Power2() will also make a large number of recursive procedure calls. Therefore, the memory space used by Power2() will be much greater than the memory space used by Power1().

Generally, we will restrict our analysis to the running time of an algorithm, and we will assume that there is sufficient memory to implement the algorithm. This is justified by noting that with current technology, computer memory is typically abundant and cheap in relation to the processor. This is not to say that issues of memory space are unimportant. For example, in certain embedded systems a processor may have a very limited amount of memory associated with it.[†] Therefore, we wish to stress that the techniques developed below for analyzing the running time of an algorithm can also be applied to the analysis of space requirements.

MEASURING RUNNING TIME. Since the running time of an algorithm may differ depending upon the input it receives, it is calculated as a function of the input size. Therefore, one approach would be to implement a given algorithm, and for various input sizes, measure the running time using a stopwatch. Computational time measured in this fashion is said to use ***wall-clock time***. This approach may give us some idea as to how an algorithm's running time changes as the size of its input is changed, but it cannot be considered very rigorous for a number of reasons. First, the speed with which a program executes depends upon the type of machine executing the program, as well as the skill of the programmer who implemented it. These factors, which are included when measuring running time using a wall clock, should not be considered when analyzing an algorithm.

We would like to be able to make judgments regarding the merit of an algorithm independent of a specific software implementation, or the hardware on which it is implemented. In order to perform this type of analysis, we must assume some general model of computation on which an implementation of the algorithm we are investigating will be executed. The most common model of computation used to

---

[†]A processor in an ***embedded system*** is only a part of a larger physical system. For example processors are now routinely embedded in automobile engines, vending machines, appliances, etc.

evaluate algorithms is the ***random-access machine (RAM)***. This model assumes the existence of a single generic processor, random-access memory, and a set of basic operations that the processor can execute. It is then assumed that the algorithm is implemented as a computer program that will execute on this RAM model using its set of basic operations, and that the instructions are executed one after another, with no concurrent operations (i.e., two or more instructions cannot be executed simultaneously). Now, to determine the running time of an algorithm we must determine the time required by each basic operation, and multiply that by how many times the operation is used when implementing the algorithm on the RAM model.

Consider the Power1() procedure presented in Section 1.6. This algorithm is now rewritten while indicating in the right hand margin the time required of each statement, and the number of times that each statement is executed:

Power1(real x, positive integer n)		*time*	*number*
1	*result* $\leftarrow x$	t_1	1
2	**for** $i \leftarrow 1$ **to** $n-1$ **do**	t_2	$n-1$
3	*result* $\leftarrow$ *result* $\cdot x$	t_3	$n-1$
4	**return** *result*	t_4	1

Thus, we can say that the running time of this algorithm is

$$T(n) = t_1 + t_2(n-1) + t_3(n-1) + t_4,$$

which may be rewritten as

$$T(n) = (t_2 + t_3)(n-1) + t_1 + t_4 \tag{2.1}$$

The actual running time of an implementation of this algorithm on a particular machine can be calculated once the values of t_1, t_2, t_3, and t_4 are known. What does this analysis tell us about the behavior of the algorithm as the size of the input grows? First, notice that lines 1 and 4 contribute a constant amount of time, $t_1 + t_4$, no matter how large the input is. Thus, the behavior of the algorithm as the input size grows is determined by the $(t_2 + t_3)(n-1)$ term in (2.1). For this reason, asymptotic analysis is normally used to express the running time of an algorithm. For example, we may write $T(n) = \Theta(n)$ since it is possible to find positive constants c_1, c_2, and n_0 such that

$$c_1 n \leq (t_2 + t_3)(n-1) + t_1 + t_4 \leq c_2 n$$

for all $n \geq n_0$. From this analysis we see that the number of multiplications performed by Power1() does in fact determine its running time.

In summary, the use of asymptotic notation in algorithmic analysis has a number of advantages. Recall that regarding an algorithm, we wish to arrive at some figure of merit that is independent of a particular software implementation or hardware platform. In the example above, the use of asymptotic notation hides the constant amounts t_1 through t_4, whose values are machine specific; and distills the most important aspect of the algorithm—that its running time will grow linearly with increasing input size. In other words, what we are interested in is the *rate of growth* of the running time, not the actual running time of an algorithm (this would require knowledge of exactly how the algorithm was to be implemented on a specific computer). Using asymptotic notation, this means that we can ignore all lower order terms in an equation that expresses the running time of an algorithm, and concentrate instead on the highest order term, since it is this term that determines the growth rate of the equation. In addition, any constant coefficient multiplying the highest order term can be ignored. Again, since this constant term generally corresponds to some implementation-specific details, a more general statement about the running time of an algorithm can be made if we ignore it. We will refer to the running time of an algorithm that is obtained in this fashion as the *asymptotic running time complexity*, or simply *time complexity* of the algorithm.

Because we are only interested in the asymptotic complexity of an algorithm, it will not be necessary to go through the analysis performed above in order to determine an algorithm's running time. Instead, the running time of a nonrecursive algorithm can be determined by simply observing the behavior of any of its loop structures. Typically, the number of iterations performed by a loop will vary with the size of the input to the algorithm. Therefore, in order to determine the running time of an algorithm, we simply count the number of basic operations that are performed inside of its loop structures. For example, the Power1() algorithm contains a loop that varies with n, and on each iteration of the loop one basic operation (multiplication) is performed. Since this loop is iterated $n - 1$ times, we can say that the running time of Power1() is $\Theta(n)$, without having to go through the analysis performed above.

For recursive algorithms we also need to count the number of basic operations that are performed—but in this case, there are no loop structures to analyze. Instead, we must perform an analysis similar to that in Section 1.6 to determine the number of operations that the recursive algorithm will implement as a function of the input size. Thus, since our analysis in Section 1.6 determined that the recursive Power2() algorithm will execute $\Theta(\log n)$ multiplications, we can say that the running time of Power2() is given by $\Theta(\log n)$.

2.1.2 Polynomial-Time and Superpolynomial-Time Algorithms

In the previous section, we introduced the notion that algorithms can be judged according to their efficiency. This idea is actually carried a step further by computer scientists when they categorize an algorithm as either being reasonable (tractable, efficient) or unreasonable (intractable, inefficient). The dividing line between these two categories is drawn as follows. If the time complexity of an algorithm can be expressed as $O(p(n))$ for some polynomial function p, where n is the input size, then this algorithm is said to be a *polynomial-time algorithm*. Any algorithm that cannot be bounded in this fashion is called a *superpolynomial-time algorithm*.

The motivation for categorizing algorithms as discussed above follows from this fact: As the size of the input n grows large, the running times of super-polynomial-time algorithms become exceedingly large, while the running times of polynomial-time algorithms generally remain reasonable. This phenomenon is clearly illustrated in Table 2.1. This table compares the running times of several polynomial

TABLE 2.1

Running times of polynomial-time and superpolynomial-time algorithms. The size of the input to an algorithm is given by n, and it is assumed that each unit of the algorithm's complexity function takes one microsecond to execute.

Algorithm complexity	Size n					
	10	**20**	**30**	**40**	**50**	**60**
polynomial						
n	.00001 sec	.00002 sec	.00003 sec	.00004 sec	.00005 sec	.00006 sec
n^2	.0001 sec	.0004 sec	.0009 sec	.0016 sec	.0025 sec	.0036 sec
n^3	.001 sec	.008 sec	.027 sec	.064 sec	.125 sec	.216 sec
n^5	.1 sec	3.2 sec	24.3 sec	1.7 min	5.2 min	13 min
super-polynomial						
2^n	.001 sec	1.0 sec	17.9 min	12.7 days	35.7 yr	366 cen
3^n	.059 sec	58 min	6.5 yr	3855 cen	$2 \cdot 10^8$ cen	$1 \cdot 10^{13}$ cen
$n!$	3.63 sec	771 cen	$8 \cdot 10^{16}$ cen	$3 \cdot 10^{32}$ cen	$1 \cdot 10^{49}$ cen	$3 \cdot 10^{66}$ cen

and superpolynomial-time algorithms. In this table it is assumed that the complexity functions express computation time in terms of microseconds. Thus, for a polynomial-time algorithm with time complexity function n^2, an input of size 20 would result in a running time of $20^2 \times 10^{-6} = 0.0004$ seconds. Notice that for small input sizes, the running times of the superpolynomial-time algorithms are fairly reasonable; but as the input size grows, the running times of these algorithms quickly become unreasonable. Such is not the case for the polynomial-time algorithms—their running times remain reasonable as n grows large. Consider an algorithm whose time complexity is given by 3^n. This algorithm requires 1.3×10^{13} centuries to compute its result with an input of size 60. To put this number in perspective, consider that dinosaurs roamed the earth some 2×10^6 centuries ago, and that the "big bang" is conjectured to have occurred some 1.5×10^8 centuries ago!

Another reason for categorizing algorithms as discussed above follows from the fact that advances in computer technology will not markedly change the situation depicted in Table 2.1. Table 2.2 illustrates the effect that improved computer technology will have on the running times of algorithms. Note that if an algorithm has a time complexity of n, then a 1000-fold increase in computer speed will allow a problem to be solved that is 1000 times larger than can be solved with current computer technology in one hour. However, if we are dealing with a superpolynomial-time algorithm that has a time complexity of 3^n, then a 1000-fold increase in computer speed only adds 6.29 units to the size of the largest problem solvable in one hour. Thus, we will not obtain a reasonable running time for a superpolynomial-time algorithm by simply waiting for improvements in computer technology.

The issues discussed above demonstrate the importance of being able to properly analyze the running times of the algorithms we develop. If we can show that an

TABLE 2.2
Effects of improvements in computer technology on the size of the largest problem solvable in one hour for several polynomial-time and superpolynomial-time algorithms.

Algorithm complexity	Size of largest problem solvable in 1 hour		
	With present computer	With computer 100 times faster	With computer 1000 times faster
polynomial			
n	N_1	$100N_1$	$1000N_1$
n^2	N_2	$10N_2$	$31.6N_2$
n^3	N_3	$4.64N_3$	$10N_3$
n^5	N_4	$2.5N_4$	$3.98N_4$
superpolynomial			
2^n	N_5	$N_5 + 6.64$	$N_5 + 9.97$
3^n	N_6	$N_6 + 4.19$	$N_6 + 6.29$

algorithm is intractable, then it makes no sense to try to solve large problems using this algorithm—even if we have a supercomputer at our disposal! Instead, we would be better served by spending time looking for a better algorithm, one that solves a special case of the problem under consideration, or one that solves the problem approximately. One of these approaches may yield an algorithm that is useful as well as tractable.

2.2 ALGORITHMIC ANALYSIS

It is important to recognize the distinction between a *problem* and an *algorithm* that solves a problem. A ***problem*** has a *single* problem statement that describes it in some general terms; however, there may be *many* different ways to solve this problem, and some of these solutions may be more efficient than others. Thus, a number of different algorithms can exist for solving a computational problem, and each of these algorithms could have a different running-time complexity.

Given a computational problem, an algorithm designer is typically interested in finding the fastest possible algorithm that solves it. In some cases, it is possible to specify a ***theoretical lower bound*** on the number of operations required to solve a problem for any possible algorithm and input instance. For instance, in Section 2.4 a theoretical lower bound of $\Theta(n \log n)$ is derived for the worst-case running time of *any* comparison-based sorting algorithm that sorts n data items. Theoretical lower bounds are typically derived by considering the information-theoretic limits imposed by the problem.

We can also talk about an obvious or ***trivial lower bound*** for the number of operations required to solve a problem. In the case of the comparison-based sorting problem, a trivial lower bound is $\Theta(n)$ since it will take this much time just to output

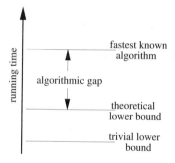

FIGURE 2.1

A graphical depiction of the algorithmic gap that may exist between the theoretical lower bound for the running time of any algorithm that can solve a given problem, and the best known algorithm that solves the problem.

the result. Likewise, the multiplication of two $n \times n$ matrices has a trivial lower bound of $\Theta(n^2)$ since at least that many operations are required just to output the result.

In many cases there is a so-called ***algorithmic gap*** between the theoretical lower bound for a problem, and the best available algorithm for solving that problem. In these cases, algorithm designers may work to close this gap by developing faster algorithms. If a faster algorithm is found, then it establishes a new lower bound for the fastest known algorithm that solves the problem. This situation is depicted in Figure 2.1.

If an algorithm is found that asymptotically matches the theoretical lower bound for a problem, then at least in an asymptotic sense, no algorithm could be faster. This is not to say that nothing can be done to improve such a solution—its asymptotic running time may be "hiding" a large constant, or the asymptotic results may only apply when the input size is extremely large. For many important problems, theoretical lower bounds have not been found. In these cases, the only basis of comparison is against the lower bound established by the fastest known algorithm for solving the problem.

In this book we will be more concerned with analyzing the behavior of specific algorithms. This approach cannot be used to judge whether such an algorithm is the "best" for a given problem. All we can do is compare the relative performance of one algorithm to another. The branch of Computer Science known as Complexity Theory is concerned with the establishment of theoretical lower bounds for the time needed to solve specific computational problems.

In order to analyze a problem in the manner discussed above, we must be able to determine the running time of any new algorithms we develop. In Section 2.1.1, we discussed how to determine the running time of an algorithm based on the number of basic operations it performs. Below we refine this idea further by considering how to handle cases where the running time of an algorithm varies depending upon the order in which the input data is supplied to it.

2.2.1 Worst-case Analysis

In many algorithms, running time will vary not only for inputs of different sizes, but also for different inputs of the *same* size. That is, we may find that the running times of an algorithm will vary for inputs of the same size, depending upon the initial ordering of the input data. For example, in Section 2.4 we will see that the running times of some sorting algorithms depend upon the initial ordering of the input data. If n input data items are presented in sorted order to an insertion sort routine, on the order of n operations are performed by the algorithm (it takes at least this much time just to check to see if the data is in fact sorted). This corresponds to a best case situation for the insertion sort. On the other hand, if the n input data items are supplied in reverse sorted order (a situation corresponding to the worst case), then this same algorithm requires on the order of n^2 operations to perform the sort. From this analysis, we have that the running time of insertion sort is given by $\Omega(n)$ and $O(n^2)$. Typically, in the analysis of algorithms, the worst-case situation is used to express running time. This convention is actually useful for a number of reasons. First, if we know the worst-case running time of an algorithm, then we have a guarantee that the algorithm will never take more than this time. Such a guarantee can be quite important in time-critical software applications that deal with, for example, air-traffic control, missile and aircraft guidance systems, or control of a nuclear power plant. In addition, it is often found in practical applications that the worst-case running time of an algorithm occurs frequently.

We define the ***worst-case running time*** of an algorithm to be the maximum running time of that algorithm over *all* possible inputs of size n. Thus, for the insertion sort algorithm discussed above, since the running time is $O(n^2)$, the worst-case running time is $\Theta(n^2)$; and for the recursive exponentiation algorithm Power2() presented in Section 1.6, the worst-case running time is $\Theta(\log n)$. Whenever we discuss running times in this text, we will be careful about stating whether we are considering worst-case behavior.

A warning should be issued at this point. In practice we might find that an algorithm whose worst-case running time is given by, for example, $\Theta(n \log n)$ usually takes longer to execute than an algorithm that accomplishes the same task, but whose worst-case running time is given by $\Theta(n^2)$. It may turn out that the $\Theta(n^2)$ algorithm almost always has a running time that is close to n, while the $\Theta(n \log n)$ algorithm may almost always have a running time that is close to $n \lg n$. In spite of this possibility, we may safely state that in the majority of cases, algorithms whose worst-case running times are better in the Θ-notation sense are also better in practice.

2.2.2   Average-case Analysis

We may also define the ***average-case running time*** of an algorithm for an input of size n, to be the value that is obtained by averaging the running times of the algorithm over all possible inputs of size n. We will indicate that the average-case running time of an algorithm is being considered by using "av" as a subscript (e.g., $T_{av}(n)$).

Although average-case analysis may appear to be better than worst-case analysis for measuring running time, it usually is not. Average-case analysis requires that we assume some underlying probability distribution for the input instances. If this assumption is violated in practice, then the average-case analysis may not be meaningful. In addition to the difficulty of determining an appropriate probability distribution function for the input data, such average-case analysis quite often becomes mathematically intractable. Nevertheless, on occasion we will find it convenient to assume that each input instance is equally likely (i.e., that the underlying probability distribution for the input data is uniform) and proceed with an analysis of the running time of that algorithm.

In summary, for the reasons stated above we will typically use the worst-case measure to express the running time complexity of an algorithm; however, we will use average-case analysis if it makes sense for a particular algorithm or application of an algorithm.

2.3 ALGORITHMIC TECHNIQUES

Below we discuss some general classes of algorithmic techniques. Each of these techniques has special properties that make them appropriate for solving certain types of problems. We stress that one should not apply these techniques blindly to any problem under consideration. The structure of the problem itself usually determines the applicability of a specific technique.

We begin by considering brute-force algorithms. For most problems, a brute-force approach represents the simplest, but most costly solution. We will often use a brute-force algorithm as a basis for comparison against alternative algorithms that are developed using the more sophisticated techniques presented below.

2.3.1   Brute-force Algorithms

Brute-force algorithms are characterized by a lack of sophistication in terms of their approach to the solution. They typically take the most direct or obvious route, without attempting to minimize the number of operations required to compute the solution. We have already seen an example of a brute-force algorithm for the exponentiation problem in Section 1.6. Recall that Power1() solved the problem by directly implementing the definition given for exponentiation.

Brute-force algorithms are considered quite often in the context of searching. In a searching problem we are required to look through a list of candidates in an attempt to find a desired object. In many cases, the structure of the problem itself allows us to eliminate a large number of the candidates without having to actually search through them. As an analogy, consider the problem of trying to find a frozen pie in an unfamiliar grocery store. You would immediately go to the frozen food aisle, without bothering to look down any of the other aisles. Thus, at the outset of your search, you would eliminate the need to search down most of the aisles in the store. Brute-force algorithms, however, ignore such possibilities and naively search through all candidates in an attempt to find the desired object. This is often called an *exhaustive search*.

2.3.2   Divide-and-conquer Algorithms

Divide-and-conquer algorithms solve a problem by breaking it down into several sub-problems that are similar to the original problem, except smaller in size. Each of the subproblems are then solved independently. Subsequently, the results obtained from solving these subproblems are combined to produce the solution to the original problem. Because each of the subproblems is similar to the original problem, a recursive approach is typically justified. The steps involved in a divide-and-conquer algorithm can be summarized as follows: First divide the original problem into a number of subproblems. Next, solve (i.e., conquer) the subproblems. If the subproblems are small enough, they should be solved directly; otherwise, they should be solved recursively. Finally, combine the solutions to the subproblems to produce the final solution.

The running times of many divide-and-conquer algorithms can be described by a recurrence relation of the form

$$T(n) = \begin{cases} \Theta(1), & \text{if } n \leq n_0 \\ aT(n/b) + \Theta(n^k), & \text{if } n > n_0 \end{cases} \tag{2.2}$$

where n is a positive integer; and $a \geq 1$, $b > 1$, $k \geq 0$, and $n_0 \geq 0$ are constants. Furthermore, since $T(n)$ is only defined on positive integer values n, we interpret the quantity n/b to mean either $\lfloor n/b \rfloor$ or $\lceil n/b \rceil$.

Recurrence 2.2 can be interpreted as follows. If the size of the problem, n, is small enough (i.e., $\leq n_0$), then a straightforward solution can be computed in constant time. However, if the size of the problem is larger (i.e., $> n_0$), then we divide the problem into a subproblems each of size n/b. The value a corresponds to the number of times the algorithm is called recursively from a given activation record, and n/b corresponds to the size of the input supplied on each of these calls. The polynomial term $\Theta(n^k)$ specifies the amount of time required to perform this decomposition, as well as the time required to combine the solutions to the subproblems in order to produce the final solution.

A closed-form solution to equation (2.2) is determined by the values of a, b, and k. Specifically, recurrence (2.2) can be bounded as follows:

$$T(n) = \begin{cases} \Theta(n^k), & \text{if } a < b^k \\ \Theta(n^k \log n), & \text{if } a = b^k \\ \Theta(n^{\log_b a}), & \text{if } a > b^k \end{cases} \tag{2.3}$$

In order to verify this result, let us first consider the case where n is a power of b—i.e., $n = b^m$ for some integer m. In this case $n/b = b^{m-1}$, $n^k = (b^m)^k = (b^k)^m$, and the second part of equation (2.2) can be rewritten as

$$T(b^m) = aT(b^{m-1}) + (b^k)^m$$

where the constant term in $\Theta(n^k)$ is assumed without loss of generality to be 1. Dividing through by a^m yields

$$\frac{T(b^m)}{a^m} = \frac{T(b^{m-1})}{a^{m-1}} + \left(\frac{b^k}{a}\right)^m \tag{2.4}$$

Letting $m = m - 1$ in this equation leads to

$$\frac{T(b^{m-1})}{a^{m-1}} = \frac{T(b^{m-2})}{a^{m-2}} + \left(\frac{b^k}{a}\right)^{m-1}$$

which can be substituted into equation (2.4), yielding

$$\frac{T(b^m)}{a^m} = \frac{T(b^{m-2})}{a^{m-2}} + \left(\frac{b^k}{a}\right)^{m-1} + \left(\frac{b^k}{a}\right)^m$$

Continuing in this fashion we obtain

$$\frac{T(b^m)}{a^m} = \frac{T(b^0)}{a^0} + \sum_{i=1}^{m} \left(\frac{b^k}{a}\right)^i$$

We can assume without loss of generality that our initial condition is $T(1) = 1$, in which case the first term on the right-hand side of the previous equation is 1 and we obtain the geometric series

$$T(n) = T(b^m) = a^m \sum_{i=0}^{m} \left(\frac{b^k}{a}\right)^i \tag{2.5}$$

Let us now consider this equation with reference to the three scenarios given in equation (2.3).

If $a < b^k$, then equation (A.19) from Appendix A can be used to obtain

$$T(n) = a^m \frac{(b^k/a)^{m+1} - 1}{(b^k/a) - 1} = \Theta(a^m (b^k/a)^m) = \Theta(b^{km})$$

$$= \Theta(n^k)$$

If $a = b^k$, then each term of the geometric series in equation (2.5) equals 1, and we can use the fact that $m = \log_b n$ to write

$$T(n) = (b^k)^m \sum_{i=0}^{\log_b n} 1 = \Theta\left((b^k)^m \log_b n\right)$$

$$= \Theta(n^k \log_b n)$$

Finally, if $a > b^k$ then each term in the geometric series is less than 1. Equation (A.21) in Appendix A demonstrates that if this were an infinite series it would converge to a constant. Thus, a finite sum of this form can be bounded by a constant. In other words, for the purposes of this analysis the geometric series in this case can be treated as a constant, which means

$$T(n) = \Theta(a^m) = \Theta(a^{\log_b n})$$

$$= \Theta(n^{\log_b a})$$

where the final result was obtained by using logarithm property (A.5) from Appendix A.

When n is not a power of b it can be shown that the use of equation (2.3) requires that for some α, $T(n)$ is monotonically nondecreasing for all $n > \alpha$.

The recursive exponentiation algorithm Power2() presented in Section 1.6 was developed using a divide-and-conquer approach. On each recursive call, Power2()

creates a subproblem that is approximately one-half the size of the previous problem. This continues until the size of the exponent is 1. Then, in the worst case, two multiplications are required to combine the results obtained at each step in the recursive process. Thus, a recurrence relation for the worst-case running time of Power2() is given by

$$T(n) = \begin{cases} \Theta(1), & \text{if } n = 1 \\ T(\lfloor n/2 \rfloor) + 2, & \text{if } n > 1 \end{cases}$$

This equation has the form of recurrence (2.2), with $a = 1$, $b = 2$, and $k = 0$. Since $a = b^k$, we have that $T(n) = \Theta(\log n)$, which agrees with our result from Section 1.6.

2.3.3 Dynamic Programming

Algorithms designed using ***dynamic programming*** are similar to those developed using divide-and-conquer in that both solve a problem by breaking it down into several subproblems that can be solved recursively. The difference between the two is that in the dynamic programming approach, the results obtained from solving smaller subproblems are *reused* in the calculation of larger subproblems. Thus, dynamic programming is a *bottom-up* technique that usually begins by solving the smallest subproblems, saving these results, and then reusing them to solve larger and larger subproblems until the solution to the original problem is obtained. This is in contrast to the divide-and-conquer approach, which solves problems in a *top-down* fashion. In this case the original problem is solved by breaking it down into increasingly smaller subproblems, and no attempt is made to reuse previous results in the solution of any of the subproblems.

It is important to realize that a dynamic programming approach is only justified if there is some degree of overlap in the subproblems. The underlying idea is to avoid calculating the same result twice. This is usually accomplished by constructing a table in memory, and filling it with known results as they are calculated. These results are then used to solve larger subproblems. Note that retrieving a given result from this table (i.e., performing a table look-up) requires $\Theta(1)$ time.

As an example, consider Exercise 1.6 which involved computing the values of the Fibonacci sequence directly from the recurrence relation that defines it, namely

$$F(n) = \begin{cases} 0, & \text{if } n = 0 \\ 1, & \text{if } n = 1 \\ F(n-1) + F(n-2), & \text{if } n > 1 \end{cases} \tag{2.6}$$

Using this brute-force approach, the final result is obtained by adding together $F(n)$ values of 1. That is, this procedure must perform at least $F(n) - 1$ additions. Since the closed form of this recurrence is $F(n) = \frac{1}{\sqrt{5}}(\phi^n - \hat{\phi}^n) = \Theta(\phi^n)$, where $\phi = (1 + \sqrt{5})/2$, the running time of the brute-force approach is superpolynomial. One thing that should be noticed about this solution is that many of the intermediate values are repeatedly calculated. For example, the value of $F(2)$ is calculated twice when computing $F(4)$ using equation (2.6).

The dynamic programming approach to the direct calculation of the Fibonacci sequence avoids the recomputation of intermediate values by storing them in a table when they are initially calculated. A one-dimensional array $f[0..n]$ containing $n+1$ storage locations is set up, and the value of $F(i)$ is stored in $f[i]$ $(i = 0, 1, \ldots, n)$. We start by storing $F(0)$ and $F(1)$. Then, $F(i)$ is computed by adding together $F(i-2)$ and $F(i-1)$ for $i = 2, 3, \ldots, n$. Since $F(i-2)$ and $F(i-1)$ can be retrieved from the table and added together in constant time, the computation of each $F(i)$ is accomplished in $\Theta(1)$ time, and the entire computation requires $\Theta(n)$ time as well as $\Theta(n)$ space. Of course $F(n)$ can be computed in constant time and space using the closed-form solution discussed above. The purpose of this example is only to demonstrate how dynamic programming can be applied.

Dynamic programming is often used to solve optimization problems. In an optimization problem, there are typically a large number of possible solutions, and each has a cost associated with it. The goal is to find a solution that has the smallest cost—this is referred to as an ***optimal solution***. For example, the problem of scheduling tasks that require the use of shared resources (e.g., determining the best order in which to execute a sequence of jobs on a computer) is an optimization problem. If an optimal solution to a problem contains within it optimal solutions to subproblems, and these subproblems overlap, then a dynamic programming approach may be appropriate.

2.3.4 Greedy Algorithms

Another approach that is often used to solve optimization problems is the greedy strategy. Most optimization problems involve a sequence of decisions that must be made appropriately if an optimal solution is to be obtained. In a ***greedy algorithm***, at each decision point the choice that has the smallest immediate (i.e., local) cost is selected, without attempting to look ahead to determine if this choice is part of an optimal solution to the problem as a whole (i.e., a global solution). By locally optimal, we mean a choice that is optimal with respect to some small portion of the total information available about a problem.

The most appealing aspect of greedy algorithms is that they are simple and efficient—typically very little effort is required to compute each local decision. However, for general optimization problems, it is obvious that this strategy will not always produce globally optimal solutions (e.g., see Exercise 2.19). Nevertheless, there are certain optimization problems for which a greedy strategy is in fact guaranteed to yield a globally optimal solution.

Consider the scenario in which a single server (e.g., a bank teller, cashier, or processor) is set up to service a sequence of customers (or tasks). Furthermore, assume that we know in advance how much time is required to service each customer. If our goal is to minimize the average time spent on each customer, then a greedy strategy is to schedule the customers in order of nondecreasing service times. That is, the remaining customer requiring the least amount of time is always serviced next. This strategy does not change the total service time, which is fixed, but it is guaranteed to minimize the average time spent per customer. For example, assume there are three customers labeled C_1, C_2, and C_3 that require 8, 4, and 6 units of time respectively.

TABLE 2.3
Average service times that result from the servicing of customers C_1 through C_3, with service times of 8, 4, and 6 respectively. The optimal solution is given by $C_2C_3C_1$.

Service order	Wait time			Avg. service time
	C_1	C_2	C_3	
$C_1C_2C_3$	8	$8+4$	$8+4+6$	12.7
$C_1C_3C_2$	8	$8+6$	$8+6+4$	13.3
$C_2C_1C_3$	4	$4+8$	$4+8+6$	11.3
$C_2C_3C_1$	4	$4+6$	$4+6+8$	10.7
$C_3C_1C_2$	6	$6+8$	$6+8+4$	12.7
$C_3C_2C_1$	6	$6+4$	$6+4+8$	11.3

The total service time for these customers is $8 + 4 + 6 = 18$ units. In Table 2.3 we calculate the average service time that results for each of the six possible orderings of these customers. In the first case C_1 is serviced first while C_2 and C_3 wait. When C_1 is finished, then C_2 is serviced while C_3 waits, and finally C_3 is serviced. The average service time for this case is 12.7. Notice that the optimal solution for this problem instance is obtained by servicing C_2 first, then C_3, and finally C_1, which yields an average service time of 10.7. This is also the order that the greedy strategy selects.

To show that this strategy will always produce a globally optimal solution for any instance of this problem, consider applying this greedy algorithm to the scheduling of n customers, and assume that the resulting ordering is $C_1, C_2, \ldots, C_n$. According to the greedy algorithm, for any $q > p$, customer C_p is serviced before customer C_q. If we let t_i represent the time required by customer C_i, then the sum of the service times for all customers is:

$$
\begin{aligned}
S(n) &= t_1 + (t_1 + t_2) + (t_1 + t_2 + t_3) + \cdots + (t_1 + t_2 + \cdots + t_n) \\
&= nt_1 + (n-1)t_2 + (n-2)t_3 + \cdots + t_n \\
&= \sum_{i=1}^{n} (n - i + 1)t_i
\end{aligned}
$$

Now suppose for some $q > p$, C_p and C_q are swapped. That is, we service C_q before C_p, even though C_q requires more time than C_p. In this case the sum of the service times for all customers is:

$$
S'(n) = (n - q + 1)t_p + (n - p + 1)t_q + \sum_{\substack{i=1 \\ i \neq p,q}}^{n} (n - i + 1)t_i
$$

Since

$$
\begin{aligned}
S'(n) - S(n) &= (n - q + 1)t_p + (n - p + 1)t_q - (n - p + 1)t_p - (n - q + 1)t_q \\
&= (q - p)(t_q - t_p)
\end{aligned}
$$

$q > p$, and $t_q \geq t_p$, we have shown that $S'(n) - S(n) \geq 0$. That is, $S'(n) \geq S(n)$. Thus if we swap customers C_p and C_q, the average time spent per customer will either stay the same or increase. Furthermore, this result holds if *any* two customers from the optimal ordering are swapped. Therefore, the ordering $C_1, C_2, \ldots, C_n$ selected by the greedy algorithm must be an optimal solution.

2.3.5 Randomized Algorithms

The behavior of a ***randomized algorithm*** is dependent not only on the input data, but also on the values produced by a random number generator. If some portion of an algorithm involves choosing between a number of alternatives, and it is difficult to determine the optimal choice, then it is often more efficient to choose a course of action at random rather than taking the time to determine the best alternative. This is particularly true in cases where there are a large number of choices, most of which are "good."

Although randomizing an algorithm will typically not improve its worst-case running time, it can be used to ensure that no particular input *always* produces the worst-case behavior. Specifically, because the behavior of a randomized algorithm is determined by a sequence of random numbers, it would be unusual for the algorithm to behave the same way on successive runs—even when it is supplied with the same inputs.

2.4 AN EXTENDED EXAMPLE: SORTING

In this example we consider sorting, a topic that arises frequently in programming. The process of sorting involves rearranging a collection of items into ascending or descending order. In computer applications, there are two general classes of sorting techniques—internal and external. ***Internal sorting*** is carried out in main memory, which means that high-speed random-access memory is used. ***External sorting***, on the other hand, makes use of slower secondary storage. External sorting is used when the number of items being sorted is too large to fit into main memory. The bottleneck in external sorting involves the movement of data items between secondary storage and main memory. We will restrict our attention in this example to internal sorting.

Before proceeding, let us define the ***sorting problem*** in more detail. It is assumed that a sequence of n items $a_1, a_2, \ldots, a_n$ is given, and that each item a_i has an associated ***key*** denoted by $key[a_i]$. A ***total ordering relationship*** is assumed to exist on the keys. This means that for any three key values $key[a_l]$, $key[a_m]$, and $key[a_n]$:

1. exactly one of the possibilities $key[a_l] < key[a_m]$, $key[a_l] = key[a_m]$, or $key[a_l] > key[a_m]$ is true; and

2. if $key[a_l] < key[a_m]$ and $key[a_m] < key[a_n]$, then $key[a_l] < key[a_n]$.

The sorting problem then involves rearranging the collection of n items so that their key values form a nondecreasing sequence. That is, an ordering $a_{p(1)}, a_{p(2)}, \ldots, a_{p(n)}$

of the n items must be found such that

$$key[a_{p(1)}] \leq key[a_{p(2)}] \leq \cdots \leq key[a_{p(n)}]$$

The sorting algorithms we will consider are ***comparison based***. This means that any decisions regarding the placement of items in the sorted sequence are based upon pairwise comparisons made between the key values of the items. It is assumed that the n items supplied to a sorting algorithm reside in an array $A[1..n]$, and that any item in this array can be accessed in $\Theta(1)$ time. Thus, the two basic operations that we will be interested in counting include:

1. *comparison*—a binary comparison made between two key values.
2. *swap*—interchanging two items in the array.

A theoretical lower bound for the comparison-based sorting problem is given by the fact that the steps taken during any algorithm that solves this problem can be represented as a binary decision tree. A binary decision tree is a binary tree in which a question is answered at each internal vertex in the tree. If the answer to a question at a given vertex is "yes," then we move to the right child of that vertex; if the answer is "no," then we move to the left child of that vertex. This continues until a leaf vertex is reached. An example of a decision tree that can be used to sort the items a_1, a_2, and a_3 is shown in Figure 2.2. This decision tree is not the only one that could be constructed for sorting these items. However, we reemphasize that the decisions (i.e., comparisons) made by any comparison-based sorting algorithm can be represented as some binary decision tree.

Note that each of the 6 possible permutations of the 3 items is listed as a leaf in the decision tree of Figure 2.2. For the general case of n items, there are $n!$ permutations of the n items, and a decision tree for this case will have at least $n!$

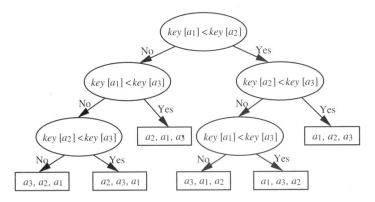

FIGURE 2.2
A binary decision tree that sorts the items a_1, a_2, and a_3. Each internal vertex contains a question (i.e., comparison). For each question, control moves to the right child of the vertex if the answer is yes, and to the left child if the answer is no. Comparisons continue until a leaf vertex is reached. The leaf vertex that terminates this process contains the sorted order of the three items.

leaves. (It is possible to have more than $n!$ leaves if there are paths from the root that lead to different leaves containing the same sorted order.) In Section B.4.2 of Appendix A we show that a perfect binary tree of height h has 2^h leaves. It follows from this that any binary tree of height h will have at most 2^h leaves. Thus, if a binary decision tree has $n!$ leaves, we can solve $n! \leq 2^h$ for h to obtain

$$h \geq \lg(n!)$$

Since the worst-case number of comparisons in any binary decision tree for sorting n numbers is given by the height of the tree, we know that at least $\lg(n!)$ comparisons must be performed. Stirling's approximation allows us to state that $\lg(n!) = \Theta(n \log n)$. Therefore, a lower bound for the comparison-based sorting problem is given by $\Theta(n \log n)$. That is, in the worst case, the running time of the best algorithm for comparison-based sorting must perform at least on the order of $n \lg n$ operations.

We now consider a number of popular sorting algorithms. First we will discuss a simple method, called insertion sort, that requires $O(n^2)$ time to sort n items. This method is most appropriate when dealing with small data sets, or with data sets that have some special structure. The sorting performed by insertion sort occurs in place. This means that the final sorted result will reside in the input array, and that only $\Theta(1)$ additional memory locations are used—in addition to those used to store the n items. Next we will examine two advanced sorting methods that are more appropriate for large data sets. The first of these, mergesort, will be shown to have a running time that matches the theoretical lower bound of $\Theta(n \log n)$; however, this sorting does not occur in place. Finally, we will investigate quicksort, a popular in place sorting algorithm that has a worst-case running time of $\Theta(n^2)$, but on average only requires $\Theta(n \log n)$ time. In subsequent chapters, we will encounter a variety of additional sorting methods.

2.4.1 Insertion Sort

Given an array $A[0..n-1]$ of items, the strategy in an insertion sort is to make n passes through the array. On the i-th pass, the item stored in $A[i-1]$ is moved to its proper location in $A[0..i-1]$. Thus, after the i-th pass, the items stored in $A[0..i-1]$ are in sorted order, and after n passes, the entire array will be sorted. An algorithm for insertion sort is given below. The parameter $A[\ ]$ is assumed to be a pointer to $A[0..n-1]$.

```
Insertion-Sort(item A[ ])
1    for i ← 1 to n − 1 do
2        for j ← i to 1 do in steps of −1
3            if key[A[j]] < key[A[j−1]] then
4                swap A[j] and A[j−1]
```

The progress of Insertion-Sort() on a specific array is demonstrated in Figure 2.3. Each iteration of the loop on line 1 of Insertion-Sort() is considered a pass. Notice that this algorithm actually makes $n - 1$ passes through the array, and on the k-th pass, the inner loop on line 2 performs k comparisons (i.e., on the first pass the

initially:	8	7	3	5	1
after pass 1:	7	8 ⋮	3	5	1
after pass 2:	3	7	8 ⋮	5	1
after pass 3:	3	5	7	8 ⋮	1
after pass 4:	1	3	5	7	8 ⋮

FIGURE 2.3
The operation of Insertion-Sort() on the array $A[0..4] = <8, 7, 3, 5, 1>$. The numbers appearing to the left of the dashed line after any given pass are in sorted order, while the numbers appearing to the right of the dashed line have not yet been tested by the algorithm.

loop variable $i = 1$, and one comparison is performed; on the second pass the loop variable $i = 2$, and two comparisons are performed; and so forth).

ANALYSIS. The number of comparisons performed on line 3 of Insertion-Sort() is given by

$$\sum_{i=1}^{n-1}\sum_{j=1}^{i} 1 = \sum_{i=1}^{n-1} i = \frac{n(n-1)}{2}$$

In the worst case, the items are supplied in reverse sorted order, and every comparison performed on line 3 yields a swap on line 4. That is, on the i-th pass, the inner loop must perform i swaps to move the $(i+1)$-th item all the way down to $A[1]$. In this case the total number of comparisons and swaps is $n(n-1) = \Theta(n^2)$.

In the best case, the items are supplied in sorted order, none of the comparisons will result in a swap, and the total number of operations is $n(n-1)/2$. Thus the running time of Insertion-Sort() is $\Theta(n^2)$. However, in practice we find that the small amount of overhead associated with this algorithm allows it to outperform more sophisticated $O(n \log n)$ algorithms when n is sufficiently small.

2.4.2   Mergesort

The mergesort algorithm uses the divide-and-conquer strategy to sort the n items in $A[0..n-1]$. First the array is divided into two subarrays, one containing $\lfloor n/2 \rfloor$ items, and the other containing $\lceil n/2 \rceil$ items. These subarrays are then sorted by recursively calling the mergesort algorithm—this is the conquer phase of the algorithm. Finally, the two sorted subarrays are combined (i.e., merged together) to produce the final sorted array. A mergesort algorithm is given below:

```
Mergesort(item A[ ], integer a, integer b)
1   if a < b then
2       p ← ⌊(a + b)/2⌋
3       Mergesort(A, a, p)
4       Mergesort(A, p + 1, b)
5       Merge(A, a, p, b)
```

where a and b are the starting and ending indices, respectively, of the portion of the array we wish to sort.

An algorithm that can be used to merge the two sorted subarrays, as required on line 5, is shown below. This algorithm is said to perform **two-way merging** since it takes two sorted subarrays as input and combines them to produce a sorted output array. This is accomplished by scanning $A[a..b]$ from the left using variables i and j. The values a and $p+1$ are initially assigned to i and j, respectively. At each step, the larger of $A[i]$ and $A[j]$ is stored in the auxiliary array $B[0..b-a]$. It is assumed that the items in subarrays $A[a..p]$ and $A[p+1..b]$ are in sorted order. The specifics of the algorithm are given below:

```
Merge(item A[ ], integer a, integer p, integer b)
1   k ← 0;    i ← a;     j ← p + 1;    n ← b − a
2   while  i < p + 1  and  j < b + 1  do
3       if  key[A[i]] < key[A[j]]  then
4           B[k] ← A[i];    i ← i + 1;    k ← k + 1
5       else
6           B[k] ← A[j];     j ← j + 1;    k ← k + 1
7   while  i < p + 1  do      ▷ copy any leftover portion of A[a..p]
8       B[k] ← A[i];    i ← i + 1;    k ← k + 1
9   while  j < b + 1  do      ▷ copy any leftover portion of A[p+1..b]
10      B[k] ← A[j];     j ← j + 1;    k ← k + 1
11  i ← a
12  for  k ← 0  to  n  do
13      A[i] ← B[k];    i ← i + 1
```

Since each of the loops in this algorithm involves n iterations, and only a constant number of operations are performed during each iteration, the running time of Merge() on an array of size n is $\Theta(n)$.

ANALYSIS. Since Mergesort() is recursive, we must come up with a recurrence relation that describes its overall running time on an input of size n in terms of its running time on smaller inputs. Specifically, we must determine the time required by each of the three phases of this divide-and-conquer algorithm. The divide phase takes $\Theta(1)$ time since all we need to do is calculate the middle item in the array. The conquer phase involves solving two subproblems, one having a size of $\lfloor n/2 \rfloor$, and the other a size of $\lceil n/2 \rceil$. Our analysis remains valid if we assume that each subproblem is simply of size $n/2$. We have already shown that the solutions to these subproblems can be combined in $\Theta(n)$ time using Merge(). Therefore, the running time of Mergesort() is given by

$$T(n) = \begin{cases} \Theta(1), & \text{if } n = 1 \\ 2T(n/2) + \Theta(n), & \text{if } n > 1 \end{cases}$$

This recurrence relation has the form of equation (2.2) with $a = 2$, $b = 2$ and $k = 1$. Therefore, equation (2.3) can be used to determine that the running time of Mergesort() is $\Theta(n \log n)$.

2.4.3 Quicksort

The quicksort algorithm also uses a divide-and-conquer strategy to sort the n items in $A[1..n]$. However, unlike the mergesort algorithm, the nonrecursive part of the quicksort algorithm involves constructing subinstances through a partitioning technique rather than combining partial solutions through merging. Specifically, quicksort partitions A into subarrays that can be sorted independently. A specific array element $A[p]$ called the **pivot** is selected, and items are rearranged so that the key values of all items in $A[1..k-1]$ are less than or equal to $key[A[p]]$, the key values of all items in $A[k+1..n]$ are greater than $key[A[p]]$, and the pivot element is moved to $A[k]$. The subarrays on either side of the pivot can now be sorted independently by recursive calls of the algorithm as shown in the following procedure:

```
Quicksort(item A[ ], integer a, integer b)
1   if  a < b  then
2       k ← Partition(A, a, b)
3       Quicksort(A, a, k − 1)
4       Quicksort(A, k + 1, b)
```

where a and b are the starting and ending indices, respectively, of the portion of the array we wish to sort.

The Partition() procedure is responsible for selecting the pivot element and rearranging the array elements as discussed above. A common approach is to select the first element in the array as the pivot, and then assign the values $a + 1$ and b to the variables *lower* and *upper*, respectively. The value of *lower* is then incremented until $key[A[lower]] > pivot$, and *upper* is decremented until $key[A[upper]] \leq pivot$. Next $A[lower]$ and $A[upper]$ are swapped. This process continues until *lower* $>$ *upper*, at which point $A[a]$ and $A[upper]$ are swapped to put the pivot element in its proper location. A procedure that implements this algorithm is given below, and a demonstration of its operation on an array is given in Figure 2.4.

```
Partition(item A[ ], integer a, integer b)
1    pivot ← key[A[a]];    lower ← a + 1;    upper ← b
2    do
3        while  key[A[lower]] ≤ pivot  and  lower ≤ upper  do
4            lower ← lower + 1
5        while  key[A[upper]] > pivot  and  lower ≤ upper  do
6            upper ← upper − 1
7        if  lower ≤ upper  then
8            swap A[lower] and A[upper]
9            lower ← lower + 1;    upper ← upper − 1
10   while  lower ≤ upper
11   swap A[a] and A[upper]    ▷ move the pivot to its proper location
12   return upper
```

Notice that *lower* and *upper* scan the array from opposite ends, and that the algorithm halts after they cross. Thus the outermost loop in the Partition() procedure can iterate no more than $\Theta(n)$ times on a subarray containing n items. Furthermore, the number of operations performed on each iteration can be upper bounded by a constant. This means that the running time of Partition() is $\Theta(n)$.

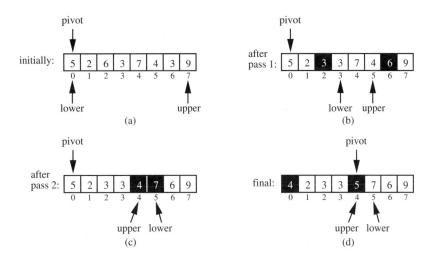

FIGURE 2.4

The operation of Partition() on the array $A[0..7] = <5, 2, 6, 3, 7, 4, 3, 9>$. (**a**) The initial arrangement. (**b**) After one pass of the outermost loop. The items shown in the shaded array locations where swapped at the end of this pass. (**c**) After two passes of the outermost loop. Note that since *upper* < *lower*, control will exit from the outermost loop. (**d**) The final arrangement of the array after the swap on line 12 of Partition() places the pivot in its proper location. At this point, all of the items to the left of *pivot* are less than or equal to *pivot*, and all of the items to the right of *pivot* are greater than or equal to *pivot*.

ANALYSIS. The running time of Quicksort() is dependent upon how evenly the pivot splits the array on each call to Partition(). In the worst case, each partitioning of an array of n elements will result in the pivot ending up in either the first or last array location. Thus at the end of each partitioning step, the subarrays will be unbalanced, with $n - 1$ elements on one side of the pivot, and no elements on the other side. Since the partitioning itself takes $\Theta(n)$ time, the recurrence relation for the worst-case running time is

$$T(n) = \begin{cases} \Theta(1), & \text{if } n = 1 \\ T(n-1) + \Theta(n), & \text{if } n > 1 \end{cases}$$

Unfolding this recurrence, we obtain

$$T(n) = T(n-1) + \Theta(n)$$
$$= T(n-2) + \Theta(n-1) + \Theta(n)$$
$$= \sum_{i=1}^{n} \Theta(i)$$
$$= \Theta\left(\sum_{i=1}^{n} i\right)$$
$$= \Theta(n^2)$$

Thus the running time of Quicksort() is $O(n^2)$. This worst-case running time will occur if Quicksort() is supplied with an initially sorted input array.

In the best case, each partitioning will split the array into two balanced sub-arrays—one containing $\lfloor n/2 \rfloor$ elements, and the other containing $\lceil n/2 \rceil$ elements. Our analysis remains valid if we assume that each subarray is simply of size $n/2$. The recurrence relation for the best case is then

$$T(n) = \begin{cases} \Theta(1), & \text{if } n = 1 \\ 2T(n/2) + \Theta(n), & \text{if } n > 1 \end{cases}$$

This is the same recurrence relation that describes the running time of mergesort. Thus the running time of Quicksort() is $\Omega(n \log n)$.

To determine the average time required by quicksort, assume that each of the $n!$ initial permutations of the array elements are equally likely, and let $T_{av}(n)$ be the average time taken by quicksort to sort an array of size n. The probability of any one element being chosen as the pivot is $1/n$. Selection of the p-th element will leave us with two subarrays of size $p - 1$ and $n - p$, respectively. Since on the order of n operations are executed during the partitioning step, we may write the following recurrence relation for the average time required by quicksort:

$$T_{av}(n) = cn + \frac{1}{n} \sum_{p=1}^{n} \left[T_{av}(p - 1) + T_{av}(n - p) \right] \tag{2.7}$$

where c is a positive constant. The second term on the right hand side of this equation includes the time required to sort all possible partitions, times the probability of each partition.

Noting that $\sum_{p=1}^{n} T_{av}(p-1) = \sum_{p=1}^{n} T_{av}(n-p)$ we can rewrite equation (2.7) as

$$T_{av}(n) = cn + \frac{2}{n} \sum_{p=1}^{n} T_{av}(p - 1) \tag{2.8}$$

This recurrence relation is said to have **full history** since it involves all of the terms $T_{av}(\alpha)$, $0 \leq \alpha \leq n - 1$. We do not consider how to handle this type of recurrence relation in Appendix A.4; however, we can reduce it to a form we do consider (i.e., containing a fixed number of terms) by performing a few simple manipulations. The general idea is to cancel all but one of the terms in the summation in equation (2.8). This can be accomplished by subtracting the quantity

$$T_{av}(n - 1) = c(n - 1) + \frac{2}{n - 1} \sum_{p=1}^{n-1} T_{av}(p - 1) \tag{2.9}$$

from equation (2.8). In order to make the algebra work properly, we will also need to perform some multiplications. Specifically, if we multiply both sides of equation (2.8) by n, and both sides of equation (2.9 by $(n - 1)$, and then subtract the two, we obtain

$$n T_{av}(n) = (n + 1) \cdot T_{av}(n - 1) + c(2n - 1)$$

The difficulty with the previous recurrence is that its coefficients are not constant; however, if we divide both sides of the equation by $n(n + 1)$ and unfold the resulting recurrence relation we get

$$\frac{T_{av}(n)}{n+1} = \frac{T_{av}(n-1)}{n} + \frac{c(2n-1)}{n(n+1)}$$

$$= \frac{T_{av}(n-2)}{n-1} + \frac{c(2(n-1)-1)}{(n-1)n} + \frac{c(2n-1)}{n(n+1)}$$

$$= \frac{T_{av}(2)}{3} + \sum_{i=3}^{n} \frac{c(2i-1)}{i(i+1)} \tag{2.10}$$

Equation (2.10) can be solved using techniques discussed in Appendix A. Specifically, since we are only concerned with an asymptotic bound, we can ignore the constant term $T_{av}(2)/3$, and concentrate on bounding the summation. The fact that $f(i) = c(2i-1)/i(i+1)$ is a monotonically decreasing function for $i > 1$ allows us to use the integral approximation technique discussed in Appendix A.3 to arrive at

$$\int_{3}^{n+1} \frac{c(2x-1)}{x(x+1)} dx \leq \sum_{i=3}^{n} \frac{c(2i-1)}{i(i+1)} \leq \int_{2}^{n} \frac{c(2x-1)}{x(x+1)} dx$$

Performing the necessary integrations allows us to determine that $\sum_{i=3}^{n} \frac{c(2i-1)}{i(i+1)} = \Theta(\log n)$. Finally, multiplying equation (2.10) by $(n+1)$ yields $T_{av}(n) = \Theta(n \log n)$.

Exercises 2.10 and 2.11 demonstrate that this asymptotic bound holds even in situations where the split produced by Partition() yields subarrays that are quite unbalanced. Furthermore, in practice the constant factor hidden in this asymptotic expression is typically smaller than the one for mergesort. This explains why quicksort is the preferred sorting method in applications that require a sorting algorithm that is usually very fast, but on occasion can have a longer running time.

Note that since the median of an array of n elements can be found in $\Theta(n)$ time (see Exercise 2.14), we can guarantee a running time of $\Theta(n \log n)$ for Quicksort() if we modify Partition() so that it first chooses the median element as the pivot before performing the partitioning. Unfortunately, the overhead associated with this approach makes it unsuitable in practice. However, we can significantly improve our chances of obtaining a good pivot, with little increase in overhead, if we use the median of a small sample taken from the array. One common approach is to choose the median of the first, middle, and last elements—this can be accomplished in $\Theta(1)$ time. The chosen element is then swapped with the first element and becomes the pivot. This approach is known as ***median-of-three partitioning***. Another technique that can be used to lessen the overhead associated with Quicksort() is to use Insertion-Sort() on subarrays when they become small enough (e.g., less than 20 elements).

EXERCISES

2.1. In general, why is the derivation of a theoretical lower bound for a problem's running time difficult to derive?

2.2. How does the running time of the matrix multiplication algorithm given in Section 1.2 compare to the obvious lower bound for the matrix multiplication problem?

2.3. What are the running times of the following procedures as a function of n? Use asymptotic notation, making your bounds as tight as possible, and state whether the procedure runs in polynomial or superpolynomial time.

(a) Moo(positive integer n)
    for $i \leftarrow 1$ **to** $n-1$ **do**
        for $j \leftarrow i+1$ **to** n **do**
            ▷ some statements requiring $\Theta(1)$ time

(b) Goo(positive integer n)
    if $n = 1$ **then**
        return 1
    else
        return Goo($n - 1$) + Goo($n - 1$)

(c) Gai(positive integer n, positive integer r)
    result $\leftarrow 0$
    for $x \leftarrow 1$ **to** n **do**
        result $\leftarrow$ *result* + Power2(x, r)
            ▷ uses Power2() from Section 1.6
    return *result*

(d) Pan(positive integer n)
    result $\leftarrow 0$
    for $i \leftarrow 2$ **to** n **do**
        result $\leftarrow$ *result* + $i \cdot$ Foo(i)
            ▷ Foo(i) requires $\Theta(\log i)$ time
    return *result*

(e) Homer(positive integer n)
    if $n = 1$ **then**
        return 1
    else
        temp $\leftarrow$ Homer($\lceil n/2 \rceil$) + Homer($\lfloor n/2 \rfloor$)
        for $i \leftarrow 1$ **to** n **do**
            temp $\leftarrow$ *temp* + i
        return *temp*

(f) Marge(positive integer n)
    if $n = 1$ **then**
        return 1
    else
        temp $\leftarrow$ Marge($\lceil n/2 \rceil$) + Marge($\lfloor n/2 \rfloor$)
        for $i \leftarrow 1$ **to** n **do**
            for $j \leftarrow 1$ **to** n **do**
                temp $\leftarrow$ *temp* + $i \cdot j$
        return *temp*

(g) Bart(positive integer n)
    if $n = 1$ **then**
        return 1
    else
        result $\leftarrow 0$
        for $i \leftarrow 2$ **to** n **do**
            result $\leftarrow$ *result* + Bart($i - 1$)
        return *result*

2.4. Construct tables of the forms given in Tables 2.1 and 2.2 for algorithms with time complexity functions $\lg n$, $n \lg n$, and $n^{\lg n}$.

2.5. What is the running time of the inorder tree traversal algorithm given in Appendix B.4.1?

2.6. Is it possible that for a particular input instance, a $O(n^2)$ algorithm that performs a specific task can actually run faster than a $O(n \log n)$ algorithm that performs the same task?

2.7. A sorting algorithm is said to be **stable** if it preserves the relative order of items with equal key values during the sort. For example, if an alphabetized class list were sorted by grade, a stable sorting algorithm would yield an output in which students receiving the same grade would appear in alphabetical order, while a non-stable sorting algorithm is not guaranteed to produce an output that has this property. Which of the sorting algorithms discussed in Section 2.4 are stable and which are non-stable?

2.8. Graphically depict the step-by-step progress of Merge() on the array $A[a..b] = \langle 3, 4, 7, 8, 2, 5, 6 \rangle$.

2.9. Write pseudocode Quicksort() and Partition() procedures that incorporate all of the improvements discussed at the end of Section 2.4.3.

2.10. Suppose that the Partition() procedure used by Quicksort() always produced a 99-to-1 proportional split. Then the running time of Quicksort() would be described by

$$T(n) = T(99n/100) + T(n/100) + \Theta(n)$$

Find a Θ-notation expression that describes the running time of Quicksort() for this situation.

2.11. Assume that the Partition() procedure used by Quicksort() alternatively produced, on successive calls, the best and worst possible splits. What would the running time of Quicksort() be in this case?

2.12. If you have solved the previous two exercises, you are probably convinced that most of the choices Partition() can make when selecting the pivot will work well. This is a good argument for picking the pivot at random. Develop a randomized version of the quicksort algorithm that chooses the pivot in this manner.

2.13. The following algorithm, known as **selection sort**, can be used to sort an array $A[0..n-1]$ of n items:

```
Selection-Sort(item A[ ])
1   for i ← 0 to n − 2 do
2       small ← i
3           for j ← i + 1 to n − 1 do
4               if key[A[j]] < key[A[small]] then
5                   small ← j
6           if i ≠ small then
7               swap A[i] and A[small]
```

Note that on the i-th pass of the outermost loop, the i-th smallest item is placed in its proper location in $A[0..n-1]$. Depict the progress of Selection-Sort() on the array $A[0..4] = \langle 8, 7, 3, 5, 1 \rangle$. What is the worst-case running time of this algorithm?

2.14. In the **selection problem** we are given an array $A[0..n-1]$, and are asked to find the k-th smallest element in the array, where $1 \leq k \leq n$. For example, the 1-st smallest is the minimum, the n-th smallest is the maximum, and the $(n+1)/2$-th smallest element is the median (assuming n is odd). If n is even, then there are two medians; these are the $n/2$-th and $(n/2+1)$-th smallest elements.

(a) An algorithm similar to Partition() can be developed for the selection problem; however, unlike Partition(), only one side of a partition needs to be examined at each step. Show that the average running time of such an algorithm is $O(n)$.

(b) If we are careful about how we choose the partition, we can obtain an algorithm for which running time is linear in the worst case. Consider an algorithm which performs the following steps:

1. Divide the n elements of A into $\lfloor n/5 \rfloor$ groups of 5 elements each, and one group made up of the remaining n mod 5 elements.
2. Find the median of each group by using the selection sort algorithm, and picking the middle element. (If the last group has an even number of elements, take the larger of the two medians.) This yields a list M of $\lceil n/5 \rceil$ medians.
3. Find the median of M and call it m, using the same approach as in step 2.
4. Use Partition(), modified to take the pivot element as input, to partition A around m.
5. Let i be the number of elements on the low side of the partition. If $k \le i$, perform the previous steps recursively on $A[0..i]$; otherwise, perform the previous steps recursively on $A[i+1..n-1]$.

Develop a recurrence relation for the worst-case running time of this algorithm, and use constructive induction to show that the closed form of your recurrence relation is $O(n)$.

2.15. In Section 1.4.1 we presented a recursive procedure for solving the Tower of Hanoi problem.

(a) If we denote a basic operation as the act of moving a single disk from one peg to another, then what is the time complexity of the Tower algorithm? Is this algorithm tractable or intractable?

(b) Legend has it that at the beginning of time, God placed a tower of 64 gold disks on top of the first of three diamond needles, and ordained that a group of Brahman priests should transfer them to the third needle using the previously stated rules for the Tower of Hanoi. When the priests complete their task, the tower will crumble and the world will end. If we assume that the priests can transfer a disk from one needle to another in one second, how long will it take them to complete their task?

2.16. Consider the problem of evaluating an n-th degree polynomial at the point $x = x_0$. For this problem we are given a set of n coefficients $a_0, a_1, \ldots, a_{n-1}$, as well as a value for x_0, and we are asked to compute

$$p(x) = a_n x^n + a_{n-1} x^{n-1} + \cdots + a_1 x + a_0 \quad \text{for } x = x_0 \quad (2.11)$$

(a) Write an algorithm that implements Equation (2.11). What is the time complexity of this algorithm?

(b) Using **Horner's rule** we may express (2.11) as

$$p(x) = a_0 + x(a_1 + x(a_2 + \cdots + x(a_{n-1} + x a_n) \cdots)) \quad (2.12)$$

Write an algorithm that implements Equation (2.12), and compare its time complexity to the algorithm developed in part (a).

2.17. Discuss how you might develop a greedy algorithm for playing chess. Would you expect this algorithm to be very successful against capable human opponents?

2.18. Consider the problem of making change for n cents using the least number of coins.

(a) Assuming you have pennies, nickels, dimes, and quarters, write a greedy algorithm that will always solve this problem in an optimal fashion.

(*b*) Is there a set of coin denominations for which the algorithm you developed in part (a) does not return an optimal solution?

2.19. In the *traveling salesman problem*, we are given a set of n cities, along with the distances between any two pairs of cities in the set, and we are asked to find the shortest path (i.e., tour) that goes through each city exactly once and returns to the city from which the tour started. Assuming the input data is provided in the form of a two-dimensional array $d[1..n, 1..n]$, with the value in row i and column j, $d[i, j]$, indicating the distance between city i and j, solve the following problems. You may also assume that $d[i, i] = 0$ and $d[i, j] = d[j, i]$, for $i, j = 1, 2, \ldots, n$.

(*a*) Develop a brute-force algorithm that will always solve this problem. What is the time complexity of your algorithm?

(*b*) Develop an algorithm that attempts to solve this problem by constructing a tour using a greedy strategy that always adds the next closest city to the tour. What is the time complexity of your algorithm? Give an example in which your greedy algorithm does not produce an optimal solution.

(*c*) Use dynamic programming to develop an algorithm that will always solve this problem. What is the time complexity of your algorithm?

2.20. *Strassen's matrix multiplication algorithm* uses a divide-and-conquer approach to multiply two $n \times n$ matrices. If we assume that n is a power of two, then two $n \times n$ matrices can be multiplied by breaking them up into four square submatrices of size $\frac{n}{2} \times \frac{n}{2}$ as follows:

$$\begin{bmatrix} A_{11} & A_{12} \\ A_{21} & A_{22} \end{bmatrix} \cdot \begin{bmatrix} B_{11} & B_{12} \\ B_{21} & B_{22} \end{bmatrix} = \begin{bmatrix} S_1 + S_2 - S_4 + S_6 & S_4 + S_5 \\ S_6 + S_7 & S_2 - S_3 + S_5 - S_7 \end{bmatrix}$$

where the As and Bs are square submatrices of size $\frac{n}{2}$, and

$$S_1 = (A_{12} - A_{22}) \cdot (B_{21} + B_{22})$$
$$S_2 = (A_{11} + A_{22}) \cdot (B_{11} + B_{22})$$
$$S_3 = (A_{11} - A_{21}) \cdot (B_{11} + B_{12})$$
$$S_4 = (A_{11} + A_{12}) \cdot B_{22}$$
$$S_5 = A_{11} \cdot (B_{12} - B_{22})$$
$$S_6 = A_{22} \cdot (B_{21} - B_{11})$$
$$S_7 = (A_{21} + A_{22}) \cdot B_{11}$$

The matrices are recursively broken up in this fashion until the base case $n = 2$ is reached. At this point the partial results are combined in order to produce the final result.

(*a*) Verify that this algorithm produces the correct result for 2×2 matrices. Exactly how many multiplications and additions/subtractions are required to obtain this result? Exactly how many multiplications and additions are required to multiply two 2×2 matrices using the straightforward $\Theta(n^3)$ algorithm?

(*b*) Derive a recurrence relation for the running time of Strassen's algorithm, and determine its closed-form. (Hint: At each step of this algorithm, seven $\frac{n}{2} \times \frac{n}{2}$ matrix multiplications, and a number of matrix additions/subtractions, are performed. Strassen's algorithm is applied recursively to each of these seven matrix multiplications, while all of the matrix additions/subtractions can be computed in $\Theta(n^2)$ time at each step.)

(c) Generalize Strassen's algorithm to handle square matrices whose sizes are not a power of 2, while at the same time maintaining the efficiency of the original algorithm.

2.21. In this exercise we consider a dynamic programming approach to the ***matrix-chain multiplication*** problem. Suppose we wish to compute the product M of a chain of n matrices: $M = M_1 M_2 M_3 \cdots M_n$, where any adjoining pair of matrices in the chain are assumed to be conformal for multiplication. Since matrix multiplication is an associative operation, the order in which these operations are performed will not affect the final result; however, the order can dramatically affect the number of scalar operations required. We will refer to each possible ordering as a ***parenthesization***. For example, one possible parenthesization for $n = 4$ is $M = (M_1((M_2 M_3)M_4))$. In this example, the product $M_{2,3} = M_2 M_3$ is computed first, followed by the product $M_{2,4} = M_{2,3}M_4$, and the final result is obtained by calculating the product of M_1 and $M_{2,4}$. Note that the optimal solution to this problem contains within it optimal solutions to subproblems. Specifically, if the best way of multiplying all matrices requires that we make the first "cut" between the i-th and $(i+1)$-th matrices (i.e., the final matrix multiplication in computing $M_1 M_2 \cdots M_n$ optimally is $M_{1,i} \cdot M_{i+1,n}$) then the optimal solution also requires that the subproducts $M_1 M_2 \cdots M_i$ and $M_{i+1}M_{i+2} \cdots M_n$ be calculated in an optimal fashion.

(a) Suppose we multiply pairs of matrices using the algorithm given in Section 1.2. How many scalar operations are required by each of the possible parenthesizations when $n = 4$? Assume M_1 through M_4 have dimensions (14×4), (4×87), (87×3), and (3×35), respectively.

(b) Discuss why it is not practical to solve this problem using a brute-force approach that finds the best parenthesization by separately calculating the number of scalar operations necessary in each possible parenthesization. (Hint: the value of the recurrence $T(n) = \sum_{i=1}^{n-1} T(i)T(n-i)$ is $\Omega(4^n/n^2)$.)

(c) Let $m[1..n, 1..n]$ be a two-dimensional array, and let element $m[i, j]$, $i \le j$, store the minimum number of scalar operations required to compute $M_i M_{i+1} \cdots M_j$. Define diagonal s of this array to be those elements $m[i, j]$ for which $j - i = s$. Starting with diagonal 1, show how the elements in diagonals $s = 2, 3, \ldots, n - 1$ can all be assigned their proper values in $\Theta(n^3)$ time. Demonstrate your approach on the matrices given in part (a). (Hint: here you should use the fact that this problem has overlapping subproblems.)

(d) Let $r[1..n, 1..n]$ be a two-dimensional array, and let element $r[i, j]$ store the value of k such that the optimal parenthesization of $M_i M_{i+1} \cdots M_j$ cuts the chain of matrices between M_k and M_{k+1}. Discuss how the elements in r can be computed at the same time the elements in m are being computed. Demonstrate your approach on the matrices given in part (a).

(e) Write a recursive pseudocode procedure that accepts a chain of matrices and the array r as input, and returns the product of the chain of matrices.

CHAPTER NOTES

An introductory level book that discusses Algorithmics in an easily accessible and engaging manner is Harel [73]. This text also includes a detailed discussion of the halting problem. A proof that no algorithm exists (or ever will) to solve the halting problem is supplied by Turing [151]. Analysis of algorithm performance based on running time was advocated by Knuth [84]. The use of asymptotic analysis as a means of comparing the relative performance of algorithms was popularized by Aho, Hopcroft, and Ullman [4]. For a discussion of the use of asymptotic notation in the analysis of algorithms see Knuth [86]. Other well-known texts that provide a treatment of the general topic of algorithms are Baase [11], Brassard and Bratley [23], Cormen, Leiserson, and Rivest [36], Horowitz and Sahni [76], Moret and Shapiro [105], Reingold, Nievergelt, and Deo [126], and Sedgewick [135]. The textbook by Motwani and Raghavan [108] treats the subject of randomized algorithms. The standard Complexity Theory reference is Garey and Johnson [63]; a more recent textbook in this area is Papadimitriou [115].

For a proof of equation (2.3) when n is not a power of b see Cormen, Leiserson, and Rivest [36]. Their result is actually more general than equation (2.3) because they replace the term $\Theta(n^k)$ in equation (2.3) with an arbitrary asymptotically positive function.

A very elegant theory has been developed, based on a discrete structure called a *matroid*, that is helpful in characterizing the types of problems that can be solved with greedy algorithms. For references on this subject, consult Lawler [90], Moret, Helman, and Shapiro [104], and Papadimitriou and Steiglitz [116].

Sorting is one of the oldest and most studied problems in computer science. A compendium of sorting techniques along with many interesting historical notes circa 1973 is given in Knuth [85]. Knuth attributes the insertion sort, selection sort, and mergesort algorithms to computing folklore; while the quicksort algorithm is attributed to Hoare [74].

Strassen's matrix multiplication algorithm is discussed in [142]. Cohen and Roth [32] show that n needs to be as large as 100, and the matrix dense, before Strassens's algorithm will multiply an $n \times n$ matrix faster than the straightforward $\Theta(n^3)$ algorithm.

CHAPTER
3

DATA STRUCTURES AND C PROGRAMS

In this chapter we present a number of important aspects of the C programming language, before discussing object-oriented programming and the C++ programming language in the next chapter. Since C++ is essentially a superset of the C programming language, it is important to understand the concepts discussed here. These concepts will surface repeatedly in our discussions of the data structures used in subsequent chapters. Furthermore, the capabilities offered by C and C++ are synergistic in the sense that the C language is "close to the machine"—allowing programmers to specify their intended actions in a simple manner that yields efficient code; while the facilities added to C in order to create C++ provide a language that is "close to the problem to be solved"—allowing programmers to express high level concepts directly and concisely.

In this chapter we discuss the use of preprocessor directives, pointers, and user-defined types in C and C++. It is assumed that the reader has a basic understanding of the C/C++ programming languages (see the notes at the end of this and the next chapter for C/C++ language references). We then demonstrate how these features can be used to implement the MATRIX ADT defined in Section 1.1.1.

3.1 THE PREPROCESSOR

C/C++ provide a number of language features through the use of a ***preprocessor*** which is automatically invoked prior to compilation. Specifically, the C/C++ preprocessor is used to modify source code before it is actually compiled. The two most commonly used preprocessor directives are `#define` and `#include`. The `#define` directive, which has the following form, is used to perform macro substitution:

```
#define   name   replacement text
```

This directs the preprocessor to replace every occurrence of the token *name* in the source file with *replacement text*.

If a constant value is used repeatedly in a source code file, then it is a good idea to give this constant a name using `#define`. This has a number of advantages. First, it is often easier, and less likely to cause errors, if we type the name of the constant rather than the constant value itself. In addition, using a name for a constant usually makes the source code more readable. Furthermore, if we wish to change the value associated with this constant name, then only a modification of the `#define` directive is required—the preprocessor ensures that this change is automatically reflected in the source code when it is recompiled. This has the desirable effect of localizing the change in the source code to a single statement. The major disadvantage of using `#define` in this manner is that it may yield erroneous results if parentheses are not used properly. For example, consider the preprocessor statement

```
#define  PI  0.14159 + 3.0
```

Due to the precedence of the operators involved, the use of this definition in the C/C++ expression

```
a = 2 * PI
```

would result in 3.28318 being assigned to a, instead of 6.28318. In C++ programs, the availability of the `const` keyword makes the use of #define in the manner discussed above obsolete.[†] This issue is discussed in more detail in the next chapter.

It is also possible to define macros that take arguments. For example, the following statement defines a macro that computes the absolute value of its argument:[‡]

```
#define abs(x) ((x) > 0 ? (x) : −(x))
```

If a, b, and c are variables, then the following statement appearing in the source code

```
c = abs(a−b);
```

[†]The `const` keyword is also supported by ANSI C compilers; however, the manner in which constant data objects are linked precludes their placement in header files. Thus, it is usually necessary to use #define for value substitution in ANSI C programs.

[‡]The syntax of the ?: operator is as follows: In the expression *exp1* ? *exp2* : *exp3*, first *exp1* is evaluated. If it is true, then *exp2* is evaluated, and the result is the value of the expression; otherwise, *exp3* is evaluated, and its result is the value of the expression.

would be expanded by the preprocessor as

```
c = ((a-b) > 0 ? (a-b) : -(a-b));
```

Although the use of `abs()` looks like a function call, it actually expands into in-line code. This means that there is no function-call overhead associated with the use of `abs()`. In many cases, the savings can be significant, if `abs()` were implemented as a simple function, the function-call overhead might be more costly than the actual computations performed in the function. Once again, the major problem associated with using `#define` in this fashion is that it can lead to problems if parentheses are not used properly (see Exercise 3.2 for an example). We will see in the next chapter that with C++, these types of macros are no longer necessary—their use is made obsolete by the availability of inline functions.

The other way in which preprocessor directives are commonly used is to perform file inclusion. If a program consists of several source files, then the usual practice is to collect all external variable declarations, function prototypes, and `#define` directives for that program in a separate file, called a ***header file***. This header file can then be included in the source files using the `#include` preprocessor directive. The reason for using header files in this fashion is that it guarantees that each of the source files in a given program will receive the same set of external declarations and definitions. The preprocessor replaces any statement of the form

```
#include <filename>
```

with the actual contents of the file *filename*. An alternate form is

```
#include "filename"
```

The only difference in the way the preprocessor interprets these two is in the order in which it searches for *filename*. If the header file name is enclosed in angle brackets, then it is assumed to be a standard header file (i.e., a header file supplied with the C/C++ compiler), and the search proceeds in some predefined order of directories. If the header file is enclosed in quotes, then the file is assumed to be a user-supplied header file, and the search begins in the current directory followed by a search of directories in some predefined order. In addition, the convention is to use a `.h` suffix in header file names.

It is not uncommon for a header file to itself contain a number of `#include` directives. Due to this nesting, it is possible for a header file to be included multiple times in a single source file. This leads to redeclaration errors during compilation. This problem can be circumvented by placing a conditional preprocessor directive in each header file. For example, in order to guarantee that the header file `my_header.h` is included only once in a given source file, we "surround" the contents of `my_header.h` with the following preprocessor statements:

```
#ifndef  MYHEADER
#define  MYHEADER
/* contents of my_header.h */
#endif
```

The conditional directive #ifndef evaluates as true only if the name that follows it has not been previously defined. Thus, the first inclusion of the file my_header.h defines the name MYHEADER, and incorporates the contents of the header file into the source file; subsequent inclusions will find this name defined and skip to the #endif, without including the contents of the file.

3.2   VARIABLES AND STORAGE CLASSES

Each variable declared in a C/C++ program has a type associated with it. In addition, every C/C++ variable is a member of a ***storage class***. A variable's storage class is determined by where it is declared and by what storage class specification, if any, is used when it is declared. The storage class of a variable determines two things: over which region of a program the variable declaration has effect, and how long the variable persists in memory. The region of a program over which a variable declaration has effect is called the ***scope*** of the declaration. Variables that only have effect within a block are said to have ***local*** scope, while variables that have effect throughout a program are said to have ***global*** scope.[†] That is, local variables are only "known" within the block in which they are defined, while global variables are "known" throughout a program.

There are two possible storage classes: automatic and static. In C/C++ programs, any variable declaration within a block creates an ***automatic variable*** if either no storage class specifier is used, or the auto or register specifier is used. The auto and register specifiers can only be used within a block. If the register specifier is used (e.g., register int var;), the compiler attempts to store the variable in a fast memory register. If the compiler is unable to do this, then the variable becomes a standard automatic variable. Note that the auto specifier is not really necessary since any variable declared within a block is by default automatic if no other storage class specification is used. An automatic variable has *local* scope. Other blocks may contain variables with the same name, but they will be independent variables stored in different memory locations. An automatic variable comes into existence each time the function that contains it is called. When the function returns control to the calling routine, the automatic variable is discarded (i.e., the memory locations where it was stored can now be used for storing other automatic variables). It is often useful to consider the model of main memory presented in Section 1.3 when discussing automatic variables. An activation record is created and pushed onto the run-time stack each time a C/C++ function is called. These activation records contain storage for the automatic variables declared in each function. If an automatic variable is not initialized, it will initially store whatever value was left over in memory from previous activation records. Thus, it is important to either initialize or assign a value to an automatic variable before using it.

The scope of a ***static variable*** may be either local to a block, or global across all blocks. In either case, the value of the static variable is retained across the boundaries

---

[†] A ***block*** in a C/C++ program is a compound statement that is enclosed by braces. For example the body of a C/C++ function is considered a block.

of blocks. That is, a static variable is initialized once, when it is declared, and the variable remains in existence throughout the duration of the program. Within a block, a static variable is declared using the specifier `static` (e.g., `static int var;`). The scope of a variable declared in this fashion is local. Any variable declared outside of all blocks is referred to as an external variable. By default, external variables that are declared without using a storage class specifier have static storage class and global scope (actually, the scope of an external variable is from the point at which it is declared, to the end of the file being compiled). With reference to the model of main memory presented in Section 1.3, static variables can be thought of as residing in static memory.

3.3 POINTERS

It is often convenient to augment our model of computer memory considered in Section 1.3, and view it as a contiguous array of n identical cells as shown in Figure 3.1. In such a model, the location of a particular cell is referred to by its *address*, shown beneath the cell. Typically, computer memory is organized according to bytes of storage. Thus, we will assume that each cell in our memory model can store a byte of information. Notice that the addresses in Figure 3.1 are mapped sequentially onto the array of storage locations. We can assume that the variables and data structures that we will declare are stored in the cells of this computer memory. Most variables will require more than a single cell to store their value. For example, a C/C++ compiler may require two bytes to store a variable of the `int` data type, and four bytes to store a variable of the `float` data type. These variables can then be used to represent integer and real (floating-point format) numbers, respectively. The variables belonging to an array of a particular data type are stored in consecutive memory locations. Thus, the C/C++ expression `int x[4]` declares an array of integer numbers that is mapped to computer memory as shown in Figure 3.2 (here we assume that an `int` is stored in two bytes). In this figure, k is said to be the base address of the array, `x[0]` is the first element in the array, and `x[3]` is the last element in the array. Thus, the expression `x[2] = 10` stores the integer value 10 in the third position of array x.

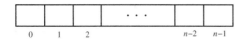

0   1   2   n-2   n-1

FIGURE 3.1
A logical model of computer memory as a one-dimensional array of storage locations or cells.

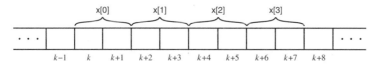

FIGURE 3.2
A schematic representation of how an array is sequentially mapped onto computer memory. The array `int x[4]` is stored in consecutive memory locations starting at the base address k.

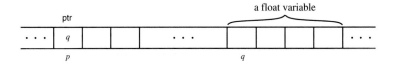

FIGURE 3.3
Schematic representation of the pointer variable `ptr`. The pointer variable `ptr` is stored in memory location p; it contains the address of another memory location, namely q. Notice that q is the address of the first byte of a `float` variable. Thus, `ptr` is said to point to the `float` variable stored at q.

A pointer variable is declared by placing an asterisk in front of a variable name. For example, `float *ptr` declares a pointer variable called `ptr` that can be used to store an address.[†] Furthermore, it is assumed that the variable stored at the location indicated by this address is of type `float`. This relationship is depicted graphically in Figure 3.3. In this figure the contents of the pointer variable `ptr`, stored at location p, are said to point to the `float` variable whose storage starts at location q.[‡] It is important to keep in mind that pointers have specific types associated with them. Thus, `ptr` is called a "pointer-to-`float`" variable.

Pointers are often used in C/C++ programs when passing parameters to a function. C implements parameter passing using pass-by-value. Thus, if a variable with local scope is passed as a parameter to a function, any modification of the parameter will not be reflected in the calling routine. In order to demonstrate this fact, consider the function `swap()` shown in Figure 3.4 which interchanges two integer arguments supplied as input. Use of the main routine shown at the bottom of this figure produces the following output:

```
main(), Before: a = 10, b = 20
swap(), Before: x = 10, y = 20
swap(), After: x = 20, y = 10
main(), After: a = 10, b = 20
```

In this example, the values supplied to the parameters x and y were interchanged by the `swap()` routine; however, because these arguments were passed by value, a and b were not interchanged in the main routine.

Pointers can be used to overcome this problem. Specifically, if we pass the *addresses* of the values we wish to interchange to a swap routine, then it can directly manipulate the storage locations of the variables we wish to interchange. This involves minor modifications to the swap and main routines given in Figure 3.4. Specifically, consider the `newswap()` function shown in Figure 3.5. The x and y parameters in this case are pointers. These pointers must be dereferenced using the ∗

[†]This is often written in the equivalent form `float* ptr` with the asterisk placed immediately after the data type name.

[‡]In Figure 3.3, the value of `ptr` is stored in a single byte. Generally, a pointer variable will require more than one byte of storage to represent an address in computer memory.

```
#include <stdio.h>  /* printf() is declared in <stdio.h> */
void swap(int x, int y)
{
  int temp;
  printf("\n swap(), Before: x = %d, y = %d", x,y);
  temp = x;
  x = y;
  y = temp;
  printf("\n swap(), After: x = %d, y = %d", x,y);
}

main()
{
  int a=10, b=20;
  printf("\n main(), Before: a = %d, b = %d", a,b);
  swap(a,b);
  printf("\n main(), After: a = %d, b = %d", a,b);
}
```

FIGURE 3.4
A function for swapping integers that does not work properly because integer numbers are passed to it by value.

```
void newswap(int* x, int* y)
{
  int temp;
  printf("\n newswap(), Before: *x = %d, *y = %d", *x,*y);
  temp = *x;
  *x = *y;
  *y = temp;
  printf("\n newswap(), After: *x = %d, *y = %d", *x,*y);
}

main()
{
  int a=10, b=20;
  printf("\n main(), Before: a = %d, b = %d", a,b);
  newswap(&a,&b);
  printf("\n main(), After: a = %d, b = %d", a,b);
}
```

FIGURE 3.5
A function for swapping integers that works properly. The addresses of integer numbers are passed as input parameters.

operator if we wish to modify the integer variables that they point to. Furthermore, since `newswap()` expects arguments of type pointer-to-`int`, the main routine must also be modified as shown in Figure 3.5. The only difference between this main routine and the previous one is that the *addresses* of a and b are passed to `newswap()`, instead of the *values* of a and b.[†] Using these modified functions, the desired result can now be obtained:

```
main(), Before: a = 10, b = 20
newswap(), Before: *x = 10, *y = 20
newswap(), After: *x = 20, *y = 10
main(), After: a = 20, b = 10
```

Note that although this example effectively performs pass-by-reference, it was accomplished with pass-by-value through the use of pointers.

There is another situation where it makes sense to use a pointer to a data object, rather than the data object itself, when passing arguments to a function. If the data object is a large structure (see Section 3.4), then a copy of this data object must be created and placed on the run-time stack every time it is passed to a function. If a pointer to the data object is passed instead, then only an address is placed on the run-time stack—depending upon the size of the data object, this can reduce the function-call overhead considerably.

3.3.1 Pointers and Arrays

In the C/C++ programming languages, pointers and arrays have a close relationship. Specifically, the name of an array is synonymous with a pointer to the memory location of the first element in the array. For the array depicted in Figure 3.2, the use of x in a program will evaluate to `&x[0]`, which in this case is the address *k*. In addition, because of the efficiency considerations discussed above, C/C++ do not allow an array to be passed as an argument to a function. Instead, a pointer to the array must be passed to functions that intend to use the array. Furthermore, after a pointer to an array is passed to a function, it can be indexed within this function using angle brackets, just like "normal" arrays. For example, the following function accepts a pointer to an integer array, as well as the length of the array as input, and returns the sum of the numbers in the array:

```
int sum(int ary[], int length)
{
  int i=0, total=0;
  for (i=0; i<length; i++)
    total += ary[i];
  return total;
}
```

[†]Recall that the C/C++ language address-of operator, &, returns the address of the variable to its right.

Notice that int ary[] is used in the argument list to denote a pointer to an integer array. A pointer to an array contains no information about the size of the array that it points to. Thus, this notation is equivalent to using int* ary. The former is usually preferred however, since it emphasizes that the pointer is also the starting address of an array. Keep in mind that any changes made to an array that is passed to a function in this manner are actually occurring in the array whose address was passed to the function. In addition, care must be taken by programmers when using arrays, since C/C++ do not provide any error checking to ensure that only valid array locations are accessed.

The reason that pointers have types associated with them becomes clear when we consider pointer arithmetic. For the array depicted in Figure 3.2, we said that the name of the array, x, is a pointer to the first element in the array. Thus, with reference to Figure 3.2, the use of x in an expression will evaluate to the address k. However, what should the expression x + 1 evaluate to? We would like this expression to yield the address &x[1]. Since pointers have types associated with them, the compiler "knows" the number of bytes required to store an int. Therefore, the compiler is able to add this number of bytes to the address k to yield the correct address $k + 2$. It should be stressed here that the number of bytes required to store a particular C/C++ data type is compiler dependent. Thus, some compilers may use, for example, four bytes to store an integer value. According to the above discussion, this will not lead to any problems when performing pointer arithmetic—the expression x + 1 will still evaluate to &x[1]. Thus, the sum() function given above could be written using pointer arithmetic as follows:

```
int sum(int ary[], int length)
{
   int i=0, total=0;
   for (i=0; i<length; i++)
     total += *(ary + i);
   return total;
}
```

Notice that the addresses calculated inside the loop must be dereferenced in order to obtain the values contained in specific array locations.

MULTI-DIMENSIONAL ARRAYS. Special consideration must be given when dealing with multi-dimensional arrays. First, it is important to understand how multi-dimensional arrays are stored in computer memory by C/C++ compilers. Each dimension is stored in turn, starting with the first dimension, in a contiguous block of computer memory. For example, the manner in which the two-dimensional array char x[2][3] would be stored is depicted in Figure 3.6. If we think of the first dimension of the array as the row dimension, and the second dimension as the column dimension, then the index of the row dimension is fixed, and the column dimension is varied in order to store each row of the two-dimensional array. It is often useful to think of two-dimensional arrays as "arrays-of-arrays." In this context, the definition char x[2][3] discussed above is considered an array of 2 arrays of 3 char

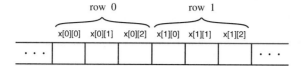

FIGURE 3.6
The layout of the two-dimensional array char x[2][3] in computer memory.

elements; x[0] is a pointer to the first element in the first array, and x[1] is a pointer to the first element in the second array. Furthermore, the name x itself is treated as a pointer to an array. The above results extend naturally to larger dimensional arrays.

Special attention must also be paid when passing a multi-dimensional array to a function. Once again, a pointer to the multi-dimensional array must be passed. Furthermore, in order for the compiler to "know" how to index the multidimensional array, each dimension beyond the first must be specified. In Figure 3.7 we extend the sum() function so that it can accept a pointer to a two-dimensional array as input. In this function, the parameter ary[][3] does contain some additional information about the type of argument it expects. Specifically, a pointer to a two-dimensional array in which the second dimension is 3 is expected. An example of how this function can be used is demonstrated in the main routine shown at the bottom of Figure 3.7.

One limitation of the sum_2d() function is that it will only work properly with arrays whose second dimension is 3. A more general function can be constructed, but it requires that we explicitly pass the second dimension of the array, and that the locations of array elements be calculated using pointer arithmetic as shown in Figure 3.8. The advantage of the newsum_2d() function shown in this figure is that it can be used with two-dimensional arrays of arbitrary dimension. As an example consider the main routine given at the bottom of Figure 3.8. Because ary is a

```
int sum_2d(int ary[][3], int row_len)
{
   int i=0, j=0, total=0;
   for (i=0; i<row_len; i++)
     for (j=0; j<3; j++)
       total += ary[i][j];
   return total;
}

main()
{
   static int total, x[2][3]=1,2,3,4,5,6;
   total = sum_2d(x,3);
   printf("\n total = %d", total);
}
```

FIGURE 3.7

The function sum_2d() which computes the sum of the integer numbers contained in a two-dimensional array. The second dimension of the input array must be 3.

```
int newsum_2d(int* ary, int row_len, int col_len)
{
  int i=0, j=0, total=0;
  for (i=0; i<row_len; i++)
    for (j=0; j<col_len; j++)
      total += *(ary + (i * col_len + j));
  return total;
}

main()
{
  int total, x[2][2]=1,2,3,4;
  total = newsum_2d(x[0],2,2);
  printf("\n total = %d", total);
}
```

FIGURE 3.8
A function that can compute the sum of the integer numbers contained in a two-dimensional array of arbitrary dimensions.

pointer-to-int, we use the argument x[0] when newsum_2d() is called. The name x would not be appropriate in this case since it is not a pointer-to-int.

3.3.2   Pointers and Dynamic Memory Allocation

Pointers are encountered whenever memory is dynamically allocated in C/C++ programs. The standard C library function malloc(n) is used to dynamically allocate *n* contiguous bytes of uninitialized memory.[†] If successful, a call to malloc() returns a pointer to the first byte of the dynamically allocated block of memory. If malloc() is unable to allocate the requested storage then the null pointer, which is the value 0, is returned.

Quite often the sizeof operator is used in conjunction with malloc(). For example, in the statements

```
float* ptr;
ptr = (float*) malloc(10 * sizeof(float));
```

a pointer-to-float variable is declared, and then malloc() is called to dynamically allocate a block of 10 floating-point numbers. Assuming that this request is satisfied, a pointer to the newly allocated block of memory is assigned to ptr. The pointer returned by malloc() must be cast into the appropriate type—thus, (float*) is used to convert this value into a pointer-to-float.[‡] Once this memory has been

---

[†]Programs using malloc() must include the header file <stdlib.h>.

[‡]The syntax of the cast operator is: (*type-name*) *expression*, where the value of *expression* is converted to the type specified by *type-name*.

allocated, `ptr` can be indexed as if it were an array. For example, `ptr[2]` will access the location of the third `float` variable in the dynamically allocated block of memory (`ptr+2` will also access this memory location).

Memory that is dynamically allocated in C/C++ programs persists until it is explicitly reclaimed. This is accomplished in C programs using `free(p)`, where `p` is a pointer that was returned by a call to `malloc()`.

3.3.3 Pointers and Strings

Strings in C/C++ are stored in character arrays. Specifically, a ***string*** in C/C++ is an array of characters in which the last "interesting" character in the array is followed by the null character (typically the ASCII value 0). For example, the definition

```
char* str="fred";
```

will cause the compiler to allocate an array of five characters, store the string constant "fred" (appended with the null character) in this array, and assign the address of the first character in this array to the pointer `str`. This situation is depicted in Figure 3.9.

Many functions for operating on strings are provided in the standard C library. These functions are declared in the `string.h` header file. Let us consider how one of these, the string length function, might be implemented. Specifically, the `strlen(s)` library function returns the number of characters (excluding the terminal null character) contained in the string argument `s`. This can be implemented as follows:

```
int strlen(char* s)
{
  int i=0;
  while(s[i] != 0)
    i++;
  return i;
}
```

This function simply steps through the character array `s` until the null value is encountered. At that point, the total number of steps that have been taken is returned as the length of the string.

A more complicated string function (not provided in the standard C library) involves swapping the contents of two strings supplied as input arguments. One approach would be to save the elements of the first string in a temporary string; and

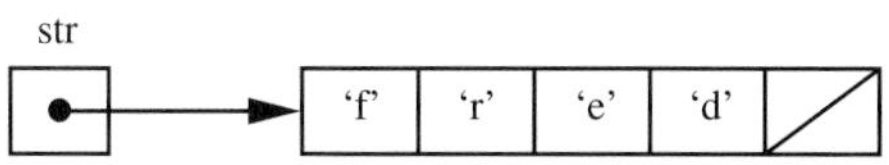

str

FIGURE 3.9
A schematic representation of how the string resulting from the expression `char* str="fred"` would be allocated in computer memory. The notation 'f' should be interpreted as the ASCII value for the character f, and the cell with the slash through it represents the null character.

then copy, on an element-by-element basis, the characters from the second string into the first string. Finally, the elements in the temporary string are copied into the second string. The major problem with this approach is that if the lengths of the two strings differ, there will not be enough room in one of the character arrays to perform the swap. Another problem with this approach is that it may involve quite a bit of copying. A more efficient approach would simply swap the pointers associated with the two input strings. Our first attempt at this approach is given in Figure 3.10. When the strswap() function shown in this figure is called using the main routine given at the bottom of the figure, the intended result is for the strings to be swapped; however, this code produces the following output:

```
Before: str1 = chicken, str2 = egg
After: str1 = chicken, str2 = egg
```

In order to understand these results, consider the strings depicted in Figure 3.11 (a). The leftmost portion of Figure 3.11 (a) depicts the arrangement of the strings in the main routine before the call to strswap(). The arguments assigned to the s1 and s2 parameters are the *values* contained in the str1 and str2 pointer variables, respectively. Inside the strswap() function these values are interchanged, as shown in the center portion of Figure 3.11 (a). Note that this swap does not effect the str1 and str2 pointers in the main routine. Thus, upon returning from strswap(), str1 and str2 are pointing to the original strings as shown in the rightmost portion of Figure 3.11 (a).

   In order to perform the desired string swap, pointers-to-pointers must be used. That is, we must pass to the string swapping routine the addresses of the pointers variables we wish to swap. This will allow us to interchange the values stored in the str1

```
void strswap(char* s1, char* s2)
{
  char* temp;
  temp = s1;
  s1 = s2;
  s2 = temp;
}

main()
  char* str1 = "chicken";
  char* str2 = "egg";
  printf("\n Before: str1 = %s, str2 = %s", str1,str2);
  strswap(str1, str2);
  printf("\n After: str1 = %s, str2 = %s", str1,str2);
}
```

FIGURE 3.10
A function for swapping strings that does not work properly.

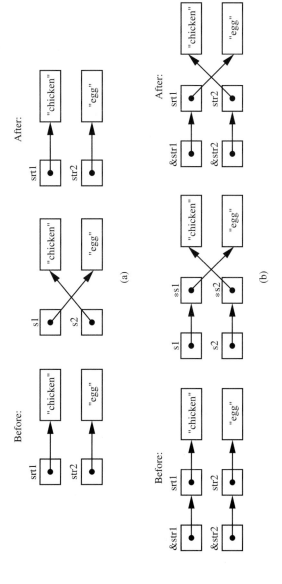

FIGURE 3.11

Schematic representations of **(a)** how the `strswap()` function given in Figure 3.10 works, and **(b)** the steps taken by the `newstrswap()` function given in Figure 3.12 to ensure that the swap actually occurs.

```
void newstrswap(char** s1, char** s2)
{
  char* temp;
  temp = *s1;
  *s1 = *s2;
  *s2 = temp;
}

main()
{
  char* str1 = "chicken";
  char* str2 = "egg";
  printf("\n Before: str1 = %s, str2 = %s", str1,str2);
  newstrswap(&str1, &str2);
  printf("\n After: str1 = %s, str2 = %s", str1,str2);
}
```

FIGURE 3.12
A function for swapping strings that works properly.

and str2 pointer variables as shown in Figure 3.11 (b). This can be accomplished by modifying the strswap() function so that it accepts pointer-to-pointer-to-char arguments as shown in Figure 3.12. Since the newstrswap() routine given in this figure expects the addresses of pointer-to-chars as input arguments, the previously given main routine should be modified accordingly. The modified main routine is given at the bottom of Figure 3.12.

COMMAND-LINE ARGUMENTS.   The C/C++ programming languages provide a means for passing arguments from the command line to a program when it begins execution. This is accomplished by supplying the main() function with a parameter list. Specifically, the complete function description for main() is:[†]

```
main(int argc, char** argv)
```

where the first parameter (traditionally called argc) is the number of command-line arguments that the program was invoked with, and the second parameter (traditionally called argv) is a pointer to an array of strings that contain the actual arguments. This arrangement is depicted in Figure 3.13. Notice that the name used to invoke the program is stored in the string argv[0], the first argument is stored in the string argv[1], the last argument is stored in the string argv[argc-1], and a null pointer is stored in argv[argc].

A simple demonstration of the use of command-line arguments is given in Figure 3.14. The function shown in this figure simply echoes the input arguments supplied on the command-line.

[†]This is often written in an equivalent form as: main(int argc, char* argv[]).

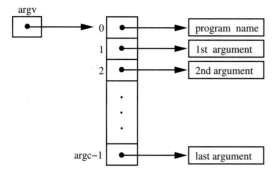

FIGURE 3.13
The manner in which command-line arguments are stored in computer memory. The parameter `argv`, which is of type pointer-to-pointer-to-`char`, points to an array of strings that hold the command line arguments.

```
main(int argc, char** argv)
{
  int i;
  for (i=1; i<argc; i++)
    printf(" %s ", argv[i]);
  printf("\n");
}
```

FIGURE 3.14
A function that prints command-line arguments on the standard output.

3.4 STRUCTURES, TYPEDEFS, AND ENUMERATED TYPES

A number of the features available in modern programming languages are provided to enhance the readability of software source code. Although they are not absolutely necessary, these features have the desired effect of making the software easier to develop, debug, and maintain.

First of all, the ability to create a composite data structure is supported in the C/C++ programming languages through the use of structures. In a number of other programming languages, structures are called "records." Specifically, a structure is a collection of one or more variables that are grouped together under a single name for convenient handling. Thus, structures allow a group of related variables to be treated as a unit instead of as separate entities.

One way of declaring a structure variable in C/C++ is as follows:

```
struct {
    member list
} structure name;
```

where *member list* is any valid list of variable declarations, and *structure name* is the variable name given to the structure. As an example, consider complex numbers. C/C++ do not provide a built-in data type for representing complex numbers. Since complex numbers contain a real and an imaginary part, it makes sense to group the two parts of such a number together when using them in a program. This can be accomplished using a structure as follows:

```
struct {
  float real;
  float imaginary;
} complex_num;
```

To gain access to individual structure members, a structure membership operator must be used. For example, the value 3.2 can be assigned to the real part of complex_num using

```
complex_num.real = 3.2;
```

If we are given the address of a structure variable, then a different structure membership operator must be used. Specifically,

```
(&complex_num)->real = 3.2;
```

will also assign the value 3.2 to the real part of complex_num.

In C/C++ programs, the typedef statement is often used in conjunction with the declaration of structure variables. The typedef statement allows you to create your own name for a data type. The principal advantage of this is that it allows the name of a data type to be made more meaningful. A typedef statement does not actually create a new type, it simply adds a new name for some existing type. When the typedef statement is used, this new name must appear in the position of a variable declaration. Thus, the declaration

```
typedef struct {
  float real;
  float imaginary;
} complex;
```

will allow us to treat the structure complex as if it were a type. Thus, in our programs we may now make variable declarations of the form

```
complex z1, z2;
```

This declares two variables, z1 and z2, of type complex.

Finally, the C/C++ programming languages provide a capability for specifying enumerated types. An *enumerated type* is defined by listing (enumerating) a set of values for objects of that type. Again, the typedef statement is often used in conjunction with enumerated types. For example, if we are writing a program to deal with the days of the week, we may define the following enumerated type to represent the days in a week:

```
typedef enum {mon, tue, wed, thr, fri, sat, sun} day_type;
```

This declaration actually associates an integer value to each of the members of this data type. Specifically, mon is assigned the value 0, tue the value 1, wed the value 2, and so on. In other words, this is simply an integer type, but it allows us to make a variable declaration of the form:

```
day_type day;
```

This variable can then be used to enhance the readability of a program. For example, a loop can be constructed that steps through each day of the week and performs some processing:

```
for (day=mon; day<=sun; day++)
  /* loop statements */
```

The use of the enumerated type here makes it clear that we are iterating through the days of the week.

An enumerated type declaration that we will make use of extensively in this text is

```
typedef enum false, true Boolean;
```

This follows the C/C++ convention that in logical expressions, 0 is treated as false, and any nonzero value is treated as true.

3.5 AN EXTENDED EXAMPLE: MATRIX ADT IMPLEMENTATION IN C

In this section we provide an extended example that demonstrates how the MATRIX ADT specification presented in Section 1.1.1 can be implemented using the C programming language. In doing so, we will make use of a number of the features available in the C programming language that were discussed in this chapter. We will also discuss some of the shortcomings of this implementation. In Section 4.3 it will be shown how many of these shortcomings can be easily addressed through the use of additional features available in the C++ programming language.

Recall from the discussion at the beginning of this chapter that we would like to implement the MATRIX ADT so that a user is able to manipulate representations of the ADT with regard to its logical viewpoint. That is, we would like programmers to be able to use matrices in their programs without having to consider how the MATRIX ADT is implemented. This will, in effect, involve creating an interface for the representation of a matrix that is stored in computer memory. This interface will consist of accessing routines that perform the operations listed in the ADT specification.

In order to make the MATRIX ADT implementation as flexible as possible, we will not place an *a priori* limit on the size of the matrix that can be represented. This will require the use of dynamic memory allocation. In addition, we will provide a means of easily changing the type of data that is stored in a matrix. The header file for the C language MATRIX ADT implementation is shown in Figure 3.15. This file contains the declaration of the data structure that will be used to store a matrix, as well as the declarations (function prototypes) of the accessing routines. First of all, notice that a `typedef` statement is used to create a new name for the `double` data type. Thus, wherever the name T occurs, the compiler will insert the word `double`. The use of this statement enables us to localize later changes to the data structure. For example, if a programmer wants to work with matrices

```
/* File: matrix.h */
#ifndef MATRIXh
#define MATRIXh

#define FORMAT "%8.3lf"

typedef double T;

typedef struct {
   int row_dim, col_dim;
   T** element;
} matrix;

/* function prototypes */
matrix create_empty(int rdim, int cdim);
matrix create_initval(int rdim, int cdim, T val);
matrix create_initvals(int rdim, int cdim, T* initval);
void destroy(matrix);
void matrix_print(matrix);
T retrieve(int row, int col, matrix m);  /* retrieve an element from m */
void assign(int row, int col, matrix*, T val);  /* assign a value to an element */
void equate(matrix* m1, matrix* m2);  /* m1 = m2 */
matrix add(matrix, matrix);
matrix subtract(matrix, matrix);
matrix negate(matrix);
matrix multiply(matrix, matrix);
matrix scalar_multiply(T scalar, matrix);
/* remaining function prototypes not shown */

#endif
```

FIGURE 3.15
The header file for the C language MATRIX ADT implementation.

whose elements are integers, then a change to the `typedef` statement so that it reads:

```
typedef int T;
```

is required. In addition, the FORMAT constant must be modified so that integer numbers can be output. This is discussed in more detail below. Once these changes are made, the program can be recompiled to work with integer matrices.

Next, notice the structure definition given for `matrix`. The `typedef` statement is used in this case so that this structure may later be referred to as `matrix` without having to use the keyword `struct`. The members of this structure consist of the integer variables `row_dim` and `col_dim`, which will be used to store the row and column dimensions of a matrix, and `element`, which will be used to store a variable of type pointer-to-pointer-to-T. For a given matrix, the variable `element` will point to an array of pointers, and each element in this array of pointers will point to another array that contains the elements belonging to a single row of the matrix. This concept is illustrated in Figure 3.16. The reason for using this type of structure is that it allows us to easily allocate memory for matrices of arbitrary dimensions, and we will be able to access the elements of these matrices as if they were stored in two-dimensional arrays. For instance, the i-th pointer in the `element` array can be accessed using `element[i]`, and since this is a pointer, it can also be indexed (see Section 3.3.1). Thus, element a_{ij} of a given matrix can be accessed using `element[i][j]`. Before discussing how this memory allocation is accomplished, let us finish our discussion of the `matrix.h` header file.

After the structure declaration in Figure 3.15, we provide a list of function prototypes. These are simply declarations of the function definitions found in the `matrix.c` file. Recall that we would like to provide a function to implement each of the operations specified by the MATRIX ADT. We have also supplied a number of additional functions. Since our goal is to allow the user to manipulate matrices without having to understand how they are represented in memory, we must supply the user with some means of creating a matrix. Thus, we have added the `create_empty()`,

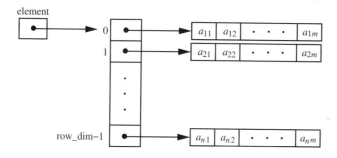

FIGURE 3.16
A logical representation of the data structure used to store the elements of an n by m matrix.

create_initval(), and create_initvals() functions. The create_empty() function can be used to create a matrix without having to specify initial matrix elements. The create_initval() function is used to create a matrix that contains the same value at every position of the matrix, and create_initvals() can be used to create a matrix that contains different values at each matrix position. We have also added the function destroy() so that the memory of previously created matrices can be reclaimed when it is no longer needed. Next, we provided a function, matrix_print(), that is used to print the elements of a matrix. Such a function allows us to "dump" the contents of our matrix representation, and is therefore quite invaluable during debugging. We will supply a similar routine for most of the ADT implementations developed in this book. The remaining function declarations shown in this figure are self-explanatory.

Let us now turn our attention to the source code required to implement the accessing routines. We must provide the function definitions for the function prototype declarations given in the matrix.h header file. These function definitions will be packaged together in the matrix.c file. We will discuss a number of these function definitions below, and then demonstrate how this MATRIX ADT implementation can be used with a simple test program.

First, consider the create_initvals() routine. The row and column dimensions of a matrix must be supplied to this function, along with a pointer to an array of data elements. The data elements must be stored in this input array in row-column order—that is, one row after the other in a single-dimensional array (i.e., initval is a pointer to the elements that will be stored in the first row of the matrix, and more generally, (initval + (cdim * i)) is a pointer to the elements that will be stored in the i-th row of the new matrix). This data will be read in by the create_initvals() routine and stored in the structure depicted in Figure 3.16. The source code for this function is given in Figure 3.17. This function declares a variable of type matrix called result. Following this statement, values are assigned to the data members of the result structure. First, the values of rdim and cdim are assigned to the structure members row_dim and col_dim, respectively. The following statement dynamically allocates the memory necessary to store the array of pointers depicted in Figure 3.16, and then assigns the resulting pointer to the structure member element.[†] Next, a loop is used to dynamically allocate memory for the arrays that will hold individual rows of the matrix data. Finally, a set of nested loops are used to assign the actual matrix data values to these arrays, and the matrix representation that was created is returned to the calling routine. Note that the create_empty() function can be implemented using these same statements if we remove the nested loops used to initialize the matrix elements.

[†]The standard C library function malloc() is used to dynamically allocate a block of memory. It takes as its arguments the number of bytes that are to be allocated, and if successful, returns the address of the first byte in the block of memory. Quite often the sizeof operator is used in conjunction with malloc(). This operator returns the number of bytes required to store the element that is supplied as its argument.

```
/* File: matrix.c */
{
   int i,j;
   matrix result;
   /* assign values to the structure members */
   result.row_dim = rdim;
   result.col_dim = cdim;
   result.element = (T**)malloc(rdim * sizeof(T*));
   for (i=0; i<rdim; i++)
     result.element[i] = (T*)malloc(cdim * sizeof(T));
   /* initialize the matrix elements */
   for (i=0; i<rdim; i++)
     for (j=0; j<cdim; j++)
       result.element[i][j] = *(initval + (cdim * i + j));
   return result;
}
```

FIGURE 3.17

Source code for the function `create_initvals()` found in the file `matrix.c`. The file `matrix.h` must be included in `matrix.c`

Given the matrix representation discussed above, it is quite easy to implement most of the remaining accessing routines. For example, the definition of the `matrix_print()` function is shown in Figure 3.18, and the routine used for adding two matrices is given in Figure 3.19. Notice how the matrix elements in these functions can be accessed as if they were stored in a two-dimensional array.

For purposes of readability, the error checking is minimal in these functions. Note, however, that the following diagnostic statement does appear in the `add()` routine of Figure 3.19:[†]

```
assert((m1.row_dim == m2.row_dim) && (m1.col_dim == m2.col_dim));
```

This statement is an assertion. Recall from Section 1.2 that assertions are used to verify relationships among specific variables in a program. In this case we want to verify that the row and column dimensions of the two matrices being passed into the `add()` function are conformal for addition. If this assertion is violated, the `assert()` macro will print an error message and terminate execution of the program. We will often use assertions in this text in place of more elaborate error handling that the reader can easily supply.

Let us now demonstrate the use of this MATRIX ADT implementation using a simple test routine. The file `test.c` shown in Figure 3.20 uses the MATRIX ADT implementation discussed above to perform some simple matrix operations. So that you may verify the correctness of this program, its output is shown in Figure 3.21.

[†]The `<assert.h>` header file must be included in order to use the `assert()` macro.

```
/* File: matrix.c */
void matrix_print(matrix m)
{
  int i,j;
  printf("\n");
  for (i=0; i<m.row_dim; i++) {
    printf("\n");
    for (j=0; j<m.col_dim; j++)
      printf(FORMAT, m.element[i][j]);
  }
  printf("\n");
}
```

FIGURE 3.18

Source code for the matrix printing function found in the file `matrix.c`. This function can be used to dump the contents of the matrix representation specified in `matrix.h`.

```
/* File: matrix.c */
matrix add(matrix m1, matrix m2)
{
  int i,j;
  matrix result;
  assert((m1.row_dim == m2.row_dim) && (m1.col_dim == m2.col_dim));
  result = create_empty(m1.row_dim, m2.col_dim);
  for (i=0; i<m1.row_dim; i++)
    for (j=0; j<m1.col_dim; j++)
      result.element[i][j] = m1.element[i][j] + m2.element[i][j];
  return result;
}
```

FIGURE 3.19

Source code for the matrix addition function found in the file `matrix.c`.

We now summarize some of the important features of this C language representation of the MATRIX ADT. The data structures used in this implementation allow us to provide a set of accessing routines that implement the MATRIX ADT operations specified in Section 1.1.1. Furthermore, the user does not have to understand how the matrix elements are stored in computer memory in order to use these accessing routines. This is clearly demonstrated in the test program shown in Figure 3.20. Therefore, we have created the wall that should exist between the user program and the ADT implementation. This wall, however, is not as impervious as we might think. Notice that a user may modify elements of the matrix, *without* using one of the supplied accessing routines, by simply using a structure

```
/* File: test.c */
#include "matrix.h"

main()
{
  static T data[] = {1,2,3,4};
  matrix a,b;
  a = create_initvals(2,2,data);
  b = create_empty(2,2);
  equate(&a,&b);
  printf("\n Matrix a:");
  matrix_print(a);
  printf("\n Matrix b:");
  matrix_print(b);
  printf("\n a+b:");
  matrix_print(add(a,b));
}
```

FIGURE 3.20

The source code of the program used to test the MATRIX ADT implementation provided in the `matrix.h` and `matrix.c` files. To obtain an executable file, the object code produced by compiling `matrix.c` must be linked to the object code produced by compiling `test.c`.

```
Matrix a:
    1.000    2.000
    3.000    4.000

Matrix b:
    1.000    2.000
    3.000    4.000

a+b:
    2.000    4.000
    6.000    8.000
```

FIGURE 3.21

The output of the executable program produced by `test.c`.

membership operator to access a given element in the `matrix` structure. There is no way to prevent users from directly accessing the matrix elements if they so desire. Thus, this implementation has the undesirable feature of allowing the wall that separates the ADT implementation from the application program to be easily circumvented.

It is also worthwhile to consider the reusability of this MATRIX ADT implementation. By simply changing the `typedef` statement and a #define statement in the header file, this implementation can be made to work with any of the built-in C data types. This implementation cannot, however, be used to represent a matrix whose elements are specified by a user-defined data type, such as a complex number data type. For example, the add() function given in Figure 3.19 would not work properly with the complex number type. In this routine, the individual matrix elements are added together inside of a nested loop. The "+" operator is used to perform this addition. In C we cannot define a new data type that uses built-in operators such as +. Therefore, the add() function in this matrix package would have to be modified in order to make it work with each built-in type we might consider using. The same is true for many of the other functions in this package.

The fact that the typedef and #define statements must be specified *a priori* also precludes the use of this matrix package with more than one built-in type in a single program. Thus, this implementation is not quite as flexible as we would like it to be. In the next chapter we will demonstrate how the C++ programming language effectively deals with these problems.

EXERCISES

3.1. Execution of the program presented below may result in the following output: Inaccurate.

```
main()
{
  float f=1.234567;
  if ((f/3.1) * 3.1 == 1.234567)
    printf("Accurate");
  else
    printf("Inaccurate");
}
```

Why does this happen?

3.2. Consider the following preprocessor statement that is intended to convert a temperature given in Celsius to one in Fahrenheit:

```
#define CtoF(t) 1.8 * (t) + 32
```

Give an example in which the use of this definition yields an erroneous result.

3.3. Draw a diagram that illustrates how the following C program variables would be stored in computer memory:

```
char val = 10;
char* ptr = &val;
char** pptr = &ptr;
```

Represent computer memory as a one-dimensional array of storage locations, and assume arbitrary values for the addresses where these variables are stored in the array.

3.4. In the following C function:

```
char* whoops() {
  char x=2;
  return &x;
}
```

the return value is referred to as a ***dangling reference***. Why?

3.5. Draw a diagram that shows how the array `char x[3][4][2]` would be stored in computer memory.

3.6. Redraw Figure 3.16 demonstrating how the matrix data structure would be stored in computer memory if computer memory was represented as a contiguous one-dimensional array of storage locations.

3.7. Functions for operating on strings are provided with the standard C string library; however, we would like to be able to treat strings in our programs as if they were a built-in type. Thus, in this exercise you are to develop a software package in C that implements the STRING ADT. This ADT should at a minimum support the following operations:

1. *Retrieve(i,s)*. Returns element i of string s.
2. *Print(s)*. Prints the contents of string s.
3. *Concatenate(s_1, s_2)*. Concatenates strings s_1 and s_2 and returns the resulting string.
4. *Copy(s_1, s_2)*. Copies the contents of string s_1 to string s_2.
5. *Compare(s_1, s_2)*. Compares string s_1 to string s_2, returning a result indicating whether or not s_1 is lexicographically greater than s_2.
6. *Length(s)*. Returns the number of characters in string s.
7. *Capacity(s)*. Returns the maximum numbers of characters that can be stored in string s.

Use your string package to perform the following tasks:
(*a*) Sort a sequence of strings provided as input.
(*b*) Determine if an input string is a palindrome.

3.8. Implement the MATRIX ADT using the C programming language. Include all of the operations given in Section 1.1.1. The following definitions may prove helpful:

- *Transpose*. Given an order $n \times m$ matrix A, the ***transpose*** of A, denoted A', is the order $m \times n$ matrix obtained by setting $a'_{ij} = a_{ji}$ for $i = 1, 2, \ldots, m$ and $j = 1, 2, \ldots, n$.
- *Determinant*. Every square (i.e., order $n \times n$) matrix A has associated with it a scalar value called its ***determinant***, which is denoted $|A|$. We can calculate $|A|$ recursively using a technique known as expansion by cofactors, but first we must define the minor of a matrix, and the cofactor of a matrix element. Given A, a ***minor*** is the determinant of any square submatrix of A, and the ***cofactor*** of element a_{ij} is the scalar obtained by taking the product of the term $(-1)^{i+j}$ and the minor of A that results from removing the i-th row and j-th column. Now, to find $|A|$ using ***expansion by cofactors*** pick any row (or column) of A, and for each element in the row (column) find its cofactor. Then multiply each element in the chosen row (column) by its cofactor and sum that results to obtain $|A|$. In order to make this recursive definition

complete we must specify how to solve the base case. Consider the 2×2 matrix

$$\begin{bmatrix} a & b \\ c & d \end{bmatrix}$$

The determinant of this matrix is calculated according to $ad - bc$.

- *Inverse.* The **inverse** of a square matrix A, denoted A^{-1}, is defined according to

$$A^{-1} = \frac{1}{|A|} A^a$$

where A^a is the adjoint of A. The **adjoint** of A is the transpose of the cofactor matrix of A, where the **cofactor matrix** of A is obtained by replacing each element of A with its cofactor. Notice from our definition that if $|A| = 0$, then A does not possess an inverse.

3.9. Systems of simultaneous equations occur frequently in engineering applications. A linear system of simultaneous equations written in the following form:

$$a_{11}x_1 + a_{12}x_2 + \cdots + a_{1m}x_m = b_1$$
$$a_{21}x_1 + a_{22}x_2 + \cdots + a_{2m}x_m = b_2 \tag{3.1}$$
$$\vdots$$
$$a_{n1}x_1 + a_{n2}x_2 + \cdots + a_{nm}x_m = b_n$$

can be rewritten in matrix form as:

$$\mathbf{Ax = b}$$

where

$$\mathbf{A} = \begin{bmatrix} a_{11} & a_{12} & \cdots & a_{1m} \\ a_{21} & a_{22} & \cdots & a_{2m} \\ \vdots & & & \\ a_{n1} & a_{n2} & \cdots & a_{nm} \end{bmatrix} \quad \mathbf{x} = \begin{bmatrix} x_1 \\ x_2 \\ \vdots \\ x_m \end{bmatrix} \quad \mathbf{b} = \begin{bmatrix} b_1 \\ b_2 \\ \vdots \\ b_n \end{bmatrix}$$

The a_{ij}'s and b_i's in this equation are known, while the x_j's are not ($i = 1, 2, \ldots, n$ and $j = 1, 2, \ldots, m$). A solution to (3.1) is a set of m numbers $x_1, x_2, \ldots, x_m$ that when substituted into (3.1) satisfies the given equations (i.e., makes all m equalities simultaneously valid). If the inverse of the $\mathbf{A}$ matrix exists, then a solution to (3.1) can be found using matrix operations as follows:

$$\mathbf{x = A^{-1}b} \tag{3.2}$$

Given this information, use the software developed in Exercise 3.8 to solve the following system of equations using the method of Equation (3.2):

$$4x_1 + 3x_2 - x_3 = -2$$
$$-2x_1 - 4x_2 + 5x_3 = 20$$
$$x_1 + 2x_2 + 6x_3 = 7$$

3.10. Given the following system of one-way streets and their corresponding traffic flows:

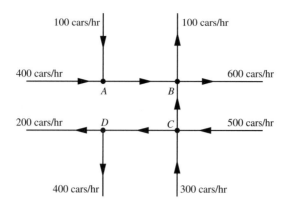

use your MATRIX ADT implementation to determine the traffic flow across branches AB, BC, and CD. (Hint: Let x_1 and x_2 equal the flow across branches AB and BC, respectively. Then, $x_1 + x_2 = 700$.)

3.11. Implement the following complex number ADT using the C programming language. The COMPLEX ADT is used to represent *complex numbers* of the form $z = \alpha + i\beta$, where α and β are real numbers and i is the imaginary number $\sqrt{-1}$. The operations supported by this ADT are:

1. *Addition*(z_1, z_2). Returns the result of performing the complex addition $z_1 + z_2$. Note that

$$(\alpha_1 + i\beta_1) + (\alpha_2 + i\beta_2) = (\alpha_1 + \alpha_2) + i(\beta_1 + \beta_2)$$

2. *Subtraction*(z_1, z_2). Returns the result of performing the complex subtraction $z_1 - z_2$. Note that

$$(\alpha_1 + i\beta_1) - (\alpha_2 + i\beta_2) = (\alpha_1 - \alpha_2) + i(\beta_1 - \beta_2)$$

3. *Multiplication*(z_1, z_2). Returns the result of performing the complex multiplication $z_1 \times z_2$. Note that

$$(\alpha_1 + i\beta_1)(\alpha_2 + i\beta_2) = (\alpha_1\alpha_2 - \beta_1\beta_2) + i(\alpha_1\beta_2 + \beta_1\alpha_2)$$

4. *Division*(z_1, z_2). Returns the result of performing the complex division z_1/z_2. Note that

$$\frac{\alpha_1 + i\beta_1}{\alpha_2 + i\beta_2} = \frac{\alpha_1\alpha_2 + \beta_1\beta_2}{\alpha_2^2 + \beta_2^2} + i\frac{\beta_1\alpha_2 - \alpha_1\beta_2}{\alpha_2^2 + \beta_2^2}$$

5. *Conjugation*(z). Returns $\bar{z}$, the complex conjugate of z. Note that

$$\bar{z} = \overline{\alpha_1 + i\beta} = \alpha_1 - i\beta$$

3.12. For any two vectors x and y of the same dimension n, we may associate a scalar, called the *inner product* of x and y. This quantity is obtained by first taking the complex conjugate of every element in y (if an element has no imaginary part, then that element and its complex conjugate are the same number). The resulting vector is denoted by $\bar{y}$. Next, multiply the corresponding elements of x and $\bar{y}$, and sum the resulting n elements.

This final scalar value is the inner product of x and y. Write a C program that makes use of the COMPLEX ADT implementation created in Exercise 3.11 to calculate the inner product of two vectors input by the user.

3.13. The representation of a complex number discussed in Exercise 3.11 is referred to as the *cartesian form*. It is also possible to represent a complex number using a *polar form*. In this case,

$$z = re^{i\theta}$$

where r is the *magnitude* of z, and θ is the *angle* or *phase* of z. Given a complex number in polar form, we can compute its cartesian form using

$$\alpha = r\cos\theta \quad \beta = r\sin\theta$$

and given a complex number in cartesian form, we may compute its polar form using

$$r = \sqrt{\alpha^2 + \beta^2}, \quad \theta = \tan^{-1}\left(\frac{\beta}{\alpha}\right)$$

We would like users to be able to deal with complex numbers in both polar and cartesian forms. Thus, we need to add some additional operations to our COMPLEX ADT. Specifically, a user should be able to create a complex number by specifying its magnitude and phase, and to retrieve the magnitude and phase of a complex number. You are to add functions to your COMPLEX ADT implementation from Exercise 3.11 that allow the user to perform these operations. (Note: Your data structure should still store a complex number using its cartesian form. The formulas above are only used for input and output of a complex number in polar form.)

CHAPTER NOTES

The C programming language was developed at AT&T Bell Laboratories in the early 1970s. In 1983, the American National Standards Institute (ANSI) formed a committee whose goal was to formalize a standard definition for the C programming language. Such standardization promotes portability of C programs across a variety of compilers and machines. As a result of this committee's work, the "ANSI C" standard was approved in 1989 [7]. Most C compilers written today follow this standard. References that are based on the ANSI standard for the C programming language include Kernighan and Ritchie [83], and Kelley and Pohl [82].

More sophisticated (and efficient) techniques for solving the system of equations given in Exercise 3.9 can be found in Press et al. [123].

CHAPTER
4

OBJECT-ORIENTED PROGRAMMING AND C++

The capabilities offered by object-oriented programming languages were provided as a means of improving the reusability of software components. The goal of object-oriented programming is to allow software systems to be easily extended to improve their functionality, or reused in other systems that require their services. Ideally, the extension or reusability of a software component does not require specific knowledge about the implementation details of the component. The ability to develop software in this manner enables software components to be packaged in such a way that they are easily incorporated into systems as needed. Such an approach facilitates the development and maintenance of software systems.

We begin this chapter by discussing the programming features that are available in any object-oriented programming language. The remainder of the chapter demonstrates how the C++ programming language supports each of these features.

4.1 FUNDAMENTAL CONCEPTS

Figure 4.1 illustrates the organization of information in the classes and objects of an object-oriented language. The meanings and implications of each of the fields in this figure are discussed in the following sections.

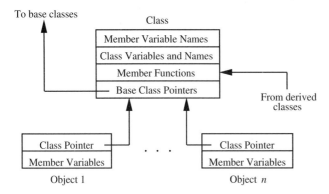

FIGURE 4.1
Organization of information in the class structure of an object-oriented language.

4.1.1 Classes and Objects

Computation in an object-oriented system involves manipulating class objects. A *class* is actually a means of packaging an ADT. That is, the class concept allows the data elements as well as the accessing routines of an ADT implementation to be encapsulated together as a single entity. Furthermore, the class controls the accessing of the data elements. An application program can only access the data elements in the class through the specified interface provided by the accessing routines. This effectively constructs the wall that should exist between an application program and the implementation level of a data type.

A class contains all the information necessary to construct separate instances of itself; these instances are referred to as *objects*. If the objects are chosen to represent objects in the real world, a more natural mapping of the problem domain to the software domain can be obtained.

It is important to understand the difference between a class and an object of that class. A class is simply a specification for creating objects. Thus, a single class may create multiple objects. As mentioned above, the objects are the actual entities that will be manipulated in a computer program. This is analogous to the difference between a data type and an instance of that data type. Multiple instances of a data type may be created in a program. These instances, not the data type itself, are then manipulated in the computer program.

Every object contains its own set of data elements, called *member variables* or *data members*, that determine the individual state of that object.[†] In addition, a class may store information that is shared among all instances of the class in *class variables*. Member and class variables are packaged in such a way that they may only be accessed through the accessing routines provided by the class. The accessing routines of a given class are shared by all objects of that particular class. In the terminology of

---

[†]Some authors use the term *instance variable* instead of member variable.

object-oriented programming, these accessing routines are called *member functions*. Note in Figure 4.1 that all instances (i.e., objects) of a class point to the same set of member functions, but each object keeps its own copy of the member variables.

4.1.2 Inheritance

The ability to structure a software system around classes provides a useful means of decomposing system components; this alone will lead to a more manageable system. However, the extendability as well as the reusability of software components is enhanced if the concept of *inheritance* is incorporated. Inheritance is the means by which objects of a class can access member variables and functions contained in a previously defined class, without having to restate those definitions. This will give us the ability to create a new class that is an extension or specialization of an existing class. In this case, the new class (i.e., the *derived class*) is said to be derived from the existing *base class*. Object-oriented programming languages must also support *multiple inheritance* in which a derived class can inherit more than one base class.

A derived class inherits member variables, class variables, and member functions from its base class. The derived class may also add new member variables, class variables, or member functions that are necessary for its specialized operations. Additionally, a derived class may redefine any member function provided by the base class by simply supplying a new member function that has the same name as the old member function in the base class. In this case, the new member function in the derived class is said to *overload* the member function with the corresponding name in the base class. This allows different meanings to be attached to the same member function name; which member function is invoked when the name is called in a program depends upon the specific class of the object being used.

The motivation for inheritance follows from the observation that in many cases new software development evolves from previous development efforts. This fact, largely ignored in classical software design, is of central concern in object-oriented design. Using inheritance, programmers are able to avoid the time consuming and error-prone task of rewriting large amounts of code that perform nearly the same tasks as some existing piece of code. Therefore, through the use of inheritance, an addition to a system often requires just that—addition and not modification.

The relationship among classes in an object-oriented program is often depicted as an *inheritance graph*. This structure pictorially represents the hierarchical organization of the classes. For example, the inheritance graph of a hierarchy of classes that can be developed for creating and manipulating graphical objects on a computer screen is shown in Figure 4.2. The base class in this hierarchy, Shape, is defined to represent the general concept of a shape. Specific shapes are then derived from Shape. Furthermore, these specific shapes can be manipulated using the interface provided by the Shape class. For example, in Figure 4.2, the Line class is derived from the Shape class, and Line in turn serves as the base class for Polygon. Since rectangles and triangles are specialized forms of polygons, the Rectangle and Triangle classes are derived from the Polygon class. Notice that more general shapes appear towards the top, and more specific shapes appear towards the bottom of the inheritance graph.

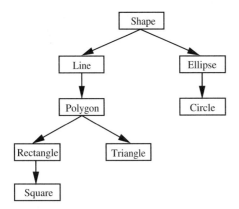

FIGURE 4.2
An inheritance graph for shapes.

By organizing shapes in this manner, we can write computer programs that manipulate general shapes without having to worry about the specific type of the shape. This means that additional shapes can be created and added through inheritance, and that previously developed code will not have to be modified in order to use these shapes.

4.1.3   Message Passing

It is often useful to think of computation in an object-oriented system as evolving around *messages*. Using this analogy, objects in the system manipulate other objects by sending messages requesting them to perform specific actions. These messages invoke the appropriate member functions in the objects' classes, possibly causing the objects themselves to change state. If a desired member function is not found in an object's immediate class, then member functions in that object's base class are searched. If it is not found there, the search continues on up the hierarchy of the object's inherited classes until either the appropriate member function is found, or the class at the root of the hierarchy is reached. If the desired member function is not found in the root class, then an error has occurred.

There is a fundamental distinction between this message passing approach and the conventional procedure calls used in procedure-oriented languages. A message can be viewed as a request of an object to perform some action. How the object responds to this request depends upon available member functions. This approach allows objects from different classes to respond appropriately to the same messages. In addition, a new object can easily replace an existing object in a software system if it responds to the same messages as the existing object. On the other hand, a procedure call specifies *how* an action should be accomplished, not *what* action is being requested.

4.1.4   Dynamic Binding and Polymorphism

When a software system determines how a particular operation is to be performed on an object, it is said to ***bind*** a specific implementation of that operation to the object.

If the system decides on which implementation of the operation to use at compile time, it performs *static binding*. If this choice is made at run time, then the system performs *dynamic binding*. That is, in static binding, the static form of an object (i.e., its form at compile time) determines which version of an operation will be used. In dynamic binding, the dynamic form of an object (i.e., its form during run time, when an operation is needed) determines which version of an operation is used.

An object-oriented programming language typically supports static binding, but it must support dynamic binding. This gives operations (i.e., messages) the important capability of being able to automatically adapt to the objects to which they are applied.

Another important feature of object-oriented languages that is directly supported by dynamic binding is *polymorphism*. Polymorphism is defined as the ability to assume various forms. In object-oriented programming this term is used to denote the ability of a single message to refer at run time to objects of different classes.

Typically a polymorphic function is declared in a base class. Then, this same function is redefined in classes that are derived from the base class (i.e., the function name is overloaded). Thus, functions with the same name as the one in the base class exist in the derived classes. Now, if an object of the base class is declared in a program, the original function definition found in the base class will be invoked when the function is called. However, if an object of a derived class is later assigned to the base class object, then the function definition for the derived class will be invoked if the same function is called.

There is a subtle but important distinction between what we have just discussed, and the simple form of function overloading introduced in Section 4.1.2. If the function in the base class was not declared as polymorphic, then static binding is performed, and the type (i.e., class) of an object at compile time determines which function definition is invoked. Thus, in the example given above, the original type of the object was that of the base class. Therefore, even if objects of different types were assigned to this object, it would still invoke the function definition found in the base class whenever the function was called. However, when the function is declared to be polymorphic, dynamic binding occurs, and the software system will check the current type of the object before invoking the appropriate function definition.

4.1.5 Putting It All Together

Taken separately, the issues discussed so far are important, but in combination they have a profound influence on the way software can be developed and used. The most significant contribution of the object-oriented paradigm involves the increase in reusability of system components; this is supported through the use of data encapsulation, message passing, polymorphism, and inheritance.

Because the data in an object can only be accessed through a well-defined external interface (i.e., the member functions) and these interface routines are packaged with the data, the implementation of the class is effectively "hidden" from the rest of the system. Thus, the class concept supports data encapsulation. Notice also that a class directly supports the implementation of ADTs. The abstract view of the data type in this case is the view provided by the member functions that manipulate the data. The ability to use data abstraction is fundamental to any design approach. Therefore, the data encapsulation and data abstraction provided by object-oriented languages allows us to develop ADTs that perform well-defined sets of operations, independent of a particular application. These ADTs may then be used as necessary in applications that require their functionality.

Additionally, through the use of inheritance, the design process may be simplified and development time reduced by adding functionality to previously developed classes. Most importantly, this additional functionality can be added to the existing class without modification to the class itself. Therefore, the consumer of the class does not need to be concerned with the implementation details of the class.[†] The consumer only needs to be familiar with the functionality provided by the external member functions.

The significance of the previous point cannot be overemphasized. Using traditional software technology, the supplier is responsible for system modification. By allowing the objects to determine how a message should be interpreted, the responsibility of implementing system modifications and additions can be shifted away from the supplier of a class to the consumers of a class. Such a fundamental change in focus supports the notion that software can be developed and packaged for later use just as hardware components are packaged for convenient use in integrated circuits (ICs). That is, class suppliers can serve the purpose of developing, debugging, and testing a set of base classes—just as corresponding IC manufacturers develop, test, and debug their hardware products. These base classes (or software ICs) are then made available to consumers for possible inclusion into their software systems.

The benefits obtained from such an approach are the same benefits obtained by hardware engineers through the use of ICs. The design and development of a system does not have to proceed through the lower levels of abstraction because fully tested sub-system components are already available. Therefore, the designers do not have to concern themselves with the detailed working of these sub-system components. Instead of starting every new development from scratch, the object-oriented approach allows the developer to use a previous working implementation that has already been thoroughly tested. The developer may then use inheritance to provide only those changes that are necessary to meet the new design specifications.

It should also be noted that these same benefits are obtained if the software components are developed and used by the same person (i.e., the supplier is the consumer). The design of applications can be simplified and the development time reduced because the developer of a class is still not required to deal with the complexities of its implementation when using the class. This means that the developer does not have to recall the implementation details of the class in order to modify and reuse the class in other applications.

[†]The *supplier* of a class is the person who implements the class, while the ***consumer*** of a class is the person who uses the class in an application program. The consumer may also add additional functionality to the class through the use of inheritance.

4.1.6 Design Philosophy

Object-oriented program design is best accomplished by analyzing the classes of objects in the physical system. This design approach consists of a successive refinement of the descriptions and interactions of these objects. Next, the collection of objects in the physical system are modeled using classes in the software system. The class structure offered by object-oriented programming languages supports this approach by allowing objects in the physical system to be modeled as the same objects in the software system. In addition, these classes can be easily extended or combined, enabling them to form more complex components. Existing classes are used whenever possible. If new classes need to be included, they are developed in a generic manner so that their services might be used in other systems. Finally, the inheritance mechanism leaves the system open for future modification or incorporation into other systems as needed, thereby placing extendability and reusability at the heart of object-oriented design.

One of the most difficult aspects of object-oriented design involves determining the organization of classes in the software system architecture. There are many different ways in which classes and objects can interact. Defining relationships between the entities that may exist in an object-oriented system often makes it easier to understand, discuss, and modify the system. We will consider the following relationships:

1. IS-A relationship: This is a *specialization* relationship which is used to indicate that one class is a variant of another class. Stating that "class B IS-A class A" indicates that the major characteristics of class B are inherited from class A.

2. HAS-A relationship: This is a *containment* relationship which is used to indicate that one class or object is part of some other class or object. While IS-A can only be used to define a relationship between classes; HAS-A can be used to define a relationship between classes, between an object and a class, or between objects. Stating that "class B HAS-A object A" indicates that object A is a component of class B. That is, class A is used as a building block in the construction of class B.

3. USES-A relationship: This is a *using* relationship which indicates that a member function of one class accepts, and therefore uses, an object of some other class as a parameter. For example, stating that "class B USES-A class A" indicates that class B objects use the facilities offered by class A objects, not that class A is used as a building block in the construction of class B.

In subsequent chapters we will use these relationships when we discuss the organization of specific classes.

4.2 THE C++ PROGRAMMING LANGUAGE

We now introduce C++, the object-oriented programming language that will be used in this book. For each of the object-oriented programming language features discussed above, we will demonstrate how that feature is implemented in C++. We begin by stating that the goal of C++ is to retain the machine level efficiency and portability of C while making program development easier through the use of object-oriented techniques. The resulting language gives us the best of both worlds—a powerful conceptual tool for use in the development process, as well as an efficient means of implementing the software design.

4.2.1 Classes and Objects

C++ supports the class construct discussed in Section 4.1.1. The development of a C++ class normally involves the creation of two separate computer files. The first file is a header file which contains the class definition that specifies how objects of the class may be created, manipulated, and destroyed. This file is incorporated into programs that use the class via the #include preprocessor directive. The second file contains the definitions of the member functions declared in the header file. This file is compiled, possibly stored in a library, and linked into an executable file when needed. In order to use a class, the consumer must only understand the interface to the class that the header file provides—not the implementation details contained in the member function definitions. The facilities provided to implement inheritance also insure that the class can be adapted as needed without explicit knowledge of how the member functions were implemented. Ideally the consumer of the class is never required to understand the actual details of the class's implementation. This capability, as well as the capabilities discussed below, make C++ an excellent candidate for use in the development of software-ICs as discussed in Section 4.1.5.

In C++, a class is an extension of the structure concept found in C. The syntax of this extended structure is shown below:

```
struct structure tag {
    private:
        private items member list
    public:
        public items member list
};
```

Specifically, C++ extends the structure concept of C by allowing functions to be declared in the *member list*. This capability is useful when implementing ADTs because it allows the functions that access the data elements to be conveniently packaged with the data elements themselves. These functions are declared in the same manner as regular C functions, except that they can access the elements of the structure without using the structure membership operators (. and $->$).

The C++ structure also provides a means of specifying the scope of items in the *member list* through the use of the public and private *access specifiers*. The keyword private is used to restrict the scope of a structure member. The private members of a structure can only be accessed by a few categories of functions— these include both functions that are declared inside the structure, as well as friend functions which are discussed later. On the other hand, the keyword public is used to specify the items in the *member list* that may be directly accessed by elements external to the structure.

If a member variable declaration is preceded by the keyword `static`, then this variable is shared among all objects of the class. In other words, if one object of the class modifies this variable, all objects of the class will "see" this modification. Thus, from the discussion in Section 4.1.1, it is clear that a private C++ variable is actually a member variable, and that a private C++ variable declared using `static` is actually a class variable. Also, recall from Section 4.1.1 that a member function was defined as a routine used to access member and class variables. Therefore, in C++ a member function would be a function declared in the public section of the class. C++ also allows a variable to be declared in the public section of the class, in which case, the variable may be accessed by consumers directly without using a member function. This tends to defeat the data encapsulation/message passing paradigm that forms the foundation of object-oriented programming. For this reason, the declaration of public variables is normally avoided. Thus, by declaring the data elements of a data type as private C++ variables, and the accessing routines as public functions, we can effectively construct the interface (wall) that should exist between an application program and a data type implementation.

C++ also provides a keyword called `class` that effectively replaces the need to use the `struct` keyword. Specifically, an alternative C++ class declaration is:

```
class class name {
    private:
        private items member list
    public:
        public items member list
};
```

There is only one difference between this construct and the structure construct presented previously. If the `private` statement is omitted in this class declaration, all member items preceding the `public` statement are assumed to be private items. In a structure, such items are `public` by default. The `class` keyword was provided so that C++ would use a terminology consistent with other object-oriented programming languages.

As an example of how an ADT can be implemented as a class, we present in Figure 4.3 a C++ class declaration that can be used to represent complex numbers, as well as the operations defined on complex numbers (the COMPLEX ADT was presented in Exercise 3.11). Note that in addition to the operators specified in Exercise 3.11, we have provided four additional functions for assigning values to the real and imaginary parts of a complex number, and for retrieving the real and imaginary parts of a complex number. Notice also that C++ has an additional comment specifier. The symbols `//` indicate that the remainder of the line on which they appear should be treated as a comment.

The implementation of the `assign_real()` member function would appear in the definition file as:

```
void Complex::assign_real(float re)    {real = re;}
```

```
class Complex {
   private:
      float real, imag;
   public:
      void assign_real(float);
      void assign_imag(float);
      float get_real();
      float get_imag();
      Complex add(Complex);
      Complex subtract(Complex);
      Complex multiply(Complex);
      Complex divide(Complex);
      // remaining member functions not shown
};
```

FIGURE 4.3
A declaration for a complex number class.

The double colon :: operator used in this definition is the scope resolution operator. Recall that the same function name may appear in more than one class. Thus, the scope resolution operator is necessary in order for the compiler to determine the class to which a given member function definition belongs. In the previous example, the scope resolution operator is used to specify that the function definition is a member of the Complex class. The implementations of the remaining member functions are left as an exercise.

Variables of type Complex can now be declared. For example,

```
Complex num1, num2, num3;
```

creates three objects of type Complex called num1, num2, and num3. Each of these objects maintains its own copy of the data elements real and imag; however, only one copy of the member functions exists. These objects may be operated on by invoking their member functions. For example, we might do the following:

```
num1.assign_real(3.2);
```

This statement uses the assign_real() member function to assign the value 3.2 to the member variable real.

The add() member function is invoked as follows:

```
num1 = num2.add(num3);
```

This adds the complex numbers represented by num2 and num3, and assigns the result to num1. A "cleaner" approach to the implementation of this addition operation will be presented later in this section when we discuss function overloading.

THE this POINTER. As demonstrated previously, class member functions may refer to other members of their class directly without using the structure membership operators. They may also refer to their class members using the this pointer.

The `this` pointer contains the address of the class object through which a member function has been invoked. When a member function accesses another member of the class, the `this` pointer is implied. Thus, the member function `assign_real()` given previously would be interpreted by the compiler as:

```
void Complex::assign_real(float re)  {this->real = re;}
```

In most cases it is not necessary for the programmer to use the `this` pointer.

INLINE FUNCTIONS. Upon reviewing the `assign_real()` member function implementation, it seems wasteful that we must invoke a function in order to assign a value to the member variable `real`. However, such an approach is necessary since we want `real` to be a private variable. This situation actually arises quite often in object-oriented programs—many member function definitions consist of only a single line of code. The problem with this approach is that the overhead associated with these function calls may actually consume more time than the operations the functions are performing.

Fortunately, C++ provides a means for eliminating the function call overhead associated with simple member functions. This is accomplished using *inline functions*. If a function is declared inline, the compiler attempts to replace every call of that function with a copy of the entire function. This is analogous to the substitution performed by the `#define` preprocessor directive. An inline function is declared by placing the keyword `inline` in front of the function declaration and definition. In addition, the resulting function definition must then be moved to the header file. For example, the `assign_real()` member function could be rewritten by placing the following definition in the header file for the complex class:

```
inline void Complex::assign_real(float re)  {real = re;}
```

C++ also provides a shorthand notation for specifying inline functions. This involves specifying the function body immediately after the function declaration in the class. For example, in the following class declaration the `assign_real()`, `assign_imag()`, `get_real()`, and `get_imag()` member functions are all implemented inline:

```
class Complex {
   private:
      float real, imag;
   public:
      void assign_real(float re)  {real = re;}
      void assign_imag(float im)  {imag = im;}
      float get_real()  {return real;}
      float get_imag()  {return imag;}
      // remaining members functions not shown
};
```

Note that in this case the keyword `inline` is not required. For purposes of clarity we will typically use the former approach.

```
#include <iostream.h>
main()
{
    int i=10;
    int& ref=i;   // ref refers to i
    cout ≪ "ref = " ≪ ref;   // prints ref = 10
    ref = 20;
    cout ≪ "i = " ≪ i;   // prints i = 20
}
```

FIGURE 4.4

A demonstration of the use of reference variables in C++. Notice that when `ref` is modified, so is the variable `i`.

Keep in mind that by declaring a function inline, we are only making a recommendation to the compiler. If the function is very large, it is unlikely that the function will actually be expanded inline.

REFERENCES.   The reference operator, &, is used to create a reference to a variable. This will allow us to pass variables to a function by reference if we so desire. (If the reference operator is not used, then a function parameter is passed by value as in the C programming language.) The syntax for declaring a reference is:

type& variable name = initialization expression;

Note that a reference to a type must be initialized by an object of the type, or by an object that can be converted to the type. The program shown in Figure 4.4 demonstrates how a reference to a variable can be used to change the value of the variable.[†]

The most common use of references is for specifying arguments and return values of functions. This allows call-by-reference. Passing an argument by reference to a function means that modifications made to the argument within the function change the actual argument, and not just a local copy of it. Thus, the swap routine given in Section 3.3 can be modified as shown in Figure 4.5 so that it uses references. Invoking this function using the main routine shown at the bottom of this figure produces the following output:

```
main(), Before: a = 10, b = 20
swap(), Before: x = 10, y = 20
swap(), After: x = 20, y = 10
main(), After: a = 20, b = 10
```

The difference between this swap routine and the one given in Figure 3.4 is in the parameter list. The `x` and `y` parameters are now references to `int`s instead of pointers-

---

[†]In Figure 4.4 the C++ header file `<iostream.h>` is included. This allows the output operator (≪) to be used to direct data to the standard output. The standard output is connected to the predefined iostream `cout`.

```
void swap(int& x, int& y)
{
    cout << "swap(), Before: x = " << x << ", y = " << y << endl;
    int temp;
    temp = x;
    x = y;
    y = temp;
    cout << "swap(), After: x = " << x << ", y = " << y << endl;
}

main()
{
    int a=10, b=20;
    cout << "main(), Before: a = " << a << ", b = " << b << endl;
    swap(a,b);
    cout << "main(), After: a = " << a << ", b = " << b << endl;
}
```

FIGURE 4.5
A function for swapping integers that accepts parameters passed by reference.

to-ints. Because of this modification the main routine does not have to pass pointers arguments to the swap routine, thereby avoiding pointer manipulations.

Another important aspect of references is that they allow large class objects to be passed as arguments to functions without a lot of overhead. Recall that when using pass-by-value, the entire object is copied with each function call. This is not the case if the object is passed by reference. If a reference argument is not going to be modified within a function, it is a good idea to declare it as a constant argument (using the keyword const). This will ensure that no accidental changes are made to the reference argument, and thus no changes will be made to the variable in the calling function to which the reference refers. The use of constant arguments is demonstrated later in this section.

FRIEND FUNCTIONS. If a function declaration in a class is preceded by the keyword friend, then that function is said to be a friend of the class. A friend function is not an actual member of the class; however, it is still permitted to access the nonpublic data members of the class. In other words, the friend mechanism can be used to give nonmembers of a class the ability to access the nonpublic members of the class. We will see an example of how friend functions can be used later in this section.

CONSTRUCTORS AND DESTRUCTORS. C++ provides a way for the class developer to specify what should happen when a new object needs to be created, or an existing object needs to be destroyed. Member functions known as constructors and destructors that accomplish these tasks can be provided by the developer of a class. A *constructor* is any member function with the same name as the class name. If a constructor is supplied in a class definition, it is invoked whenever an object of that class needs to be created. This may occur when a class object is declared, or when a class object is dynamically allocated using the new operator.[†] As with primitive data types, the compiler is responsible for allocating memory for class data elements. The constructor, however, can be used to initialize this allocated memory, and to assign dynamically allocated memory to pointer variable members of the class. A class may contain more than one constructor; however, each constructor must differ from the others in either the type or the number of parameters (this is discussed in more detail below).

Two forms of constructors have been given special names. The *default constructor* for a class is one that can be called without any arguments, and the *copy constructor* for a class is one that can be called with a single argument that has the same type as the class. Furthermore, this argument must be passed by reference. The default constructor is called whenever an array of objects needs to be created. The copy constructor can be called to make a copy of a class object. These two constructors are considered so basic that the compiler will automatically generate them if they are not supplied by the class developer. It is important to note, however, that such compiler-generated constructors will only create the class data members *without* initializing them.

Conversely, a *destructor* is used to destroy (i.e., reclaim) data pointed to by an object's data members immediately before the object itself is destroyed. A destructor is a member function with the same name as the class prefixed with a tilde. A class may contain only one destructor, and this destructor function must have an empty parameter list. The destructor is automatically called whenever an object goes out of scope. In addition, the delete operator will invoke the destructor associated with an object, prior to reclaiming the object.[‡] Thus, a destructor is typically not needed in a class unless the objects of the class have data members that point to dynamically allocated memory.

Below we add a constructor to the Complex class presented previously:

```
class Complex {
    private:
        float real, imag;
    public:
        Complex(float re=0, float im=0) {real=re; imag=im;}
        // remaining member functions not shown
};
```

The constructor for this class is the member function named Complex. Notice that a constructor does not supply a return value. In this example the constructor is imple-

---

[†]The new operator is used in C++ to perform dynamic memory allocation. It can be used in place of the malloc() function that is typically used in C programs.

[‡]The delete operator is used in C++ to reclaim dynamically allocated memory. It can be used in place of the free() function that is typically used in C programs. It should be invoked through a pointer to an object that was returned by the new operator.

mented inline. This example also illustrates another feature of the C++ programming language—the ability to supply default values for function parameters. In this case, both the real and imaginary parts of the complex number will be assigned the value zero if no parameter values are specified when the constructor is called. Examples of how this constructor can be called are given below. In this example, three objects of type `Complex` are declared and initialized differently depending upon how the constructor is called.

```
Complex num1;              // num1.Re=0.0   num1.Im=0.0
Complex num2(3.2);         // num2.Re=3.2   num2.Im=0.0
Complex num3(5.1, 2.7);    // num3.Re=5.1   num3.Im=2.7
```

Because the constructor for the `Complex` class does not initialize any data members to point to dynamically allocated memory, it is not necessary to supply a destructor. In other words, when objects of type `Complex` go out of scope, the compiler is able to reclaim all of the memory that was allocated when the object was created, without the use of a destructor. We will see a destructor used in the example presented in Section 4.3.

FUNCTION OVERLOADING. The parameter list of a function is often referred to as the *signature* of the function because it can be used to distinguish between two functions that have the same name. If two or more functions having the same scope share the same name, then this name is said to be *overloaded*. In C++, such functions may share the same name as long as each function has a unique signature. A signature is considered unique if it differs from other signatures in either the number, type, or ordering of its arguments. Note that functions differing only in the return type may not share the same name.

In C++, operators themselves can be overloaded; which proves quite useful when developing classes with operations that have arithmetic definitions. What we are talking about is actually a special type of function overloading called *operator overloading*. Most of the existing C++ operators can be overloaded. However, a new operator, such as `**` for exponentiation, cannot be introduced by the designer of a class—and the meaning of operators supplied with built-in data types cannot be changed. In addition, the predefined precedence of operators is preserved when they are overloaded. Furthermore, unary C++ operators must be overloaded as unary operators, and binary C++ operators must be overloaded as binary operators.

An operator function may either be a member function or a friend function; in both cases, at least one of the function arguments must be an object of the class itself. (Note, however, that the =, (), [], and —> operators may only be overloaded as member functions.)

An operator function is defined in the same manner as other functions, except that the function name (in this case, an operator symbol) must be preceded by the keyword `operator`. Consider the previous class developed to represent complex numbers. The + and += operators can be overloaded to perform addition of two

```
class Complex {
   private:
      float real, imag;
   public:
      Complex(float re=0, float im=0)  {real=re; imag=im;}
      //  operator overloading using member functions
      Complex operator+(const Complex&);
      Complex operator+=(const Complex&);
      //  remaining member functions not shown
};

Complex Complex::operator+(const Complex& z)
{return Complex(real + z.real, imag + z.imag);}

Complex Complex::operator+=(const Complex& z)
{real += z.real;  imag += z.imag;  return *this;}
```

FIGURE 4.6
Operator overloading using member functions.

complex numbers as shown in Figure 4.6. In this figure, the operator functions are member functions, and the implied first argument to these functions is the `this` pointer. In other words, the object that invokes the member function will serve as the operand on the left-hand side of the + or += operator, and the `Complex` object being passed to the function will serve as the operand on the right-hand side. Notice that this operand is passed as a constant reference. Definitions for the member operator functions are given below the class declaration. Since these are member function definitions, the scope resolution operator is used. Also note that the argument of the return statement in the + function definition invokes the constructor for the complex class, passing the real and imaginary parts of the resulting number as parameters.

If `Complex` objects A, B, and C are declared, the operator functions given in Figure 4.6 may be invoked using a member function call as follows:

```
C = A.operator+(B);
```

However, we may also invoke these member functions using:

```
C = A+B;
```

Another alternative is to overload these operators using a friend function as shown in Figure 4.7. Because these operators are being overloaded as friend functions (i.e., the functions are not members of the `Complex` class), the scope resolution operator is not needed in the function definitions shown below the class declaration. Notice also that these operator functions are able to directly access the private parts of the objects that are passed to them as parameters.

```
class Complex {
    private:
        float real, imag;
    public:
        Complex(float re=0, float im=0)  {real=re; imag=im;}
        // operator overloading using a friend function
        friend Complex operator+(const Complex&, const Complex&);
        friend Complex operator+=(Complex&, const Complex&);
        // remaining member functions not shown
};

Complex operator+(const Complex& z1, const Complex& z2)
{return Complex(z1.real + z2.real, z1.imag + z2.imag);}

Complex operator+=(Complex& z1, const Complex& z2)
{return Complex(z1.real += z2.real, z1.imag += z2.imag);}
```

FIGURE 4.7
Operator overloading using friend functions.

Given the same `Complex` objects declared previously, this friend operator function may be invoked using:

```
C = operator+(A,B);
```

or in an equivalent manner using:

```
C = A+B;
```

Note that in these examples, if the operator function is invoked without using the keyword `operator`, then from the user's point of view there is no difference between the member function or the friend function approach. However, there is a difference between these two approaches if both of the operands supplied are not objects of type `Complex`. First, consider the friend function implementation. If A and B are objects of type complex, then we may write the following:

```
B = 1+A;
```

The function prototype for the friend operator function given in Figure 4.7 states that both operands will be treated as complex objects. Thus, this statement is interpreted by the compiler as:

```
B = operator+(1,A);
```

This forces the value 1 to be converted to a `Complex` before it is added to A. How is this done? The compiler automatically converts 1 to a `Complex` using the constructor that is supplied with the class. The value one is treated as the first argument to the constructor, and the default value of zero is supplied as the second argument. Thus, 1 is converted into a complex object with its real part equal to one, and its imaginary part equal to zero.

Now consider what happens when the member operator function is used in the same statement. In this case, the compiler interprets the statement as:

```
B = 1.operator+(A);
```

and since 1 is not an object of type `Complex`, it cannot invoke the member operator function, resulting in an error.

From this discussion it can be concluded that friend functions should be used whenever you want the overloaded operator to treat its arguments symmetrically. Note, however, that the compiler must be able to convert these arguments to the appropriate type when using either automatic type conversion, or a constructor. A friend function is more desirable in the example discussed above because we would like the expressions `B = 1+A` and `B = A+1` to yield the same result.

CLASS TEMPLATES. The ability to create parameterized classes is provided by the template facility in C++. A *parameterized class* is a class in which the types of various members are specified using formal parameters when the class is declared, and actual values for these parameters are used to specify the missing type information when the class is used. Parameterized classes can be used to construct *container classes*— these are classes designed to operate on collections of elements of some unspecified type. The designer of a container class is interested in specifying how the container class operations should be performed, without considering what type of elements the class will contain. Thus, the designer of the container class specifies the type of the contained elements using a parameter, and users of the class can create different instances of the container class by supplying appropriate arguments for this parameter. The implementation of the MATRIX ADT can be thought of in terms of a container class. We would like to specify matrix operations without worrying about what type of elements the matrix might contain. We will demonstrate how the MATRIX ADT can be implemented as a class template in Section 4.3.

The template class syntax requires that the `template` keyword begin every forward declaration and definition of a template class. This keyword must be followed by a formal template parameter list that is surrounded by angle brackets. For example, in Section 4.3 we will declare a matrix class using

```
template<class T>
class Matrix {
   private:
       // private members
   public:
       Matrix(int rdim, int cdim, const T& initval)
       // remaining member functions
};
```

The use of the keyword `class` in the template parameter list indicates that the parameter that follows represents a type parameter. Thus, in the example above, `T` represents a formal type parameter that can be used throughout the class declaration. For example, this name appears as one of the arguments to the constructor. Outside the class declaration, however, the programmer must once again explicitly state the template parameters. For example, the constructor shown above would be defined using

```
template<class T>
Matrix<T>::Matrix(int rdim, int cdim, const T& initval)
{
    body of constructor
}
```

Note that the first occurrence of `Matrix` in this definition is modified with the template parameter list since it represents the name of the class template, while the second occurrence of `Matrix` is *not* modified with the template parameter list since it represents the name of a member function. Matrix objects can be created using this constructor as follows:

```
Matrix<int> my_matrix(2,3,1);
```

This statement creates a 2×3 matrix of integer elements called `my_matrix`, and initializes each element in the matrix to 1.

4.2.2   Inheritance

In C++, as in other object-oriented languages, a derived class inherits member variables, class variables, and member functions from the base class. The derived class may also add new member variables, class variables, or member functions that are necessary for its specialized operations. Additionally, a derived class may redefine any member function provided by the base class by simply supplying a new function that has the same name as the old member function in the base class. That is, the new member function in the derived class overloads the member function with the corresponding name in the base class. This allows different meanings to be attached to the same member function name; which member function is invoked when the member function name is used in a program depends upon the particular class being referenced.

The class syntax for C++ presented in Section 4.2.1 was actually not quite complete. In order to incorporate the capability of inheriting existing classes, the syntax of the class specification must be modified. The complete syntax is as follows:

```
class class name : derivation list   {
    private:
        private items member list
    protected:
        protected items member list
    public:
        public items member list
};
```

where the *derivation list* specifies the base classes that the class being defined will inherit, as well as the access control that will be applied to these inherited classes. The access specifier `protected` is used to restrict the scope of the items that follow it. Specifically, protected members behave as public class members to derived classes; but to clients of the class, the protected class members are private.

The syntax for the derivation list is a comma-separated list of the base class names prefixed by a keyword that controls the access to each base class:

`keyword` *base_class_name1*, `keyword` *base_class_name2*, . . .

The keywords that may be used in this derivation list are `public` and `private`. If a keyword is not given for a specific base class, it is assumed to be `private`. Below we discuss how the use of these keywords in the derivation list affects the members of derived classes, as well as the objects created from derived classes.

The inherited members of a public base class (i.e., a base class inherited using the `public` keyword) maintain their specified access levels within the derived class. In this case, private members of the base class may not be accessed by members of the derived class; however, protected and public members of the base class are also treated as protected and public members in the derived class. In addition, any class that is derived from this derived class using the keyword `public` will have access to the protected and public members of the original base class. Furthermore, objects created using the derived class will only have access to the public members of the base class.

If a derived class is created using a private base class, then the protected and public members of the base class essentially become private members in the derived class. The derived class may access these members, but any other class derived from this derived class may not. Furthermore, objects created using the derived class will not have access to *any* members of the base class.

To illustrate these concepts, consider the classes shown in Figure 4.8. In this figure, we first declare a class named `base` that contains three data members. Next, we declare another class called `derived_1` that inherits `base` as a private base class. The fact that `base` is inherited as a private class has no effect on the member functions specified in `derived_1`. The member functions supplied in this example verify this fact. Notice that the member functions in `derived_1` may directly access the protected and public member, but not the private member of `base`. Specifically, the `derived_1::assign_x()` member function will yield an error during compilation since it attempts to access a private member of the base class. In addition, objects of type `derived_1` are not allowed to access any of the members of `base`.

Finally, a third class called `derived_2` is created that inherits `derived_1`. This means that the accessing routines in `derived_2` may access the protected and public member of `derived_1`, but not the private member of `derived_1`, or any of the members of `base`, since `base` was inherited as a private class by `derived_1`. Objects of type `derived_2` would only be allowed access to the public members of `derived_1` and `derived_2`.

Note that if `base` were inherited by `derived_1` using the `public` keyword, then the `derived_2::print_y()` and `derived_2::print_z()` members functions would also be valid. In addition, objects of type `derived_2` would have access to the public members of `base`.

```
class base {
    private:
        int x;
    protected:
        int y;
    public:
        int z;
};

class derived_1 : private base {
    private:
        int a;
    protected:
        int b;
    public:
        void assign_x()   {x=a;}   // cannot access base::x
        void assign_y()   {y=a;}   // o.k.
        void assign_z()   {z=a;}   // o.k.
};

class derived_2 : public derived_1 {
    public:
        void print_a()   {cout << a;}   // cannot access derived_1::a
        void print_b()   {cout << b;}   // o.k.
        void print_x()   {cout << x;}   // cannot access base::x
        void print_y()   {cout << y;}   // cannot access base::y
        void print_z()   {cout << z;}   // cannot access base::z
};
```

FIGURE 4.8
A demonstration of inheritance and access control in C++. Note that there are a number of errors in this code.

4.2.3 Polymorphism Through Virtual Functions

Recall from our discussion in Section 4.1.4 that object-oriented programming languages support polymorphism through the use of dynamic binding, and that polymorphism allows an operation to be applied to objects of different classes at run time. In C++, a polymorphic function is called a *virtual function*. A virtual function is declared in a base class by using the keyword virtual in front of its declaration. As with other member functions, a virtual member function may be overloaded in derived classes by simply providing a new member function with the same name as the virtual member function in the base class. However, a member function that overloads a virtual member function is treated differently. The use of the keyword virtual signifies that implementation of the member function provided in the base class is a default which will only be used by derived classes when they do not supply their own implementation for the virtual function. If a derived class overloads the virtual function, then it will be used.

```
class base {
   private:
      int x;
   public:
      base()    {x=5;}
      virtual void print()   {cout ≪ "x=" ≪ x ≪ endl;}
};

class derived : base {
   private:
      int y;
   public:
      derived()   {y=10;}
      void print()   {cout ≪ "y=" ≪ y ≪ endl;} // overloads base::print()
};

main()
{
   base* bptr;
   base obj1;
   derived obj2;
   obj1.print();   // prints x=5
   obj2.print();   // prints y=10
   bptr = &obj1;
   bptr—>print();   // prints x=5
   bptr = &obj2;
   bptr—>print();   // prints y=10
}
```

FIGURE 4.9
A demonstration of a polymorphic function in C++. Notice that the keyword `virtual` is used in the base class, but not in the derived class.

Specifically, if a pointer to an object of the base class is declared, then pointers to objects of the derived class may be assigned to this base class pointer. Now, if a virtual member function is invoked, the type (i.e., class) of the object that is currently assigned to the base class pointer will determine which member function implementation is used. We illustrate this with an example in Figure 4.9. In this figure, a virtual function called `print()` is declared in the class named `base`. Next, we declare another class called `derived` that inherits `base`. This class provides a member function that overloads the virtual member function in its base class. Next, we use these classes in the main routine shown at the bottom of the figure. The significance of this example is that we were able to refer to the derived class through a pointer to the base class in the last member function call in `main()`. If the `base::print()` function had not been declared virtual, then this last member function call would have printed `x=5` instead of `y=10`.

The advantage offered by using virtual functions is that we can write more general programs. This results from the fact that we are not forced to restrict the classes of objects that the program may work with to only those that are known at compile time. Through the use of inheritance we may add additional objects that respond to messages in the program in a different manner. That is, the program satisfies the so-called ***open-closed principle*** in which the software is considered both open and closed at the same time. A program is said to be open if it is still available for extension, and it is said to be closed if it is available for use.

4.3 AN EXTENDED EXAMPLE: MATRIX ADT IMPLEMENTATION IN C++

We now demonstrate how the MATRIX ADT presented in Section 1.1.1 can be implemented in C++. Although this example does not require the use of inheritance or virtual functions, it is instructive to compare this implementation to the one given in Section 3.5 which uses the C programming language. We will use the same data structure as before (see Figure 3.16) to store the matrix data elements; however, the use of C++ will facilitate the construction and manipulation of this data structure. By using the resulting class, we will be able to write application programs that manipulate matrix objects with statements that look like mathematical expressions instead of function calls. At the conclusion of this example we will provide a set of guidelines that were used during the construction of this example, the use of which will greatly simplify the implementation of other ADTs.

The header file for the C++ MATRIX ADT implementation is shown in Figure 4.10. The `Matrix` class is declared in this file. This class contains the declarations for the private member variables that are used to store the row and column dimensions of a matrix, as well as a variable that points to the data structure containing the actual matrix elements. This class also provides a set of member functions that can be used to create and access the matrix data elements. As was discussed in Section 3.1, the contents of this header file are surrounded by the `#ifndef`—`#endif` preprocessor directives. From this point forward in the text, it will be understood that every header file we present contains these preprocessor statements, even if they are not shown in our source code listsings.

Four different constructors are provided (notice that each has a different signature). The first constructor, which takes no arguments, is the default constructor. An inline definition of this function is provided at the bottom of the figure. It is necessary to supply this constructor so that the data members of initially empty `Matrix` objects will be properly initialized. The second constructor is used to create a matrix object whose dimensions are initialized, but not its elements. The third constructor in this class is used to create a matrix object of specific dimensions, and assign initial values to all of the elements in the matrix. These initial values must be stored in an array in row-column order, and a pointer to the first element in this array is passed to the constructor. An implementation of this constructor is given in Figure 4.11. This constructor serves essentially the same purpose as the `create()` function discussed in Section 3.5. The final constructor provided by the `Matrix` class is the copy constructor. A definition for this function is given in Figure 4.12. As discussed previously, this is a special constructor that is used whenever a class object is initialized with

```
/* File: matrix.H */
#ifndef MATRIXH
#define MATRIXH

template<class T>
class Matrix {
  private:
    int row_dim, col_dim;
    T** element;
  public:
    inline Matrix(); // default constructor
    Matrix(int rdim, int cdim); // constructor
    Matrix(int rdim, int cdim, T* initval); // constructor
    Matrix(const Matrix<T>&); // copy constructor
    ~Matrix(); // destructor
    inline int Row() const; // returns the row dimension
    inline int Col() const; // returns the column dimension
    Matrix<T>& operator=(const Matrix<T>&);
    friend ostream& operator<<(ostream& os, const Matrix<T>&);
    friend Matrix<T>& operator+(const Matrix<T>&, const Matrix<T>&);
    friend Matrix<T>& operator*(const Matrix<T>&, const Matrix<T>&);
    friend Matrix<T>& operator*(const T& scalar, const Matrix<T>&);
    friend Matrix<T>& Transpose(const Matrix<T>&);
    // remaining member functions not shown
};

template<class T>
inline Matrix<T>::Matrix() {row_dim=col_dim=0; element=0;}

// remaining inline member function definitions not shown

#endif
```

FIGURE 4.10
The header file for the C++ MATRIX ADT implementation.

another class object. Once again, it is important that we supply this constructor so that object data members will be properly initialized whenever it is called. Consider the following statements:

```
Matrix X(2,2,data);
Matrix Y=X;
```

The first statement declares an object X of type Matrix and calls the constructor given in Figure 4.11. The next statement declares another object Y of type Matrix, and it uses the copy constructor to *initialize* the object. If a copy constructor were not provided, then the initialization would simply copy the values of all of the data members in X to the data members in Y. In this case the data member element in X and Y would both point to the same memory location. This situation is depicted

```
/* File: matrix.C */
template<class T>
Matrix<T>::Matrix(int rdim, int cdim, T* initval)
{
  row_dim = rdim;
  col_dim = cdim;
  element = new T* [row_dim];
  for (int i=0; i<rdim; i++)
    element[i] = new T[col_dim];
  // initialize the matrix elements
  for (i=0; i<rdim; i++)
    for (int j=0; j<cdim; j++)
      element[i][j] = *(initval + (cdim * i + j));
}
```

FIGURE 4.11
A constructor for the Matrix class.

in Figure 4.13 (a). We can avoid this problem by supplying a copy constructor as is demonstrated in Figure 4.13 (b).

It is important to notice the distinction between *initialization* and *assignment*. For example, the statement B=A in Figure 4.17 *assigns* the data members in object A to those in object B—this statement does *not* invoke the copy constructor! However, it is clearly the case that the situation depicted in Figure 4.13 will also result unless the = operator is overloaded. Thus, in Figure 4.10 we see that a member function declaration that overloads this operator is supplied. The definition of this member function will be nearly identical to the copy constructor definition, except that the

```
/* File: matrix.C */
template<class T>
Matrix<T>::Matrix(const Matrix<T>& m)
{
  row_dim = m.row_dim;
  col_dim = m.col_dim;
  element = new T* [row_dim];
  for (int i=0; i<row_dim; i++)
    element[i] = new T[col_dim];
  for (i=0; i<row_dim; i++)
    for (int j=0; j<col_dim; j++)
      element[i][j] = m.element[i][j];
}
```

FIGURE 4.12
The definition for the copy constructor of the Matrix class. This constructor dynamically allocates a set of matrix elements for the new object.

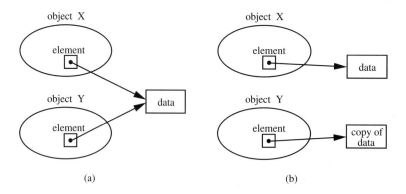

(a)   (b)

FIGURE 4.13
Assignment of `Matrix` object X to `Matrix` object Y when **(a)** the copy constructor is not provided, and **(b)** the copy constructor is provided.

= operator must return an object. Specifically, this function should return the object that called it (i.e., `return *this;`).

The `Matrix` class also declares a destructor. The destructor is necessary here because we must specify how the memory that is dynamically allocated by the constructors will be reclaimed. The `Matrix` destructor definition is shown in Figure 4.14. Note that in order to reclaim an array that was dynamically allocated with the `new` operator, the form

> `delete []` *expression*

must be used. In this case, *expression* is the pointer returned by the `new` operator when the array was dynamically allocated.

Referring back to Figure 4.10 we see that the `Row()` and `Col()` member functions are defined inline. The next member function declaration overloads the ≪ output operator. This operator will be used to output the elements of a matrix. Its definition is given in Figure 4.15. We also supply the definition for the matrix addition function in Figure 4.16. Notice that this function dynamically allocates a matrix using

```
/* File: matrix.C */
template<class T>
Matrix<T>::~Matrix()
{
   for (int i=0; i<row_dim; i++)
     delete [] element[i];
   delete [] element;
}
```

FIGURE 4.14
The destructor for the `Matrix` class.

```
/* File: matrix.C */
template<class T>
ostream& operator≪(ostream& os, const Matrix<T>& m)
{
  for (int i=0; i<m.row_dim; i++) {
    for (int j=0; j<m.col_dim; j++) {
      os ≪ "element(" ≪ i ≪ "," ≪ j ≪ ") = ";
      os ≪ m.element[i][j] ≪ endl;
    }
  }
  return os;
}
```

FIGURE 4.15

The definition for the overloaded operator function used to output a matrix. Note that the use of this operator requires an `ostream` (e.g., `cout`) as the left-hand operand, and a `Matrix` object as the right-hand argument.

the `new` operator, and assigns the resulting pointer to the variable `result`. The use of the `new` operator in this case will result in the construction of a `Matrix` object using the second constructor given in Figure 4.10. It is necessary to dynamically allocate this matrix so that the memory associated with it will not be reclaimed after the function call is completed and all local variables go out of scope.

Finally, the test program shown in Figure 4.17 demonstrates how this matrix class can be used. Four different matrix objects are created: A, B, C, and D. Matrices A and B store integer elements, while matrix C stores floating-point numbers. Matrix object D stores elements that are themselves matrices. Specifically, each element in D is initialized to the matrix C. It is important to supply a space between the angle brackets in this declaration; otherwise, the compiler cannot distinguish them from the ≫ operator. In the last line of this program, the overloaded form of the

```
/* File: matrix.C */
template<class T>
Matrix<T>& operator+(const Matrix<T>& m1, const Matrix<T>& m2)
{
  assert((m1.row_dim == m2.row_dim) && (m1.col_dim == m2.col_dim));
  Matrix<T>* result = new Matrix<T>(m1.row_dim, m1.col_dim);
  for (int i=0; i<m1.row_dim; i++)
    for (int j=0; j<m1.col_dim; j++)
      result->element[i][j] = m1.element[i][j] + m2.element[i][j];
  return *result;
}
```

FIGURE 4.16

The definition for the overloaded operator function used to perform addition using `Matrix` objects.

```
/* File: test.C */
#include "matrix.H"

main()
{
   static int data1[4] = {1,2,3,4};
   static float data2[4] = {0.1,0.3};
   Matrix<int> A(2,2,data1);
   Matrix<int> B(2,2);
   Matrix<float> C(2,1,data2);
   Matrix< Matrix<float> > D(2,2,C);  // spacing between angle brackets is required
   cout.precision(4);  // 4 digits of precision
   cout.setf(ios::showpoint);  // display the decimal point
   B = A;
   cout << "A + B = " << endl;
   cout << A + B << endl;
   cout << "D = " << endl;
   cout << D << endl;
}
```

FIGURE 4.17

The source code of the program used to test the MATRIX ADT implementation provided in the matrix.H and matrix.C files. To obtain an executable file, the object code produced by compiling matrix.C must be linked to the object code produced by compiling test.C.

output operator provided in the matrix class will be used to output each element of matrix D.

Notice how the ability of C++ to essentially add new data types to the language allows us to make the test file shown in Figure 4.17 much more readable than the one shown in Figure 3.20. That is, we can perform operations on matrix objects as if they were variables associated with a built-in data type. In addition, by packaging this ADT in a class, we can ensure that the data elements are only accessed through the accessing routines.

GUIDELINES FOR ADT IMPLEMENTATION. Building good classes for nontrivial ADT implementations is a difficult task. In order to simplify the work involved, we now provide the set of guidelines that was followed when constructing the MATRIX ADT implementation. This set of rules will guide the construction of all other ADT implementations given in this text. We also encourage the reader to use them since they take much of the "guesswork" out of the development process, and they lead to the development of code that is directly understood and supported by C++. This supports the production of efficient and safe code, even when the ADT being implemented is quite complex.

The principal idea behind these guidelines is to construct ADT implementations in such a way that they can be treated just like built-in C++ types. This means that the objects created using these rules can be assigned, declared, and passed as arguments to functions in the same manner as variables associated with built-in types. The reader is encouraged to review the application of each of the rules that follow in the MATRIX ADT example given at the beginning of this section. The guidelines are as follows:

1. Provide an appropriate set of constructors for initializing class objects. Specifically, every constructor should initialize objects in such a way that the class destructor can always be invoked on them. It is particularly important to supply the default and copy constructors for the following reasons. Recall that the default constructor is called automatically by the compiler when a constructor is needed that takes no arguments, or to initialize the members of an array of objects. If a default constructor is not provided, the compiler will provide one on the developer's behalf. A compiler-supplied default constructor will only initialize those data members which also have default constructors, and all other members will be left uninitialized.

    Recall that the copy constructor is used to construct an exact copy of an object. This constructor is called automatically by the compiler whenever an object is passed by value as a parameter, and is sometimes invoked when the value of an object is returned by a function. If a copy constructor is not provided by the class developer, a default copy constructor is provided by the compiler which simply copies the values of all data members in the input object (on a member-by-member basis) to the newly constructed object. Use of the compiler-supplied copy constructor will not copy any dynamically allocated data associated with pointer members. The problems this can lead to were depicted in Figure 4.13.

2. Provide an overloaded assignment operator. Once again, if this member function is not supplied, the compiler simply copies the data members of the object on the right-hand side of the assignment operator, on a member-by-member basis, to the data members of the object on the left-hand side. Notice that this operator is similar to the copy constructor, except that it is used for assignment, not initialization. Furthermore, this operator returns a value, whereas the copy constructor does not. The return type should be a reference to an object of the class. This eliminates the overhead associated with the creation of a temporary object. Furthermore, because the return value has the same type as input parameter, multiple object assignments in a single statement are allowed—e.g., A = B = C. Because this member function replaces the contents of one object with another, it must reclaim any memory dynamically allocated by the object being copied over (i.e., the left-hand operand). Failure to reclaim memory before pointer variables are reassigned can lead to dynamically allocated memory that is not referenced by *any* pointer. This problem is referred to as a ***memory leak***.

3. Provide a destructor to reclaim any memory that an object acquired through the execution of one of its constructors. The reason for supplying a destructor in this case is obvious—if one is not supplied, then the default destructor is invoked, and only the memory associated with data members is reclaimed. Thus, all pointers to memory dynamically allocated by the constructors will be lost. This again leads to memory leaks. Furthermore, if the previous guidelines have been followed, then we know that every object has been created by a constructor in such a way that

the destructor can be invoked on them. This is why we assigned the null pointer to the `element` data member in the default constructor for the `matrix` class (see Figure 4.10). Supplying the delete operator used in the `matrix` destructor (Figure 4.14) with the null pointer is perfectly valid—as we wish, nothing will happen. However, if `element` were left uninitialized, then whatever value it happened to store when it was created would be used by the delete operator as if it were a pointer to dynamically allocated memory.

4. Develop and test a class without using templates first. Once the class has been debugged and is working properly, make the modifications/insertions necessary to turn it into a parameterized class. This can often be done by using the typedef facility on the class data members that you wish to parameterize (e.g., see the C MATRIX ADT implementation given in Section 3.5). These data members can then be changed into the formal parameters of the template class.

Note that these guidelines only make sense if pointers and dynamic memory allocation are involved. This will be the case for nearly every ADT implementation presented in this book, and for almost every nontrivial class encountered in practice. We should also mention that in addition to these basic guidelines, it may be necessary to add constructors that allow objects of one class to be automatically converted to objects of another class that wish to use their data. The application under consideration will help determine the need for such constructors.

EXERCISES

4.1. What is the reason for not allowing member function declarations to be added to a class outside of the class declaration?

4.2. Write a string swapping routine that uses reference parameters to swap two strings. The function prototype for this function should look like:

```
void str_swap(char*& str1, char*& str2);
```

Use this function to perform a string swap in a test program. Note that C++ follows the C convention that the last "interesting" character in a string is followed by the null character.

4.3. What does the friend declaration in the class `bbb` below mean? That is, which members can objects of class `aaa` and class `bbb` access?

```
class aaa {
   private:
      // private members
   public:
      // public members
};

class bbb {
   friend class aaa;
   private:
      // private members
   public:
      // public members
};
```

4.4. Is it possible to gain access to the nonpublic members of a class by simply declaring a function to be a friend of that class, and then using this function to access the nonpublic class members? Explain your answer.

4.5. Given the following class declarations:

```
class cls_a {
    private:
        int w;
    protected:
        int x;
    public:
        cls_a() {w=1; x=2;}
        void foo() {cout << "w=" << w << endl;}
        virtual void bar() {cout << "x=" << x << endl;}
};

class cls_b : public cls_a {
    private:
        int y;
    protected:
        int z;
    public:
        cls_b() {y=3; z=4;}
        void foo() {cout << "y=" << y << endl;}
        void bar() {cout << "z=" << z << endl;}
};
```

what does the following program print? Explain your answer.

```
main()
{
    cls_a A;
    cls_b B;
    cls_a* bptr = &A;
    A.foo();
    A.bar();
    B.foo();
    B.bar();
    bptr->foo();
    bptr->bar();
    bptr = &B;
    bptr->foo();
    bptr->bar();
}
```

4.6. Implement the STRING ADT presented in Exercise 3.7 using the C++ programming language. Operating overloading should be used wherever it makes sense. For example, the + and += operators should be overloaded to perform string concatenation, and operators such as ==, <, >, and != should be overloaded to perform comparison operations. Use your string class to:

(*a*) Sort a sequence of strings provided as input.

(*b*) Determine if an input string is a palindrome.

4.7. In Figure 3.19, the C implementation of the MATRIX ADT addition operator uses a local variable of type `matrix` called `result`; however, in Figure 4.16, this same operator is implemented in C++, but `result` is now of type pointer-to-`Matrix`. Why was it necessary to make `result` a pointer variable in the C++ version?

4.8. The following program was developed using a version of the MATRIX ADT implementation presented in Section 4.3 in which the = operator was *not* overloaded:

```
#include "matrix.H"
main()
{
    static int data1[] = {1,2,3,4};
    static int data2[] = {1,1,1,1};
    Matrix<int> A, B;
    Matrix<int> *C, *D;
    C = new Matrix<int>(2,2,data1);
    A = *C;
    delete C;
    D = new Matrix<int>(2,2,data2);
    B = A + *D;
    cout << B << endl;
}
```

One execution of this program yielded the following output:

```
2        2
2        2
```

Why?

4.9. Implement the MATRIX ADT, including the *Determinant* and *Inverse* operations, using the C++ programming language.

4.10. Implement the COMPLEX ADT presented in Exercises 3.11 and 3.13 using the C++ programming language.

4.11. In this exercise you are to implement a C++ template ARRAY ADT class that can be used in place of built-in array types. Built-in array types in C/C++ possess a number of features that can make them difficult to use, including:

1. The size of a built-in array must be declared using a constant expression. A more flexible approach would allow the size of an array to be specified (or even modified) during run time.

2. There is no range checking when accessing built-in arrays. A safer approach would check the index when accessing an array to make sure it falls within the array bounds.

3. It is inconvenient that built-in arrays cannot be copied using a single assignment statement.

4. The size of a built-in array is not stored with it. Thus, when passing an array to a function, it is also necessary to pass an extra argument containing the size of the array.

Your ARRAY implementation should address each of the problems discussed above. A sample declaration for such a class is given next:

```
template <class T>
class Array {
  protected:
    int size;
    T* array;
    void Init(const T* bi_array, int sz_bi);
    // bi_array is a built-in array
  public:
    Array() {}
    inline Array(int sz);
    inline Array(const T* bi_array, int sz_bi);
    Array(const Array<T>&);
    inline ~Array();
    inline int Size() const;
    void Grow(int new_sz);
    void Shrink(int new_sz);
    Array<T>& operator=(const Array<T>&);
    inline T& operator[](int index);
    friend ostream& operator<<(ostream&, const Array<T>&);
};
```

4.12. Use the `Array` class developed in the previous exercise to implement the MATRIX ADT. The private member `element` should be declared using `Array`.

4.13. The ability to generate random numbers from various probability distributions is required in a variety of computing applications. Assume you are given a base class, `pdf`, whose declaration is given in Figure 4.18. By itself, this class will not be useful—only through inheritance will it obtain sufficient functionality. The `Draw()` member function is used to select a random value from a probability distribution. The manner in which this function is implemented will depend upon the specific distribution. For this reason, `Draw()` is declared as a virtual function. Since we used `=0` when declaring `Draw()`, it

```
/* file: pdf.H */
#include <stdlib.h>  // random() and srandom() are declared here

class pdf {
  protected:
    const double MAX;    // 2^31 − 1, random() returns a value in [0, MAX]
    const double TWOPI;  // 2π
  public:
    pdf() : MAX(2147483647.0), TWOPI(6.2831852) {}
    void SetRand(int seed) {srandom(seed);}
    virtual double Draw()=0;  // a pure virtual function
    virtual void Type()=0;    // prints name of distribution & associated parameters
};
```

FIGURE 4.18
The declaration of the base probability class `pdf`.

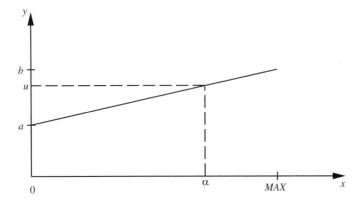

FIGURE 4.19
The mapping of a $(0, MAX)$–uniform random number α to an (a, b)–uniform random number u.

```
/* file: pdf.H */
class uniform_pdf : public pdf {
  protected:
    double a,b;
  public:
    uniform_pdf(double arg1=0, double arg2=1) {a=arg1; b=arg2;}
    inline double Draw();
    inline void Type();
};

inline double uniform_pdf::Draw()
{double slope = (b-a)/MAX; return slope * random() + a;}
```

FIGURE 4.20
A C++ class that can be used to generate (a, b)–uniform random numbers.

is actually a ***pure virtual function***, which means that every class which inherits `pdf` must supply its own overloaded version of `Draw()`. The member function `SetRand()`, when initialized with an appropriate seed, is used to initialize the random number generator associated with this class. Initializing the random number generator to a given seed will always cause it to produce the same sequence of numbers.[†] Figure 4.19 demonstrates how an (a, b)–uniform random number (i.e., a uniform random number in the range $[a, b]$) can be created from a $(0, MAX)$–uniform random number. In Figure 4.20 we demonstrate how a class that is used to draw random numbers from a uniform distribution can be created. Pseudorandom numbers from virtually any distribution can be

---

[†]This appears to be a contradiction. How can a sequence of numbers be random if it is completely determined by the seed? The answer is that the sequence is not *truly* random, instead it is said to be ***pseudorandom***. By this we mean that the sequence satisfies certain statistical tests of "randomness," and therefore appears to be random. For simplicity, however, we shall call the sequence random.

obtained through the transformation of uniform pseudorandom numbers. In this exercise we consider the generation of pseudorandom numbers from a number of distributions that provide good mathematical models for many different physically observed pseudorandom phenomena. For each of the distributions discussed here, develop a class that can be used to draw pseudorandom numbers from that distribution. The `pdf` class should serve as the base class for each implementation. Test your classes by separately plotting the mathematical representation of each distribution, and overlaying them with a histogram of pseudorandom numbers drawn from an object of the corresponding class.

(*a*) The mathematical representation of the ***normal*** (or ***Gaussian***) ***distribution*** is given by

$$f(x) = \frac{e^{-(x-\mu)^2/2\sigma^2}}{\sigma\sqrt{2\pi}} \qquad \text{for } -\infty < x < \infty$$

where μ and σ are the mean and standard deviation, respectively. If we let U_1 and U_2 represent two $(0, 1)$–uniform random numbers, then two standard normal (i.e., normal with $\mu = 0$ and $\sigma = 1$) variables Z_1 and Z_2 can be obtained by setting

$$Z_1 = \cos(2\pi U_1)\sqrt{-2\ln(U_2)}$$

$$Z_2 = \sin(2\pi U_1)\sqrt{-2\ln(U_2)}$$

This technique is known as the ***Box-Muller method***. A normal random variable X can be obtained from a standard normal random variable Z using $X = Z\sigma + \mu$.

(*b*) The mathematical representation of the ***exponential distribution*** is given by

$$f(x) = \lambda e^{-\lambda x} \qquad \text{for } x \geq 0$$

where $1/\lambda$ is the mean. If U is a $(0, 1)$–uniform random number, then an exponentially distributed random variable X can be obtained by using $X = -\ln(1 - U)/\lambda$.

(*c*) The mathematical representation of the ***Poisson distribution*** is given by

$$f(x) = \frac{e^{-\theta}\theta^x}{x!} \qquad \text{for } x = 0, 1, 2, \ldots$$

where the mean and variance are both θ. A Poisson random variable X can be generated from $(0, 1)$–uniform random variables using the following procedure:

```
Draw()
1    X ← 1    m ← e^θ
2    while m ≥ 1 do
3        U ← (0, 1)–uniform random number
4        X ← X + 1    m ← mU
5    return X
```

4.14. Suppose that a continuous signal has been discretized into a finite-duration sequence $x[n] =< x(0), x(1), \ldots, x(n-1) >$ by sampling it at n equally spaced intervals. The ***discrete Fourier transform*** (***DFT***) of this sequence is given by:

$$X(k) = \frac{1}{n}\sum_{i=0}^{n-1} x(n)e^{-jk(2\pi/n)i}, \qquad k = 0, 1, \ldots, n-1 \tag{4.1}$$

The set of values, $X(0), X(1), \ldots, X(n-1)$, determined by this equation are called the discrete Fourier transform samples of $x[n]$. They represent the spectral samples of $x[n]$.

One of the most important features of the DFT is that it can be used to perform the convolution of two finite-duration sequences. This operation is commonly performed when processing digital signals, and can also be used to multiply two polynomials. Equation (4.1) can be rewritten in matrix-vector form as:

$$
\begin{bmatrix} X(0) \\ X(1) \\ X(2) \\ \vdots \\ X(n-1) \end{bmatrix} = \frac{1}{n} \begin{bmatrix} 1 & 1 & 1 & \cdots & 1 \\ 1 & e^{-j(2\pi/n)} & e^{-j(4\pi/n)} & \cdots & e^{-j(2\pi/n)(n-1)} \\ 1 & e^{-j(4\pi/n)} & e^{-j(8\pi/n)} & \cdots & e^{-j(4\pi/n)(n-1)} \\ \vdots & & & & \\ 1 & e^{-j(2\pi/n)(n-1)} & e^{-j(4\pi/n)(n-1)} & \cdots & e^{-j(2\pi/n)(n-1)(n-1)} \end{bmatrix}
$$

$$
\times \begin{bmatrix} x(0) \\ x(1) \\ x(2) \\ \vdots \\ x(n-1) \end{bmatrix}
$$

Use C++ implementations of the COMPLEX and MATRIX ADTs to compute the discrete Fourier transform samples of the following sequence:

$$
x(0) = \frac{1}{2}, \quad x(1) = 1, \quad x(2) = \frac{3}{2}, \quad x(3) = 2, \quad x(4) = \frac{3}{2}, \quad x(5) = 1, \quad x(6) = \frac{1}{2}
$$

with $x(n) = 0$ for all $n > 6$.

CHAPTER NOTES

Peterson [118] presents a collection of papers that discuss the concepts of object-oriented programming. An introductory level text that treats this subject matter, and provides numerous examples using a variety of different object-oriented languages, is Budd [25]. The introductory chapters of Cox [37] and Meyer [101] provide excellent discussions regarding the motivation for object-oriented programming. In particular, Cox expounds the idea of treating classes as software ICs. There is also a journal entitled the *Journal of Object-Oriented Programming*, which is devoted entirely to the subject of object-oriented programming. The text by Booch [21] provides an excellent treatment of object-oriented design with examples in a number of languages, including C++. Booch also introduces a number of diagrammatic techniques that can be used to graphically depict the structure and temporal relationships between entities in an object-oriented system. These techniques are useful in the development of very large software systems.

The concept of embedding abstract data types in a programming language can be traced to the class construct found in the SIMULA 67 language [19]. In fact, Stroustrup [143] states that the C++ language was originally invented because he "wanted to write some event-driven simulations for which SIMULA 67 would have been ideal, except for efficiency considerations." C++ language references include Stroustrup [144] and Lippman [93], with the latter being more tutorial in nature. These references also discuss how to call C functions from within C++ programs. Additional references that prove quite useful are Meyers [102] and Coplien [35].

For a discussion of random numbers, pseudorandom numbers, and the derivation of nonuniform random numbers, see Knuth [87] and Devroye [41].

A detailed development of the discrete Fourier transform, along with demonstrations of its applicability to various problem domains, is provided by Oppenheim, Willsky, and Young [112]. The continuous-time Fourier transform has a long history dating back to the work of Jean Baptiste Joseph Fourier in the early 1800s; however, much of the mathematical theory involved predates Fourier's work. The extension of Fourier analysis to discrete-time signals (which lead to the development of the DFT) occurred in the 1940s and 1950s, and parallels the development of digital computers. From equation (4.1), it is easy to see that the computational cost of an n-point DFT is $\Theta(n^2)$. In 1965 Cooley and Tukey [34] revolutionized the field of digital signal processing by demonstrating that an n-point DFT could be computed in $\Theta(n \log n)$ time using a divide-and-conquer algorithm which is now called the *fast Fourier transform* (*FFT*).

PART
II

BASIC DATA STRUCTURES

INTRODUCTION TO PART II

The set is a fundamental structure in mathematics that is used to group objects together. The concept of a set can also serve as the basis for a wide variety of useful abstract data types. Indeed, a large number of computer applications involve the manipulation of sets of data elements. Thus, it makes sense to investigate data structures and algorithms that support efficient implementation of various operations on sets.

It is important to distinguish between the mathematical concept of a set (discussed in Appendix B), and the sets considered here. A set in mathematics is unchanging, while the sets we will consider change over time as data elements are added or deleted. Thus, we will refer to them as *dynamic sets*. In addition, we will assume that each element in a dynamic set contains an identifying field called a *key*, and that a total ordering relationship exists on these keys (the total ordering relationship was discussed in Section 2.4). In order to simplify analysis we will assume that no two elements of a dynamic set contain the same key, unless we explicitly state otherwise. In practice this restriction is typically quite easy to remove, at the expense of additional checks in the source code.

Following the approach outlined in Chapter 1, we will specify the concept of a dynamic set as an ADT—that is, as a collection of data elements, along with the legal operations defined on these data elements—and we will consider different approaches to implementing this DYNAMIC SET ADT. If the DYNAMIC SET ADT is implemented properly, application programmers will be able to use dynamic sets without having to understand their implementation details. As discussed in Chapter 1, the use of ADTs in this manner simplifies design and development, and promotes reusability of software components.

Below we supply a list of general operations for the DYNAMIC SET ADT. In each of these operations, S represents a specific dynamic set.

1. *Search*(S, k). Returns the element with key k in S, or the null value if an element with key k is not in S.
2. *Insert*(S, x). Adds element x to S. If this operation is successful, the boolean value true is returned; otherwise, the boolean value false is returned.
3. *Delete*(S, k). Removes the element with key k in S. If this operation is successful, the boolean value true is returned; otherwise, the boolean value false is returned.
4. *Minimum*(S). Returns the element in dynamic set S that has the smallest key value, or the null value if S is empty.
5. *Maximum*(S). Returns the element in S that has the largest key value, or the null value if S is empty.
6. *Predecessor*(S, k). Returns the element in S that has the largest key value less than k, or the null value if no such element exists.
7. *Successor*(S, k). Returns the element in S that has the smallest key value greater than k, or the null value if no such element exists.

In addition, when considering the DYNAMIC SET ADT (or any modifications of this ADT) we will assume the following operations are available:

1. *Empty*(S). Returns a boolean value, with true indicating that S is an empty dynamic set, and false indicating that S is not.
2. *MakeEmpty*(S). Clears S of all elements, causing S to become an empty dynamic set.

Since these last two operations are often trivial to implement, they generally will not be considered in our analysis.

In many instances an application will only require the use of a few DYNAMIC SET operations. In fact, some groups of these operations are used so frequently that they are given special names. For example, the ADT that supports *Search*, *Insert*, and *Delete* operations is called the DICTIONARY ADT. We will also introduce the STACK, QUEUE, and PRIORITY QUEUE ADTs, which are all special types of dynamic sets.

Chapters 5 through 9 describe a variety of data structures that can be used to implement either the DYNAMIC SET ADT, or ADTs that support specific subsets of the DYNAMIC SET ADT operations. Each of the data structures described will be analyzed in order to determine how efficiently they support the implementation of these operations. In each case, our analysis will be performed in terms of n, the number of data elements stored in the dynamic set. This analysis will demonstrate that there is no optimal data structure for implementing dynamic sets. Rather, the best implementation choice will depend upon which operations need to be supported, the frequency with which specific operations are used, and possibly many other factors. As always, the more we know about how a specific application will use data, the better we can fine tune the associated data structures so that this data can be accessed efficiently.

The list data structure is introduced in Chapter 5, along with two different approaches to storing lists in computer memory—sequential mapping and linked lists. We then demonstrate how all of the DYNAMIC SET ADT operations listed previously can be implemented in $O(n)$ time using either of these representations. In the extended example for this chapter we revisit the MATRIX ADT, demonstrating how sparse matrices can be efficiently implemented using lists.

In Chapter 6 we consider stacks and queues, two special dynamic sets that are used so frequently in computer applications that we will define ADTs for them. Stacks and queues are examples of dynamic sets that only support a subset of the DYNAMIC SET ADT operations. In addition, insertions into and deletions from stacks and queues are defined to occur in a specific order. The list data structures developed in the previous chapter will be used, through inheritance, to implement the STACK and QUEUE ADTs. The extended example in this chapter shows how to simulate a queueing system.

The binary search tree data structure, discussed in Chapter 7, is a binary tree in which the vertices must obey a specific order. A binary search tree can be used to implement all of the DYNAMIC SET ADT operations in $O(h)$ time, where h is the height of the tree. In the worst case, h equals n, and this data structure is no better than a list; however, we use average-case analysis in this chapter to argue that a binary search tree is likely to have a height closer to $\log n$. Binary search trees also serve as the basis for a number of more sophisticated data structures presented in Chapter 11. These data structures use subtree rotations to ensure that the height of a binary search tree is $O(\log n)$.

Chapter 8 introduces the hash table, a data structure that is used to implement the DICTIONARY ADT. Although the worst-case time to perform the DICTIONARY ADT operations using a hash table is $O(n)$, it is possible to show, using a probabilistic analysis, that the expected time to perform these operations is $O(1)$. An application of hash functions in cryptography is given at the conclusion of this chapter.

The priority queue, introduced in Chapter 9, is another dynamic set variation that is frequently used in computer applications. The PRIORITY QUEUE ADT is used to store elements in a dynamic set and retrieve them based upon the priority of their keys. In this chapter we demonstrate how such an ADT can be used to perform discrete-event simulation. Next we consider data structures that can be used to efficiently implement the special operations required by the PRIORITY QUEUE ADT. We conclude this chapter with a discussion of Huffman codes, which are commonly used in data compression.

CHAPTER
5

LISTS

A list is one of the most fundamental data structures used to store a collection of data items. In fact, lists are used so frequently that it makes sense to define a LIST ADT. The importance of the LIST ADT is that it can be used to implement a wide variety of other ADTs. That is, the LIST ADT often serves as a basic building block in the construction of more complicated ADTs. In this chapter, we will define the LIST ADT and investigate techniques for representing lists in computer memory. We will then demonstrate how lists can be used to implement the DYNAMIC SET ADT, as well as a number of other ADTs.

5.1 THE LIST ADT

A list may be defined as a dynamic ordered n-tuple:

$$L = (l_1, l_2, \ldots, l_n) \tag{5.1}$$

where l_i is the i-th element in the list. The use of the term *dynamic* in this definition is meant to emphasize that the elements in this n-tuple may change over time. Notice that these elements have a linear order that is based upon their position in the list. The first element in the list, l_1, is called the **head** of the list; while the last element, l_n, is referred to as the **tail** of the list. The number of elements in a list L is denoted by $|L|$, which we will also refer to as the length of the list. Thus the empty list, represented by (), has length 0. For the list given in equation (5.1) $|L| = n$.

We will not place any restrictions on the type of elements that a list may store. If all of the elements stored in a list are of the same type, then the list is said to be ***homogeneous***. However, if different types of elements are stored in the list (e.g., one element is an integer and another is a real number), then the list is said to be ***heterogeneous***. In many applications it is also useful to work with lists of lists. In this case, each element of the list is itself a list. For example, consider the list

$$L = ((3), (4, 2, 5), (12, 7, (8, 4), 1), ())$$

This list contains four elements. The first element is a list containing a single element 3. The next element is a list containing the elements 4, 2, and 5. The third element in L is a list containing four elements—the first element is 12, the second element is 7, the third element is a list containing the elements 8 and 4, and the last element is 1. The last element in L is an empty list.

The operations we will define for accessing list elements are given below. For each of these operations, L represents a specific list. It is also assumed that a list has a current position variable that refers to some element in the list. This variable can be used to iterate through the elements of a list.

1. *Insert*(L, x, i). Adds element x to L at position i, causing elements $l_i, l_{i+1}, \ldots, l_n$ to become elements $l_{i+1}, l_{i+2}, \ldots, l_{n+1}$, and the length of the list to become $n + 1$. If this operation is successful, the boolean value true is returned; otherwise, the boolean value false is returned.

2. *Append*(L, x). Adds element x to the tail of L, causing the length of the list to become $n + 1$. If this operation is successful, the boolean value true is returned; otherwise, the boolean value false is returned.

3. *Retrieve*(L, i). Returns the element stored at position i of L, or the null value if position i does not exist.

4. *Delete*(L, i). Deletes the element stored at position i of L, causing elements $l_{i+1}, l_{i+2}, \ldots, l_n$ become elements $l_i, l_{i+1}, \ldots, l_{n-1}$, and the length of the list becomes $n - 1$. If this operation is successful, the boolean value true is returned; otherwise, the boolean value false is returned.

5. *Length*(L). Returns $|L|$, the length of L.

6. *Reset*(L). Resets the current position in L to the head (i.e., to position 1) and returns the value 1. If the list is empty, the value 0 is returned.

7. *Current*(L). Returns the current position in L.

8. *Next*(L). Increments and returns the current position in L. That is, if the current position is i, the current position becomes $i + 1$, and the value $i + 1$ is returned.

Note that only the *Insert*, *Delete*, *Reset*, and *Next* operations modify the lists to which they are applied. The remaining operations simply query lists in order to obtain information about them. Of course these are only a small number of the operations that can be defined on lists. Nevertheless, we will find them quite useful when constructing other ADTs that are based on the LIST ADT.

Let us now demonstrate how the LIST ADT can be used in the design of another ADT, the POLYNOMIAL ADT. Polynomials of the form

$$p(x) = a_n x^n + a_{n-1} x^{n-1} + \cdots + a_1 x + a_0$$

can be represented using a list as follows: Each element of the list stores the coefficient and exponent of a particular term in the polynomial. For example, the first element in the list will contain the value of the coefficient a_n and the exponent n. If $a_{n-1} \neq 0$, then the second element in the list will contain a_{n-1} and $n - 1$. If $a_{n-1} = 0$ and $a_{n-2} \neq 0$, then the second element in the list will contain a_{n-2} and $n - 2$, and so on. Thus, only terms that have nonzero coefficients are stored in the list. For example, the polynomial $p(x) = 5x^3 + 10x - 7$ would be represented by a list with compound data elements: $l_1 = 5, 3$; $l_2 = 10, 1$; and $l_3 = -7, 0$.

Now, assume that we have two polynomials $p_1(x)$ and $p_2(x)$ stored in lists L_1 and L_2, respectively, and we wish to create a third list that contains the polynomial $p_3(x)$, where $p_3(x) = p_1(x) + p_2(x)$. We begin by examining the elements at the head of L_1 and L_2. If their exponents are equal, then their coefficients are added and stored in a new element, along with the exponent of L_1 and L_2. This new element is then appended to the tail of the third list; call it L_3. However, if the exponent of the first element in L_1 is greater than that of the corresponding element in L_2, then a duplicate of the first element in L_1 is created and appended to the tail of L_3. Conversely, if the exponent of the first element in L_1 is less than that of the corresponding element in L_2, then a duplicate of the first element in L_2 is created and appended to the tail of L_3. This continues until all elements in lists L_1 and L_2 have been examined. For example, if we wish to add the polynomials $2x^4 - x + 10$ and $x^3 + x + 5$, we would first represent them in lists L_1 and L_2 as follows:

$$L_1 : \ l_1 = 2, 4; \ l_2 = -1, 1; \ l_3 = 10, 0$$
$$L_2 : \ l_1 = 1, 3; \ l_2 = 1, 1; \quad l_3 = 5, 0$$

Next, we examine the elements at the head of each list. Since the term $2x^4$ has a larger exponent than the term x^3, an element containing the coefficient 2 and the exponent 4 is appended to L_3. Continuing in this fashion until both L_1 and L_2 have been traversed yields the following result:

$$L_3 : \ l_1 = 2, 4; \ l_2 = 1, 3; \ l_3 = 15, 0$$

An algorithmic description of these steps using the LIST ADT operations is given in Figure 5.1. The implementation of this algorithm, as well as the implementation of additional POLYNOMIAL ADT operations, are left as exercises.

We would like to store the items belonging to a list in a manner that allows them to be accessed as efficiently as possible. In the following sections, we will investigate two basic approaches. One stores the list elements in contiguous memory locations, and the other uses pointers to connect list elements that reside in noncontiguous memory locations. The efficiency of both of these approaches is considered in detail below.

PolyAdd(LIST L_1, LIST L_2)
```
1    Reset(L₁);    Reset(L₂)
2    while Current(L₁) ≤ Length(L₁) and Current(L₂) ≤ Length(L₂) do
3        term₁ ← Retrieve(L₁,Current(L₁));    term₂ ← Retrieve(L₂,Current(L₂))
4        if term₁[exp] = term₂[exp] then    ▷ exponents of terms are equal
5            term₃[coef] ← (term₁[coef] + term₂[coef]);    term₃[exp] ← term₁[exp]
6            Next(L₁);    Next(L₂)
7        else if term₁[exp] > term₂[exp] then
8            term₃ ← term₁;    Next(L₁)
9        else    ▷ L₁ term exponent < L₂ term exponent
10           term₃ ← term₂;    Next(L₂)
11       if term₃[coef] ≠ 0 then    ▷ is the resulting coefficient nonzero?
12           Append(L₃, term₃)
13   while Current(L₁) ≤ Length(L₁) do    ▷ copy any leftover portion of L₁
14       Append(L₃,Retrieve(L₁,Current(L₁)));    Next(L₁)
15   while Current(L₂) ≤ Length(L₂) do    ▷ copy any leftover portion of L₂
16       Append(L₃,Retrieve(L₂,Current(L₂)));    Next(L₂)
17   return L₃
```

FIGURE 5.1

Polynomial addition using the LIST ADT. The variables $term_1$, $term_2$, and $term_3$ are used to store compound data objects that represent polynomial terms. These compound data objects have a coefficient field, $coef$, and an exponent field, exp.

5.2 SEQUENTIAL MAPPING

If all of the elements that comprise a given data structure are stored one after the other in consecutive memory locations, we say that the data structure is ***sequentially mapped*** into computer memory. Sequential mapping makes it possible to access any element in the data structure in constant time. Given the starting address of the data structure in memory, we can find the address of any element in the data structure by simply calculating its offset from the starting address. An array is an example of a sequentially-mapped data structure. Because it takes the same amount of time to access any element, a sequentially-mapped data structure is also called a ***random access data structure***. That is, the accessing time is independent of the size of the data structure, and therefore requires $\Theta(1)$ time.

The LIST ADT may be implemented using sequential mapping by allocating an array of memory locations at compile time that is big enough to hold all of the list elements. Figure 5.2 demonstrates how the elements of a list would be stored in the array $a[0..n-1]$. Note that list element l_i is stored in array location $a[i-1]$, and that successive list elements are stored in consecutive array locations. The advantages

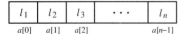

FIGURE 5.2

The sequential mapping of a list into an array.

offered by this approach include its simplicity, as well as the efficiency with which the LIST ADT operations can be implemented. The main disadvantage that results from allocating the array at compile time is that an *a priori* limit must be placed on the number of elements that can be stored in the list. This can lead to problems at run time. If the size of the list grows beyond the maximum specified size, then an obvious error situation arises. Since in many applications it is not known how large a list may grow, one approach is to choose the maximum size very large in order to ensure that this error situation does not occur. This can lead to inefficiencies, in terms of wasted memory, if the size of the list turns out to be quite small at run time. Another approach overcomes this size restriction by dynamically allocating the array, and resizing it as necessary during run time. This approach is discussed in more detail in the following section.

5.2.1 List Operations

Let us now consider the efficiency with which the LIST ADT operations can be implemented when using an array. Since this approach allows us to randomly access the data structure, the *Retrieve* operation can be implemented in $\Theta(1)$ time. However, the *Insert* operation takes $O(n)$ time, since the integrity of the sequential mapping must be maintained after an insertion. If an element is inserted at the i-th position of a list, the elements stored in array locations $i-1$ through $n-1$ must all be shifted "up" one array location. In the worst case, the new element is inserted at the head of the list, and n shifts are required. If we store the length of the list in a variable, then the *Length* operation can be implemented in constant time. Likewise a list can be checked to see if it is empty in constant time by testing if this length variable is zero, and a list can be made empty by setting its length variable equal to zero. Because the *Append* operation adds an element to the end of the array, no shifting is required, and it can be accomplished in $\Theta(1)$ time (assuming the array has enough room to store another element). It is also easy to see that a variable can be used to store the current position in a list, allowing the *Reset* and *Next* operations to be implemented in $\Theta(1)$ time.

We still must handle the situation in which an *Insert* or *Append* operation causes the list to exceed available array memory. This must either be treated as an error, or handled by allocating more memory. Before discussing one common strategy for allocating more memory, let us first define the **load factor** of an array to be the number of elements stored in the array, divided by the size of the array (if an array has a size of zero, we assign it a load factor of 1). Based on this definition, the strategy is as follows: dynamically allocate a new array that is twice the size of the current array whenever the load factor reaches 1, and then copy all of the elements stored in the current array into the new array. Furthermore, in order to minimize unused memory, dynamically allocate a new array that is one-half the size of the current array whenever the load factor is reduced to one-fourth or below, and then copy the elements stored in the current array into the new array. Note that the copying associated with these cases does not change the asymptotic complexity of the *Insert* or *Delete* operations, but it does cause the running time of the *Append* operation to become $O(n)$ instead of $\Theta(1)$.

5.2.2   Array Implementation

We now consider a C++ implementation of the LIST ADT using a dynamically-allocated random-access data structure which we shall refer to as a ***dynamic list***. Since we would like this list to be able to hold arbitrary types of elements, we will implement it as a parameterized class by using the template facility. Figure 5.3 shows the portion of the header file containing the declaration of the class DynList. Notice the forward declaration for the template class called DynListIterator. This forward declaration informs the program that the template class DynListIterator exists, and that its definition will occur somewhere else in the program. The DynList-Iterator class is an auxiliary class that will be used to implement some of the LIST

```
/* File: dynlist.H */
// forward declaration for iterator class
template <class Type> class DynListIterator;

template<class T>
class DynList {
  friend class DynListIterator<T>;
  private:
    int length, size;
    T* element;
  public:
    inline DynList();
    inline DynList(const T&);
    DynList(const DynList<T>&);
    inline ~DynList();
    DynList<T>& operator=(const DynList<T>&);
    friend ostream& operator<<(ostream&, const DynList<T>&);
    Boolean Insert(const T&, int);
    Boolean Append(const T&);
    T& Retrieve(int) const;
    Boolean Delete(int);
    inline int Length() const;
    inline Boolean Empty() const;
    inline void MakeEmpty();
};

template<class T>
inline DynList<T>::DynList(const T& elm)
{size = 2; element = new T[size]; element[0]=elm; length=1;}

template<class T>
inline DynList<T>::~DynList() {delete [] element;}

// remaining inline function definitions not shown
```

FIGURE 5.3
The C++ declaration of the DynList class.

ADT operations. This class is discussed in more detail below. This forward declaration is necessary because a type argument is supplied with the `DynListIterator` class when it is declared a friend inside the `DynList` class declaration. Specifically, the first friend declaration inside the `DynList` class states that for every instantiation of `DynList` to a particular type, all corresponding `DynListIterator` instantiations are its friend. For example, only integer `DynListIterator` objects can be friends of integer `DynList` objects. If the type argument were not specified in this friend declaration, then any instantiation of the `DynListIterator` would be a friend of a `DynList` object. This would allow, for example, an integer `DynListIterator` object to be a friend of a character `DynList` object, which is not appropriate for this implementation.

The private data members of the `DynList` class include the integer variables `length` and `size`, which are used to store the number of elements contained in the list, and the current size of the array that contains the list elements, respectively. The remaining private data member is the pointer variable `element` that points to the dynamically-allocated array containing the list elements.

The declarations of the member functions used to implement the LIST ADT accessing routines are given in the public section of the `DynList` class declaration. Many of these members are quite simple and are therefore implemented as inline functions. Notice that three constructors are provided—the default constructor, a constructor that takes a single list element as an argument, and the copy constructor. The default constructor sets the initial array size to zero, while the constructor which accepts a single list element dynamically allocates a two element array. As an example of a more complicated member function, let us consider the definition of `Insert()` shown in Figure 5.4. The first conditional statement in this function checks whether the integer supplied as an input parameter is a valid list position. Next, a conditional statement determines if this insertion will cause the load factor to reach 1. If it does, then a new array that is twice the size of the old one is created, and the elements contained in the old array are copied over to the newly created array, taking care to insert the new element in its proper location. After this is completed, the memory used by the old array is reclaimed, and `element` is made to point to the new array. If the load factor is less than 1, then there is enough room in the current array to store the new element. Thus, the appropriate elements are shifted up one array location, and the new element is added to the array in its proper location.

We also show in Figure 5.5 how the output operator can be overloaded to print the elements of a list. Note that individual list elements are output using the ≪ operator. Thus, the ≪ operator must be defined for any element stored in the list if this member function is to be used. Implementation of the remaining member function definitions is left as an exercise.

ITERATOR CLASSES. In Chapter 1 we discussed the advantages offered by data abstraction in software design. Similarly, it is often useful to abstract the control aspects of a data type. This will typically be accomplished by supplying an iterator with a data type implementation. An *iterator* embodies the control abstraction of

```
template<class T>
Boolean DynList<T>::Insert(const T& elm, int pos)
{
  if (pos <= 0 || pos > length)
    return false;
  if (length == size) { // load factor is 1
    size *= 2; // double the size of the array
    T* new_array = new T[size];
    if (new_array == 0)
      return false;
    for (int i=0; i<pos-1; i++) // copy 1st part of old array to new array
      new_array[i] = element[i];
    new_array[pos-1] = elm; // place elm in new array
    for (i=pos; i<=length; i++) // copy last part of old array to new array
      new_array[i] = element[i-1];
    delete [] element; // get rid of old array
    element = new_array;
  }
  else { // load factor is < 1
    for (int i=length; i>=pos; i--)
      element[i] = element[i-1];
    element[pos-1] = elm;
  }
  length++;
  return true;
}
```

FIGURE 5.4
A definition for the `Insert()` member function in the dynamic list class `DynList`.

```
/* File: dynlist.C */
template<class T>
ostream& operator<<(ostream& os, const DynList<T>& lst)
{
  os << "(";
  for (int i=0; i<lst.length; i++)
    os << lst.element[i] << ",";
  os << "\b)";
  return os;
}
```

FIGURE 5.5
Overloading of the output operator ≪ in the `DynList` class.

sequencing through the elements of the data type. This allows us to maintain an abstract view of the flow of control in our data type implementations.

The class declaration for the iterator used with `DynList` is shown in Figure 5.6. This class is responsible for implementing the LIST ADT operations that deal with iterating through list elements; specifically, the *Current, Reset,* and *Next* operations. The `DynListIterator` class contains two private data members: `current`, which stores an integer value representing the current position in the list; and `list`, which stores a constant pointer to the `DynList` object to which a particular iterator object is bound. Therefore a HAS-A relationship exists between an iterator and a particular list. All of the member functions for `DynListIterator` are defined inline as shown in Figure 5.6. The *Next* operation is implemented by overloading the increment operator `++`. Both the prefix and postfix forms of this operator are overloaded. In the postfix form, a dummy integer argument must appear in the function header, but it does not have to be used in the body of the function definition.

```
/* File: dynlist.H */
template<class T>
class DynListIterator {
  private:
    int current;
    const DynList<T>* list;
  public:
    inline DynListIterator(const DynList<T>&);
    inline int Reset();
    inline int Current() const;
    inline int operator++(); // prefix
    inline int operator++(int); // postfix
};

template<class T>
inline DynListIterator<T>::DynListIterator(const DynList<T>& lst)
{lst.length==0 ? current=0 : current=1; list = &lst;}

template<class T>
inline int DynListIterator<T>::Current() const {return current;}

template<class T>
inline int DynListIterator<T>::Reset()
{return list->length == 0 ? current=0 : current=1;}

template<class T>
inline int DynListIterator<T>::operator++() {return ++current;}

template<class T>
inline int DynListIterator<T>::operator++(int) {return ++current;}
```

FIGURE 5.6
The iterator class used to iterate through the sequentially-mapped dynamic-list implementation.

5.2.3 Dynamic Set Operations

It is not difficult to see how a sequentially-mapped list implementation of the LIST ADT can be used to implement the DYNAMIC SET ADT. The elements of the dynamic set are stored as list elements, and the DYNAMIC SET ADT operations are implemented using the LIST ADT operations. The *Maximum* (*Minimum*) operation can be implemented in $\Theta(n)$ time by starting at the head of a list and traversing through every element, saving the one with the largest (smallest) key value. The remaining DYNAMIC SET ADT operations can be implemented in a similar fashion. For instance, the *Search* would be implemented as follows:

```
SeqMapList::Search(LIST L, key k)   ▷ sequential search
1    for i ← 1 to Length(L) do
2        elem ← Retrieve(L,i)
3        if k = elem[key] then
4                return elem   ▷ a successful search
5    return NULL   ▷ an unsuccessful search
```

Notice that we have attached the prefix SeqMapList:: to the name of this pseudocode procedure. This is done to make explicit the form of the data structure being used in this procedure.

The statement on line 5 of SeqMapList::Search() will only be executed if an element with key k is not found in the list. Since the list is assumed to be random access, each *Retrieve* operation on line 2 takes $\Theta(1)$ time. In the worst case, the entire list would have to be searched before the desired element is found. The entire list would also have to be searched in order to determine that an element is not in the list—we will call this an unsuccessful search. Thus if the list contains n elements, the *Search* operation requires $O(n)$ time using the implementation given above. This brute-force approach is referred to as either a ***linear*** or ***sequential search***.

BINARY SEARCH. We can implement the *Search* operation more efficiently if we assume that the dynamic set elements are stored in an *ordered* sequentially-mapped list (i.e., the list elements are stored in sorted order). In this case, a technique known as ***binary search*** can be used to reduce the search time to $O(\log n)$. A binary search begins by comparing the middle element in the ordered list to the search key. This effectively splits the list into two parts, a lower half and an upper half. Since the list is ordered, the key of each element in the lower half of the list must be smaller than the key of each element in the upper half of the list. If the search key equals the key of the middle element, then we have found the desired element, and the search is terminated. However, if the search key is smaller than the key of the middle element, then the middle element in the lower half of the list is examined. Otherwise the search key must be larger than the key of the middle element, and the middle element in the upper half of the list is examined. The list is continually divided in this fashion until either the desired element is found, or the entire list is searched. An example of this process is given in Figure 5.7. In this figure, the dynamic set elements are fifteen integers stored in a sequentially-mapped ordered list, and the key of each element is assumed to be its integer value. The sequence of steps taken during the search for

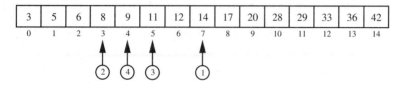

3	5	6	8	9	11	12	14	17	20	28	29	33	36	42
0	1	2	3	4	5	6	7	8	9	10	11	12	13	14

FIGURE 5.7
A binary search for the element with key value 9. The order in which the elements are examined during the search is shown in circles below the array.

element 9 is shown below the array. The middle element in the array is examined first. The key of this element is 14—which is greater than 9—so the next step is to examine the middle element in the lower half of the list. Notice that the desired element is found after four comparisons.

A recursive procedure for performing a binary search on an ordered sequentially-mapped list L is given below:

```
OrderedList::BinarySearch(LIST L, key k, integer first, integer last)
1    if first > last then
2        return NULL    ▷ an unsuccessful search
3    middle ← ⌊(last−first)/2⌋ + first
4    elem ← Retrieve(L, middle)
5    if k = elem[key] then
6        return elem    ▷ a successful search
7    else if k < elem[key] then
8        result ← BinarySearch(L, k, first, middle−1)
9    else    ▷ k > elem[key]
10       result ← BinarySearch(L, k, middle+1, last)
11   return result
```

This procedure can be used to implement the dynamic set *Search* operation as follows:

```
OrderedList::Search(LIST L, key k)    ▷ binary search
1    return BinarySearch(L, k, 0, Length(L)−1)
```

For the general case of n elements, the worst-case running time for binary search occurs during an unsuccessful search. This also upper bounds the running time of a successful search, since the number of comparisons performed during a successful binary search can be no greater than the number of comparisons performed during an unsuccessful binary search. Let us first determine the running time of an unsuccessful search when n is assumed to be one less than a power of two. This corresponds to the best-case situation for an unsuccessful binary search. In this case, after each comparison the list will be split into two equal parts, each containing an odd number of elements. Specifically, the first comparison will be performed on a list of size $2^k - 1$, the next comparison will be performed on a list of size $\lfloor \frac{2^k-1}{2} \rfloor$, and so forth. Therefore the running time obeys the following divide-and-conquer recurrence relation:

$$T(n) = \begin{cases} T(\lfloor \frac{2^k-1}{2} \rfloor) + 1, & \text{if } k > 1 \\ 1, & \text{if } k = 1 \end{cases} \tag{5.2}$$

Using equation (2.3), this recurrence relation can be bounded by $\Theta(\log n)$.

The worst-case running time for an unsuccessful binary search occurs when n is a power of two, and the search proceeds through the larger of the two lists resulting from each comparison. To see this, note that if n is even, then the index of the middle element must be chosen as either $\frac{n}{2}$ or $\frac{n}{2} - 1$. In either case, the list will be split into two unequal parts, one containing $\frac{n}{2}$ elements and the other containing $\frac{n}{2} - 1$ elements. We are assuming that the binary search proceeds through the part containing $\frac{n}{2}$ elements. Therefore, the number of comparisons performed in the worst case during an unsuccessful search obeys:

$$T(n) = \begin{cases} T(2^{k-1}) + 1, & \text{if } k > 0 \\ 1, & \text{if } k = 0 \end{cases} \tag{5.3}$$

Once again, equation (2.3) bounds this recurrence relation by $\Theta(\log n)$. Thus, we have shown that the running time of a binary search is $O(\log n)$.

The *Insert* operation of the DYNAMIC SET ADT can be implemented in $\Theta(1)$ time if the array is large enough to store the new element, and we are not concerned with maintaining an ordered list. We simply use the LIST ADT *Append* operation to add each new element to the tail of the list. However, if the binary search technique is to be used for the *Search* operation, then the sorted order of the list must be preserved after the insertion of each new element. One approach involves two steps: First we perform a binary search to determine where the new element should be added in the array. Specifically, the array location of the last element examined during an unsuccessful binary search is where the new element should be added. We have already determined that this requires $O(\log n)$ time. Next, if we assume the new element is added at array location i, then the elements stored in array locations $i + 1$ through $n - 1$ must all be shifted "up" one array location. In the worst case, the new element is added at the head of the list, and n elements must be shifted. This means that the running time for the DYNAMIC SET *Insert* operation is $O(n)$ if we must maintain a sorted list. The *Delete* operation will also require $O(n)$ time since the element we wish to delete must be found, and in the worst case it is found at the head of the list.

SELF-ORGANIZING LISTS. Another approach used to reduce the time required by the DYNAMIC SET *Search* operation involves reordering the list elements according to heuristic rules that are intended to place the most frequently requested elements towards the front of the list.[†] A sequential search, starting at the head of the list, is then employed to find a specific element. The goal is to organize the list elements so

---

[†]A *heuristic* is a rule of thumb, strategy, or method that aids in the solution of a problem, but its use cannot be rigorously justified.

that the total time of a sequence of sequential search operations will be as small as possible. We will refer to each of the sequential search operations in this sequence as a *request*.

If we know the probability of requesting each element, and each request is independent of the other requests in the sequence, then from a statistical point of view, the best approach is to store the list elements in nonincreasing order of request probabilities, and never reorder them. This arrangement is referred to as the **optimum static ordering**. Of course in practice we rarely know these probabilities, and other techniques must be developed to dynamically reorder the list elements as requests are occurring. Techniques that reorder list elements based solely on the sequence of requests that have occurred so far are referred to as **self-organizing heuristics**. Three commonly used heuristics are:

1. *Move-to-front.* After a successful search for a key, move the corresponding element to the front (head) of the list, without changing the relative order of the other elements. If an element is inserted, place it at the front of the list.
2. *Transpose.* After a successful search for a key, exchange the corresponding element with the element immediately in front of it in the list. If an element is inserted, place it at the front of the list.
3. *Frequency count.* Maintain a frequency count for each element. The count for each element (which is initially zero) is incremented when an element is inserted, or whenever the element is returned from a search request. This count is set to zero when the element is deleted. The list is maintained so that the elements appear in nonincreasing order by frequency count.

Note that the first two approaches do not require any additional memory, but the third technique requires an additional count field for each list element.

The worst-case running time for a sequential search operation on lists that uses any of these heuristics is $\Theta(n)$. This is no better than a sequential search on lists that does not use these heuristics. However, in practice, these strategies often lead to improved search times. In support of this observation, average-case analysis has been used to demonstrate specific conditions under which self-organizing search heuristics improve search time (see the Chapter Notes for references). We will also use amortized analysis in Section 10.5 to compare the performance of move-to-front to other self-organizing heuristics.

5.3 LINKED LISTS

Another approach to implementing the LIST ADT uses a **linked list**, which allocates memory for storing list elements as it is needed during run time, and connects list elements together using pointers. Memory is then de-allocated whenever a list element is no longer needed. Schematically, a linked list is represented by a sequence of nodes connected by links, as is depicted in Figure 5.8 (a). Because each node in the list is connected to the next by a single link, this data structure is called a **singly-linked list**. A node in a singly-linked list contains two fields: *data*, which holds a list element,

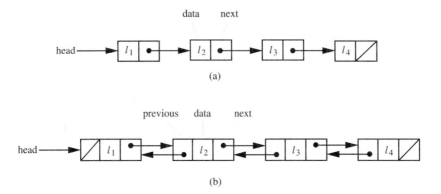

FIGURE 5.8
Schematic representations of **(a)** a singly-linked list and **(b)** a doubly-linked list.

and *next*, which stores a link (i.e., pointer) to the next node in the list. Notice also that we gain access to the list itself through a pointer to the head of the list. As shown in Figure 5.8 (a), the next field of the last node in a singly-linked list contains a special symbol that indicates the end of the list. We will assume that this is the null pointer.

A more sophisticated data structure known as a ***doubly-linked list*** can also be used to implement the LIST ADT. Each node in a doubly-linked list contains three fields—as shown in Figure 5.8 (b), one field stores a list element, and the other two store links to the preceding and succeeding nodes in the list. Notice that null pointers are used to mark both ends of the list in this case.

It is also possible to augment these data structures with various useful features. For example, in a ***circularly-linked list***, instead of placing the null pointer in the next field of the tail node, we store a pointer to the head of the list (for doubly-linked lists, we would also need to store a pointer to the tail node in the previous field of the head node). In addition, dummy nodes called ***sentinels*** are often added to linked lists. Sentinels can be used to store information about a list, or to simplify the testing of boundary conditions in a list.

Below we consider the efficiency of LIST ADT operations assuming the use of singly- and doubly-linked list data structures.

5.3.1 List Operations

The first thing to note about linked lists is that we no longer have direct access to arbitrary elements in the list. In order to access the i-th element, we must traverse the list, beginning at the head, until the desired element is located. Thus, any LIST ADT operation that involves a list position (e.g., *Insert*, *Retrieve*, and *Delete*) will in the worst case traverse the entire list in order to find the desired position in the linked list. However, if we are dealing with a doubly-linked list, once the desired position is located, each of these operations only requires $\Theta(1)$ additional time to complete its task. Figure 5.9 demonstrates how the *Insert* and *Delete* operations are performed in a doubly-linked list. Figure 5.9 (a) shows the initial configuration of the doubly-linked list. In Figure 5.9 (b), an insertion is performed at position i. The node at position i prior to the insertion is located at position $i + 1$ after the insertion. In Figure 5.9 (c), the node at position i is deleted. Thus, the node at position $i + 1$ prior to the deletion is now located at position i. For both operations, once we are given the address of the node at position i, we are able to move forward (using the pointer contained in the next field) or backward (using the pointer contained in the previous field) to other nodes in the list in order to perform the necessary pointer manipulations.

In singly-linked lists it is not possible to move backwards to other nodes in the list. This makes it difficult to perform the necessary pointer reassignments during an *Insert* or *Delete* operation. For example, in Figure 5.10 (a), we show a singly-linked list in which we wish to insert a node at position i. If we have access to the node at position $i - 1$, then it is a simple matter to "splice" the new node into the list, as shown in Figure 5.10 (b). Similarly, deleting a node from the singly-linked list requires that we modify the next field of the node at position $i - 1$ when we "cut" the appropriate node out of the list. Thus, with singly-linked lists, it is necessary to keep

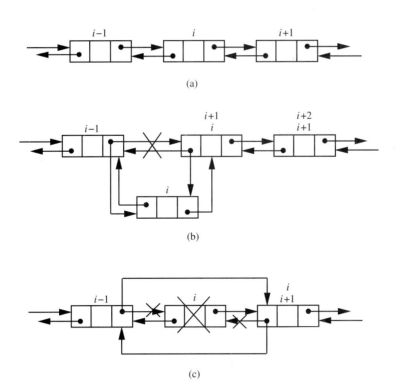

(a)

(b)

(c)

FIGURE 5.9
Performing the LIST ADT *Insert* and *Delete* operations using a doubly-linked list. **(a)** The initial doubly-linked list prior to an insertion or deletion at position i. **(b)** Pointer manipulations necessary to insert a node at position i, and **(c)** to delete the node at position i.

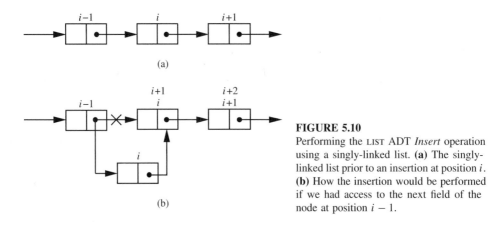

FIGURE 5.10

Performing the LIST ADT *Insert* operation using a singly-linked list. **(a)** The singly-linked list prior to an insertion at position i. **(b)** How the insertion would be performed if we had access to the next field of the node at position $i - 1$.

track of the previous node in the list as the traversal associated with an insertion or deletion is being performed. The following pseudocode details how to determine the address of the node at position $i - 1$ in $O(n)$ time.

```
LinkedList::Traverse(LIST L, positive integer i)
1    prev_node ← current_node ← head[L]   ▷ head[L] is a pointer
2    if  i ≠ 1  then
3         current_node ← ↓current_node[next]
4         for  i ← 2 to i  do
5              prev_node ← current_node
6              current_node ← ↓current_node[next]
7    return prev_node
```

The pointer variables prev_node and current_node are initially assigned the address contained in the pointer variable head. If the desired position is 1, then a pointer to the head of the list is immediately returned on line 7; otherwise, current_node is assigned the address of the second node in the list, and a loop is used to traverse the list until position i is reached. On each iteration, prev_node and current_node are incremented by one node position, with prev_node lagging one node behind current_node. (Note that the current_node pointer must be dereferenced in lines 3 and 6 in order to gain access to the next field of the node it is pointing to.) When the loop is completed, current_node points to the node at position i, and prev_node points to the node at position $i - 1$. Finally, the address contained in prev_node is returned. Given this pointer, an insertion or deletion at position i can easily be completed in $\Theta(1)$ time.

The *Append* operation takes $\Theta(n)$ to implement in either form of a linked list since we must traverse the entire list before adding the node. However, if we use an extra pointer to keep track of the tail, then this operation can be implemented in $\Theta(1)$ time.

It is interesting to contrast the efficiency of the LIST ADT *Insert* and *Delete* operations when using a linked list versus sequentially-mapped data structures. Finding the appropriate position in a linked list takes $O(n)$ time, but only $\Theta(1)$ time in a sequentially-mapped data structure; while actually performing the insertion or deletion takes $\Theta(1)$ time in a linked list, and $O(n)$ time in a sequentially-mapped data structure. Although each of these data structures can handle certain aspects of these operations more effectively than the other, the overall time complexity using either approach is $O(n)$.

5.3.2 Linked List Implementation

Below we consider a C++ implementation of the LIST ADT using a circular singly-linked list data structure. Once again we will make use of the template facility in order to provide a parameterized class. Figure 5.11 shows the portion of the header file containing the declaration of the class used to implement a node in the singly-linked list. There are two forward declarations for the template classes SlList and SlListIterator that are subsequently declared as friends of SlNode. We also make an overloaded version of the output operator a friend of the class so that it can output the data field of an SlNode. The private member data is the parameterized variable that stores the data field, while the private member next stores the next field. Finally, two constructors are provided: a default constructor, and a constructor that takes a single data element as an input parameter. The interesting thing to note here is that the constructors are private member functions. This effectively encapsulates the SlNode class, allowing only SlList and SlListIterator objects (which are friends of the SlNode class) to construct SlNode objects.

Figure 5.12 demonstrates how the SlNode class is used in the construction of the SlList class. Specifically, note that SlList HAS-A pointer to an SlNode object called tail. Since an SlListIterator object must access the private data in an SlList object in order to traverse its associated list, the SlListIterator class is

---

```
/* File: sl_list.H */
// forward references for template classes
template <class Type> class SlList;
template <class Type> class SlListIterator;

template<class T>
class SlNode {
  friend class SlList<T>;
  friend class SlListIterator<T>;
  friend ostream& operator≪(ostream&, const SlList<T>&);
  private:
    T data;
    SlNode<T>* next;
    SlNode() {}
    inline SlNode(const T&);
};
```

FIGURE 5.11
The declaration of the SlNode class used to store data elements in a singly-linked list.

made a friend of the SlList class. The private member variable tail is used to store a pointer to the last node in the list, and it is assumed that tail—>next contains a pointer to the head node, thus forming a circularly linked list. This means that we only need to keep a pointer to the tail node—every other node in the list can be reached from this node. The member function declarations for the constructors, a destructor, and the LIST ADT operations are provided in the public section of this class.

Figure 5.13 shows the member function definition for the *Insert* operation. This code implements the sequence of steps depicted in Figure 5.10 (b), and traverses the list using the technique described in the LinkedList::Traverse() pseudocode of Section 5.3.1. Implementation of the remaining member function definitions is left as an exercise.

We also supply an iterator for the SlList class as shown in Figure 5.14. It should be noted, however, that iterators cannot be used as efficiently by SlList

```
/* File: sl_list.H */
template<class T>
class SlList {
  friend class SlListIterator<T>;
  protected:
    int length;
    SlNode<T>* tail; // tail—>next is the head of the list
  public:
    inline SlList();
    SlList(const T&);
    SlList(const SlList<T>&);
    inline ~SlList();
    SlList<T>& operator=(const SlList<T>&);
    friend ostream& operator≪(ostream&, const SlList<T>&);
    void Insert(const T&, int);
    void Append(const T&);
    T& Retrieve(int) const;
    void Delete(int);
    inline int Length() const;
    inline Boolean Empty() const;
    void MakeEmpty();
};

template<class T>
inline SlList<T>::SlList() {length=0; tail=NULL;}

template<class T>
inline SlList<T>::~SlList() {MakeEmpty();}

// remaining inline function definitions not shown
```

FIGURE 5.12
The declaration of the SlList class that implements a circular singly-linked list.

```
/* File: sl_list.C */
template<class T>
void SlList<T>::Insert(const T& elm, int pos)
{
  assert((pos > 0) && (pos <= length));
  SlNode<T>* prev_node;
  SlNode<T>* current_node;
  prev_node = current_node = tail->next;
  SlNode<T>* new_node = new SlNode<T>(elm); // create the new node
  if (pos == 1) {
    new_node->next = tail->next;   tail->next = new_node;
  }
  else {
    current_node = current_node->next;
    for (int i=2; i<pos; i++) {
      prev_node = current_node;   current_node = current_node->next;
    }
    prev_node->next = new_node; // splice the new node into the list
    new_node->next = current_node;
  }
  length++;
}
```

FIGURE 5.13
The definition of the `Insert()` function in the `SlList` class.

objects as they can by `DynList` objects. Specifically, since our iterator operations return a list position, the element stored at a specific position can be accessed directly by a random-access data structure—but accessing a specific position requires a list traversal when using a linked list. This is easily rectified by modifying the `SlListIterator` so that its operations return a pointer to an `SlNode` object rather than a list position. This, however, means that the *Insert*, *Retrieve*, and *Delete* operations must be modified in the `SlList` class so that they accept an `SlNode` pointer, instead of a list position, if they are to use the iterator effectively. We have already shown that given the appropriate pointer, each of these operations can be implemented in $\Theta(1)$ time using a linked list. These modifications, however, mean that the `DynList` and `SlList` classes can no longer be used interchangeably in application programs. The pros and cons involved in these trade-offs must be judged within the framework of the constraints facing the programmer who must use these classes in an application program.

5.3.3 Dynamic Set Operations

Let us now investigate how a linked list implementation of the LIST ADT can be used to implement the DYNAMIC SET ADT. The pseudocode for the *Search* operation given in Section 5.2.3 assumed that L was a sequentially-mapped list. This procedure also works correctly if L is assumed to be a linked list, although the efficiency will

```
/* File: sl_list.H */
template<class T>
class SlListIterator {
  private:
    int current;
    const SlList<T>* list;
  public:
    SlListIterator() {}
    SlListIterator(const SlList<T>* lst);
    int Reset();
    inline int Current() const;
    int operator++();    // prefix
    int operator++(int); // postfix
};
```

FIGURE 5.14
The iterator class for the circular singly-linked list implementation.

change from $O(n)$ to $O(n^2)$. This is because the *Retrieve* operation on line 2 only takes $\Theta(1)$ time if L is a sequentially-mapped list, but this same operation takes $\Theta(i)$ time to retrieve the i-th element if L is a linked list. In order to implement the DYNAMIC SET ADT *Search* operation in $O(n)$ time using a linked list, we need to access the linked list directly. Specifically, if we implement the DYNAMIC SET ADT by *inheriting* the singly-linked list class, then we can access the list directly using the DYNAMIC SET implementation, and only one list traversal is required in order to determine if the desired item is in the list.

The binary search technique used with sequentially mapped sorted lists does not make sense in linked lists, since random access is necessary in order to obtain a $O(\log n)$ search time. However, the self-organizing heuristics discussed in Section 5.2.3 all use sequential search. Thus, they can be exploited by a DYNAMIC SET ADT implementation that uses a linked list. In fact, the move-to-front heuristic can be implemented more efficiently than it could with a sequentially-mapped data structure, since the element being moved is simply spliced onto the head of the linked list.

SKIP LISTS. A clever adaptation of binary search can be used to overcome the major weakness of linked lists, namely, the inability to randomly access arbitrary list elements during a search. Skip lists improve search time by adding extra pointers to certain list nodes. These pointers "skip" ahead a fixed number of nodes in the lists. If the list is kept sorted, these skip pointers can be used to perform a type of binary search.

Consider, for instance, the skip list shown in Figure 5.15 (a), in which every other node contains a pointer to the node two places ahead of it in the list, and the list elements are stored in sorted order. In addition we have placed a sentinel node at the head of the list that contains only pointers. The dashed line in this figure shows the search path for the element with key value 19. The strategy involves following the path of pointers that skip nodes until we encounter a node that points to an element

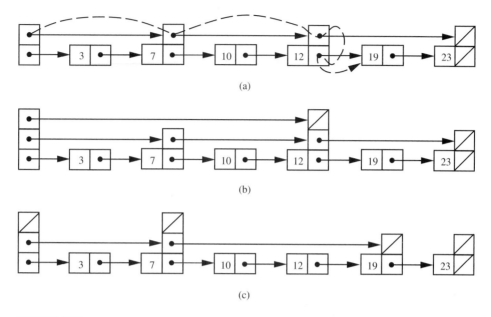

FIGURE 5.15
Three different examples of skip lists; in each, list elements are stored in sorted order. **(a)** A 6-node skip list containing only level 1 and 2 nodes. The search path for the element with key value 19 is shown with a dashed line. **(b)** A 6-node complete skip list. **(c)** A randomly constructed 6-node skip list.

whose key is larger than the search key. At that point, we start traversing the skip list a single node at a time. It is not difficult to see that using this approach, the maximum number of nodes that must be examined during a search of an n-node skip list constructed in the manner of Figure 5.15 (a) is $\lceil n/2 \rceil + 1$.

We can extend our searching strategy to skip lists containing even more pointers, but first we must define some terminology. Let us define a node containing i pointers as a *level i node*, and note that such a node contains level $1, 2, \ldots, i$ pointers. For instance all of the nodes in a standard singly-linked list are level 1 nodes, containing only level 1 pointers. In Figure 5.15 (a) three nodes are at level 1 (containing only level 1 pointers), and the remaining nodes are at level 2 (containing level 1 and 2 pointers). In an n-node *complete skip list* every 2^i-th node is at level i, for $i = 1, \ldots, \lceil \lg n \rceil$. This at most doubles the number of pointers as compared to a singly-linked list. An example complete skip list is shown in Figure 5.15 (b).

If the maximum level of any node in a skip list is i, then we will call it a *level i skip list*. In order to search a level i skip list for a given key k, we first traverse the level i pointers, starting at the head. If a key is found that is larger than k, then we drop down to the level $(i - 1)$ pointers and continue searching, and so on, in this manner, until no further progress can be made on level 1 pointers. The algorithm we have just described is implemented in the following pseudocode procedure. In this procedure, we use $x[\text{next}(i)]$ to denote the level i pointer in node x.

```
SkipList::Search(LIST L, key k)
1    x ← head[L]
2    for i ← level[L] to 1 do    ▷ level[L] is the max node level in L
3        while (↓x[next(i)]) ≠ NULL and (↓x[next(i)])[key] < k do
4            x ← ↓x[next(i)]    ▷ jump to the next level i node
5    x ← ↓x[next(1)]
6    if x[key] = k then
7        return x    ▷ successful search
8    else
9        return NULL    ▷ unsuccessful search
```

Notice that it is not necessary for a node to store its level in order to perform the search; however, a single variable is needed to store the level of the list. For an n-element complete skip list, the analysis of SkipList::Search() is very similar to the previous analysis of binary search, yielding a running time of $O(\log n)$.

Although a complete skip list allows rapid searches, maintaining its required structure after an *Insert* or *Delete* operation is prohibitively expensive, requiring $O(n)$ pointer reassignments. If, however, the level of a node is chosen randomly during insertion, then these operations can be performed using only local pointer modifications. This is accomplished by using a randomized algorithm to choose the level of a node according to its proportion in a complete skip list. In a complete skip list, 50 percent of the nodes are at level 1, 25 percent are at level 2, and in general $(100/2^i)$ percent are at level i. An example of a randomly constructed skip list is given in Figure 5.15 (c).

The randomized insertion of a node is accomplished as follows: First a search is conducted using SkipList::Search() to determine the insertion point in the list. During this search, we must also maintain an array of pointers—let us call it update—where update[i] stores the rightmost node of level i or higher that is to the left of the insertion point. Next a random number is drawn to determine the level of the node, and memory for the node is allocated. Using the update array, this new node is then spliced into the skip list. A similar approach is used to splice a node out of a skip list during a *Delete* operation. The details of these procedures are left as Exercise 5.14.

Since the *Insert* and *Delete* operations we describe only require local pointer modifications, their running times are bounded by the time required to find the insertion/deletion point; because the skip list is no longer guaranteed to be complete, this can take linear time. In practice, however, the running time of a search in a randomly constructed skip list is typically logarithmic. Furthermore, because this data structure is relatively simple to implement, and the algorithms which access it have low overhead (as compared to the balanced tree data structures in Chapter 11), it is an attractive choice in applications requiring fast performance on average.

5.4   MEMORY MANAGEMENT

We now briefly discuss memory management, an important application area in which linked lists are commonly used. Memory management involves the administration of a limited memory resource through the use of various strategies.

Up until this point in the text, we have been content with allowing the compiler to handle most aspects of memory management through the use of the `new` and `delete` operators. Although users are explicitly allocating and de-allocating memory when they use these operators, the free store is viewed as a "black box." By this we mean that the free store responds to the `new` operation by reserving (i.e., allocating) some portion of its memory, and it responds to the `delete` operation by freeing (i.e., de-allocating) some portion of its memory. The user, however, is completely unaware of how the free store is actually managing its memory when it performs these tasks.

By allowing the user to overload the `new` and `delete` operators, C++ provides a way for the programmer to take over some of the memory management responsibility normally handled by the compiler. In order to motivate the need to do this, let us point out that by taking control of memory management in this fashion, the programmer can usually outperform the compiler-supplied routines. This is particularly true in cases for which we have some *a priori* knowledge about the memory needs of a program—for example, when large numbers of small objects are continually allocated and de-allocated, or when numerous memory chunks of the same size must be managed. The following caveat should be added to this discussion: A program should always be profiled to determine its memory management overhead *before* trying to optimize it away with user-supplied routines.

It is easy to attach a user-supplied memory manager to an existing class by overloading the `new` and `delete` operators. Assuming we have an existing class X, the memory manager can be added by modifying the declaration of X, as shown in Figure 5.16. The basic idea involves storing objects of type X in a linked list; but rather than allocating these objects one at a time, we will ask the free store for a pool of objects. Limiting the number of calls in this fashion can greatly increase the speed of a program—it is much more efficient to call the compiler-supplied allocator

```
/* File: X.H */
#include <stddef.h> // size_t is defined here

class X {
  private:
    // existing private members not shown
    const int chunk;
    static X* pool; // pool is a class variable
    X* next;
  public:
    // existing public members not shown
    void* operator new(size_t); // overload the new operator
    void operator delete(void*, size_t); // overload the delete operator
};
```

FIGURE 5.16
Modifications to the declaration of class X that allow the incorporation of a simple user-supplied memory manager.

once, asking for a pool of 100 objects, than to call it 100 times for the individual objects. The extra objects we obtain by grabbing these large chunks of memory will be stored in a linked list, where the used user-supplied memory management routines can make use of them.

In the class shown in Figure 5.16, the variable `pool` stores a pointer to the head of a list of available objects. Since we want *all* objects of type X to use this one list, `pool` is made a class variable by preceding its declaration with the keyword `static` (see Section 4.2.1). The private data member `next` is also added to class X. Whenever an object of class X resides in the `pool` list, its `next` variable will store a pointer to the next available object of class X in the list.

In order to overload the compiler-supplied `new` and `delete` operators, function declarations of the form shown in the public section of class X in Figure 5.16 must be used. Notice that both of these operators require an argument of type `size_t`, which is an integer type defined in the system header file `<stddef.h>`. This argument is automatically initialized by the compiler with the size in bytes of class X.

Implementations of the overloaded `new` and `delete` operations are shown in Figure 5.17. Notice that our `new` operator first checks to see if the pool is empty prior to using the compiler-supplied `new` operator to grab a chunk of additional

```
/* File: X.C */
#include "X.H"

//initialize static members
X* X::pool = 0;
const int X::chunk = 1024;

void* X::operator new(size_t sz) {
  X* p;
  if (pool == 0) { // pool is empty, grab a chunk of memory from the free store
    pool = (X*) new char[chunk * sz]; // using the system allocator
    for (p=pool; p!=pool[chunk-1]; p++) // link objects together
      p->next = p+1;
    pool[chunk-1].next = NULL; // pointer of last object in list
  }
  p = pool;
  pool = pool->next; // strip off head of list
  return p; // and return it
}

void X::operator delete(void* p, size_t) {
  ((X*)p)->next = pool; // add freed object to head of pool list
  pool = (X*)p; // reassign head pointer
}
```

FIGURE 5.17

Implementation of the `X::operator new()` and `X::operator delete()` functions in class X.

memory. The compiler-supplied `new` operator should be called in the manner we have shown, since calling it using `new X[chunk]` would lead to infinite recursion if the constructor for `X` uses the `new` operator.

The overloaded `delete` operator shown in Figure 5.17 is very simple. Whenever an object of class `X` is deleted, its memory is *not* returned to the compiler-supplied allocator; rather, it is added to the head of the `pool` list. This object can now be returned by a subsequent call to class `X`'s `new` operator. Only when the destructor for the `Pool` object is invoked will it actually hand back memory to the free store.

The method we have described for adding a user-supplied memory manager to a class is so general that it makes sense to write a generic memory manager class that can be incorporated into any class. The implementation of such a class is the topic of Exercise 5.8.

5.5 AN EXTENDED EXAMPLE: SPARSE MATRICES

In Sections 3.5 and 4.3 we considered MATRIX ADT implementations that stored the elements of a matrix in a sequentially-mapped data structure. Recall that an array was dynamically allocated for each row in the matrix, and that the number of elements in each array was determined by the column dimension of the matrix. This storage method can be quite wasteful if the matrices we are dealing with are sparse. A *sparse matrix* contains relatively few nonzero elements. Thus, most of the storage in this case is taken up by 0 entries.

In this section we consider an alternative approach that uses lists to store only the nonzero matrix elements. The memory that is saved using this approach can be considerable. For example, storing every element of a 1000×1000 matrix would require allocating memory for 1 million elements. However, if this matrix only contained $20,000$ nonzero elements, and the list approach is used, then only $20,000$ elements would be stored. Compared to the array implementation of the MATRIX ADT, this implementation will require more work to access a particular element, but computation time is saved when performing operations on sparse matrices, since only the nonzero elements are considered. Thus, a large number of useless arithmetic operations (e.g., addition of zero, or multiplication by zero) can be avoided.

Let us begin our discussion of the sparse matrix implementation by first noting that a vector can be represented as a list of two-element sublists. For example, the eight-element row vector [8 3 0 0 1 0 2 0] can be represented as a list containing four elements:

$$((1, 8), (2, 3), (5, 1), (7, 2))$$

Each element in this list is itself a two-element list containing the index and the corresponding value of a nonzero entry in the vector. The first thing we will do is

```
/* File: spmatrix.H */
#include "dynlist.H"
// forward declarations
template <class Type> class SpVector;
template <class Type> class SpMatrix;

template<class T>
class SpElem {
  private:
    int index;
    T value;
  public:
    SpElem() {}
    inline SpElem(int, T);
    friend ostream& operator≪(ostream&, const SpElem<T>&);
};
```

FIGURE 5.18

The declaration of the SpElem class used to represent the elements in a sparse vector or matrix.

construct a class that can be used to represent the elements of a sparse vector. This class, called SpElem, is shown in Figure 5.18. The private member variables index and value are used to store the index and value of a nonzero vector element. This class is then used to construct the sparse vector class shown in Figure 5.19. The private member variables in the SpVector class include index, which will later be used by a sparse matrix class, and rep, which is the list of elements representing the sparse vector. Specifically, SpVector HAS-A DynList object that has been instantiated to work with SpElem objects. We overloaded the operators in the SpVector class as member functions. These operators are able to access the private members of Spelem objects since SpVector is declared as a friend inside of the Spelem class. Notice that the − operator is overloaded twice, once for vector negation, and another time for vector by vector subtraction. In addition, the + operator is overloaded to perform vector addition, and the * operator is overloaded three times. The first form is used when we wish to multiply a vector by a scalar, the second form is used to compute the inner product of two vectors, and the third form is used to compute a vector by matrix product.[†] It is not necessary to supply a copy constructor for this class since none of its data members are initialized to point to dynamically allocated memory.

In Figure 5.20 we supply a definition for the vector addition operation. The approach taken here is very similar to the one used in Section 5.1 to add two polynomials. Two iterators, it1 and it2, are declared and then reset so that it1 initially refers to the first element in the list stored by the left-hand sparse vector operand,

---

[†]The **inner product** of two real valued vectors $[x_1, x_2, \ldots, x_n]$ and $[y_1, y_2, \ldots, y_n]$ is given by the scalar quantity $\sum_{i=1}^{n} x_i \cdot y_i$.

```
/* File: spmatrix.H */
template<class T>
class SpVector {
  friend class SpMatrix<T>;
  private:
    int index;
    DynList< SpElem<T> > rep;
  public:
    SpVector() {}
    inline SpVector(int);
    inline SpVector(int, const DynList< SpElem<T> >&);
    friend ostream& operator«(ostream&, const SpVector<T>&);
    SpVector<T>& operator-();
    SpVector<T>& operator-(const SpVector<T>&);
    SpVector<T>& operator-=(const SpVector<T>&);
    SpVector<T>& operator+(const SpVector<T>&);
    SpVector<T>& operator+=(const SpVector<T>&);
    SpVector<T>& operator*(const T&); // vector by scalar product
    T& operator*(const SpVector<T>&); // inner product
    SpVector<T>& operator*(const SpMatrix<T>&); // vector by matrix product
    // remaining member functions not shown
};
```

FIGURE 5.19

The declaration of the `SpVector` class used to implement sparse vectors.

and `it2` initially refers to the first element in the list stored by the right-hand sparse vector operand. We then iterate through the elements of the two lists, constructing a third list as we go. At each step, the index fields of the elements pointed to by `it1` and `it2` are checked. If they are equal, a new element containing the index of these elements, along with the sum of their values fields, is appended to the third list, and both iterators are incremented. (The new element is only appended to the third list if the sum does not equal zero.) If the index values are not equal, then a copy of the element with the smaller index is appended to the third list, and only the iterator associated with the list that this element came from is incremented. When both iterators reach the end of their respective lists, the final result will be contained in the third list. Most of the other operands are implemented in a similar fashion. Of particular interest is the operator that is overloaded to perform vector by matrix multiplication. Before discussing the implementation of this operator, we must consider how sparse matrices will be implemented.

A matrix can be constructed by using the sparse vector representation discussed above to store each row of a given matrix. We simply create a list that stores a row index, along with the vector associated with that row. For example, the 4×4 identity matrix can be represented by the following list:

$$((1, ((1, 1))), \ (2, ((2, 1))), \ (3, ((3, 1))), \ (4, ((4, 1))))$$

```
/* File: spmatrix.C */
template<class T>
Spvector<T>& SpVector<T>::operator+(const SpVector<T>& v)
{
  DynListIterator< SpElem<T> > it1(rep);
  DynListIterator< SpElem<T> > it2(v.rep);
  assert((it1.Reset() != 0) && (it2.Reset() != 0));
  SpElem<T> elem1, elem2, elem3;
  SpVector<T>* result = new SpVector<T>(index);
  while (it1.Current() <= rep.Length() && it2.Current()
                                        <= v.rep.Length()) {
    elem1 = rep.Retrieve(it1.Current());
    elem2 = v.rep.Retrieve(it2.Current());
    if (elem1.index == elem2.index) {
      elem3.index = elem1.index;
      elem3.value = elem1.value + elem2.value; it1++;    it2++;
    }
    else if (elem1.index < elem2.index) {
      elem3 = elem1;    it1++;
    }
    else { // elem2.index < elem1.index
      elem3 = elem2;    it2++;
    }
    if (elem3.value != 0)
      result->rep.Append(*(new SpElem<T>(elem3)));
  }
  while (it1.Current() <= rep.Length()) { // copy what's left of LH operand
    result->rep.Append(*(new SpElem<T>(rep.Retrieve(it1.Current()))));
    it1++;
  }
  while (it2.Current() <= v.rep.Length()) { // copy what's left of RH operand
    result->rep.Append(*(new SpElem<T>(v.rep.Retrieve(it2.Current()))));
    it2++;
  }
  return *result;
}
```

FIGURE 5.20
The addition operation for sparse vectors in the `SpVector` class.

The declaration of a class that stores sparse matrices in this fashion is given in Figure 5.21. The private member variable `rep` in this class is used to store a list of vectors. That is, `Matrix` HAS-A `DynList` object that has been instantiated to work with `SpVector` objects. Thus we have now used `DynList` objects to store two different kinds of objects in the same application. The ability to do so was facilitated by developing `DynList` as a template class. Also notice that the class `SpVector` is made a friend of this class because the vector by matrix multiplication operation defined in the `SpVector` class will need to access private members of `Smatrix` objects.

```
/* File: spmatrix.H */
template<class T>
class SpMatrix {
  friend class SpVector<T>;
  private:
    int row_dim, col_dim;
    DynList< SpVector<T> > rep;
  public:
    SpMatrix() {}
    SpMatrix(int rdim, int cdim);
    SpMatrix(int rdim, int cdim, const T&);
    SpMatrix(int rdim, int cdim, T*);
    inline int Row() const;
    inline int Col() const;
    friend ostream& operator<<(ostream&, const SpMatrix<T>&);
    SpMatrix<T>& operator-();
    SpMatrix<T>& operator-(const SpMatrix<T>&);
    SpMatrix<T>& operator+(const SpMatrix<T>&);
    friend T& operator*(T& scalar, const SpMatrix<T>&);
    SpMatrix<T>& operator*(const SpMatrix<T>&);
    SpMatrix<T>& Transpose();
    // remaining member functions not shown
};
```

FIGURE 5.21
The declaration of the SpMatrix class used to implement sparse matrices.

Given this representation, the addition of two sparse matrices is performed using roughly the same approach that was used to add two vectors. That is, we iterate through both matrices on a row-by-row basis. If at any point the two indices pointed to by the iterators are the same, then the vector addition operator given in Figure 5.20 can be used to add the two rows together. Otherwise we simply append the row with the smaller index to the resultant matrix, and proceed.

Implementing the vector by matrix multiplication operation in the SpVector class does not appear to be as simple as this. Recall that this operation involves forming the inner product of the vector with each *column* of the matrix. However, our sparse matrix implementation is not set up to allow efficient column access. Fortunately, there is an alternative way to perform this operation using previously developed SpVector operations. Specifically, if we multiply the i-th row of the matrix by the i-th vector component using the scalar by vector multiplication operation, and then we sum all rows of the matrix using the vector by vector addition operation, we also obtain the product of the vector and matrix. For example, the result of the following vector-matrix product

$$[3\ 2\ 0\ 1] \cdot \begin{bmatrix} 1 & 2 & 1 \\ 3 & 1 & 0 \\ 4 & 2 & 1 \\ 0 & 3 & 2 \end{bmatrix}$$

```
/* File: spmatrix.C */
template<class T>
SpVector<T>& SpVector<T>::operator*(const SpMatrix<T>& m)
{
   DynListIterator< SpElem<T> > v_it(rep);
   DynListIterator< SpVector<T> > m_it(m.rep);
   assert(v_it.Reset() != 0 && m_it.Reset() != 0);
   SpElem<T> scalar;
   SpVector<T> vector, result;
   while (v_it.Current() <= rep.Length() &&
          m_it.Current() <= m.rep.Length()) {
     scalar = rep.Retrieve(v_it.Current());
     vector = m.rep.Retrieve(m_it.Current());
     if (scalar.index == vector.index) {
       result += (vector * scalar.value);
       v_it++; m_it++;
     }
     else if (scalar.index < vector.index)
       v_it++;
     else // vector.index < scalar.index
       m_it++;
   }
   return *(new SpVector<T>(index, result.rep));
}
```

FIGURE 5.22
The sparse vector by sparse matrix multiplication operation in the SpVector class.

can be expressed as

$$3 \cdot [1\ 2\ 1] + 2 \cdot [3\ 1\ 0] + 1 \cdot [0\ 3\ 2] = [9\ 11\ 5]$$

The implementation of these steps as an SpVector operator function is given in Figure 5.22. Once again notice how iterators are used to traverse the two operands. Furthermore, the availability of the overloaded vector operators makes this operation fairly easy to implement.

The vector by matrix multiplication operation can now be used to implement the matrix by matrix multiplication operation. First recall that the element in row i and column j of the matrix that results from multiplying two matrices M_1 and M_2, is given by the inner product of row i in M_1 and column j in M_2. Note, however, that once again we can avoid accessing the columns of M_2. Specifically, the i-th row of the resultant matrix can also be computed by taking the product of the i-th row of M_1 and the matrix M_2. This can be done using the vector by matrix multiplication operation we have already developed. This approach is demonstrated in Figure 5.23. Thus, the implementation of the matrix by matrix multiplication operation is fairly easy, given the previously developed vector by matrix multiplication operator.

```
/* File: spmatrix.C */
template<class T>
SpMatrix<T>& SpMatrix<T>::operator*(const SpMatrix<T>& m)
{
  assert(col_dim == m.row_dim);
  DynListIterator< SpVector<T> > it(rep);
  assert(it.Reset() != 0);
  SpMatrix<T>* result = new SpMatrix<T>(row_dim, m.col_dim);
  SpVector<T> vector;
  while (it.Current() <= rep.Length()) {
    vector = rep.Retrieve(it.Current());
    vector = vector * m;
    if (vector.rep.Empty() == false)
      result->rep.Append(*(new SpVector<T>(vector)));
    it++;
  }
  return *result;
}
```

FIGURE 5.23
The multiplication operation for sparse matrices in the SpMatrix class.

EXERCISES

5.1. Write a nonrecursive pseudocode procedure for the binary search algorithm assuming that the data elements are stored in a sequentially-mapped list L.

5.2. Implement the DYNAMIC DICTIONARY ADT by:
(*a*) inheriting the DynList class,
(*b*) using the SlList class.

5.3. Describe strategies that a malicious adversary could use to defeat each of the self-organizing list strategies described in Section 5.2.3.

5.4. Create C++ DYNAMIC DICTIONARY classes that implement each of the self-organizing heuristics presented in Section 5.2.3. Each of these classes should inherit the SlList class.

5.5. Develop a C++ class called DlList that implements each of the LIST ADT operations using a doubly-linked list data structure.

5.6. Rewrite the SlList class so that its member functions use pointers to data objects, rather than list positions, as was discussed at the end of Section 5.3.3.

5.7. A common improvement to binary search involves trying to make a better guess at the location of the interval that contains the key being sought (rather than blindly starting at the midpoint of an interval at each step). This method, called *interpolation search*, is similar to the technique most of us use when looking up a word in a dictionary. For instance, when looking up the word *didactic*, we begin by opening the dictionary toward the beginning, but if the word is *xeric* we would start by opening the dictionary toward the end. That is, when we perform such a search, we take advantage of additional information and estimate the approximate location of a word. Modify the OrderedList::BinarySearch() algorithm given in Section 5.2.3 so that it uses this strategy. You may assume that the keys stored in a dynamic set are numerically uniformly distributed. Illustrate the performance of your algorithm on the example given in Figure 5.7.

5.8. In Section 5.4 we demonstrated how to add a user-supplied memory manager to an existing class X by defining the functions `X::operator new()` and `X::operator delete()`. In this exercise you are to develop a generic memory management class called `Pool` that can be incorporated into any class Y as follows:

```
class Y {
    private:
        // existing private members
        static Pool Ypool(sizeof(Y));
    public:
        // existing public members
        void* operator new(size_t) {return Ypool.Alloc();}
        void operator delete(void* p, size_t) {Ypool.Free(p);}
};
```

(Hint: A portion of the header file for your class might look like:

```
class Pool {
    private:
        class Link {Link* next;};
        Link* head;
        const unsigned elm_size;
        void Grow(); // grabs a chunk, called by Alloc()
    public:
        inline Pool(unsigned elm_sz);
        ~Pool();
        void Free(void*);
        void* Alloc();
};)
```

5.9. The operators in the `SpVector` and `SpMatrix` classes, shown in Figures 5.19 and 5.21 respectively, were overloaded as member functions. This creates a number of problems. For instance, we cannot compute a scalar by vector product (where the left-hand operand is a scalar) using the `SpVector` class. Rewrite both of these classes so that all operators treat their arguments symmetrically (i.e., so that cases such as the one discussed above are handled).

5.10. Show that the technique for multiplying two sparse matrices discussed in Section 5.5 is correct by demonstrating that it yields the same results as the standard matrix multiplication algorithm given in Figure 1.2.

5.11. The POLYNOMIAL ADT is used to represent polynomials of the form

$$p(x) = a_n x^n + a_{n-1} x^{n-1} + \cdots + a_1 x + a_0$$

and supports three types of operations: query operations, numerical operations, and algebraic operations.

   1. *Evaluate*$(p(x), z)$. A numerical operation that uses Horner's rule (see Exercise 2.16 (b)) to evaluate the polynomial $p(x)$ at the point $x = z$ and returns the result.

   2. *Add*$(p_1(x), p_2(x))$. An algebraic operation that returns the polynomial that results when $p_1(x)$ is added to $p_2(x)$.

3. *Subtract*($p_1(x)$, $p_2(x)$). An algebraic operation that returns the polynomial that results when $p_1(x)$ is subtracted from $p_2(x)$.

4. *Multiply*($p_1(x)$, $p_2(x)$). An algebraic operation that returns the polynomial that results when $p_1(x)$ is multiplied by $p_2(x)$.

5. *Differentiate*($p(x)$, z). An algebraic operation that returns the polynomial that results when $p(x)$ is differentiated z times.

6. *Order*($p(x)$). A query operation that returns the order of polynomial $p(x)$.

(*a*) Consider the *Multiply* operation, and assume that polynomials are represented using lists. If one of the input polynomials contains m terms and the other n, where $m \leq n$, use the LIST ADT operations to write a pseudocode procedure that multiplies these polynomials in $\Theta(m^2n^2)$ time. Your output polynomial should have at most one term of any power. Can you derive an algorithm that solves this problem in $\Theta(m^2n)$ time?

(*b*) Develop a C++ class that implements the POLYNOMIAL ADT by using a LIST ADT implementation as a private class member.

5.12. Use the POLYNOMIAL ADT implementation developed in the previous problem to find a real root of a given polynomial using the ***Newton-Raphson method***. For a given function $f(x)$, the Newton-Raphson iteration function is defined as follows:

$$x_k = x_{k-1} - \frac{f(x_{k-1})}{f'(x_{k-1})}, \quad k = 1, 2, \ldots \tag{5.4}$$

If $f(x)$, $f'(x)$, and $f''(x)$ are continuous near the root r, and $f'(r) \neq 0$, then if the initial approximation x_0 is chosen close enough to r, the sequence $< x_k >$ defined in (5.4) will converge to r. Test your program on the polynomial

$$p(x) = x^5 - 6x^4 + 8x^3 + 8x^2 + 4x - 40$$

starting with the initial approximations $x_0 = 3$.

5.13. This exercise considers performing calculations with very large integers, a common problem in cryptography. Specifically, the integer values of interest in this case are too large to be represented by a built-in integer data type. Furthermore, it is assumed that the calculations must be exact, which rules out representing such numbers in floating-point format. One approach involves treating a large integer as a polynomial, the coefficients of which must be integers in the range 0–9. For instance, the 20-digit integer 80210030809011042003 can be represented as the following polynomial:

$$8x^{19} + 2x^{17} + x^{16} + 3x^{13} + 8x^{11} + 9x^9 + x^7 + x^6 + 4x^4 + 2x^3 + 3$$

Given this representation, we can use the POLYNOMIAL ADT operations (see Section 5.1 and Exercise 5.11) to manipulate large integers. Assuming that large integers are represented as polynomials:

(*a*) Discuss how the coefficients of a polynomial can be adjusted after a polynomial operation (e.g., addition or multiplication) so that they remain in the range 0–9.

(*b*) Give an algorithm for computing the mod operation.

(*c*) Construct an C++ class that implements the INTEGER ADT for arbitrarily large integers.

5.14. Given the skip list data structure:

(*a*) Write pseudocode procedures for the randomized insertion algorithm as well as the deletion algorithm discussed in Section 5.3.3. Demonstrate the operation of your procedures on the example skip list given in Figure 5.15 (c).

(*b*) Using the randomized insertion algorithm discussed in Section 5.3.3, there is a small chance that the level of a new node will be much larger than the level of any other node in the list. If this happens, subsequent operations will entail a lot of useless effort traversing the null pointers in this node. One solution is to let the level of the list increase by at most one on any insertion. That is, if the randomly generated level is more than one greater than the current largest node level in the list, we make the new node's level one greater than the maximum. Modify your pseudocode from part (a) to incorporate this heuristic.

CHAPTER NOTES

Overviews of the heuristics used in self-organizing lists are given in Knuth [85] and Rivest [127]. Yao and Yao [157] present a complex combinatorial argument showing that the average running time of interpolation search is $\Theta(\log \log n)$. A survey of the literature concerning the interpolation search algorithm, along, with a discussion regarding its implementation and complexity, is given by Gonnet, Rogers, and George [66]. Perl and Reingold [117] provide a pseudo-interpolation search algorithm which on average performs roughly $2.4 \lg \lg n$ comparisons, but is easier to analyze.

Skip lists were introduced by Pugh [125]. In his paper, Pugh showed that the average-case running time of a search in a randomized skip list is $O(\log n)$. He also compared the experimental performance of randomized skip lists to several balanced tree data structures (see Chapter 11) and found that skip lists were superior as long as the computational cost of key comparison was not too high. Munro, Papadakis, and Sedgewick [109] subsequently devised a more complicated version of the skip list data structure in which a search can be performed in worst-case logarithmic time.

Sparse matrices appear in many engineering and scientific problems. For example, the numerical solution of partial differential equations by either finite difference or finite element methods typically requires the solution of large sparse matrices. See Press et al. [123] for a discussion of these methods.

The straightforward way (alluded to in Exercise 5.11(a)) of implementing the *Multiply* operation in the POLYNOMIAL ADT requires $\Theta((mn)^2)$ time. The fast Fourier transform can be used to reduce the time needed to multiply these polynomials to $\Theta(mn \lg(mn))$. A explanation of this method is provided in Cormen, Leiserson, and Rivest [36]. For a more detailed discussion of the convergence of sequence (5.4) given in Exercise 5.12, the reader is referred to Press et al. [123].

CHAPTER
6

STACKS AND QUEUES

In this chapter we investigate stacks and queues, two special types of dynamic sets that are frequently encountered in computer applications. Before discussing them, it is useful to define the terms FIFO and LIFO. A *FIFO* is a first-in-first-out structure; which means that the first item stored in this type of structure will be the first item retrieved from it. An example of a FIFO structure is the line that forms at the front of a cashier at a grocery store check-out line. The first person who enters this line will be the first person served. A *LIFO*, on the other hand, is a last-in-first-out structure. In this case, the last item that is stored in the structure will be the first item retrieved from it. An example of a LIFO structure is a stack of trays at a cafeteria. Typically, clean trays are placed on top of this stack, and trays are removed from the top of this tray stack as well. Thus, the last tray placed on the stack will be the first tray removed by a customer.

6.1   THE STACK AND QUEUE ADTS

A *stack* is a dynamic set that obeys the LIFO property, while a *queue* is a dynamic set that obeys the FIFO property. This means that the temporal order of insertions into these sets completely determines the order in which elements are retrieved from them.

We now present the collection of operations that define the STACK and QUEUE ADTs. Although these operations are extremely simple, they prove to be quite useful in a large number of applications. In order to demonstrate this fact, we present a number of examples. The example considered in Section 6.2 describes how stacks are used to evaluate mathematical expressions, while the example in Section 6.3 discusses how stacks can be used to eliminate recursive function calls. We will have the opportunity to use the QUEUE ADT in the queueing system simulation discussed in Section 6.5.

6.1.1   Stack Operations

Since a stack is just a special type of dynamic set, the operations associated with the LIST ADT can be used to implement a stack. However, these operations are given special names when they are applied to stacks. In each of the STACK ADT operations given below, x represents a data element, and S an arbitrary stack.

1. *Push(S, x)*. Inserts x into S.

2. *Top(S)*. Returns the data element that was most recently inserted into S.

3. *Pop(S)*. Deletes the data element that was most recently inserted into S.

In practice the *Pop* operation is often implemented so that it returns the most recently inserted element before deleting it. We will assume that performing a *Pop* or *Top* operation on an empty stack yields an error.

It is often helpful to think of a stack using the cafeteria tray analogy discussed previously. For example, Figure 6.1 shows how a stack of integer numbers would be represented. The only element we have access to is the most recently inserted one, which is referred to as the top-of-stack. In Figure 6.1 the most recently inserted element is 8, and the element that has resided on the stack the longest is 2.

It is not difficult to implement both the *Push* and *Pop* operations in $\Theta(1)$ time using either a sequentially-mapped or a linked list. For either form of list we have two basic choices: we can keep the top-of-stack at the head or tail of the list. With a sequentially-mapped list, it is most efficient to keep the top-of-stack at the tail of the list. In this case, we simply append a new element to the tail of the list on a *Push* operation, and delete an element from the tail of the list on a *Pop* operation. Since a sequentially-mapped list allows random access, both of the operations can

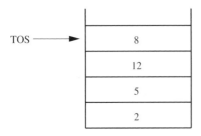

FIGURE 6.1
A logical view of a stack of integer numbers. The TOS (top-of-stack) variable points to the most recently inserted element.

be implemented in $\Theta(1)$ time. In Section 6.4 we demonstrate a C++ implementation that uses this approach.

Keeping the top-of-stack at the head of a sequentially-mapped list does not allow the STACK ADT operations to be implemented as efficiently. To see why, recall that inserting a new element at the head of a list requires that the elements at positions 1 through n be shifted up to positions 2 through $n + 1$, an operation requiring $\Theta(n)$ time. Furthermore, a deletion from the head of the list also takes $\Theta(n)$ time since the elements in positions 2 through n must be shifted down. Therefore, both the *Push* and *Pop* operations would require $\Theta(n)$ time in this case.

In a linked list implementation, elements can be stored at either the head or tail of the list (assuming we store a pointer to the tail), and both *Push* and *Pop* can be implemented in $\Theta(1)$ time.

6.1.2 Queue Operations

The operations provided by a LIST ADT implementation can also be used to implement the QUEUE ADT. The special names for the QUEUE accessing routines are given below. In each operation, x once again represents a data element, and Q an arbitrary queue.

1. *Enqueue*(Q, x). Inserts x into Q.
2. *Head*(Q). Returns the list element that has resided in Q the longest.
3. *Dequeue*(Q). Deletes the list element that has resided in Q the longest.

In practice, the *Dequeue* operation is typically implemented so that it returns an element before deleting it. We will assume that performing a *Head* or *Dequeue* operation on an empty stack yields an error, and we will refer to the items that have resided in a queue for the longest and shortest periods of time as the *head* and *tail* of the queue, respectively.

Implementing the QUEUE ADT involves adding elements to one end of the list during an *Enqueue* operation, and removing them from the other end of the list during a *Dequeue* operation. This guarantees that elements are accessed in FIFO order. This strategy can be efficiently implemented using a linked list, since inserting an element at position 1 of a linked list only takes $\Theta(1)$ time, as does appending an element to the tail of a linked list (assuming we keep a pointer to the tail node as discussed in Section 5.3.1).

Implementing the aforementioned strategy using a sequentially-mapped list, however, is rather inefficient. If the head of the queue is fixed at the head of the list, then each *Dequeue* operation would involve shifting $n - 1$ elements down one position in the list. Likewise, fixing the tail of the queue at the tail of the list causes each *Enqueue* operation to perform $n - 1$ shifts.

One way around these problems is to let the head and tail of the queue move through the list. That is, treat the head and tail of the queue as variables which may point to any position in the list. As we shall see, this essentially turns the queue into a circular structure that is able to "wrap around" the ends of the list. It is easiest to demonstrate this strategy with an example. Consider the implementation of a queue in the initially empty four-element array Q shown below:

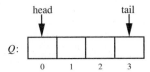

Notice that we have initialized two variables, called head and tail, so that they point to array locations 0 and 3, respectively. Assuming that three elements with keys 8, 3, and 5 were enqueued (i.e., inserted using *Enqueue*) in the order given, the queue would now look like:

$$
\begin{array}{c}
\text{head} \qquad \text{tail} \\
Q:\ \boxed{\ 8\ |\ 3\ |\ 5\ |\ \ } \\
\ \ 0\ \ \ 1\ \ \ 2\ \ \ 3
\end{array}
$$

Before each *Enqueue* operation, the tail variable was incremented modulo the size of the array (see Appendix A.1.2 for a discussion of the mod operator) before inserting the new element at the position pointed to by this variable.

A *Dequeue* operation would return the element with key 8, and modify the data structure as follows:

$$
\begin{array}{c}
\text{head} \ \text{tail} \\
Q:\ \boxed{\ \ |\ 3\ |\ 5\ |\ \ } \\
\ \ 0\ \ \ 1\ \ \ 2\ \ \ 3
\end{array}
$$

Let us now perform three more operations—*Enqueue*$(Q, 7)$, *Dequeue*(Q), and *Enqueue* $(Q, 2)$. After these operations, the queue would look like:

$$
\begin{array}{c}
\text{tail} \qquad \text{head} \\
Q:\ \boxed{\ 2\ |\ \ |\ 5\ |\ 7\ } \\
\ \ 0\ \ \ 1\ \ \ 2\ \ \ 3
\end{array}
$$

The interesting thing to note here is that the queue now wraps around the end of the array.

The specific location in the array of a given queue element can be easily calculated using the mod operator. Specifically, if h denotes the array index where the head of the queue is stored in an n-element array, and t denotes the array index where the tail of the queue is stored, then the queue elements (starting from the head) are stored in array locations

$$h, \ (h + 1) \bmod n, \ (h + 2) \bmod n, \ \ldots, \ t$$

Furthermore, by observing the initial state of the queue in the previous example, we can see that one necessary condition for determining whether the queue is empty is

$$h = (t + 1) \bmod n \tag{6.1}$$

However, this condition is not sufficient, as can be demonstrated by continuing with the previous example. If an element with key 8 is enqueued, the queue would look like:

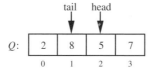

At this point the array is full. Furthermore, condition (6.1) holds. In general, condition (6.1) will hold whenever the queue is empty or the array is full. To distinguish between these two states, checking one additional condition will suffice. Specifically, if condition (6.1) holds, then the type of operation that last modified the queue can be used to determine the state of the queue. The only way a queue can become empty is if the last operation that modified the queue was a *Dequeue*.[†] If condition (6.1) holds, and the last operation to modify the queue was an *Enqueue*, then the array must be full. A C++ implementation that makes use of this strategy is given in Section 6.4.

6.2 STACKS AND EXPRESSION EVALUATION

We now consider the use of the STACK ADT in the evaluation of mathematical expressions found in source code. This section is meant to provide only a glimpse at the techniques used by compilers to perform this task. For more details, the reader may wish to consult one of the references given in the Chapter Notes.

6.2.1 Postfix Expressions

First let us consider the evaluation of mathematical expressions given in *postfix form* (i.e., reverse Polish notation). In this notation, mathematical operators follow their operands. For instance, the postfix expression

$$a \ b + c *$$

is equivalent to the standard (i.e., **infix**) expression

$$(a + b) * c$$

[†]Strictly speaking, this does not hold for an initially empty queue; however, this is easily handled by artificially assuming that a *Dequeue* operation occurred immediately prior to the queue's creation.

Note that parentheses are not necessary in postfix notation, but they are often necessary to ensure the correct order of evaluation with infix expressions.

If we evaluate a postfix expression by reading it from left to right, operands are encountered before their associated operators. Thus, whenever an operator is read, we must be able to backtrack to find the proper operands. The easiest way to do this is to use a stack: The postfix expression is scanned from left to right, and each time an operand is encountered it is pushed onto the stack. Whenever an operator is found, it is applied to the two operands most recently pushed onto the stack. For example, the postfix expression

$$4\ 8\ 7\ 3 + * 2 / +$$

is evaluated as follows: The first four operands are pushed onto the stack in the order they are encountered. This yields

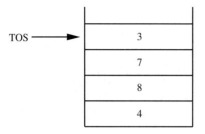

Next the '+' operand is read, so the top two elements are popped from the stack and their sum, 10, is pushed back onto the stack as shown below:

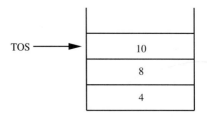

The next symbol read is the '*' operand, so 10 and 8 are popped from the stack and their product, 80, is pushed back onto the stack:

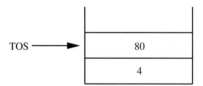

Next a 2 is pushed onto the stack:

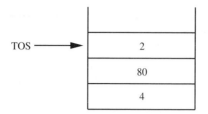

Then the '/' operand is encountered, so 80 and 2 are popped from the stack, and $80/2 = 40$ is pushed onto the stack:

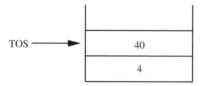

Finally, a '+' is read and 40 and 4 are popped from the stack, and the final result $40 + 4 = 44$ is pushed onto the stack:

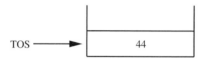

Notice that postfix expressions are easy to evaluate because rules of precedence do not have to be applied during the evaluation—the same cannot be said for infix expressions. There is, however, a straightforward way of converting an infix expression into a postfix expression. The technique we have just presented can then be used to evaluate the resulting postfix expression.

6.2.2 Infix-to-Postfix Conversion

The conversion process we are about to discuss accepts an infix expression as input, and produces a postfix expression as output. The general idea is to use a stack to store operands as they are encountered, and to later pop these operands according to their precedence. Specifically, the infix expression is scanned from left to right and processed according to the following rules:

1. Whenever an operand is encountered it is passed to the output.
2. Each time an operator is read, the stack is continually popped, and operands are passed to the output, until an operator is reached that has a lower precedence than

the most recently read operator. The most recently read operator is then pushed onto the stack.

3. When the end of the infix expression is reached, all symbols remaining on the stack are popped and passed to the output.

4. Since parentheses can be used to change the order of evaluation in infix expressions, we must incorporate them into the conversion process. This is accomplished by treating parentheses as operators that have higher precedence than any other operator. In addition, we do not allow right parentheses to be pushed onto the stack, and we only allow a left parenthesis to be popped after a right parenthesis has been read. Note, however, that parentheses should not be passed to the output when they are popped from the stack since they do not appear in postfix expressions.

As a demonstration of this conversion process, consider the infix expression

$$a * (b + c) + d/e$$

The first symbol read is a; since it is an operand, it is passed through to the output. Next, the '$*$' operator is read. Because the stack is currently empty, no operators are popped, and '$*$' is pushed onto the stack. Thus we have

Output: a

Next a '(' is read, and since all operators have a lower precedence than a left parenthesis, it is immediately pushed onto the stack. Then 'b' is read and passed to the output. This yields

Output: a b

The next symbol read is the '$+$' operator. Although '(' has a higher precedence than this operator, it cannot be popped from the stack until a ')' has been read. Thus, nothing is popped, and the '$+$' operator is pushed onto the stack. Following this, 'c' is read and passed to the output:

Output: a b c

A ')' is read next. Since '+' has a lower precedence than this operator, nothing is popped from the stack. The ')' symbol is discarded; however, when the situation arises, we will now be able to pop the left parenthesis, since its corresponding right parenthesis has been read. The next symbol encountered is the '+' operator. Reading this symbol causes all of the currently stored symbols to be popped from the stack (none of these operators has a lower precedence than a '+'), but only the '+' and '∗' operators are passed through to the output. The most recently read operator, '+', is then pushed onto the stack:

Output: a b c + ∗

Next a '*d*' is read (and output) followed by a '/'. Since addition has a lower precedence than division, the '/' operator is pushed onto the stack:

Output: a b c + ∗ d

The final symbol read is '*e*', which is output. Then the remaining operators stored on the stack are popped and passed through to the output as shown below:

Output: a b c + ∗ d e / +

The final output is the correct postfix expression.

6.3   STACKS AND RECURSION

Recall that our model of computer memory presented in Section 1.3 included a run-time stack that stored activation records. If we refer back to the recursion tree for Tower() given in Figure 1.9, we see that the recursive calls "bottom out" at the left-most child in the tree. At that point, control passes to the activation record represented by the parent of this child. This involves backtracking to the last activation record placed on the run-time stack. It is not too difficult to convince ourselves that the sequence of activation records are accessed in LIFO order off the run-time stack, allowing program control to return to the proper location after the completion of each recursive call.

A common technique used to improve the run-time performance of a program involves eliminating procedure calls. This is due to the fact that a significant amount of information is stored in the activation records produced by a procedure call (see Section 1.3). In the case of recursive calls, instead of relying on the system run-time stack, we can create a stack in our program and manually perform the bookkeeping associated with each recursive call. The elimination of the function call overhead associated with these recursive calls may reduce the running time, as well as the amount of memory required by the program. In this section we present a technique that uses a stack to systematically convert a recursive procedure into a nonrecursive (i.e., iterative) one.

It should first be mentioned, however, that a recursive call appearing on the last line of a procedure can be removed without the use of a stack. Specifically, this type of recursive call, called *tail recursion*, can be replaced with a loop. Tail recursion is so easy to identify that it is often automatically removed by compilers. In spite of this, it is good programming practice to manually remove it from your code. Consider, for instance, the Quicksort() routine given in Section 2.4.3:

Quicksort(**item** $A[\ ]$, **integer** a, **integer** b)
1   **if** $a < b$ **then**
2       $k \leftarrow$ Partition(A, a, b)
3   Quicksort($A, a, k - 1$)
4   Quicksort($A, k + 1, b$)   ▷ tail recursion

The statement on the last line of this procedure is tail recursive since no code follows it. Thus we can rewrite it using a loop:

Quicksort1(**item** $A[\ ]$, **integer** a, **integer** b)
1   $k \leftarrow$ Partition(A, a, b)
2   **while** $a < b$ **do**
3   Quicksort1($A, a, k - 1$)
4       $a \leftarrow k + 1$
5       $k \leftarrow b + 1$

On each iteration of the loop, Quicksort1() is first called recursively on the lower portion of a subarray. On the next iteration, the index locations are modified so that Quicksort1() is called recursively on the upper portion of the same subarray.

It is easy to verify (e.g., by drawing recursion trees) that Quicksort() and Quicksort1() produce exactly the same sequence of recursive calls. Thus, nothing is saved, in terms of the number of recursive calls, unless we can also eliminate the other recursive call that appears on line 3. This can be accomplished by employing a user-supplied stack as shown below:

Quicksort2(**item** $A[\ ]$, **integer** a, **integer** b)
1   STACK S
2   $Push(a, S)$ $Push(b, S)$
3   **do**
4       $b \leftarrow Pop(S)$ $a \leftarrow Pop(S)$
5   **while** $a < b$ **do**
6           $k \leftarrow$ Partition(A, a, b)
7           $Push(k + 1)$ $Push(b)$
8           $b \leftarrow k - 1$
9   **while** $Empty(S) =$ false

In this procedure, after each call to Partition() the index locations corresponding to the upper portion of the current subarray are pushed onto the stack. On the next iteration, the Partition() procedure is called with inputs corresponding to the index locations of the lower portion of the subarray. Thus, we can think of the stack in this procedure as saving for subsequent processing the upper portions of all subarrays, while the lower portions of the subarrays are being partitioned.

For the initial recursive procedure, the number of activation records stored on the run-time stack at any one time may be as large as $\Theta(n)$. The size of the stack used in the final nonrecursive procedure would also be as large as $\Theta(n)$ for the worst-case partitioning. However, in Quicksort2() the maximum stack size can be reduced to $\Theta(\log n)$ if we are careful about which subarray is processed first. Specifically, instead of always placing the index locations of the upper portion of a subarray on the stack, place the index locations of the larger subarray array on the stack. The smaller subarray is then partitioned on each iteration. In Exercise 6.6 you are asked to prove that this approach results in a worst-case stack size of $\Theta(\log n)$.

6.4 STACK AND QUEUE IMPLEMENTATION

The implementation of both the STACK and QUEUE ADTs is easily accomplished by inheriting one of the previously developed list classes discussed in Chapter 5. Specifically, in Figure 6.2 we demonstrate a STACK ADT implementation that makes use of the singly-linked list class developed in Section 5.3.2. The fact that the base class SlList in this figure is a parameterized (i.e., template) class complicates the inheritance slightly. If we had wanted to declare a stack class that only stored a specific type of element (e.g., integers), then the class declaration would have looked like

```
class IntStack : private SlList<int> {···}
```

In this case the integer instantiation of the template class SlList serves as a private base class for the nontemplate class IntStack. However, we want to implement the stack as a template class so that it will be able to store elements of arbitrary type. Thus, in Figure 6.2 the class declaration appears as

```
template <class T>
class SlStack : private virtual SlList<T> {···}
```

Note that in order to parameterize the SlStack class, the keyword virtual must appear in its derivation list. With this declaration, each instantiation of a SlStack object to a specific type will result in the instantiation of a base class SlList object of the same type. For example,

```
SlStack<int> s;
```

generates an integer instance of the SlList class, which is used to create an integer instance of the SlStack class. Furthermore, a user will be unable to invoke the member functions of the SlList class directly since it was inherited as a private base class. This restricts the user to the interface provided by the SlStack class, thereby imposing the desired LIFO properties on the list.

```
/* File: stack.H */
#include "sl_list.H"

template<class T>
class SlStack : private virtual SlList<T> {
  public:
    SlStack(const T& elm) : SlList<T>(elm) {}
    SlStack() : SlList<T>() {}
    inline void Push(const T& elm);
    T& Pop();
    inline Boolean Empty() const;
    inline void MakeEmpty();
    friend ostream& operator<<(ostream& os, const SlStack<T>& stk)
    {return operator<<(os, (SlList<T>)stk);}
};

template<class T>
inline void SlStack<T>::Push(const T& elm) {Append(elm);}

template<class T>
inline Boolean SlStack<T>::Empty() const {return SlList<T>::Empty();}
```

// remaining inline function definitions not shown

FIGURE 6.2
The declaration of the SlStack class.

Notice the ease with which the member functions in Figure 6.2 are implemented. The fact that the SlStack class IS-A SlList means that only a minimal amount of new code needs to be supplied. For instance, the Push() member function is implemented by using the Append() member function in the SlList class to add new elements at the tail of the list. The Pop() member function can then be implemented by simply retrieving the element stored at the tail of the list. The ≪ operator is overloaded as an inline function by casting an SlStack object to a SlList object, and then using the SlList ≪ operator to output the list. Notice also that the Empty() member function in Figure 6.2 has the same name as the member function it calls in the SlList class. In order for the compiler to determine which member function it should invoke, the member function call in the inline definition of this function must be fully qualified with the base class name as shown in the figure. Leaving the base class name off this call would cause the Empty() member function in the SlStack class to continually call itself recursively since there is no termination condition.

Finally, notice that a destructor is not provided in the SlStack class. In C++ destructors are not inherited; however, if a derived class does not declare a destructor, then the compiler will automatically generate one that calls the destructor for the base, as well as the destructors for the members of the derived class. Since the SlList is actually performing all of the dynamic memory allocation for the SlStack, this compiler-supplied destructor will suffice.

The STACK ADT can also be implemented by inheriting the sequentially-mapped dynamic list class discussed in Section 5.2.2. In fact, this implementation simply involves replacing every appearance of the class name SlList in the declaration given in Figure 6.2 with the class name DynList.

As discussed in Section 6.1.2, the QUEUE ADT is also easily and efficiently implemented by inheriting the SlList class; however, implementing this ADT using a sequentially-mapped data structure is a little more difficult. Below, we consider the implementation of the QUEUE ADT using the circular array strategy discussed in Section 6.1.2. Instead of trying to use the DynList class to implement this strategy, we will build a new class from "scratch."

In Figure 6.3 we provide the class declaration for the SmQueue class. The circular array in this class is dynamically allocated by one of the constructors, and a pointer to the array is stored in the protected member element. Notice that a new type called op_type is declared using the typedef facility, and that a variable called

```
/* File: sm_queue.H */
typedef enum {enque, deque} op_type;

template<class T>
class SmQueue {
  protected:
    int head, tail, size;
    op_type last_op;
    T* element;
  public:
    SmQueue(int sz, const T& elm);
    SmQueue(int sz);
    SmQueue(const SmQueue<T>& que);
    SmQueue() {}
    inline ~SmQueue();
    SmQueue<T>& operator=(const SmQueue<T>&);
    void Enqueue(const T& elm);
    T& Dequeue();
    Boolean Empty() const;
    inline void MakeEmpty();
    friend ostream& operator<<(ostream& os, const SmQueue<T>& que);
};

template<class T>
inline SmQueue<T>::~SmQueue() {delete [] element;}

template<class T>
inline void SmQueue<T>::MakeEmpty() {head=0; tail=size-1;
last_op=deque;}
```

FIGURE 6.3
The declaration of the SmQueue class.

```
/* File: sm_queue.C */
template<class T>
void SmQueue<T>::Enqueue(const T& elm)
{
  if (head == (tail+1) % size)
    assert(last_op != enque); // enqueue into a full array
  last_op = enque;
  tail = (tail+1) % size;
  element[tail] = elm;
}

template<class T>
T& SmQueue<T>::Dequeue()
{
  if (head == (tail+1) % size)
    assert(last_op != deque); // dequeue from an empty queue
  last_op = deque;
  T* temp = new T(element[head]);
  head = (head+1) % size;
  return *temp;
}
```

FIGURE 6.4

Implementation of the Enqueue() and Dequeue() operations in the SmQueue class.

last_op of type op_type appears as a protected member of the class. As discussed in Section 6.1.2, this variable will be used to distinguish between an empty queue and a full array. The use of this variable in the *Enqueue* and *Dequeue* operations is demonstrated in Figure 6.4

6.5   AN EXTENDED EXAMPLE: QUEUEING SYSTEM SIMULATION

One of the areas in which object-oriented programming (and computers for that matter) have had the greatest impact is in simulation. The goal of a simulation program is to model some *physical system* (e.g., a chemical reaction, a weather system, or an assembly line) so that we may analyze and predict its behavior. The physical system may be thought of as a collection of interdependent elements, or entities, that operate and interact to accomplish some task. A collection of *state variables* is used to represent the state of the physical system. Quite often the state variables of a system are defined to be the states of the entities involved. For example, in the simulation of airplane traffic at an airport, a given plane would be an entity in the system under consideration, and its state might be defined as in the air, on the ground, landing, or taking off.

Typically, we wish to model a system stochastically; in this case, one or more of the state variables are assigned values according to a probability distribution.

For example, in the aforementioned airport simulation, we might model the probability that an airplane will be unable to take off due to a malfunction according to a probability distribution that closely matches observed data. In addition, the changes in system state are normally measured versus time. In a ***continuous system simulation*** the state of the system is continuously evolving with time. On the other hand, in a ***discrete system simulation*** the state variables are only allowed to change at specific points in time. It is important to distinguish between *simulated time*, which is the time in the physical system, and the *computing time* required to execute the program. For large complicated systems, hours of computing time may be required to simulate a few seconds of time in the physical system. In other situations, the computing time should be much less than the simulated time—for example, we would certainly like this to be the case in weather forecasting programs!

The major difficulty that arises in implementing a computer simulation involves bridging the conceptual gap that exists between the physical system and its computer representation. This involves determining what data structures can be used to model the components of the physical system. In this regard, object-oriented programming lends itself quite naturally to simulation. The components of the physical system are represented by class objects, and the interaction of components in the physical system is simulated by passing messages between objects in the simulation system. One advantage of this approach is that it encapsulates in a class object the information associated with a component, and the object itself determines how it should respond to specific events.

In this example we will focus on modeling ***queueing systems***, that is, systems with waiting lines. A large number of physical systems can be modeled in this manner; consider, for instance, the waiting lines that form at the front of bank tellers, or at the check-out lane of a grocery store. Customers entering these lines are served on a first-come-first-serve basis. This resembles the FIFO property of a queue. The same can be said for vehicles awaiting service at a gas station, airplanes awaiting clearance from an airport control tower for take off, and message transmission in a computer communication network.

In its simplest form, a queueing system consists of a single server that services a single queue. This situation is depicted in Figure 6.5. In order to simulate this system, the following information must be specified:

1. The distribution of customer interarrival times. Customers are assumed to arrive according to a known probability distribution $A(t)$. Specifically, $A(t) = Pr\{$time between consecutive arrivals $\leq t\}$.

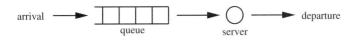

FIGURE 6.5
A single-server queueing system.

2. The service time distribution. The service time of an individual customer is assumed to vary according to a known probability distribution $S(t)$. Specifically, $S(t) = Pr\{\text{customer service time} \leq t\}$.

Given this scenario, one is typically interested in determining (via simulation in our case) the distribution of queue length and customer waiting times, and the efficiency of the server.

It is easy to extend this general idea to more complicated scenarios. For example, Figure 6.6 (a) depicts a system in which s servers are set up to service k queues; a typical approach to servicing customers taken by banks. Figure 6.6 (b) shows a collection of queues and servers set up as a network. This type of system might be used to model the production of parts in a manufacturing plant.

Below we consider the construction of a rudimentary program for simulating queueing systems. This will involve the creation of three classes: a customer queue class that models the waiting line (we will simply call this the queue); a server class that services these customers; and a scheduler class that schedules the events that occur during the simulation. The following pseudocode gives a general overview of how the scheduler will function in this simulation. In this pseudocode, a single-server queueing system is simulated by initializing the simulation clock t, and then incrementing it by the fixed amount Δt on every iteration.

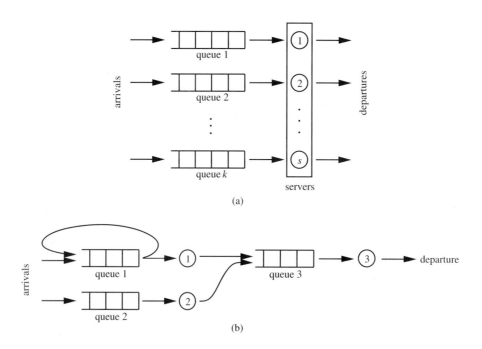

FIGURE 6.6
(a) A multiple-queue multiple-server queueing system. **(b)** A queueing network.

Simulate_TimeDriven(time t_{start}, time t_{end})
1   initialize system state and simulation clock
2   **while** $(t < t_{end})$ **do**
3        $t \leftarrow \Delta t$
4   **if** $t \geq t_{arrival}$ **then**
5   add a customer to queue and update statistics
6            $t_{arrival} \leftarrow t + A(t)$ $\triangleright$ generate next customer arrival time
7   **if** $t \geq t_{done}$ **then**
8            $server\_state \leftarrow$ idle
9   **if** $server\_state =$ idle **and** customers are in the queue **then**
10   remove a customer from queue and update statistics
11            $server\_state \leftarrow$ busy
12            $t_{done} \leftarrow t + S(t)$ $\triangleright$ generate service time

On each iteration of the loop over lines 2–12, several conditional statements are used to check if any events have occurred during the previous time interval. For instance, if a customer arrived during the previous time interval, the statement on line 4 will evaluate true, causing the customer to be added to the queue, and the arrival time of the next customer to be generated.

We now consider an object-oriented implementation of this general model. The declaration for the customer queue class is shown in Figure 6.7. This class is responsible for keeping track of the statistics related to the waiting line. These

```
/* File: que_sys.H */
#include "sm_queue.H"
#include "pdf.H" // see Exercise 4.13

class CustomerQueue : private SmQueue<double> {
  private:
    int length, max_queue_size, total_customers, lost_customers;
    double last_event_time, total_wait_time, max_wait_time, total_queue_size;
    virtual Boolean Balk();
  public:
    inline CustomerQueue();
    void Enter(double current_time);
    void Exit(double current_time);
    inline Boolean Empty();
    void PrintStats(double current_time);
};

inline CustomerQueue::CustomerQueue()
{length=max_queue_size=total_customers=
 lost_customers=0; total_wait_time=max_wait_time=total_queue_size=0;}

inline Boolean CustomerQueue::Empty() {return SmQueue<double>::Empty();}
```

FIGURE 6.7
The declaration of the CustomerQueue class.

include the average and maximum size of the queue during the simulation, and the average customer wait time in the queue. It is assumed that customers enter the queue according to a known probability distribution. In Figure 6.7, the private data members `max_queue_size` and `total_customers` are used to keep track of the maximum size that the queue attains, and the total number of customers served during the simulation, respectively.

In certain cases we would also like to allow the possibility of a customer declining to enter the queue—for example, if the line is too long. This situation is referred to as a ***balk***. In the `CustomerQueue` class, the virtual member function `Balk()` is used to determine if a customer balks, and a running total of the number of customers that have balked during a simulation is stored in the `lost_customers` member variable.

The time at which the last enqueue or dequeue operation was performed on the queue is stored in `last_event_time`, and the cumulative wait time for all customers is stored in `total_wait_time`. The longest wait that any customer experienced in the queue is stored in `max_wait_time`. Finally, the data member `total_queue_size` is used to calculate the average queue size. This data member stores the cumulative sum of products of the size of the queue times the amount of time that the queue was a particular size. Thus the average queue size can be determined by dividing the value stored in `total_queue_size` by the total simulation time.

The only member functions that can change any of the data members of a `CustomerQueue` object are the `Enter()` and `Exit()` operations, the definitions of which are shown in Figure 6.8. In order to compute the various statistics associated with the queue, it is only necessary to store in the queue the times at which customers enter. Notice also that in the `Enter()` function we check for a balk before enqueuing a customer.

The server class is responsible for compiling statistics related to the service time. These include the total number of customers serviced during the simulation and the average service time per customer, as well as the percentage of time that the server was busy. It is assumed that the service time for an individual customer is determined by a known probability distribution.

The interface to this class is shown in Figure 6.9. The private data members `customers_served` and `total_service_time` are used to store the number of customers that have been served by a server, and the amount of time it has taken to perform this service, respectively. The `busy_until` variable is used to store the time at which a server will switch from the busy state to the free state. A server object is in the busy state whenever it is servicing a customer, and in the free state whenever it is available to service a customer. The data member `distribution` is used to store a pointer to the class `pdf`—a probability distribution class developed in Exercise 4.13. Also, the member function `NextAvailable()` is declared as private because only the `ServiceCustomer()` member function needs to use it. The `NextAvailable()` function is responsible for computing the time at which the server will be available to service customers—that is, the time at which the server changes from the busy state to the free state. As shown in the definition of the `ServiceCustomer()` function in Figure 6.10, `NextAvailable()` is used to determine the value of `busy_until`.

```
/* File: que_sys.C */
void CustomerQueue::Enter(double current_time)
{
  total_customers++;
  total_queue_size += length * (current_time - last_event_time);
  last_event_time = current_time;
  if (Balk() == true)
    lost_customers++;
  else {
    Enqueue(current_time);
    length++;
    if (length > max_queue_size)
      max_queue_size = length;
  }
}

void CustomerQueue::Exit(double current_time)
{
  total_queue_size += length * (current_time - last_event_time);
  length--;
  last_event_time = current_time;
  double wait = current_time - Dequeue();
  if (wait > max_wait_time)
    max_wait_time = wait;
  total_wait_time += wait;
}
```

FIGURE 6.8

The `Enter()` and `Exit()` member function definitions in the `CustomerQueue` class.

We would like to be able to specify at run time which probability distribution function the `Server` class will use. The advantage of this approach is that it does not constrain the `Server` class to a predefined set of probability distribution functions. Therefore, we have the capability of using additional probability distributions without being forced to modify and recompile the `Server` class. This is accomplished by using the polymorphic (i.e., virtual) functions developed in Exercise 4.13. The key to this approach is that a pointer to a derived class may be assigned to a pointer of the base class, and if member functions have been declared virtual, then the functions of the derived class can be invoked through the base class pointer. Thus, in the `Server` class we have the declaration

```
pdf *distribution;
```

A user program may make the declaration

```
uniform_pdf uniform_distribution(a,b);
```

where a and b are the parameters of the uniform distribution, and the constructor for the `Server` class can then be called using

```
server teller(&uniform_distribution);
```

```
/* File: que_sys.H */
class Server {
  private:
    int customers_served;
    double busy_until, total_service_time;
    pdf* distribution;
    inline double NextAvailable(double current_time);
  public:
    inline Server(pdf *Dist);
    inline Boolean Busy(double current_time);
    void ServiceCustomer(double current_time);
    inline double FractionTimeBusy(double current_time);
    void PrintStats(double current_time);
};

inline double Server::NextAvailable(double current_time)
  {return (current_time + distribution->Draw());}

inline Boolean Server::Busy(double current_time)
  {return (current_time > busy_until ? false : true);}

// remaining inline member functions not shown
```

FIGURE 6.9
The declaration of the Server class.

```
/* File: que_sys.C */
void Server::ServiceCustomer(double current_time)
{
  assert(Busy(current_time) == false);
  busy_until = NextAvailable(current_time);
  total_service_time += busy_until - current_time;
  customers_served++;
}
```

FIGURE 6.10
The ServiceCustomer() member function in the Server class.

This creates an object called teller of class Server. Invoking the ServiceCustomer() function as follows

```
        teller.ServiceCustomer(time);
```

will cause this function to compute the time that the teller object is next available based upon a random number in the range $[a, b]$ drawn according to the uniform distribution.

Finally, as discussed previously, the scheduler class keeps track of the simulated time and is responsible for enqueuing and dequeuing customers. The declaration

```
/* file: que_sys.H */
class Scheduler {
  private:
    double start, done_time;
    CustomerQueue* que;
    Server* server;
    pdf* arrival_dist;
  public:
    inline Scheduler(CustomerQueue* line, pdf* dist, Server* asst);
    void Simulate(double start_time, double end_time);
    void PrintStats(double current_time);
};
```

FIGURE 6.11
The declaration of the Scheduler class.

of the Scheduler class is shown in Figure 6.11. Once a Scheduler object has been properly constructed, the Simulate member function can be called to actually perform a simulation. This member function executes a sequence of steps that are generally described by the Simulate_TimeDriven() pseudocode given previously in this section. This will cause the CustomerQueue and Server objects to collect a set of statistics that can be output using the PrintStats member function.

As a demonstration of the use of the classes presented here, consider a server who services customers (from a queue) who arrive according to a Poisson distribution with a mean interarrival time of 50 seconds. Assume that the service time is exponentially distributed with a mean of 60 seconds. Furthermore, let us assume that if there are n customers already in the queue, an arriving customer will balk with the following probability:

$$Pr(balk) = \begin{cases} 0, & \text{if } n \leq 4 \\ 0.5, & \text{otherwise} \end{cases}$$

The results obtained from simulating this scenario three different times are shown in Table 6.1.

TABLE 6.1
Results of the queueing system simulation on three different runs. On each run, customers arrived according to a Poisson distribution with a mean interarrival time of 50 seconds, and the service time had a normal distribution with a mean of 60 seconds and a standard deviation of 35 seconds.

Customers served	Customers lost	Avg queue size	Max queue size	Max wait in queue (sec)	Avg service time (sec)	% Server busy
239	10	3.33742	8	463	58.7112	95.612
251	1	2.14639	5	314	55.7578	96.592
241	6	1.79783	7	415	55.3761	91.773

EXERCISES

6.1. Write pseudocode procedures that use the STACK ADT operations to implement

(*a*) the evaluation of a postfix expression supplied as input, and

(*b*) the conversion of an infix expression supplied as input into a postfix expression.

6.2. Write a pseudocode procedure that takes as input a C++ source code file and checks to make sure that the following symbols appear "balanced" in the source file: { }, /* */, [ ], ( ).

6.3. Rewrite the inorder traversal algorithm given in Section B.4.1, removing tail recursion.

6.4. Write nonrecursive versions of the exponentiation algorithm Power-RC() presented in Section 1.6

(*a*) using a stack, and

(*b*) without using a stack.

6.5. To verify that the first two versions of quicksort given in Section 6.3 produce the exact same sequence of recursive function calls, draw the recursion tree that results when each of these procedures is used to sort an array containing 15 elements. Assume that in each procedure, Partition() produces a perfect split each time it is called.

6.6. Notice that the two recursive calls performed in the Quicksort() procedure given in Section 6.3 are independent of each other, and that no additional code follows them. Thus, either call can be executed before the other. We took advantage of this fact in Section 6.3 when we discussed the implementation of a nonrecursive version of quicksort that always saved the larger portion of a subarray on a user-supplied stack for subsequent processing.

(*a*) Prove that in this nonrecursive implementation of quicksort the maximum stack size is $\Theta(\log n)$.

(*b*) Can this same strategy be used to reduce the maximum number of activation records stored on the run-time stack to $\Theta(\log n)$ for the fully recursive version?

6.7. Write a nonrecursive procedure that solves the Tower of Hanoi problem discussed in Section 1.4.1.

6.8. In this exercise you are to develop a program that can traverse a maze. This technique requires that alternative paths through the maze be saved at decision points (points in the maze where it is possible to move in more than one direction). When a dead end is reached in the maze, we simply return to the last decision point and move in a different direction. This search technique is known as *backtracking*. Since backtracking requires remembering decision points in LIFO order, a stack should be used to save and recall them. Your program should be able to handle input in the form of a maze represented by an $n \times m$ character array of 1s and 0s, with an "*E*" placed in the entry location. You may move vertically or horizontally (but not diagonally) in any direction that contains a 0; you may not move to a location that contains a 1. If you move to a border location that contains a 0, you have found an exit. (Note: you are allowed to "mark" locations in the maze with some other character value after you have visited them.) Use the program you develop to traverse the following mazes:

```
1 1 1 1 E 1 1 1 1 1      0 1 1 E 1 1 0 1 1 1
1 0 0 1 0 1 0 0 0 1      1 0 1 0 0 0 1 0 0 1
1 0 0 1 0 0 0 1 0 1      1 0 0 0 1 0 0 0 0 1
1 1 0 1 0 1 1 1 0 1      1 0 1 0 1 0 1 0 1 0
1 1 0 1 0 0 1 1 0 1      1 0 0 0 0 0 1 0 0 1
1 0 0 1 0 0 0 0 0 1      1 0 1 1 0 0 1 0 1 1
1 0 1 1 0 1 0 1 1 1      1 0 0 1 1 0 1 0 1 0
1 0 0 1 1 1 0 0 0 1      1 0 1 0 0 0 1 0 0 1
1 0 0 0 0 0 0 1 0 1      1 0 0 1 1 0 1 0 0 1
1 1 1 1 1 1 0 1 1 1      1 1 1 1 1 1 1 1 1 1
```

6.9. In the *eight queens problem* you are asked to place eight queens on a chessboard (an 8×8 grid) so that no queen is in a position to take any other queen. (A queen may take any other queen that is on the same row, column, or diagonal.)

(*a*) A brute-force algorithm for solving this problem systematically checks all possible ways of placing eight queens on a chessboard to see if a solution has been found. How many possibilities are there?

(*b*) The brute-force approach checks some arrangements that we can immediately rule out. For instance we know that no two queens can appear in the same row. Thus a solution can always be represented using a vector $P[1..8]$, where $P[i]$ is the column placement of the queen in the i-th row, and therefore the actual queen positions are given by $(1, P[1])$, $(2, P[2])$, ... , $(8, P[8])$. We say that the vector P is k-feasible if none of the queens in positions $(1, P[1])$, $(2, P[2])$, ..., $(k, P[k])$ can take any other queen in these postions. Develop a backtracking search algorithm that solves the eight queens problem by systematically producing k-feasible vectors, for $k = 1, 2, \ldots, 8$. Extend your algorithm so that it produces *all* solutions to this problem. (Hint: Vector P is k-feasible if for every $i \neq j$ between 1 and k, $P[i] - P[j] \notin \{i - j, 0, j - i\}$.)

(*c*) This problem can be generalized to n queens on an $n \times n$ chessboard. What is the running time of the algorithm you developed in part (b) for the n queens problem? Are there values of $n > 3$ for which no solutions exist?

6.10. Consider a puzzle consisting of four six-sided cubes, where each face of a cube is painted either red, green, blue, or white. The cubes must be placed side by side on a table so that when the cubes are viewed from above, front, or back, all four colors are seen (i.e., if the cubes are viewed from above, we should see each of the four colors on the top surfaces of the cubes; if they are viewed from the front, we should see each of the four colors on the front surfaces of the cubes, and so on). Develop an algorithm that solves this problem using a backtracking search.

6.11. Modify the `SmQueue` class given in Section 6.4 so that it expands the size of the array `element` (a la the `DynList` class) whenever the load factor reaches 1, and contracts the size of the array whenever the load factor reaches $1/4$.

6.12. A double-ended queue (deque) is a list that combines the properties of a stack and a queue. The DEQUE (pronounced "deck") ADT operations include:

1. *Push*(x, D). Adds x to D as the new first element, making the old i-th element be the $(i + 1)$-th.

2. *Pop*(D). Deletes and returns the first element in D, making the old i-th element ($i \geq 2$) the $(i - 1)$-th. If D is empty, this yields an error.

3. *Inject*(x, D). Adds x to D as the new last element.

4. *Eject*(D). Deletes and returns the last element in D. If D is empty, this yields an error.

Given the C++ class in Section 5.8 that implements the LIST ADT using a singly-linked list, create an implementation of the DEQUE ADT through the inheritance of this class. Each DEQUE operation should run in $\Theta(1)$ time.

6.13. The Second National Bank of the RTC would like to improve its customer service. The bank is considering two different approaches to servicing customers at its teller windows. You have been hired as a consultant by the bank president to determine which of these approaches is most efficient. The president would like you to develop a simulation that computes the relevant statistics for each model. The two approaches under consideration are:

(*a*) A single line of customers is formed. If one or more tellers is unoccupied, the customer at the front of the line is serviced. If more than one teller is free, the choice of teller is determined at random, with each teller having an equal likelihood of being chosen.

(*b*) Each teller has a separate waiting line. If a customer enters the bank and one or more tellers is free with no waiting line, then the choice of teller is random, with each teller having an equal likelihood of being chosen. In the event that all tellers are occupied, the customer joins the shortest line. If two or more of the shortest lines have the same number of customers, the customer joins one of these lines at random, with each of the lines having an equal likelihood of being chosen.

For each of these scenarios, it is assumed that there are three tellers available for servicing customer requests, and that the servicing time for each of these is uniformly distributed, with Teller 1 requiring between 0.5 and 1.5 minutes, Teller 2 requiring between 0.5 and 2 minutes, and Teller 3 requiring between 0.5 and 2.5 minutes to service a customer. The arrival times of the customers are also uniformly distributed, with a mean interarrival time of 1.5 minutes, and the following balk probability:

$$Pr(balk) = \begin{cases} 0, & \text{if } n \leq 3 \\ 0.25, & \text{if } 4 < n \leq 8 \\ 0.5, & \text{otherwise} \end{cases}$$

Simulate each of these models for an entire working day (for bankers, this is seven hours) and report the results. Remember to continue servicing the customers that were already in line when the bank closed.

6.14. The take-out counter at Mickey D's Burger Palace is serviced by two employees, one making hamburgers, and the other wrapping and selling them. Customers are served in the order of their arrival. A cook produces hamburgers at a steady rate in a time uniformly distributed between 30 and 50 seconds; hamburgers that are ready but have not been sold yet are stored under a heat lamp. Customers arrive according to an exponential distribution, with a mean interarrival time of 2 minutes. Arriving customers seeing more than three people in line will go elsewhere 25 percent of the time. The number of hamburgers ordered by a customer has the following distribution:

number of hamburgers	1	2	3	4	5	6
probability	0.4	0.25	0.15	0.1	0.075	0.025

It takes a fixed time of 45 seconds, plus 10 seconds per hamburger, to wrap a customer's order and collect their money. Furthermore, a customer's order can only be serviced when all required hamburgers are available. Simulate this system for a period of 4 hours to determine:

(*a*) the total number of customers arriving, and the total number of customers lost.

(*b*) the average time a customer must wait for his or her order.

(*c*) the percentage of time the servers are productive.

CHAPTER NOTES

For a more detailed discussion of the translation of infix to postfix expressions, as well as compiler design in general, see Aho, Hopcraft, and Ullman [5]. Most books dealing with operating systems discuss the use of queues in process scheduling (e.g., Silberschatz and Peterson [136]). Bratley, Fox, and Schrage [24] provide a nice overview of simulation. Dequeues are discussed in Tarjan [147].

CHAPTER
7

BINARY
SEARCH TREES

In Chapter 5 we considered the implementation of the DYNAMIC SET ADT using lists. Recall that using a linked list implementation meant that many of the operations associated with this ADT would require $O(n)$ time, where n is the number of data elements stored in the list. If a sorted sequentially mapped list was used, then the *Search* operation could be reduced to $O(\log n)$ time using binary search, at the expense of increasing the running time of *Insert* to $O(n)$. In this chapter, we will study a data structure based on the binary tree that will allow us to implement each of the DYNAMIC SET ADT operations in $O(h)$ time, where h is the height of the binary tree.

7.1 DEFINITIONS

A binary tree is a special type of tree in which every vertex has either no children, one child, or two children. The terminology associated with binary trees is presented in Appendix B.4.2. You are encouraged to review that appendix before proceeding.

In this chapter we will construct a data structure that is based on the binary tree, and use it to store DYNAMIC SET elements. Specifically, a compound data object will be stored at each vertex of the binary tree. This data object will contain a DYNAMIC SET element along with its associated key, and pointers to each child of the vertex (a pointer will be null if a child does not exist). In addition, we will place constraints on how these data elements can be stored in the tree. Specifically, the data items must be stored in the tree in such a way that the key values in the left subtree of the root are less than the key value of the root, and the key value of all vertices in the right subtree of the root are greater than the key value of the root. Furthermore, this same relationship must hold at any other vertex in the tree. This leads to the following definition:

> **Definition 7.1.   Binary Search Tree.** A binary search tree is a data structure whose data elements are organized as a binary tree. The vertices of this tree are ordered such that for any vertex x in the tree, if y is any vertex in the left subtree of x, then $\text{key}[y] < \text{key}[x]$, and if y is any vertex in the right subtree of x, then $\text{key}[x] < \text{key}[y]$.

We will refer to the ordering imposed on the vertices of a binary search tree as the ***binary search tree property***. An important consequence of this property is that an inorder traversal on a binary search tree will always visit the vertices of the tree in sorted order.

Two example binary search trees are shown in Figure 7.1. The alphabetic keys associated with the data elements are shown inside of the vertices. The same key values appear in both of the trees in this figure; however, the binary search tree in part (a) has a height of 2, while the binary search tree in part (b) has a height of 4. By inspection, it is easy to verify that these trees satisfy the binary search tree property.

The maximum height obtainable in an n-vertex binary search tree occurs when the tree degenerates to a linked list, as shown in Figure 7.1 (b). The height of such a tree is $n - 1$. On the other hand, the minimum height of $\lceil \lg n \rceil$ occurs when the binary search tree is a complete binary tree. Intuitively, one can think of the tree in Figure 7.1 (a) as being more "balanced" than the tree in Figure 7.1 (b). In Chapter 11 we will more formally consider this notion of balance. For the present chapter, however, we will somewhat loosely speak of a binary tree whose height close to $\lg n$ as being balanced, and a binary tree whose height is close to n as being unbalanced.

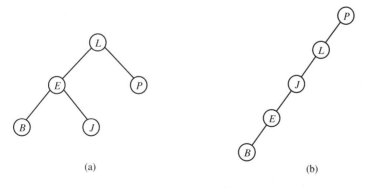

(a)   (b)

FIGURE 7.1
(a) A binary search tree that has a height of 2. **(b)** A binary search tree with the same keys, but whose height is 4.

7.2   DYNAMIC SET OPERATIONS

Let us now consider how the binary search tree data structure supports the implementation of the DYNAMIC SET ADT. We will first consider DYNAMIC SET ADT query operations. These operations do not change the composition of the data elements being stored, they simply request some information regarding the data elements. Next, insertions and deletions will be considered.

In the pseudocode used throughout the remainder of this chapter, we will let BST represent an arbitrary binary search tree. We will also use left[v] and right[v] to denote the left and right children, respectively, of vertex v in a binary tree.

7.2.1   Query Operations

Below we will show that each of the DYNAMIC SET ADT query operations can be implemented in $O(h)$ time in a binary search tree, where h is the height of the binary search tree. We have already demonstrated that in the worst case, this height is $n-1$. Thus it appears that nothing is gained by using this data structure, rather than a linked list. However, in Section 7.4 we will demonstrate that in a randomly constructed binary search tree (i.e., a tree created via a random sequence of insertions), the average running time of all DYNAMIC SET ADT query operations is $\Theta(\log n)$. Furthermore, if some means of restricting the height of a binary search tree to $\Theta(\log n)$ can be devised, then we can always guarantee logarithmic running times for the DYNAMIC SET ADT operations. Methods for restricting the height of a binary search tree in this fashion are presented in Chapter 11.

SEARCH OPERATION.   Given a binary search tree, we search for the key k by first checking to see if the root stores an element with this key. If not, then we must determine if the key we are searching for might be in the left or right subtree of the root. Specifically, if k is less than the key stored at the root, then due to the binary search property, our search can be limited to the left subtree of the root. Likewise, if k is greater than the key stored at the root, our search can be limited to the right subtree of the root. This leads to the following recursive algorithm:

```
BST::Search(BST B, key k)
1    v ← root[B]
2    if v = NULL or k = key[v] then
3        return v
4    if k < key[v] then
5        BST::Search(left-subtree[v], k)
6    else
7        BST::Search(right-subtree[v], k)
```

The conditional statement on line 2 determines when the search terminates. If a vertex is found whose key matches k, then this vertex is returned on line 3. If key k is not in the binary search tree (i.e., the search is unsuccessful), line 3 will return the null value.

The vertices encountered during any search form a path downward from the root towards a leaf. In the worst case, a search will proceed down the longest such path all the way to a leaf. Since this path determines the height of the tree, the running time of BST::Search() is $O(h)$. A useful analogy can be drawn to the binary search technique discussed in Section 5.2.3. At each point in the search process in a binary search tree we move either to a left or right child, while in binary search we move to either the left or right half of an array. In a binary search each such move will always cut the search space in half, guaranteeing a running time of $O(\log n)$; it is important to note that this is not the case in binary search trees. However, if a binary search tree is constructed so that the left subtree of every vertex has the same number of vertices as its right subtree (within one), then the tree will emulate the behavior of binary search.

MAXIMUM AND MINIMUM OPERATIONS.   Implementation of the *Maximum* and *Minimum* operations is quite easy in binary search trees due to the binary search tree property. Specifically, this property guarantees that the minimum key in any binary search tree is the leftmost child of the tree, and that the maximum key tree is the rightmost child of the tree. Thus we can implement the *Maximum* operation by starting at the root and continually moving to the right child of a vertex until a leaf is reached, as is shown below:

```
BST::Maximum(BST B)
1    v ← root[B]
2    while right[v] ≠ NULL do
3         v ← right[v]
4    return v
```

Notice that the null value will be returned if the binary search tree is empty.

The *Minimum* operation is implemented in a symmetric fashion by starting at the root and continually moving to the left child of a vertex. Once again, since both of these algorithms can only trace a path downward in a binary search tree, their running times are given by $O(h)$.

PREDECESSOR AND SUCCESSOR OPERATIONS.   Due to the binary search tree property, it is also possible to easily determine the vertex in a binary search tree whose key value immediately precedes or succeeds a vertex v with key k (if such a vertex exists). Furthermore, the only key comparisons required to implement these operations are a subset of those that were used to initially find v.

We first consider the *Predecessor* operation. Suppose that a vertex v with key k has been located, and that this vertex has a left subtree; then the binary search tree property guarantees that all vertices with keys less than k must appear in this left subtree. Therefore, all that remains is to find the vertex with the largest key in the left subtree of v. This is easily accomplished by employing the previously discussed *Maximum* operation on the left subtree of v.

If vertex v does not have a left subtree, then the binary search tree property guarantees that if its predecessor exists, it can be found by tracing a path from v back towards the root until a vertex is found whose left subtree does not contain v. This vertex is the predecessor of v. To see why this must be so, consider the portion of the binary search tree shown in Figure 7.2, and assume we must find the predecessor

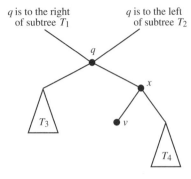

q is to the right
of subtree T_1

q is to the left
of subtree T_2

FIGURE 7.2

A portion of a binary search tree in which the predecessor of vertex v, whose left subtree is empty, must be found. The vertex q in this tree can either be a left child, a right child, or the root.

of the vertex labeled v. The vertex labeled q in this figure is the first vertex on the path back to the root that does not contain v in its left subtree. Because this is a binary search tree, we know that

$$\text{key}[q] < \text{key}[v] < \text{key}[x] \tag{7.1}$$

This means that the key value of q precedes that of v. However, we must show that q is the *immediate* predecessor of v.

If we let keys[T] denote the key values of all vertices in subtree T, then the binary search tree property implies that in Figure 7.2

$$\text{keys}[T_3] < \text{key}[q] < \text{key}[v] \tag{7.2}$$

and

$$\text{key}[q] < \text{key}[v] < \text{keys}[T_4] \tag{7.3}$$

Thus, the predecessor of v cannot be in subtrees T_3 or T_4.

If q is not the root, then we must also consider its ancestors. Specifically, if q is a left child, then with reference to Figure 7.2

$$\text{key}[q] < \text{key}[v] < \text{keys}[T_2]$$

Together with equations (7.1), (7.2), and (7.3), this implies that q is the predecessor v. On the other hand, if q is a right child, then

$$\text{keys}[T_1] < \text{key}[q] < \text{key}[v]$$

and once again, combining this result with equations (7.1), (7.2), and (7.3) implies that q is the predecessor of v. It is not difficult to generalize this analysis to cases in which the path from v to x contains additional vertices.

As an example, consider the binary search tree in Figure 7.1 (a). We see that vertex J has no left subtree. Upon tracing a path back towards the root, the first vertex found whose left subtree does not contain J is the one labeled E, which is in fact the immediate predecessor of J in this tree.

Pseudocode for the *Predecessor* operation is shown below. An algorithm that performs the *Successor* operation can be developed in a nearly symmetric fashion.

BST::Predecessor(BST B, key k)
1    $v \leftarrow$ BST::Search(B,k) $\triangleright$ find the vertex with key k
2   **if** left[v] $\neq$ NULL **then**
3   **return** BST::Maximum(left-subtree[v])
4    $p \leftarrow$ parent[v]
5   **while** $p \neq$ NULL **and** $v =$ left[p] **do**
6        $v \leftarrow p$
7        $p \leftarrow$ parent[p]
8   **return** p

Lines 2 and 3 of this procedure consider the case in which v has a left subtree, and lines 4–8 treat the case in which it does not. In line 4 we are assuming that if v is storing the null value, then parent[v] is also null. The reader should verify that this procedure behaves properly if either the vertex with key k or its predecessor do not exist (in which case the null value should be returned).

7.2.2   Insertion and Deletion

In this section we consider the standard techniques used to insert and delete vertices in a binary search tree. The procedures presented here have the advantage of being relatively simple to implement; their use, however, may lead to the construction of unbalanced trees. In Chapter 11 we will study more complicated procedures concerned with the maintenance of specific balance conditions within binary trees.

INSERT OPERATION.   The standard technique used to insert a new data element into a binary search tree involves three steps. First, a compound data object containing the data element and key must be created. Next, the insertion point in the binary search tree must be determined. This is easily accomplished by searching for the key in the binary search tree. If the key is not in the tree (which is a prerequisite for a successful insertion), this search will encounter a null pointer at one of the leaf vertices. This is the location at which the new data object should be inserted. Thus, the final step involves assigning the address of the new data object to the variable containing the null pointer encountered during the search. If the key is found, then a false value is returned and the operation is terminated. Note that with this approach data elements will always be inserted as leaves. Furthermore, this approach guarantees that the insertion itself does not destroy the binary search tree property.

In the binary search tree insertion algorithm given next, we assume that a vertex has been created and initialized, and that it is passed in as the parameter u. Lines 2 and 3 of this algorithm check to see if the insertion is being performed on an empty tree; if so, vertex u becomes the root of the tree. In the loop over lines 4–11, the variable v is used to trace a path to the insertion path. During this traversal, we also maintain a variable p that stores the parent of v. If an insertion point is found (i.e., v is set to NULL), then u will be inserted either as the left or right child of p, depending upon the outcome of the test performed on line 12. Since the number of loop iterations performed is determined by the height of the tree, the running time of BST::Insert() is $O(h)$.

BST::Insert(BST B, vertex u)
```
1    v ← root[B]
2    if v = NULL then    ▷ an empty tree
3        root[B] ← u
4    while v ≠ NULL do
5        if key[u] = key[v] then
6            return false    ▷ element with key[u] already in tree
7        p ← v
8        if key[u] < key[v] then
9            v ← left[v]
10       else
11           v ← right[v]
12   if key[u] < key[p] then
13       left[p] ← u
14   else
15       right[p] ← u
16   return true
```

DELETE OPERATION.   Given the key of an element we wish to delete, the first step in the *Delete* operation is to search for this key in the binary search tree. If a vertex with the key is found, then the steps taken during the next step of the operation will differ depending upon the number of children the vertex being deleted has. Three cases can be distinguished:

1. Deleting a vertex with *no* children (i.e., a leaf). This deletion is simply a matter of setting the appropriate pointer of the parent vertex to the null value, and then disposing of the leaf vertex. This case is demonstrated in Figure 7.3 (a) where vertex D is deleted.

2. Deleting a vertex with *one* child. This only involves a simple pointer reassignment. That is, the appropriate pointer stored in the parent of the vertex we wish to delete must be made to point instead to the child of the vertex being deleted. In

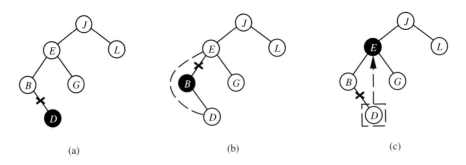

(a)   (b)   (c)

FIGURE 7.3
Deleting a binary search tree vertex that has **(a)** no children, **(b)** one child, and **(c)** two children. In each case the vertex being deleted is black.

Figure 7.3 (b) vertex B is deleted. This involves a reassignment of the left child pointer (shown with a dashed line) of vertex E.

3. Deleting a vertex with *two* children. The simplest approach in this case is to replace the vertex we wish to delete with its inorder predecessor. This strategy is guaranteed to maintain the binary search tree property. The problem then becomes one of deleting the vertex vacated by the inorder predecessor. However, this problem reduces to either a case 1 or case 2 deletion for the following reason. Since the vertex v being removed from the tree has two children, its inorder predecessor must be the vertex with maximum key value in its left subtree. Therefore, the inorder predecessor of v cannot have a right child; however, it may contain a left child. A symmetric argument can be employed to demonstrate that the inorder successor will also work as the replacement vertex. An example is given in Figure 7.3 (c) where vertex E is deleted. Vertex E is replaced with its inorder predecessor, vertex D, and a case 1 deletion is performed on the vertex that formerly stored D.

A binary search tree deletion algorithm that handles each of these cases is given below:

```
BST::Delete(BST B, key k)
1    v ← BST::Search(B,k)   ▷ find the vertex with key k
2    if v = NULL then
3        return false   ▷ element with key k not in tree
4    if left[v] = NULL or right[v] = NULL then   ▷ case 1 or 2
5        if left[parent[v]] = v then
6            c ← left
7        else
8            c ← right
9        if left[v] ≠ NULL then   ▷ case 2, v has a left child
10           c[parent[v]] ← left[v]
11       else if right[v] ≠ NULL then   ▷ case 2, v has a right child
12           c[parent[v]] ← right[v]
13       else   ▷ case 1
14           c[parent[v]] ← NULL
15       reclaim v
16   else   ▷ case 3
17       p ← BST::Maximum(left-subtree[v])   ▷ p is the predecessor of v
18       data[v] ← data[p]
19       BST::Delete(B, key[p])
20   return true
```

Line 4 of this algorithm determines if either a case 1 or 2 deletion is required. If so, then on lines 5–8 we determine if the vertex being deleted is a left or right child of its parent. Thus, either left or right will be stored in the variable c. Lines 9–12 and lines 13–14 are responsible for handling the pointer reassignments in case 2 and 1 deletions, respectively. Finally, lines 16–19 treat a case 3 deletion. On line 18, the dynamic set element stored in the predecessor vertex p is copied to vertex v. Line 20 then calls BST::Delete() recursively to delete vertex p. Notice that for a tree of height h, this algorithm has a worst-case running time of $\Theta(h)$.

7.3   BINARY SEARCH TREE IMPLEMENTATION

In order to implement a binary search tree class, we will first construct a binary tree class to serve as the base class. The declaration of class `BinaryTree` is shown in Figure 7.4. This class is constructed using the now familiar technique of first creating a `Bnode` that will be used to store the data elements, and then creating a `BinaryTree` class that HAS-A pointer to the root `Bnode` object.

```
/* File: bintree.H */
typedef enum {left, right} Child;

// forward references for template classes
template <class Type> class BinaryTree;
template <class Type> class BST;

template<class T>
class Bnode {
  friend class BinaryTree<T>;
  friend class BST<T>;
  friend ostream& operator<<(ostream&, const BinaryTree<T>&);
  protected:
    T data;
    Bnode<T>* parent;
    Bnode<T>* lchild;
    Bnode<T>* rchild;
  public:
    Bnode() {}
    Bnode(const T& elm) : data(elm), parent(0), lchild(0), rchild(0) {}
    friend ostream& operator<<(ostream& os, const Bnode<T>& v);
};

template<class T>
class BinaryTree {
  protected:
    Bnode<T>* root;
  public:
    BinaryTree() : root(0) {}
    BinaryTree(const T& elm);
    inline ~BinaryTree();
    Boolean InsertLeaf(const T& elm, Bnode<T>* prnt, Child lr);
    void InorderSubtreePrint(ostream& os, Bnode<T>*) const;
    friend ostream& operator<<(ostream& os, const BinaryTree<T>& tree);
    // remaining member functions not shown
};
```

FIGURE 7.4

The C++ declaration of a binary tree class that will serve as the base class for a binary search tree class. Objects of the `Bnode` class act as vertices in the `BinaryTree` class.

An important member function in the `BinaryTree` class is `InsertLeaf`, which is shown in Figure 7.5. The input parameters of this function are a data element, a pointer to the vertex where the insertion will take place, and a flag indicating whether the new vertex will be inserted as a left or right child of its parent. This function will be used by the binary search tree class `BST` to perform insertions.

The header file for the `BST` class is shown in Figure 7.6. Note that `BST` IS-A `BinaryTree`. Since we have not provided a destructor for `BST`, the compiler will automatically generate a default destructor that calls the destructor in the base class `BinaryTree`.

Three utility functions are supplied as protected members in `BST`. The `SubtreeMin` and `SubtreeMax` functions return pointers to the minimum and maximum vertices, respectively, of the subtree rooted at the vertex pointer supplied as input. As we saw in the previous section, many of the DYNAMIC SET ADT operations in a binary search tree involve first searching for a specific vertex. Thus we have supplied

```
/* File: bintree.C */
template<class T>
Boolean BinaryTree<T>::InsertLeaf(const T& elm, Bnode<T>* prnt, Child lr)
{
  Bnode<T>* new_node = new Bnode<T>(elm);
  if (prnt == 0) // inserting the root
    root = new_node;
  else {
    new_node->parent = prnt;
    if (lr == left) { // inserting a left child
      if (prnt->lchild == 0)
        prnt->lchild = new_node;
      else { // prnt already has a left child
        delete new_node;
        return false;
      }
    }
    else { // inserting a right child
      if (prnt->rchild == 0)
        prnt->rchild = new_node;
      else { // prnt already has a right child
        delete new_node;
        return false;
      }
    }
  }
  return true;
}
```

FIGURE 7.5
The `InsertLeaf` member function in the `BinaryTree` class.

```
/* File: bst.H */
#include "bintree.H"

template<class T>
class BST : private virtual BinaryTree<T> {
  protected:
    Bnode<T>* SubtreeMin(Bnode<T>*) const;
    Bnode<T>* SubtreeMax(Bnode<T>*) const;
    Bnode<T>* Search(Bnode<T>*, int key, Boolean& success) const;
  public:
    BST() : BinaryTree<T>() {}
    BST(const T& elm) : BinaryTree<T>(elm) {}
    T& Search(int key, Boolean& success) const;
    Boolean Insert(T item);
    Boolean Delete(int key);
    T& Minimum(Boolean& success) const;
    T& Maximum(Boolean& success) const;
    T& Predecessor(int key, Boolean& success) const;
    T& Successor(int key, Boolean& success) const;
    BST<T>& operator=(const BST<T>&);
    friend ostream& operator<<(ostream& os, const BST<T>& tree)
    {return operator<<(os, (BinaryTree<T>)tree);}
    // remaining member functions not shown
};
```

FIGURE 7.6

The C++ declaration of a binary tree class BST.

a protected member function called Search whose definition is shown in the upper portion of Figure 7.7.

This function accepts three parameters as input. The first parameter is a pointer to the vertex from which the search should commence, the second parameter is the search key, and the final parameter is a Boolean flag passed in by reference. If the search is successful this flag will be set to true, and a pointer to the vertex containing the search key will be returned. If, on the other hand, the search is unsuccessful then the flag will be set to false, and the last vertex examined prior to reaching a null pointer will be returned.

In the spirit of object-oriented programming, we assume that the data elements manipulated by BST objects are also represented using objects, and that the key value of any data element can be obtained by applying the member function Key() to it. In other words, it is the responsibility of data element objects to supply their key values whenever they are requested using the proper accessing routine.

The code given in the lower portion of Figure 7.7 demonstrates how the public member function Search, which performs the DYNAMIC SET ADT *Search* operation, is implemented by overloading (and at the same time using) the protected Search function. This function has two formal parameters: key, which is the search key,

```
/* File: bst.C */
template<class T>
Bnode<T>* BST<T>::Search(Bnode<T>* u, int key, Boolean& success) const
{
  Bnode<T>* v = u;
  while (v != 0 && key != v->data.Key()) {
    u = v; // copy v to u before moving to a child
    if (key < v->data.Key())
      v = v->lchild;
    else
      v = v->rchild;
  }
  if (v != 0)
    success = true;
  else {
    success = false;
    v = u; // v gets last vertex visited prior to the null pointer
  }
  return v;
}

template<class T>
T& BST<T>::Search(int key) const
{
  Bnode<T>* v = Search(root, key, success);
  if (success == true)
    return v->data;
  else
    return *(new T); // unsuccessful search, return a dummy value
}
```

FIGURE 7.7
Implementation of the Search member functions in the BST class.

and success, which is a Boolean value. When we defined the DYNAMIC SET ADT
on page 128, we stated that the *Search* operation should either return an element if
the search was successful, or the null value if it was not. Since a C/C++ function
can only have a return value of a single type, we pass the Boolean variable success
into Search by reference. If a search is successful, a value will be returned by the
public member function Search, and the Boolean variable passed to this function
by reference will be set to true; otherwise, a dummy value is returned, and the
reference parameter is set to false. Thus it is good practice to always check the
value of the reference parameter prior to using any values returned by Search.

A further illustration of the use of the protected Search function is given in
Figure 7.8. In this function, a new vertex will only be inserted in the binary search
tree if the search is unsuccessful; in this case, the InsertLeaf function given in
Figure 7.5 is used to add the vertex at the appropriate location.

```
/* File: bst.C */
template<class T>
Boolean BST<T>::Insert(T item)
{
  Boolean found;
  Bnode<T>* new_node = new Bnode<T>(item);
  if (root == 0)
    root = new_node;
  else {
    Bnode<T>* v = Search(root, item.Key(), found);
    if (found == true) { // item is already in tree
      delete new_node;
      return false;
    }
    if (item.Key() < v->data.Key())
      BinaryTree<T>::InsertLeaf(new_node->data, v, left);
    else
      BinaryTree<T>::InsertLeaf(new_node->data, v, right);
  }
  return true;
}
```

FIGURE 7.8
The Insert member function in the BST class.

7.4   RANDOM BINARY SEARCH TREES

We have shown how each of the DYNAMIC SET ADT operations can be implemented in $O(h)$ time in a binary search tree, where h is the height of the tree. We have also discussed the fact that in the worst case h equals n, which results in very poor running times for each of these operations. In practice, however, this type of performance can often be avoided. Thus, we would like to use average-case analysis to say something about the average running time of the DYNAMIC SET ADT operations in a binary search tree.

In this section we will make the assumption that all binary search trees on n vertices are equally likely. This is equivalent to assuming that an initially empty binary search tree was constructed via the random insertion of n data elements. Here we are making the standard uniformity assumption that each of the $n!$ insertion orders is equally likely. We will refer to such a tree as a randomly constructed binary search tree. Although it is naive to believe that in practice all binary search trees will appear with equal likelihood, astute practitioners can still use the results of this section to their advantage. For instance, if a sequence of data elements must be inserted, then randomizing the order of insertion will make the construction of an "average case" tree more likely—especially since data sets are often provided in sorted order.

Given an n-vertex randomly constructed binary search tree, we will consider the average time of both a successful search, which we denote by $S(n)$, and an unsuccessful search, which we denote by $U(n)$. The average time taken under each of these scenarios can then be used to calculate the average running times of all the DICTIONARY ADT operations in a binary search tree. For example, the *Search* operation will obviously have one of these two outcomes. The *Insert* operation given in Section 7.2.2 can be thought of as an unsuccessful search to locate the insertion point, followed by a constant amount of work to splice the new vertex into the tree. The *Delete* operation can be thought of as a successful search, followed by a constant amount of work to remove a specific vertex.

For the purposes of this analysis, we will create an augmented binary search tree by placing an additional vertex at the position of each null pointer in a binary search tree. For instance, the binary search trees in Figure 7.1 would be modified as shown in Figure 7.9, where the shaded vertices correspond to null pointers in the original trees. For a binary search tree containing n vertices, this construction will always lead to the addition of $n + 1$ external vertices. Furthermore, the n vertices in the original tree will become internal vertices in the augmented tree. Thus, a successful search in the original binary search tree corresponds to an internal vertex in the augmented binary search tree. Likewise, an unsuccessful search in the original binary search can now be thought of as a successful search that terminates at an external vertex in the augmented binary search tree.

The average time of a successful search is given by the average depth of an internal vertex in a randomly constructed binary search tree that has been augmented in the manner we have discussed. In order to determine this average depth, we will first determine the average internal path length of such a tree. The internal path length $I(n)$ of an n-vertex binary tree is the sum of the path lengths from the root to each internal vertex in the tree. If we assume that there are n_l vertices in the left subtree of the root, then there must be $n_r = n - n_l - 1$ vertices in the right subtree of the root. The depth of each vertex in the full tree (except the root, which is 0) will be

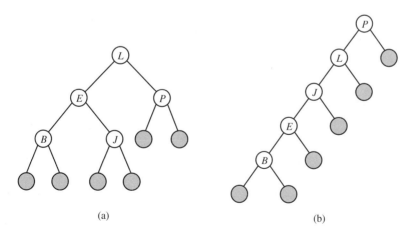

(a)   (b)

FIGURE 7.9
The augmented binary search trees created by adding additional vertices (shaded) at the position of each null pointer in the original binary search trees given in Figure 7.1.

one greater than its depth in the left or right subtree. Since there are $n - 1$ vertices in both subtrees, we can write the following recurrence:

$$I(n) = I(n_l) + I(n_r) + n - 1 \tag{7.4}$$

According to the assumption stated previously, all subtree sizes are equally likely. Together with equation (7.4) this assumption allows us to derive a recurrence for $I_{av}(n)$, the average internal path length of a randomly constructed n-vertex binary search tree:

$$I_{av}(n) = \frac{1}{n} \left(\sum_{i=0}^{n-1} (I_{av}(i) + I_{av}(n - i - 1)) + n - 1 \right) \tag{7.5}$$

This is a full-history recurrence since it includes all previous values of I_{av}. As we saw in Section 2.4.3, where we analyzed Quicksort(), a full-history recurrence can usually be reduced to a form containing a fixed number of previous terms by subtracting the value of the recurrence evaluated at $n - 1$ from its value at n. Since the goal of this strategy is to cancel the lower-order terms, we may also need to modify the coefficients appropriately. With equation (7.5) this is accomplished by subtracting $(n - 1) \cdot I_{av}(n - 1)$ from $n \cdot I_{av}(n)$, which yields

$$nI_{av}(n) - (n - 1)I_{av}(n - 1) = 2I_{av}(n - 1) + 2n - 2$$

Collecting like terms, we obtain

$$nI_{av}(n) = (n + 1)I_{av}(n - 1) + 2(n - 1) \tag{7.6}$$

The difficulty with this recurrence is that its coefficients are not constant. The approach we will take is to divide equation (7.6) by $n(n + 1)$:

$$\frac{I_{av}(n)}{n + 1} = \frac{I_{av}(n - 1)}{n} + \frac{2(n - 1)}{n(n + 1)} \tag{7.7}$$

Evaluating equation (7.7) at $n - 1$ yields

$$\frac{I_{av}(n - 1)}{n} = \frac{I_{av}(n - 2)}{n - 1} + \frac{2(n - 2)}{n(n - 1)} \tag{7.8}$$

Substituting equation (7.8) into equation (7.7) we get

$$\frac{I_{av}(n)}{n + 1} = \frac{I_{av}(n - 2)}{n - 1} + \frac{2(n - 1)}{n(n + 1)} + \frac{2(n - 2)}{n(n - 1)}$$

Continued substitution leads to

$$\frac{I_{av}(n)}{n + 1} = \frac{I_{av}(1)}{2} + 2 \left(\frac{n - 1}{n(n + 1)} + \frac{n - 2}{n(n - 1)} + \frac{n - 3}{(n - 1)(n - 2)} + \cdots + \frac{1}{6} \right)$$

$$= \frac{I_{av}(1)}{2} + 2 \sum_{i=1}^{n} \frac{i - 1}{i(i + 1)}$$

But for $i > 3$ it is easy to show that

$$\frac{1}{i + 3} < \frac{i - 1}{i(i + 1)} < \frac{1}{i + 2}$$

which allows us to write

$$\frac{I_{\text{av}}(n)}{n+1} = \Theta\left(\sum_{i=1}^{n} \frac{1}{i}\right)$$

The summation in this equation is $H(n)$, the n-th harmonic number, which is shown in Appendix A.3 to be $\Theta(\log n)$. Therefore, multiplying through by $(n+1)$ yields the average internal path length of a randomly constructed n-vertex binary search tree:

$$I_{\text{av}}(n) = \Theta(n \log n) \tag{7.9}$$

We are now able to determine the average time of a successful search. Since there are n internal vertices in an augmented binary search tree:

$$S(n) = \frac{I_{\text{av}}(n)}{n} = \Theta(\log n)$$

Since an unsuccessful search corresponds to a search to an external vertex in the augmented binary search tree, the average time of an unsuccessful search is given by the average depth of an external vertex in the augmented tree. This can be obtained by dividing the average external path length by the total number of external vertices. The external path length $E(n)$ of an n-vertex binary tree is the sum of the path lengths from the root to each external vertex in the tree. Because the augmented tree is a full binary tree, we may use the fact that $E_{\text{av}}(n_i) = I_{\text{av}}(n_i) + 2n_i$, where n_i is the number of internal vertices (see Exercise B.20 in Appendix B). For the augmented tree, $n_i = n$, and

$$U(n) = \frac{E_{\text{av}}(n)}{n+1} = \frac{\Theta(n \log n) + 2n}{n+1}$$
$$= \Theta(\log n)$$

In summary, since the average time of both a successful and an unsuccessful search in a randomly constructed binary search tree is $\Theta(\log n)$, all DYNAMIC SET ADT operations will have an average running time of $\Theta(\log n)$ when using this data structure. It can also be shown, through a much more difficult analysis (see the Chapter Notes for a reference), that the average *height* of a binary search tree constructed with n random insertions is $O(\log n)$. The reader should recognize, however, that the derivation given in this section cannot be used to demonstrate this fact (Exercise 7.15 may help to convince you of this).

Unfortunately, it is difficult to analytically determine the average running time of DYNAMIC SET ADT operations in a binary search tree when an arbitrary sequence of insertions and deletions were used to create it. This is because if deletions are allowed, we can no longer assume that all binary search trees on n vertices are equally likely. To understand why, let us assume that the BST::Delete() algorithm given in Section 7.2.2 is used to perform all deletions. Whenever this algorithm performs a case 3 deletion of a vertex v, it replaces v with its inorder predecessor p. Since p will always appear in v's left subtree, the tendency is for the height of left subtrees to become smaller than the height of right subtrees. In this case, a reasonable remedy is to randomly choose between the inorder predecessor and successor when performing a case 3 deletion. The use of this strategy should on average lead to more balanced trees; this, however, has yet to be substantiated analytically.

7.5   OPTIMAL BINARY SEARCH TREES

In some applications it may be possible to determine the frequency with which the individual data elements of a dynamic set are accessed (i.e., are the "target" of a DYNAMIC SET ADT operation). Or it may be possible to estimate these frequencies by observing the operation of the dynamic set on sample inputs taken from the application domain. Given this type of information, a reasonable strategy would be to construct a binary search tree that minimizes the average search time. In this section we define an *optimal binary search tree* as one that minimizes the average search time, given the access frequency of each data element. In Section 5.2.3 we discussed the optimum static ordering of elements in a list, which involved placing the most frequently requested elements towards the head of the list. An analogous strategy in binary search trees would be to place the most frequently accessed elements closer to the root of the tree. This is essentially the same idea we will use to encode messages using a prefix code in Section 9.5. However, there is one major difference: in binary search trees the vertices must also obey the ordering imposed by the binary search tree property. Next we consider two approaches that can be used to construct an optimal binary search tree: the first is brute force, and the second makes use of dynamic programming.

A brute-force algorithm that checks all possible binary search trees on n vertices to find an optimal one is not feasible. To see why, first let $B(n)$ denote the number of different binary search trees on n vertices. Since each subtree of a binary search tree is also a binary search tree, we can write

$$B(n) = \sum_{i=0}^{n-1} B(i)B(n-1-i) \tag{7.10}$$

That is, if the left subtree of the root of an n-vertex binary search tree has i vertices, where i can be between 0 and $n-1$, then its right subtree must have $n-1-i$ vertices. Recurrence (7.10) defines the n-th Catalan number (discussed in Exercise B.8); therefore $B(n) = \binom{2n}{n}/(n+1) = \Omega(4^n/n^{3/2})$. This means that the number of binary search trees that would have to be checked by a brute-force algorithm is exponential in the number of vertices.

Before proceeding to a dynamic programming solution, let us set up this problem more formally. We can assume, without loss of generality, that the keys have been sorted in nondecreasing order and labeled according to $k_1, k_2, \ldots, k_n$, with k_1 being the smallest key and k_n the largest. Given this ordering, if a binary search tree has k_r at the root, its left subtree must contain $k_1, k_2, \ldots, k_{r-1}$ and its right subtree must contain $k_{r+1}, k_{r+2}, \ldots, k_n$. Now let p_i denote the access frequency of key k_i $(1 \le i \le n)$, and assume that these frequencies are fixed with $\sum_{i=1}^{n} p_i = 1$ (this implies that all searches will be successful). If we let $C(1, n)$ denote the average search time for a tree containing keys $k_1, k_{l+1}, \ldots, k_n$, and recognize that the number of comparisons needed to access a data element at a depth d in the tree is $d + 1$, then

$$C(1, n) = \sum_{i=1}^{n} p_i(d_i + 1) \tag{7.11}$$

where d_i is the depth of key k_i in the tree. Our problem can now be restated as that of minimizing the function $C(1, n)$ in the previous equation.

An important feature of this problem is that it can only be solved optimally if its subproblems (i.e., subtrees) are also constructed optimally; otherwise, any nonoptimal subtree could be replaced with a better one, leading to a better overall solution. Let us define $C(l, m)$ to be the average search time for a subtree containing keys $k_l, k_{l+1}, \ldots, k_m$. That is,

$$C(l, m) = \sum_{i=l}^{m} p_i(d_i + 1) \tag{7.12}$$

where $C(l, m) = 0$ if $l > m$, and d_i is the depth of key k_i with respect to the subtree roots. Notice that equation (7.12) includes equation (7.11) as a special case. Now let $\hat{C}(l, m)$ denote an optimal solution to equation (7.12), i.e., a subtree containing keys $k_l, k_{l+1}, \ldots, k_m$ constructed so as to minimize the average access time of the keys. Taking the required optimality of subtrees into account, and letting k_r denote the key stored in the root, we can write the optimal solution to our problem as

$$\hat{C}(1, n) = \min_{k_1 \le k_r \le k_n} \left\{ p_r + \hat{C}(1, r - 1) + \hat{C}(r + 1, n) + \sum_{\substack{i=1 \\ i \ne r}}^{n} p_i \right\}$$

where the summation term accounts for the fact that all keys (except k_r) are one level deeper with respect to k_r than they are with respect to their subtree root. Combining the first and last term in the previous equation leads to

$$\hat{C}(1, n) = \min_{k_1 \le k_r \le k_n} \left\{ \hat{C}(1, r - 1) + \hat{C}(r + 1, n) + \sum_{i=1}^{n} p_i \right\}$$

More generally, if k_r is the key stored in the root of some subtree containing keys $k_l, k_{l+1}, \ldots, k_m$, we can write

$$\hat{C}(l, m) = \min_{k_l \le k_r \le k_m} \left\{ \hat{C}(l, r - 1) + \hat{C}(r + 1, m) + \sum_{i=l}^{m} p_i \right\} \tag{7.13}$$

The final ingredient of this problem, which makes a dynamic programming solution applicable, is that there is a large degree of overlap in the subproblem calculations in equation (7.13). Specifically, all possible subtrees of a given subtree include many duplicate subtrees. For a given collection of keys, we would like to calculate the $\hat{C}$ value once, store it in a table, and then reuse this value whenever a larger collection of keys (i.e., subtrees) are being considered.

A dynamic programming solution to this problem proceeds by constructing a table using the two-dimensional array $\hat{C}[1..n, 1..n]$, where entry $\hat{C}[i, j]$ stores $\hat{C}(i, j)$. The entries are filled in diagonal by diagonal, starting with the main diagonal and working toward the diagonal containing the single entry $\hat{C}[1, n]$. Note that since $\hat{C}(i, j) = 0$ if $i > j$, all entries below the main diagonal will store 0. The entries in the main diagonal, where $i = j$, are also easy to fill in since $\hat{C}(i, i) = p_i$. Each successive diagonal can then be filled in by using the entries from the previous diagonal to perform the calculation in equation (7.13).

As an example, consider the keys, along with their associated frequencies, as shown in Figure 7.10 (a). The p_i values are stored along the main diagonal of the table given in Figure 7.10 (b). The next diagonal considers all subtrees containing two vertices. For instance,

$$\hat{C}[2, 3] = \min\{(C[2, 1] + C[3, 3] + 0.1 + 0.3), (C[2, 2] + C[4, 3] + 0.1 + 0.3)\}$$
$$= \min\{0.7, 0.5\}$$

and since the minimum occurs when k_3 is stored at the root, the values 0.5 and (3) are stored in this entry. After all entries are filled in, an optimal tree (as shown in Figure 7.10 (c)) is constructed by starting at $\hat{C}[1, 5]$ and working backwards in the table.

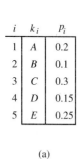

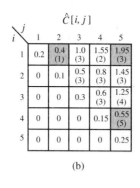

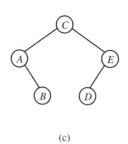

(a) (b) (c)

FIGURE 7.10
(a) Five example keys along with their access frequencies. (b) The table $\hat{C}[1..5, 1..5]$ produced by using the dynamic programming solution. If an entry $\hat{C}[i, j]$ includes a number (r) in parentheses, then key k_r should be placed at the root of the subtree containing keys $k_i, k_{i+1}, \dots, k_j$ in order to obtain an optimal subtree. (c) An optimal binary search tree constructed using the table in part (b). Since entry $\hat{C}[1, 5]$ contains (3), $k_3 = C$ is placed at the root of the tree. The roots of the left and right subtrees of vertex C are now obtained by examining $\hat{C}[1, 2]$ and $\hat{C}[4, 5]$, respectively.

The running time of this solution is directly proportional to the time it takes to fill in the entries of table $\hat{C}[1..n, 1..n]$. Since there are $n - s$ entries to compute in diagonal s, and each of these computations involves a summation containing s terms, the total running time of the dynamic programming solution is

$$\sum_{s=1}^{n-1}(n - s)s = n\sum_{s=1}^{n-1}s - \sum_{s=1}^{n-1}s^2$$

$$= (n^3 - n)/6 = \Theta(n^3)$$

It is easy to see that the space requirements of this algorithm are $\Theta(n^2)$.

7.6   AN EXTENDED EXAMPLE: CONSTRUCTING AN INDEX

In this section we consider the problem of automatically creating a rough index for an electronic document. Given an input file in ASCII format, we would like to produce an output file that contains an alphabetical list of keywords, along with the page numbers on which they appear in the input document. Such an output would prove useful as a "first cut" in the process of generating a final index. In fact, the methods developed in this example assisted in the construction of the index for this book.

One way of producing an index would be to read through the entire document, storing each novel word that is encountered in a list. Next a user would remove from the list those words that should not appear in the index. Finally the document would be read again, noting the pages on which each word in the list appears. The process we describe requires two passes through (i.e., readings of) the input document.

It is possible to construct an index in a single pass by keeping track of the page numbers on which words occur as they are encountered. The problem with this approach is that the user is not given the opportunity to cull words from the list, which means that commonly occurring words (e.g., "and," "the," and "it") would appear in the index.

To solve this problem we will augment our one-pass method with a dictionary containing words that should *not* appear in the index. Let us call this dictionary *LeaveOut*. The question then becomes: What words should appear in *LeaveOut*? Obviously, words such as "and," "the," and "it" should appear in *LeaveOut*, and the user can add many other common words to this dictionary. However, certain words such as "tree" and "algorithm," which occur frequently in a book such as this one, may occur very infrequently in a document on another subject. In the former case we would not want to keep track of every occurrence of these words, but in the latter case we would. To handle this situation, we will add a new word to *LeaveOut* whenever the number of occurrences of that word in the input document exceeds a prespecified threshold.

Let us assume that we are storing the words we wish to include in our index in a dictionary called *Master*, and that along with a word, we store the list of page numbers on which it occurs, and also the number of times it occurs. The modified one-pass approach then works as follows. Each time a word is read from the input document, we first check to see if it appears in *LeaveOut*. If it does, then ignore this word and read the next one. If it does not, then we first search *Master* to see if it contains this word. If the word is not present, we add it to *Master*, along with the page number on which it appeared, and we initialize its number of occurrences to one. If the word we are searching for is found in *Master*, then we simply update the list of page numbers on which the word occurs, and increment the number of occurrences by one. After this we check to see if the number of occurrences of the word has exceeded the threshold. If it has, then we delete the word from *Master* and add it to *LeaveOut*.

The method we have just described entails quite a bit of time searching the *LeaveOut* and *Master* dictionaries. For this reason, we will implement these dictionaries using binary search trees, which should perform much better than lists in this application.

Pseudocode for our one-pass index creation method is given next. In this pseudocode we are assuming that *Master* and *LeaveOut* store compound data objects consisting of a key (which is a function of a word), a list called *pages*, which stores page numbers, and a variable *occur*, which keeps track of the number of occurrences of a given word. This pseudocode also assumes that a special word, PgBk, will be used in the input document to indicate a page break.

Index(**file** *document*, BST *LeaveOut*)
1   BST *Master*
2   *current_page* ← 1
3   **while** (*word* ← next word in *document*) ≠ NULL **do**
4   **if** *word* = PgBk **then**
5   *current_page* ← *current_page* + 1
6   **else if** *Search*(*LeaveOut*, *word*) = NULL **then**   ▷ *word* ∉ *LeaveOut*
7   **if** (*result* ← *Search*(*Master*, *word*)) = NULL **then**   ▷ *word* ∉ *Master*
8   *Insert*(*Master*, *word*)
9   **else if** *occur*[*result*] < *threshold* **then**
10   *Append*(*pages*[*result*], *current_page*)
11   *occur*[*result*] ← *occur*[*result*] + 1
12   **else**   ▷ *word* occurs too many times
13   *Insert*(*LeaveOut*, *word*);   *Delete*(*Master*, *word*)
14   Write *Master* to the output file using an inorder traversal

The loop spanning lines 3–14 of Index() performs a single pass through the input document, implementing the steps we have just described. Specifically, line 3 reads the words in the input document sequentially until it reaches the end of the file (i.e., encounters a null value). If the current word is not in *LeaveOut*, then *Master* is searched on line 7. If the result of this search is the null value (which means the word is not currently in *Master*) then the word is inserted in *Master*. If the search on line 7 is successful and the number of occurrences of the word does not exceed the threshold, then the list of page numbers is updated on line 10, and the

```
/* File: index.H */
#include <iostream.h>  // <iostream.h> and <fstream.h> are needed for
#include <fstream.h>   // connecting a file to a program for input
#include <string.h>    // strcpy() and strcmp() are declared in <string.h>
#include <ctype.h>     // toupper() is declared in <ctype.h>
#include "dynlist.H"
#include "bst.H"

class WordRecord {
  private:
    char word[40];
    int key, occur;
    DynList<int> pages;
  public:
    inline WordRecord();
    inline WordRecord(char* wd);
    inline int Key();
    friend int MakeKey(char*);
    inline int Occurrences();
    inline void UpdatePages(int current_pg);
    friend ostream& operator<<(ostream& os, const WordRecord& wd);
};

inline WordRecord::WordRecord(char* wd)
{strcpy(word,wd); key = MakeKey(wd); occur=0;}

inline void WordRecord::UpdatePages(int current_pg)
{pages.Append(current_pg); occur++;}

// remaining inline function definitions not shown
```

FIGURE 7.11
The C++ declaration of the class used for storing word records.

number of occurrences is incremented on line 11. If, on the other hand, the number of occurrences of the current word exceeds the threshold, then this word is inserted into *LeaveOut*, and deleted from *Master* on line 12. After all words in the input document have been processed, the *Master* dictionary is written to an output file using an inorder traversal. If we choose the key values for our words appropriately, this will output the words in alphabetical order.

In order to implement our simple index creation method in C++, we first created the class WordRecord shown in Figure 7.11. In this class, the character array word will be used to store a string. We have also declared variables for storing a key and for the number of occurrences of a word, as well as for a page list. An implementation of one of the WordRecord constructors is also shown in Figure 7.11. Notice that it uses the strcpy() function to copy the input string wd to the private member word, and then it calls the function MakeKey(), which is a friend of WordRecord.

```
/* File: index.C */
int MakeKey(char* s)
{
  int n=0;
  for (int i=0; i<5 && s[i]!=0; i++)
    n += (toupper(s[i])-65) * power(26,4-i);
  return n;
}
```

FIGURE 7.12
The C++ definition of the function MakeKey() which produces a radix-26 integer from an input string.

The MakeKey() function is responsible for creating an integer key out of an input string. Its definition is shown in Figure 7.12. The power() function used in MakeKey() is an implementation of the recursive exponentiation algorithm discussed in Section 1.6.

For simplicity, MakeKey() only considers the first five characters in a word, which are processed as follows. First the toupper() function is used to obtain the ASCII value for the uppercase version of a character. Next, since the ASCII character set encodes the uppercase letters A, B, ..., Z with the values 65, 66, ..., 91, we subtract 65 from the value returned by toupper(). This value is multiplied by $26^{(4-i)}$, where i is the position of the character in the word array, and the result is added to n. This creates a key which is a radix-26 integer.[†]

Our C++ implementation of the Index() pseudocode is shown in Figure 7.13. In order to simplify the code, we are not passing LeaveOut in as a parameter; instead, we only add elements to it as Index() is running. Thus, the only words that will appear in LeaveOut are those that occur too often. In Exercise 7.19, you are asked to modify Index() so that the user may supply a file of words for inclusion in LeaveOut.

Another concept demonstrated in Index() is the manipulation of files in C++. The statement

```
ifstream InFile(document, ios::in);
```

opens the file document, and since we are using ios::in it is opened in input mode. The object InFile, which is of type ifstream, is used to tie document to our program for input.

Words are read from the input document by Index() using the function ReadWord(), which is shown in Figure 7.14. The first loop in ReadWord() is used to skip over any leading white space (i.e., blanks, newlines, and tabs), and also

---

[†]The **radix** is simply the base of a number system. For example, the binary number system is radix-2, the octal number system is radix-8, and the decimal number system is radix-10. The digits of a radix-r number system must lie in the range 0 to $r - 1$. For example, the decimal number 3945 can be expressed as $(3 \times 10^3) + (9 \times 10^2) + (4 \times 10^1) + (5 \times 10^0)$.

```
/* File: index.C */
void Index(char* document)
{
  char word[40];
  const int threshold = 12;
  int current_page = 1;
  Boolean success;
  WordRecord* temp;
  BST<WordRecord> Master, LeaveOut;
  ifstream InFile(document, ios::in);  // open the document file
  while (ReadWord(InFile,word) != 0) {
    if (!strcmp(word, "PgBk"))  // page break?
      current_page++;
    else {
      LeaveOut.Search(MakeKey(word), success);
      if (success == false) {  // word is not in LeaveOut
        temp = &(Master.Search(MakeKey(word), success));
        if (success == false) {  // word is not in Master
          temp = new WordRecord(word);
          temp->UpdatePages(current_page);
          Master.Insert(*temp);
        }
        else if (temp->Occurrences() < threshold)
          temp->UpdatePages(current_page);
        else {
          LeaveOut.Insert(word); Master.Delete(MakeKey(word));
        }
      }
    }
  }
  cout << Master << endl;
}
```

FIGURE 7.13
The C++ definition of the function Index().

checks to make sure the end of file character (EOF) has not been read. The second loop actually reads the characters of a word. Notice that we add the null value to the end of a word after we finish reading it into the buf array. This allows the array to be treated as a string when control returns to Index().

Finally, notice in Figure 7.13 that after Master is searched, we assign the address of the returned WordRecord object to the variable temp. Thus, if the search was successful, temp will point to some WordRecord object stored in Master, and we are able to modify this object (using its accessing routines) through temp. If we instead declared temp as a WordRecord, and we assigned an actual object (rather than a pointer) to it, then any modifications to temp would not modify an object stored in Master—they would only modify temp, which is a *copy* of an object in Master.

```
/* File: index.C */
char* ReadWord(ifstream& file, char buf[])
{
  char ch;
  int i=0;
  do { // check for end of file, and skip over any leading whitespace
    if ((ch = file.get()) == EOF)
      return 0;
  } while (ch == ' ' || ch == '\n' || ch == '\t');
  do {
    buf[i++] = ch;
    file.get(ch);
  } while (ch != ' ' && ch != '\n' && ch != '\t' && ch != EOF
                              && ch != ',' && ch != '.');
                    // each of these characters indicates the end of a word
  buf[i] = 0; // add null value to end of string
  return buf;
}
```

FIGURE 7.14
The C++ definition of the function ReadWord().

In order to demonstrate our code, consider the following excerpts from *On the Pulse of Morning* by Maya Angelou:

```
Each of you, descendant of some passed
On traveler, has been paid for.
PgBk
So say the Asian, the Hispanic, the Jew
The African, the Native American, the Sioux,
The Catholic, the Muslim, the French, the Greek,
The Irish, the Rabbi, the Priest, the Sheik,
The Gay, the Straight, the Preacher,
The privileged, the homeless, the Teacher.
They hear. They all hear
The speaking of the Tree.
PgBk
History, despite its wrenching pain,
Cannot be unlived, but if faced
With courage, need not be lived again.
PgBk
Lift up your eyes upon
This day breaking for you.
Give birth again
To the dream.
```

When this text was processed using Index(), it produced the following output:

```
(African, (2), again, (3,4), all, (2), American, (2), Asian, (2), be,
(3,3), been, (1), birth, (4), breaking, (4), but, (3), Cannot, (3),
Catholic, (2), courage, (3), day, (4), descendant, (1), despite, (3),
dream, (4), Each, (1), eyes, (4), faced, (3), for, (1,4), French, (2),
```

```
Gay, (2), Give, (4), Greek, (2), has, (1), hear, (2,2), Hispanic, (2),
History, (3), homeless, (2), if, (3), Irish, (2), its, (3), Jew, (2),
Lift, (4), lived, (3), Muslim, (2), Native, (2), need, (3), not, (3),
of, (1,1,2), On, (1), paid, (1), pain, (3), passed, (1), Pulse, (4),
Preacher, (2), Priest, (2), privileged, (2), Rabbi, (2), say, (2),
Sheik, (2), Sioux, (2), So, (2), some, (1), speaking, (2), Straight,
(2), Teacher, (2), They, (2,2), This, (4), To, (4), traveller, (1),
Tree, (2), unlived, (3), up, (4), upon, (4), With, (3), wrenching,
(3), you, (1,4), your, (4))
```

The only word that appeared frequently enough in these excerpts to be left out was "the." Notice that some of the page listings contain duplicate entries. This is another problem you are asked to eliminate in Exercise 7.19.

EXERCISES

7.1. Draw the binary search tree that is formed by inserting data elements with key values $A, Z, B, Y, C, X, D, W, E$, and V in the order given.

7.2. Assume that the following key values are encountered (in the order given) while performing a *Search* on a binary search tree: E, K, M, R, P, J, T. Why must there be an error?

7.3. Remove all recursive calls from the BST::Search() algorithm given in Section 7.2.

7.4. Write a pseudocode algorithm that uses the *Insert* and *Minimum* operations on a binary search tree to sort a collection of n items. What is the running time of your algorithm?

7.5. Consider a binary search tree implementation of the DYNAMIC SET ADT in which elements with equal keys are allowed. One strategy involves keeping a list at each vertex that stores elements with equal keys. Modify the BST class so that it implements this strategy. The *Search* (*Delete*) operation should return (delete) all elements that possess the search key.

7.6. Modify the BST class given in Section 7.3 so that it employs a user-supplied memory manager as discussed in Section 5.4.

7.7. Is the deletion algorithm BST::Delete() given in Section 7.2.2 commutative? That is, if this algorithm is used to delete a vertex u and then v, will the same tree result if the vertices are deleted in the order v and then u? Suppose BST::Delete() were changed so that all deletions were performed by replacing a vertex with its inorder predecessor. Is this implementation commutative?

7.8. Implement the binary search tree data structure in C++, adding a member function which computes the height of a tree as discussed in Exercise B.17. Then write a program to empirically evaluate the following strategies for performing case 3 deletions in a binary search tree (i.e., deleting a vertex v that has two children):

(*a*) Always replace v with its inorder predecessor, and then perform the appropriate case 1 or 2 deletion of the vertex vacated by the inorder predecessor. This is the strategy used by the BST::Delete() algorithm given in Section 7.2.2.

(*b*) Alternate between replacing v with its inorder predecessor and inorder successor, and then perform the appropriate case 1 or 2 deletion of the vacated vertex.

(*c*) Randomly choose between replacing v with its inorder predecessor or inorder successor whenever a case 3 deletion is required, and then perform the appropriate case 1 or 2 deletion of the vacated vertex.

Your experiments should involve the creation of binary search trees, containing large numbers of nodes, from random insertions and deletions. From these experiments, determine which strategy leads to the best trees in terms of balance, and which strategy is most efficient (in terms of processing time).

7.9. Use induction to prove that an inorder traversal of a binary search tree visits the data elements stored in the tree in sorted order.

7.10. In this exercise we consider adding the *RangeSearch* operation to the DICTIONARY ADT. For this operation we are given two keys k_1 and k_2, with $k_1 < k_2$, as input, and we must return all elements x in the DICTIONARY ADT such that $k_1 \leq key[x] \leq k_2$.

(*a*) Write a pseudocode algorithm that performs this operation in $O(n)$ time.

(*b*) Write a pseudocode algorithm that performs this operation in $O(K \cdot h)$ time on a height-h binary search tree, where K is the number of elements returned.

Discuss the advantages and disadvantages of both approaches.

7.11. Show that for any leaf v in a binary search tree, if u is the parent of v, then either key[v] is the largest key in the tree smaller then key[u], or key[u] is the smallest key in the tree larger than key[v].

7.12. When implementing certain operations using binary search trees, we often found it necessary to gain access to the parent of a vertex. Thus, the binary search tree implementation given in this chapter allocates storage for a left child, a right child, and a parent pointer in every vertex. If storage is expensive, there are a number of ways (discussed below) to reduce the number of pointers per vertex from three to two. For each of these techniques, write pseudocode algorithms that implement the DICTIONARY ADT operations, and determine the additional computational overhead incurred by using them.

(*a*) Auxiliary stack method. Each vertex stores left and right child pointers only. When tracing a path down the tree from the root, a stack is used to store the return path back to the root.

(*b*) Pointer reversal method. Each vertex stores left and right child pointers only. When tracing a path down the tree from the root, the return path back to the root is encoded in the data structure itself. For example if the $v_a \rightarrow v_b \rightarrow v_c \rightarrow v_d$ is taken down the tree, all along right children, then when moving from v_b to v_c, v_b's right child is made to point to v_a. Next, when moving from v_c to v_d, v_c's right child is made to point to v_b, and so on. These pointers are reassigned their appropriate values during a retracing of the path back up the tree. Note that one bit per vertex must be used to keep track of the direction of the path. This bit vector is used during retracing to determine whether the left or right child pointer was made to point to the parent of a vertex.

(*c*) Leftmost-child-right-sibling representation. Each vertex stores a pointer to its leftmost child and to its right sibling. If a vertex does not have a right sibling, the second pointer will point instead to the parent. For example, the binary tree shown on the left would be represented using the pointer arrangement shown on the right:

7.13. A binary search tree on n vertices stores $n+1$ pointers that contain the null value. Thus, half of the pointers in these trees are not utilized. A ***threaded binary search tree***, on the other hand, uses these pointers in the following manner: If a vertex does not have a left child, make its left child pointer point to its inorder predecessor, and if vertex does not have a right child, make its right child pointer point to its inorder successor. These modified pointers are called ***threads***.

(*a*) How can threads be distinguished from other pointers in the binary search tree?

(*b*) Write pseudocode procedures that implement all of the DYNAMIC SET ADT operations using a threaded tree.

(*c*) What advantages do threaded trees offer?

7.14. In a randomly *chosen* binary search tree, each possible binary search tree on n vertices is considered to be equally likely. Discuss how this probabilistic assumption differs from the one made in Section 7.4 when defining randomly constructed binary search trees. (Hint: For both assumptions, list the probabilities when $n = 3$.)

7.15. What is the largest possible height of an n-vertex binary search tree having an average depth of $\Theta(\log n)$?

7.16. Develop a pseudocode algorithm that implements the dynamic programming solution to the optimal binary search tree problem given in Section 7.5. This solution should involve two procedures, one for constructing the table $\hat{C}[1..n, 1..n]$, and one that uses this table to construct an optimal binary search tree.

7.17. The matrix-chain multiplication problem discussed in Exercise 2.21 is very similar to the problem of constructing an optimal binary search tree. If you have not done so already, work Exercise 2.21 using this knowledge.

7.18. Generalize the dynamic programming solution to the optimal binary search tree problem given in Section 7.5 by taking into account the possibility of a request for a key that is not in the tree. As before, let p_i denote the probability of accessing key k_i, $(1 \le i \le n)$. In addition, let q_i denote the probability of requesting a key not in the tree, but whose value is between k_i and k_{i+1}, $(1 \le i \le n)$; in this case, $\sum_{i=1}^{n} p_i + \sum_{i=1}^{n} q_i = 1$. An optimal tree for this problem is one that minimizes the average search time assuming both successful and unsuccessful searches.

7.19. Modify the Index() function given in Section 7.6 so that it accepts an input file containing a list of words. The words in this file should be added to *LeaveOut* prior to processing the input document. In addition, modify Index() so that it prints a specific page number only once when it prints the page list for a given word, and writes the dictionary *Master* to disk after processing a document.

CHAPTER NOTES

The binary search tree data structure is generally attributed to computing folklore (it appears to have been independently discovered by a number of researchers in the late 1950s). For an analysis of the behavior of binary search trees when random insertions and deletions are allowed, see Jonassen and Knuth [80]. Eppinger [50] used simulation to demonstrate that on average, binary search trees tend to perform well. See Culberson [39] for some additional simulation results. Cormen, Leiserson, and Rivest [36] provide a proof that the average height of a randomly constructed binary search tree on n vertices is $O(\log n)$.

CHAPTER
8

HASHING

A hash table is a data structure that is often used to implement the DICTIONARY ADT. Indeed, hash tables are typically one of the most efficient means of implementing the DICTIONARY ADT, particularly if we have some knowledge about the distribution of key values in a given application. Hash tables do not, however, efficiently support any operations that rely on the relative ordering of data elements. For example, an efficient traversal algorithm for outputting hash table elements in sorted order is generally not possible, nor are there efficient algorithms for implementing the *Minimum* and *Maximum* operations found in the more general DYNAMIC SET ADT. One of the most common uses of hash tables is to implement the symbol table of a compiler. A symbol table is a specific form of the DICTIONARY ADT, which compilers use to keep track of various pieces of symbolic information that must be accessed when generating executable code.

Worst-case analysis does not lead to any insights when studying hash tables since all dictionary operations require $\Theta(n)$ in the worst case for any hash table storing n elements. If the use of hash tables is to be justified, it must be done through probabilistic analysis. Thus, in Section 8.6 we show that under relatively mild probabilistic assumptions, hash tables lead to an average running time of $\Theta(1)$ for all DICTIONARY ADT operations.

As a word of warning, let us stress at this point that much of what we will discuss in this chapter is either heuristic in nature, or based on certain probabilistic assumptions about the data. Therefore it is always a good idea to test how the hashing techniques you develop perform on actual data taken from the intended application domain.

8.1 HASH TABLES

Let us denote the set of all possible key values (i.e., the universe of keys) used in a dictionary application by U. Suppose an application requires a dictionary in which elements are assigned keys from the set of small natural numbers. That is, $U \subset \mathbb{Z}^+$ and $|U|$ is relatively small. If no two elements have the same key, then this dictionary can be implemented by storing its elements in the array $T[0..|U| - 1]$. This implementation is referred to as a ***direct-access table*** since each of the requisite DICTIONARY ADT operations—*Search*, *Insert*, and *Delete*—can always be performed in $\Theta(1)$ time by using a given key value to index directly into T, as shown in Figure 8.1. In this figure, empty locations (i.e., slots) in the table store the null value.

Given this data structure, the DICTIONARY ADT operations are trivially implemented as follows:

DirectAccessTb::Search(array T, key k) $\triangleright$ T is a direct-access table
1   **return** $T[k]$

DirectAccessTb::Insert(array T, element x)
1    $T[\text{key}[x]] \leftarrow x$

DirectAccessTb::Delete(array T, key k)
1    $T[k] \leftarrow$ NULL

The obvious shortcoming associated with direct-access tables is that the set U rarely has such "nice" properties. In practice, $|U|$ can be quite large. This will lead to wasted memory if the number of elements actually stored in the table is small relative to $|U|$. Furthermore, it may be difficult to ensure that all keys are unique. Finally, a specific application may require that the key values be real numbers, or some symbols which cannot be used directly to index into the table.

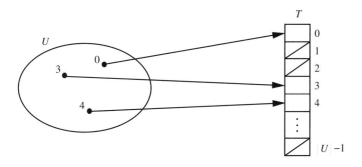

FIGURE 8.1
A direct-access table implementation of the DICTIONARY ADT. The key values drawn from U are used to index directly into table T.

An effective alternative to direct-access tables are hash tables. A ***hash table*** is a sequentially mapped data structure that is similar to a direct-access table in that both attempt to make use of the random-access capability afforded by sequential mapping. However, instead of using a key value to directly index into the hash table, the index is *computed* from the key value using a ***hash function***, which we will denote using h. This situation is depicted in Figure 8.2. In this figure $h(k_i)$ is the index, or ***hash value***, computed by h when it is supplied with key $k_i \in U$. We will say that k_i ***hashes*** to slot $T[h(k_i)]$ in hash table T. If we can ensure that all keys have unique hash values, then the DICTIONARY ADT operations can be implemented as follows:

HashTb::Search(array T, key k)   ▷ T is a hash table
1   **return** $T[h(k)]$

HashTb::Insert(array T, element x)
1   $T[h(\text{key}[x])] \leftarrow x$

HashTb::Delete(array T, key k)
1   $T[h(k)] \leftarrow$ NULL

The advantages of this approach are that, if we pick the hash function properly, the size of the hash table m can be chosen so as to be proportional to the number of elements actually stored in the table n, and the key values will not be restricted to the set of small natural numbers. Furthermore, if the hash function itself can be computed in $\Theta(1)$ time, then each of the DICTIONARY ADT operations can be implemented in $\Theta(1)$ time. Of course, this strategy relies on proper selection of the hash function. In order to understand where problems may arise, let us consider hash functions in more detail.

An ***ordinary hash function*** h performs a mapping from the universe of keys U to slots in the hash table $T[0..m-1]$:

$$h : U \to \{0, 1, \ldots, m-1\}$$

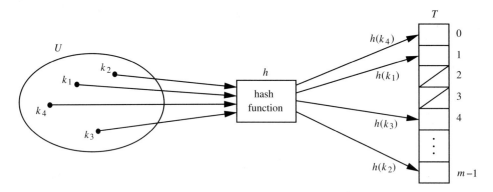

FIGURE 8.2

A hash table implementation of the DICTIONARY ADT. A key value drawn from U is passed through the hash function h, which computes an index into table T. Notice that $h(k_1) = 1$, $h(k_2) = m-1$, $h(k_3) = 4$, and $h(k_4) = 0$.

Since $|U|$ is generally much larger than m, h is unlikely to perform a one-to-one mapping. In other words, it is very probable that for two keys k_i and k_j, where $i \neq j$, $h(k_i) = h(k_j)$. This situation, where two different keys hash to the same slot, is referred to as a ***collision***. Since two elements cannot be stored in the same slot in a hash table, the *Insert* operation must resolve collisions by relocating an element so that it can be found by subsequent *Search* and *Delete* operations. This will increase the running time of all three operations.

There is an interesting space-time tradeoff associated with hash tables. By making the table size m larger, the chances of collisions are generally reduced. However, if m is too large most of the hash table slots will never be utilized. In general, m should be proportional to n, the number of elements that must be stored in the hash table. If we let α denote the load factor of a hash table (i.e., the ratio of the number of elements currently stored in the table, to the size of the table), then a rule of thumb that works well in practice is to choose m so that α never exceeds 0.8 while using the hash table.

The development of efficient strategies for resolving collisions is an important issue that will be taken up in Section 8.3. But first let us discuss some issues related to the design of "good" hash functions, and also consider various methods for creating them.

8.2 HASH FUNCTIONS

The most important properties of a good hash function are that it can be computed very quickly (i.e., only a few simple operations are involved), while at the same time minimizing collisions. After all, any hash function that never yields a collision, and whose computation takes $\Theta(1)$ time, can be used to implement all DICTIONARY ADT operations in $\Theta(1)$ time.

In order to minimize collisions, a hash function should not be biased towards any particular slot in the hash table. Ideally, a hash function will have the property that each key is equally likely to hash to any of the m slots in the hash table. This behavior is referred to as ***simple uniform hashing***. More formally, simple uniform hashing implies that if $P(k)$ is the probability of independently drawing the key k from U, and s_j is the set of all key values that hash to slot j (i.e., $s_j = \{k \in U \mid h(k) = j\}$), then

$$\sum_{k \in s_j} P(k) = \frac{1}{m} \quad \text{for } j = 0, 1, \ldots, m - 1$$

We will show in Section 8.6 that if this condition holds, then the average running time of any DICTIONARY ADT operation is $\Theta(1)$. The difficulty in designing good hash functions is that we usually do not know the probability distribution P.

For each of the hashing methods discussed next we will let k represent an arbitrary key, m represent the size of the hash table, and n represent the number of elements stored in the hash table. We will also assume that the universe of keys is some subset of the natural numbers. If the key values associated with a particular application do not have this property, it is typically quite easy to devise an appropriate scheme for transforming them. For example, keys that are character strings can be transformed by treating the ASCII value of each character in the string as one digit in a radix-128 integer. This is essentially the approach we used in Section 7.6. For instance, since "p" = 112, "t" = 116, and "r" = 114 in the ASCII character set, the string "ptr" becomes $(112 \times 128^2) + (116 \times 128^1) + (114 \times 128^0) = 1,849,970$. Of course, we must be careful not to make the size of the transformed key too large; otherwise we may not be able to easily store it in memory. A common remedy for this situation involves *folding* the resulting key into a smaller value. This can be accomplished by breaking the transformed key into chunks, and then combining these chunks via some operation such as integer addition or bit-wise exclusive-or.

Let us now consider a number of specific techniques used to create hash functions. Although a wide variety of hash functions have been suggested, the ones presented next have proved to be most useful in practice.

8.2.1 Division Method

Hash functions that make use of the *division method* generate hash values by computing the remainder of k divided by m:

$$h(k) = k \bmod m$$

With this hash function, $h(k)$ will always compute a value that is an integer in the range $0, 1, \ldots, m - 1$.

The choice of m is critical to the performance of the division method. For instance choosing m as a power of 2 is usually ill-advised, since $h(k)$ is simply the p least significant bits of k whenever $m = 2^p$. In this case, the distribution of keys in the hash table is based only on a portion of the information contained in the keys. Unless all bits of the keys are truly random, this will bias the hash function toward particular slots. For similar reasons, choosing m as a power of 10 should be avoided. In this case, when $m = 10^p$, $h(k)$ is simply the last p digits in the decimal representation of k.

In general, the best choices for m when using the division method turn out to be prime numbers that do not divide $r^l \pm a$, where l and a are small natural numbers, and r is the radix of the character set we are using (typically $r = 128$ or 256). If the table size m violates this condition, a large number of the hash values tend to be simple superpositions of the key digits. A particularly bad choice is $m = r - 1$ (note that $l = a = 1$ in this case). In order to see why this is a poor choice, let us assume keys are transformed into radix-r numbers using

$$k = \sum_{i=0}^{b-1} c_i r^i$$

where b is the number of characters in the key, and the c_i's are the character values (this is precisely how the string "ptr" was transformed in the previous section). The hash values in this case are given by

$$h(k) = \left(\sum_{i=0}^{b-1} c_i r^i \right) \bmod (r - 1) \tag{8.1}$$

Using the results of Exercise A.7 in Appendix A, this can be rewritten as

$$h(k) = \left[\sum_{i=0}^{b-1} \left(c_i r^i \bmod (r-1) \right) \right] \bmod (r-1)$$

and since $r^i \bmod (r-1) = 1$ for any i (see Exercise A.8),

$$h(k) = \left(\sum_{i=0}^{b-1} c_i \right) \bmod (r-1) \tag{8.2}$$

The summation in equation (8.2) only involves the character values themselves. Consequently equation (8.1) yields the same value for *any* permutation of the characters $c_0, c_1, \ldots, c_{b-1}$. The reader may wish to check this by verifying that all permutations of characters in the string "abc" will hash to the same location if we transform the string using radix-128 notation, and choose $m = 127$.

As an example of a properly chosen value for m, consider an application in which we must store $n = 725$ alphabetic strings, where each character is encoded using its ASCII representation. If we wish m to be proportional to n, then a reasonable table size is $m = 907$, since this is a prime number which is not close to a power of 128, and the load factor will be roughly 0.8 when all strings have been stored.

8.2.2 Multiplication Method

Although the division method has the advantages of being simple and easy to compute, its sensitivity to the choice of m can be overly restrictive. The principal advantage of the multiplication method is that the choice of m is not critical—in fact, m is often chosen to be a power of 2 in fixed-point arithmetic implementations (this will be discussed in more detail shortly).

Hash functions that make use of the ***multiplication method*** generate hash values in two steps. First the fractional part of the product of k and some real constant A, where $0 < A < 1$, is computed. This result is then multiplied by m before applying the floor function to obtain the hash value:

$$h(k) = \lfloor m \left(kA - \lfloor kA \rfloor \right) \rfloor$$

Note that $kA - \lfloor kA \rfloor$ yields the fractional part of the real number kA. Since the fractional part must be greater than or equal to 0, and less than 1, the hash values must be integers in the range $0, 1, \ldots, m-1$. One choice for A that often does a good job of distributing keys throughout the hash table is the inverse of the golden ratio

$$A = \phi^{-1} \approx 0.61803399$$

The multiplication method exhibits a number of nice mathematical features. Because the hash values depend on all bits of the key, permutations of a key are no more likely to collide than any other pair of keys. Furthermore, keys such as "ptr1" and "ptr2" that are very similar, and therefore have transformed key values that are numerically close to each other, will yield hash values that are widely separated.

As an example of this method, consider a hash table of size $m = 1024$, and $A \approx \phi^{-1}$. Then an element with key $k_1 = 1849970$ would hash to slot

$$h(k_1) = \left\lfloor 1024 \left(1849970\phi^{-1} - \lfloor 1849970\phi^{-1} \rfloor \right) \right\rfloor = 348$$

while an element with key $k_2 = 1849971$ would hash to slot

$$h(k_2) = \lfloor 1024 \left(1849971\phi^{-1} - \lfloor 1849971\phi^{-1} \rfloor \right) \rfloor = 981$$

A particularly nice property of the multiplication method is that it can be easily approximated using fixed-point arithmetic. In order to grasp the significance of this point, let us digress a moment and discuss how real numbers are stored in memory. First let us denote the b-bits of a memory word w using $w_0, w_1, \ldots, w_{b-1}$, where w_0 is the most significant bit, and w_{b-1} is the least significant bit. There are two common ways of representing real numbers in such memory words. In a *fixed-point* representation, the position of the decimal point is assumed to be the same for all numbers. Thus, it is not necessary to store decimal point positions with the numbers. If the decimal point is assumed to be between bits w_{q-1} and w_q, where $0 \leq q \leq b$, then the real number stored in w is computed by dividing its integer representation by 2^q. As an example, let $b = 4$ and assume that the decimal point is fixed between bits w_1 and w_2. Then the decimal number represented by the binary bit pattern 1011 is $11/2^2 = 5.5$. Note that if the decimal point is assumed to appear at the left end of the word (i.e., $q = 0$), all numbers will be fractions; and if the decimal point is assumed to appear at the right end of the word (i.e., $q = b$), all numbers will be integers.

A *floating-point* representation, on the other hand, does not assume that the placement of the decimal point is fixed. Thus, at least two machine words are required: one to store the actual number, and the other to store the position of the decimal point in the number. In most computers, computations involving numbers stored in a fixed-point format are much faster than those involving numbers represented in a floating-point format. In fact, some computers (e.g., ones found in embedded systems) may not even support floating-point arithmetic. Digression completed, let us get back to the task of implementing the multiplication method using fixed-point arithmetic.

It is not difficult to show that the product of a b-bit fixed-point fraction x and an integer k, where $0 \leq k \leq 2^b - 1$, yields a $2b$-bit result. The integer part of this result will reside in the high-order b bits, and the fractional part in the low-order b bits. Thus the floor of the $2b$-bit product is simply the high-order b bits. Furthermore, multiplication of a number stored in fixed-point format by an integer number $m = 2^p$ can be accomplished by simply shifting the fixed-point number p bits to the left, while filling in the p vacated bits with 0's.

This suggests the following approach for computing hash values using the multiplication method. If b is the number of bits in a machine word, choose the table size to be a power of 2 such that $m = 2^p$, where $p \leq b$. Represent key values using b-bit integers, and approximate A as a b-bit fixed-point fraction. Perform the fixed-point multiplication kA saving only the low-order b-bit word. The high-order p bits of this word, when interpreted as an integer, is the hash value $h(k)$. This procedure is depicted in Figure 8.3.

8.3 COLLISION RESOLUTION STRATEGIES

Although we should strive to construct hash functions that minimize collisions, in most applications it is reasonable to assume that collisions will occur. Therefore the manner in which we resolve collisions will directly affect the efficiency of the

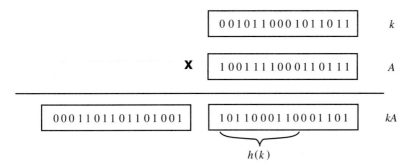

FIGURE 8.3
Implementation of the multiplication method using fixed-point arithmetic and 16-bit words. In this figure, $k = 11355$ and $A \approx 0.61803399$. If the table size $m = 1024$, then $p = 10$, and the hash value is given by the 10 most significant bits in the low-order word of the result. In this case the hash value is the binary bit pattern 1011000110, which is the decimal number 710.

DICTIONARY ADT operations. It is also important to recognize that a given collision resolution strategy has a more subtle impact on efficiency—if collision resolution is not handled intelligently, it may actually cause additional collisions in the future, thereby impacting the running time of future operations.

In this section we consider a number of important collision resolution strategies. The strategies discussed in Section 8.3.1 involve constructing additional data structures for storing the data elements, and then attaching these data structures to the hash table in some fashion. In Section 8.3.2 we will consider collision resolution strategies that assume that all data elements must be stored in the hash table itself. When considering the running times of the DICTIONARY ADT operations under these various collision resolution strategies, we will assume that the associated hash functions are computed in $\Theta(1)$ time.

8.3.1 Separate Chaining

One of the simplest collision resolution strategies, called *separate chaining*, involves placing all elements that hash to the same slot in a linked list (i.e., a chain). Thus every element stored in a given linked list will have the same key. In this case the slots in the hash table will no longer store data elements, but rather pointers to linked lists, as shown in Figure 8.4. This strategy is easily extended to allow for any dynamic data structure, not just linked lists. Note that with separate chaining, the number of items that can be stored is only limited by the amount of available memory.

Next we demonstrate how each of the DICTIONARY ADT operations can be implemented using hashing with chaining. In these operations, $T[h(k)]$ is a pointer to some dynamic data structure that can also be used to implement the DICTIONARY ADT. For example, if the hash table slots stored pointers to doubly-linked lists, then the statement $Search(T[h(k)], k)$ implies a sequential search of the doubly-linked list pointed to by $T[h(k)]$ for the element with key k.

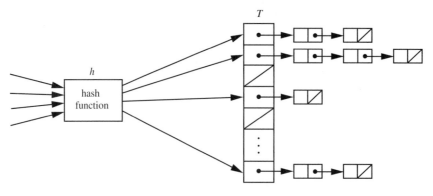

FIGURE 8.4
Collision resolution by separate chaining. Each hash slot contains a pointer to a dynamically allocated linked list which stores all elements that hash to that slot.

HashChain::Search(array T, key k)   ▷ separate chaining
1   **return** $Search(T[h(k)], k)$

HashChain::Insert(array T, element x)
1    $Insert(T[h(key[x])], x)$

HashChain::Delete(array T, key k)
1    $Delete(T[h(k)], k)$

If unordered linked lists are used in this strategy, then the *Insert* operation can be implemented in $\Theta(1)$ time, independent of collisions—each new element is simply added to the head of a specific list. The same cannot be said for the *Search* and *Delete* operations. It is easy to see that in the worst case, both of these operations will take time that is proportional to the length of the longest list. That is, in the worst case, all n elements hash to the same slot, and the element we are searching for (or deleting) is stored at the tail of this list. This leads to worst-case running times of $\Theta(n)$ for both of these operations. Of course, hash tables should not be selected for a given application based on their worst-case performance. In Section 8.6 we will demonstrate that under the assumption of simple uniform hashing, both the *Search* and *Delete* operations can be implemented in $\Theta(n/m)$ time when collisions are resolved using separate chaining.

8.3.2   Open Addressing

In **open addressing** all data elements are stored in the hash table itself. In this case, collisions are resolved by computing a sequence of hash slots. This sequence is successively examined, or **probed**, until an empty hash table slot is found in the case of *Insert*, or the desired key is found in the case of *Search* or *Delete*. The advantage of this approach is that it avoids the use of pointers. The memory saved by not storing pointers can be used to construct a larger hash table if necessary. Thus, using the same amount of memory we can construct a larger hash table, which potentially leads to fewer collisions and therefore faster DICTIONARY ADT operations.

In open addressing, the ordinary hash functions discussed in Section 8.2 are modified so that they use both a key and a probe number when computing a hash value. This additional information is used to construct the probe sequence. More specifically, in open addressing, hash functions perform the mapping

$$h : U \times \{0, 1, \ldots, \infty\} \rightarrow \{0, 1, \ldots, m-1\}$$

and produce the ***probe sequence***

$$< h(k, 0), h(k, 1), h(k, 2), \ldots >$$

Because the hash table contains m slots, there can be at most m unique values in a probe sequence. Note, however, that for a given probe sequence we are allowing the possibility of $h(k, i) = h(k, j)$ for $i \neq j$. Therefore it is possible for a probe sequence to contain more than m values.

Inserting an element using open addressing involves probing the hash table using the computed probe sequence until an empty array slot is found, or some stopping criteria is met, as shown in the following pseudocode:

```
OpenHash::Insert(array T, element x)    ▷ open addressing
1    i ← 0
2    do
3        idx ← h(key[x], i)
4        i ← i + 1
5        stop ← f(i)    ▷ stopping criteria is some function of i
6    while T[idx] ≠ EMPTY or T[idx] ≠ DELETED or stop = false do
7    if stop = true then    ▷ an unsuccessful search
8        return false
9    else    ▷ a successful search
10        T[idx] ← x
11        return true
```

Initially all hash table locations store the EMPTY value; however, if an element is stored in the table and later deleted, we will mark the vacated slot using the DELETED symbol rather than the EMPTY symbol.

Searching for (or deleting) an element involves probing the hash table until the desired key is found. Note that the same sequence of probes used to insert an element must also be used when searching for (or deleting) it. The use of DELETED (rather than EMPTY) to mark locations that have had an element deleted increases the efficiency of future *Search* operations. To see why, note that if these locations were instead marked with the EMPTY symbol, we would always have to assume that an element had been deleted and continue probing through the entire probe sequence whenever an EMPTY was encountered. However, if the DELETED symbol is used, then a search can terminate whenever an EMPTY value is encountered. In this case, we know that the element being searched for is not in the hash table.

Because the hash functions used in open addressing produce a sequence of values, rather than a single value, we will extend the idea of simple uniform hashing to a sequence. Specifically, we will use the term ***uniform hashing*** to refer to the assumption that a probe sequence contains m unique elements, and that each of the $m!$ possible probe sequences are equally likely. Let us now consider a number of specific open addressing strategies.

LINEAR PROBING.   This is one of the simplest probing strategies to implement; however, its performance tends to decrease rapidly with increasing load factor. It is also instructive to study linear probing since it is easy to demonstrate with this approach the pathological conditions which may arise when using open addressing.

If the first location probed is j, and c_1 is a positive constant, the probe sequence generated by linear probing is

$$< j, (j + c_1 \cdot 1) \bmod m, (j + c_1 \cdot 2) \bmod m, \dots >$$

Given any ordinary hash function $h' : U \to \{0, 1, \dots, m - 1\}$, a hash function that uses linear probing is easily constructed using

$$h(k, i) = (h'(k) + c_1 i) \bmod m \qquad (8.3)$$

where $i = 0, 1, \dots, m - 1$ is the probe number. Thus the argument supplied to the mod operator is a linear function of the probe number.[†]

It should be noted that some choices for c_1 and m work better than others. For example, if we choose m arbitrarily and $c_1 = 1$, then every slot in the hash table can be examined in m probes. However, if we choose m to be an even number and $c_1 = 2$, then only half the slots can be examined by any given probe sequence. In general, c_1 needs to be chosen so that it is relatively prime to m if all slots in the hash table are to be examined by the probe sequence.[‡]

The use of linear probing leads to a problem known as ***clustering***—elements tend to clump (or cluster) together in the hash table in such a way that they can only be accessed via a long probe sequence (i.e., after a large number of collisions). This results from the fact that once a small cluster emerges in the hash table, it becomes a "target" for collisions during subsequent insertions. To see why, assume simple uniform hashing (i.e., $h(k, 0)$ is equally likely to be any slot in the hash table), and consider the case where $c_1 = 1$. In this case, if an empty slot $T[j]$ is preceded by i occupied slots, then the probability of inserting the next element at $T[j]$ is given by $(i + 1)/m$. That is, if the element being inserted initially hashes to $T[j]$, or to any of the i slots preceding $T[j]$, it will end up being stored in $T[j]$. On the other hand, if the slot immediately preceding $T[j]$ is empty, the probability of inserting

---

[†]This is actually a more general form of linear probing than most authors consider. Typically, in linear probing it is assumed that $c_1 = 1$, and the probe sequence becomes $< h'(k), h'(k) + 1, \dots, m - 1, 0, 1, \dots, h'(k) - 2, h'(k) - 1 >$.

[‡]Two integers are said to be ***relatively prime*** if their only common divisor is 1. For example, 8 and 15 are relatively prime. The divisors of 8 are 1, 2, 4, and 8, while the divisors of 15 are 1, 3, 5, and 15, and their only common divisor is 1.

the next element at $T[j]$ is simply $1/m$. Thus, small clusters are likely to form larger clusters, which in turn offer larger targets to subsequent insertions. Notice that this problem is particularly severe if m is relatively small compared to n. This analysis is easily extended to other values of c_1 with similar results.

There are two factors in linear probing that lead to clustering. First, every probe sequence is related to every other probe sequence by a simple cyclic shift. Specifically, if we interpret a given probe sequence as a q-permutation ($q \leq m$) of hash table locations, then every other probe sequence can be generated via a modulo q shift of this permutation. This leads to a specific form of clustering called *primary clustering*: because any two probe sequences are related by a cyclic shift, they will overlap after a sufficient number of probes. A less severe form of clustering, called *secondary clustering*, results from the fact that if two keys have the same initial hash value $h(k_1, 0) = h(k_2, 0)$, then they will generate the same probe sequence— $h(k_1, i) = h(k_2, i)$ for $i = 1, 2, \ldots, m - 1$.

We have observed that the probe sequence in linear probing is completely determined by the initial hash value, and since there are m of these, the number of unique probe sequences is m. This is far fewer than the $m!$ possible unique probe sequences over m elements. This fact, coupled with the clustering problems, conspire to make linear probing a poor approximation to uniform hashing whenever n approaches m.

QUADRATIC PROBING.   This is a simple extension of linear probing in which one of the arguments supplied to the mod operation is a quadratic function of the probe number. More specifically, given any ordinary hash function h', a hash function that uses quadratic probing can be constructed using

$$h(k, i) = (h'(k) + c_1 i + c_2 i^2) \bmod m \tag{8.4}$$

where c_1 and c_2 are positive constants. Once again, the choices for c_1, c_2, and m are critical to the performance of this method.

Since the left-hand argument of the mod operation in equation (8.4) is a non-linear function of the probe number, probe sequences cannot be generated from other probe sequences via simple cyclic shifts. This eliminates the primary clustering problem, and tends to make quadratic probing work better than linear probing. However, as with linear probing, the initial probe $h(k, 0)$ determines the entire probe sequence, and the number of unique probe sequences is m. Thus, secondary clustering is still a problem, and quadratic probing only offers a good approximation to uniform hashing if m is large relative to n.

DOUBLE HASHING.   Given two ordinary hash functions h'_1 and h'_2, double hashing computes a probe sequence using the hash function

$$h(k, i) = (h'_1(k) + i h'_2(k)) \bmod m \tag{8.5}$$

Note that the initial probe $h(k, 0) = h'_1(k) \bmod m$, and that successive probes are offset from previous probes by the amount $h'_2(k) \bmod m$. Thus the probe sequence depends on k through both h_1' and h_2'. This approach alleviates primary and secondary clustering by making the second and subsequent probes in a sequence independent of the initial probe. Even if $h(k_1, 0) = h(k_2, 0)$, it is unlikely that $h(k_1, i) = h(k_2, i)$ on any given probe i, if h_2' is selected properly.

Ideally the values produced by h_1' and h_2' vary independently over m, in which case there are m^2 possible probe sequences. Specifically, for a given k, the probe sequence is completely determined by the pair $(h_1'(k), h_2'(k))$. Since there are at most m^2 such pairs, we have at most m^2 possible probe sequences. The probe sequences produced by this method have many of the characteristics associated with randomly chosen sequences, which makes the behavior of double hashing a good approximation to uniform hashing.

COALESCED HASHING.   This form of collision resolution is similar to the separate chaining approach, except that all data elements are stored in the hash table itself. This is accomplished by allowing each slot in the hash table to store not only a data element, but also a pointer. These pointers may store either the null value, or the address of some other location within the hash table. Thus, starting from a pointer stored in any non-empty slot, a chain is formed by following this pointer to the slot it points to, reading the pointer contained in the new slot, and continuing in this fashion until a null pointer is reached.

During an insertion, a collision is resolved by inserting the data element into the largest-numbered empty slot in the hash table, and then linking this element to the end of the chain that contains its hash address. An example of this strategy is shown in Figure 8.5.

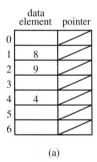 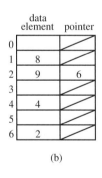 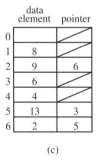

(a)   (b)   (c)

FIGURE 8.5
Coalesced hashing using the hash function $h(k) = k \bmod 7$. **(a)** Data elements with key values 4, 8, and 9 have been inserted. **(b)** A data element with key value 2 is inserted next, resulting in a collision at location 2 in the hash table. Thus the data element is stored in location 6, and the address 6 is written to the pointer stored at location 2. **(c)** A data element with key value 13 is inserted next, resulting in a collision at location 6. The data element is stored at location 5, and the address 5 is written to the pointer stored at location 6. Finally, a data element with key value 6 is inserted, resulting in a collision at location 6. Following the pointer stored in location 6 leads us to location 5, and another collision. The data element is finally stored in location 3, and the address 3 is written to the pointer stored at location 5.

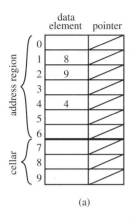

FIGURE 8.6
Coalesced hashing with a cellar using the hash function $h(k) = k$ mod 7. **(a)** Data elements with key values 4, 8, and 9 have been inserted. **(b)** A data element with key value 2 is inserted next, resulting in a collision at location 6. The data element is stored at location 9 in the cellar, and the address 9 is written to the pointer stored at location 2. **(c)** A data element with key value 13 is inserted next without causing a collision. Finally, a data element with key value 6 is inserted, causing a collision that is resolved by placing the data element at location 8 in the cellar, and storing the address 8 in the pointer at location 6.

A variation on coalesced hashing sets aside a portion of the hash table, called the **cellar**, for handling collisions. The portion of the hash table that is not part of the cellar is referred to as the **address region**. A hash function is selected so that its range is restricted to the address region. Whenever a collision occurs during an insertion, it is resolved by storing the data element in the next available slot in the cellar. In practice, this approach appears to slightly improve search time; however, the difficulty of determining the appropriate size for the cellar is introduced. Empirical studies have shown that allocating 14 percent of the hash table to the cellar leads to good performance. An example of this strategy is shown in Figure 8.6.

8.4 TABLE OVERFLOW

Up to this point, we have assumed the hash table size m will always be large enough to accommodate the data sets we are working with. In practice, however, we must consider the possibility of an insertion into a full table (i.e., table overflow). If separate chaining is being used, this is typically not a problem since the total size of the chains is only limited by the amount of available memory in the free store. Thus we will restrict our discussion to table overflow in open address hashing.

Two techniques that circumvent the problem of table overflow by allocating additional memory will be considered. In both cases, it is best not to wait until the table becomes completely full before allocating more memory; instead, memory will be allocated whenever the load factor α exceeds a certain threshold which we denote by α_t.

8.4.1 Table Expansion

The simplest approach for handling table overflow involves allocating a larger table whenever an insertion causes the load factor to exceed α_t, and then moving the contents of the old table to the new one. The memory of the old table can then be reclaimed. In Section 5.2.1 we used a similar strategy in our array-based implementation of the LIST ADT. Using this technique with hash tables is complicated by the fact that the output of hash functions is dependent on the table size. This means that after the table is expanded (or contracted), every data element needs to be "rehashed" into the new table. The additional overhead due to rehashing tends to make this method too slow. An alternative approach is considered next.

8.4.2 Extendible Hashing

Extendible hashing limits the overhead due to rehashing by splitting the hash table into blocks. The hashing process then proceeds in two steps: The low-order bits of a key are first checked to determine which block a data element will be stored in (i.e., all data elements in a given block will have identical low-order bits), and then the data element is actually hashed into a particular slot in that block using the methods discussed previously in Section 8.3.2. The addresses of these blocks are stored in a directory table, as shown in Figure 8.7. In addition, a value b is stored with the table—this gives the number of low-order bits to use during the first step of the hashing process.

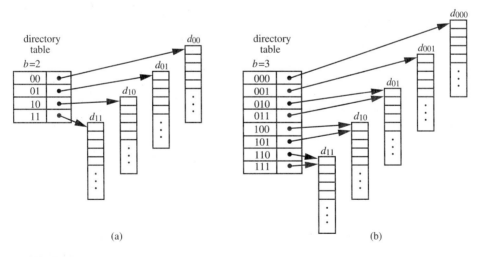

(a)   (b)

FIGURE 8.7

(a) A diagram of the data structure used in extendible hashing. The value stored in the variable b determines the number of low-order bits to use when hashing to one of the blocks. Each entry in the directory table stores one of the 2^b possible arrangements of low-order bits, along with a pointer to the block containing all data whose b low-order bits match that particular arrangement of low-order bits. **(b)** The hash table is extended by doubling the size of the directory table whenever a block d exceeds its load factor α_{t_d}. In this example, the data stored in block d_{00} from part (a) is now stored in blocks d_{000} and d_{001}.

Table overflow can now be handled as follows. Whenever the load factor α_{t_d} of any one block d is exceeded, an additional block d' the same size as d is created, and the elements originally in d are rehashed into both d and d' using $b + 1$ low-order bits in the first step of the hashing process. Of course, the size of the directory table must be doubled at this point, since the value of b is increased by one. This process is demonstrated in Figure 8.7 (b), where the block d_{00} from part (a) has been split into two blocks: d_{000} and d_{001}. Notice that only those data elements initially stored in d_{00} will need to be rehashed.

If the block sizes are kept relatively small, the extendible hashing approach will greatly reduce the overhead due to rehashing. Of course, this comes at the expense of the additional time that is spent comparing low-order bits in the directory table during the first step of the hashing process.

8.5 HASH TABLE IMPLEMENTATION

The hash table classes developed in this section were all derived from a single base class called HashTb. Thus, by specifying this base class in an application program that needs to use hashing, we leave open the possibility of using any hashing technique that was (or could be) derived from the base class. The class declaration for HashTb is shown in Figure 8.8. Notice that the protected member variable table in this class

```
/* File: HashTb.H */
template<class T>
class HashTb {
  protected:
    int m;
    void* table;
    virtual int Hash(int key, int i) const = 0;
    virtual ostream& Output(ostream& os, int i) = 0;
  public:
    HashTb() {}
    HashTb(int size);
    inline virtual ~HashTb();
    virtual Boolean Insert(T item) = 0;
    virtual T& Search(int key, Boolean& success) const = 0;
    virtual Boolean Delete(int key) = 0;
    virtual HashTb<T>& operator=(const HashTb<T>&);
    friend ostream& operator<<(ostream& os, const HashTb<T>& tb);
};

template<class T>
inline HashTb<T>::~HashTb() {delete [] table;}
```

FIGURE 8.8

The C++ declaration of the HashTb class that serves as the base class for all hashing strategies implemented in this chapter.

is of type pointer-to-void. This type of pointer may be assigned the address of an object of *any* data type. The ability to do this allows HashTb to serve as a base class for collision resolution strategies based on chaining as well as on open addressing. In the former case, table will store a pointer to an array of lists, and these lists will store the actual data elements; while in the latter case, table will store a pointer to an array of data elements.

In order for HashTb to serve in the capacity we have described, all of its member functions (except for the constructors) need to be virtual. In classes that use open addressing, the protected virtual function Hash() will be overloaded so that it can be used to compute the function $h(k, i)$, where k is a given key and i is the probe number. In classes that use separate chaining, Hash() is overloaded so that it can be used to compute the function $h(k)$ for a given key k. In this case, the second integer parameter, i, is simply ignored.

Because the table pointer is treated differently depending upon the type of collision resolution strategy being used, it is difficult to write a general purpose routine in the HashTb class for outputting the data elements stored in a hash table. This difficulty arises because the output operator ($\ll$) cannot be specified as a virtual function—only functions that are members of some class can be declared virtual. We overcome this problem by having the output operator call the virtual function named Output() in HashTb, as shown in Figure 8.9. Derived classes can now overload the Output() function differently, depending upon the collision resolution strategy being used, and the $\ll$ operator can be applied to any class derived from HashTb.

Let us first consider how HashTb can be used to develop a class that uses separate chaining. The declaration for a class called HashChain is shown in Figure 8.10. This class uses dynamic list objects to build the chains that will be associated with hash table slots. Thus we are using the #include preprocessor directive to read in the DynList class declaration discussed in Section 5.2.2. Notice also that we have implemented the Hash() function inline using the division method, and that the Output() function has been overloaded so that the $\ll$ operator may be applied to objects of class HashChain. In the implementation of Output(), we are simply indexing into the i-th location of the table array, and writing the information con-

```
/* File: HashTb.C */
template<class T>
ostream& operator≪(ostream& os, const HashTb<T>& tb)
{
   for (int i=0; i<tb.m; i++)
     os ≪ "Slot " ≪ i ≪ ": " ≪ tb.Output(os, i) ≪ endl;
   return os;
}
```

FIGURE 8.9
The definition of the output operator for the HashTb class. This virtual function Output() called by this operator will be overloaded in derived classes.

```
/* File: Chain.H */
#include "HashTb.H"
#include "dynlist.H"

template<class T>
class HashChain : public virtual HashTb<T> {
  protected:
     inline int Hash(int key, int i=0) const;
     inline ostream& Output(ostream& os, int i);
  public:
     HashChain() : HashTb<T>() {}
     HashChain(int size);
     Boolean Insert(T item);
     T& Search(int key, Boolean& success) const;
     Boolean Delete(int key);
};

template<class T>
inline int HashChain<T>::Hash(int key, int i) const
{return (key % m);} // division method

template<class T>
inline ostream& HashChain<T>::Output(ostream& os, int i)
{os << (*((DynList<T>*)table+i)); return os;}
```

FIGURE 8.10
The declaration of class `HashChain`, which is derived from the `HashTb` class to implement the separate chaining collision resolution strategy.

tained there to the output stream `os`. If `table` was not declared as a `void` pointer, the indexing could be accomplished using `table[i]`. However, because `table` is a `void` pointer, we must explicitly cast it to the appropriate type before using it. This leads to the use of more complicated pointer arithmetic in the implementation of `Output()`.

In the constructor for `HashChain`, shown in Figure 8.11, an array of `DynList` objects is dynamically allocated, and a pointer to this array is assigned to the variable `table`. Once again, because `table` is a `void` pointer, it is necessary to explicitly perform a cast of the pointer returned by the `new` operator.

We also demonstrate in Figure 8.11 how the *Insert* operation can be implemented. Once again, we assume that the data elements are represented using objects, and that their key values can be obtained using the `Key()` member function. Notice that if the index `idx` returned by `Hash()` does not fall within the hash table, then the `false` value is returned; otherwise, the data element is appended to some list using the `DynList::Append()` function. If this append operation is successful, then the `true` value will be returned. The `Search()` and `Delete()` functions are implemented similarly, so their implementations are left to the reader.

```
/* File: Chain.C */
#include "Chain.H"

template<class T>
HashChain<T>::HashChain(int size)
{
  assert(size > 0);
  m = size;
  table = (DynList<T>*) new DynList<T> [m];
}

template<class T>
Boolean HashChain<T>::Insert(T item)
{
  Boolean success;
  int idx = Hash(item.Key());
  if (idx < 0 || idx ≥ m)
    success = false;
  else
    success = ((DynList<T>*)table+idx)—>Append(item);
  return success;
}
```

FIGURE 8.11
The definition of a constructor and the Insert() member function in class Chain.

Next we show how the HashTb class can be used to develop a class that uses open addressing to resolve collisions. The class declaration for OpenHash is given in Figure 8.12. No particular probing strategy is specified in the OpenHash class; rather, these will be specified in classes derived from OpenHash. Notice that three protected member variables have been added in the OpenHash class. The integer variable limit can be set so that a search in the hash table will be terminated if the probe length exceeds this value. The variables empty and deleted will point to Boolean arrays that are the same size as the hash table. A true entry in empty[i] indicates that the hash table location table[i] has never stored a dictionary element, while a true entry in deleted[i] indicates that the hash table location table[i] is currently empty due to a deletion. The reason for keeping track of this information was discussed in Section 8.3.2.

The definition for one of the constructors in the OpenHash class is shown in Figure 8.13. The probe limit is set to the size of the table in this constructor. In practice, it makes sense to supply a member function that would allow the user of the class to set this value. Next, the array that will store the hash table elements is allocated, and a pointer to it is assigned to table. The instructions in the remainder of the constructor are concerned with the allocation and initialization of the empty and deleted arrays.

We also show in Figure 8.13 how the Insert() member function is implemented. The function Hash() is repeatedly called inside of a while loop until a

```
/* File: OpenHash.H */
#include "HashTb.H"

template<class T>
class OpenHash : public virtual HashTb<T> {
  protected:
    int limit; // probe length limit
    Boolean* empty;
    Boolean* deleted;
    inline ostream& Output(ostream& os, int i);
  public:
    OpenHash() : HashTb<T>() {}
    OpenHash(int size);
    Boolean Insert(T item);
    T& Search(int key, Boolean& success) const;
    Boolean Delete(int key);
};

inline ostream& OpenHash<T>::Output(ostream& os, int i)
{os << (*((T*)table+i)); return os;}
```

FIGURE 8.12

The declaration of class OpenHash, which is derived from the HashTb class. This class will be used to implement the open addressing collision resolution strategy; however, it does not specify a particular probing strategy.

suitable table index is found. Specifically, the loop will iterate until either an empty slot is found (this includes slots that are empty due to deletion), or the probe limit is reached. At this point, if the probe limit is reached, then a false value is returned; otherwise the data element is stored in the hash table, and the true value is returned.

In order to implement a specific probing strategy, we simply need to inherit the OpenHash class, and overload the virtual member function Hash(). An example is shown in Figure 8.14. The OpenHashLinear class shown in this figure implements the linear probing strategy of equation (8.3), where $h'(k)$ is the division method, and c_1 defaults to 1 unless specified otherwise when an object is constructed.

8.6 ANALYSIS OF UNIFORM HASHING

Of all the data structures discussed in this text, the justification for using hash tables is most heavily dependent upon average-case analysis. Indeed, a programmer who uses hash tables had better believe in probability theory. This is because the worst-case behavior of hashing is very poor—$\Theta(n)$ for all DICTIONARY ADT operations. In practice, however, this type of performance is typically not encountered, particularly if one is careful about using any available information regarding the distribution of key values in a given application. Therefore, in this section we justify the use of

```
/* File: OpenHash.C */
template<class T>
OpenHash<T>::OpenHash(int size)
{
  assert(size > 0);
  m = limit = size;
  table = (T*) new T[m];
  empty = new Boolean[m];
  deleted = new Boolean[m];
  for (int i=0; i<m; i++) {
    empty[i] = true;
    deleted[i] = false;
  }
}

template<class T>
Boolean OpenHash<T>::Insert(T item)
{
  int idx, i=0;
  do
    idx = Hash(item.Key(), i++);
  while(empty[idx]==false && deleted[idx]==false && i<limit);
  if (i >= limit)
    return false;
  else {
    *((T*)table+idx) = item;
    empty[idx] = deleted[idx] = false;
    return true;
  }
}
```

FIGURE 8.13
Definitions for a constructor and the `Insert()` member function in the `OpenHash` class.

hashing via average-case analysis. A completely general analysis of most hashing techniques is an extremely difficult task. Thus, we will restrict our analysis to special cases that simplify analysis, but whose behavior is close to what we strive for in practice.

Specifically, in this section, we consider the analysis of both separate chaining and open addressing strategies under the assumptions of simple uniform hashing and uniform hashing, respectively. Our analysis will be in terms of the load factor α. In either strategy we will consider the average time it takes to search for an element with a given key during both a successful search, which we denote $S(\alpha)$, and an unsuccessful search, which we denote $U(\alpha)$, of a hash table with load factor α. The average time taken under each of these search scenarios can be used to calculate the average running times of all DICTIONARY ADT operations in a hash table. The *Search* operation will obviously have one of these two outcomes, while the *Delete* operation can be thought of as a successful search for the element we wish to delete, followed

```
/* File: OpenHashLinear.H */
#include "OpenHash.H"

template<class T>
class OpenHashLinear : public virtual OpenHash<T> {
  protected:
    float c1;
    inline int Hash(int key, int i) const;
  public:
    inline OpenHashLinear(float param=1);
    inline OpenHashLinear(int size, float param=1);
};

template<class T>
inline OpenHashLinear<T>::OpenHashLinear(float param) :
OpenHash<T>()
{c1 = param;}

template<class T>
inline OpenHashLinear<T>::OpenHashLinear(int size, float param) :
OpenHash<T>(size)
{c1 = param;}

template<class T>
inline int OpenHashLinear<T>::Hash(int key, int i) const
{return ((int)((key % m) + c1 * i) % m);}
```

FIGURE 8.14

The C++ declaration of the `OpenHashLinear` class which inherits the `OpenHash` class. This class performs linear probing in an open address hash table.

by the actual deletion. The *Insert* operation, on the other hand, can be thought of as an unsuccessful search (we probe until an empty slot is found), followed by the actual insertion. We will assume that the time to compute the hash function itself is independent of n and m. Specifically, we assume that the time required by h is $\Theta(1)$, which is the case in any reasonable hashing strategy.

Consider first the separate chaining strategy. For the case of simple uniform hashing, each key is equally likely to hash to any one of the m hash table locations on any given insertion. Thus, the average length of each list will be $n/m = \alpha$. During an unsuccessful search for an element with key k, the first probe accesses hash table slot $T[h(k)]$, which stores a list header (see Figure 8.4), and then the search proceeds through the entire list pointed to by $T[h(k)]$. Therefore

$$U(\alpha) = 1 + \alpha$$

The analysis of $S(\alpha)$ is slightly more difficult. Since the items contained in each list are assumed to be uniformly distributed, a successful search on average will examine half of the items in a single list. Specifically, for a list of length l, the probability of any elements in the list being the object of our search is $1/l$, and the average number of elements examined during a successful search is

$$\frac{1}{l}\sum_{i=1}^{l} i = \frac{l+1}{2}$$

Since the average number of elements in a list is α, we have that

$$S(\alpha) = 1 + \frac{\alpha+1}{2}$$

Given these results, we see that for the separate chaining strategy if n is proportional to m (which makes α a constant), then $T_{av}(n) = \Theta(1)$ for the *Search*, *Insert*, and *Delete* operations.

We now consider open addressing under the uniform hashing assumption. In the probe sequence of any unsuccessful search, every probe except the last results in a collision, and the last probe is to an empty slot. Thus we need to calculate the average number of probes needed to find an empty slot. We let q_i denote the probability of *at least i probes* (i.e., $i-1$ collisions), and p_i the probability of *exactly i probes* during an unsuccessful search of a hash table with load factor α. The average number of probes is therefore

$$\sum_{i=1}^{\infty} i \cdot p_i \tag{8.6}$$

Since a probe sequence may involve repeated visits to a given slot, we cannot be sure it will terminate in finite time. Thus, the sum in equation (8.6) is taken to ∞.

The p_is in equation (8.6) are difficult to obtain directly, however, they can be obtained from the q_is. Specifically, the probability of at least i probes is given by the sum of the probabilities of exactly j probes, for $i \le j < \infty$:

$$q_i = \sum_{j=i}^{\infty} p_i$$

Furthermore, since

$$\sum_{i=1}^{\infty} q_i = \sum_{i=1}^{\infty}\sum_{j=i}^{\infty} p_i$$

$$= \sum_{i=1}^{\infty} i \cdot p_i$$

our problem reduces to finding the q_is. Let us take a closer look. We are certain to have at least one probe (the initial hash location), so $q_1 = 1$. The probability of at least two probes is simply the probability of a collision on the first probe, which implies $q_2 = \alpha = n/m$. The probability of three probes is given by the product of the probabilities of collisions on the first and second probes. Since the second probe is to one of the $m-1$ unprobed slots, $n-1$ of which are occupied, we have

$$q_2 = \left(\frac{n}{m}\right) \cdot \left(\frac{n-1}{m-1}\right)$$

In general, for $i > 1$ the probability of at least i probes is

$$q_i = \left(\frac{n}{m}\right) \cdot \left(\frac{n-1}{m-1}\right) \cdots \left(\frac{n-i+2}{m-i+2}\right)$$

$$\leq \left(\frac{n}{m}\right)^{i-1}$$

$$= \alpha^{i-1} \tag{8.7}$$

Equation (8.6) can now be evaluated using the upper bound for q_i given in equation (8.7):

$$\sum_{i=1}^{\infty} i \cdot p_i = \sum_{i=1}^{\infty} q_i$$

$$\leq \sum_{i=1}^{\infty} \alpha^{i-1}$$

$$= \sum_{i=0}^{\infty} \alpha^i$$

If $n < m$, then $\alpha < 1$, and we can use equation (A.19) in Appendix A to show that the average number of probes in a unsuccessful search is

$$U(\alpha) = \sum_{i=1}^{\infty} i \cdot p_i$$

$$\leq \frac{1}{1-\alpha} \tag{8.8}$$

Since an element can only be inserted in a hash table that uses open addressing if $\alpha < 1$, we conclude that the average running time of the *Insert* operation is $O(1/1 - \alpha)$.

Since the search for an element in an open-address hash table follows the exact same sequence of probes used to insert that element, we can use the results obtained for an unsuccessful search to determine the average number of probes during a successful search.

Assume we are searching for an element that was the $(i+1)$-th element inserted into the table. Then from equation (8.8) we have that the expected number of probes made during the search for this element is at most

$$\frac{1}{1-i/m} = \frac{m}{m-i}$$

Averaging this result over all n possible elements yields the average number of probes in a successful search:

$$S(\alpha) = \frac{1}{n} \sum_{i=0}^{n-1} \frac{m}{m-i}$$

$$= \frac{m}{n} \left(\sum_{i=1}^{m} \frac{1}{i} - \sum_{i=1}^{m-n} \frac{1}{i} \right)$$

$$= \frac{1}{\alpha}\left(H_n - H_{m-n}\right) \tag{8.9}$$

$$\leq \frac{1}{\alpha}\left(\ln n - \ln(m-n)\right) \tag{8.10}$$

$$= \frac{1}{\alpha}\left(\ln\left(\frac{n}{m-n}\right)\right)$$

$$= \frac{1}{\alpha}\ln\left(\frac{1}{1-\alpha}\right) \tag{8.11}$$

where H_i in equation (8.9) is the i-th harmonic number, and in equation (8.10) we are using the fact that $H_i \leq \ln i + 1$ (see Exercise A.13).

As one would expect, the average number of probes needed to find an element (successful search) is less than the number needed to insert it (unsuccessful search). For example, equation (8.8) tells us that on average, the number of probes needed to insert an element into an open-address hash table with load factor $\alpha = 0.75$ is no greater than 4. While equation (8.11) demonstrates that the average number of probes needed to locate any element in a table with the same load factor is not greater than 1.85.

Finally, note that if n is proportional to m, then equations (8.8) and (8.11) show that $T_{\mathrm{av}}(n) = \Theta(1)$ for the *Search*, *Insert*, and *Delete* operations in open-address hash tables.

8.7 AN EXTENDED EXAMPLE: CRYPTOGRAPHY

The extended example from the previous chapter (Section 7.6) considered the use of the DICTIONARY ADT in an application. A hash table implementation can easily be substituted for the binary search tree data structure in that application. Therefore, rather than present another example that uses the DICTIONARY ADT, this example demonstrates the use of hash functions in cryptography, an area of immense importance in the modern computing world.

Cryptography is concerned with methods for ensuring the secrecy and authenticity of messages. The essence of cryptography is captured in the following problem: Two parties (the tradition is to call them *Alice* and *Bob*) wish to communicate over a public communication channel in the presence of a malevolent eavesdropper (the tradition here is to call the eavesdropper *Eve*).

If Alice and Bob want the contents of their messages to remain unknown to Eve, then the issue is one of *secrecy*. In this case, rather than sending their messages unaltered, Alice and Bob first use an ***encryption algorithm*** to modify their messages in such a way that they become unintelligible to Eve. When Alice or Bob receives such an encrypted message, they apply a ***decryption algorithm*** to it in order to extract the original message. This situation is depicted in Figure 8.15, in which we refer to the unencrypted messages M_A and M_B as ***plaintext***, and to the encrypted messages C_A and C_B as ***ciphertext***.

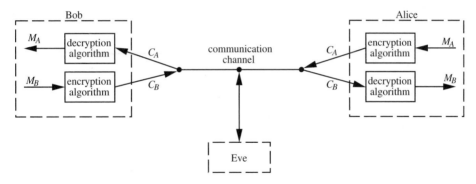

FIGURE 8.15
The cryptography problem. Alice and Bob wish to transmit their plaintext messages, M_A and M_B respectively, to each other. To do this over a public communication channel (monitored by Eve), they encrypt their messages using an encryption algorithm, producing the ciphertext messages C_A and C_B respectively. Alice and Bob use a decryption algorithm to decrypt the ciphertext messages they receive. We assume that Eve only "sees" ciphertext messages.

There are many situations in which the critical security issue is not so much the *secrecy* of the message itself, but determining whether the message is *authentic*, in which case one is concerned with determining whether or not a message has been altered since it left the sender, or if the sender has been misrepresented. We now discuss some specific cryptographic protocols. For each of these, we will consider how the secrecy and authentication issues are addressed.

SECRET-KEY CRYPTOGRAPHY. In secret-key cryptography, it is assumed that Alice and Bob both use some piece of information in their encrypting and decrypting algorithms (i.e., the secret key) that is not known to Eve. As an example, consider the following protocol based on exponentiation. First Alice and Bob select a large prime number p, and then they choose a secret key $K_s \in \{1, 2, \ldots, p-1\}$ that is relatively prime to $p - 1$. Now Alice encrypts the plaintext message M_A using the function

$$C_A = f(M_A) = (M_A)^{K_s} \bmod p \qquad (8.12)$$

Bob decrypts this ciphertext using

$$M_A = f^{-1}(C_A) = (C_A)^I \bmod p \qquad (8.13)$$

where I is the multiplicative inverse of K_s modulo $p-1$ (i.e., $(I \cdot K_s) \bmod (p-1) = 1$). If K_s is known, I can be easily calculated using Euclid's algorithm (see Exercises 8.12 and 8.13). In order to verify that $f^{-1}(f(M_A)) = M_A$ requires some number-theoretic results that are beyond the scope of this book (please see the Chapter Notes for references).

The secret key K_s can also be calculated from C_A (which Eve knows) by solving equation (8.12) for p. This, however, requires the calculation of discrete logarithms module p; at present, the best algorithms for performing this operation take time that is exponential in p. Thus by choosing p large, Alice and Bob make it computationally infeasible for Eve to determine M_A without knowing K_s. This effectively addresses the secrecy issue.

As for the authenticity of messages under the previous protocol, the fact that Eve does not know K_s also makes it impossible for her to misrepresent herself. For instance, she will not be able to use equation (8.12) to encrypt a rogue message such as "Bob, Please give Eve the $1024 dollars you owe me. Thanks, Alice." Likewise, any ciphertext C_A altered by Eve (without knowing K_s) will most likely be detected by Bob. The alteration will simply lead to garbled plaintext when Bob uses equation (8.13) to decipher C_A.

In summary, for both secrecy and authentication, the major security issue in secret-key cryptography involves keeping the secret key K_s unknown to Eve. This requirement also leads to the major shortcoming of secret-key cryptography since Alice and Bob must somehow agree in advance on a K_s that will be known to themselves, and no one else. This generally means that they must meet in person (or arrange some secure communication channel) in order to determine K_s. It is not difficult to see the impracticality of using this approach among a large collection of people.

PUBLIC-KEY CRYPTOGRAPHY. Modern cryptography is based on the idea of *public-key cryptography*, in which there is no longer a single secret key shared by Alice and Bob; rather, both of them have two keys, one of which is made public and the other of which is kept secret (i.e, neither Alice nor Bob needs to know the other's secret key). Therefore, it is not necessary for Alice and Bob to meet privately in order to exchange secret information, making cryptography viable among a network of many users.

The most widely used public-key cryptosystem is the *RSA cryptosystem*, which we describe next. Suppose Alice wishes to communicate secretly with Bob, whom she has never met. Bob first generates two large (e.g., 200 digit) prime numbers p and q, and forms the product

$$m = pq$$

Next, he chooses a small arbitrary integer E which is relatively prime to

$$\varphi(m) = (p - 1)(q - 1)$$

and then uses Euclid's algorithm to compute D as the multiplicative inverse of E, modulo $\varphi(m)$. That is,

$$(E \cdot D) \bmod \varphi(m) = 1$$

The pair (E, m) constitutes Bob's public key, and D is his secret key. Alice constructs her public and secret keys in a similar fashion.

Alice encrypts her plaintext message M_A using only Bob's public key through

$$f_B(M_A) = (M_A)^E \bmod m \tag{8.14}$$

to produce C_A. Bob decrypts C_A using his secret key through

$$f_B^{-1}(C_A) = (C_A)^D \bmod m \tag{8.15}$$

An important property of equations (8.14) and (8.15) is that they are inverses of one another, i.e., $f_B^{-1}(f_B(M)) = f_B(f_B^{-1}(M)) = M$. We will make use of this property shortly.

Secrecy in the RSA cryptosystem relies on the fact that the easiest known way to infer a secret key from a public key involves factoring m to find p and q, a problem that appears to require superpolynomial time. Authentication, on the other hand, is not as easy to guarantee in public-key cryptography. Since everybody knows everybody else's public key, Eve can easily send a message to Bob claiming to be Alice.

DIGITAL SIGNATURES. One way to address the authentication problem in public-key cryptography is to attach a *digital signature* to the end of each message that can be used to verify the sender of the message. Specifically, if Alice is sending a message to Bob, she first uses her own secret key to encrypt her digital signature S_A according to $f_A^{-1}(S_A)$ given in equation (8.15). Since this involves the use of Alice's secret key, only she can produce $f_A^{-1}(S_A)$. She then appends her encrypted digital signature to her message M_A to produce the signed message $M_A \cdot f_A^{-1}(S_A)$, where the dot denotes concatenation. Next Alice applies equation (8.14) to her signed message, using Bob's public key. The ciphertext message she transmits to Bob is $C_A = f_B(M_A \cdot f_A^{-1}(S_A))$.

When Bob receives C_A he first applies equation (8.15) using his secret key to produce $f_B^{-1}(C_A) = M_A \cdot f_A^{-1}(S_A)$. Thus, the message M_A will appear, along with a portion of gibberish at the end of the message. To authenticate M_A, Bob uses Alice's public key to perform $f_A(f_A^{-1}(S_A))$. If Alice's digital signature appears, he knows the message is authentic.

The only remaining issue involves selecting the digital signature S_A. If Alice uses the same digital signature in every message, Eve will be able to detect this by looking for common strings among Alice's transmissions. Even though by doing this Eve will only discover $f_A^{-1}(S_A)$, this is all she needs in order to sign a rogue message and misrepresent herself as Alice to Bob.

Therefore, it is important for Alice to use a different S_A in every message. One strategy is to make S_A depend on the message M_A. Hash functions are commonly used to implement this strategy. In this setting a public hash function h is required to transform a variable-length message into a fixed-length *message fingerprint* F, i.e.,

$$h : M_A \to F$$

Alice's ciphertext message to Bob is encrypted using

$$C_A = f_B(M_A \cdot f_A^{-1}(F))$$

After applying f_B^{-1} to this ciphertext, Bob can authenticate it by first computing $f_A(f_A^{-1}(F)) = F$, and then comparing this result to the result he obtains by applying the hash function h to M_A.

We have already mentioned that there are many instances in which the main security issue is authentication and not secrecy. For example, a financial institution may be content with sending and receiving their transactions unencrypted, as long as they can guarantee that these transmissions are not altered. The digital signature strategy we have considered is easily used in this mode. Specifically, if Alice sends the messages $M_A \cdot f_A^{-1}(F)$ to Bob, then even though Eve can read M_A, she will not be able to alter it unless she is able to determine F.

In order for a public hash function h to be effective, it must possess at least the following two properties. First, since h is known to all, for any y it must be computationally intractable to find an M_A such that $h(M_A) = y$. In other words, Eve should have great difficulty in trying to invert h in order to obtain M_A. Second, it should be computationally intractable to find messages that collide. To see why, assume we have a hash function h that does not satisfy this property. Now suppose *Eve* constructs two messages M_A and M_A' such that $h(M_A) = h(M_A')$, and Alice is perfectly happy to sign M_A but not M_A'. If Eve can convince Alice to sign M_A, then Eve will also be able to achieve her fraudulent goal of signing M_A' with Alice's digital signature.

Many digital hashing schemes are based on the following idea. Let h' be a hash function that maps s-bit keys to k-bit values, for some fixed $s > k$. From h' we construct a public hash function that produces a k-bit message fingerprint by first breaking the message M_A into t blocks $M_{A_1}, M_{A_2}, \ldots, M_{A_t}$, each containing $s - k$ bits. Next let

$$F_i(M_{A_i}) = h'(F_{i-1} \cdot M_{A_i})$$

where the dot denotes concatenation, and F_0 is a k-bit initializing value, often chosen as all zeros. The message fingerprint is then given by F_t.

EXERCISES

8.1. Develop a C++ class that implements the DICTIONARY ADT using hashing with separate chaining of doubly-linked lists. This class should have a USES-A relationship with the DlList class developed in Exercise 5.5.

8.2. The OpenHash::Insert() algorithm given in Section 8.3.2 stops probing if some unspecified stopping criteria is met. Discuss various criteria that can be used in order to determine when to stop probing. These should depend, among other things, on the probing strategy being employed.

8.3. A nice extension of linear probing that tends to reduce collisions lets c_1 in equation (8.3) vary according to k. Develop a hash function that implements this strategy. In general, what properties should such a hash function possess?

8.4. Compare the amount of memory used by an open-address hash table (with load factors $\alpha = 0.95, 0.75$, and 0.5) versus a binary search tree. Then compare the average amount of time required to perform the DICTIONARY ADT operations using both of these data structures under the same load factors. You may assume that each probe in the hash table, and each comparison in the binary search tree, take unit time.

8.5. Determine the average case running times of the DICTIONARY ADT operations under the assumption of uniform hashing when the dynamic data structure used in separate chaining is:

(*a*) an ordered list.

(*b*) a binary search tree.

8.6. Describe the expected behavior of double hashing if we choose $h'_2(k) = 1$ for all k.

8.7. Assume that a sequence of n data elements need to be sorted, and that the range of key values associated with these data elements is known (and not too large). A technique known as **bucket sorting**, which uses hashing with chaining, is often a good choice in this case. The chains, which are called buckets, are represented using queues. The hash function for bucket sorting is given by

$$h(k) = \left\lceil \frac{k - a + 1}{\lceil (b - a + 1)/m \rceil} \right\rceil$$

where all key values are assumed to fall in the range $[a, b]$, and $m \approx n$. This hash function guarantees that the data elements stored in any one bucket will be contiguous in the final sorted sequence. Thus, all that remains is to sort the data elements in each individual bucket, and then concatenate the data stored in successive buckets.

(*a*) Making the assumption that all permutations of the n data elements are equally likely, prove that the expected sorting time is $\Theta(n)$.

(*b*) Is this a stable sorting algorithm?

8.8. In Section 8.4 we restricted our discussion of table overflow to open address hashing. This was justified by the fact that the amount of data that can be stored when using separate chaining is only limited by the amount of available memory. However, the performance of separate chaining will obviously deteriorate as the number of data elements increases, and the chains become longer. A generalization of separate chaining, called **linear hashing**, addresses this problem by keeping the expected length of the chains within prespecified bounds. Assume that we start with a table of size m, and the initial hash function is $h_0(k) = k \bmod m$. During insertion, linear hashing may expand the table size as follows. Whenever the load factor (which in this case is defined as the average chain length) reaches a prespecified limit, slot m is added to the table, and the data stored in the chain at slot 0 is rehashed using $h_1(k) = k \bmod 2m$. The next expansion will add slot $m + 1$, and will cause a rehashing of the chain stored at slot 1, and so on. Once the table expands to a size of $2m$, the next slot to be rehashed will once again be slot 0, but this time the rehashing will continue through to slot $2m - 1$ using hash function $h_2(k) = k \bmod 4m$, and so on. Similarly, deletion can cause a table contraction if the load factor falls below a prespecified limit. In this case, if the chain at slot i was the last one rehashed, and m is the current table size, then the chains at slots i and m are merged, and the table size is reduced by one.

(*a*) Demonstrate the operation of linear hashing when m is initially 3, the lower bound on the load factor is $\alpha_{t_l} = 1$, and the upper bound is $\alpha_{t_u} = 2$. Insert the following data elements in the order given, and then delete them in the same order: 6, 5, 14, 20, 12, 18, 7, 15, 8, 9, 1.

(*b*) Assume that a linear hash table is constructed using insertions only. Making the standard uniformity assumption, determine the average time for a successful and an unsuccessful search in such a table as a function of α_{t_u}.

8.9. In the STATIC DICTIONARY ADT only the *Search* operation is used. Thus, it is assumed that all data elements are known *a priori*, and we have the freedom to arrange them in whatever data structure we might be using.

(*a*) If we use a binary search tree to implement the STATIC DICTIONARY ADT, what will the worst-case search time be?

(b) A hash function $h : U \to \{0, 1, \ldots, m - 1\}$ is said to be **perfect** for the set $S \subseteq U$ if none of the elements in S collide when using h. In a perfect hash function the STATIC DICTIONARY ADT *Search* operation is implemented in $\Theta(1)$ worst-case time. Can a perfect hash function be constructed for *any* set S of size at most m? What is the maximum number of bits needed to represent a perfect hash function?

8.10. Although a given hash function may perform well on most set of inputs, there is always the possibility that a particular set of inputs will cause poor performance. Worse yet, it may turn out that a particular application repeatedly uses these "bad" inputs. A strategy called **universal hashing** attempts to overcome this problem by randomly picking the hash function at run time from a set of carefully chosen hash functions. A set H of hash functions is said to be universal if for *every* hash function $h \in H$, the probability of *any* two keys colliding is $1/m$. In other words, for any pair of keys $k_i, k_j \in U$, $i \neq j$, the expected number of hash functions $h \in H$ for which $h(k_i) = h(k_j)$ is exactly $|H|/m$.

(a) Let us define the following indicator function for a collision between any two keys $k_i, k_j \in U$, $i \neq j$, under the hash function h

$$\delta(k_i, k_j, h) = \begin{cases} 1, & \text{if } h(k_i) = h(k_j) \\ 0, & \text{otherwise} \end{cases}$$

Next define $\delta(k_i, k_j, H) = \sum_{h \in H} \delta(k_i, k_j, h)$. Note that $\delta(k_i, k_j, H) \leq |H|/m$. Show that the set H of universal hash functions is in some sense optimal by proving that for $m \ll |U|$

$$\delta(k_i, k_j, H) > \frac{|H|}{m} - \frac{|H|}{|U|}$$

(b) Assume n data elements need to be stored in a hash table. Choose a prime number $p \geq n$, and then choose a and b at random from the set $\{0, 1, \ldots, p - 1\}$. Next define the set of hash functions

$$h_{a,b}(k) = f_{a,b}(k) \bmod m \tag{8.16}$$

where $f_{a,b}(k) = ak + b \bmod p$. Making the standard uniformity assumption, prove that the set constructed using equation (8.16) is a universal set of hash functions.

8.11. An **anagram** is a word produced by transposing the letters of some other word. In this exercise you are to develop a C++ class (that uses any hashing strategy you desire) which stores the words in an english language dictionary, and use this class to develop a program that unscrambles anagrams. Specifically, given an anagram as input, your program should generate all permutations of the letters in an anagram, and then search your dictionary of words to see how many of these permutations are in the dictionary. Test your program on the following anagrams: erpedec, tpaels, gnaarma, tatnscrlanoninet, thyca, abnieohpox, rwlhothiwe, ulbelenrva, isicudstive, aebod, tniaitaulri, laitsvrcouervnate, aainnooprrsttt, iocnsiceoocom, dczaio. (Hint: Many UNIX systems keep a dictionary of words in the file /usr/dict/words.)

8.12. Given two positive integers a and b, both not zero, the **greatest common divisor** of a and b, denoted $\gcd(a, b)$, is the largest common divisor of a and b. For instance, $\gcd(10, 15) = 5$, $\gcd(10, 13) = 1$, and $\gcd(5, 0) = 5$. One way of determining $\gcd(a, b)$ is to first perform factorizations of a and b, and then find the largest number that appears in both factorizations. However, using the best known algorithms for factoring, it is computationally infeasible to factor a large (e.g., 200 digit) arbitrary integer. Fortunately the simpler method given next, known as **Euclid's algorithm**, allows us to find $\gcd(a, b)$ without factoring a and b.

```
Euclid(positive integer a, positive integer b)   ▷ returns gcd(a, b)
1    if b = 0 then
2           return a
3    else
4           return Euclid(b, a mod b)
```

(a) Prove the correctness of this algorithm. (Hint: show that gcd(a, b) = gcd(b, a mod b).)

(b) Show that the running time of Euclid() is $O(\log(\max(a, b)))$. (Hint: First use induction to show that if $a > b$ and the invocation of Euclid(a, b) performs k recursive calls, then $a \geq F_{k+2}$ and $b \geq F_{k+1}$, where F_k is the k-th Fibonacci number.)

8.13. Euclid's algorithm, discussed in the previous exercise, can be extended so that it also computes the (possibly negative) integer coefficients x and y in the equation

$$d = \gcd(a, b) = ax + by \tag{8.17}$$

Specifically,

```
ExtendedEuclid(positive integer a, positive integer b)
1    if b = 0 then
2           return (a, 1, 0)
3    (d', x', y') ← ExtendedEuclid(b, a mod b)
4    (d, x, y) ← (d', y', x' − y'⌊a/b⌋)
5    return (d, x, y)
```

(a) Prove that the values returned by ExtendedEuclid() satisfy equation (8.17). (Hint: The results of the previous exercise show that $d = \gcd(a, b)$. If we make the induction hypothesis $d = ax + by$, then assuming the induction hypothesis is true, line 3 implies $d' = bx' + (a \bmod b)y'$.)

(b) What is the running time of ExtendedEuclid()?

(c) If gcd(a, b) = 1, then the quantity x in the equation $ax \bmod b = 1$ is called the *multiplicative inverse* of a, modulo b. Prove that if gcd(a, b) = 1, then the integer x returned by ExtendedEuclid(a,b) is the multiplicative inverse of a, modulo b.

CHAPTER NOTES

For comprehensive references on hashing, we refer the reader to Knuth [85] and Gonnet [65]. Important early papers on this subject include Morris [106] and Peterson [119]. A thorough treatment of coalesced hashing is given in Vitter and Chen [153]. The linear hashing method was developed by Litwin [94]. When a hash table is too large to fit in main memory, an extension of linear hashing discussed by Larson [89] is often an excellent choice for implementing an external hash table in secondary storage. A comparative survey that considers some additional hashing methods not presented here can be found in Lum, Yuen, and Dodd [96]. The choice of $A \approx \phi^{-1}$ in the multiplication method is justified in Knuth [85]. Use of the term uniform hashing originated in Peterson [119], while the term simple uniform hashing is used by Cormen, Leiserson, and Rivest [36]. Perfect hash functions were defined by Sprugnoli [141]; Fredman and Komlós [58] discuss methods for efficiently constructing them. Universal hashing was first described by Carter and Wegman [27].

Our presentation of cryptography in Section 8.7 is fairly rudimentary. For a more elaborate treatment that considers some of the deeper issues in modern cryptography, the reader should consult Simmons [137]. The notions of public-key cryptography and digital signatures, introduced by Diffie and Hellman [43], are also addressed in the Simmons text. The RSA cryptosystem was proposed by Rivest et al. [128]. Because the RSA cryptosystem is relatively slow at encrypting and decrypting messages, it is often used in a hybrid mode. In this mode of operation, the RSA cryptosystem is used to establish a secret key between two users. This secret key is then used in a secret-key cryptosystem (which will generally be faster) to encrypt and decrypt messages.

We did not consider one method that Eve can use to compromise a public-key cryptosystem. Prior to using a public-key cryptosystem, Alice and Bob must exchange their public keys. If Eve is able to convince Bob that she is Alice, then he will be tricked into using a bogus public key that Eve has supplied (claiming that it is Alice's), and Bob would unwittingly divulge his secrets to Eve. To avoid this problem, rather than having users directly exchange public keys, a "trusted authority" is often put in charge of issuing public keys to all users. By making the public key of the trusted authority known to all, users can authenticate the digital signature of the trusted authority to ensure they are receiving valid public keys.

For an introduction to elementary number theory, the reader may wish to consult Niven and Zuckerman [111]. Euclid's algorithm, discussed in Exercises 8.12 and 8.13, is one of the most famous number theoretic algorithms, dating back to at least 300 B.C. when it was described in the *Elements* of Euclid.

CHAPTER
9

PRIORITY
QUEUES

This chapter introduces the PRIORITY QUEUE ADT, another specialization of the DYNAMIC SET ADT that has proved useful in a variety of computing applications. Specifically, it is often useful to think of the key values associated with dynamic set elements as being *priorities*. In this case, since the keys obey a total ordering relationship, we can identify those elements with highest (or lowest) priorities. One application of priority queues is in scheduling jobs (processes) on a multiuser computer system. One simple approach is to use a queue to service jobs on a first-come-first-serve basis. This approach does not work well, however, when short jobs get "trapped" in the queue behind long running jobs. It is generally best to let short jobs run first (see the discussion of greedy algorithms in Section 2.3.4). If we assign priorities to jobs based on the amount of CPU time they require, then a priority queue can be used to schedule jobs such that the pending job requiring the least amount of time will always execute next. In this chapter, we will also investigate how priority queues can be used in discrete-event simulations, as well as in the development of optimal prefix codes.

9.1 THE PRIORITY QUEUE ADT

The scheduling problem we just considered occurs in a number of other settings as well. For example, the most prevalent operation performed at each step in a greedy solution to an optimization problem involves determining the best (i.e., highest priority) choice from some competing collection of choices; "best" in this sense is typically defined to mean the choice that yields the largest improvement in some cost function. In these applications, the collection of choices can be stored in a dynamic set, where the priority of a choice is represented by the value of its key.

The common theme in the applications discussed above is that we must be able to repeatedly select the element in a dynamic set that has the maximum (or minimum) key value. If all of the elements in this dynamic set are known in advance, and their key values remain unchanged, then this problem is easily solved by sorting the elements and retrieving them in order. In the applications discussed above, however, it is often necessary to insert new elements into the dynamic set as other elements are being processed. This leads to the set of priority queue operations given below. In each of these operations, P is assumed to be an arbitrary priority queue.

1. *Insert*(P, x). Adds element x to P.
2. *FindMin*(P). Returns the element in P with highest priority (lowest key value). If P is empty this operation yields an error.
3. *DeleteMin*(P). Removes and returns the element in P with highest priority (lowest key value). If P is empty this operation yields an error.

These operations actually specify what is called the MIN-PRIORITY QUEUE ADT, the obvious complement of which is the MAX-PRIORITY QUEUE ADT. For mainly historical reasons, when we use the term priority queue we will be referring to the former. That is, the convention is to designate the element with the smallest key value as having the highest priority.

In applications that make use of priority queues it is often the case that two or more elements have the same priority; we will allow this possibility in the implementations we consider by assuming *FindMin* and *DeleteMin* break ties arbitrarily.

DISCRETE-EVENT SIMULATION. Before considering priority queue implementations, let us discuss one of their most prevalent applications areas. A priority queue can be used to handle the time-advance mechanism for the simulation clock in discrete-event simulations. Recall in Section 6.5, where discrete-event simulation was introduced, that we used a fixed-increment time advance to update the simulation clock. With this approach, a value Δt is chosen, and the simulation clock is updated Δt units on each iteration. After each update, a check is made to determine whether any events should have occurred during the previous interval of Δt time. If one or more events were scheduled to have occurred, they are treated as if they occurred at the *end* of this interval, and the system state (and counters) are updated accordingly. The disadvantages associated this approach involve the computer time wasted by processing time intervals in which no events occur, the error introduced by processing events at the end of the interval in which they occur, and the problem of deciding which event to process first when two or more occur in the same time interval. The severity of these latter two problems can be reduced by decreasing Δt; however, this may drastically accentuate the first problem, particularly when the time between successive events is very irregular.

As an alternative to the fixed-increment time-advance mechanism, we will now consider an approach that always advances the simulation clock to the time of the next event. This approach eliminates the disadvantages discussed above by updating the simulation clock from one event time to the next, thereby skipping over periods of system inactivity. Using a next-event time-advance mechanism involves first initializing the simulation clock, and then determining the occurrence times of future events. The simulation clock is then advanced to the time of the first (earliest) event, and the system state is updated to account for the occurrence of this event. The processing of this event may lead to the generation of additional future events. The simulation proceeds by advancing the clock to the next event, updating the system state, and possibly generating new future events, and so on, until some stopping criteria is met. This type of simulation approach is sometimes referred to as being *event-driven* rather than *time-driven*.

The PRIORITY QUEUE ADT is well suited for use in event-driven simulations. This involves storing events in the priority queue, with the priorities determined by the occurrence time of events. With this approach, the next event can always be determined using a *DeleteMin* operation, and new events are easily incorporated into the priority queue using the *Insert* operation.

A general overview of the event-driven approach in simulating a single-server queueing system is given in the following pseudocode. In this pseudocode, E_c and E_s are used to denote events corresponding to a customer arrival and a server completing service, respectively.

Simulate_EventDriven(time t_{start}, time t_{end})
```
1   PRIORITY QUEUE P
2   initialize system state and simulation clock
3   while (t < t_end) do
4       event ← DeleteMin(P)    ▷ event is the next event
5       t ← time[event]    ▷ update simulation clock
6       if type[event] = E_c then
7           add a customer to customer queue
8       else if type[event] = E_s then
9           server_state ← idle
10      if server_state = idle and Empty(Q) = false then
11          remove a customer from customer queue and service them
12          server_state ← busy
13          Insert(P, E_c)    ▷ time[E_c] = time of next customer arrival
14          Insert(P, E_s)    ▷ time[E_s] = time when server next becomes idle
```

On line 2 of this algorithm, we are assuming the simulation clock t is initialized, and that events corresponding to the first customer arrival and the time at which the server is first available are inserted in the priority queue P. After this, the loop over lines 3–14 repeatedly removes the next event from P and processes it accordingly. Observe that the simulation clock is updated on each iteration to the time of the next event. We are assuming that the customer queue and the server keep track of the appropriate statistics related to their use.

9.2 BALANCED TREES

We will first investigate an implementation of the PRIORITY QUEUE ADT using a data structure designed to implement the full complement of DYNAMIC SET ADT operations. In the following sections we will consider simpler data structures that admit efficient implementations of only those operations required by the PRIORITY QUEUE ADT.

Using a balanced binary search tree, which we shall study in Chapter 11, we can ensure that the height of an n-element binary search tree never exceeds $O(\log n)$. Recall that the minimum key value in a binary search tree is stored at the leftmost leaf. Thus, using a balanced binary search tree to store the elements of a priority queue makes it easy to implement the *Insert*, *FindMin*, and *DeleteMin* operations in $O(\log n)$ time. Moreover, the maximum key in a binary search tree can be found with equal efficiency; allowing operations such as *FindMax* and *DeleteMax* to be interspersed with *FindMin* and *DeleteMin* operations, without affecting their efficiency. An ADT supporting all of these operations is often called a DOUBLE-ENDED PRIORITY QUEUE.

Using a balanced binary search tree to implement the standard PRIORITY QUEUE ADT operations is really "overkill"—the binary search tree property is maintained when it is not actually needed. In addition, rebalancing operations tend to add significant overhead to the run times of these operations.

Although we will not be able to obtain better asymptotic running times using other data structures, we can reduce the overhead significantly using the simpler data structure considered in the following sections.

9.3 BINARY HEAPS

A binary heap is a simple data structure that efficiently supports the PRIORITY QUEUE ADT operations. It is defined as follows:

> **Definition 9.1. Heap.** A binary heap (or simply heap) is a complete binary tree in which the key value stored at any vertex is less than or equal to the key values of its children.

We will refer to the ordering of vertices specified in this definition as the ***partial ordering property***, and a binary tree that obeys this property at every vertex will be called a ***partially ordered tree***. Another way to think about this property is that for any direct path from a leaf back to the root, key values must be encountered in nonincreasing order. This means that an item with the smallest key value must be stored at the root vertex of a heap. Thus, the *FindMin* operation can be trivially implemented in $\Theta(1)$ time by simply returning a copy of the element stored in the root. We will also use the term ***heap shape*** to refer to the fact that a heap is a complete binary tree (see Appendix B.4.2 for the definition of a complete binary tree).

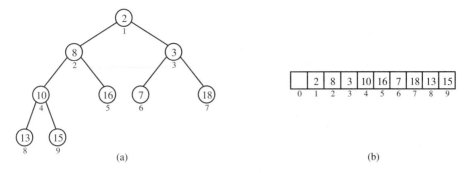

FIGURE 9.1
(a) An example heap with vertices numbered from left to right in level order, and key values displayed inside of the vertices. (b) The manner in which this heap can be stored in an array.

Figure 9.1 (a) shows a heap in which the vertices have been numbered in level order from left to right. Notice that, unlike a binary search tree, there is no particular order between the key values of vertices on the same level. Note also that the minimum key is stored at the root, as it must be if partial ordering is to be satisfied.

The fact that a heap is a complete binary tree makes it easy to represent in a sequentially-mapped data structure as demonstrated in Figure 9.1 (b). In this figure, the number of a vertex becomes its array index, which means that array location zero is not used. However, with this mapping it is easy to calculate the array location of a vertex given its parent's location (and vice versa). Specifically, the heap shape property implies that if a vertex is stored at location i, its left child (if there is one) is at location $2i$, its right child is at location $2i + 1$, and its parent is at location $\lfloor i/2 \rfloor$. Furthermore, $2i$ and $\lfloor i/2 \rfloor$ are easily (and rapidly) calculated by performing a left or right bit shift, respectively, on the binary representation of i.

This sequentially-mapped approach is more space efficient than a linked approach since there is no need to store pointers. It may also offer a time advantage if these index calculations take less time than the associated pointer dereferences in a linked representation. For these reasons, the array representation is the preferred approach for implementing heaps.

9.3.1 Maintaining a Heap

The *Insert* and *DeleteMin* operations do not have trivial implementations in a heap. In either case, the major concern will be with ensuring that a heap maintains both its heap shape and partial ordering after these operations are performed.

THE INSERT OPERATION. Due to the heap shape property, performing this operation on an n element heap must result in an $n + 1$ vertex complete binary tree. That is, we know that the new vertex must be added as the rightmost leaf on the last level of the tree, which is position n. Let us store the element being inserted in this vertex. Although this will guarantee heap shape, it may result in a tree that is not partially ordered. However, the following simple algorithm can be used to restore partial order-ing: If the new element, which was inserted at position n, is smaller than the key of its parent, swap these two elements. Continue swapping the inserted element up towards the root of the tree until it reaches a position in which its key is smaller than that of its parent. Thus, every time an element is inserted, it needs to "sift up" the tree until it reaches its appropriate level. A demonstration of this operation is given in Figure 9.2.

The process of sifting the inserted element up the tree is guaranteed to restore partial ordering to the entire tree for the following reasons. Consider a heap with root v_r whose left and right subtrees are labeled T_L and T_R, respectively. Let us assume, without loss of generality, that the new vertex v_l is added to T_L; T_R will not be affected by this operation. We must show that after sifting the inserted element up the tree, the path from any leaf in T_L back to v_r still encounters keys in nonincreasing order. The sifting process itself ensures that the path $v_l \leadsto v_r$ satisfies this property. In addition, only the vertices along this path can be swapped during the sift-up process. All other paths from leaves in T_L to v_r will share some vertices (possibly only v_r) in

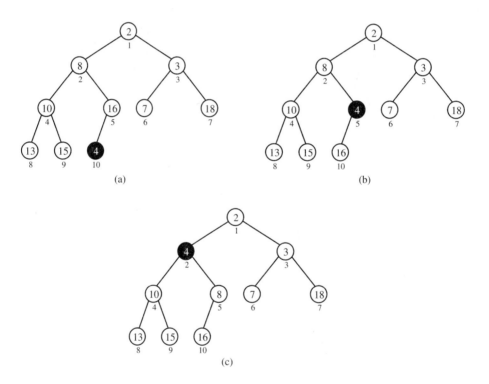

FIGURE 9.2
The result of performing an *Insert* on the heap shown in Figure 9.1. **(a)** A new vertex containing the element (with key 4) is initially inserted as the rightmost leaf on the last level of the tree (i.e., position 10). This maintains heap shape. **(b)** Since the key of the element stored at position 10 is smaller than its parent's key (position 5), these two elements are swapped. **(c)** A final swap between the elements stored at positions 5 and 2 produces a partially ordered tree.

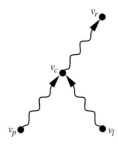

FIGURE 9.3

A heap with root vertex v_r in which a new vertex, v_l, has been added as the rightmost leaf on the last level. During the sift-up process only vertices on the path $v_l \rightsquigarrow v_r$ can be swapped, but this cannot destroy the property that keys appear in nonincreasing order along any other path $v_p \rightsquigarrow v_r$.

common with the path $v_l \rightsquigarrow v_r$. Without loss of generality, choose a leaf vertex v_p in T_L that is different from v_l. This situation is depicted in Figure 9.3, where v_c is the first vertex in common between the paths $v_l \rightsquigarrow v_r$ and $v_p \rightsquigarrow v_r$. If during the sift-up process the element stored at v_c is swapped with the new element, then the new element must have a smaller key than the one stored in v_c. This implies that the path $v_p \rightsquigarrow v_c$ will encounter keys in nonincreasing order after this swap. Continued swapping may cause the new element to move up the path $v_c \rightsquigarrow v_r$, the final result being that $v_c \rightsquigarrow v_r$ encounters keys in nonincreasing order. Since $v_p \rightsquigarrow v_c$ and $v_c \rightsquigarrow v_r$ now both satisfy this property, and v_c is common to both paths, the entire path $v_p \rightsquigarrow v_r$ must encounter keys in nonincreasing order at the completion of this operation.

THE DELETEMIN OPERATION. As discussed above, determining which element needs to be returned is a simple matter since the partial ordering property guarantees that an element with minimum key is stored at the root. Furthermore, due to the heap shape property we know that performing this operation on an n element heap must result in an $n - 1$ vertex complete binary tree. In this case, the rightmost leaf on the last level, which is at position n, must be removed from the tree. These constraints lead to the following algorithm: First, return the element stored at the root. Next, move the element stored at position n to the root, and delete the vertex it has vacated. This approach will maintain the heap shape; however, it may result in the loss of partial ordering. Therefore, if the key of the root is smaller than the key of either of its children, swap it with the smaller of the two. Continue swapping in this manner until partial ordering is restored. That is, the element that was moved to the root must "sift down" in the tree until it reaches its appropriate level. A demonstration of this operation is given in Figure 9.4.

In order to show that this approach will restore partial ordering to the entire tree, we make the following inductive argument. Consider a heap with root vertex v_r whose left and right subtrees are labeled T_L and T_R, respectively. In the *DeleteMin* implementation discussed above, the element in the rightmost leaf on the last level of T_R is moved to the root. It is easy to see that T_L and T_R will still be heaps after this move; however the entire tree may no longer be partially ordered. If it is necessary, the next step involves swapping the element now stored at v_r with the smaller of its two children. Let us assume, without loss of generality, that the elements stored in v_r and root$[T_R]$ are swapped. For this to occur, it must be the case that prior to the swap key[root$[T_R]$] $\leq$ key[root$[T_L]$]. Thus, not only is subtree T_L still a heap

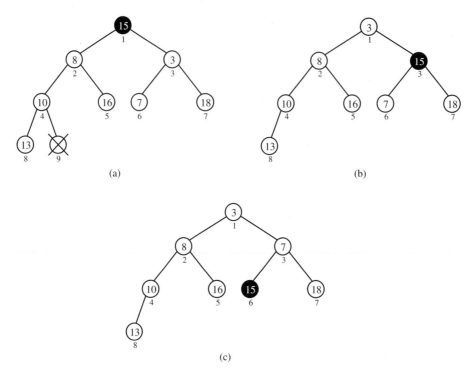

FIGURE 9.4

The result of performing a *DeleteMin* on the heap shown in Figure 9.1. **(a)** The element stored at the root is removed and the element stored at vertex position 9 is placed in the root. The vertex at position 9 is then deleted. This maintains heap shape. **(b)** The element at the root has a larger key value than both of its children; therefore, it is swapped with the element in the child vertex containing the smaller key. **(c)** The key of the element at position 3 is still larger than the key of its left child, so these elements are swapped. This swap produces a partially ordered tree.

after this swap, but the key now stored in v_r must be as small as any key in T_L. At this point subtree T_R may no longer be partially ordered; however, the left and right subtrees of the root of T_R must still be. Thus, subtree T_R now has the form of the original problem, except that it is smaller in size.

9.3.2 Heap Construction

In applications, it is often the case that a heap needs to be created from some existing collection of n elements. Using the heap operations currently at our disposal, this can be accomplished by successively inserting each element into an initially empty heap. Each of these *Insert* operations takes $O(\log n)$ time; so the entire process can be completed in $O(n \log n)$ time. This approach is often referred to as ***top-down heap construction***.

Using a ***bottom-up*** approach, however, it is actually possible to create a heap in linear time. Assuming n elements, this process involves two phases:

1. Create an n vertex complete binary tree, and arbitrarily store the n elements in this tree.

2. Starting at vertex number $\lfloor n/2 \rfloor$ (the lowest numbered vertex on the second-to-last level), and processing in decreasing order to vertex number 1, *heapify* (i.e., create a heap out of) the subtree rooted at each vertex by sifting down the element stored at the subtree's root until it reaches its appropriate level.

An example is given in Figure 9.5. Part (a) of this figure shows an initial arrangement of nine elements in a complete binary tree. Parts (b)–(e) depict the sequence of steps taken during the heapify phase of the algorithm. In Figure 9.5 (a), the white vertices form single element heaps. The processing at each subsequent step involves the creation of a heap from two subtrees that are already heaps. Let us assume that we are currently processing vertex v. Only if the element stored at v is smaller than either of its children will partial ordering be violated for the subtree rooted at v. In this case, partial ordering can be restored by simply sifting the element initially stored at v down until it reaches its appropriate level.

It is clearly the case that Phase 1 of the bottom-up heap construction algorithm takes $\Theta(n)$ time. Thus, to ensure linear-time heap creation we must show that Phase 2 can be completed in $O(n)$ time. In order to demonstrate this fact, recall that the maximum number of vertices in a binary tree of height h is $2^{h+1} - 1$. Such a tree has 2^h vertices on level h (these are leaves), 2^{h-1} vertices on level $h - 1$, and so on. Let $f(n)$ denote the maximum number of swaps performed during Phase 2 of the algorithm on the aforementioned tree. Since the 2^h vertices on level h each form single element heaps, we do not need to perform any swaps to heapify them. For each of the 2^{h-1} vertices on level $h - 1$, at most one swap is needed to heapify the subtrees rooted at these vertices. For each of the 2^{h-2} vertices on level $h - 2$, at most two swaps are needed to heapify the subtrees rooted at these vertices. Continuing in this fashion, at most h swaps will be needed to heapify the entire tree when the root vertex is reached. Thus,

$$f(n) = 2^h \cdot 0 + 2^{h-1} \cdot 1 + \cdots + 2^1 \cdot (h-1) + 2^0 \cdot h$$

$$= \sum_{i=0}^{h} 2^i (h - i)$$

$$= h \sum_{i=0}^{h} 2i - \sum_{i=0}^{h} i2^i$$

$$= h \left(\frac{2^{h+1} - 1}{2 - 1} \right) - \left((h-1)2^{h+1} + 2 \right)$$

$$= 2^{h+1} - h - 2$$

Using the fact that $h = \lg(n+1) - 1$, we have shown that $f(n) = n - \lg(n+1)$. Since the worst-case running time of Phase 2 is proportional to $f(n)$, this demonstrates that the worst-case running time of bottom-up heap construction is $\Theta(n)$.

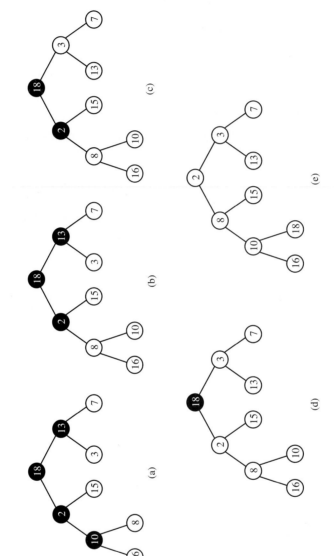

FIGURE 9.5
The bottom-up heap construction algorithm. (a) The initial arrangement of elements as a complete binary tree (Phase 1). (b)–(e) The processing during the heapify (Phase 2) portion of the algorithm. At each step, the vertices that have not yet been processed are black.

9.3.3 Heap Implementation

We have already mentioned that a binary heap can be easily represented using a sequentially-mapped data structure. Therefore, we will use the previously developed dynamic list class `DynList` to create a binary heap class called `HeapPQ`. The declaration of this class is shown in Figure 9.6. Observe that class `HeapPQ` IS-A `DynList`, and recall that `DynList` objects use an array called `element` to store the elements of a list. The first list element is stored in `element[0]`, the second in `element[1]`, and so on. Thus, in agreement with the representation shown in Figure 9.1, `DynList::Retrieve(2)` will return the root element.

The member functions `SiftUp()` and `SiftDown()`, which are declared in the protected section of `HeapPQ`, are used to perform the sift-up and sift-down operations discussed in Section 9.3.1. These member functions will be used to implement many of the public member functions of this class.

The definition of `SiftUp()` is given in Figure 9.7. Because the element being sifted up is involved in each swap, a large amount of unnecessary data movement can be avoided if we store this element in a temporary variable, and perform only one half of each swap. Thus the first statement in `SiftUp()` stores the element being sifted up in the variable `elm`. In effect, an empty vertex is created in the tree at location `i`. Then, on each iteration of the loop, this empty vertex is moved up the tree one level via the assignment statement `element[p] = element[i]`, where `p` is the location of the parent of the vertex stored at location `i`. After the loop terminates, the empty

```
/* File: heap_pq.H */
template<class T>
class HeapPQ : private virtual DynList<T> {
  protected:
    void SiftUp(int i);   // i is index of heap element to be sifted up
    void SiftDown(int i); // i is index of heap element to be sifted down
  public:
    HeapPQ(const T& elm);
    HeapPQ(T* elms);
    HeapPQ() {}
    void Insert(const T& elm);
    T& FindMin();
    T& DeleteMin();
    Boolean Empty() const;
    inline void MakeEmpty();
    friend ostream& operator<<(ostream& os, const HeapPQ<T>& pque);
};

template<class T>
inline T& HeapPQ<T>::FindMin() {return Retrieve(2);}
```

FIGURE 9.6
The C++ declaration of the binary heap class `HeapPQ`.

```
/* File: heap_pq.C */
template<class T>
void HeapPQ<T>::SiftUp(int i) {
  T elm = element[i]; // store sifted element until final placement
  int p = i/2; // index of parent of i
  while (elm < element[p] && i>1) {
    element[p] = element[i]; // move parent down one level
    i = p; // consider next level up
    p = i/2;
  }
  element[i] = elm; // final placement of sifted element
}
```

FIGURE 9.7
Implementation of the SiftUp() protected member function in the HeapPQ class.

vertex is "filled" with the sifted element by the assignment element[i] = elm. Using this approach, no data element is moved more than once.

Notice that the test for loop termination involves testing two different conditions: the first checks to see if partial ordering has been obtained, and the second (a boundary test) checks to make sure the sifted vertex has not reached the root (which is stored at element[1]). It is possible to remove this second test, thereby eliminating two operations on every iteration, if we know in advance all values that priorities may assume. If this is the case, and p_{min} is the minimum possible priority in an application, then we simply initialize element[0] to contain an element with priority $p_{min} - 1$ and remove the second test. Since $p_{min} - 1$ must be smaller than any priority in the tree, this element will serve as a sentinel, guaranteeing that the sifting process will always terminate if it reaches the root.

The sift-down process is slightly more difficult to implement, since at each step we must check the direction (left or right child) that the sifted element may take down the tree. Further complications arise at the second-to-last level of the tree where a vertex may have zero, one, or two children. We leave the implementation of SiftDown() as an exercise for the reader.

Given the SiftUp() and SiftDown() functions, the remaining PRIORITY QUEUE ADT operations are trivial to implement. For example, implementations of the *Insert* and *FindMin* operations are given in Figure 9.8.

9.4   LEFTIST HEAPS

We have shown that heaps efficiently support the PRIORITY QUEUE ADT *Insert* and *DeleteMin* operations. Another useful operation involves the ability to merge two priority queues into a single priority queue. We will use this operation in Chapters 12 and 14. This merging operation, which we will call *Meld*, is defined as follows:

- *Meld*(P_1, P_2). Merges priority queues P_1 and P_2 into a single priority queue and returns the resulting priority queue. P_1 and P_2 are destroyed in the process.

```
/* File: heap_pq.C */
template<class T>
void HeapPQ<T>::Insert(const T& elm) {
  Append(elm);
  SiftUp(length);
}

template<class T>
T& HeapPQ<T>::DeleteMin() {
  assert(length > 1); // check for empty tree
  T* min = new T(FindMin());
  element[1] = element[length];
  Delete(length);
  if (Empty() == false)
    SiftDown(1);
  return *min;
}
```

FIGURE 9.8
Implementation of the `Insert()` and `DeleteMin` member functions in the `HeapPQ` class.

We should point out that this operation is not efficiently supported by priority queues implemented as heaps. The best we can do with heaps is to place the elements of P_2 below those of P_1 in a complete binary tree. The heapify process can then be applied to the elements originally in P_2, and the entire process takes linear time. With this approach, however, we are not able to take advantage of the fact that P_2 is a heap.

It is possible to perform this operation in logarithmic time, while maintaining logarithmic running times for *Insert* and *DeleteMin*, using a data structure known as a leftist heap; but first we must define a leftist tree. When defining this data structure, it is convenient to use the term ***nonfull vertex*** to refer to a binary tree vertex with less than two children. A ***leftist tree*** is a binary tree that obeys the following property at each vertex v in the tree: the path length from v's right child to the nearest nonfull vertex never exceeds that of v's left child to the nearest nonfull vertex.[†] We will refer to the restriction on path lengths in this definition, which tends to make the binary tree "left heavy," as ***leftist shape***. Given the previous definition we may now define the leftist heap:

Definition 9.2. Leftist Heap. A leftist heap is a partially ordered leftist tree.

Examples of leftist heaps are shown in Figure 9.9.

[†]If a vertex does not have a left or right child, then the path length from the missing child to a nonfull vertex is assumed to be -1. Thus, a binary tree consisting of only a root vertex and a right subtree is not a leftist tree.

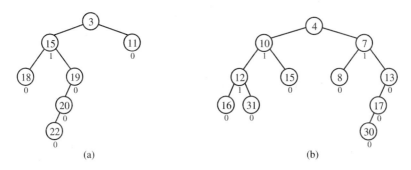

(a)   (b)

FIGURE 9.9

Example leftist heaps with key values shown inside vertices, and the path length to the nearest nonfull vertex (i.e., vertex with less than two children) shown directly below each vertex.

An immediate consequence of the leftist shape property is that the shortest path from the root to a nonfull vertex in a leftist tree must repeatedly follow right children. Furthermore, in an n-vertex leftist tree, this rightmost path contains at most $\lfloor \lg(n+1) \rfloor$ vertices. This fact can be demonstrated using induction: The relationship is satisfied if $n = 1$; now assume it holds true for all values between 1 and $n - 1$. Next, consider a leftist tree T with $\lfloor \lg(n+1) \rfloor$ vertices on its rightmost path. The right subtree of T will have $\lfloor \lg(n+1) \rfloor - 1$ vertices on its rightmost path, and the left subtree of T must also have at least $\lfloor \lg(n+1) \rfloor - 1$ vertices on its rightmost path (otherwise T would not satisfy the leftist property). Some algebraic manipulation reveals that $\lfloor \lg(n+1) \rfloor - 1 = \lfloor \lg((n-1)/2 + 1) \rfloor$, which puts this quantity in a form that allows us to use the induction hypothesis. That is, according to the induction hypothesis, each of T's subtrees (which are also leftist trees) has at least $(n-1)/2$ vertices. These vertices plus the root add to a total of at least n vertices in T, which concludes the proof.

Since a leftist heap obeys partial ordering, an element with minimum key must once again reside at the root, making *FindMin* trivial to implement. We now demonstrate how the remaining PRIORITY QUEUE ADT operations can be efficiently implemented using this data structure. The general idea involves performing all operations on the rightmost path, since it is guaranteed to be short. The difficulty is that partial ordering and leftist shape must also be maintained as a result of performing these operations.

Consider first the *Meld* operation. To meld two leftist heaps, we simply merge the subtrees along their rightmost paths. Specifically, we treat the subtrees encountered along the rightmost paths as two sorted sequences (according to the key value of the subtree root), one sequence for each tree. These two sequences are then merged by repeatedly taking the smallest remaining tree from each sequence and combining them so as to produce a partially ordered tree.

An example of this merging process is given in parts (a) through (e) of Figure 9.10, in which the two leftist heaps given in Figure 9.9 are melded. Part (a) shows the trees to be merged. These were produced by traversing the rightmost paths of both trees in Figure 9.9, forming a tree out of the left subtree rooted at each vertex encountered. In part (b) a partially ordered tree is formed by merging the first two trees. The tree whose root vertex has the larger key is simply attached as the right subtree of the root vertex with the smaller key. This continues until all trees in part (a) have been processed. The result is a single partially ordered tree, as shown in part (e). This tree may violate leftist shape at any vertex along its rightmost path. In order to restore leftist shape, we start at the rightmost vertex and trace a path back to the root. If at any point we encounter a vertex that violates leftist shape, we swap its left and right subtrees. This will restore leftist shape to the subtree rooted at that vertex. For example, in Figure 9.10 (e), the first vertex encountered that violates leftist shape is the root of the entire tree; by swapping its left and right subtrees, we create the leftist heap shown in part (f).

The need for a final backward walk up the rightmost path suggests that *Meld* can be implemented recursively. Consider the following pseudocode:

LeftistHeap::Meld(LeftistHeap H_1, LeftistHeap H_2)
```
1    if key[root[H₁]] > key[root[H₂]] or root[H₁] = NULL then
2        swap H₁ and H₂   ▷ H₁ will have the smaller root
3    if root[H₁] ≠ NULL then
4        right-subtree[H₁] ← LeftistHeap::Meld(right-subtree[H₁], H₂)
5        if length[left[root[H₁]]] < length[right[root[H₁]]] then
6            swap left-subtree[root[H₁]] and right-subtree[root[H₁]]
7        length[root[H₁]] ← length[right[root[H₁]]] +1
8    return H₁
```

In this procedure we are assuming that each vertex v in a leftist heap keeps a variable that stores the path length to the nearest nonfull vertex, and that this variable is accessed using length[v]. The recursive call on line 4 implements the merging process, and the (possible) swap on line 2 ensures that the tree with the larger root is always attached to the right subtree of the tree with the smaller root. Lines 5 and 6 take care of the backward walk up the tree in order to obtain leftist shape.

In Section 2.4 we analyzed the two-way merging process, showing that it can be accomplished in time that is linear in the number of elements being merged. Let us assume LeftistHeap::Meld() is being applied to two leftist heaps containing n vertices each. For each tree, the rightmost path has at most $\lfloor \lg(n+1) \rfloor$ vertices, meaning that $O(\log n)$ vertices will be involved in the merging process. In addition, there can be no more than $O(\log n)$ subtree swaps after they are merged. Therefore the total time for performing a *Meld* of two n-vertex leftist heaps is $O(\log n)$.

Given an implementation of the *Meld* operation, all other PRIORITY QUEUE ADT operations are easily implemented. For instance, the *Insert* operation can be performed by a *Meld* of the current leftist heap with a one-vertex leftist heap containing the new element. Likewise, *DeleteMin* is a *Meld* of the left and right subtrees of the root of a leftist heap, after the root has been deleted. The declaration of a leftist heap class Leftist is shown in Figure 9.11; observe that Leftist IS-A BinaryTree.

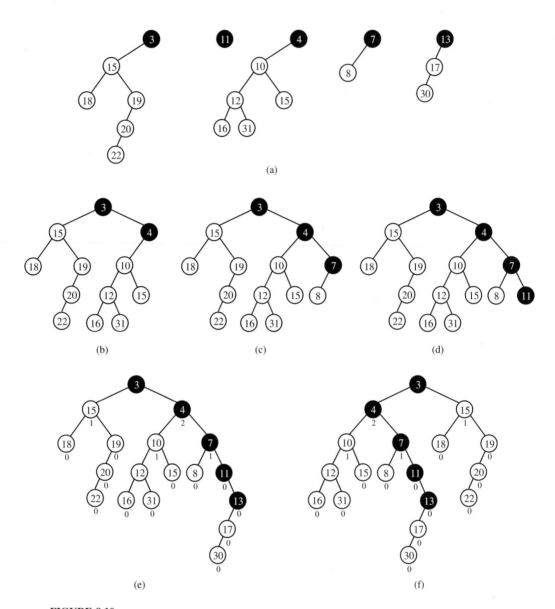

(a)

(b)

(c)

(d)

(e)

(f)

FIGURE 9.10

Performing the *Meld* operation on the two leftist heaps in Figure 9.9. **(a)** A forest of leftist heaps is formed by making trees out of the subtrees rooted at each vertex along the rightmost paths of both trees. The black vertex in each tree will be treated as the key value for that tree when merging them. **(b)–(e)** The merging process. The resulting tree is partially ordered, but may not have leftist shape. **(f)** In order to restore leftist shape, a path is traced from the rightmost vertex back to the root of the tree shown in part (e). The first vertex where leftist shape is violated is at the root. Thus the two subtrees of the root are swapped to produce a leftist heap.

```
/* File: leftist.H */
template<class T>
class Leftist : private virtual BinaryTree<T> {
  public:
    Leftist(const T& elm);
    Leftist(T* elms);
    Leftist() {}
    Leftist<T>& Meld(Leftist<T>& H1, Leftist<T>& H2);
    void Insert(const T& elm);
    T& FindMin();
    T& DeleteMin();
    Boolean Empty() const;
    inline void MakeEmpty();
    friend ostream& operator<<(ostream& os, const Leftist<T>& pque);
};
```

FIGURE 9.11
The C++ declaration of the leftist heap class `Leftist`.

9.5   AN EXTENDED EXAMPLE: DATA COMPRESSION AND HUFFMAN CODES

Data compression involves the transformation of a string of characters from some alphabet into a new string that contains the same information, but whose length is smaller than the original string. This requires the design of a *code* that can be used to uniquely represent every character in the input string. More precisely, a code is said to map *source messages* into *codewords*. The process of using a code to transform a source message into codewords is referred to as *encoding*, while the process of transforming codewords back into a source message is referred to as *decoding*. The design of efficient coding schemes for data compression is very important because they can significantly reduce the amount of memory required to store a data file, as well as the amount of time required to transmit the data file.

If a *fixed-length code* is used, then all codewords will have the same length. The ASCII code is an example of a fixed-length code that maps 256 different characters into 8-bit codewords. Note that if there are p possible characters in an input string, then each codeword in a fixed-length code will require at least $\lceil \lg p \rceil$ bits to encode each character. For instance, if the only characters that can appear in an input string are a, b, c, d, e, and f, then 3 bits would be required to represent each of these six characters using a fixed-length code. One possibility is: a = 000, b = 001, c = 010, d = 011, e = 100, and f = 110. If we let n denote the number of characters that must be encoded, then the total number of bits required by this coding scheme is $3 \cdot n$. Furthermore, $3 \cdot n$ bits are required regardless of the frequency in which these characters appear in the data file.

It is possible to significantly reduce the number of bits required to represent source messages if a *variable-length code* is used. In this case, the number of bits required can vary from character to character. The objective is to encode characters that occur more frequently using shorter bit strings, and characters that occur less frequently using longer bit strings. However, when characters are encoded using varying numbers of bits, some method must be used to determine the start and end bits of a given codeword. For example, assume once again that the only characters appearing in an input string are a, b, c, d, e, and f, and that these characters are encoded using the following codewords: a = 00, b = 111, c = 0011, d = 01, e = 0, and f = 1. This code is not *uniquely decodable* because every codeword is not identifiable when immersed in a sequence of codewords. For example, the string 010001 could be interpreted as deed, deaf, daef, deeef, and so on. One way to guarantee that an encoded bit string only corresponds to a single sequence of characters is to ensure that no codeword appears as the first part of any other codeword in the code. That is, if no codeword appears as a proper prefix of any other codeword, then the corresponding code is uniquely decodable. A code that has this property is called a *prefix code* (or *prefix-free code*). The variable-length code given above is not a prefix code since some codewords are proper prefixes of other codewords—for instance, the codeword for a appears as a proper prefix in the codeword for c. Not only are prefix codes uniquely decodable, they also have the desirable property of being *instantaneously decodable*. This means that a codeword in a coded message can be decoded without having to look ahead to other codewords in the message. The codeword set {1, 1000, 00} is not instantaneously decodable. To see this, assume we are given the message 1001. The first codeword of this message must be 1, but this cannot be determined until the last bit in the message is read. If the last bit in this message was instead a 0, then the first bit would have been part of the codeword 1000.

To demonstrate the usefulness of prefix codes, let us again assume that the only characters appearing in an input string are a, b, c, d, e, and f. Furthermore, let us assume that the size of this input message is 10000 characters, and that a appears 3000 times, b appears 1000 times, c appears 500 times, d appears 500 times, e appears 3500 times, and f appears 1500 times. If we encode this message using a fixed-length code, then $10000 \cdot 3 = 30000$ bits are required. However, if we encode this input message using the variable-length prefix code a = 00, b = 101, c = 1000, d = 1001, e = 01, and f = 11, then

$$(3000 \cdot 2) + (1000 \cdot 3) + (500 \cdot 4) + (500 \cdot 4) + (3500 \cdot 2) + (1500 \cdot 2) = 23000 \text{ bits}$$

are required. A technique that can be used to construct optimal prefix codes will be presented shortly, when we discuss Huffman codes.

One method of data compression involves calculating the frequencies of all the characters in a given message before the message is stored or transmitted. Next, a variable-length prefix code is constructed, with more frequently occurring characters encoded with shorter codewords, and less frequently occurring characters encoded with longer codewords. Then the compressed message is stored or transmitted, along with the code used to encode the message. Note that the code must be included with the encoded message; otherwise the message could not be decoded.

A convenient way of representing prefix codes is to use a binary tree. Using this approach, each character is stored as a leaf in the binary tree, and the codeword

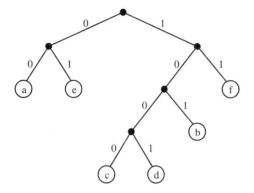

FIGURE 9.12

The binary tree corresponding to the coding scheme a = 00, b = 101, c = 1000, d = 1001, e = 01, and f = 11.

for a particular character is given by the path from the root to the leaf containing the character. For each bit in the codeword, a "0" means "go to the left child" and a "1" means "go to the right child." For example, a binary tree representation of the variable-length prefix code developed above for the characters a through f is shown in Figure 9.12.

The requirement that all characters reside in the leaves of the tree ensures that no codeword is a prefix of any other codeword. Specifically, since there is only one path from the root to any leaf, and only the leaves can store characters, the code is uniquely decodable. Furthermore, it is quite simple to decode a message using this binary tree representation. Starting with the first bit in the encoded message, move left from the root of the binary tree if this bit is "0," and right if it is "1"; continue reading bits and moving left or right in this fashion until a leaf is reached. The value stored in this leaf is output, and we move back to the root of the binary tree to start decoding the next character.

It is useful to think of data compression as an optimization problem in which the goal is to minimize the number of bits required to encode a message. Given a message M consisting of characters from some alphabet Γ, and a binary tree T corresponding to a prefix code for the same alphabet, let $f_M(c)$ denote the frequency of character c in M and $d_T(c)$ the depth of the leaf that stores c in T. Then the *cost* (i.e., the number of bits required) to encode M using T is

$$C_M(T) = \sum_{c \in \Gamma} f_M(c) d_T(c) \qquad (9.1)$$

Minimization of this cost function will yield an optimal prefix code for M. We will refer to the binary tree that represents this optimal prefix code as an optimal tree.

We now present a well-known greedy algorithm that uses a priority queue to create an optimal prefix code for a message. The resulting optimal tree is called a Huffman tree, and the corresponding prefix code is called a *Huffman code*. Recall that the advantage of using a greedy approach is that it generally leads to efficient algorithms. It is not difficult to recognize that this is an important factor when transmitting data; if data compression takes too long, we gain no advantage over transmitting data in its uncompressed form.

In the following pseudocode, we assume that for each character $c \in \Gamma$, the frequency $f_M(c)$ has been calculated. The reader should see that these frequencies can be calculated in time that is linear in the size of the message $|M|$. Next, for each $c \in \Gamma$ with a nonzero value of $f_M(c)$, a binary tree vertex is created and its data field is initialized to $f_M(c)$. We will refer to this set of vertices as Γ_M. The data field of each vertex $v \in \Gamma_M$ can be accessed via $f_M[v]$. This collection of vertices forms a forest of single-vertex binary trees. The basic idea then involves constructing a $|\Gamma_M|$-vertex binary tree in bottom-up fashion by repeatedly forming a larger tree from the two trees in the forest with highest priority. The priority of a tree is given by the sum of the frequencies of the characters stored at its leaves. This is a greedy strategy since at each step, only the two subtrees with lowest cost are considered.

```
Huffman(vertex set Γ_M)
1    PRIORITY QUEUE P ← Γ_M
2    for i ← 1 to |Γ_M| − 1 do
3        v ← create a new binary tree vertex
4        left[v] ← DeleteMin(P)
5        right[v] ← DeleteMin(P)
6        f_M[v] ← f_M[left[v]] + f_M[right[v]]
7        Insert(P, v)
8    return DeleteMin(P)
```

Line 1 of Huffman() creates a priority queue and initializes it to contain a forest of $|\Gamma_M|$ single-vertex binary trees. The loop over lines 2–7 repeatedly removes the two trees from the priority queue that have the lowest priorities (i.e., frequencies). These two trees become the left and right subtrees (it does not matter in which order) of a new binary tree with root vertex v. The priority of this tree, which is stored in the data field of v, is then set to the sum of the priorities of its subtrees. This new tree (actually its root) is then inserted into the priority queue. It is easy to see that after $|\Gamma_M| - 1$ iterations, the only item remaining in the priority queue will be a $|\Gamma_M|$-vertex binary tree. This binary tree is returned on line 8. We will shortly prove that this tree corresponds to an optimal prefix code for the string M. Figure 9.13 shows the subtrees produced at each iteration of Huffman() for an example message.

It is interesting to note that by swapping lines 4 and 5 in Huffman(), a different optimal tree can be produced for a message. Thus, optimal prefix codes are not unique for any given message. Notice also that this algorithm will always produce full binary trees, since at each step it always creates a new tree with nonempty left and right subtrees.

For the analysis of Huffman(), we assume that the priority queue P is implemented using a heap. Let us also assume that $|\Gamma| = n$. We have already mentioned that the set Γ_M can be constructed in $O(n)$ time, and that in the worst case $|\Gamma_M| = n$. In this case, the loop over lines 2–7 is executed exactly $n - 1$ times. On each iteration three priority queue operations are performed, each requiring $O(\log n)$ time. So the loop contributes $O(n \log n)$ to the total running time. The overall running time of Huffman() is therefore $O(n \log n)$.

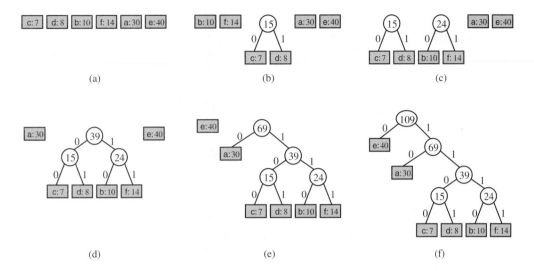

FIGURE 9.13

The subtrees produced by Huffman() on a message containing the characters a, b, c, d, e, and f with frequencies of 30, 10, 7, 8, 40, and 14, respectively. **(a)** The initial set of 6 single-vertex subtrees. The priority of each, which is shown inside the vertex, is the frequency of each character. **(b)–(e)** The subtrees formed during the intermediate stages. **(f)** The final tree. The binary values encountered on each path from the root to a leaf is the codeword for the character stored in that leaf.

To show that Huffman() produces an optimal tree, we must demonstrate that the sequence of greedy choices it makes leads to a prefix code that minimizes the cost function C_M given in equation (9.1). We will do so using induction on n, where n is the size of the vertex set Γ_M. The base case is trivial; it is easy to verify that Huffman() produces an optimal tree when n equals 1 or 2. Our induction hypothesis is that Huffman() produces an optimal tree for all messages in which $|\Gamma_M|$ is not more than $n - 1$. The extension step involves showing that if Huffman() produces an optimal tree when $|\Gamma_M| = n - 1$, it must also produce an optimal tree when $|\Gamma_M| = n$. We will demonstrate this step in an equivalent manner by showing that if Huffman() produces an optimal tree when $|\Gamma_M| = n - 1$, it cannot produce a nonoptimal tree when $|\Gamma_M| = n$.

Consider a message in which $|\Gamma_M|$ equals n, and assume Huffman() returns a nonoptimal tree T. Let T_{opt} be an optimal tree for the same message, with x and y being the characters with the first and second lowest frequencies, respectively, in M. We know that x must appear as a leaf with maximal depth in T_{opt}—if this were not the case, we could exchange this leaf with the lowest leaf in the tree, thereby decreasing C_M and contradicting the optimality of T_{opt}. Moreover, we can always exchange vertices in T_{opt}, without affecting C_M, so that the vertices storing x and y become siblings (proof of this fact is left as an exercise). These two vertices must also appear as siblings in T—they are paired together on the first iteration of Huffman(). Now consider the two trees T' and T'_{opt} produced by replacing these two siblings and their parent with a single vertex containing a new character z whose frequency equals $f_M[x] + f_M[y]$. Note that Huffman() would produce T' on the message M' obtained by replacing all occurrences of x and y in M with z. Except for x and y, the depth of every character in these new trees is the same as it was in the old trees. Furthermore, in both T' and T'_{opt} the new character z appears one level higher than both x and y did in T and T_{opt}, respectively. Thus, using equation (9.1) we have that

$$C_{M'}(T'_{\text{opt}}) = C_M(T_{\text{opt}}) - f_M[x] - f_M[y] \tag{9.2}$$

and

$$C_{M'}(T') = C_M(T) - f_M[x] - f_M[y] \tag{9.3}$$

Since we have assumed that $C_M(T_{\text{opt}}) < C_M(T)$, it follows from equations (9.2) and (9.3) that $C_{M'}(T'_{\text{opt}}) < C_{M'}(T')$. But T' is a Huffman tree in which $|\Gamma| = n-1$, so this latter inequality contradicts our induction hypothesis. This contradiction implies that Huffman() cannot produce a nonoptimal tree when $|\Gamma_M| = n$, if it produces an optimal tree when $|\Gamma_M| = n - 1$. This verifies the extension step, and therefore completes the proof that Huffman() produces an optimal prefix code for any message.

EXERCISES

9.1. The *heapsort algorithm* uses a heap to sort a collection of n data elements by first constructing a heap in $O(n)$ time, and then performing n *DeleteMin* operations. Since each *DeleteMin* operation takes $O(\log n)$ time, the worst-case running time of this algorithm is $\Theta(n \log n)$. What advantage does this algorithm have over the mergesort algorithm discussed in Section 2.4?

9.2. If data elements are processed in the same order, will the top-down and bottom-up heap construction techniques always produce the same heaps?

9.3. Rewrite the simulations in Exercises 6.13 and 6.14 using an event-driven approach.

9.4. Write an efficient C++ implementation of the `HeapPQ::SiftDown()` operation that does not use any sentinels. Discuss how adding a sentinel element to your implementation would simplify your code.

9.5. A d-heap is a complete d-ary tree that has heap order (i.e., a binary heap is a 2-heap). What are the advantages and disadvantages of using a d-heap, $d > 2$, as opposed to a binary heap, when implementing the PRIORITY QUEUE ADT.

9.6. Prove that the shortest path from the root to a leaf in a leftist tree is the rightmost one.

9.7. The selection problem was described in Exercise 2.14. Describe how a heap can be used to solve this problem in $O(k \log n)$ time. Can you modify your approach to solve this problem in $O(n \log k)$ time?

9.8. Assume you are given a collection of n elements arranged into m sorted sequences. Describe how these sequences can be merged into a single sorted sequence in $O(n \log m)$ time.

9.9. Develop a linear-time leftist heap construction algorithm that takes as input a collection of n elements, and produces as output a single leftist heap containing these elements.

9.10. The QUEUE-WITH-HEAP-ORDER ADT is simply the QUEUE ADT in which one additional operation, *FindMin*, is supported. Describe a queue-with-heap-order implementation that allows *Enqueue*, *Dequeue*, and *FindMin* all to be implemented in $\Theta(1)$ time. (Hint: Use a standard queue along with an auxiliary stack. The stack should contain only those queue elements x such that $key[x] \leq key[y]$, for every y "behind" x in the queue.)

9.11. Draw the binary tree associated with the coding scheme: a $= 00$, b $= 111$, c $= 0011$, d $= 01$, e $= 0$, and f $= 1$. Use this tree to discuss why the code is not uniquely decodable.

9.12. Must a binary tree corresponding to an optimal prefix code always be full?

9.13. Given a message M in which x and y are the two characters in M having the lowest frequencies, show that there always exists an optimal prefix code for M in which x and y appear as siblings with maximal depth in the corresponding binary tree.

9.14. Are there some optimal prefix codes which cannot be produced by the Huffman() algorithm? Does your answer hold if we assume that no two characters have the same frequency in the message?

9.15. Assume you are given a Huffman tree that encodes a certain message. Suppose now that the frequency of one of the (existing) characters in the message is changed. Describe an algorithm for updating the tree so that it becomes optimal with respect to the new message.

CHAPTER NOTES

Heaps were first introduced for use in the heapsort algorithm by Williams [156]. Floyd [56] subsequently introduced the linear-time heap construction algorithm as a means of speeding up heapsort. Although these papers are concerned with using heaps in sorting, both authors point out the usefulness of heaps in implementing priority queues. Crane [38] invented the leftist heap data structure, while Knuth [85] first used the term "leftist" to describe it. Huffman [77] introduced the codes that bear his name. Queues-with-heap-order have applications in pagination and routing (see Cole and Siegel [33] and Diehr and Faaland [42]). Lelewer and Hirschberg [91] discuss prefix codes and present an excellent survey of data compression techniques.

The topic of heaps will be revisited in Chapter 12, but only after we have had the opportunity to study amortized analysis in Chapter 10.

PART
III

ADVANCED
DATA
STRUCTURES

INTRODUCTION TO PART III

In this part we introduce a number of advanced data structures and algorithms, along with a new analysis technique called amortized analysis. Amortized complexity analysis is one of the most exciting and ingenious recent developments in the field of data structures and algorithms. It is generally the case that the user of a data structure will apply a number of ADT operations to the data structure—not just one. Using amortized analysis we seek worst-case bounds on the running time of such a *sequence* of ADT operations, rather than on the running time of a single operation. The key point is that the amortized bounds are often tighter than ones obtained by simply summing the worst-case running times of each individual operation in a sequence. The reason for this is simple: The operations in a sequence are often correlated in such a way that if one operation achieves its worst-case running time, a subsequent operation cannot. Amortized analysis gives us a means of discovering these dependencies between the operations in a sequence, and allows us to exploit them in our derivations of worst-case running time bounds.

We should also point out that amortized analysis gives us another way of thinking about the design of data structures and their associated algorithms. In other words, this technique is not only useful as an analysis tool, but it can also lead to the development of new data structures. In fact, many of the data structures introduced in this

275

part are recent discoveries, whose justifications are mainly supported by amortized analysis.

After a detailed description of amortized analysis in Chapter 10, balanced binary search trees are introduced in Chapter 11. These data structures are able to maintain good balance by reorganizing their subtrees after certain operations are performed. The method used for reorganizing subtrees is described first. Next, two balanced search tree data structures are presented that are able to achieve worst-case $\Theta(\log n)$ running times for any of the DYNAMIC SET ADT operations. A simpler balanced search tree data structure is also presented that has these same running time bounds, but this time in an amortized sense.

The MELDABLE PRIORITY QUEUE ADT, an extension of the PRIORITY QUEUE ADT first mentioned in Section 9.4, is considered in Chapter 12. The data structures used to implement the MELDABLE PRIORITY QUEUE have been studied quite extensively using amortized analysis. This chapter considers a number of the more important implementations, as well as the Fibonacci heap, a data structure of considerable theoretical importance. We will demonstrate in Chapter 14 how the Fibonacci heap can be used to improve the worst-case running time of certain graph algorithms.

In Chapter 13 we first consider adding an operation for range searching to the DYNAMIC SET ADT. For one-dimensional keys, the binary search tree can efficiently implement this operation. We also introduce the trie data structure, which is often a good alternative to binary search trees in applications where key comparisons are expensive. Next, the important topic of multidimensional keys is introduced. We describe how lists can be used to store multidimensional data, and then an assortment of new data structures that more effectively support multidimensional searching are considered. This chapter also introduces the DISJOINT SET ADT, and studies it using amortized analysis. We will use this ADT to implement Kruskal's algorithm in Chapter 14.

The final chapter treats the important topic of graphs, which are discrete structures used in many areas of study. The ability of graphs to model many important physical phenomena is first demonstrated, followed by a discussion of efficient graph representation in computer memory. The remainder of the chapter is concerned with various algorithms for solving graph related problems. These algorithms will make use of a large number of data structures considered in previous chapters.

CHAPTER
10

AMORTIZED
ANALYSIS

When an ADT implementation is used in an application program, a sequence of operations is typically performed on the data type, rather than just a single operation. Until now, however, we have only been concerned with analyzing the running times of individual operations. The two techniques we have considered are worst- and average-case analysis (see Section 2.2). It is not difficult to extend worst-case analysis to a sequence of operations. This is accomplished by simply determining the worst-case running time for each operation in the sequence, relative to the data structure used in the implementation, and then summing these to produce a bound for the worst-case running time of the entire sequence. This approach, however, may yield an overly pessimistic upper bound in situations where the operations in the sequence are correlated in some fashion. Specifically, it is often the case that performing one operation in a sequence will modify the underlying data structure in such a way that the worst-case running time of some future operation in the sequence cannot occur. In this case, the actual worst-case running time of a sequence of operations may be much lower than the bound obtained by summing over the individual operation's worst-case running times. Amortized complexity analysis provides a means for arriving at these tighter bounds. This type of analysis is most often used with self-adjusting data structures—we have already seen some of these in Section 5.2.3 when we discussed self-organizing lists. We will see a number of other self-adjusting data structures in this and subsequent chapters.

10.1   AN OVERVIEW

The general idea in amortized complexity analysis involves averaging (i.e., amortizing) the time for each operation in a worst possible sequence, over the time required by the entire sequence. Although a single operation in the sequence may be quite expensive, averaging its cost over the entire sequence may significantly reduce its overall affect.

It is important to understand the difference between this approach and average-case analysis. If we wish to compute the average-case running time for an entire sequence of operations, then some probabilistic assumptions about the operations must be made. Next, the average running times for the individual operations would have to be computed, and summed together, to arrive at the expected running time for the sequence. We must acknowledge, however, that certain sequences may have running times that are much worse than this expected result, and that the analysis is only valid as long as the probabilistic assumptions hold. In contrast, amortized analysis does not involve probabilities. Furthermore, with amortized analysis we can guarantee that the running time we arrive at will not be exceeded by *any* sequence of operations.

In the following sections we present two approaches used to perform amortized complexity analysis. The first approach, called the accounting method, takes the "banker's view" by relating running time to cost. That is, the individual operations in a sequence assign credits or debits to a balance sheet. Certain types of operations may "over pay" (i.e., assign more credits to the balance sheet than they actually cost) so that more expense operations may later use these extra credits to help pay for themselves.

The second approach, called the potential method, takes the "physicist's view" by relating running time to potential energy. In this case, the individual operations are thought of as increasing or decreasing the potential energy in a system (where the system is the data structure). Once again, certain types of operations may put more energy into the system than they actually consume. This is stored as potential energy, which can be released for use by other operations. As an analogy consider the physical system given in Figure 10.1, in which a ball has a potential energy related to its height above ground level. In our analogy the physical system represents a data structure that is implementing some ADT, and the force being applied to the ball denotes individual ADT operations. If the force is sufficient it will push the ball uphill a short distance, increasing its potential energy. That is, each operation consumes some amount of energy, and any leftover energy is transferred to the ball in the form of potential energy. At some point, a small amount of additional force (i.e., one operation) will push the ball over a hill, releasing some potential energy as kinetic energy. This corresponds to an operation that uses some of the potential energy stored by earlier operations.

In both approaches, each operation in a sequence has two values c and $\hat{c}$ associated with it; these values are called the actual and amortized running times of

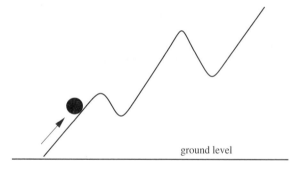

FIGURE 10.1
A physical system that is used as an analogy for the potential method of amortized analysis. Force is applied in the direction of the arrow.

ground level

the operation, respectively. As we mentioned previously, the actual running time of a given operation may depend upon the operations that have proceeded it in a sequence. In amortized complexity analysis, however, the amortized running time of an operation will be fixed, and therefore independent of any previous operations.

If we let c_i and $\hat{c}_i$ denote the actual and amortized running times of the i-th operation in a sequence of n operations, then the actual and amortized running times of the *sequence* are $\sum_{i=1}^{n} c_i$ and $\sum_{i=1}^{n} \hat{c}_i$, respectively. The key idea in both approaches to amortized complexity analysis involves upper bounding the actual running time of the sequence by the amortized running time of the sequence. Specifically, we will want to ensure that

$$\sum_{i=1}^{n} \hat{c}_i \geq \sum_{i=1}^{n} c_i \tag{10.1}$$

We would like to emphasize here that the accounting and potential methods are equivalent. You should use whichever one feels most natural, or gives you the most insight into the problem under consideration. Finally, the reader should understand that these techniques are used for analysis purposes only. Neither a balance sheet, nor a potential energy variable (used in the context discussed above) should ever appear in your data structures.

10.2 ACCOUNTING METHOD

Since the running time of an operation is thought of as having a monetary value with this approach, we will use the terms ***amortized running time*** and ***amortized cost*** interchangeably.

With the accounting method, if the amortized cost of an operation exceeds its actual cost, the positive difference is recorded as a credit on a balance sheet. Likewise, if the amortized cost of an operation is less than its actual cost, the negative difference is recorded as a debit. Accumulated credits can later be used to help pay for operations that register debits on the balance sheet. Furthermore, similar to the United States government, deficit spending is allowed. However, any such deficits must eventually be paid off using the credits allocated to other operations in the sequence. If this condition is met, then the sum of the amortized costs of the operations in the sequence will provide an upper bound on the actual cost of the sequence. In particular, condition (10.1) will have been met.

The reader should recognize that a sufficient (but not necessary) condition for satisfying equation (10.1) is that the balance sheet never becomes negative. The reader may also find it useful to think of the idea of storing extra credits on the balance sheet as allowing us to average forward over time, and using these credits to help pay for future operations as allowing us to average backward over time.

10.2.1   Stack Operations and Linked Lists

In order to get a feel for the accounting method, let us first present a fairly simple example based on the STACK ADT implementation given in Section 6.4. Recall that *Push* and *Pop* can be implemented in $\Theta(1)$ time using a linked list implementation. Therefore, in order to make the analysis nontrivial, let us also include the *MakeEmpty* operation. For a stack containing $n \geq 0$ elements, *MakeEmpty* requires $\Theta(n)$ time in a linked list implementation, since the memory associated with each of the n elements must be reclaimed. The actual costs of these operations are proportional to:

Operation	Actual Cost (c)
Push	1
Pop	1
MakeEmpty	n

We are assuming, as in Chapter 6, that *Pop* will not be applied to an empty stack.

If we must perform a sequence of m operations, then in the worst case each would be a *MakeEmpty* operation requiring $\Theta(n)$ time, and the running time for an entire sequence would be $\Theta(mn)$. It is obvious that this worst-case analysis ignores the correlated effects of the STACK ADT operations: the *MakeEmpty* operation takes $\Theta(n)$ time only if there are $\Theta(n)$ elements on the stack, but at least $\Theta(n)$ *Push* operations must have been performed to get $\Theta(n)$ elements on the stack. Using the accounting method we can incorporate this information into our analysis. Specifically, an element cannot be removed from a stack using a *Pop*, unless it has been previously placed on the stack using a *Push*. As noted above, the same restriction applies to *MakeEmpty*. Thus, whenever a *Push* operation is performed, we add an extra credit to the balance sheet. This credit can be used later to pay for the element's removal during either a *Push* or *MakeEmpty* operation. Therefore let us assign the following amortized costs to the STACK ADT operations:

Operation	Amortized Cost ($\hat{c}$)
Push	2
Pop	0
MakeEmpty	0

It is not difficult to argue that, starting with an empty stack, any sequence of STACK ADT operations can be paid for using these amortized costs. In particular, according to the actual costs and to the choices for the amortized costs, if the stack is initially empty, the balance sheet can never become negative.

Given that any sequence of operations can be paid for by the amortized costs shown above, all that remains is to determine the amortized cost of a worst-case sequence of m operations. This will occur if all m are *Push* operations, yielding a worst-case amortized cost of $2m$. In conclusion, since we have previously shown that the amortized cost of such a sequence provides an upper bound on the actual cost of the sequence, we now know that any sequence of m STACK ADT operations can be performed in $\Theta(m)$ time, and that the average cost of each operation is given by $2m/m = \Theta(1)$.

10.2.2 Stack Operations and Dynamic Lists

We can also use the accounting method to study the behavior of a sequence of STACK ADT operations when the stack is implemented using the dynamic list data structure presented in Section 5.2.2. Recall that the load factor of a nonempty dynamic list is defined as the length of the list divided by the current size of the array that stores the list (an empty dynamic list has a load factor of 1); that whenever an operation causes the load factor of a dynamic list to reach 1, a new array that is twice the size of the current array is allocated; and that whenever the load factor reaches $1/4$, a new array that is one-half the size of the current array is allocated. We will refer to the former as an expansion, and to the latter as a contraction. In either case, the elements stored in the current array are then moved to the new array before deleting the current array.

All of the STACK ADT operations can be implemented in $\Theta(1)$ time if they do not cause an expansion or contraction. However, in the worst case, a single *Push* or *Pop* would lead to an expansion or contraction, respectively. It is reasonable to assume that the cost of moving elements in these cases will dominate the cost of allocating and deallocating memory. Thus, when using this data structure, in the worst case *Push* and *Pop* require $\Theta(n)$ time, where $n \geq 0$ is the number of elements currently stored on the stack. Therefore, a worst-case analysis on m operations would lead to a running time of $\Theta(mn)$.

Once again we can do better by using amortized analysis. First, let us write down the actual costs of the stack operations:

Operation	Actual Cost (c)
Push	1 or n
Pop	1 or $(n-1)$
MakeEmpty	1

Notice that with a dynamic list implementation of the STACK ADT, the *Push* and *Pop* operations can be expensive, while in the linked list implementation it was the *MakeEmpty* operation that was expensive.

Next let us attempt to come up with some amortized costs for these operations. These costs must be chosen so that their use on any sequence of operations will yield a nonnegative balance sheet after the completion of all m operations in the sequence.

We will show that the following choices accomplish this goal:

Operation	Amortized Cost ($\hat{c}$)
Push	3
Pop	2
MakeEmpty	1

If no expansion or contraction occurs, then it is easy to see that these charges are adequate. In fact there will be two leftover credits for each *Push*, and one leftover credit for each *Pop* in this case. Next we will demonstrate that these amortized costs are also sufficient to pay for any expansions or contractions of the dynamic list.

To see why the amortized cost of *Push* must be 3, consider what happens if more than one expansion occurs while executing the sequence of operations. For instance, assume a *Push* operation is performed on a dynamic list containing $n = 2^k$ elements, and that this leads to an expansion as shown in the top portion of Figure 10.2. Immediately prior to the first expansion shown in this figure, the array has a size of 2^k and is storing 2^k list elements. Let us assume the balance sheet contains 2^k credits. After this expansion, the array has a size of 2^{k+1} and is storing $2^k + 1$ list elements. The *Push* that caused the expansion will contribute 2 credits to the balance sheet, but 2^k credits must be used to cover the cost of copying the 2^k elements to the new array. Thus, the balance sheet will contain 2 credits immediately after this operation.

After the first expansion, assume 2^k additional *Push* operations are performed, leading to the second expansion shown in Figure 10.2. These *Push* operations will contribute 2^{k+1} credits, so immediately prior to the second expansion the balance sheet will contain $2^{k+1} + 2$ credits. Of these, 2^{k+1} credits must be used to pay for the copying required immediately after the second expansion. Thus, we can think of the 3 credits associated with each of these 2^k *Push* operations as being allocated in the following fashion: One credit is immediately used to pay for the *Push* operation itself, another credit is placed on the balance sheet to pay for moving one of

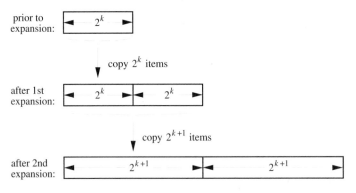

FIGURE 10.2

Two expansions of a dynamic list. The copying costs associated with the first expansion are 2^k, and with the second expansion they are 2^{k+1}.

the 2^k elements inserted after the first expansion, and the final credit is placed on the balance sheet to pay for moving one of the 2^k elements that was stored in the array prior to the first expansion. Note that if *Pop* operations are interspersed with these *Push* operations, and no contractions occur, then the analysis remains valid since these *Pop* operations will actually increase the number of credits stored on the balance sheet.

Next let us examine the cost of *Pop* operations that lead to contractions of the dynamic list. Assume 2^k stack elements are stored in a dynamic list with 2^k storage locations, and that 2^k consecutive *Pop* operations are performed. The *Pop* operation that causes the number of stack elements to be reduced to 2^{k-2} will lead to the first contraction (since the load factor will be 1/4). Since the previous *Pop* operations payed for themselves, the balance sheet must contain at least 2^{k-2} credits to pay for the copying costs associated with moving the 2^{k-2} stack elements to the new smaller array. The next contraction will occur when the stack is reduced to 2^{k-4} elements. Thus, 2^{k-4} credits are needed for this contraction, and so on. If we let $C(2^k)$ denote the number of credits needed for a sequence of 2^k *Pop* operations when there are 2^k elements on the stack, then we can write the following recurrence relation[†]

$$C(2^k) = \begin{cases} C(2^{k-2}) + 2^{k-2}, & \text{if } k > 1 \\ 0, & \text{otherwise} \end{cases}$$

The exact solution of this equation is

$$C(2^k) = \frac{2^k}{3} + \frac{(-1)^k}{6} - \frac{1}{2}$$

which is strictly less than 2^k. Thus, 2^k credits are sufficient to pay for this sequence of *Pop* operations. Note that if *Push* operations are interspersed with these *Pop* operations, and no expansions occur, the analysis remains valid since each *Push* can only increase the number of credits stored on the balance sheet.

To see why the amortized cost of *Pop* must be 2 instead of 1, we must consider what happens when *Push* operations are interspersed with the sequence of *Pop* operations, and an expansion occurs. Assume an expansion has just occurred so that the array has size 2^k, and that only 2 credits remain on the balance sheet. (In our analysis of a sequence of *Push* operations we demonstrated that if there are at least 2^{k-1} credits available prior to this *Push*, then there will be 2 credits on the balance sheet after the expansion.) A contraction will occur only if the number of stack elements stored in the array is reduced to 2^{k-2}. In order to reduce the number of stack elements by this amount, at least 2^{k-2} credits must be added to the balance sheet. That is, in the worst case 2^{k-2} *Pop* operations follow the expansion, each contributing 1 credit to the balance sheet. These credits are sufficient to cover the copying costs associated with the ensuing contractthen ion.

In summary, we have shown that if the length of the dynamic list is 2^k, $k \geq 1$ (which implies that the stack size is between $2^{k-2} + 1$ and 2^k), and if the

---

[†]This is actually an upper bound since we are not accounting for the fact that each *Pop* operation prior to the contraction also contributed 1 credit to the balance sheet.

balance sheet contains at least 2^k credits, then any sequence of STACK ADT operations can be payed for by the amortized costs listed previously. The only remaining work involves showing that starting from an empty stack, there are at least 2 credits on the balance sheet when the stack size reaches 2. This fact can be easily verified by the reader. Since we have bounded the amortized cost of each STACK ADT operation by a constant, it follows that any sequence of m STACK ADT operations can be completed in $\Theta(m)$ time.

10.3   POTENTIAL METHOD

Given a data structure D, let us denote its initial configuration (i.e., its configuration before any operations have been applied) using D_0, and its i-th configuration (i.e., its configuration after the i-th operation) as D_i. Next let us define a *potential function* Φ, which performs the mapping $\Phi : D \rightarrow \mathbb{R}$. That is, a potential function maps a data structure configuration into a real number. The potential method then works as follows: The amortized running time of an operation on data structure D is defined with respect to Φ as

$$\hat{c} = c + \Delta\Phi(D) \tag{10.2}$$

where $\Delta\Phi(D)$ represents the change in potential that resulted from operation c. Therefore, the amortized running time of a sequence of m operations is

$$\sum_{i=1}^{m} \hat{c}_i = \sum_{i=1}^{m} (c_i + \Phi(D_i) - \Phi(D_{i-1}))$$

$$= \sum_{i=1}^{m} c_i + \Phi(D_m) - \Phi(D_0) \tag{10.3}$$

From equation (10.3) it is easy to see that the amortized running time of the sequence will bound the actual running time of the sequence (i.e., condition (10.1) will be satisfied) as long as $\Phi(D_m) \geq \Phi(D_0)$. Furthermore, a sufficient (but not necessary) condition for satisfying equation (10.1) is that $\Phi(D_i) \geq \Phi(D_{i-1})$ for $i = 1, 2, \ldots, m$.

10.3.1   Stack Operations and Linked Lists

As an example of the potential method, consider again the linked list STACK ADT implementation given in Section 6.4. Let us choose the potential function for this data structure to be the number of elements stored in the stack. Starting with an empty stack, we have $\Phi(D_0) = 0$. Furthermore, since the number of elements stored in a stack can never be negative, it must be the case that for a sequence of m operations, $\Phi(D_m) \geq \Phi(D_0)$. Therefore, the amortized running time of such a sequence of operations will represent an upper bound on the actual running time of the sequence of operations.

Given this potential function, we can derive the amortized running times of the individual stack operations. If a *Push* is performed on a stack containing n elements, then the change in potential is

$$\Delta\Phi(D) = (n+1) - n$$
$$= 1$$

Substituting this result into equation (10.2) yields an amortized running time of $\hat{c} = 1 + 1 = 2$ for the *Push* operation. Using the aforementioned potential function, the change in potential resulting from a *Pop* is -1. Therefore, the amortized running time of the *Pop* operation is $\hat{c} = 1 + (-1) = 0$. Finally, if the *MakeEmpty* operation is applied to a stack containing n elements, then the change in potential will be $-n$. Thus, the amortized running time of the *MakeEmpty* operation is $\hat{c} = n + (-n) = 0$.

These are the same amortized running times that were used for this data structure when we considered the accounting method. Using these amortized running times, we showed in Section 10.2.1 that any sequence of m STACK ADT operations can be performed in $\Theta(m)$ time.

10.3.2 Stack Operations and Dynamic Lists

Given a dynamic list D that is being used to implement the STACK ADT, we will use $size[D]$ to denote the current size of the array used to store the stack elements, and $length[D]$ to denote the actual number of elements stored in this array. Next, consider the following potential function

$$\Phi(D) = \begin{cases} 2 \cdot length[D] - size[D], & \text{if } \alpha(D) \geq 1/2 \\ size[D]/2 - length[D], & \text{otherwise} \end{cases} \tag{10.4}$$

where $\alpha(D)$ is the load factor of D. By showing that this potential function is initially 0 (when the stack is empty), and that it can never become negative, we will demonstrate that the amortized running time of any sequence of STACK ADT operations will upper bound its actual running time.

Initially, $size[D] = length[D] = 0$, which implies $\Phi(D_0) = 0$. Furthermore, because of the way dynamic lists are implemented, it must be the case that $1/4 < \alpha(D) \leq 1$ after any operation. From equation (10.4) we see that if $1/4 < \alpha(D) < 1/2$, the minimum value that the potential function may assume is 0. Similarly, if $1/2 \leq \alpha(D) \leq 1$, the minimum value that the potential function may assume is 0. Thus we have shown that $\Phi(D_m) \geq \Phi(D_0)$, which is a sufficient condition for satisfying condition (10.1). Potential function (10.4) can now be used to derive amortized running times for each of the STACK ADT operations.

If we assume that the i-th operation is a *Push*, and that this operation does not cause an expansion, then $size[D_{i-1}] = size[D_i]$ and there are three cases to consider: If $\alpha(D_{i-1})$ and $\alpha(D_i)$ are both less than $1/2$, then according to equation (10.2) the amortized cost of this operation is

$$\hat{c}_i = c + \Phi(D_i) - \Phi(D_{i-1})$$
$$= 1 + (size[D_i]/2 - length[D_i]) - (size[D_{i-1}]/2 - length[D_{i-1}])$$
$$= 1 - length[D_i] + length[D_{i-1}]$$
$$= 0$$

If $\alpha(D_{i-1}) < 1/2$ and $\alpha(D_i) = 1/2$, then $length[D_i] = size[D_i]/2$, and

$$\hat{c}_i = c + \Phi(D_i) - \Phi(D_{i-1})$$

$$= 1 + (2 \cdot length[D_i] - size[D_i]) - (size[D_{i-1}]/2 - length[D_{i-1}])$$

$$= 1 + 2 \cdot length[D_i] - size[D_i] - size[D_i]/2 + length[D_i] + 1$$

$$= 1 + 2 \cdot length[D_i] - 2 \cdot length[D_i] - length[D_i] + length[D_i] + 1$$

$$= 2$$

Finally, if both $\alpha(D_{i-1})$ and $\alpha(D_i)$ are greater than or equal to $1/2$, then the amortized cost of this operation is given by

$$\hat{c}_i = c + \Phi(D_i) - \Phi(D_{i-1})$$

$$= 1 + (2 \cdot length[D_i] - size[D_i]) - (2 \cdot length[D_{i-1}] - size[D_{i-1}])$$

$$= 1 + 2(length[D_{i-1}] + 1) - 2 \cdot length[D_{i-1}]$$

$$= 3$$

If on the other hand the *Push* operation causes an expansion, then the value of $size[D_{i-1}]$ is one-half that of $size[D_i]$, $size[D_{i-1}] = length[D_{i-1}] = length[D_i] - 1$, and the amortized cost of the operation is

$$\hat{c}_i = c + \Phi(D_i) - \Phi(D_{i-1})$$

$$= length[D_i] + (2 \cdot length[D_i] - size[D_i]) - (2 \cdot length[D_{i-1}] - size[D_{i-1}])$$

$$= 3 \cdot length[D_i] - 2 \cdot length[D_{i-1}] - size[D_i] + size[D_{i-1}]$$

$$= 3(size[D_{i-1}] + 1) - 3 \cdot size[D_{i-1}]$$

$$= 3$$

Thus, fixing the amortized running time of *Push* at 3 is sufficient to cover all possible scenarios under which this operation can be used.

A similar analysis demonstrates that the amortized running time of *Pop* needs to be at most 3, and the amortized running time of *MakeEmpty* is at most 2. Since the amortized running time of each STACK ADT operation is constant, we have once again demonstrated that any sequence of m STACK ADT operations requires at most $\Theta(m)$ time when using the dynamic list data structure.

10.4 THE BINARY COUNTER ADT

As another illustration of amortized analysis we will examine the n-bit BINARY COUNTER ADT, which counts upward from 0 to $2^n - 1$, and supports the following operations:

1. *Increment(C)*. Adds 1 modulo 2^n to the current value of counter C and returns the resulting binary value.
2. *Reset(C)*. Sets each bit in counter C to 0.

In Chapter 12 we will find that operations associated with certain heap data structures can be thought of in terms of a binary counter.

Let us consider implementing the n-bit BINARY COUNTER ADT using an array $b[0..n-1]$ of bits, where $b[0]$ stores the least significant bit and $b[n-1]$ stores the most significant bit of the counter. Given this data structure, we can implement the *Increment* operation using the following algorithm which is based on ripple-carry addition:

```
RC-Increment(bit array b[0..n-1])
1   i ← 0
2   while i < n and b[i] = 1 do
3         b[i] ← 0
4         i ← i + 1
5   if i < n then
6         b[i] ← 1
```

A demonstration of how this algorithm operates on a 5-bit counter that is incremented from 0 to 15 is shown in Figure 10.3.

For a single *Increment*, the running time of RC-Increment() is given by the number of bits that must be flipped from 1 to 0, or from 0 to 1. In the worst case, every bit is flipped, and RC-Increment() takes $\Theta(n)$ time on an n-bit counter. In Figure 10.3 we have shaded the bits that must be flipped in order to obtain the current counter value from the previous one. Notice that RC-Increment() terminates whenever a bit is flipped from 0 to 1. This suggests some sort of correlation between successive *Increment* operations, which we examine next using amortized analysis.

We will show that starting from a counter value of 0, a sequence of m *Increment* operations requires at most $\Theta(m)$ rather than $\Theta(mn)$ time when using RC-Increment(). Let us assign an amortized cost of 2 to set a bit to 1. Thus whenever a bit is set, we use 1 credit, and save the other on the balance sheet. This means that at any point in time, every 1 bit in C has a credit on the balance sheet. Therefore nothing needs to be charged to set a bit back to 0; instead, one of the credits on the

$b[0..4]$	counter value
0 0 0 0 0	0
0 0 0 0 1	1
0 0 0 1 0	2
0 0 0 1 1	3
0 0 1 0 0	4
0 0 1 0 1	5
0 0 1 1 0	6
0 0 1 1 1	7
0 1 0 0 0	8
0 1 0 0 1	9
0 1 0 1 0	10
0 1 0 1 1	11
0 1 1 0 0	12
0 1 1 0 1	13
0 1 1 1 0	14
0 1 1 1 1	15

FIGURE 10.3

A 5-bit binary counter as it is incremented from a value of 0 to 15. The bit values in the array $b[0..4]$ are shown to the left, and the corresponding counter value is shown to the right. The bits that must be flipped in order to obtain the current counter value from the previous one are shown shaded.

balance sheet can be used to pay for this. Since RC-Increment() is only flipping bits from 1 to 0 within the loop (lines 2–4), and only flips a bit from 0 to 1 once (on line 6), its amortized cost is 2. If we start from a counter value of 0, the balance sheet can never go negative, and therefore the amortized cost of m *Increment* operations is $\Theta(m)$.

In Exercise 10.9 you are asked to show that any sequence of m *Increment* and *Reset* operations can also be executed in $\Theta(m)$ time.

10.5 AN EXTENDED EXAMPLE: COMPETITIVE ANALYSIS OF THE MTF HEURISTIC

Now that we have examined a number of simple data structures using amortized analysis, let us consider the context in which amortized analysis is most often used— to analyze ***self-adjusting data structures***. In order to understand the difference between self-adjusting data structures and rebalancing data structures, such as AVL and red-black trees (which we discuss in Chapter 11), we make the following distinction. The form of any data structure is modified in *direct* response to certain operations. For instance, the shape of a binary search tree is always modified in response to an *Insert* or *Delete* operation. This is also the case in AVL and red-black trees, the only difference being that certain rebalancing steps may also occur as a direct result of these operations. In a self-adjusting data structure, however, modifications to the data structure may occur as a side effect of performing some operation (e.g., *Search*) that does not directly change the data structure.

We have already seen examples of self-adjusting data structures in Section 5.2.3 where several self-organizing list heuristics were presented. In this section we will use amortized analysis to demonstrate that one of these, the move-to-front (MTF) heuristic, is nearly as good as any other self-organizing list implementation of the DICTIONARY ADT. Before stating this result more precisely, let us present some preliminary information.

Recall that the operations of interest in the DYNAMIC DICTIONARY ADT are *Search*, *Insert*, and *Delete*. We will assume that any self-organizing list implementation either returns, adds, or removes the desired element before rearranging the list. Thus we can define the following minimum running times for each of these operations: If an element with the key we are looking for is located at position i in the list, then the sequential search used by the *Search* operation requires at least i time. The *Delete* operation also has a minimum running time of i in this case, since we must find an element before we can delete it. If the list has a length of i, then *Insert* has a minimum running time of $i + 1$, since we must scan the entire list to make sure the key is not already present before appending the element to the end of the list.

Specific self-organizing list algorithms may have additional costs associated with each of these operations that involve rearranging the list. We assume that for any algorithm, all rearrangement is done by exchanging pairs of consecutive list elements, and that all exchanges involve the element that was initially accessed. For example if a *Search* finds the desired element at position i, then each subsequent exchange performed after the search must involve the element stored at position i prior to the search. Thus, the first exchange after the search can either be between the elements stored at positions i and $i - 1$, or between the elements stored at positions i and $i + 1$. We can distinguish between two different types of exchanges. If a *Search* or *Insert* occurs at position i in a list, then any sequence of at most i exchanges that occur immediately after these operations, on elements located at positions prior to i, are referred to as ***free exchanges***. Note that free exchanges do not asymptotically increase the running time of a *Search* or *Insert*. All other exchanges that occur after an operation are referred to as ***paid exchanges***. Since the MTF algorithm always performs a sequence of exchanges that moves an element to the head of the list, all of the exchanges it performs are free. However, other self-organizing list algorithms may involve paid exchanges.

We are now ready to state the main result more precisely: For any self-organizing list algorithm A and any sequence of m operations starting with an empty list,

$$\sum_{i=1}^{m} c_i^{MTF} \leq 2\sum_{i=1}^{m} c_i^{A} + X^{A} - F^{A} - m \tag{10.5}$$

where c_i^{MTF} and c_i^{A} are the running times of the i-th operation when using algorithms MTF and A, respectively; while X^{A} and F^{A} are the number of paid and free exchanges, respectively, performed by A during the sequence of operations.

Before we proceed with the proof of equation (10.5), notice that we must use amortized analysis in a different way than we have previously. In previous sections of this chapter we have derived *absolute* worst-case bounds on the running time of a sequence of ADT operations. In this case we must derive a ***competitive bound***. That is, we must bound the running time of a sequence of DICTIONARY ADT operations when using the MTF algorithm, by the running time of any other possible self-organizing list algorithm on the same sequence. In this case we are comparing the MTF algorithm to an infinite number of other self-organizing list algorithms. This analysis is actually quite remarkable because it will tell us that for any sequence of operations, the MTF algorithm is nearly as good as the optimum algorithm—even if we do not know what the optimum algorithm is!

In order to use amortized analysis to prove equation (10.5), assume we simultaneously maintain two initially empty lists over the sequence of operations—one using MTF, and the other using A. Furthermore, assume that any DICTIONARY ADT operation that takes place at position β in A's list occurs at position μ in MTF's list. We will first assume that no exchanges are performed in A's list and then show, using the potential function approach, that the amortized running time of any operation in MTF's list is at most $2c^{A} - 1$, where c^{A} is the actual running time (i.e., the minimum running time derived above) of the same operation in A's list. We will subsequently extend our analysis to account for exchanges in A's list. This will allow us to arrive at the desired bound.

Let us choose as our potential function the number of inversions in MTF's list with respect to A's list. An inversion is defined as follows: For any two lists containing the same elements, an ***inversion*** in one list with respect to the other list is a 2-set of list elements $\{x, y\}$ such that x appears before y in one list, but after y in the other. For instance, consider the lists

$$L_1 : a, \ b, \ c$$
$$L_2 : a, \ c, \ b$$

Of the three possible 2-sets $\{a, b\}$, $\{a, c\}$, and $\{b, c\}$, only $\{b, c\}$ is an inversion. Note that with this potential function, the initial potential is zero since we start with empty lists, and the final potential must be nonnegative since the number of inversions is always greater than or equal to zero.

First we consider the *Search* operation. Let I_β be the element stored at position β in A's list; and let x_β be the number of elements that precede I_β in MTF's list, but follow I_β in A's list. For example if we have

$$A : \ a, \ c, \ e, \ f, \ b, \ d, \ g$$
$$MTF : \boxed{d}, \ a, \ e, \ c, \boxed{b}, \ f, \ g$$

and $\beta = 4$, then $I_\beta = f$, $\mu = 6$, $x_\beta = 2$, and the total number of inversions is 7. The elements enclosed in boxes are the ones that precede f in MTF's list, but follow it in A's list. Note that the number of common elements preceding I_β in both lists is given by $\mu - 1 - x_\beta$ (these are elements a, c, and e in the example given above). Thus if we move I_β to the front of MTF's list we create $\mu - 1 - x_\beta$ new inversions, but we remove x_β other inversions. Since the actual running time of this operation in MTF's list is μ, the amortized running time of a *Search* in MTF's list is

$$\hat{c}^{MTF} = \mu + \underbrace{(\mu - 1 - x_\beta) - x_\beta}_{\Delta\Phi}$$
$$= 2(\mu - x_\beta) - 1 \qquad (10.6)$$

However, the number of elements preceding I_β in A's list that are common to the elements preceding I_β in MTF's list (before any exchanges) can be no greater than the total number of elements preceding I_β in A's list. That is, $\mu - 1 - x_\beta \leq \beta - 1$, so we can substitute β for $\mu - x_\beta$ in equation (10.6) and upper bound the amortized running time of a *Search* in MTF's list by $2\beta - 1$. Since β is the actual running time for this operation in A's list, the amortized running time of a *Search* in MTF's list is

$$\hat{c}^{MTF} \leq 2c^A - 1 \qquad (10.7)$$

Next consider the *Insert* operation, and assume that the lists have length β prior to this operation. In this case let $I_{\beta+1}$ be the element we are inserting. Since $I_{\beta+1}$ is appended to the end of both lists, when $I_{\beta+1}$ is moved to the front of MTF's list, β new inversions are created, and none are removed. Thus the amortized running time of an *Insert* in MTF's list is

$$\hat{c}^{MTF} = (\beta + 1) + \beta$$
$$= 2c^A - 1 \qquad (10.8)$$

Finally consider the *Delete* operation, where the element being deleted is located at position β in A's list. Since no exchanges will take place in either list, no new inversions are created, and only those x_β inversions that involve the element being deleted will be removed. Therefore the amortized running time of a *Delete* in MTF's list is

$$
\begin{aligned}
\hat{c}^{MTF} &= \mu - x_\beta \\
&\leq \beta \\
&= c^A \\
&\leq 2c^A - 1
\end{aligned}
\tag{10.9}
$$

Equations (10.7), (10.8), and (10.9) demonstrate that if no exchanges occur in A's list, each of the DICTIONARY ADT operations in the MTF algorithm has an amortized running time upper bounded by $2c^A - 1$. Since the amortized running time of the sequence bounds the actual running time, it follows that

$$
\begin{aligned}
\sum_{i=1}^{m} c_i^{MTF} &\leq \sum_{i=1}^{m} (2c_i^A - 1) \\
&= \sum_{i=1}^{m} 2c_i^A - m
\end{aligned}
$$

Now we must consider what happens when exchanges are allowed in A's list. First note that each individual exchange in A's list has no actual cost in MTF's list. Each exchange in A can only increase the amortized running time of an operation on the MTF list by the number of inversions it causes (i.e., by the amount it changes the potential function). Furthermore, a single exchange will only increase or decrease the number of inversions (with respect to MTF's list before it performs any exchanges) by 1. Specifically, if there is a free exchange in A, the potential will decrease by 1; and if there is a paid exchange in A, the potential will increase by 1 (the reader should verify this on some examples). Factoring this into our sequence of operations we obtain

$$
\sum_{i=1}^{m} c_i^{MTF} \leq 2 \sum_{i=1}^{m} c_i^A + X^A - F^A - m
$$

which proves the main result of this section—the MTF algorithm is nearly optimal among self-organizing list implementations of the DICTIONARY ADT.

EXERCISES

10.1. Can amortized analysis be used to show that any sequence of m LIST ADT operations can be implemented in $\Theta(m)$ time when using a linked list?

10.2. Using the potential function given in equation (10.4) show that the amortized running time of a *Pop* operation is at most 2.

10.3. Would the amortized analysis performed in Sections 10.2.2 and 10.3.2 still hold if the dynamic list data structure was modified so that (*a*) a list contraction (by $1/2$) occurred whenever the load factor reached $1/2$ instead of $1/4$.

(*b*) a list contraction (by $2/3$) occurred whenever the load factor reached $1/3$.

If your answer is no in either case, give a specific sequence of operations that supports your claim.

10.4. A sequentially-mapped QUEUE ADT implementation that made use of the list expansion and contraction idea was discussed in Exercise 6. 11. What are the amortized costs of the QUEUE ADT operations when this data structure is used?

10.5. The DEQUE ADT was introduced in Exercise 6.12. Discuss how each of the operations supported by this ADT can be implemented in constant amortized time.

10.6. Using the binary heap data structure, we demonstrated in Section 9.3 that the *Insert* and *DeleteMin* operations had worst-case running times of $\Theta(\log n)$ when applied to an n-element priority queue. Use the potential function approach to show that for any sequence of PRIORITY QUEUE ADT operations, the amortized costs of *Insert* and *DeleteMin* are $\Theta(\log n)$ and $\Theta(1)$, respectively.

10.7. A sequence of m operations is performed on a data structure. The running time of the i-th operation is given by:

$$c_i = \begin{cases} i, & \text{if } i = 2^k, \text{ integer } k \\ 1, & \text{otherwise} \end{cases}$$

Determine the amortized running time per operation.

10.8. Develop a potential function for the n-bit BINARY COUNTER ADT that allows you to show that a sequence of m *Increment* operations requires at most $\Theta(m)$ time.

10.9. Show how to implement both the *Increment* and *Reset* operations in the n-bit BINARY COUNTER ADT using a bit-array data structure so that any sequence of m operations requires at most $\Theta(m)$ time. (Hint: Keep track of the high-order 1.)

10.10. In this exercise we consider an implementation of the DICTIONARY ADT using a list of arrays. In Section 5.2.3 we discussed how binary search on an n-element ordered array leads to a worst-case time of $\Theta(\log n)$ for the *Search* operation, but that maintaining an ordered array results in a $\Theta(n)$ worst-case running time for the *Insert* operation. Instead of using a single array, consider the following data structure which uses k arrays $A_0, A_1, \ldots, A_{k-1}$, where $k = \lceil \lg(n + 1) \rceil$, and the length of A_i equals 2^i for $i = 0, 1, \ldots, k - 1$. With this implementation, each array will be either completely empty or completely full. Specifically, if we let $< n_{k-1}, n_{k-2}, \ldots, n_0 >$ denote the binary representation of n, then A_i will be full if $n_i = 1$; otherwise it will be empty. Furthermore, assume that the data elements in each array are kept sorted, but that no particular ordering exists between the data elements in different arrays.

(*a*) Describe how a *Search* can be implemented on this data structure with a worst-case running time of $\Theta(\log n \log n) = \Theta(\log^2 n)$.

(*b*) Using this data structure, describe an efficient scheme for *Insert* that has an amortized running time of $\Theta(\log^2 n)$.

(*c*) Does this data structure support an efficient *Delete* operation?

10.11. The DEQUE-WITH-HEAP-ORDER ADT is simply the DEQUE ADT (discussed in Exercise 6.12) in which each data item has a key and one additional operation, *FindMin*, is supported. Describe a deque-with-heap-order implementation that allows all operations to be implemented in $\Theta(1)$ amortized time. (Hint: Extend the hint given in Exercise 9.10.)

10.12. In the analysis performed in Section 10.5, we assumed that for any access to the element stored at position i, algorithm A could only perform a sequence of exchanges between this element and elements it is adjacent to (prior to an exchange) in the list. Does the analysis still hold if we allow *any* pair of elements in A's list to be exchanged?

10.13. Generalize the analysis performed in Section 10.5 to the case in which MTF's and A's lists are not initially empty. (Hint: Make the initial number of list inversions a parameter in your analysis.)

10.14. We can generalize the result given in equation (10.5) by considering what happens when the MTF algorithm moves an accessed element some fixed fraction of the way towards the head of the list, instead of all the way to the head of the list. Specifically, prove that if $MTF(d)$ ($d \geq 1$) is an algorithm that takes an element at position μ and moves it $p = \lceil \mu/d \rceil - 1$ elements closer to the front of the list after a *Search* or *Insert* operation, then

$$\sum_{i=1}^{m} c_i^{MTF(d)} \leq d \left(2 \sum_{i=1}^{m} c_i^A + X^A - F^A - m \right)$$

where A is any self-organizing list algorithm that obeys the assumptions given in Section 10.5. Note that when $d = 1$, this is equation (10.5).

CHAPTER NOTES

The survey article by Tarjan [148] provides the basis for much of the material presented in this chapter. For more information on the amortized analysis of self-organizing lists see Sleator and Tarjan [138], and also Bentley and McGeoch [18]. Allen and Munro [6] were able to show that the move-to-front heuristic leads to an average-case running time that is within a constant factor of minimum, but their analysis assumes that the probabilities of accessing various data elements are fixed and independent. The DEQUE-WITH-HEAP-ORDER ADT was invented by Tarjan [147].

It is interesting to note that although amortized analysis is a fairly recent idea, the notion of having a data structure adjust itself based on the pattern of operations applied to it is not. For example, the move-to-front heuristic is, in essence, the strategy employed by nearly all virtual memory management algorithms. In a computer system that uses virtual memory, the addressable memory is broken into blocks called pages. Only a fraction of these pages will fit into main memory, with the remainder being placed in secondary storage. A list of page locations, called the **page table**, is kept and repeatedly searched by the memory management hardware to determine whether or not a page is in main memory. In order to reduce the time spent searching, the elements of the page table are organized so that the location of the most recently used page is at the head of the list, and the least recently used is at the tail. If a memory location that has been mapped to secondary storage must be accessed, the page that contains it is first swapped with the least recently used page in main memory. As a result of the locality of reference that typically occurs in programs, this self-adjusting page-swapping strategy, called the **least recently used (LRU)** algorithm, is usually very effective.

CHAPTER
11

BALANCED
SEARCH TREES

In this chapter we investigate the use of balanced trees to implement dynamic sets. In Chapter 7 we implemented this ADT using a binary search tree. Our analysis of the binary search tree demonstrated that in the worst case, any operation would require $\Theta(n)$ time. This resulted from the fact that in the worst case, the height of an n vertex binary search tree is $n - 1$. Furthermore, this worst-case height occurs whenever the dictionary elements are inserted into the binary search tree in either increasing or decreasing order—a situation that is likely to occur in practice. In this chapter we introduce a number of balanced search tree data structures that can be used to avoid building binary search trees that have this undesirable property.

The first data structure we consider, the AVL tree, comes with a worst-case $\Theta(\log n)$ running time guarantee for any DYNAMIC SET ADT operation on an n vertex tree. This is the first time in this book that we are able to make such a guarantee. The next data structure we discuss, the red-black tree, also has a worst-case $\Theta(\log n)$ running time bound for these operations. However, we will use amortized analysis to argue that this data structure is superior to the AVL tree. The final data structure we present in this chapter is the self-adjusting splay tree, which is easier to implement than the previous two data structures. We will use amortized analysis to show that any sequence of m DYNAMIC SET ADT operations can be completed in a worst-case time of $\Theta(m \log n)$ in a splay tree.

294

11.1 ROTATIONS

All of the balanced search trees we consider in this chapter are special cases of binary search trees—i.e., they have the structure of a binary tree, and obey the binary search tree property. This means that the searching strategy developed in Section 7.2.1 directly applies to these data structures. The balanced search trees discussed here are considered special cases due to the additional constraints they place on a binary search tree. Although the types of constraints they impose are quite different from one another, they all serve the general purpose of restricting the height of the resulting binary tree. In other words, the imposition of these constraints leads to the construction of balanced trees.

One property shared by all of the balanced search tree data structures we consider is that in order to satisfy their various constraints, they will reorganize their subtrees using rotations. Each of the rotation patterns we will consider is constructed by using one or more of the basic rotation operations shown in Figure 11.1. Starting with the subtree on the left in this figure, a right-rotate operation at the root vertex p proceeds by making v the new root, and p the new right child of v. The old right subtree of v is then made the new left subtree of p. The end result is the subtree shown on the right in Figure 11.1. This figure also demonstrates that the left-rotate operation is the mirror image of the right-rotate operation.

The most important feature of these basic rotation operations is that they do not destroy the binary search tree property in the subtrees they are performed on. This is easy to verify by studying the subtrees shown in Figure 11.1. Specifically, the left-to-right ordering of subtrees T_a through T_c is not changed by these rotation operations. Furthermore, most of the subtrees to the left (or right) of vertices v and p remain to the left (or right) of these vertices after either rotation. The only exceptions are subtrees T_a after a right-rotate(p), and subtree T_c after a left-rotate(v). These cases are easy to check. Consider the subtree on the left in Figure 11.1. Prior to the right-rotate(p) operation T_a is to the left of vertex p, but afterwards it is not. In fact, the vertices in T_a are no longer descendents of vertex p after this rotation. However, the subtree on the left implies key[p] > key[v] > keys[T_a], and it is easy to verify that these inequalities are not violated after the rotation. A similar argument can be made for subtree T_c after a left-rotate(v) operation. Finally, the vertices v and p do not violate the binary search tree property (with respect to each other) as a result of either rotation.

FIGURE 11.1
The two basic rotation operations used to implement all on the rotation patterns discussed in this chapter. The right-rotate(p) operation starts with the subtree on the left and produces the subtree on the right, while the left-rotate(v) operation starts with the subtree on the right and produces the one on the left.

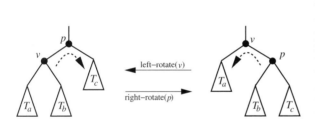

11.2 AVL TREES

The first balanced search tree data structure we consider is the AVL tree, which is defined as follows:

> **Definition 11.1. AVL Tree.** An AVL tree is a binary search tree in which the height of the left and right subtrees of any vertex differ by at most 1.

We will refer to the constraint placed on the height of subtrees in an AVL tree as the **AVL tree property**. This constraint is depicted in Figure 11.2, where v_r is the root of some subtree in a binary search tree, with left and right subtrees T_L and T_R, respectively. If T_L has a height of h, then according to the AVL tree property, T_R must have a height of either $h - 1$, h, or $h + 1$. This relationship must hold at every vertex in a binary search tree for it to be an AVL tree.

Given Definition 11.1, it is possible to prove that the height of an AVL tree containing n vertices is $\Theta(\log n)$. In order to prove this, it is sufficient to show that the longest possible path in an AVL tree from the root to a leaf is $\Theta(\log n)$. First, let $n(h)$ represent the fewest possible number of vertices in an AVL tree of height h. For example, $n(0) = 1$, $n(1) = 2$, and $n(2) = 4$. Next, let T_h be any AVL tree containing $n(h)$ vertices, where $h \geq 2$. A tree in the set T_h is a worst-case AVL tree in the sense that it has the maximum height possible on n vertices. An example of an AVL tree from the set T_4 is shown in Figure 11.3. The difference in height between the two subtrees of any vertex in this tree is one. Also note that the ordering of the

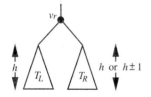

FIGURE 11.2
A subtree in a binary search tree with root vertex v_r, left subtree T_L, and right subtree T_R. Since the height of T_L and T_R differ by at most 1, this subtree obeys the AVL tree property.

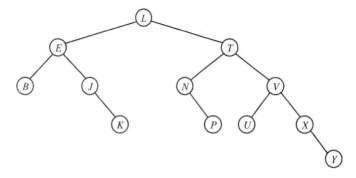

FIGURE 11.3
A worst-case AVL tree from the set of trees in T_4. By counting the number of vertices in this tree, we have that $n(4) = 12$.

alphabetic key values shown inside the vertices obeys the necessary binary search tree property.

Since a tree in T_h is an AVL tree, its left and right subtrees must also be AVL trees. Furthermore, since a tree in T_h is an AVL tree with the fewest possible number of vertices, one of the subtrees of the root must have height $h - 1$, and the other must have height $h - 2$. Thus, the number of vertices in a worst-case AVL tree of height h is given by

$$n(h) = 1 + n(h - 1) + n(h - 2)$$

If we assume that $n(h) = 0$ when $h < 0$, then the first few values of this recurrence relation are $1, 2, 4, 7, 12, 20, \ldots$, and in general

$$n(h) = F(h + 2) - 1$$

where $F(i)$ is the i-th Fibonacci number. Since $F(i) = \frac{1}{\sqrt{5}}(\phi^i - \hat{\phi}^i)$, we have that

$$n(h) = \frac{\phi^{h+2}}{\sqrt{5}} - \frac{\hat{\phi}^{h+2}}{\sqrt{5}} - 1$$

Notice that $|\hat{\phi}| = |(1 - \sqrt{5})/2|$ is less than 1. Thus the second term in the above equality approaches zero as h grows large, and the asymptotic behavior of $n(h)$ is given by $n(h) = \Theta(\phi^{h+2})$. Taking the logarithm base ϕ of this expression yields $\log_\phi n(h) = h + 2$, and solving for h we obtain

$$h = \log_\phi n(h) - 2$$

Since $n(h)$ is the number of vertices in the "worst" AVL tree of height h, we know from the above analysis that the height of any AVL tree on n vertices is $O(\log n)$. We also showed in Chapter 7 that the height of the "best" binary search tree containing n vertices is $\Theta(\log n)$. Taken together, these bounds establish that the height of any AVL tree containing n vertices is $\Theta(\log n)$.

11.2.1 Dynamic Set Operations

An AVL tree is represented in the same manner as a binary search tree—that is, as vertices containing pointers to their parent, and to their left and right children. A vertex in an AVL tree must also store an additional field that indicates the **balance** of the vertex. The balance of a vertex is determined by examining its left and right subtrees. Specifically, the balance of a vertex is given by the height of its right subtree minus the height of its left subtree. Thus, the balance of a vertex in an AVL tree is either -1, 0, or $+1$. A -1 indicates that the height of the right subtree of a vertex is one *less* than the height of its left subtree, a 0 indicates that the left and right subtrees of a vertex have the *same* height, and a $+1$ indicates that the height of the right subtree of a vertex is one *more* that the height of its left subtree. Figure 11.4 shows an example of an AVL tree with the balance of each vertex given beside it.

QUERY OPERATIONS. Because an AVL tree is a special type of binary search tree, it must maintain the binary search tree property. This means that we can use the same algorithms developed for binary search trees to perform query operations

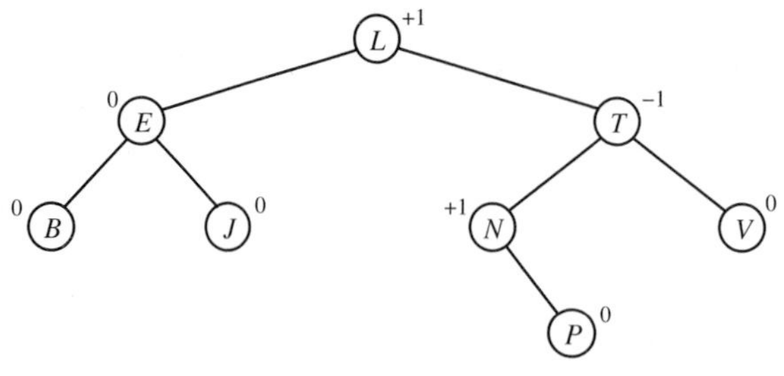

FIGURE 11.4
An example AVL tree with the balance of each vertex shown beside the vertex.

in an AVL tree. Furthermore, since we have shown that the height of an n-vertex AVL tree is $\Theta(\log n)$, we have a guarantee that in the worst case, each of these operations runs in only $\Theta(\log n)$ time. Implementing *Insert* and *Delete*, however, are not as straightforward in AVL trees as they were in binary search trees because these operations may cause the balance of a vertex to become something other than 0 or ± 1. Consider the AVL tree in Figure 11.4. If a vertex with key Q were inserted in this tree, then the balance of vertex N would become $+2$. Likewise, if vertex V were deleted, then vertex T would have a balance of -2. In either case, the tree would no longer be an AVL tree. Thus, the *Insert* and *Delete* operations used in binary search trees must be modified so that an AVL tree is *rebalanced* whenever these operations lead to an "unbalanced" tree.

INSERT OPERATION.   The *Insert* operation is accomplished as follows in an AVL tree. First, using the insertion algorithm developed for binary search trees in Section 7.2.2, trace a path from the root vertex and insert the new vertex as a leaf. This portion of the operation takes $O(\log n)$ time since the height of the tree is $\Theta(\log n)$. Next, retrace this path back to the root, updating balances along the way. If a vertex is encountered during this retracing whose balance becomes ± 2, then adjust the subtrees of this vertex so that the tree becomes a binary search tree with balance 0 or ± 1 at each vertex. The manner in which the subtrees of a vertex are adjusted during the retracing process is discussed next.

   Although it appears that a large number of possibilities would have to be considered when determining how to adjust various subtrees during rebalancing, the remarkable fact is that only two general cases need be considered. The subtrees of any vertex can be rebalanced by either performing a single rotation pattern or a double rotation pattern.

   The steps required to perform a ***single rotation pattern*** are illustrated in Figure 11.5. Part (a) of this figure shows a subtree of an AVL tree denoted by T_a. Subtree T_a contains within it two vertices with keys E and J, and three subtrees labeled T_b, T_c, and T_d, each of height h. Notice that the balance of vertex J is 0, and the balance of vertex E is $+1$. Assume that an *Insert* operation is performed, and that a new element is added to subtree T_d causing its height to become $h + 1$. As shown in Figure 11.5 (b), this insertion causes the balance of vertex J to become $+1$, and the balance of vertex E to become $+2$. Therefore, the tree no longer has the AVL tree property. In order to restore this property, a left-rotate(E) operation is performed. Figure 11.5 (c) depicts the results of this operation. In AVL trees, this rotation pattern is referred to as a ***single left rotation***.

Of course we could easily construct a subtree that is a symmetric mirror image of T_a. In this case, the balance of vertex E is -1 before the insertion, and the balances of vertices E and J are -2 and -1, respectively, after the insertion. A ***single right rotation*** pattern is required to restore the AVL tree property to this tree. In either case, the rebalancing can be implemented in $\Theta(1)$ time by simply reassigning three pointers.

If the new vertex in Figure 11.5 was added to subtree T_c instead of subtree T_d, then a single left rotation pattern would not restore the proper balance to the vertices in subtree T_a. In this case, a double rotation pattern is required. The steps required to perform a ***double rotation pattern*** are illustrated in Figure 11.6. In this figure we

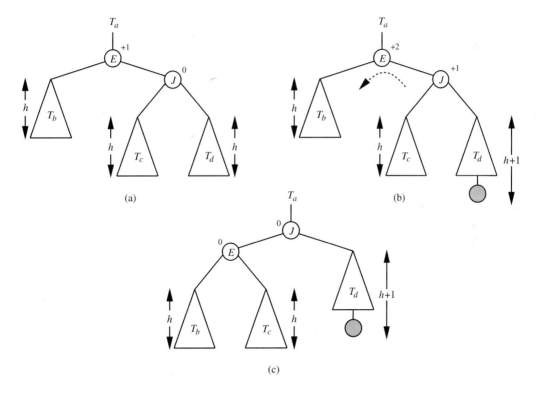

FIGURE 11.5

A single left rotation pattern applied at subtree T_a in an AVL tree. (a) Subtree T_a prior to insertion. The height of subtrees T_b through T_d are h, and the height of T_a as a whole is $h+2$. The balance of vertices E and J are $+1$ and 0, respectively. (b) Insertion of a vertex that results in the height of subtree T_d changing from h to $h+1$. This causes the balance of vertex E to become $+2$, necessitating a rebalancing of T_a. Subtree T_a is rebalanced by performing a left-rotate(E) operation. (c) Subtree T_a after rebalancing. Vertex E now has left subtree T_b, right subtree T_c, and appears to the left of vertex J. The balance of vertices E and J are now 0, and the height of T_a as a whole is $h+2$.

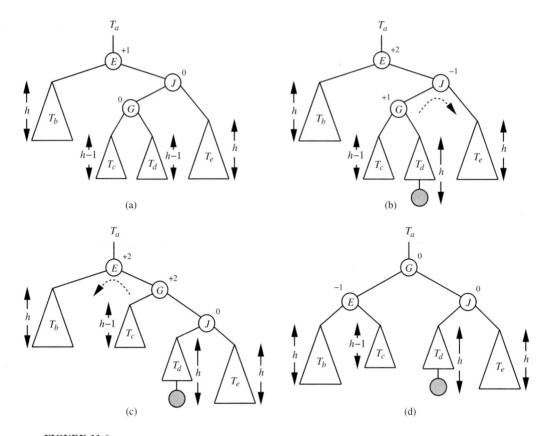

(a)   (b)   (c)   (d)

FIGURE 11.6
A double RL rotation performed after the insertion of an element in subtree T_a of an AVL tree. This
rotation pattern consists of a right-rotate operation followed by a left-rotate operation.

have broken down the subtree T_c from the previous figure into a subtree whose root
vertex is G, and whose left and right subtrees are labeled T_c and T_d respectively. We
stress that the subtrees shown in Figures 11.5 (a) and Figure 11.6 (a) are equivalent.
The only difference between these two figures is in where the new vertex is added.
Specifically, in Figure 11.6 (a) we show subtree T_a of an AVL tree that contains
within it three vertices with keys E, J, and G, and four subtrees labeled T_a, T_b,
T_c, and T_d. Notice that the balance of vertex E is $+1$. In Figure 11.6 (b), a new
vertex has been inserted into the right subtree of vertex G. This causes the balance
of vertex J to become -1 and the balance of vertex E to become $+2$. In order
to restore the AVL tree property, a right-rotate(J) is performed (the result of this
operation is shown in Figure 11.6 (c)), followed by a left-rotate(E). The resulting
subtree is shown in Figure 11.6 (d). This rotation pattern is referred to as a ***double RL
rotation***. Observe that T_a does not have the AVL tree property after the first rotation
operation since both vertices E and G have a balance of $+2$ at that point.

If the new vertex was added to the left subtree of G instead of the right subtree, then the final tree would be the same as the one in Figure 11.6, except the new vertex would be attached to subtree T_c, and the balances of vertices E and J would be 0 and $+1$ respectively. Notice that the double rotation pattern performed in Figure 11.6 can also be implemented in $\Theta(1)$ time by simply rearranging the appropriate pointers.

Once again, we could easily construct a subtree that is a symmetric mirror image of T_a, in which the balance of vertex E is initially -1, and the balances of vertices E and J are -2 and $+1$, respectively, after an insertion. In this case, the rotation pattern consists of a left-rotate(J) followed by a right-rotate(E), and we call the rotation pattern a **double LR rotation**.

An important aspect of both the single and double rotation patterns illustrated in Figures 11.5 and 11.6 is that they do not change the height of subtree T_a. In both cases, before the insertion of the new vertex, the height of T_a is $h + 2$, and after the insertion and rebalancing, the height is also $h + 2$. This observation is important because it means that the balance of the remainder of the vertices in an AVL tree are not affected by a single or a double rotation.

Thus, during the retracing step of the AVL insertion procedure, all we need to do is find the first vertex whose balance changes from ± 1 to ± 2. We will call this vertex the **pivot**. For instance, in Figures 11.5 and 11.6 the pivot is E. Once the pivot is found (if there is one) the appropriate rotation is performed, and the height of the subtree rooted at the pivot vertex will be restored to the value it had before the insertion. This means that every vertex in the tree will once again have a balance of 0 or ± 1.

We can actually simplify the retracing step further by noting that the first vertex encountered during the retracing whose balance is ± 1 is the only vertex that can possibly serve as the pivot (proof of this fact is left as Exercise 11.5). We will refer to this vertex (if it exists) as the **potential pivot**. If the balance of the potential pivot is not changed to ± 2 by the insertion, then the tree will not have to be rebalanced. Furthermore, since every vertex below the potential pivot has a balance of 0, the subtree rooted at the potential pivot must either have the form given in Figure 11.5 (a) (or its mirror image), or the form given in Figure 11.6 (a) (or its mirror image). We have already shown that any insertion leading to an unbalanced vertex in either of these subtrees can be remedied by performing either a single or a double rotation pattern. Thus, we have proven that either a single or a double rotation pattern is sufficient to rebalance the subtree rooted at a pivot (which rotation pattern is used depends upon where the new vertex is added), and that at most one of these rotation patterns is ever necessary to rebalance an entire AVL tree after an insertion.

It is not difficult to recognize when a single or a double rotation pattern should be applied during this retracing step. If the balance of the pivot is $+2$, and the balance of this vertex's right child is $+1$, then a single left rotation pattern is required (e.g., Figure 11.5); otherwise, the balance of the pivot's right child is -1, and a double RL rotation pattern is required (e.g., Figure 11.6). Similarly, if the balance of the pivot becomes -2, and the balance of this vertex's left child is -1, then a single right rotation pattern is required; otherwise, the balance of the pivot's left child is $+1$, and a double LR rotation pattern is required.

In summary, the total time required to implement the *Insert* operation in an AVL tree is $\Theta(\log n)$ in the worst case. This is due to the fact that it takes $O(\log n)$ time to add the new vertex, $O(\log n)$ time to retrace the path in order to find the pivot, and $\Theta(1)$ time to perform any necessary rebalancing.

DELETE OPERATION. Assume we wish to delete the vertex with key k. The AVL tree deletion algorithm first uses the deletion algorithm developed for binary search trees in Section 7.2.2 to remove the appropriate vertex from the tree. Recall that this may actually be the vertex that stores the inorder predecessor (or successor) of k. Next, the path from the deleted vertex's parent is retraced back to the root, updating balances along the way. If a vertex is encountered whose balance becomes ± 2, then either a single or double rotation pattern is used to restore balance.

The height of a subtree is not preserved after a deletion and rebalancing. Thus, unlike *Insert*, the *Delete* operation may require more than one rebalancing step. In the worst case, the shallowest leaf in any worst-case AVL tree (e.g., vertex B in Figure 11.3) is deleted, and every vertex along the path back to the root must be rebalanced. However, since the number of rebalancing steps is bounded by $\Theta(\log n)$, the AVL tree deletion algorithm only requires $\Theta(\log n)$ time in the worst case.

It is not always necessary to traverse the entire path back to the root during the retracing portion of this algorithm. If as a result of deleting a vertex, the balance of the deleted vertex's parent changes from 0 to ± 1, then the algorithm can terminate since the height of the subtree rooted at the parent vertex was not changed by the deletion. This fact is demonstrated on an example AVL tree in Figure 11.7. In part (a) of this figure we show an example AVL tree. In part (b) the vertex with key Z is deleted. This causes the balance of the parent vertex V to change to -1, as shown in part (c). Notice, however, that the height of the subtree rooted at V did not change. Thus the balances of any vertices further up in the tree cannot change.

Another case to consider is if the balance of the parent of the deleted vertex changes from ± 1 to 0. In this case the height of the subtree rooted at the parent's parent (i.e., grandparent) vertex will change, and a rebalancing operation may or may

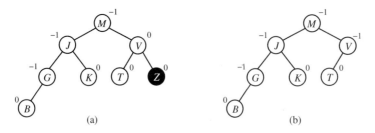

FIGURE 11.7
(a) An example AVL tree before a *Delete* operation, and **(b)** immediately after the vertex with key Z is deleted. Observe that the height of the subtree rooted at V is 1, before as well as after the deletion. Since the height of this subtree was not changed, no rebalancing is necessary; however, the balance of vertex V must be adjusted.

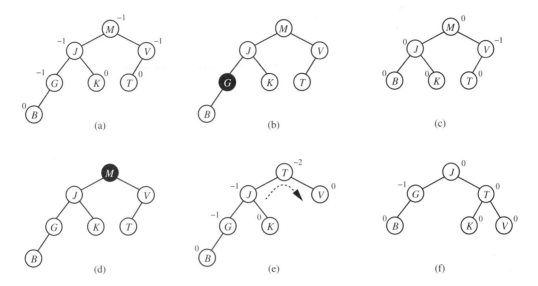

FIGURE 11.8

(a) An example AVL tree prior to any deletions. **(b)** Performing a deletion on vertex G leads to the balanced tree shown in **(c)**, and no rebalancing is required. **(d)** Deleting instead vertex M from the tree given in part (a) leads to the unbalanced tree shown in **(e)**. A single right rotation pattern restores the AVL tree property as shown in **(f)**.

not be necessary. For example, consider the tree in Figure 11.8 (a). If the vertex with key G is deleted as shown in part (b), then the balance of the parent vertex J becomes 0, and the height of the subtree rooted at the grandparent vertex (i.e., M) changes from 3 to 2. A rebalancing step is not necessary in this case since the balance of M is changed to 0 as shown in part (c). If the vertex with key M is deleted instead, as shown in part (d), then the inorder successor T is copied to the vertex that stores M, and the leaf vertex that previously stored T is deleted. Thus, the parent vertex in this case is V. Note that the balance of the parent vertex changes to 0, and that the balance of the grandparent vertex changes to -2 as shown in part (e). Thus a single right rotation pattern is required. The resulting balanced tree is shown in part (f).

The only remaining case to consider is when the balance of a vertex changes from ± 1 to ± 2 as a result of a deletion. Of course, at least one rebalancing step will always be necessary in this case.

11.3   RED-BLACK TREES

In the red-black tree data structure we adopt a coloring convention for the vertices in a binary search tree. Specifically, each vertex in a red-black tree is colored either red or black. The coloring of vertices in trees, and graphs in general, is a common practice often used to facilitate the discussion or analysis of these structures.

In order to facilitate our discussion of red-black trees, we will also assume that vertices have been added at the position of every null pointer in a binary tree. As we discussed in Section 7.4, this creates an augmented binary search tree by adding $n + 1$ external vertices (i.e., leaves) to an n-vertex binary search tree. We stress that these external vertices are needed for analysis purposes only; in practice it is not necessary to allocate memory for them. With this in mind, red-black trees are defined as follows:

> **Definition 11.2. Red-Black Tree.** A red-black tree is an augmented binary search tree in which every vertex is colored either red or black, and the arrangement of vertices obeys the following constraints:
>
> **1.** (Black rule) Every leaf is colored black.
> **2.** (Red rule) If a vertex is red, then both of its children are black.
> **3.** (Path rule) Every path from the root to a leaf contains the same number of black vertices.

We will say that a tree obeys the ***red-black properties*** if it satisfies the rules listed in this definition. An example red-black tree is shown in Figure 11.9.

It is important to note that if an augmented binary tree obeys the path rule, then this same rule is automatically satisfied at the root of every subtree in the tree as well. In other words, in a red-black tree, every path from a vertex to any descendent leaf must contain the same number of black vertices, and therefore, every subtree in a red-black tree is itself a red-black tree. We will refer to the number of black vertices on any path from, but not including, a given vertex v to a descendent leaf as the ***black-height*** of v, denoted $bh(v)$.

To what extent do the constraints imposed by the red-black properties restrict the height of red-black trees? We will show that a red-black tree with n internal vertices has a height of at most $2 \lg(n + 1)$. In order to do this, we will first prove that the subtree rooted at any vertex v in a red-black tree contains at least $2^{bh(v)} - 1$ internal vertices. This claim can be established using induction on the black-height of v. For the base case, v is a leaf; therefore it has a black-height of 0, the number of internal vertices is 0, and $2^0 - 1 = 0$. Now consider a vertex v that has a black-height of at least 1, which means it must be an internal vertex. Each child of v must have a black-height of either $bh(v)$, if it is red, or $bh(v) - 1$, if it is black. Using the induction hypothesis, we can write that the subtree rooted at v has at least $(2^{bh(v)-1} - 1) + (2^{bh(v)-1} - 1) + 1 = 2^{bh(v)} - 1$ internal vertices, which establishes our claim.

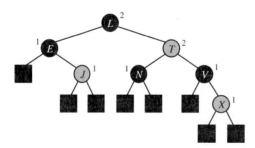

FIGURE 11.9

An example red-black tree in which the black vertices are shown darkened, the red vertices are shaded, and the external vertices are drawn as boxes. The black-height of each vertex, which is the number of black vertices in any path from, but not including, a given vertex to a descendent leaf, is shown beside it. The black-height of this tree is 2 since this is the black-height of the root vertex.

Now, the red rule implies that at least half of the vertices on any path from the root to a leaf in a red-black tree must be black. Therefore if an n-vertex red-black tree has a height of h, its root must have a black-height of at least $h/2$. Combining this with the previous claim means that

$$n \geq 2^{h/2} - 1$$

and solving for h yields

$$h \leq 2\lg(n + 1)$$

which demonstrates that a red-black tree with n internal vertices has a height of at most $2\lg(n + 1)$.

11.3.1 Dynamic Set Operations

Once again, we will assume that a red-black tree is represented in the same manner as a binary search tree, except that each vertex must store an additional field that indicates its color. Because two different colors can be uniquely encoded using one bit, a red-black tree implementation will require only one additional bit of storage per vertex, as compared to a standard binary search tree implementation.

QUERY OPERATIONS. Just like in AVL trees, the fact that red-black trees satisfy the binary search trees property means that we can use the previously developed binary search tree algorithms to perform all DYNAMIC SET ADT query operations. And since we have shown that the height of a red-black tree is $O(\log n)$, the worst-case running time for each of these operations is $\Theta(\log n)$. However, the insertion or deletion of a vertex in a red-black tree may cause some of the red-black properties to be violated. Next we consider how the red-black properties can be restored, after performing an insertion or deletion, via a sequence of rotation and recoloring steps.

INSERT OPERATION. Once again the binary search tree insertion algorithm is used to perform the actual insertion of a vertex in red-black trees. However, for analysis purposes, you should think of this vertex as a subtree consisting of a red vertex (containing the data element we wish to insert) and two black children. Recall that with the binary search tree insertion algorithm, all vertices are inserted as leaves. Therefore, an insertion in a red-black tree can be thought of as the replacement of an external black vertex with a subtree consisting of a red root and two black children. For instance, if we inserted an element with key G into the red-black tree shown in Figure 11.9, the new subtree would replace the external vertex at the left child of J, as shown in Figure 11.10 (a). This strategy guarantees that the black and path rules remain satisfied in the resulting tree; however, it may cause the red rule to be violated, which is in fact the case in Figure 11.10 (a).

In order to demonstrate how the red-black properties can be reestablished, while at the same time maintaining the binary search tree property, let us consider the general case in which a vertex labeled v has been inserted into a red-black tree

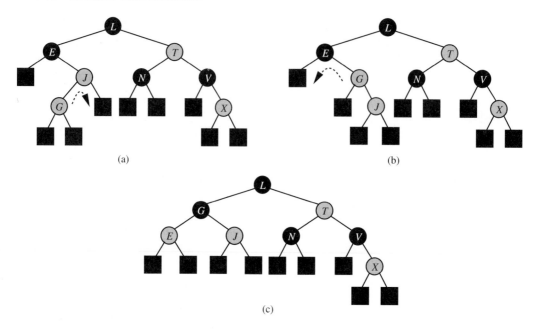

FIGURE 11.10

The *Insert*(*G*) operation in the red-black tree given in Figure 11.9. **(a)** A subtree consisting of the red vertex *G* and two black children replaces the external vertex that was previously at the left subtree of vertex *J*. This leads to a violation of the red rule at vertex *J*. Since *G*'s grandparent is black, *J* is to the right of *E*, and *G* is to the left of *J*, we must perform the (symmetric version of the) double rotation shown in Figure 11.11 (c). **(b)** The result of the first rotation, a right-rotate(*J*). **(c)** The final red-black tree that results from the second rotation, a left-rotate(*E*), and a recoloring.

T, and let us label *v*'s parent with a *p*, *v*'s grandparent with a *g*, and *v*'s uncle (i.e., *p*'s sibling) with a *u*. For example in Figure 11.10 (a), if *v* is the vertex with key *G*, then *p* is the vertex with key *J*, *g* is the vertex with key *E*, and *u* is the external vertex that is the left child of the vertex with key *E*.

If *v* is the root then *T* automatically satisfies the red-black properties. Likewise, if *p* is black, then *T* remains a red-black tree after inserting *v*, and nothing more needs to be done. If on the other hand *p* is red, then *T* must be modified in order to reestablish the red rule. These modifications require a recoloring of the vertices, and may also involve subtree rotations.

First let us consider the case in which *p* is the root, and it is red. By simply recoloring *p* black we reestablish the red rule, turning *T* back into a red-black tree. More generally *p* will not be the root, and there are only three cases that we need to distinguish: one involving recoloring only, and two involving rotations and recoloring (each having a symmetric variant). First note that since *p* is red, the red rule implies that its parent *g* must be black, and since red-black trees are augmented binary trees, the vertex we labeled *u* must also exist. It is the color of *u* that determines whether a recoloring pattern or a rotation/recoloring pattern needs to be performed.

If u is red, as shown on the left side of Figure 11.11 (a), then the recoloring pattern shown on the right side of Figure 11.11 (a) will reestablish the red rule in the subtree rooted at g. We have not indicated whether v is the left or right child of p; in either case the same recoloring pattern will be performed. Furthermore, if g's parent is black, this recoloring is all that is needed to turn T back into a red-black tree. However if g's parent is red, T once again violates the red rule, but this time at g's parent rather than at p. We are then back to the original problem—only it occurs two levels higher up in the tree. Thus in the worst case this recoloring pattern will propagate all the way back to the root of T.

The next two cases, which occur when u is black, lead to an adjustment pattern involving either one or two rotations, depending upon whether v is the left or right child of p. When v is a left child, as shown on the left side of Figure 11.11 (b), a right-rotate(g) followed by the recoloring shown on the right side of Figure 11.11 (b) suffices to reestablish the red rule in this subtree. Furthermore, since the subtree root ends up being black, the entire tree T must now satisfy the red-black properties.

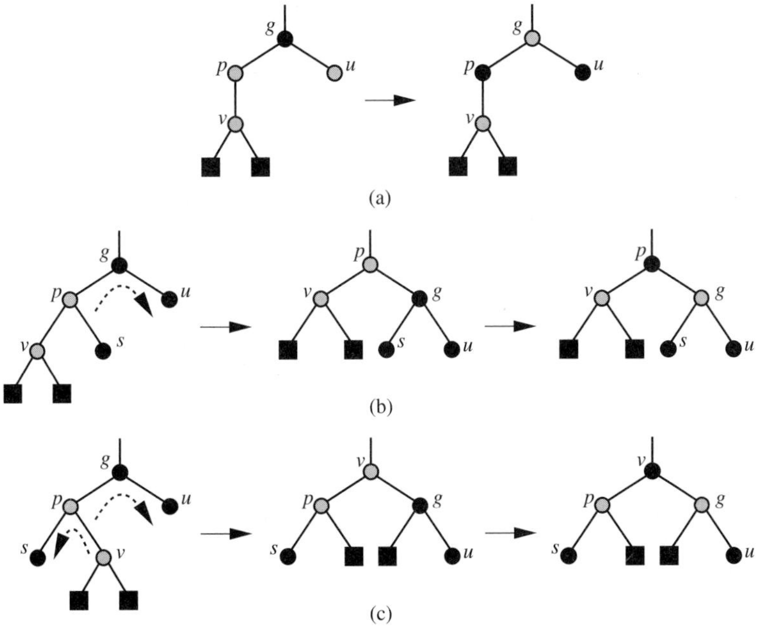

(a)

(b)

(c)

FIGURE 11.11
The three adjustment patterns that may be necessary after the insertion of a vertex v in a red-black tree. Adjustments are only necessary when p is red. The labels are used for identification purposes only; they are *not* keys. **(a)** When u is red only a recoloring is needed. This may propagate up the tree, leading to additional rotations and/or recolorings. **(b)** If u is black and v is a left child we apply a right-rotate(g) operation (middle) followed by a recoloring (right). This will stop propagation. **(c)** If u is black and v is a right child we apply a double rotation consisting of a left-rotate(p) followed by a right-rotate(g) operation (middle), and then recoloring (right). This will also stop propagation.

The third adjustment pattern occurs when v is a right child, as shown in Figure 11.11 (c). A left-rotate(p) followed by a right-rotate(g) leads to the subtree shown in the middle of Figure 11.11 (c). A recoloring step then produces the red-black subtree shown on the right. Since the root of the subtree becomes black, we know that T now satisfies the red-black properties.

Returning to the insertion shown in Figure 11.10 (a), since G's grandparent is black, J is to the right of E, and G is to the left of J, we must perform the (symmetric version of the) adjustment pattern shown in Figure 11.11 (c). The result of the first rotation is shown in Figure 11.10 (b), and the result of the second rotation and recoloring is shown in Figure 11.10 (c).

In summary, since each of these adjustment patterns takes $\Theta(1)$ time, and in the worst case they will propagate back to the root, the worst-case running time of an insertion in a red-black tree is $\Theta(\log n)$.

DELETE OPERATION. The initial portion of the red-black tree deletion algorithm uses the binary search tree deletion algorithm to remove the appropriate vertex from the tree. In Section 7.2.2 we showed that this will always result in the removal of a vertex u containing at most one child (i.e., eventually either a case 1 or case 2 deletion). Since we are dealing with red-black trees, this means that at least one of u's children is an external black vertex, and we can think of a deletion as the replacement of u with either an external vertex (case 1) or an internal vertex (case 2) that may have a subtree attached to it. In either case, let us label the replacement vertex v.

If u is a red vertex, then according to the red rule v must be black, and the replacement of u with v will lead to a tree that still satisfies the red-black properties. The red-black properties will also remain satisfied, no matter what the color of u, if u is the root. However if u is a non-root black vertex, then replacing it with v will lead to a tree that no longer satisfies the black rule—any path from v to a descendent leaf will now be deficient one black vertex. If we were somehow able to give v an extra unit of black color (i.e., if v were "doubly black"), then the black rule would be restored. We cannot actually make a vertex doubly black, but thinking of it in these terms will help us derive some adjustment patterns that reestablish the black rule. Specifically, if u is black, then after its deletion we can think of v as containing an extra unit of black color that must be absorbed by one of its ancestors.

There are only four general cases (each having a symmetric variant) that need to be distinguished when v is a non-root black vertex. The adjustment patterns needed to restore the black rule for each of these cases is shown in Figure 11.12. Each part in this figure shows a subtree in a red-black tree T immediately *after* vertex u has been replaced with vertex v. A vertex containing an extra unit of black color is identified using a "+" superscript.

To determine the appropriate adjustment pattern, we first look at the color of v's sibling vertex s. If s is red, then according to the red rule both of its children as well as its parent must be black. This situation is shown on the left side of Figure 11.12 (a). For this case, the first step in the adjustment pattern is a left-rotate(p) operation. In the resulting subtree, shown in the middle of the figure, n_r has lost one of its black ancestors. By recoloring s black and p red in this subtree,

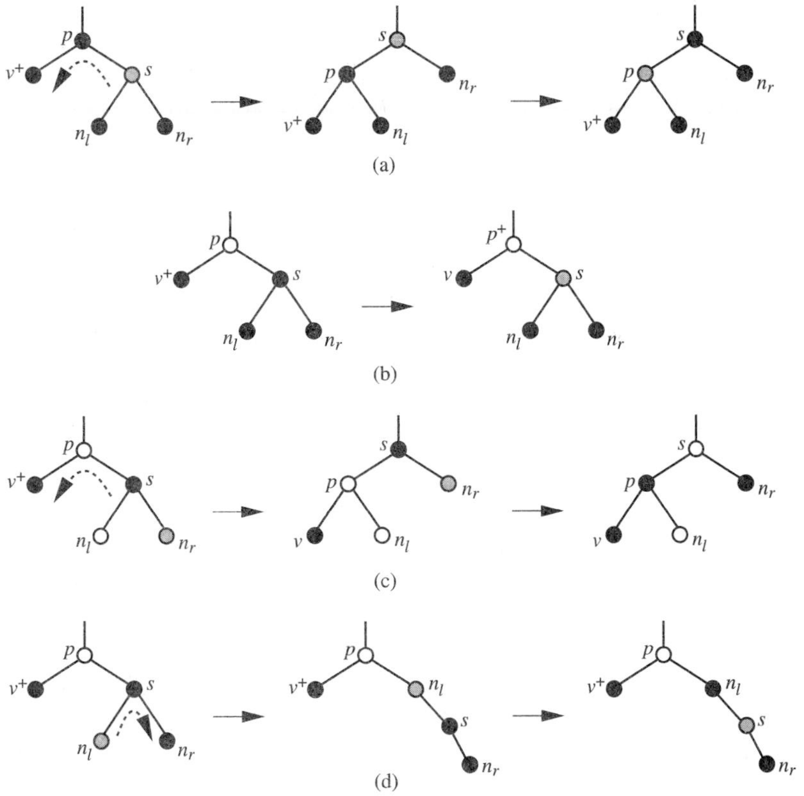

FIGURE 11.12

The four adjustment patterns that may be necessary after the deletion of a vertex u from a red-black tree. The vertex that replaced u is labeled v. Adjustments are needed only if v is a nonroot black vertex. The labels are used for identification purposes only; they are *not* keys. A vertex containing a label with a "+" superscript has an extra unit of black color. **(a)** If s is red a left-rotate(p) operation (middle), followed by the recoloring shown on the right, transforms this case into one of the other three cases. **(b)** If s and its two children are black, only a recoloring is needed. This may propagate up the tree. **(c)** If s is black and its right child is red we apply a left-rotate(p) operation (middle), followed by the recoloring shown on the right. This restores the black rule in the tree. **(d)** If s and its right child are black, and its left child is red, we apply a right-rotate(s) operation (middle) followed by the recoloring shown on the right. This case is now transformed into the one shown in part (c).

n_r will obtain the proper number of black ancestors; however, v still retains the extra unit of black color, as shown in the rightmost subtree of Figure 11.12 (a). We have now changed the problem into one where v's sibling (now labeled n_l) is black, and this case is handled by one of the three remaining adjustment patterns shown in Figure 11.12.

If s is black, the necessary rotations are completely determined by the colors of s's children, and are independent of the color of p. For this reason p is drawn as a empty circle in the initial subtrees of parts (b)–(d) in Figure 11.12. The empty circle can be treated as either a red or black vertex. The three possible adjustment patterns that can occur when s is black are discussed next.

For the case shown in Figure 11.12 (b), both of s's children are black. The adjustment pattern for this case involves recoloring only. Specifically, s is recolored red, as shown on the right side of Figure 11.12 (b), which means that both n_l and n_r now have one too few black ancestors. Observe that the extra unit of black color has been passed along to p. If p is red, then the black rule is reestablished in T by recoloring p black (i.e., by letting p absorb the extra unit of black color). If, however, p was originally black, then the extra unit of black color cannot be absorbed by p, and adjustments must propagate up the tree. In the worst case a sequence of recolorings propagates all the way back to the root of T.

The next case, shown in Figure 11.12 (c), occurs when n_r is red, independent of the color of n_l. The adjustment proceeds by first performing a left-rotate(p) operation, the result of which is shown in the middle of the figure. Since v now has an additional black ancestor in this subtree, the extra unit of black color has been absorbed. In the recoloring shown on the right side of this figure n_r is made black, and the colors of s and p were swapped (this part is only necessary if p is red). This will restore the black rule in T.

The final case, shown in Figure 11.12 (d), occurs when n_l is red, and n_r is black. First a right-rotate(s) operation is performed. The resulting subtree is shown in the middle of the figure. This subtree is recolored as shown on the right side of the figure. Notice that v retains its extra unit of black color; however, its new sibling (labeled n_l) now has a red right child (labeled s). Therefore we have reduced this case to the previous case.

In summary, since each of these adjustment patterns takes $\Theta(1)$ time, and in the worst case a sequence of adjustments can propagate back to the root, the worst-case running time of a deletion in a red-black tree is $\Theta(\log n)$.

11.3.2   Amortized Analysis

We have shown that red-black trees, like AVL trees, have a logarithmic guarantee on the worst-case running time of any DYNAMIC SET ADT operation. However, red-black trees possess another important property that can be revealed using amortized analysis—namely that the sum of the adjustment patterns that may occur during any single *Insert* or *Delete* operation has an amortized complexity of $\Theta(1)$. Using this fact, we can argue that the constants associated with the logarithmic running times of these operations are small.

In order to define a potential function for a red-black tree T, let V_b denote the set of black vertices in T. Next define the functions

$$f_b(v) = \begin{cases} 1, & \text{if both of vertex } v\text{'s children are black} \\ 0, & \text{otherwise} \end{cases}$$

and

$$f_r(v) = \begin{cases} 1, & \text{if both of vertex } v\text{'s children are red} \\ 0, & \text{otherwise} \end{cases}$$

A potential function for T can then be defined as

$$\Phi(T) = 2 \sum_{v \in V_b} f_r(v) + \sum_{v \in V_b} f_b(v) \tag{11.1}$$

In other words, the potential of T is given by twice the number of black vertices with two red children, plus the number of black vertices with two black children. According to this definition, the potential of a red-black tree can never be negative, and the potential of an empty red-black tree is zero. Thus equation (11.1) is a valid potential function.

Except for pattern (a) in Figure 11.11 and pattern (b) in Figure 11.12, any single adjustment pattern that may occur during an insertion or deletion takes $\Theta(1)$ actual time. Furthermore, it is not difficult to use equation (11.1) to show that these constant-time adjustment patterns can only change the potential of a red-black tree by a constant amount (see Exercise 11.14).

The actual worst-case running time of a sequence of adjustments during an insertion or deletion is $\Theta(\log n)$. But this can only happen during an insertion if g's parent is red on repeated applications of pattern (a) in Figure 11.11, and during a deletion if p is black on repeated applications of pattern (b) in Figure 11.12. Equation (11.1) can be used to show that any time adjustment pattern (a) in Figure 11.11 is applied, the change in potential will be -1. Likewise, any time adjustment pattern (b) in Figure 11.11 is applied, the change in potential will be -2. Thus the cost of any application of pattern (a) in Figure 11.11 or pattern (b) in Figure 11.12 is covered by the release of potential energy. Therefore the amortized cost of any sequence of adjustment patterns following an insertion or deletion is $\Theta(1)$.

11.4 SPLAY TREES

Another interesting data structure that supports all of the DYNAMIC SET ADT operations is the splay tree. A splay tree is a binary search tree in which all of the DYNAMIC SET ADT operations are implemented using a restructuring scheme called a *splay*. This self-adjusting heuristic involves moving a given vertex v to the root of the splay tree via a sequence of rotations. Like the move-to-front heuristic in self-organizing lists, the motivation behind splaying is to reduce the total time spent accessing data elements by moving the most frequently accessed ones toward the root of the tree, where they can be found more quickly.

It is interesting to compare this strategy to the one underlying AVL and red-black trees. With AVL and red-black trees, the access history of data elements is not explicitly utilized; the goal instead is to ensure that the tree never becomes unbalanced, thereby guaranteeing that any one access never requires more than $O(\log n)$ time. With splay trees we are not so much concerned with the cost of a single access, which may be as bad as $O(n)$; rather we want to ensure that this type of behavior cannot happen repeatedly. The result is that it is not necessary to store any type of balance information in the vertices of splay trees, making them more space efficient while at the same time simplifying their implementation.

The manner in which a vertex is rotated to the root must be considered carefully if we wish to derive efficient amortized running times. Splaying uses the following strategy: At each step of the splay process, one of three basic rotation patterns is used. Let us assume a splay is being performed at vertex v, whose parent and grandparent vertices (if they exist) are labeled p and g, respectively. Then the three cases (each having a symmetric variant) to consider at each step are:

1. Zig pattern—If p is the root of the tree and v is a left child, perform a right-rotate(p) operation as shown in Figure 11.13 (a). This case always terminates the splay since v will have reached the root.
2. Zig-zig pattern—If p is not the root, and v and p are both left children, perform a right-rotate(g) followed by a right-rotate(p) as shown in Figure 11.13 (b).
3. Zig-zag pattern—If p is not the root, p is a left child and v is a right child, perform a left-rotate(p) followed by a right-rotate(g) as shown in Figure 11.13 (c).

Figure 11.14 demonstrates how these rotation patterns are used in a typical splay. In this example, observe how the tree becomes more balanced as a result of performing the splay.

11.4.1 Dynamic Set Operations

As mentioned previously, a splay tree can be represented in exactly the same manner as a binary search tree, i.e., without storing any additional information at the vertices. However, unlike the AVL and red-black trees, *any* DYNAMIC SET ADT operation in a splay tree may lead to a modification of the underlying data structure.

QUERY OPERATIONS. The *Search* operation in a splay tree can now be described. Assume we are searching for an element with key k. Since a splay tree obeys the binary search tree property, we can use the same technique used in binary search trees to look for the element. If a vertex v containing an element with key k is found, the tree is splayed at v and the element is returned. If, on the other hand, the search is unsuccessful, then the last vertex examined prior to reaching a null pointer is splayed and the null value is returned. In this case, the vertex moved to the root will contain either the inorder successor or predecessor of the key we are searching for. Since the path taken up the tree during the splay is the reverse of the one followed down the tree by the search, the running time of the entire operation is proportional to (i.e., within a constant factor of) the time taken splaying the tree.

All other DYNAMIC SET ADT query operations are implemented in a similar fashion. For each of these operations, if the target of the query is found, the vertex containing it is splayed. On the other hand, if a query is unsuccessful, then the form of the query determines which vertex is splayed. Again, the key idea is to make sure that the running time of the entire operation is proportional to the splaying time. Thus, for the *Maximum* and *Minimum* operations, the last vertex examined before determining that the query was unsuccessful is the one that is splayed to the root.

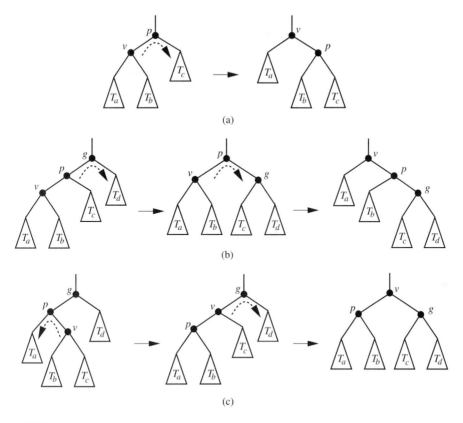

(a)

(b)

(c)

FIGURE 11.13
The three rotation patterns that can be used during a splay. Each case has a symmetric variant that is not shown. In each case, the splay is being performed at vertex v, whose parent and grandparent vertices are labeled p and g, respectively (v, p, and g are *not* the key values of these vertices). **(a)** Vertex p is the root; this leads to a zig rotation pattern which will terminate the splay process. **(b)** Vertices v and p are both left children; thus a zig-zig rotation pattern is performed. **(c)** Vertex v is a right child and vertex p is a left child; thus a zig-zag rotation pattern is performed.

For the *Predecessor* operation, two cases must be considered. Assume we are trying to find the predecessor of a vertex v with key k. If this vertex does not exist, then the search for it will lead to a null pointer. The last vertex examined prior to reaching this null pointer should be splayed. If v does exist, but it does not have a predecessor in the tree, then v should be splayed. Referring to the pseudocode for BST-Predecessor() given in Section 7.2.1 it is easy to see that in this latter case, v will be the deepest vertex accessed in the tree and therefore determines the running time of the operation. The *Successor* operation is implemented in a similar fashion.

INSERT OPERATION. An *Insert* is implemented using a simple modification to the standard binary search tree insertion method discussed in Section 7.2.2. That is, we

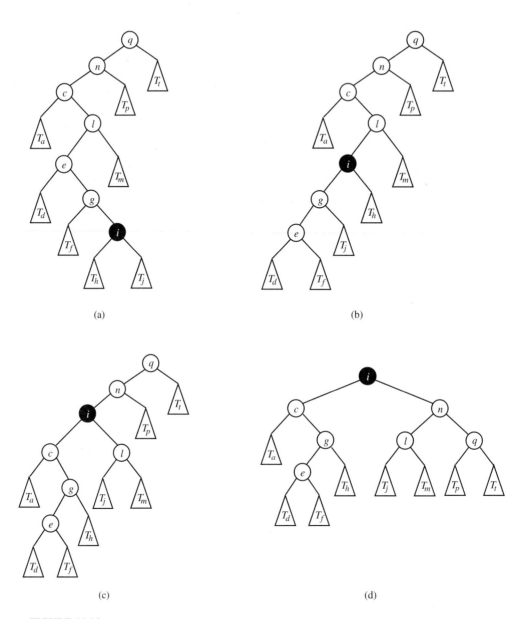

FIGURE 11.14

The sequence of steps taken during a splay of the vertex with key i. (a) The initial splay tree. (b) The splay tree after the first step (a zig-zig). (c) The splay tree after the second step (a zig-zag). (d) The final step, which is a zig-zig, causes the vertex being splayed to reach the root.

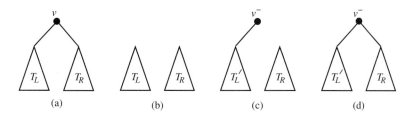

FIGURE 11.15
Deletion of vertex v from a splay tree. **(a)** The tree after splaying v to the root. **(b)** Deletion of v leads to two separate splay trees T_L and T_R. **(c)** Performing the *Maximum* operation on T_L causes the inorder predecessor of v, denoted v^-, to be splayed to the root. **(d)** Making T_R the right child of v^- completes the operation.

start by searching for the insertion point; if a null pointer is encountered the new vertex is added, as before, to the tree at this point as a leaf. The new vertex is then splayed. However, if an element with the key we are looking for already exists in the tree, then it is splayed.

DELETE OPERATION.   A *Delete* is the most complicated operation to implement since it involves two splays. First the vertex we wish to delete must be found (if it cannot, then the last vertex encountered by this search is splayed). Let us assume the key we are looking for is found at vertex v. Then v is splayed to the root (as shown in Figure 11.15 (a)) and then removed. This leaves us with two separate splay trees as shown in Figure 11.15 (b), and the binary search tree property ensures that every key in T_L is less than every key in T_R. To join these two trees back together we rearrange one of the trees, say T_L, by performing a *Maximum* on it. This will cause the inorder predecessor of v, denoted v^-, to move to the root of T_L as shown in Figure 11.15 (c). Since v^- contains the maximum key in T_L it will not have a right child, and the operation is completed by making the root of T_R the right child of v^-. If we wish instead to rearrange T_R, then a *Minimum* would be performed on T_R prior to adding T_L to it.

11.4.2   Amortized Analysis

Although the running time of any DICTIONARY ADT operation can be as much as $\Theta(n)$ when applied to an n-element splay tree, we will show that any sequence of m such operations that starts from an empty tree and grows to a maximum size of n takes at most $\Theta(m \log n)$ time. In order to do this, we will define a potential function that leads to an amortized running time of $\Theta(\log n)$ for performing all of the rotations in any given splay. Define $w(v)$, the weight of vertex v, to be the number of descendents of vertex v (including v itself) and define $r(v)$, the rank of vertex v, to be $\lg w(v)$. Using this notation, a potential function that accomplishes our goal is given by the sum of the vertex ranks in a splay tree T:

$$\Phi(T) = \sum_{v \in T} r(v) \qquad (11.2)$$

We will use primes to distinguish the rank (or weight) of a vertex after the completion of a rotation step from its rank (or weight) prior to the rotation step. For instance, if we are splaying vertex v, and k rotation steps are needed to move v to the root, then the rank of v prior to each step in the splay is given by the sequence $r(v), r'(v), r''(v), \ldots, r^{(k-1)}(v)$. Furthermore, if there are n vertices in the tree then $r^{(k)}(v)$, the rank of v after the rotation that causes it to reach the root, equals $\lg n$.

We will subsequently show that the actual cost of a single zig-zig or zig-zag rotation pattern applied at vertex v, plus the change in potential due to this step, is no greater than $3(r'(v) - r(v))$. In the case of the zig pattern this quantity will be no greater than $3(r'(v) - r(v)) + 1$. If these bounds can be established, it follows that the amortized cost of the splay process is $O(\log n)$. Specifically, in a k-step splay

$$
\begin{aligned}
\hat{c} &< 3\left(r'(v) - r(v)\right) + 3\left(r''(v) - r'(v)\right) + \cdots + 3\left(r^{(k)}(v) - r^{(k-1)}(v)\right) + 1 \\
&= 3\left(r^{(k)}(v) - r(v)\right) + 1 \\
&= 3\left(\lg n - r(v)\right) + 1 \\
&= O(\log n)
\end{aligned}
\tag{11.3}
$$

Since we have previously shown that the running time of each DYNAMIC SET ADT operation is proportional to the running time of a splay, it follows that any sequence of m DYNAMIC SET ADT operations, requires at most $\Theta(m \log n)$ time.

Let us now concentrate on establishing the bounds used to derive the amortized complexity of a splay in equation (11.3). We will consider each of the three rotation patterns separately:

1. Referring to Figure 11.13 (a) we see that only vertices v and p can change rank. According to equation (11.2) this means that $\Delta\Phi(T) = (r'(p) - r(p)) + (r'(v) - r(v))$. Since the actual running time for the zig pattern is proportional to 1 (i.e., it only involves one rotation), using equation (10.2) we can write

$$
\begin{aligned}
\hat{c}^{\text{zig}} &= 1 + \left(r'(p) - r(p)\right) + \left(r'(v) - r(v)\right) \\
&< 1 + r'(v) - r(v) \\
&< 1 + 3(r'(v) - r(v))
\end{aligned}
$$

where we are using the fact that $r(p) > r'(p)$ to obtain the inequality on the second line, and the fact that $r'(v) > r(v)$ to obtain the last inequality.

2. Referring to Figure 11.13 (b) we see that the change in potential resulting from the zig-zig pattern is due entirely to the change in ranks of vertices v, p, and g. The actual running time of this pattern is proportional to 2 since it involves two rotations; thus we have

$$
\begin{aligned}
\hat{c}^{\text{zig-zig}} &= 2 + \left(r'(g) - r(g)\right) + \left(r'(p) - r(p)\right) + \left(r'(v) - r(v)\right) \\
&= 2 + r'(g) + r'(p) - r(p) - r(v) \\
&< 2 + r'(g) + r'(v) - 2r(v) \\
&< 3(r'(v) - r(v))
\end{aligned}
$$

where we used the fact that $r'(v) = r(g)$ to establish the equality on the second line, and the fact that $r(p) > r(v)$ and $r'(v) > r'(p)$ to obtain the inequality on the third line. The last inequality requires some additional explanation. Let us start by noting that the last two lines,

$$2 + r'(g) + r'(v) - 2r(v) \; < \; 3(r'(v) - r(v))$$

can be simplified to

$$2 + r'(g) + r(v) \; < \; 2r'(v) \tag{11.4}$$

In order to verify that the zig-zig pattern satisfies equation (11.4) let us return to Figure 11.13 (b); with a little thought, the reader should see that $w'(g) + w(v) < w'(v)$. Using the fact that if $x + y < z$, and x and y are both positive integers, then $\lg x + \lg y < 2 \lg z - 2$, we can write $\lg w'(g) + \lg w(v) < 2 \lg w'(v) - 2$. Finally, using the definition of rank this becomes $2 + r'(g) + r(v) < 2r'(v)$, which confirms the desired bound in equation (11.4).

3. Referring to Figure 11.13 (c) we see that once again only three vertices can change rank, and that the actual running time of the zig-zag pattern is proportional to 2. This implies

$$
\begin{aligned}
\hat{c}^{\text{zig-zag}} &= 2 + \big(r'(g) - r(g)\big) + \big(r'(p) - r(p)\big) + \big(r'(v) - r(v)\big) \\
&< 2 + r'(p) + r'(g) - 2r(v) \\
&< 2(r'(v) - r(v)) \\
&< 3(r'(v) - r(v))
\end{aligned}
$$

where the second line follows from the fact that $r'(v) = r(g)$ and $r(v) < r(p)$, and the second-to-last inequality is established using a technique similar to the one used in the previous case. Specifically, from Figure 11.13 (c) we see that $w'(g) + w'(p) < w'(v)$, which implies $2 + r'(g) + r'(p) < 2r'(v)$. Substituting this result into the second line leads to the inequality $\hat{c}^{\text{zig-zag}} < 2(r'(v) - r(v))$, which is upper bounded by the quantity on the last line.

Thus, we have verified the assumptions used to derive the $O(\log n)$ amortized running time for splay in equation (11.3). Furthermore, by changing the definition of vertex weight, it is possible to use the potential function given in equation (11.2) to demonstrate some additional desirable properties of splay trees (see, for instance, Exercise 11.18).

11.5 AN EXTENDED EXAMPLE: PERSISTENT DATA STRUCTURES

Consider a data structure that has a sequence of operations applied to it. Let us define the state of the data structure after the i-th operation as the form that it has after operations $1, 2, \ldots, i$ have been performed. With the DYNAMIC SET ADT we have made a distinction between those operations that update the form of a data structure, namely insertion and deletion, and those that do not, namely the query operations. In all of the various data structures we have used to implement the DYNAMIC SET ADT, performing even a single update operation makes it essentially impossible to determine the previous states of the data structure. In many applications, such as text editing or computational geometry, it is often necessary to access the previous states of a data structure. This capability is also useful in database applications; consider, for instance, a customer who is no longer serviced by a particular company, but who is disputing a transaction that occurred in the past.

A *persistent data structure* allows ADT operations to be applied to previous states. The data structure is *partially persistent* if all previous states can be accessed via query operations, but only the current state can have update operations applied to it. In a *fully persistent* data structure any operation can be performed on any state of the data structure. In this extended example we will focus on implementing partially persistent data structures. We will refer to a non-persistent data structure as an ordinary data structure.

One brute-force approach to the implementation of persistent data structures simply saves a complete copy of an ordinary data structure (along with a corresponding time stamp) prior to performing any update operation. If an AVL or red-black tree is used for the ordinary data structure, and $\Theta(m)$ operations are performed, then any operation can be performed on any state of the data structure in $O(\log m)$ time. Here binary search is used to find the appropriate state in $O(\log m)$ time, and this is followed by an $O(\log m)$ time search in the resulting tree. Each update operation will also increase by $\Theta(m)$ the amount of space used by this persistent data structure. Thus the space requirements of this approach are $O(m^2)$.

An alternative is to store the actual sequence of operations, and no copies of the ordinary data structure. In this case the i-th state of the data structure is rebuilt by starting from the initial configuration of the data structure, and performing the first i operations. Using this approach with a balanced search tree requires only $\Theta(m)$ storage, but accessing the i-th state takes $O(m \log m)$ time.

A space-time compromise involves storing the entire operation sequence, and every j-th state of the data structure, for some suitably chosen value of j. With this approach, accessing state i of the data structure requires that we rebuild it starting from state $j \lfloor i/j \rfloor$. However, no matter how j is chosen, it is not possible for a balanced search tree data structure to simultaneously use $O(m \log m)$ space and still require only $O(\log m)$ time per operation. The approach we consider next does achieve these bounds using a technique called *path copying*.

Initially we will consider how the *Insert* and *Delete* operations can be implemented in a persistent binary search tree using path copying. We will then demonstrate how rotations can also be implemented. The key idea we use is that only the access path in the binary search tree needs to be stored after each update operation. For an insertion, the access path is the one followed from the root to the leaf where the new element will be inserted. The access path for a deletion starts from the root and traces a path downward in the tree to the vertex that is actually deleted.

Consider the binary search tree shown in Figure 11.16 (a). A pointer to the root of this tree, labeled v_r^i, indicates that this is the i-th state of the data structure.

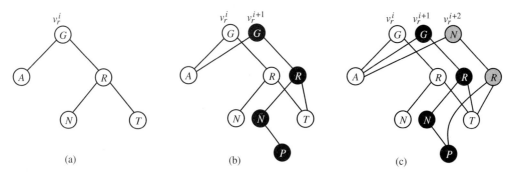

FIGURE 11.16

A persistent binary search tree implemented using path copying. **(a)** The binary search tree after the i-th operation has been performed. This tree is pointed to by v_r^i. **(b)** The $(i+1)$-th operation, *Insert*(P), produces a tree that is accessed through v_r^{i+1}. The vertices produced by this operation are shown blackened. The previous state can still be accessed through v_r^i. **(c)** The tree produced when the next operation is *Delete*(G). Vertex G is replaced by its inorder successor N, and the access path is traced from N back to the root. The new tree is accessed through v_r^{i+2}, and the vertices produced by this operation are shown shaded.

Assume that the next operation is *Insert*(P). The insertion point in the tree is first determined, via searching, to be to the right of vertex N. Next the access path is followed back up the tree to the root. For each vertex on this path, a new vertex is created, as shown in Figure 11.16 (b). This creates a new binary search tree that is accessed through the pointer v_r^{i+1}. Observe, however, that any vertex that was not on the access path will be shared by both trees. A deletion is implemented similarly. Figure 11.16 (c) demonstrates the tree that results when the next operation is *Delete*(G). Notice that the tree pointed to by v_r^{i+2} shares vertices with the trees pointed to by v_r^i and v_r^{i+1}.

Since all of the work in path copying is done along the access path, the time required to perform an update operation is $O(h)$, where h is the maximum height of the trees pointed to by $v_r^0, v_r^1, \dots$. Furthermore, each update operation will also increase the space of the data structure by $O(h)$.

A query operation on the j-th state is implemented by first finding the pointers v_r^i and v_r^{i+1} such that $i \le j < i+1$, and then performing the query on the ordinary binary search tree pointed to by v_r^i. Once v_r^i is found, the query operation takes $O(h)$ time. The search for v_r^i can be implemented in $O(\log m)$ time using binary search. Therefore the query operations can be implemented in $O(\log m + h)$ time using path copying.

An annoying feature of the path copying approach is that the parent pointers of a vertex can grow in an unbounded fashion. For instance, vertex A in Figure 11.16 (c) stores three parent pointers. In order to make the vertices uniform, the parent pointers will be eliminated. These pointers, however, where used to trace the access path back up the tree after an update operation. The auxiliary stack or pointer reversal methods discussed in Exercise 7.12 can be used to perform this function without using parent pointers.

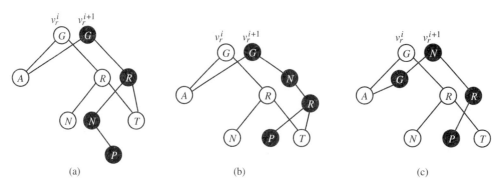

(a) (b) (c)

FIGURE 11.17
Implementing a rotation pattern in a persistent AVL tree that uses path copying. **(a)** The AVL tree immediately after vertex P is inserted. Note that v_r^i points to an AVL tree, but currently v_r^{i+1} does not since the balance at the black vertex G is $+2$. Because the balance of the black vertex R is -1, a double RL rotation pattern is required. **(b)** The result of the first rotation, a right-rotate(R). **(c)** The final AVL tree is obtained by performing a left-rotate(G).

The rotation patterns required by AVL and red-black trees can be implemented in the persistent binary search tree data structure we have just considered. The fact that there are no parent pointers makes this a little more difficult, but the auxiliary stack or pointer reversal methods can still be used to gain access to the appropriate parent or grandparent pointers. Figure 11.17 demonstrates an insertion that results in a double RL rotation in an AVL tree. Observe that only the current state of the data structure is affected by the rotations.

Because the AVL and red-black tree properties will restrict the height of any tree in the collection to $O(\log m)$, any operation can be performed in $O(\log m)$ time when these data structures are made partially persistent using path copying. In addition, the space required by these persistent data structures will be $O(m \log m)$. With red-black trees it is possible to reduce the storage requirements to $O(m)$ amortized space. The technique used to do this is discussed in Exercise 11.20.

EXERCISES

11.1. Show that an arbitrary n-vertex binary search tree can be transformed into any other binary search tree on n vertices using $O(n)$ basic rotation operations. (Hint: First show that an n-vertex binary search tree consisting of a root and right children only can be transformed in this fashion.)

11.2. A *treap* is a partially ordered binary tree that simultaneously satisfies the binary search tree property. Each vertex in a treap stores a search key and also a priority key.

   (*a*) Assuming that all search keys and all priority keys are distinct, show that any set $\{(k_1, p_1), (k_2, p_2), \ldots, (k_n, p_n)\}$ of search-priority key pairs can be represented as a treap. (Hint: The shape of the tree is determined by the priority keys.)

(*b*) Write pseudocode procedures for the DICTIONARY ADT *Search*, *Insert*, and *Delete* operations that run in $\Theta(\log n)$ time in a treap. (Hint: Use rotations to restore the partial ordering property after an insertion or deletion.)

(*c*) In a ***random treap*** the *Insert* operation is randomized by picking the priority of the inserted element at random according to the uniform distribution. Prove that the average-case running times of the *Search*, *Insert*, and *Delete* operations are $\Theta(\log n)$ in a random treap. Next show that the expected number of rotations during an insertion or deletion is at most 2 in a random treap. (Hint: Review the analysis of randomly constructed binary search trees in Section 7.4.)

11.3. Draw the sequence of rotations required to perform a single right rotation and a double LR rotation in an AVL tree.

11.4. With reference to Figure 11.6, draw the sequence of subtrees resulting from the rotations that occur during a double RL rotation in which the new vertex is inserted in subtree T_c as opposed to subtree T_d.

11.5. Prove that the first vertex encountered during the retracing step of the AVL tree insertion algorithm whose balance is ± 1 is the only vertex that can possibly serve as the pivot.

11.6. Consider an AVL tree with height 5 that belongs to the set of worst-case AVL trees. Draw the sequence of rebalancing operations that occur when the shallowest leaf in this tree is deleted.

11.7. Discuss how an AVL tree can be used to sort a sequence of n elements in $O(n \log n)$ time.

11.8. Given a collection of data items with alphabetic keys A, B, C, D, E, F, G, H, I, and J, show the AVL, red-black, and splay trees that result after these items are inserted, in the order given, into initially empty trees.

11.9. Use induction (on tree height) to show that every red-black tree of height h can be recolored so that there are exactly $\lfloor h/2 \rfloor$ black vertices on every path from the root to a leaf, and that the root is black if and only if h is even.

11.10. Describe how any AVL tree can be represented as a red-black tree (without changing the tree shape). Can every red-black tree be represented as an AVL tree (once again, without changing the tree shape)?

11.11. Explicitly state the conditions under which the insertion of a vertex in a red-black tree will result in a sequence of recoloring steps that terminate with the root changing color.

11.12. Will the root of a red-black tree always be black after performing a *Delete* operation?

11.13. Consider an initial red-black tree T. If a data element is inserted into T, and then it is deleted on the very next operation, will the resulting tree always be the same as the initial tree.

11.14. Using equation (11.1) list the changes in potential for every individual adjustment pattern that may occur during an insertion or deletion in a red-black tree.

11.15. Write pseudocode procedures for the *Insert* and *Delete* operations in red-black trees.

11.16. Implement a splay tree class in C++ by inheriting the binary search tree class developed in Section 7.3.

11.17. One variation on splaying, called *semisplaying*, modifies the zig-zig rotation pattern by performing only the first rotation:

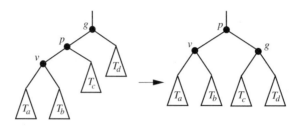

The splaying steps are then continued using vertex p rather than v. Whether semisplaying offers an improvement over splaying depends on the actual sequence of operations.

(a) Show that the amortized cost of each step in a semisplay is the same as that of the splay, except that the constant factor can be reduced from 3 to 2.

(b) Under what conditions would you expect semisplaying to perform better than splaying, and vice versa.

11.18. Consider a sequence of m operations on an n-vertex splay tree, where $f(i)$ is the frequency at which vertex i is accessed (i.e., is the "target" of an operation) while executing the sequence of operations. A standard result from information theory (see the Chapter Notes for a reference) states that for any fixed search tree, if every vertex is accessed at least once, then the running time of the sequence is $\Omega(m + \sum_{i=1}^{n} f(i) \log(m/f(i)))$. Show that in an asymptotic sense, a splay tree is as efficient as any fixed search tree, including an optimal tree for the sequence of operations. (Hint: Assign a fixed weight of $f(i)/m$ to vertex i.)

11.19. The *B-tree* is a balanced search tree data structure designed for use with large data sets in secondary storage. It is generally considered the best method for implementing the DYNAMIC SET ADT on a disk drive. A B-tree of degree d is a tree having the following properties:

- The root is either a leaf, or it has between 2 and d children.
- All internal vertices (except the root) have between $\lceil d/2 \rceil$ and d children.
- All data elements are stored in the leaves, and all leaves have the same depth.

An example B-tree of degree four is shown below:

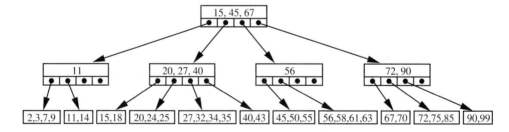

Notice that the internal vertices store pointers to at most four subtrees, and they also store at most three keys; these are the smallest keys in the descendents of the three rightmost subtrees of the vertex. These keys are used to determine which subtree needs to be searched. A typical disk drive contains a number of *tracks*, with each track being divided into a fixed number of equally-sized **blocks**. The time required to position the read/write head on a specific track, and to wait for the desired block to pass under the head (i.e., the **disk access time**), is generally large—on the order of tens of milliseconds. However, once the read/write head is positioned, the time needed to read or write a block is much smaller. In order to minimize disk access time, the degree of a B-tree should be selected as the largest possible value that allows a maximum size leaf to fit in one block.

(a) Assuming a block size of b, what is the maximum number of disk accesses needed to find a data element in an n-element B-tree?

(b) Describe $O(\log n)$ time techniques for inserting and deleting data elements in a B-tree. (Hint: When a vertex becomes too full, it should be split into two vertices. This may propagate up the tree.)

11.20. The space requirements of a partially persistent red-black tree can be reduced by using a technique called **limited-node copying**. With this approach each vertex stores three pointers: a left and right child pointer, and an overflow pointer that is initially empty. Rather than copying a vertex during an update operation, we first check to see if the parent of that vertex has an empty overflow pointer. If it does, then the time of the update operation, and the child to which it applies, is stored in this overflow pointer. If the parent's overflow pointer is not empty, the parent vertex must be copied. In the worst case this can propagate up the entire length of the access path.

(a) Use amortized analysis to show that m update operations can cause at most $O(m)$ total vertices to be copied.

(b) Because the times at which updates occurred are now stored in the red-black tree itself (in the overflow pointers), the search technique used in Section 11.5 no longer applies. Write a pseudocode algorithm that performs a search in this data structure in $O(\log m)$ time.

CHAPTER NOTES

The idea of balancing a search tree using rotations was first proposed by Adel'son-Vel'skiĭ and Landis when they introduced the AVL tree [3]. The B-tree was proposed by Bayer and McCreight [14], and the red-black tree by Bayer [13]; however, he referred to it as a "symmetric binary B-tree." Guibas and Sedgewick introduced the red/black coloring convention in a paper that examined the properties of these trees [71].

Prior to the introduction of the splay tree by Sleator and Tarjan [139], Allen and Munro [6] and Bitner [20] proposed two other binary search tree restructuring heuristics. The first, called **single rotation**, involves rotating a vertex v with its parent p and then stopping (rather than rotating v all the way to the root, as in splaying). This strategy is similar to the transpose heuristic used in self-organizing lists. The second, called **move-to-front**, involves repeatedly rotating v with its parent until it reaches the root. However, neither of these heuristics are efficient, in an amortized sense, because with each approach there exist sequences such that the time per operation is $O(n)$ in an n-element tree (see Allen and Munro [6]). For more details on the information theoretic bound discussed in Exercise 11.18, the reader may consult Abramson [1].

Driscoll et al. [47] discusses techniques for making general linked data structures persistent.

CHAPTER
12

HEAPS

One of the ADTs that is most closely tied to amortized analysis is the MELDABLE PRIORITY QUEUE. This is an extension of the PRIORITY QUEUE ADT that includes two additional operations: *Meld*, which was discussed in Section 9.4, and *DecreaseKey*, which is defined in the following section. These operations are useful in the solution of many optimization problems, including one that we will see in Chapter 14 called the minimum spanning tree problem. Using amortized analysis as a design tool, a number of interesting heap-based data structures have been developed that can implement the MELDABLE PRIORITY QUEUE ADT operations with remarkable efficiency. These data structures, and their corresponding analysis, are the subject of this chapter.

12.1 MELDABLE PRIORITY QUEUE ADT

The MELDABLE PRIORITY QUEUE ADT is a collection of dynamic set elements on which the following operations may be performed:

- All operations available in the PRIORITY QUEUE ADT (see Section 9.1). These include *Insert*, *FindMin*, and *DeleteMin*.

- *Meld*(P_1, P_2). Combines meldable priority queues P_1 and P_2 into a single meldable priority queue and returns it, destroying P_1 and P_2 in the process.
- *DecreaseKey*(P, x, k). Changes the key value of element x in meldable priority queue P to k, where k is assumed to be no greater than the current key value of x.

With the *DecreaseKey* operation, it is assumed that a pointer to the element whose key is being decreased is supplied. Therefore we are not required to perform a search for the key prior to decreasing it. This operation is used extensively in many optimization problems associated with graphs.

We will investigate a variety of different implementations of this ADT in the following sections. Each of the data structures we discuss are heap-based (i.e., each contains trees that obey the partial ordering property). We will see that certain data structures support specific subsets of the MELDABLE PRIORITY QUEUE ADT operations more efficiently than others. We emphasize here that if only the standard PRIORITY QUEUE ADT operations are required in an application, then the binary heap discussed in Section 9.3 is almost always the best choice. In a binary heap, *FindMin* requires $\Theta(1)$ time, while *Insert* and *DeleteMin* can be implemented in $O(\log n)$ time; furthermore, the constants involved in these asymptotic terms are very small since a random-access data structure (i.e., an array) can be used to implement a binary heap.

In the following sections a progression of data structures are considered that eventually allow us to show how all MELDABLE PRIORITY QUEUE ADT operations, except *DeleteMin*, can be implemented in $\Theta(1)$ amortized time using a Fibonacci heap. The *DeleteMin* operation will require $O(\log n)$ amortized time using this data structure. Although the Fibonacci heap is of considerable theoretical importance, its practical usefulness is rather specious. The complexity and excessive overhead associated with Fibonacci heaps make them an unwise choice for almost any application. Nevertheless, by showing that these time bounds are obtainable, it is reasonable to believe that a data structure with the same time bounds, but more amenable to implementation, may be discovered.

12.2 NONAMORTIZED DATA STRUCTURES

Before considering amortized data structures in the following sections, let us first consider how the heap data structures encountered in Chapter 9 can be used to implement a meldable priority queue. First we discuss how the binary heap efficiently supports all meldable priority queue operations, except *Meld*. Next we show that the more elaborate leftist heap data structure can implement all MELDABLE PRIORITY QUEUE ADT operations in $\Theta(\log n)$ worst-case time, except *FindMin*, which only takes $\Theta(1)$ worst-case time.

12.2.1 Binary Heaps

In Section 9.4 we discussed the difficulty of implementing the *Meld* operation using binary heaps. We showed that for two binary heaps containing $\Theta(n)$ elements each, the best we can do is meld them in $O(n)$ time. The *DecreaseKey* operation, on the other hand, can be easily and efficiently implemented using this data structure. The decreased key is simply sifted up in the binary heap until partial order is restored. Since the height of a binary heap is $\Theta(\log n)$, this operation takes $O(\log n)$ time.

12.2.2 Leftist Heaps

In Section 9.4 we also showed how to implement the *Meld* operation using leftist heaps in $O(\log n)$ time. Since a leftist heap also obeys partial order, we can implement *DecreaseKey* as we did in the binary heap by sifting up the decreased key. The problem with this data structure, however, is that its leftist shape only gives us a guarantee that the rightmost path will be short. Since the height of an n-element leftist tree is $O(n)$, the running time of *DecreaseKey* using this approach will be $O(n)$. What we need is a strategy that exploits the short rightmost paths in leftist heaps.

Consider applying *DecreaseKey* to a vertex v with parent p in a leftist heap. If we remove the edge (p, v), we are left with two trees. If v is the right child of p then both of these trees are leftist heaps, and we can create a new leftist heap out of them in $O(\log n)$ by simply performing a *Meld*. On the other hand, if v is a left child, then one of the trees formed by removing (p, v) must retain its leftist shape, while the other might not. For instance, consider the tree shown in Figure 12.1 (a), where key 12 has been decreased to 3. Removal of the edge between the vertex with key 3 and its parent leads to the two subtrees shown in part (b). The subtree on the left in this figure is a leftist heap, but the one on the right is not since it violates leftist shape at the root. This subtree can always be turned into a leftist heap by swapping the subtrees of the vertex at which leftist shape is violated, as shown in part (c) of the figure. These two leftist heaps are then melded to create the final leftist heap shown in part (d). So, as promised, here we have a data structure that allows all of the MELDABLE PRIORITY QUEUE ADT operations to be implemented in $O(\log n)$ time.

The data structure considered next is the binomial heap. In an asymptotic sense, this data structure does not improve upon the running times obtained using leftist heaps; however, two of the amortized data structures studied in the following sections are based on the binomial heap.

12.2.3 Binomial Heaps

Binomial heaps are composed of a forest of binomial trees, where binomial trees are defined recursively as follows:

Definition 12.1. Binomial Tree. A binomial tree B_k is an ordered tree where[†]

- B_0 consists of a single vertex.
- B_k is composed of two trees from B_{k-1}, where one of the two is attached to the root of the other as a rightmost child.

[†]Ordered trees are defined in Appendix B.4.1.

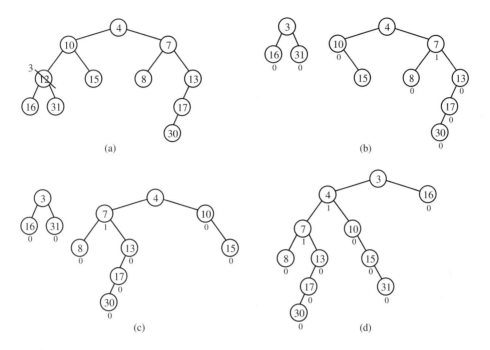

FIGURE 12.1

Performing the *DecreaseKey* operation in a leftist heap. **(a)** The vertex with key 12 has its key value decreased to 3. **(b)** Removal of the edge between the vertex whose key was decreased and its parent creates two subtrees. The one on the left is a leftist heap, but the one on the right is not. **(c)** The subtree on the right is turned into a leftist heap by swapping the subtrees of the vertex at which leftist shape is violated. **(d)** A *Meld* operation joins the two subtrees to create the final leftist heap.

Binomial trees B_0 through B_4 are shown in Figure 12.2. Notice that when going from tree B_{k-1} to B_k we add a single subtree to the root, which doubles the number of vertices and increases the tree height by one. From this it follows immediately that B_k has height k, contains 2^k vertices, and has a root vertex with exactly k children. Furthermore, induction can be used to prove that the number of children in B_k at a depth of i ($0 \le i \le k$) is the binomial coefficient $\binom{k}{i}$, which led to the naming of this data structure.

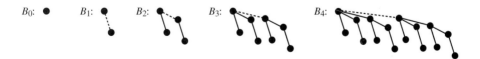

FIGURE 12.2

The binomial trees B_0 through B_4. Binomial tree B_k is constructed by linking two trees from B_{k-1}, where the edge added to link the trees is drawn as a dashed line.

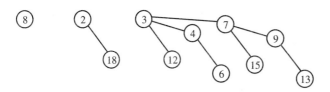

FIGURE 12.3
An 11-element binomial heap containing three heap-ordered binomial trees, B_0, B_1, and B_3.

A binomial heap can now be defined as follows:

Definition 12.2. Binomial Heap. A binomial heap is a forest of binomial trees that obey the following properties:

- Each individual binomial tree is partially ordered, but no particular ordering is assumed between elements in different binomial trees.
- A tree from B_k appears at most once in the forest.

A 11-element binomial heap is shown in Figure 12.3; notice that it contains the three partially-ordered binomial trees B_0, B_1, and B_3.

A number of interesting properties of binomial heaps are uncovered by relating this data structure to the binary number system. Consider an n-element binomial heap, and let $b_m b_{m-1} \dots b_1 b_0$ denote the binary representation of the number n. Recall that the value of n is obtained from its binary representation using $n = 2^m \cdot b_m + 2^{m-1} \cdot b_{m-1} + \cdots + 2 \cdot b_1 + b_0$. Using the fact that a tree in B_k contains exactly 2^k elements, we have a way of determining which binomial trees must be included in an n-element binomial heap: First write the binary representation of the number n, then include only those binomial trees B_i for which $b_i = 1$. In Appendix A.1.2 we show that $m = \lfloor \lg n \rfloor$, which means that $O(\log n)$ binomial trees are needed in an n-element binomial heap. Given this information, a convenient way to represent binomial heaps is as an array of $\lfloor \lg n \rfloor + 1$ pointers, where location i of the array contains either a pointer to a partially-ordered binomial tree in B_i or the null value.

We now show how each of the MELDABLE PRIORITY QUEUE ADT operations can be implemented in a binomial heap. Since each binomial tree in a binomial heap is partially ordered, the *FindMin* operation simply involves a search through roots of these trees to find the smallest one. In an n-element binomial heap this takes $O(\log n)$ time using binary search; however, by maintaining a pointer to the tree with the smallest root, we can implement this operation in $\Theta(1)$ time using only $\Theta(1)$ additional memory.

Consider next a *Meld* of a p-element binomial heap H_1 with a q-element binomial heap H_2, where $p + q = n$. First of all it is easy to determine which binomial trees are in the resulting tree by looking at the binary representation of $p + q$. This suggests that we base the implementation of *Meld* on a binary addition algorithm.

An algorithm based on ***ripple-carry binary addition*** starts by checking if binomial tree B_0 is present in either H_1 or H_2. If B_0 is present in one heap, but not the other, then this tree is copied to the result heap H_3. If it is present in both heaps, then a partially-ordered binomial tree with the shape of B_1 is created by attaching the larger of the two vertices as the right child of the other. Finally, if B_0 is not contained in either heap, then we check to see if B_1 is, and continue. Note that in these subsequent iterations, we must check to see if a tree has been "carried" forward from a previous iteration. At the completion of this operation, the resulting heap will contain at most $\lfloor \lg p \rfloor + \lfloor \lg q \rfloor + 2 \leq \lfloor \lg n \rfloor + 2$ binomial trees. So the time needed to perform a *Meld* operation is $O(\log n)$. As discussed previously, the *Insert* and *DeleteMin* operations are easily implemented using *Meld*. Thus *Insert* and *DeleteMin* can also be implemented in $O(\log n)$ time in a binomial heap.

Finally, the *DecreaseKey* operation can be implemented by sifting up the appropriate data element, within its binomial tree, until partial order is restored. In the worst case an n-element binomial heap consists of a single binomial tree, and the element being sifted up is the rightmost leaf. Such a tree will have a height of $\lg n$, and the running of the *DecreaseKey* operation would be $\Theta(\log n)$.

12.3 AMORTIZED DATA STRUCTURES

In the following sections we present, and use amortized analysis to study, three different data structures that support the MELDABLE PRIORITY QUEUE ADT operations. The first of these is a self-adjusting data structure known as a skew heap. We will show that the amortized costs for the MELDABLE PRIORITY QUEUE ADT operations in a skew heap are the same as the worst-case costs of these operations in a leftist heap. The advantage of skew heaps is that they are easier to implement.

The next data structure we present is the lazy binomial heap, an extension of the binomial heap considered in the previous section. The running times we obtain with lazy binomial heaps are much better than the ones we derived for binomial heaps: $\Theta(1)$ time for *Insert*, *FindMin*, and *Meld*; $O(\log n)$ amortized time for *DeleteMin*; and $O(\log n)$ time for *DecreaseKey*.

Finally we will study the Fibonacci heap, which is an extension of the lazy binomial heap. We will show that this data structure supports all of the MELDABLE PRIORITY QUEUE ADT operations in $\Theta(1)$ time (for *DecreaseKey* this is amortized time), except *DeleteMin*, which requires $O(\log n)$ amortized time.

Although we use amortized analysis to study lazy binomial heaps and Fibonacci heaps, they are not true self-adjusting data structures; with both of them, explicit "balance" information must be stored at their vertices. This complexity makes them less suitable for use in applications. It remains an open problem as to whether a true self-adjusting data structure can be devised with the same amortized time bounds as the Fibonacci heap.

12.3.1 Skew Heaps

A *skew heap* is an amortized variation on the leftist heap (see Section 9.4) that is easier to implement due to the use of a self-adjusting heuristic. Recall that in leftist heaps the *Meld* operation is performed in two steps by first performing a top-down walk along the rightmost paths of the two trees in order to merge them; next, a bottom-up walk along the rightmost path of the resulting tree is used to restore leftist shape by swapping left and right subtrees of any vertex at which this condition is violated.

The heuristic employed in skew heaps involves unconditionally performing the swap at *all* vertices along the rightmost path during the bottom-up walk (except for the rightmost vertex—since it does not have a right child, it makes no sense to give it one). This leads to a simpler implementation for the following reasons. First, it is no longer necessary to store and maintain a depth field at each vertex. Second, since no tests are required to determine if a child should be swapped, a *Meld* can now be performed during a single top-down walk of the rightmost paths. The *Meld* operation on skew heaps is illustrated in Figure 12.4. Part (a) of this figure shows the two skew heaps that will be melded. Part (b) shows the tree that results

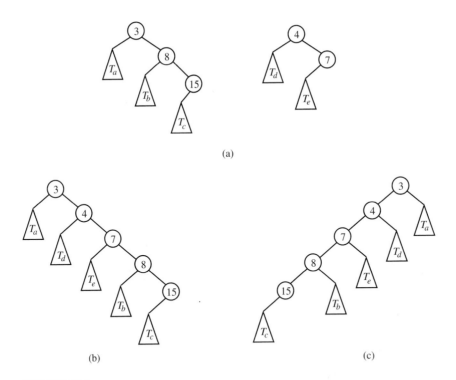

(a)

(b)   (c)

FIGURE 12.4
Performing the *Meld* operation on two skew heaps. **(a)** The two skew heaps that will be melded. **(b)** The result of merging the subtrees of the trees in part (a) along their rightmost paths. **(c)** The final skew heap that results by starting at the root of the tree in part (b), and swapping the subtrees rooted at every vertex (except the last) along the rightmost path. Parts (b) and (c) can actually be accomplished during a single traversal of the rightmost paths of the original skew heaps.

from merging the subtrees along the rightmost paths of the trees in part (a), prior to any swaps. Part (c) shows the final tree after all swaps have been performed. As we have noted, when implementing this operation the merging and swapping can actually be accomplished during a single top-down traversal of the rightmost paths of the trees being melded. You are asked to develop an algorithm for this in Exercise 12.2.

The most important property of an n-vertex leftist tree, which was proved in Section 9.4, is that it has $O(\log n)$ vertices on its rightmost path. Since melding only involves traversals of rightmost paths, this property guarantees that the running time of a *Meld* of two n-vertex leftist heaps is $O(\log n)$. It is not difficult to see that the leftist shape property may no longer hold in skew heaps, and thus we cannot guarantee a $O(\log n)$ time for a single *Meld*. In fact, since skew heaps have no restrictions on their shape, it is possible that all of the vertices in two skew heaps lie along their rightmost paths, leading to a running time of $O(n)$ for the *Meld* operation. However, we will show next that the amortized running time of the *Meld* operation in a skew heap is $O(\log n)$.

Since the melding of two skew heaps only involves a traversal of their rightmost paths, intuitively we know that the shorter the rightmost paths are, the better. What we need is a potential function that captures this notion. As was done with splay trees, let us start by defining the weight, $w(v)$, of a vertex v in a binary tree to be the number of descendents of v (including v itself). Now, let us call v *heavy* if its weight is greater than half the weight of its parent; otherwise v is said to be *light*. Since the root does not have a parent, we define it to be light. Two interesting observations can be made at this point:

1. For any vertex in a binary tree, if one of its children is heavy, the other must be light. Consider a heavy vertex v with parent vertex p and sibling vertex s. Since v is heavy, $w(v) > w(p)/2$, and v's descendents constitute more than half of the vertices in the subtree rooted at p. Thus, less than half of p's descendents remain available for placement in the subtree rooted at s. By definition, this means that v's sibling s is light, i.e., $w(s) \leq w(p)/2$. Note that the converse does not hold, i.e., a vertex may have two children that are both light.

2. Any path from the root to a leaf in an n-vertex binary tree contains at most $\lfloor \lg n \rfloor$ light vertices. Consider a light vertex v with parent vertex p, and assume $w(p) = n$. Since v is light we know that $w(v) \leq \lfloor n/2 \rfloor$. So if we start tracing a path from the root, then in the worst case, each time we encounter a light vertex we assume it has half the number of descendents as its parent (within one). But n can be successively halved in this fashion at most $\lfloor \lg n \rfloor$ time before the value 1 is reached, and a vertex with one descendent is a leaf. Thus an n-vertex tree may contain at most $\lfloor \lg n \rfloor$ light vertices on any path from an ancestor to a descendent.

Let us choose as our potential function the number of heavy vertices that are also right children in a skew heap. Starting from an empty tree, the initial potential is 0, and after m operations the potential must be greater than or equal to 0. Thus, according to equation (10.1), the amortized costs of operations obtained using this potential function will bound their actual costs.

To derive the amortized cost of the *Meld* operation, assume H_1 and H_2 are two skew heaps with l_1 and l_2 light vertices on their rightmost paths, and h_1 and h_2 heavy vertices on their rightmost paths, respectively. Since H_1 has $l_1 + h_1$ vertices on its rightmost path, while H_2 has $l_2 + h_2$ vertices on its rightmost path, the actual time for the *Meld* operation is $l_1 + l_2 + h_1 + h_2$. Let us now consider how the light/heavy status of the right children vertices in skew heaps are changed by this operation. First of all, only the children of vertices initially on the rightmost paths of H_1 or H_2 will have their left/right child status changed due to a swap. Because of the way we defined the potential function, we are only interested in left children that are changed to right children due to such a swap. Consider first a vertex on the rightmost path whose right child was heavy prior to being swapped. The first skew heap observation tells us that this vertex will have a light right child after the swap. Next consider a vertex on the rightmost path whose right child was light prior to being swapped. After the swap, the right child of this vertex may or may not become heavy. In the worst case, though, all such right children will become heavy, causing the largest possible increase in potential. In this case, the change in potential due to such a *Meld* is $l_1 + l_2 - h_1 - h_2$. Therefore, the amortized cost of this operation is

$$
\begin{aligned}
\hat{c} &= (l_1 + l_2 + h_1 + h_2) + (l_1 + l_2 - h_1 - h_2) \\
&= 2(l_1 + l_2)
\end{aligned}
$$

i.e., two times the total number of light vertices originally on rightmost paths. By the second skew heap observation, we know that the number of light vertices on any path from the root to a leaf is $O(\log n)$. From this it follows that the amortized cost of the *Meld* operation is $O(\log n)$.

In summary, the worst-case time for a *FindMin* is $\Theta(1)$ in a skew heap, and the amortized time for *Meld* is $O(\log n)$. This means that the *Insert*, *DeleteMin*, and *DecreaseKey* operations can also be implemented in $O(\log n)$ amortized time in a skew heap by using the *Meld* operation.

12.3.2 Lazy Binomial Heaps

If we are comfortable with amortized running times, then it is possible to considerably improve upon the running times obtained so far for the MELDABLE PRIORITY QUEUE ADT operations by using a *lazy binomial heap*. Like the binomial heap, a lazy binomial heap consists of a collection of partially-ordered binomial trees; however, in lazy binomial heaps the second structural constraint given in Definition 12.2 is relaxed. Specifically, a lazy binomial heap may contain two or more partially-ordered binomial trees of the same size. As we shall see, this simple change makes the implementation of most of the MELDABLE PRIORITY QUEUE ADT operations trivial. But first, let us consider the representation of a lazy binomial heap.

Because a lazy binomial heap may contain more than one binomial tree of a given size, it is no longer possible to represent this data structure using an array of $\lfloor \lg n \rfloor + 1$ pointers-to-binomial-trees. Instead we must keep a list of all the partially-ordered binomial trees that comprise the lazy binomial heap—each entry in the list will contain a pointer to the root of one of the partially-ordered binomial trees. In addition a pointer to the list entry containing the binomial tree with the smallest root needs to be maintained. This allows the *FindMin* operation to be implemented in $\Theta(1)$ time.

If a doubly-linked list is used, then the *Meld* operation is easily implemented in $\Theta(1)$ time by appending the list associated with one lazy binomial heap to the tail of the other list. Since no effort is made to maintain the more rigid structure of binomial heaps (by merging trees of like size), this operation is thought of as being lazy. Likewise, an *Insert* is performed in $\Theta(1)$ time by creating a one-vertex binomial tree and appending it to the list associated with the existing lazy binomial heap. When performing *DecreaseKey* on an n-vertex lazy binomial heap, the worst case again occurs when there is a single binomial heap. Thus, the *DecreaseKey* operation still requires $O(\log n)$ time.

The *DeleteMin* operation is where this data structure finally pays for its laziness. Finding and returning the minimum element is easy since we are keeping a pointer to the smallest root. After deleting the minimum root, its children are then split off to form separate binomial trees. The problem now is to determine which root, out of the entire collection of binomial trees, has the new minimum. It is not difficult to conceive of a scenario in which there will be $\Theta(n)$ trees in an n-element lazy binomial heap, e.g., after n successive *Insert* operations. Therefore, the search for the new minimum requires $O(n)$ time. However, we can obtain a $O(\log n)$ amortized cost for this operation if one additional step is performed: After finding the new minimum, merge all trees of like size until a standard binomial heap is created.

An implementation of this merging step is given in the following algorithm. In this algorithm we assume that each vertex keeps a **rank** field r, which stores the number of children that the vertex has. The rank of a binomial tree is given by the rank of its root. Thus if the root has rank i, it must be a tree from B_i.[†]

LazyBinomHeap::Merge(binomial heap H)
1   create an array of lists $L[0..r_{max}]$ where $L[i]$ contains all trees of rank i
2   **for** $i \leftarrow 0$ **to** r_{max} **do**
3   **while** $L[i] \geq 2$ **do**
4   remove and merge two trees from $L[i]$
5   add the new tree to $L[i + 1]$

At the completion of this algorithm, there is at most one binomial tree of any given

[†]For the root vertex of a binomial tree, this definition of rank is equivalent to the one given in Section 11.4 for splay trees, where the rank was defined as the base 2 logarithm of the weight of a vertex. In binomial trees, by definition, the number of children of a root is exactly the base 2 logarithm of the tree weight.

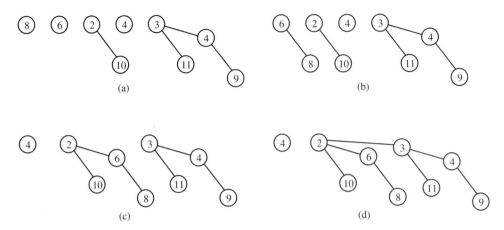

(a) (b)

(c) (d)

FIGURE 12.5

A demonstration of the LazyBinomHeap::Merge() algorithm that is used during the *DeleteMin* operation in lazy binomial heaps. **(a)** A forest of binomial trees immediately after the minimum vertex has been deleted. **(b)** The trees of rank 0 are merged first. **(c)** Next the trees of rank 1 are merged. **(d)** The final binomial tree is obtained by merging the trees of rank 2.

rank. We have used r_{max} to denote the maximum rank of any binomial tree prior to performing the merge. For an n-element binomial heap, we have already discussed the fact that $r_{max} = \lfloor \lg n \rfloor$. A demonstration of LazyBinomHeap::Merge() is given in Figure 12.5.

For the sake of analysis, let T be the number of binomial trees in a lazy binomial heap of size n immediately prior to performing LazyBinomHeap::Merge(). Line 1 of this algorithm creates an array of lists, each containing all binomial trees of a given size. Since there are T trees, this step takes $O(T)$ time; after it is completed, though, the size of array L can be no larger than $\lfloor \lg n \rfloor + 1$. Thus, the loop over lines 2–5 only needs to iterate $\lfloor \lg n \rfloor + 1$ times. On each iteration of the loop over lines 3–5, the number of trees in the forest is reduced by 1 in $\Theta(1)$ time. Since we can reduce the number of trees at most $T - 1$ times, the total time for lines 2–5, as well as the entire algorithm, is proportional to $T + \lfloor \lg n \rfloor$. Using worst-case analysis we know that T can be as large as n, leading to a worst-case running time for *DeleteMin* of $\Theta(n)$. The key to the usefulness of the merging step is that it only adds a constant amount to the cost of *DeleteMin*—it was already a $O(n)$-time operation due to the search. At the same time, the reorganization it performs will generally reduce the time needed to perform any future *DeleteMin* operations.

We now show that the amortized running time for the *DeleteMin* operation in a lazy binomial heap is $O(\log n)$, while at the same time maintaining the superior time bounds derived previously for all of the other MELDABLE PRIORITY QUEUE ADT operations (but this time they will be amortized bounds).

Let the potential function for a lazy binomial heap be T, the number of binomial trees it contains. Starting from an empty lazy binomial heap, we see that this potential function will be nonnegative after any sequence of operations. Thus the amortized running times we derive will upper bound the actual running times. Notice that the change in potential due to a *FindMin*, *Meld*, or *DecreaseKey* operation is 0, and that for an *Insert* operation it is 1. Thus, according to equation (10.2), the amortized times for each of these operations equal their worst-case bounds derived previously.

For the *DeleteMin* operation, consider an n-element lazy binomial heap containing T binomial trees, and let i be the rank of the binomial tree with minimum root. After this vertex is deleted, i new binomial trees are created out of its children, and the total number of trees is now $T + i - 1$. These trees will be merged into at most $\lfloor \lg n \rfloor + 1$ binomial trees using LazyBinomHeap::Merge() in actual time that is proportional to $(T + i - 1) + \lfloor \lg n \rfloor$. Therefore, the amortized time for *DeleteMin* is proportional to

$$\hat{c} = T + i - 1 + \lfloor \lg n \rfloor + \underbrace{\lfloor \lg n \rfloor + 1 - T}_{\Delta \Phi}$$

$$= 2\lfloor \lg n \rfloor + i$$

Since all trees in the forest are binomial trees, it must be the case that $i \leq \lfloor \lg n \rfloor$. Substituting this into the previous equation leads to an amortized time of $O(\log n)$ for the *DeleteMin* operation.

Thinking about this data structure from the "accountant's" perspective, we see that *Insert* operations add extra credits to the balance sheet whenever they are performed. These accumulated credits can then be used to help pay for future *DeleteMin* operations. The reader should also observe that this is not a true self-adjusting data structure since we now must maintain rank information at each vertex.

12.3.3 Fibonacci Heaps

The **Fibonacci heap** is an extension of the lazy binomial heap. Specifically, it is implemented as a forest of trees in which the *Meld*, *Insert*, *FindMin*, and *DeleteMin* operations are implemented exactly as in lazy binomial heaps. In addition, it "borrows" an idea from the leftist heap data structure in order to improve the amortized running time of *DecreaseKey* to $\Theta(1)$. As in leftist heaps, Fibonacci heaps implement *DecreaseKey* by making a cut between the vertex whose key is being decreased, and its parent. Assume we are decreasing the key of vertex v whose parent is p. The first step, which is the same as in leftist heaps, involves making v the root of a new tree by removing edge (p, v). However, the manner in which the original tree is rearranged (the one containing p) is different. In Fibonacci heaps we keep an extra bit field (which is initially 0) called *mark* at each vertex, and then use the following rules during the rearranging step of the *DecreaseKey* operation:

1. The first time a nonroot vertex loses a child (due to a cut), set *mark* to 1. We will refer to this as a **marked vertex**.

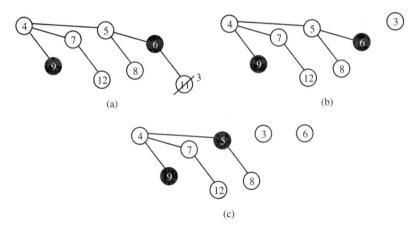

FIGURE 12.6
Performing the *DecreaseKey* operation in a Fibonacci heap. Marked vertices are black. **(a)** The initial
Fibonacci heap consists of a single tree. The vertex with key 11 has its key value decreased to 3. **(b)**
The vertex whose key was decreased is cut from the tree. **(c)** Because the parent of the vertex cut from
the tree is marked, it must also be cut from the tree. The parent of this vertex (the one with key 5) is
then marked, which completes the operation.

2. If a marked vertex v loses a child, then cut it from its parent, making v the root
of a new tree.

3. A vertex is unmarked whenever it becomes a root.

Note that each cut due to the second rule will result in either an unmarked vertex
being marked (which terminates the operation), or another marked vertex being cut
from the tree. Since a sequence of cuts may cascade up the tree, they are known
as ***cascading cuts***. An example *DecreaseKey* operation is shown in Figure 12.6.
Observe that unlike leftist heaps, there is no final melding step to create a single
tree. Rather, like lazy binomial heaps, pointers to the roots of the three trees shown
in Figure 12.6 (c) will be stored in a doubly-linked list.

It is not difficult to see that certain cuts during a *DecreaseKey* operation can
result in the formation of trees that are not binomial trees. For instance, in Figure 12.6 (c) the tree with six vertices is not a binomial tree. This does not matter
though; we prove next that each of the MELDABLE PRIORITY QUEUE ADT operations,
except *DecreaseKey*, can still be implemented exactly as they were in lazy binomial
heaps with no loss of efficiency. We will also show that the *DecreaseKey* operation
requires $\Theta(1)$ amortized time in a Fibonacci heap.

The fact that the *DeleteMin* operation can be implemented using the algorithm
developed for lazy binomial heaps, namely LazyBinomHeap::Merge(), requires some
explanation. As before, let us define the rank of a vertex to be the number of children associated with it, and the rank of a tree in a Fibonacci heap to be the rank

of its root vertex.[†] Given these definitions, it is not difficult to see that the LazyBinomHeap::Merge() algorithm will also work with Fibonacci heaps. However, in this case the size of array L can be larger than $\lfloor \lg n \rfloor + 1$, so the loop over lines 2–5 must be adjusted accordingly.

A key fact that we will need to use in our amortized analysis of Fibonacci heaps is that each tree in an n-vertex Fibonacci heap has rank $O(\log n)$. In order to prove this, we begin by noting that the rules given previously for performing cascading cuts during a *DecreaseKey* operation will tend to limit the number of children a vertex may have. To see exactly how much, let c_i be the i-th youngest child of a vertex v in a Fibonacci heap, where $i > 1$. This means that v has $i - 1$ children, $c_1, c_2, \ldots, c_{i-1}$, that were merged with v (during *DeleteMin* operations) prior to the time that c_i became a child of v. We will show that the rank of c_i must be at least $i - 2$. Recall that only trees of equal rank can be merged while performing a *DeleteMin* operation. Thus when c_i was merged with v, c_i must have also had $i - 1$ children. Since this merge, it could have lost at most one child due to a *DecreaseKey* operation; otherwise, it would have been cut from v (this is the only way a vertex can lose a child). Thus c_i must have at least $i - 2$ children, and hence a rank of at least $i - 2$.

We can use this bound on the rank to show that any tree of rank r in a Fibonacci heap has at least $F(r + 2)$ descendents, where $F(r + 2)$ is the $(r + 2)$-th Fibonacci number discussed in Exercise 1.6. To do this, let $T(r)$ be the smallest tree of rank r in a Fibonacci heap. It is easy to see that $T(0) = 1$, $T(1) = 2$, and $T(2) = 3$. Now consider the r children of $T(r)$ when r is greater than 2. Except for the oldest child (i.e., c_1), which must have rank at least 0, we can use the result we have just derived to show that the remaining children have ranks of at least $r - 2, r - 1, \ldots, 0$. If we include the root vertex, then $T(r)$ is defined recursively as

$$T(r) = 2 + \sum_{i=0}^{r-2} T(i) \qquad \text{for } r > 2$$

From this it is easy to show that $T(r) = F(r + 2)$, for r greater than or equal to 0.

Consider next an arbitrary n-vertex tree in a Fibonacci heap that has an unknown rank of r. The root of this tree has exactly n descendents, but we also know that since it has a rank of r, it has at least $F(r + 2)$ descendents. This implies $F(r + 2) \leq n$. Two important facts to note at this point are that $F(r + 2)$ increases exponentially with r, and that a logarithmic function is the inverse of an exponential function. Thus by taking logarithms in the previous inequality we obtain $r = O(\log n)$, completing the proof that each tree in an n-vertex Fibonacci heap has rank $O(\log n)$.

Now that we have shown that $r_{max} = O(\log n)$ in a Fibonacci heap, we can use amortized analysis to derive the running times of the MELDABLE PRIORITY QUEUE ADT operations. Given a Fibonacci heap H, let T denote the number of trees in its forest, and m the number of marked vertices. The potential function we will use for

---

[†]Here the rank of the tree is no longer equivalent to the definition used with splay trees.

analyzing Fibonacci heaps is the number of trees in its forest, plus twice the number of marked vertices:

$$\Phi(H) = T + 2m \tag{12.1}$$

Using this potential function, the change in potential due to a *FindMin* or *Meld* operation is 0, and for an *Insert* operation it is 1.

Consider next the *DeleteMin* operation, and assume that a vertex v with rank i is the one being deleted. This operation cannot create any new marked vertices, and only those children of v that are marked prior to this operation can become unmarked (because they will become root vertices). The act of splitting the children of v will create i new trees, and the total number of trees will now be $T + i - 1$. Next, the LazyBinomHeap::Merge() algorithm will merge these into at most r_{max} trees in actual time that is proportional to $(T + i - 1) + r_{max}$. Therefore the amortized time for *DeleteMin* is proportional to:

$$\hat{c} = T + i - 1 + r_{max} + \underbrace{(r_{max} + 2m) - (T + 2m)}_{\Delta\Phi}$$

$$= 2r_{max} + i - 1$$

Finally, since $i \le r_{max}$ and $r_{max} = O(\log n)$, we arrive at an amortized time of $O(\log n)$ for the *DeleteMin* operation.

To show that the amortized time for the *DecreaseKey* operation is $\Theta(1)$, let C be the number of cascading cuts implemented while performing this operation. The actual cost of this operation is proportional to the number of cascading cuts, plus one for the first cut. This first cut creates a new tree, which increases the potential by at most 1. Each cascading cut also increases the number of trees by one, but also decreases the number of marked vertices by one, leading to a net loss of 1 unit of potential for each cascading cut. In the worst case the last cascading cut will convert an unmarked vertex to a marked one, increasing the potential by 2. Thus, using potential function (12.1) the amortized time for the *DecreaseKey* operation is proportional to:

$$\hat{c} = C + 1 + \underbrace{3 - C}_{\Delta\Phi}$$

$$= 4$$

which means that *DecreaseKey* has an amortized running time of $\Theta(1)$ in Fibonacci heaps.

Thinking about this data structure from the "accountant's" perspective, we see that each *Insert* operation adds a credit to the balance sheet, and these credits are used to pay for future *DeleteMin* operations. If cascading cuts do not occur, the *DecreaseKey* operation will also add 2 credits to the balance sheet when it marks a vertex. Since a cascading cut can only occur when a marked vertex loses a child, these 2 credits are always available to pay for it. One credit is used to pay for the actual cut, and the other is used to offset the unit increase in potential that occurs when the cascading cut creates a new tree.

TABLE 12.1
A summary of the running times for the MELDABLE PRIORITY QUEUE ADT operations using the data structures discussed in this chapter. A starred entry denotes amortized time.

Operation	Data structure					
	Binary heap	Leftist heap	Binomial heap	Skew heap	Binomial heap (lazy)	Fibonacci heap
Insert	$O(\log n)$	$O(\log n)$	$O(\log n)$	$O(\log n)^*$	$\Theta(1)$	$\Theta(1)$
FindMin	$\Theta(1)$	$\Theta(1)$	$\Theta(1)$	$\Theta(1)$	$\Theta(1)$	$\Theta(1)$
DeleteMin	$O(\log n)$	$O(\log n)$	$O(\log n)$	$O(\log n)^*$	$O(\log n)^*$	$O(\log n)^*$
Meld	$O(n)$	$O(\log n)$	$O(\log n)$	$O(\log n)^*$	$\Theta(1)$	$\Theta(1)$
DecreaseKey	$O(\log n)$	$O(\log n)$	$O(\log n)$	$O(\log n)^*$	$O(\log n)$	$\Theta(1)^*$

The running time results we have obtained for the MELDABLE PRIORITY QUEUE operations using the various heap data structures discussed in this chapter are collected in Table 12.1.

12.4 AN EXTENDED EXAMPLE: APPROXIMATION ALGORITHMS

In Chapter 9 it was mentioned that priority queues are commonly used in the context of optimization algorithms. For a large number of important optimization problems, polynomial-time algorithms do not exist. In many applications, however, an approximate solution to these problems may suffice. In this extended example a famous optimization problem called the traveling salesman problem is presented that (as far as anyone knows) does not possess a polynomial-time algorithmic solution. (This problem was first discussed in this text in Exercise 2.19.) We then present a polynomial-time algorithm that produces an approximate solution using a meldable priority queue. Before considering this problem and the associated algorithm, it is necessary to discuss how we will judge the goodness of an approximation algorithm.

Assume that the potential solutions associated with an optimization problem all have positive cost, and that one with minimum possible cost is optimal.[†] An approximation algorithm is said to have a **_ratio bound_** of $\rho(n)$ if for any input of size n, the cost C of the solution output by the approximation algorithm is within a factor $\rho(n)$ of the optimal solution C_{opt}:

$$\frac{C}{C_{\text{opt}}} \leq \rho(n) \tag{12.2}$$

Notice that $\rho(n)$ can never be less than 1. Obviously, we would like to develop approximation algorithms that have small ratio bounds.

[†]This is a minimization problem. For a maximization problem, there are obvious analogues to the definitions given in this section.

Returning to the traveling salesman problem, assume we are given a set Γ of n cities $c_1, c_2, \ldots, c_n$, along with the distances between any two pairs of cities in this set. The optimal solution to this problem is the shortest path (i.e., tour) that goes through each city exactly once, and returns to the city from which the tour started. The distance between cites c_i and c_j will be denoted by $d(c_i, c_j)$. We will also assume that for $i, j = 1, 2, \ldots, n$ the following conditions hold: $d(c_i, c_j) = d(c_j, c_i)$, $d(c_i, c_j) \geq 0$, and $d(c_i, c_j) + d(c_j, c_k) \geq d(c_i, c_k)$. The third condition, referred to as the ***triangle inequality***, is very important. If the distances are not constrained by the triangle inequality, then it is believed that a polynomial-time approximation algorithm with a fixed ratio bound does not exist for the traveling salesman problem.

It is often useful to think of an instance of the traveling salesman problem as a graph, where the cities are vertices and the distances between cities are weighted edges (weighted graphs are discussed in Appendix B.4). With this in mind, any tour containing more than one city can be thought of as a cycle, and the length of the tour is the sum of the weighted edges in its corresponding cycle.

An important observation to make at this point is that by removing any one edge from a cycle in a graph, a tree is created. In Chapter 14 we will study the minimum spanning tree problem, which involves trying to find a tree T_{MST} whose edges span all of the vertices in a graph, and whose total weight is minimal. Let us denote the weight of T_{MST} using $w(T_{\text{MST}})$. If we consider the cycle associated with an optimal tour for an n-city traveling salesman graph, it is easy to show that the longest edge in this cycle must have a length of at least C_{opt}/n. By removing this edge, a tree with weight $C_{\text{opt}} - C_{\text{opt}}/n$ is created. By definition, the weight of a minimal spanning tree for this graph cannot exceed this amount. Thus we can write

$$w(T_{\text{MST}}) \leq \left(1 - \frac{1}{n}\right) C_{\text{opt}} \tag{12.3}$$

In this extended example we will construct an approximate tour by starting with an initial tour that contains a single city, and then adding one city at a time until all cities are included. The cities in the tour at time m will be denoted by the ordered m-tuple $\tau_m = (\alpha_1, \alpha_2, \ldots, \alpha_m)$, where $\alpha_1, \alpha_2, \ldots, \alpha_m$ denotes a permutation of the cities in Γ. Specifically, this tour starts at city α_1, then goes to city α_2, and so on until city α_m is reached, and then returns to city α_1. Given a tour τ_m and a city $c_j \notin \tau_m$, the distance $d(\tau_m, c_j)$ between τ_m and c_j is defined as

$$d(\tau_m, c_j) = \min\{d(c_i, c_j) \mid c_i \in \tau_m\}$$

That is, $d(\tau_m, c_j)$ is the minimum distance between any city in the tour τ_m, and city c_j which is not in the tour.

The ***nearest insertion method*** starts by choosing an arbitrary city to be α_1 in the tour τ_1. At each subsequent step, the closest city to the current tour is added to create the next tour. Specifically, at step m, the city α_m which satisfies

$$\min\{d(\tau_{m-1}, c_j) \mid c_j \in \Gamma - \tau_{m-1}\} \tag{12.4}$$

is added to τ_{m-1} to create τ_m. When m is greater than 2, the position of α_m in τ_m is determined by the two cities c_i and c_j in τ_{m-1} which minimize

$$d(c_i, \alpha_m) + d(\alpha_m, c_j) - d(c_i, c_j) \tag{12.5}$$

City α_m is placed between cities c_i and c_j in τ_m. A demonstration of this method is given in Figure 12.7.

An algorithm that implements the nearest insertion method is given next. In this algorithm a key is attached to each city in Γ. A meldable priority queue is then used to find the city in $\Gamma - \tau_i$ that is nearest to the tour τ_i. Initially all cities are placed in the priority queue with a key value of ∞, except for some starting city c_s, which is assigned a key value of 0.

```
ApproxTSP(array d[1..n, 1..n])      ▷ nearest insertion method
1   τ₁ ← an arbitrary starting city cₛ
2   for each cᵢ ∈ Γ do
3       key[cᵢ] ← ∞
4   key[cₛ] ← 0
5   MakePriorityQueue(P, C)      ▷ P is a meldable priority queue
6   for i ← 1 to n − 1 do
7       c ← DeleteMin(P)
8       nearest ← ∞      ▷ reinitialize nearest
9       for each x ∉ τᵢ do      ▷ determine which city is nearest to τᵢ
10          if d[c, x] < key[x] then
11              DecreaseKey(P, x, d[c, x])
12          if d[c, x] < nearest then
13              nearest ← d[c, x]
14              c_near ← x
15      τᵢ₊₁ ← τᵢ ∪ c_near      ▷ add city c_near to τᵢ using equation (12.5)
16  return τₙ
```

The city returned by the first *DeleteMin* operation on line 7 of ApproxTSP() will be c_s. The *DecreaseKey* operation is then used to decrease the key values of all other cities in such a way that the next city returned by the *DeleteMin* operation on line 7 will be the nearest city to c_s. This nearest city is added to the tour, and the process is repeated until all cities have been included. Because the *DecreaseKey* operation is being used, on subsequent iterations of the loop over lines 9–15, the nearest city to *any* city in the current tour τ_i is always located.

Assume that a Fibonacci heap is used in ApproxTSP(). With this data structure, the heap itself can be constructed in $\Theta(n)$ time, while the *DeleteMin* and *DecreaseKey* operations can be implemented in $O(\log n)$ and $O(1)$ amortized time, respectively. The fact that both *DeleteMin* and *DecreaseKey* will be executed numerous (i.e., at least $n - 1$) times in this algorithm means that we are actually deriving worst-case bounds, not amortized bounds. Since $n - 1$ *DeleteMin* operations are always performed, they take $O(n \log n)$ time. On each iteration of the loop over lines 9–14, $O(n)$ *DecreaseKey* operations can be performed; so the total time spent performing *DecreaseKey* operations is $O(n^2)$. Thus by using a Fibonacci heap, the running time of ApproxTSP() on n cities is $O(n^2)$.

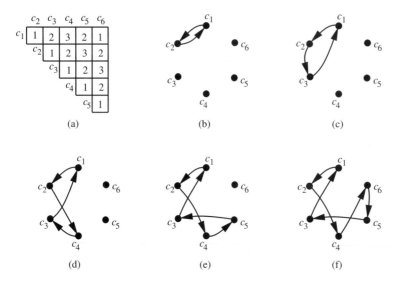

FIGURE 12.7
(a) An instance of the traveling salesman problem given by a chart containing the distances between any two pairs of cities in the collection c_1, c_2, c_3, c_4, c_5, and c_6. **(b)** In the nearest insertion method an arbitrary city, c_1, is chosen first, and then a closest city to c_1, c_2 in this case, is added to create the tour $\tau_2 = (c_1, c_2)$. **(c)** A closest city to τ_2 is added to create the tour $\tau_3 = (c_1, c_2, c_3)$. **(d)** Next city c_4 is added. Equation (12.5) is minimized by either $\tau_4 = (c_1, c_2, c_3, c_4)$, or $\tau_4 = (c_1, c_2, c_4, c_3)$. We assume here that c_4 is placed between c_2 and c_3. **(e)** The addition of city c_5, where once again there are multiple placements of c_5 that satisfy equation (12.5). **(f)** The final nearest insertion tour $\tau_6 = (c_1, c_2, c_4, c_6, c_5, c_3)$. The length of τ_6 is 10. An optimal tour, e.g., $\tau_{\text{opt}} = (c_1, c_2, c_3, c_4, c_5, c_6)$, has length 6.

Next we will prove that the ratio bound of any tour produced by the nearest insertion method can never exceed 2. We will use $C_{\text{NI}}(m)$ to denote the cost (i.e., length) of a tour τ_m constructed by the nearest insertion method. If we let $\Delta C_{\text{NI}}(m)$ denote the difference in cost between τ_{m-1} and τ_m, then

$$C_{\text{NI}}(m) = C_{\text{NI}}(m-1) + \Delta C_{\text{NI}}(m)$$

According to equation (12.5), if τ_{m-1} contains at least two cities, then

$$\Delta C_{\text{NI}}(m) = d(c_i, \alpha_m) + d(\alpha_m, c_j) - d(c_i, c_j) \qquad (12.6)$$

where, from the graph point of view, τ_m is constructed from τ_{m-1} by removing the edge (c_i, c_j), and adding the edges (c_i, α_m) and (α_m, c_j). From this it follows that the total cost of an n-city tour produced by the nearest insertion method is

$$C_{\text{NI}}(n) = \sum_{i=1}^{n} \Delta C_{\text{NI}}(i) \qquad (12.7)$$

To complete our proof we need to establish a relationship between a nearest insertion tour, and the edges of a minimal spanning tree in the corresponding traveling salesman graph. First consider the cost associated with the insertion of a single city. We can show that the cost of inserting city α_m using the nearest insertion method is bounded by:

$$\Delta C_{NI}(m) \leq 2 \cdot d(\alpha_m, c_j) \tag{12.8}$$

where c_j is any city in τ_{m-1}. For the case when $m = 2$, equation (12.8) is easy to verify. For $m > 2$, first note that the triangle inequality allows us to write

$$d(\alpha_m, c_j) \geq d(c_i, \alpha_m) - d(c_i, c_j) \tag{12.9}$$

Substituting equation (12.9) into equation (12.6) leads to equation (12.8).

Using equation (12.8), equation (12.7) can be rewritten as

$$C_{NI}(n) \leq \sum_{i=1}^{n} 2 \cdot d(\alpha_i, c_j) \tag{12.10}$$

where c_j is always a member of τ_i, and α_i is not. Now, thinking about the distances between cities as weighted edges, the bound in equation (12.10) must hold even when the edges $(\alpha_1, \alpha_2), (\alpha_2, \alpha_3), \ldots, (\alpha_{n-1}, \alpha_n)$ selected by the nearest insertion method form a minimum spanning tree. In other words,

$$C_{NI}(n) \leq 2 \cdot w(T_{MST}) \tag{12.11}$$

Substituting equation (12.3) into equation (12.11) yields

$$\frac{C_{NI}(n)}{C_{opt}} \leq 2 \cdot \left(1 - \frac{1}{n}\right) \tag{12.12}$$

which proves that the ratio bound for the nearest insertion method is at most 2.

EXERCISES

12.1. Prove that the number of children at a depth of i in binomial tree B_k, $0 \leq i \leq k$, is $\binom{k}{i}$.

12.2. Write a pseudocode procedure for performing a *Meld* of two skew heaps using only a single traversal of their rightmost paths.

12.3. Develop a pseudocode algorithm for the *Insert* operation in a binomial heap that does not use *Meld*. (Hint: See Section 10.4.)

12.4. Draw a diagram that illustrates the arrangement of all the pointers and associated data structures needed in:
(*a*) A binomial heap implementation.
(*b*) A Fibonacci heap implementation.

12.5. Exhibit a sequence of MELDABLE PRIORITY QUEUE ADT operations that lead to the construction of an n-vertex Fibonacci heap containing a single tree having a height of exactly $n - 1$.

12.6. In Section 12.3.3 we denoted the smallest tree of rank r in a Fibonacci heap using $T(r)$. Prove that $T(r) = F(r + 2)$, where $F(r + 2)$ is the $(r + 2)$-th Fibonacci number.

12.7. The *DecreaseKey* operation can be generalized as follows:

- *ChangeKey(P, x, k)*. Changes the key value of element x in meldable priority queue P to k, where no assumptions are placed on k.

Develop an efficient implementation of this operation using the Fibonacci heap data structure that does not change the running times of any of the other MELDABLE PRIORITY QUEUE ADT operations.

12.8. Show that the approximation method discussed in part (b) of Exercise 2.19 has a ratio bound of $1/2\lceil \lg n \rceil + 1/2$.

12.9. In line 15 of ApproxTSP() given in Section 12.4 we use $\tau_{i+1} \leftarrow \tau_i \cup c_{near}$ to denote that city c_{near} is added to tour τ_i, but we do not give the specifics of how this is done. Modify this algorithm so that it explicitly handles the placement of a new city according to equation (12.5).

12.10. Give an instance of the traveling salesman problem where equation (12.12) is achieved with equality by the nearest insertion method.

12.11. The *cheapest insertion method* for approximating the traveling salesman problem is a variation on the nearest insertion method. Rather than using equation (12.4) to select the next city, the cheapest insertion method uses

$$\min\{\Delta C_{NI}(m) \mid c \in \Gamma - \tau_{m-1}\}$$

Equation (12.5) is then used to determine the placement of this city.

(a) Show that the ratio bound remains at most $2 \cdot (1 - 1/n)$ using this approach.

(b) Develop an algorithm for implementing the cheapest insertion method that runs in $O(n^2 \log n)$ time.

12.12. Assume that the cities in an instance of the traveling salesman problem are points in the plane, and that for $i, j = 1, 2, \ldots, n$, $d(c_i, c_j)$ is the Euclidean distance between cities c_i and c_j. Prove that an optimal tour for such an instance never crosses itself.

12.13. In the *vertex cover problem* we are given a graph $G = (V, E)$, and we are asked to find a set of vertices $C \subseteq V$ such that for each edge in E at least one of its endpoints is in C. It is believed that a polynomial-time algorithm does not exist for this problem.

(a) If a vertex has high degree, by definition it covers many edges. This leads to the following greedy approximation algorithm which starts with $C = \emptyset$. While there are still edges remaining in E, choose the vertex in V that has the largest degree. This vertex is added to C, and deleted from V. All edges incident from the selected vertex are also deleted from E. Show that the ratio bound for this algorithm is $O(\log n)$.

(b) A simpler algorithm, which also starts with $C = \emptyset$, repeatedly chooses a random edge (u, v) from E, and adds u and v to C. Every edge incident on u or v is then removed from E. Show that the ratio bound for this algorithm is 2.

CHAPTER NOTES

Binomial heaps were introduced by Vuillemin [154]. Skew heaps were introduced by Sleator and Tarjan [140]. In their paper they also discuss a variation of skew heaps called ***bottom-up skew heaps*** in which the amortized running time of *Insert* and *Meld* are $\Theta(1)$, and the amortized running time of *DeleteMin* is $O(\log n)$. Fibonacci heaps are discussed by Fredman and Tarjan in [59]. Driscoll et al. [46] have developed a data structure called the ***relaxed heap*** in which *DecreaseKey* can be made to run in $\Theta(1)$ worst-case (not amortized) time, and *DeleteMin* can be made to run in $\Theta(\log n)$ worst-case time. These authors demonstrate that relaxed heaps have some advantages over Fibonacci heaps when they are used in parallel algorithms. An experimental comparison between binary heaps, leftist heaps, binomial heaps, skew heaps, splay trees, and some additional data structures (but not lazy binomial heaps and Fibonacci heaps) was performed by Jones [81]. The model for generating operation sequences in this study was based on the use of a priority queue in discrete-event simulation; thus, only *Insert* and *DeleteMin* were used. Under this scenario, the running times using each of these data structures were very similar, with splay trees performing slightly better than the others.

Although in each of the data structures we have considered, at least one of the standard PRIORITY QUEUE ADT operations requires $O(\log n)$ time, there is reason to believe that within the context of certain optimization algorithms, better performance may be obtained; Fredman and Tarjan [59] discuss this issue.

The traveling salesman and vertex cover problems belong to a large class of important problems that are said to be ***NP-complete***. It is strongly believed that polynomial-time algorithms do not exist for solving NP-complete problems, although this has yet to be proven. A detailed discussion of the issues associated with NP-completeness can be found in Garey and Johnson [63], and Papadimitriou [115]. Analysis of the ApproxTSP() algorithm appears in Rosenkrantz, Stearns, and Lewis [132]; a number of other polynomial-time approximation algorithms for the traveling salesman problem are also given in their paper.

CHAPTER
13

DYNAMIC SETS
WITH SPECIAL
OPERATIONS

Although the DYNAMIC SET ADT has proven quite useful in a wide variety of computing applications, in practice you are likely to encounter situations where the operations
we have defined (in the introduction to Part II) are not sufficient. In many cases, an
existing data structure can be modified to fit the needs of the application. In some
cases, however, entirely new data structures are necessary. In this chapter we first
consider adding an operation for range searching to the DYNAMIC SET ADT. For one-
dimensional data, this operation is easily and efficiently implemented in binary search
trees; however, for certain applications a new data structure called the trie is a better
choice. Next, data structures for storing multidimensional data are considered. Some
simple, but rather inefficient, solutions to the multidimensional searching problem are
presented, followed by a number of data structures developed specifically with this
searching problem in mind. Finally, we consider a data structure for implementing
the DISJOINT SET ADT, which is another specialization of the DYNAMIC SET ADT that
is used to maintain equivalence relations.

13.1 RANGE SEARCHING

An important operation often required in DYNAMIC SET ADT applications is range searching. Recall that the *Search* operation involves either finding an element with a given key value, or reporting that no such element exists. The *RangeSearch* operation is a generalization of *Search* to a range of key values. This operation was first discussed in Exercise 7.10. Its definition is repeated below:

- *RangeSearch(S, k_1, k_2)*. Returns all elements x in the dynamic set S such that $k_1 \leq \text{key}[x] \leq k_2$, or the null value if there are no such elements.

In practice this operation is often modified so that it returns a pointer to where the data elements within the range can be found, rather than the data elements themselves.

13.1.1 Binary Search Trees

It is easy to implement a range search in a binary search tree. First, search the binary search tree for the key k_1. Let v be the vertex at which k_1 is found, or the last vertex on the search path with key value greater than k_1 if a vertex with key k_1 does not exist. The vertices with key values in the appropriate range are now found by repeatedly performing *Successor* operations, starting with v, until a vertex with key value greater than k_2 is reached. Since all of the data elements may fall within the range of the search, the running time of this algorithm is $O(n)$ in an n-vertex binary search tree. Furthermore, this same argument leads trivially to a running time of $\Omega(n)$ for *any* range searching algorithm.

In order to more accurately ascertain the performance of range searching algorithms, it is necessary to include the size of the output (i.e., number of elements returned) as a parameter in our analysis. For instance, if we let K denote the number of elements with key values in the range $[k_1, k_2]$ in an n-vertex binary search tree, then the algorithm we just described runs in $O(K + h)$ time if the binary search tree has height h. This running time can be improved to $O(K + \log n)$ by using one of the balanced binary search trees discussed in Chapter 11. Furthermore, if it is only necessary to report where the data elements can be found, then the running time for a range search in a balanced binary search tree is $O(\log n)$.

13.1.2 Tries

In binary search trees, data elements are stored at each vertex in the tree. Thus, searching for a specific key in a binary search tree involves a key comparison at *each* vertex along the corresponding search path. If the keys in an application are large (e.g., strings), these comparisons can add significant overhead to the cost of searching. In this section we present a data structure called the trie (pronounced "try") that can significantly reduce this overhead. Tries support the full complement of DYNAMIC SET ADT operations, as well as the *RangeSearch* operation. For this reason, they should be considered as an alternative to binary search trees in any application requiring the DYNAMIC SET ADT, not just in ones requiring the *RangeSearch* operation.

In order to define a binary trie, consider a path $v_0 \leadsto v_m$ from the ancestor vertex v_0 to the descendent vertex v_m in a binary tree, and without loss of generality assume vertices are encountered along this path in the order $v_0, v_1, \ldots, v_m$. A binary number $b_0, b_1, \ldots, b_{m-1}$, which we shall call the **binary path label** of $v_0 \leadsto v_m$, can be constructed by choosing b_i to be either 0 or 1 according to whether v_{i+1} is to the left or right, respectively, of v_i. Assuming each key k in a dynamic set is represented as a binary number $k_0, k_1, \ldots$ (with k_0 being the most significant bit), the binary trie can now be defined as follows:

> **Definition 13.1. Binary Trie.** A binary trie is a binary tree in which all data elements are stored in external vertices, and the keys of the data elements obey the following property. If the binary path label b from the root to external vertex v has p bits, then the first p (most significant) bits of the key stored in v equal b.

An example binary trie is shown in Figure 13.1. From Definition 13.1 it follows that there can only be one binary trie corresponding to a given set of binary keys. Note that the Huffman trees we constructed in Section 9.5 are in fact binary tries, as is any binary tree representation of a prefix code.

A binary trie is searched very much like a binary search tree. Starting from the most significant bit of the search key we move left (on a 0 bit) or right (on a 1 bit) down the tree until either an external vertex or a null pointer is reached. If a null pointer is encountered, then the search was unsuccessful. If an external vertex is reached, then we must compare the remainder of the search key to the one stored at the external vertex in order to determine if the search was successful or unsuccessful. Since only a single bit needs to be examined at each internal vertex along the search path, this portion of the search operation can be accomplished using successive right bit-shift operations. Thus, using the bit-wise operators available in C/C++, the total number of bit comparisons required in a search of a binary trie equals the total number of bit operations required in a single key comparison. This means that if the maximum key size is m, the *Search* operation has a running time of $O(m)$, independent of the number of data elements stored in the binary trie.

The use of tries is not restricted to the case when keys are treated as binary strings. The idea used in binary tries will also work if the keys are character strings. The difference is that each vertex in the resulting data structure will have d children,

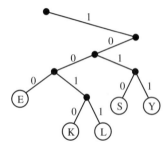

FIGURE 13.1
The binary trie for the keys E, K, L, S and Y, with ASCII values 1000101, 1001011, 1001100, 1010011, and 1011001, respectively.

where d is the size of the alphabet the character strings are drawn from. For obvious reasons, this data structure is referred to as a ***multiway trie***. Thus, in applications where key comparisons are expensive, or the keys have varying lengths, tries are a good alternative to binary search trees.

It is now clear that a search in a trie can be thought of as a successive partitioning of the search (i.e., key) space. In the case of a binary trie, the left subtree of the root contains all keys whose most significant bit is 0, and the right subtree contains all keys whose most significant bit is 1. As we move down levels in a trie, finer and finer partitions are obtained. The same can be said for multiway tries, except that the partitioning occurs d ways at each level. In general, data structures that support searching operations can be placed into one of two categories: those that partition the search space according to the data—we will refer to this as ***data decomposition***; and those that partition the search space in a regular fashion, independent of the data—we will refer to this as ***spatial decomposition***. From our previous discussions, it is clear that tries are based on the idea of spatial decomposition, while all of the other data structures studied prior to this point in the text use data decomposition. This is clearly evident, for example, in binary search trees, where the data being stored determines the shape of the tree.

An insertion is performed in a trie by first searching it in the manner we have just described. If a null pointer is encountered, the new vertex (containing the data element being inserted) is attached as a child of the internal vertex visited immediately prior to encountering the null pointer. If, however, the search leads to an external vertex, then the minimal number of internal vertices needed to distinguish between the search key and the key stored in the external vertex are added to the trie. For instance, if the key D is inserted in the binary trie shown in Figure 13.1, two internal vertices would need to be added as shown in Figure 13.2.

To delete a data element from a trie, the tree is searched for the desired key. If the key is found, it will be at an external vertex. In this case we remove the external vertex, along with all the internal vertices that are needed to distinguish the vertex being deleted from all other external vertices. For example, deleting the vertex with

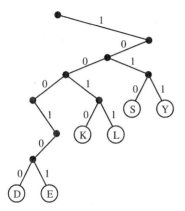

FIGURE 13.2
Insertion of a data element with key D (1000100) into the binary trie shown in Figure 13.1.

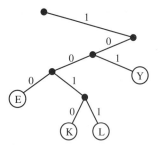

FIGURE 13.3
Deletion of the data element with key S from the binary trie shown in Figure 13.1.

key S in Figure 13.1 would lead to the removal of a single internal vertex as shown in Figure 13.3.

The *RangeSearch* operation in a trie is implemented by first searching for the data element on the lower boundary of the range using key k_1, and then searching for the data element on the upper boundary using key k_2. All external vertices between these two extremes fall within the search range. The details of this operation are left as Exercise 13.2

By observing Figure 13.2, one of the major shortcomings of tries becomes evident: If the keys of data elements agree in many of the leading bit positions, most of the paths to external vertices in the corresponding trie will be long, and search times in such a trie will be poor. The PATRICIA trie, discussed next, addresses this issue.

PATRICIA TRIES. In the PATRICIA trie data structure, every internal vertex stores a *skip count* field that is used to eliminate nonessential branches. In essence, the PATRICIA trie is a compressed version of a trie. Specifically, if the skip count field of vertex v is i, then the next i characters in each of the keys that are stored in descendent vertices of v are not needed to distinguish between these keys. In a trie, these nonessential branches correspond to internal vertices with only one child. For example, in Figure 13.2 the paths to the vertices with keys D and E both traverse the same two single-child internal vertices. This means that there are three edges that are common to these paths only, and therefore nonessential. The binary PATRICIA trie containing the keys used in Figure 13.2 is illustrated in Figure 13.4. During a search of a PATRICIA trie, the skip count field is utilized as follows. If we are currently processing k_i, the i-th character of search key k, and the current internal vertex v has a skip count of j, then character k_{i+j} determines which child of vertex v should be searched.

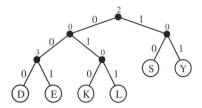

FIGURE 13.4
The binary PATRICIA trie corresponding to the binary trie shown in Figure 13.2. The skip count of each internal vertex is shown immediately above it.

A shortcoming associated with PATRICIA tries (as well as the tries discussed previously) follows from the fact that their vertices are not homogeneous; the internal vertices do not store data (other than pointers and a skip count), while the external vertices do. This complicates the implementation of tries since it requires the type of vertex to be checked at every step of the search algorithm. An implementation that addresses this shortcoming is given in Exercise 13.5.

13.2 MULTIDIMENSIONAL SEARCHING

Up to this point in the text we have restricted our attention to ADT operations involving at most one key. In essence we can think of the data elements associated with these ADTs as having one-dimensional attributes (their key values), and any operation involving a key search as a one-dimensional point search. More generally, the data associated with an application will have multiple attributes, each of which needs to be examined during a search operation. This type of operation is needed in computer graphics and image processing, database management systems, geographic information systems (GIS), and computational geometry applications, just to name a few.

One fact that immediately complicates the implementation of data structures for multidimensional point data is that, unlike one-dimensional point data, the total ordering relationship does not necessarily exist between the data elements. Thus the DYNAMIC SET operations *Minimum*, *Maximum*, *Successor*, and *Predecessor* are not well defined. For this reason we will only consider the DICTIONARY ADT operations, and also the *RangeSearch* operation. Particular emphasis will be placed on range searching due to its ubiquitousness in applications involving multidimensional data.

In this section we will focus on data elements with two-dimensional attributes; however, the data structures we present can all be extended to d-dimensions. It is often useful to think in geometric terms when studying multidimensional searching. For example, in two dimensions the *RangeSearch* operation will require four keys as input rather than two. In the two-dimensional search space, these keys define the corners of a rectangle, which we will refer to as the *query rectangle*. We are interested in finding all data points that lie on or inside the query rectangle.

We will first consider some rather simple approaches that use lists to store two-dimensional data. Next we will consider two tree-based data structures, the quad tree and the 2-d tree, that are organized using data decomposition. Finally, we will examine grid files, which use spatial decomposition. The two-dimensional data points shown in Figure 13.5 will be used to illustrate the organization of these data structures. We will only briefly touch on the implementation details of these data structures, leaving many of the specifics for exercises.

13.2.1 List-Based Data Structures

Similar to one-dimensional data, the simplest way to store d-dimensional data is in a list. The fact that a total ordering relationship may not exist means that the binary search technique cannot be directly extended to d dimensions. Thus, implementing

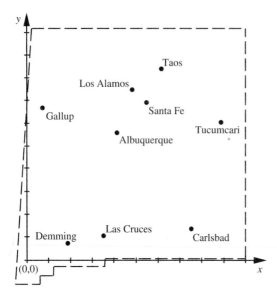

FIGURE 13.5
A map of the state of New Mexico. By overlaying the x-y coordinate system shown in this figure, the following coordinates are obtained: Albuquerque, (42,56); Carlsbad, (75,13); Demming, (19,7); Gallup, (7,67); Las Cruces (36,11); Los Alamos (49,75); Santa Fe (55,69); Taos (62,83); Tucumcari (90,60).

either the *Search* or *RangeSearch* operation in a list requires that we examine every data element (and each key attribute), leading to an $O(n \cdot d)$ running time if there are n data points. In cases where most of the keys fall within the query rectangle, this approach performs well.

An alternative approach doubles the storage requirements by keeping two lists, which are referred to as ***inverted lists***. The first list is sorted according to the x coordinate, and the second is sorted according to the y coordinate. Figure 13.6 shows the inverted lists that result from the data in Figure 13.5. Searching for a single key in inverted lists can be accomplished in $O(\log n)$ time by performing two binary searches—one for each coordinate in the key.

x coordinate	y coordinate
Gallup	Demming
Demming	Las Cruces
Las Cruces	Carlsbad
Albuquerque	Albuquerque
Los Alamos	Tucumcari
Santa Fe	Gallup
Taos	Santa Fe
Carlsbad	Los Alamos
Tucumcari	Taos

FIGURE 13.6
The inverted lists for the data in Figure 13.5. The list on the left is obtained by projecting the data onto the x axis, and the list on the right by projecting the data onto the y axis.

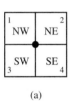

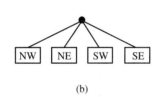

(a)   (b)

FIGURE 13.7
(a) Drawing a vertical and horizontal line through a two-dimensional key quarters the plane into the northwest (NW), northeast (NE), southwest (SW), and southeast (SE) quadrants. **(b)** The four children of a vertex in a quad tree are ordered according to these compass directions, with the leftmost child being NW, and the rightmost being SE.

The *RangeSearch* operation is implemented by performing two binary searches on one list, say the x-coordinate list, in order to find all keys satisfying the x range. Each of these keys must then be searched for in the other list, using binary search, to check if it also falls within the y range. Alternatively, two binary searches can be performed on both lists, saving the one that returns fewer keys. These keys are then searched for in the other list. With either approach, the running time is $O(n \log n)$ when there are n keys, which may actually be worse than the single-list approach. However, we can expect the inverted lists approach to outperform the single-list approach when only a few keys fall within one of the coordinate ranges.

13.2.2   Quad Trees

A generalization of binary search trees to two-dimensional attributes leads to the quad tree data structure. In a binary search tree there are at most two children per vertex; in a quad tree there are at most four. These four children are ordered according to the compass directions shown in Figure 13.7. Thus, if we consider the two-dimensional key stored in the root v_r of a quad tree, all data elements that have keys in the northwest quadrant (with respect to v_r) should be in the NW (i.e., leftmost) subtree of v_r, all data elements that have keys in the northeast quadrant should be in the NE subtree, and so on. A quad tree that stores the data given in Figure 13.5 is shown in Figure 13.8. Notice that the first partitioning produces the root of the tree, and that subsequent partitionings occur in a given quadrant only if there is more than one data point in that quadrant.

The approach used to search a quad tree is nearly identical to the one used to search a binary search tree, the only difference being that two comparisons are needed at a vertex in order to determine which of the four subtrees of that vertex need to be searched next. The *Insert* operation in quad trees is also a straightforward extension of the way it is implemented in binary search trees. Because we are not able to define the predecessor or successor of a vertex, an efficient implementation of the *Delete* operation in quad trees is rather complex. A simple, but inefficient, approach is to simply reinsert all vertices in the subtree of the deleted vertex. In Exercise 13.8 you are asked to develop a more efficient deletion algorithm, and in

Exercise 13.9 a method for maintaining balance after insertions or deletions is suggested. The *RangeSearch* operation is relatively easy to implement in quad trees. Letting R denote the query rectangle, we first check to see if any of the four children of the root overlap with R. Each of the children that do overlap are then recursively searched in the same manner.

The fact that it is impossible to quarter any collection of four collinear points (at least two quadrants must be empty) means that certain arrangements of data points

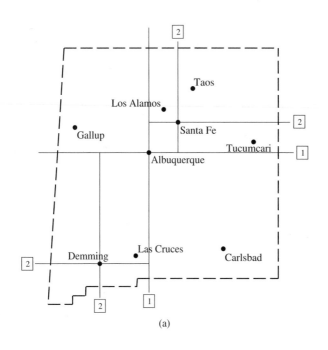

(a)

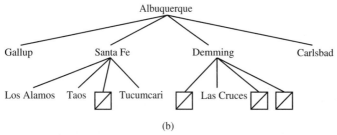

(b)

FIGURE 13.8

(a) Successive quartering of the two-dimensional data given in Figure 13.5. The first quartering occurs at Albuquerque, as indicated by the $\boxed{1}$ s. At the next step, the SW and NE quadrants of the initial quartering are partitioned through Santa Fe and Demming, as indicated by the $\boxed{2}$ s. **(b)** The quad tree corresponding to the partitioning in part (a). The boxes with diagonal lines through them indicate null pointers.

lead to better (i.e., more balanced) quad trees than others. However, given a set of n distinct points in the plane, a quad tree of height $O(\log n)$ can always be constructed in $O(n \log n)$ time. In order to do this, first sort the data primarily by their x values, and secondarily by their y values (i.e., only if some of the data points have the same x coordinate). Next, recursively split the data in half about the x median. Since at each step we are dividing the remaining points into at least two halves, the resulting quad tree will have a worst case height proportional to $\log_2 n$. This worst case occurs when all of the data points are collinear. The reader should also see that a perfect quad tree has height $\log_4 n$, and $2^{\log_4 n} = 2^{\log_2 n / \log_2 4} = \sqrt{n}$ external vertices.

13.2.3 k-d Trees

In quad trees, each internal vertex corresponds to a partitioning through both dimensions of the search space. However, in k-d trees each internal vertex corresponds to a partition through only a single dimension. This will always produce a binary tree. In a 2-d tree, the vertices on one level of the binary tree correspond to vertical partitions, and on the next level to horizontal partitions. Figure 13.9 demonstrates one such partitioning of the data points given in Figure 13.5, along with the resulting 2-d tree. Notice that for the horizontal partitions, those cities above the partition line are placed in the left subtree, and the cities below the partition line are placed in the right subtree.

The *Search* operation in 2-d trees is a generalization of this operation in binary search trees. The only difference is that as we move down the tree, we alternate between the x and y coordinates of the search key. The *Insert* operation is also generalized in the obvious way from the one used with binary search trees. Deletions are complicated in 2-d trees because, unlike binary search trees and quad trees, not every subtree in a 2-d tree is itself a 2-d tree. Unfortunately, the structure of 2-d trees also makes it difficult to implement rotation operations that maintain balance after insertions or deletions. The *RangeSearch* operation in 2-d trees is only slightly different from the one described for quad trees.

Given a collection of n distinct points in the plane, a 2-d tree of height $O(\log n)$ can be constructed in $O(n \log n)$ time by first finding the median of the n points according to their x coordinates. The median is made the root. Next a vertical line is drawn through the median, and the medians of the point sets on either side of this line are found, this time according to their y coordinates. These medians are made the left and right children of the root. This process continues until there are no points left to partition. The reader should verify that this construction technique is able to partition certain point sets more effectively than the quad tree—which is its major advantage over the quad tree. Indeed, the worst case in 2-d trees only occurs when all data points are collinear, *and* the line that runs through these points is parallel to one of the coordinate axes.

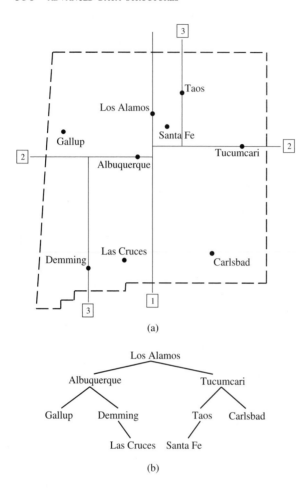

(a)

(b)

FIGURE 13.9
(a) A successive partitioning of the data given in Figure 13.5. The first partition through the x dimension splits the search space in half at Los Alamos, as indicated by the ☐1☐. These two halves are then independently partitioned, as indicated by the ☐2☐s. The final partitions, indicated by the ☐3☐s, occur once again through the x dimension. **(b)** The 2-d tree corresponding to the partitioning in part (a).

13.2.4 Grid Files

The grid file is a data structure commonly used in geographic information systems. The search space is divided into grid blocks using grid lines. Figure 13.10 demonstrates one such division of the two-dimensional data given in Figure 13.5. If a data point falls on the boundary of two or more grid blocks, it is placed in the grid block to the north, east, or northeast. The grid lines drawn in this figure have equal spacing in both the x and y dimensions, but this is not necessary. Note also that if the grid line spacing is fixed *a priori*, then spatial decomposition is being employed. We will assume this is the case. It is also possible to implement grid files using data decomposition (see Exercise 13.11).

The grid file is a two-level data structure. On the first level a grid directory is maintained, storing one pointer for each grid block. Each of these pointers in turn points to a separate data structure storing the data that falls within its corresponding

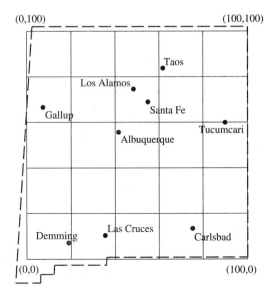

FIGURE 13.10

A partitioning of the data given in Figure 13.5 using a grid. Grid lines are drawn every 20 units in both the x and y dimensions, producing a 5×5 grid, and 25 grid blocks.

grid block. If the data points are uniformly distributed throughout the grid, with most grid blocks containing at least one data point, then a two-dimensional array is a good choice for implementing the grid directory. If this is not the case, a more space efficient approach involves using some data structure that implements the DICTIONARY ADT—a good choice is the hash table. With this approach, only grid blocks that actually contain data points are stored in the grid directory. In either case, the construction of a grid file from a collection of n data points is a straightforward exercise.

The *Search* operation in a grid file is implemented by translating the coordinates of the search key into the address of a grid block. The pointer stored in this grid block would then be dereferenced in order to search the associated data structure for the search key. The *RangeSearch* operation is a simple extension of this idea, the only difference is that multiple grid blocks may need to be examined. Specifically, any grid blocks that overlap with the query rectangle must be searched to see if the data elements in their associated data structures fall within the query rectangle. Insertions and deletions in a grid file involve a search for the appropriate grid block, followed by the actual insertion or deletion in the associated data structure.

In practice, the best grid line spacing in a grid file depends on the size and shape of the query rectangles used in an application. In many applications, however, the size and shape of the query rectangles are fixed, and only their locations are unknown. In these cases, choosing the grid block size to be the same as the query rectangle leads to good performance. Grid files also work well with large data sets that require the use of secondary storage. In these cases, the grid directory can be stored in main memory, and the data associated with a given grid block can be stored in contiguous blocks on a disk drive. This approach allows rapid searching of the grid directory, and also minimizes disk access time.

13.3   THE DISJOINT-SET ADT

An abstract data type that we will find useful in the next chapter is the DISJOINT SET ADT. Given a dynamic set S, this ADT maintains a partitioning of S into a collection of disjoint subsets. That is, if a disjoint set is storing the subsets $S_1, S_2, \ldots, S_k$, then these subsets must satisfy $S_1 \cup S_2 \cup \cdots \cup S_k = S$, and $S_i \cap S_j = \emptyset$ whenever $i \neq j$. Furthermore, the elements belonging to any given subset S_i are assumed to be "equivalent" in some sense. Specifically, if the *Find* operation, which will be defined shortly, returns the same value when applied to two different elements of S, then these elements must belong to the same subset. As a simple mathematical example of this concept, let S be a set of integers, and partition each element $x \in S$ according to $x \bmod n$. In this case all elements of S that are congruent modulo n will belong to the same subset, and each element will belong to exactly one subset.

When processing disjoint sets, it is convenient to refer to an entire subset using a single label. By default, the dynamic set elements belonging to a given subset all have labels (i.e., their keys); however, the subset itself does not. Thus each subset will choose one of its elements to serve as its ***representative element***. In many applications it will not matter which elements are chosen as the representatives, as long as a given subset always returns the same element whenever repeated requests are made for its representative (assuming the subset has not been modified between these requests). In other cases, the representatives will need to be chosen according to some specific rule; e.g., we may require that the smallest element in a subset be the representative. With this in mind, we define the DISJOINT SET ADT as a collection of dynamic set data elements S that may be operated on using:

1. *Create*(S). Creates a trivial partitioning of S into $|S|$ subsets, one for each element in S.

2. *Union*(S, x, y). Merges the two subsets containing the representative elements x and y. If this operation is successful, the true value is returned; otherwise the false value is returned.

3. *Find*(S, a). Returns (the representative element of) the subset of S to which a belongs, or the null value if $a \notin S$.

13.3.1   Up-Trees

One of the simplest data structures for implementing a single subset of a disjoint set stores each dynamic set element in a vertex, with each of these vertices containing a pointer to the vertex storing the representative element. Because the direction of the pointers is from child to parent, this data structure is called an ***up-tree***. The

DISJOINT SET ADT is then represented as a forest of up-trees. Notice that there is no particular ordering between the vertices in an up-tree, and the vertex containing the representative element points to itself.

Figure 13.11 (a) shows two subsets that have been represented in this fashion, one with representative element x, and the other with representative element h.

If the *Union* operation is not used, then the *Find* operation can be efficiently implemented using up-trees having the form shown in Figure 13.11 (a). Given a pointer to any element a, only a single pointer needs to be dereferenced to find the representative of the subset to which a belongs; and because the root contains a pointer to itself, no special processing of the representative vertex needs to be considered.

Allowing the *Union* operation complicates matters. If the up-tree created as a result of this operation is to have a height of one (as they do in Figure 13.11 (a)), then every pointer in one of the up-trees would have to be changed so that they point to the representative vertex of the other up-tree. However, since we only have access to the representative vertex stored in each up-tree, the other members of the subset cannot be reached, making it impossible to change these pointers. One way around this problem is to allow the representative vertex to store pointers back to each of its children. Not only does this introduce additional storage requirements, but it makes the data structure "nonuniform" in that the representative vertex must store more pointers than the other vertices in the up-tree.

Another alternative is to implement the *Union* operation in $\Theta(1)$ time by simply changing the representative vertex of one up-tree so that it points to the representative vertex of the other. For instance, if this approach is applied to the two subsets shown in Figure 13.11 (a), it might produce the up-tree shown in Figure 13.11 (b). This eliminates the need for any additional pointers, at the expense of additional pointer dereferencing during *Find* operations. In the worst case, a sequence of n such *Union* operations will lead to the construction of a degenerate up-tree having

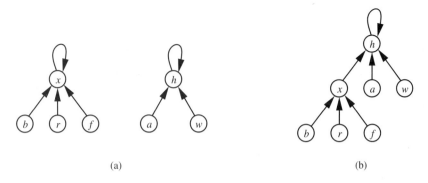

(a) (b)

FIGURE 13.11
(a) The up-tree data structure for two subsets, one with representative element x, and the other with representative element h. (b) The resulting data structure after a *Union*(S, x, h) operation.

height $n - 1$ (i.e., a linked list), and a *Find* operation would require $O(n)$ time in this tree.

If we are careful about how we merge two up-trees when performing a *Union*, the construction of degenerate up-trees can be avoided. Rather than merging up-trees in some prespecified (or random) order, let us use *weight*(x) to denote the number of vertices in the subtree rooted at x (including x), and assume up-trees are merged during a *Union* operation according to the following rule:

> **Definition 13.2. Union-by-Weight Heuristic.** When implementing *Union*(S, x, y) using up-trees, if *weight*(x) $\leq$ *weight*(y), then make the up-tree rooted at x a subtree of the one rooted at y; otherwise, make the up-tree rooted at y a subtree of the one rooted at x.

Therefore, if *weight*(x) $\leq$ *weight*(y), y will be the representative element in the resulting tree; otherwise, x will be the representative element of the new up-tree. Intuitively this heuristic tends to create up-trees in which larger-weight subtrees are closer to the root. Notice that the up-tree in Figure 13.11 (b) was *not* created using this heuristic. In Figure 13.11 (b) there are three vertices at a distance of 2, and four vertices at a distance of 1 from the root (including the root itself); however, if union-by-weight were used, there would be two vertices at a distance of 2, and five vertices at a distance of 1 from the root, as shown in Figure 13.12 (a).

It turns out that by using the union-by-weight heuristic, the running time of *Find* is actually improved to $O(\log n)$, without changing the $\Theta(1)$ time of the *Union* operation. We prove this by showing that if this heuristic is used, then the longest path from any vertex to the root in an n-element up-tree is at most $\Theta(\log n)$. Let us denote the length of the longest path in the subtree rooted at x using *rank*(x). Induction will be used to establish the inequality

$$2^{rank(x)} \leq weight(x) \tag{13.1}$$

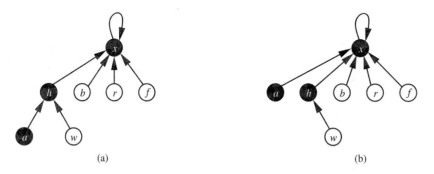

(a)   (b)

FIGURE 13.12
(a) An example up-tree formed by using the union-by-weight heuristic on the two up-trees shown in Figure 13.11 (a). The vertices encountered during a *Find*(S, a) operation are drawn black. **(b)** The resulting data structure after the path-compression heuristic has been applied during a *Find*(S, a) operation.

If an up-tree with representative element x contains n vertices, then taking logarithms of both sides of inequality (13.1) leads to the desired result:

$$rank(x) \leq \lg n \tag{13.2}$$

For the base case, a single vertex up-tree, inequality (13.1) clearly holds. Now consider applying $Union(S, x, y)$ to two up-trees, and without loss of generality assume the up-tree with representative vertex y is attached as a subtree to the one with representative vertex x. If we use primes to denote the rank and weight of the resulting tree, then $rank'(x)$ will either be $rank(x)$, or $rank(y) + 1$. The latter case will occur if the up-tree with representative vertex y contains a path that is as long as any of the paths in the initial up-tree with representative vertex x. In the former case $2^{rank'(x)} = 2^{rank(x)}$, and $weight'(x) = weight(x) + weight(y)$, so inequality (13.1) is preserved in the new up-tree. If the latter case occurs, then

$$
\begin{aligned}
2^{rank'(x)} &= 2^{rank(y)+1} \\
&= 2^{rank(y)} + 2^{rank(y)} \\
&\leq weight(y) + weight(y) \\
&\leq weight(x) + weight(y) = weight'(x)
\end{aligned}
$$

where the induction hypothesis was used on the third line. On the fourth line we used the fact that the up-tree with representative vertex y will only be attached as a subtree to the one with representative vertex x if $weight(y) \leq weight(x)$. Exercise 13.13 demonstrates that this result is tight.

Obviously, an up-tree implementation that uses this heuristic would need to keep track of the weight of each vertex. If each vertex uses a variable to store its current weight, then the weight of the root vertex after a $Union(S, x, y)$ operation can be calculated in $\Theta(1)$ time by adding the weights stored in vertices x and y.

The results we have obtained for the union-by-weight heuristic still hold if we store the rank, rather than the weight, of each vertex, and modify the heuristic so that it checks $rank(x) \leq rank(y)$ rather than $weight(x) \leq weight(y)$. We leave the proof of this fact as Exercise 13.15 (a), and we refer to this modification as the **union-by-rank** heuristic.

In an effort to further improve the running time of the *Find* operation, another heuristic can be introduced. Suppose a forest of up-trees is being used to maintain a partitioning of S, and that the $Find(S, a)$ operation returns representative element x; then there must exist a path $a \rightsquigarrow x$ in one of the up-trees. Let us refer to this path as the **find path** of $Find(S, a)$. For instance, the find path obtained by applying this operation to the up-tree shown in Figure 13.12 (a) is a, h, x. The vertices in this path are black in this figure.

Now, consider the following self-adjusting heuristic, which modifies the pointers associated with vertices on the find path:

Definition 13.3. Path-Compression Heuristic. When implementing $Find(S, a)$ using up-trees, make the pointer of each vertex along the find path point directly back to the representative vertex.

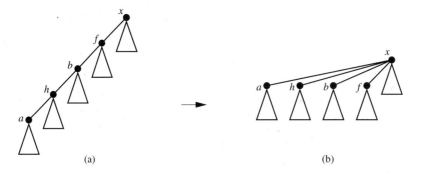

FIGURE 13.13
(a) An up-tree in which a *Find(S, a)* yields the find path $a \rightsquigarrow x$. (b) The effect of path compression on the tree.

Figure 13.12 (b) demonstrates how this heuristic affects the shape of the up-tree originally given in part (a) of the figure. Specifically, more vertices are now at a distance of 1 from the representative vertex. The intuition here is that this tree is more like our original definition of an up-tree (e.g., Figure 13.11 (a)), where *every* vertex is adjacent to the root. Figure 13.13 demonstrates that in addition to changing the depth of every vertex on the find path to 1, this heuristic "pulls up" the subtrees attached to the find path vertices. A crucial point is that, since all pointer manipulations associated with the path-compression heuristic occur along the find path, they do not increase the asymptotic running time of the *Find* operation. Furthermore, if no *Union* operations occur in the mean time, then any future *Find* operations involving vertices on this find path will take constant time.

ANALYSIS OF UNION-BY-RANK WITH PATH-COMPRESSION. The reader may have already concluded that the most sensible thing to do at this point is to use the union-by-weight (or rank) and path-compression heuristics simultaneously in an up-tree implementation. It is easy to see that running time of the *Union* operation will still be $\Theta(1)$ under this scenario. The remarkable fact, which we shall prove, is that the amortized time per *Find* operation is very nearly $\Theta(1)$ over a sequence of DISJOINT SET ADT operations.

Specifically, we will demonstrate that if the union-by-rank and path-compression heuristics are employed simultaneously on an initially trivial partitioning of n elements, then any sequence of m DISJOINT SET ADT operations, where $m > n$, can be completed in $O(m \lg^* n)$ time, where $\lg^* n$ is the *iterated logarithm function* defined as

$$\lg^* n = \min\{i \geq 0 \mid \lg^{(i)} n \leq 1\}$$

with $\lg^{(i)} n$ denoting a composition of the logarithm function i times. That is,

$$\lg^{(i)} n = \underbrace{\lg(\lg(\lg(\cdots (n) \cdots)))}_{i \text{ times}}$$

This function does *not* denote the logarithm of n raised to the i-th power, which is often written as $\lg^i n$. Thus, $\lg^* n$ denotes the number of times the (base 2) logarithm needs to be applied in succession, starting with n, until the result is less than or equal to 1.

In order to gain a better understanding of the $\lg^* n$ function, below we list its value for a number of arguments:

$$\lg^* 2 = 1$$
$$\lg^* 4 = 2$$
$$\lg^* 16 = 3$$
$$\lg^* 65536 = 4$$
$$\lg^* 2^{65536} = 5$$

Notice how slowly this function grows, and that its value only exceeds 5 when n is greater than 2^{65536}. In order to appreciate the enormity of this number, consider that it is larger than the number of atoms in the observable universe! With this in mind, it is safe to say that growth rates of $O(m \lg^* n)$ and $O(m)$ are indistinguishable in practice.

We now concentrate on proving the $O(m \lg^* n)$ running time bound on any sequence of m DISJOINT SET ADT operations implemented using a forest of up-trees, along with the union-by-rank and path-compression heuristics. The analysis is complicated by the fact that although path compression will not alter the weights of any vertices, it can reduce the ranks of vertices along the find path; furthermore, these ranks are difficult to calculate. In order to circumvent this problem, our analysis will use the rank value that a vertex would obtain if path compression were not used, noting that this value always upper bounds the rank of the vertex when path compression is used. In essence we are redefining the rank of a vertex x to be the longest path that has *ever* existed from any leaf y to x. This assumes that at some point in time there was a path $y \rightsquigarrow x$; however, due to path compression it may no longer exist. Using our new definition, a vertex can only change rank when it is the root of an up-tree, and this change in rank can only happen as a result of a *Union* operation. Thus the rank of any vertex will increase monotonically over time until it "loses" in a *Union* operation, at which point its rank can never change, even though it may lose children during path compression. This new definition also maintains a natural property associated with our previous definition for the rank of an up-tree vertex—starting from any vertex and tracing a path back to the root yields a sequence of ranks that is strictly increasing. You are asked to prove this in Exercise 13.15 (b). It is easy to see that, because of path compression, the new definition of rank does *not* always satisfy inequality (13.1). The reader can, however, verify that at the time a vertex changes rank, this inequality will be satisfied.

One additional property that we will find useful in our forthcoming analysis is that in an n-vertex forest of up-trees, at most $\lfloor n/2^r \rfloor$ vertices of rank r can exist simultaneously. To see why, choose a particular value for r and assume that whenever a vertex x attains the rank of r, we color each vertex in the up-tree rooted at x black. According to equation (13.1), at least 2^r vertices will be colored black each time this happens. Furthermore if x later changes rank, we know that it must be to a value larger than r, and that it can never change back to r. This means that each of the n vertices can be colored at most once. Now assume that some n-vertex forest of up-trees contains more than $\lfloor n/2^r \rfloor$ vertices of rank r. This forest of up-trees must contain at least $(\lfloor n/2^r \rfloor + 1) \cdot 2^r > n$ black vertices. But this is a contradiction—we only have n vertices available, so therefore the number of vertices of rank r must be at most $\lfloor n/2^r \rfloor$.

In the following amortized analysis we will group the n vertices in a forest of up-trees according to their rank. Specifically, we define the j-th rank group as

$$G_j = \left\{ x \mid \lg^{(j+1)} n < rank(x) \le \lg^{(j)} n \right\}$$

Notice that the lower rank groups contain the vertices with higher rank. Also, since $\lg^{(\lg^* n+1)} n \le 0$ for any positive n, j ranges from 1 to at most $\lg^* n + 1$ in this definition. Finally, since ranks are integer values, the number of different ranks in G_j is given by $\lfloor \lg^{(j)} n \rfloor - (\lfloor \lg^{(j+1)} n \rfloor + 1)$.

Using the fact that there are at most $\lfloor n/2^r \rfloor$ vertices of rank r, we can calculate an upper bound on the number of vertices in each rank group:

$$|G_j| \le \sum_{i=\lfloor \lg^{(j+1)} n \rfloor + 1}^{\lfloor \lg^{(j)} n \rfloor} \frac{n}{2^i}$$

$$< \frac{n}{\lg^{(j)} n} \sum_{i=0}^{\infty} \left(\frac{1}{2} \right)^i$$

$$= \frac{2n}{\lg^{(j)} n}$$

The bound on the second line follows from the fact that the largest term in the original sum is smaller than $n/2^{\lg^{(j+1)} n} = n/2^{\lg(\lg^{(j)} n)} = n/\lg^{(j)} n$, and each succeeding term is half the previous one. Equation (A.21) from Appendix A.3 is then applied to obtain the final result.

The key idea we need to exploit in our amortized analysis is that path compression happens less frequently as more *Find* operations are performed. Thus we will spread a portion of the work performed during path compression in earlier *Find* operations to the initial *Union* operation. Specifically, we will assign the following amortized costs to the DISJOINT SET ADT operations:

Operation	Amortized Cost ($\hat{c}$)
Create	$n + \Theta(n \lg^* n)$
Union	1
Find	$\lg^* n + 2$

Using these charges, the initial *Create* operation pays for itself, and leaves $\Theta(n \lg^* n)$ credits on the balance sheet. Any subsequent *Union* operation is able to pay for itself using the single credit available to it.

To pay for a *Find*, we will need one credit for each vertex on the find path. Equation (13.2) shows that this can be as much as $\lg n$ credits; however, we only have $\lg^* n + 2$ credits available per *Find* operation. To see how we will spend these credits, assume the find path is $v_0, v_1, \ldots, v_l$, where v_l is a root. Tracing the path $v_0 \rightsquigarrow v_l$ we will encounter vertices in order of strictly increasing rank. Let us allocate one credit to the *last* vertex belonging to each rank group encountered along this path, and one credit to v_{l-1}, the child of the root. There can be vertices from at most $\lg^* n + 1$ different rank groups on any find path, so there will always be enough credits to pay for these vertices. For each of the remaining vertices on the find path, we register one debit on the balance sheet.

The number of credits consumed by m *Find* operations is at most $m(\lg^* n + 2)$, and there are $\Theta(n \lg^* n)$ credits left over from the initial *Create* operation. Therefore we must only show that the total number of debits due to *Find* operations is $O(n \lg^* n)$.

First note that once a vertex $v_i \neq v_{l-1}$ on the find path uses a credit, due to being the last vertex in a rank group encountered on the find path, it can never again cause a debit to appear on the balance sheet. To see why, observe that each time path compression occurs, the rank of v_i remains the same, but the rank of its parent must increase. This means that once v_i and its parent are in different rank groups (and they must be if v_i used a credit), they will always be in different rank groups, and v_i will always be the last vertex in its rank group on any find path that contains it.

Now if a vertex on a find path ever records a debit, it will be moved by path compression and get a new parent of higher rank than its old parent. Thus a vertex in rank group G_j can be moved at most $\lfloor \lg^{(j)} n \rfloor - (\lfloor \lg^{(j+1)} n \rfloor + 1)$ times before its parent will move out of rank group G_j. After this point, as we have just discussed, the vertex will not be able to register any additional debits.

Therefore the maximum number of debits due to vertices in a *single* rank group is given by the product of the maximum number of vertices in that rank group, and the maximum number of debits due to a single vertex in the rank group. It follows that the maximum number of debits for all *Find* operations, which we denote by D, is obtained by summing this product over all rank groups:

$$D = \sum_{j=1}^{\lg^* n + 1} \frac{2n}{\lg^{(j)} n} \cdot \left(\lfloor \lg^{(j)} n \rfloor - \left(\lfloor \lg^{(j+1)} n \rfloor + 1 \right) \right)$$

$$\leq \sum_{j=1}^{\lg^* n + 1} \frac{2n}{\lg^{(j)} n} \cdot \lg^{(j)} n$$

$$= \sum_{j=1}^{\lg^* n + 1} 2n$$

$$= 2n(\lg^* n + 1)$$

$$= O(n \lg^* n)$$

This demonstrates that the total number of debits registered by *Find* operations is

$O(n \lg^* n)$, and therefore the total running time of any sequence of $m \geq n$ DISJOINT SET ADT operations is $O(m \lg^* n)$.

13.4   AN EXTENDED EXAMPLE: COMPUTATIONAL GEOMETRY

Computational geometry is concerned with the design and analysis of algorithms for computing various properties associated with geometric objects. These geometric algorithms are often employed in conjunction with the data structures we considered for multidimensional searching in Section 13.2. A few of the areas in which computational geometry is routinely applied include VLSI design, robot path planning, and computer-aided design. In this extended example, the scope of our discussion is necessarily limited to a few fairly simple problems. However, the algorithms we consider often serve as building blocks in the design of more complicated geometric algorithms. We will once again restrict our attention to two dimensions, and note that the resulting algorithms can often be extended to higher dimensions.

Before proceeding, it is necessary to define a few terms. As before, we will denote a *point* p in the plane using x and y coordinates (i.e., $p = (x, y)$). The *line segment* between points p_1 and p_2 is denoted by $\overline{p_1 p_2}$. A *polygon* is a collection of line segments $\overline{p_1 p_2}, \overline{p_2 p_3}, \ldots, \overline{p_{n-1} p_n}, \overline{p_n p_1}$. The points $p_1, p_2, \ldots, p_n$ are referred to as the *vertices* of the polygon. In a *simple polygon* none of a line segments that comprise it intersect. A simple polygon therefore encloses some portion of the plane, which we say is inside the polygon; the remainder of the plane is outside the polygon. Finally, in a *convex polygon*, a line segment connecting any two points inside the polygon must itself lie inside the polygon.

INTERSECTION OF LINE SEGMENTS.   We start with a simple problem, determining whether two line segments intersect. To solve this problem in $O(1)$ time we simply compute the line equation for each segment using $y = mx + b$. Next we find the point of intersection of these two lines, and check to see if this point is on both line segments. Of course, before solving for the intersection point, we should check for the special case of parallel lines.

The handling of special cases is not something that is new to us; we have dealt with them on a number of occasions prior to this point in the text. Computational geometry problems, however, typically have an abundance of special cases to consider. In order to streamline our presentation, we will often defer these to exercises.

POINT INSIDE A POLYGON.   Determining whether a point is inside a simple polygon appears to be an easy problem at first glance, but when convex polygons are involved (such as the one in Figure 13.14), the problem does not seem as trivial. Furthermore, in the example of Figure 13.14 we are given the benefit of a pictorial representation. When we consider that this polygon would actually be represented in computer memory as a collection of vertices, this problem seems even less trivial. There is, however, a fairly straightforward algorithm for determining if a point lies inside a polygon.

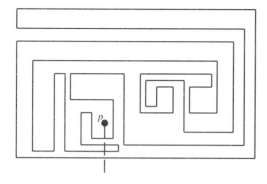

FIGURE 13.14
Does the point p lie inside the polygon?

Notice in Figure 13.14 that a dashed line has been drawn from a region that is definitely outside the polygon, to the point p. Starting from outside the polygon, and tracing along the dashed line, we know that the first line we cross will put us inside the polygon. Crossing the next line will move us outside the polygon, and so forth. Upon reaching p, if the total number of line intersections is odd, then p is inside the polygon; otherwise, p is outside the polygon. The following algorithm implements this strategy:

```
PointInPolygon(point p, polygon Q)
1   pick a point s outside of Q
2   count ← 0
3   for each  p_i p_j ∈ Q  do
4       if  sp intersects p_i p_j  then
5           count ← count +1
6   if  count mod 1 = 0  then    ▷ is count odd?
7       return true    ▷ p is inside Q
8   else
9       return false
```

Finding a point s outside the polygon Q is not a difficult task. By reading through the line segments in Q once, we can find the vertices with minimum x and y coordinates. Any point whose x and y coordinates are smaller than these will due for s. Therefore, if Q consists of n line segments, this algorithm runs in $O(n)$ time.

There are a number of special cases that can cause trouble in PointInPolygon(). First, we must treat the case where $\overline{sp}$ completely overlaps some segment of Q. In addition, if $\overline{sp}$ intersects a vertex of Q, the count may not need to be incremented, as demonstrated in Figure 13.15. We leave the detection and treatment of these special cases as Exercise 13.18.

CONVEX HULLS. The convex hull of a collection of points is the smallest convex polygon that encloses the points. This problem is very common in computational geometry since it is an easy way of finding a reasonably small region that encloses a set of points. One way to think about this problem is that the points are a package that needs to be wrapped with a string. This analogy leads to the so-called **_package-wrapping algorithm_**, which builds the convex hull one vertex at a time. This algorithm

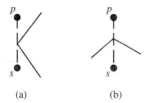

(a)   (b)

FIGURE 13.15
The two ways in which the line segment $\overline{sp}$ can intersect a vertex of Q. **(a)** The count is not incremented in this case. **(b)** The count is incremented in this case.

FIGURE 13.16
(a) The convex hull constructed using the package-wrapping algorithm. The vertices on the convex hull are labeled according to the order they were added by the algorithm. The first point added is the one with minimum y coordinate. The string is tied to this point and rotated clockwise until it hits the next point, and so on. **(b)** The angle calculations required to determine which point should be added third. The minimum angle is denoted by θ.

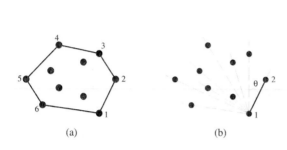

(a)   (b)

starts by finding an extreme point (in either the x or y dimension). This point is guaranteed to be a vertex on the convex hull. The string is tied to this point, and then rotated until it hits another point. This is the next vertex added to the convex hull. This process continues until the string wraps back around to the starting point. Figure 13.16 (a) illustrates this method.

Although the package-wrapping algorithm is easy to explain by analogy, it is more difficult to code. Implementation of the iterative step in this algorithm involves finding the point p_k such that $\overline{p_i p_k}$ forms the minimum angle with $\overline{p_i p_j}$, where p_i and p_j are next to last and last points, respectively, added to the convex hull as it is being constructed. Figure 13.16 (b) demonstrates the angle calculations that are required after the second point has been added to the convex hull. In the following pseudocode for the package-wrapping algorithm, the angle between line segments $\overline{pq}$ and $\overline{pr}$ is denoted by $\angle(\overline{pq}, \overline{pr})$.

```
PackageWrapping(point set P = {p1, p2, ..., pn})
1  C ← ∅
2  find s ∈ P with minimum y coordinate
      ▷ (if there is more than one, pick the one with maximum x coordinate)
3  C ← s
4  let L be the line containing s that is parallel to the x axis
5  while C is not complete do
6     find q ∈ P such that ∠(sq, L) is minimized
7        C ← C ∪ q
8     let L be the line through sq
9        s ← q
10 return C
```

The loop over lines 5–9 will iterate m times, where m is the number of vertices on the convex hull. On each iteration, at most n points need to be examined. Therefore, the running time of PackageWrapping() is $O(nm)$.

EXERCISES

13.1. Write pseudocode algorithms that implement the *Minimum, Maximum, Predecessor,* and *Successor* operations in a binary trie.

13.2. Write an efficient pseudocode algorithm for the *RangeSearch* operation in a multiway trie. Rewrite your algorithm assuming a pointer to each level in the trie is available. Under what circumstances would you expect this algorithm to outperform the range searching algorithm we described for binary search trees?

13.3. Assuming that each bit in a key is equally likely to be a 0 or 1, and that the bit strings corresponding to any two keys are independent, what is the average time for a successful and an unsuccessful search in a binary trie?

13.4. The idea used in binary tries of comparing a bit at a time during searches can be extended to sorting. Specifically, if the keys being sorted are treated as binary bit strings, then comparison-based sorting can be implemented using bit comparisons. This leads to two different sorting techniques depending on the order in which bits are processed:

    (*a*) In the ***radix sort*** bits are processed in order from least significant bit to most significant bit.

    (*b*) In the ***radix exchange sort*** bits are processed in order from most significant bit to least significant bit.

Develop pseudocode algorithms for both of these sorting techniques. (Hint: Radix exchange sort is similar to quicksort.)

13.5. By using backward pointers it is possible to implement PATRICIA tries using only a single type of vertex, as demonstrated below:

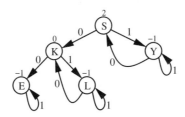

Arrowheads have been added to the edges in order to distinguish between forward and backward pointers. During a search, the data element stored in a vertex is ignored until a negative skip count is encountered. At this point, processing the current character will cause the traversal of a backward pointer, and the vertex pointed to by this backward pointer either contains the desired key, or the search is unsuccessful.

    (*a*) For a given set of key values, are the PATRICIA tries constructed in this manner unique?

    (*b*) Develop pseudocode algorithms for the *Search, RangeSearch, Insert,* and *Delete* operations using this data structure.

13.6. In the inverted lists data structure, is it necessary for the keys within each list to be unique in order to obtain a $O(\log n)$ running time for the *Search* operation?

13.7. What are the running times of the *Insert* and *Delete* operations in the single list and inverted lists data structures storing d-dimensional keys?

13.8. Develop a pseudocode algorithm for the *Delete* operation in quad trees that minimizes the reinsertion of vertices. (Hint: Assume the vertex v we wish to delete has key coordinates (x_v, y_v). Replace v with some vertex u, having key coordinates (x_u, y_u), where the region between the lines $x = x_u$ and $x = x_v$ and the region between the lines $y = y_u$ and $y = y_v$ are empty.)

13.9. Develop rotation patterns for the quad tree that are analogous to the single and double rotation patterns in AVL trees.

13.10. In Section 13.2 we focused on multidimensional point data. The ***region quad tree*** data structure was developed for dealing with multidimensional region data. The region quad tree is based on the idea of recursively subdividing a two-dimensional region into four equally-sized quadrants. In this sense it can be thought of as an extension of tries to two dimensions. Region quad trees are often used to represent image data. Consider the 8×8 binary image shown on the left below, where a black pixel denotes a 1, and a white pixel a 0. The region quad tree for this image, shown on the right, is constructed by continually quartering the image into equally-sized regions until homogeneous quadrants (i.e., containing only 0s or 1s) are obtained. These homogeneous quadrants are denoted by black (1) or white (0) external vertices. Thus the root of the region quad tree represents the first quartering, the vertices in the next level represent the quarterings of the four quadrants produced by the first quartering, and so on.

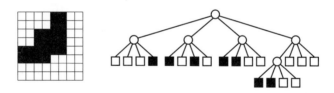

(*a*) Develop a pseudocode algorithm that takes a two-dimensional binary array $b[1..n, 1..n]$ as input, and produces a region quad tree as output.

(*b*) Develop a pseudocode algorithm for performing a range search in a region quad tree. Your algorithm should return all black pixels that intersect with the query rectangle.

13.11. A grid file can be organized using data decomposition if we let the insertion and deletion of data elements determine the number of grid blocks, and the grid directory is implemented using a dynamic two-dimensional array. Initially the grid file is empty, and there is only one grid block, which corresponds to the entire search space. The data structure associated with this grid block is able to store a fixed maximum number of data elements; after this point the grid block is split in half. Similarly, if the number of data elements stored in a grid block becomes too small, it should be merged with one of its neighboring grid blocks if possible. Elaborate as to exactly how this strategy should be employed in grid files to implement the *Search*, *Insert*, *Delete*, and *RangeSearch* operations.

13.12. An important operation in many database applications involves finding all keys that do *not* satisfy a given property. For example, in the *Co-RangeSearch* operation we are given two keys k_1 and k_2, with $k_1 < k_2$, as input and asked to return all elements x in a

DICTIONARY ADT outside the range $[k_1, k_2]$. Develop efficient pseudocode algorithms for performing this operation in the following data structures:

(*a*) A binary search tree.

(*b*) A binary trie.

(*c*) A quad tree.

(*d*) A 2-d tree.

(*e*) A grid file.

13.13. Consider an up-tree implementation of the DISJOINT SET ADT that uses only the union-by-weight heuristic. Show that a sequence of *Union* operations exists which leads to an up-tree that has a longest path that is logarithmic in the weight of the tree.

13.14. In the ***weighted quick-find heuristic*** a *Union*(S, x, y) operation is implemented using up-trees by making the children of x point to y, assuming $weight(x) \le weight(y)$; otherwise the children of y are made to point to x. With this approach, a *Find* operation only requires $\Theta(1)$ time. Show that if there are n dynamic set elements, the amortized time per *Union* operation is $O(\log n)$ when this heuristic is used.

13.15. Assume that each vertex in an up-tree stored its rank instead of its weight; then the union-by-weight heuristic would need to be modified so that it tested for $rank(x) \le rank(y)$, rather than $weight(x) \le weight(y)$.

(*a*) Show that the running time of the *Find* operation remains $O(\log n)$ when this union-by-rank heuristic is used (without using the path-compression heuristic).

(*b*) Now consider what happens when the path-compression heuristic is also used. Path compression does not alter the weight of any vertex, but it can change the rank. Let us assume the ranks of vertices are *not* updated during path-compression operations. Show that in this case the rank value stored at a vertex always upper bounds its true rank, and that the sequence of stored ranks encountered on any path from a vertex (other than the root) to the root is strictly increasing. Finally, argue that if this method of updating ranks is used, the union-by-rank heuristic will work properly in conjunction with the path-compression heuristic (i.e., an up-tree rooted at x with (true) rank larger than the up-tree rooted at y will never become a subtree of y during a *Union*(S, x, y) operation).

13.16. The ***path-halving heuristic*** is a modification to the path-compression heuristic in which every other vertex on the find path is made to point to its grandparent (whenever possible), rather than to the root, as shown below.

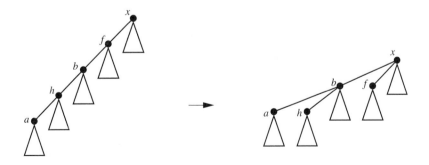

The advantage of this approach is that the find path must only be traversed once in order to implement path-halving. Show that any sequence of m DISJOINT SET ADT operations that starts with an initially trivial partitioning of n dynamic set elements can still be implemented in $O(m \lg^* n)$ time when this heuristic is used in conjunction with the union-by-rank heuristic.

13.17. Develop a $O(n \log n)$-time algorithm for determining whether an n-vertex polygon, specified as a collection of line segments, is simple.

13.18. Modify PointInPolygon() so that it explicitly detects and handles all special cases.

13.19. The following technique can be used to improve the running time of almost any convex hull algorithm, particularly when the point set is large. Pick four extreme points (which must be on the convex hull), and remove all points that lie inside the quadrilateral formed by these four points. Incorporate this technique into PackageWrapping().

CHAPTER NOTES

The name trie was coined because this data structure is commonly used for data re*trie*val. Sussenguth [145] is credited with inventing the trie, and the PATRICIA trie is attributed to Morrison [107], who coined the term PATRICIA as an acronym for Practical Algorithm To Retrieve Information Coded In Alphanumeric. The modified PATRICIA trie in Exercise 13.5 that uses backward pointers is discussed in Sedgewick [135].

Samet [134] has written a comprehensive textbook on data structures for multidimensional data sets. His companion text [133] considers the use of these data structures in a number of important application areas. Samet attributes the quad tree to Bentley and Finkel [55], the k-d tree to Bentley [16], and the grid file to Nievergelt, Hinterberger, and Sevcik [110]. The data structure proposed by Nievergelt, Hinterberger, and Sevcik is actually more similar to the one described in Exercise 13.11. An excellent survey article on range searching was written by Bentley and Friedman [17]; a more recent survey is provided by Matoušek [100]. The development of data structures for implementing the STATIC DYNAMIC SET ADT, in which only query operations are defined, is generally much easier than the development of data structures that must support the full complement of DYNAMIC SET ADT operations. This is particularly true if multidimensional data is involved. A technique known as *dynamization* can often be used to turn data structures developed for the static problem into data structures that also support insertions and deletions. A number of specific dynamization techniques are presented in Overmars [114].

Galil and Italiano [60] provide a survey of the data structures and algorithmic techniques that have been proposed for the DISJOINT SET ADT, along with some variations of this ADT. They attribute the idea of representing disjoint sets as rooted trees, as well as the union-by-weight heuristic, to Galler and Fischer [61]. They attribute the path-compression heuristic to Hopcroft and Ullman [75], the union-by-rank heuristic to Tarjan and van Leeuwen [149], and the path-halving heuristic to van Leeuwen and van der Weide [152].

Hopcroft and Ullman [75] derived an $O(m \lg^* n)$ bound for a sequence of $m \geq n$ DISJOINT SET ADT operations implemented using path-compression and union-by-weight. This bound was later improved by Tarjan [146] to $O(m\alpha(m, n))$, where $\alpha(m, n)$ is the functional inverse of Ackermann's function (see Exercise 1.9) which actually grows at a slower rate than $\lg^* n$. Tarjan also demonstrated that the bound is tight by showing that there are sequences of operations that take $\Omega(m\alpha(m, n))$ time. Tarjan and van Leeuwen [149] subsequently showed that the $O(m\alpha(m, n))$ bound holds when either union-by-weight or union-by-rank is used with either the path-compression or path-halving heuristics.

Mannila and Ukkonen [97] consider adding a *Deunion* operation to the DISJOINT SET ADT, which allows the most recently performed *Union* operation which has not yet been undone to be undone. This operation proves useful in the implementation of interpreters for logic programming languages such as Prolog. Westbrook and Westbrook [155] derived an amortized bound of $\Theta(\log n / \log \log n)$ for an n-element up-tree implementation that includes the *Deunion* operation.

The literature in the area of computational geometry is extensive. The texts by Preparata and Shamos [122], and Edelsbrunner [48] provide good starting points for study in this area. The package-wrapping algorithm was proposed by Jarvis [79], and is sometimes referred to as the ***Jarvis march***. Another algorithm for computing convex hulls is the Graham scan [67]. If the number of vertices m on the convex hull of a set of n points is such that $m = \Omega(\log n)$, then the Graham scan will run asymptotically faster than the package-wrapping algorithm.

CHAPTER
14

GRAPHS

Up to this point in the text we have primarily been concerned with using graphs to organize the data elements in various data structures. In this regard, we have mainly focused on graphs that were formed as binary trees. Graphs are also commonly used to model physical situations involving discrete entities that are related in some fashion. For instance, graphs are routinely used to represent and study transportation networks, communication networks, parallel computer architectures, and electrical circuits. This final chapter concentrates on the study of graphs that are used in these modes. Specifically, given a graph that is modeling some physical entity, we will want to infer something about this entity by studying the properties of its corresponding graph. In doing so, we will make use of many data types considered in previous chapters.

We begin in Section 14.1 by formalizing a number of important problems associated with graphs. Discussions of how each of these graph problems can be used to model specific physical situations are also given. Most of the problems we consider here are easy to solve given a small pictorial representation of the associated graph; however, using them to model realistic problems often leads to very large graphs, with far too many vertices and edges to allow a useful pictorial representation. Thus, in Section 14.2, we consider storing graphs in computer memory using techniques that allow the graph elements to be efficiently accessed when solving large graph-related problems. In the remaining sections of this chapter, specific algorithms are presented for solving the problems presented in Section 14.1. If the reader is unfamiliar with the terminology associated with graphs, Appendix B.4 should be reviewed prior to proceeding.

14.1 GRAPH PROBLEMS

Graph theory has been used to study problems arising in a wide variety of application areas including computer science, electrical engineering, chemistry, operations research, political science, and economics, just to name a few. In order to use graph theory in these areas, it is first necessary to represent the physical structure of the problem as a graph. A few representative examples are considered next.

Some of the easiest physical structures to model using graphs are those that can be thought of as networks. Examples include communication networks, transportation networks, electrical circuits, parallel computer interconnection networks, and so on. Consider, for instance, a collection of people, computers, or any other entities, that are able to communicate. To model such a communicate network as a graph, we represent each member of the collection as a vertex, and we draw a directed edge between two vertices if it is possible to communicate directly between their corresponding members (if the communication is bi-directional, the edge will be undirected). An example communication network is shown in Figure 14.1. If the capacities of the communication channels between the members of the collection are known, they can be modeled in the graph as weighted edges, the result being a weighted graph.

Transportation networks are similarly modeled; in this case, though, the vertices correspond to locations between which we would like to move goods or people. Depending on the precise problem, the locations may represent cities, warehouses, airports, terminals in an oil pipeline, and so on. Once again, a weighted graph can be used if we wish to model the amount of cargo that can be transported between locations, or the distances between locations.

Graphs are also commonly used to model precedence relationships that may exist between the tasks that are necessary to complete some job. In this case each task is represented by a vertex, and a directed edge is incident from vertex v_1 to vertex v_2 if the task associated with v_1 must be completed before the task associated with v_2. For instance, a precedence graph that describes the construction of a home is shown in Figure 14.2. Precedence graphs can also be used to model computation. In this case the vertices denote the operations that need to be performed, and the edges denote dependencies between the operands. Given a precedence graph, a common problem is that of producing a viable scheduling of the tasks involved.[†]

After the structure of a problem has been cast as a graph, the next step involves restating the physical problem of interest as a graph problem. The use of graphs in this manner leads to geometric interpretations of physical problems that are often easier to analyze. Furthermore, if we are able to pose a physical problem as a graph

---

[†]Indeed, the reader may be actively pursuing a solution to a physical problem that can be thought of in these terms. After all, the course work that must be completed in order to obtain a university degree can be organized as a precedence graph!

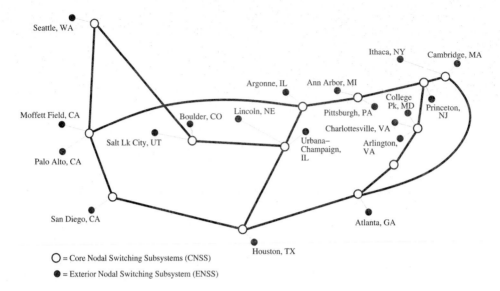

○ = Core Nodal Switching Subsystems (CNSS)

● = Exterior Nodal Switching Subsystem (ENSS)

FIGURE 14.1

A graphical representation of the NSFNET (circa 1993), the high-speed network which forms the backbone of the United States portion of the Internet. The Internet is a "network of networks"—various networks around the country gain access to the backbone through an exterior nodal switching subsystem. Messages can then be sent via high-speed links (shown as dark lines) to other networks connected to the backbone.

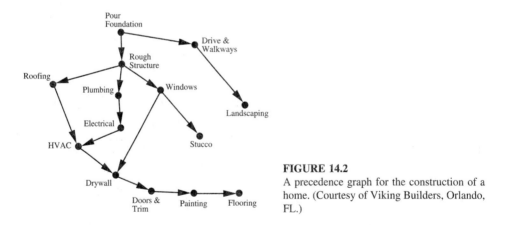

FIGURE 14.2

A precedence graph for the construction of a home. (Courtesy of Viking Builders, Orlando, FL.)

problem, we may be able to make use of existing graph-theoretic results to solve the problem. It should also be noted that a single graph problem can often be used to model problems in a large number of application areas; this makes the issue of finding efficient algorithms for solving common graph problems extremely important.

We will now discuss some of the most common graph problems, and demonstrate how each of them can be used to model physical situations. In the sections that follow, we will investigate algorithms that efficiently solve the common graph problems given here.

CONNECTEDNESS AND COMPONENTS.   One of the most basic questions one may ask regarding a graph is whether or not it is connected. Furthermore, if a graph is not connected, it may be useful to know how many different connected components it does have (in the case of directed graphs, we may also be interested in determining the number of strongly connected components). Many graph algorithms first seek answers to these questions prior to performing their main function. For instance, if the running time of a graph algorithm increases rapidly in proportion to the size of the input graph, it may be more efficient to separately apply the graph algorithm to the (smaller) components of the graph.

It is not difficult to see the practicality of the ***connectedness problem***. When examining a communication network, a common question to ask is: Can every person send a message to every other person? In a transportation network, this is equivalent to asking: Is it possible for every vehicle to move from one location to any other location? The answers to these questions will be "yes" only if the corresponding graphs are connected (or strongly connected if the problems are modeled using directed graphs).

REACHABILITY AND SHORTEST PATHS.   A problem closely related to connectedness is that of determining whether one vertex in a graph can be reached from some other vertex. Specifically, in the ***reachability problem*** we are given a graph $G = (V, E)$, a source vertex $s \in V$, and a destination vertex $d \in V$, and we are asked to determine if there exists a path from s to d.[†] In terms of a communication network, a solution to this problem is equivalent to answering the question: Can one person send a message to another person? In a transportation network, the question becomes: Is it possible for a vehicle to move from one location to another?

Even if we have determined that d is reachable from s, it may be of considerable practical importance to find the shortest path by which this can be done; in an unweighted graph, this corresponds to a path $s \leadsto d$ with the smallest number of edges, and in a weighted graph it corresponds to a path $s \leadsto d$ with the smallest total weight. In either case, we refer to this problem as the ***single-pair shortest-path problem***. For any graph $G = (V, E)$ there are actually a number of variants to this problem. In the ***single-source shortest-paths problem*** we are given a source vertex $s \in V$, and asked to find a shortest path from s to *every* vertex $v \in V$. Obviously, an algorithm that solves this problem also solves the single-pair shortest-path problem. However, even though the single-pair shortest-path problem appears easier, no algorithm has been found for it that is asymptotically faster than the best algorithm for the single-source shortest-paths problem. Finally, in the ***all-pairs shortest-paths problem***, for every pair of vertices $u, v \in V$, we are asked to find

---

[†] If G is undirected, and we have already determined that it is connected, then this problem is already solved since any two vertices are reachable from each other in this case.

a shortest path from u to v. Although this problem can be solved by solving the single-source shortest-paths problem on every vertex $v \in V$, there are other ways to solve it that are generally faster.

SPANNING TREES. Another classic problem in graph theory is that of finding a spanning tree. Given a connected undirected graph $G = (V, E)$, an acyclic set of edges $T \subseteq E$ that connects (i.e., spans) all vertices of G is called a *spanning tree*. If the graph is also weighted, then rather than finding any spanning tree, one is often interested in finding a minimum spanning tree. Specifically, given G, a *minimum spanning tree* is a spanning tree T of G whose total weight, defined as

$$w(T) = \sum_{(u,v) \in T} w(u, v)$$

is minimal. The problem of determining this tree is referred to as the *minimum spanning tree problem*. A minimum spanning tree of a weighted graph is shown with darkened edges in Figure 14.3 (a).

Given a spanning tree T of $G = (V, E)$, we will make use of the following fact later in this chapter: It is always possible to partition V into two sets V_1 and V_2 such that only a single edge in T connects a vertex in V_1 to one in V_2. One such partitioning of the vertices in the graph given in Figure 14.3 (a) is shown in Figure 14.3 (b). Given any spanning tree T, it is easy to see that there are at least $|V|$ of these partitions. These can be constructed as follows. For each vertex $v \in V$, place v in V_1, and all other vertices in V_2. Since T is a tree, it cannot contain a cycle; therefore we know that only one edge in T can join v to any of the vertices in V_2.

In order to relate the minimum spanning tree problem to a physical problem, assume we are given a map, and then asked to design a railroad transportation system that connects all cities on the map using the smallest possible amount of track. It is easy to see that this problem can be solved by first modeling the map as an undirected

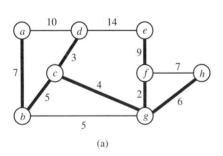

(a)

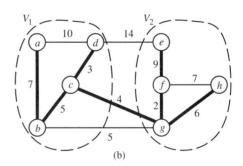

(b)

FIGURE 14.3
(a) An example weighted graph in which the edges belonging to a minimum spanning tree for the graph are shown darker. The weight of this minimum spanning tree is 36. (b) A partitioning of the graph into two sets of vertices V_1 and V_2 such that only one edge belonging to the minimum spanning tree crosses between the sets.

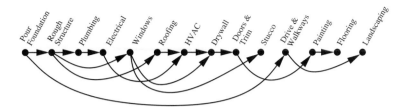

FIGURE 14.4
A redrawing of the precedence graph from Figure 14.2 so that all vertices lie on a horizontal line, and every edge is directed from left to right.

weighted graph (with the weight of an edge denoting the distance between the cities it connects), and then finding a minimum spanning tree.

TOPOLOGICAL SORTING. We mentioned previously that given a precedence graph, we are often interested in producing a viable scheduling of the tasks involved. Performing a topological sort on the precedence graph is one way of obtaining such a schedule (or of determining that no viable schedule is possible). Specifically, in the ***topological sorting problem*** a directed acyclic graph $G = (V, E)$ is supplied as input, and we are asked to produce a linear ordering of V such that if E contains a directed edge (u, v), then u appears before v in the ordering. (Note that if G contains a cycle, no such ordering is possible.) From this definition it follows that if we write the vertices in V along a horizontal line according to the ordering produced by a topological sort, every edge in E must be directed from left to right. For instance, the precedence graph in Figure 14.2 can be drawn as shown in Figure 14.4. Thus, a viable schedule is produced by simply executing these tasks in order from left to right.

14.2 GRAPH REPRESENTATION

In order to solve a graph problem using a computer, we must be able to store graphs in computer memory. Thus we need to consider the representation of a graph as a data structure. The two most common ways of doing this involve using either an adjacency matrix or an adjacency list. An ***adjacency-matrix*** representation of a graph $G = (V, E)$ is stored in a two-dimensional array $A[1..|V|, 1..|V|]$, where

$$A[i, j] = \begin{cases} 1, & \text{if } (i, j) \in E \\ 0, & \text{if } (i, j) \notin E \end{cases}$$

An example graph is shown in Figure 14.5 (a), and its corresponding adjacency matrix is shown in Figure 14.5 (b). This representation is easily extended to weighted graphs by replacing each "1" entry in the adjacency matrix corresponding to edge (u, v) with the weight $w(u, v)$ associated with that edge.

Adjacency matrices of undirected graphs possess a number of interesting properties. Since self loops are not allowed in undirected graphs, the main diagonal

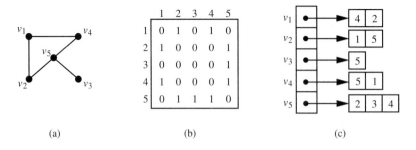

(a)   (b)   (c)

FIGURE 14.5
(a) An example undirected graph along with (b) its adjacency-matrix representation, and (c) its adjacency-list representation.

contains zeros only. Moreover, since (i, j) and (j, i) represent the same edge in an undirected graph, the adjacency matrix of an undirected graph is symmetric about its main diagonal. These properties obviously do not apply to directed graphs. Notice also that the adjacency matrix representation of graph $G = (V, E)$ requires $\Theta(|V|^2)$ memory locations (which we shall write as $\Theta(V^2)$), independent of both the number of edges in G, and whether G is directed or undirected.

An *adjacency-list* representation of a graph $G = (V, E)$ consists of an array of $|V|$ list pointers, one for each vertex in the graph. The list associated with each vertex $u \in V$ contains the labels of all vertices in the graph adjacent from u (i.e., all vertices $v \in V$ such that $(u, v) \in E$), with the ordering of the vertex labels in each list typically arbitrary. The adjacency-list representation of the graph shown in Figure 14.5 (a) is given in Figure 14.5 (c). This representation is also easily adapted to weighted graphs by adding a single data field to each list element for storing the weight associated with that edge. The total number of list pointers used in this representation is $|V|$, and the sum of the lengths of all the adjacency lists is $|E|$ in a directed graph, and $2|E|$ in an undirected graph—for each edge (u, v) in an undirected graph the label for u appears in v's list and the label for v appears in u's list. Thus the memory required for the adjacency-list representation of a graph $G = (V, E)$ is $O(\max(V, E)) = O(V + E)$.

Although more complicated due to its use of pointers, the adjacency-list representation of a graph may require asymptotically less memory than its adjacency-matrix representation. In the case of *sparse* graphs, where $|E| \ll |V|^2$, the memory requirements are $\Theta(V)$ for the adjacency matrix representation. For *dense* graphs, where $|E| \approx |V|^2$, the adjacency matrix representation is often preferred. The adjacency-matrix representation offers another distinct advantage: Determining whether a given edge (u, v) is present in a graph requires $\Theta(1)$ time. In an adjacency-list representation this same operation requires that we search for v's label in u's adjacency list, an operation requiring $O(E)$ time.

Which representation should you use? In an asymptotic sense, when analyzing the running times of most graph algorithms it turns out that the graph representation is not important. We will typically make use of the adjacency-list representation.

In practice, it is useful to provide the capability of switching between these two representations. It is not difficult to see that an algorithm that produces one graph representation given the other as input will require $\Theta(V^2)$ time.

14.3 BASIC SEARCH TECHNIQUES

Solving almost any nontrivial graph problem requires the examination of every edge (and in the process every vertex) of an input graph. For instance, this is necessary when trying to determine if a graph is connected—ignoring even a single edge may cause us to falsely conclude that a graph is not connected, when in fact this edge is joining two otherwise disconnected components.

One systematic way of examining a graph uses a search algorithm that maintains a set $S \subseteq V$ of vertices in the following manner: Initially all vertices in V are unmarked, except a source vertex s, and $S = \{s\}$. On each iteration of the algorithm, a vertex u is removed from S and processed as follows: For each edge (u, v) incident from u, if vertex v is unmarked, then it is marked and added to S. This process continues until S becomes empty, at which point any vertex that remains unmarked cannot be reached from a path that starts from s. A new source vertex can now be selected from any remaining unmarked vertices, and the search process can continue until no unmarked vertices remain.

The only portion of the aforementioned search algorithm not completely specified is the order in which vertices are removed from S. If we treat S as a queue, always removing the vertex that has remained in S the longest, then the vertices in V will be searched from s in a breadth-first fashion. That is, all vertices adjacent to s will be searched first, then the vertices adjacent to these vertices will be searched, and so on. On the other hand if S is treated as a stack, always removing the most recently added vertex, then the vertices in V will be searched from s in a depth-first fashion. These two basic approaches lead to the two algorithms discussed next. These algorithms not only search a graph in the manners discussed above, but each collects additional information along the way. We will show how this information can be used to discover specific properties about a graph. Many of the problems discussed in Section 14.1 can be efficiently solved using simple variations or extensions of one of these two basic search techniques.

14.3.1 Breadth-First Search

In the breadth-first search algorithm given here, an array $d[1..|V|]$ is used to keep track of the marked and unmarked vertices in V. With this scheme, a vertex i is considered unmarked if $d[i]$ is storing a specially designated value, which we denote by ∞, and marked if it is storing any other value. At the completion of the algorithm, for each marked vertex $i \in V$, $d[i]$ will store the minimum number of edges in any one path from the source to i. Thus, given any input graph, this algorithm can be used to solve the reachability problem, and it also solves the single-source shortest-paths problem for unweighted graphs. Furthermore, vertices that are not reachable from the source are not marked by this algorithm. Thus if the input graph is undirected, we can easily determine if it is connected by running BFS(), and then checking to see if any ∞ entries remain in the d array at the completion of the run.

```
BFS(GRAPH G = (V, E), vertex s)    ▷ s is the source
1   for each  v ∈ V  do
2       d[v] ← ∞   ▷ unmark all vertices
3   d[s] ← 0   ▷ mark the source
4   Enqueue(Q, s)
5   while  Empty(Q) = false  do
6       v ← Dequeue(Q)
7       for each  u ∈ adjacent[v]  do
8           if  d[u] = ∞  then   ▷ is vertex u unmarked?
9               d[u] ← d[v] + 1   ▷ mark vertex u
10              Enqueue(Q, u)
```

Lines 1–3 of BFS() perform the task of marking the source vertex, and initially designating all other vertices as unmarked. In the remainder of the algorithm, a vertex at a time is removed from the queue, starting with the source s. For each vertex v removed, every adjacent and unmarked vertex u is first marked on line 9, and then inserted in the queue on line 10. Figure 14.6 depicts the progress of BFS() on an example directed graph. This algorithm can also be applied to undirected as well as weighted graphs.

Because a queue is being used in this algorithm, we know that all vertices at a distance k from the source will be marked prior to marking any vertex at a distance of $k + 1$. We will subsequently prove that if the minimum number of edges in any path $s \rightsquigarrow v$ is stored in $d[v]$, and u is an unmarked vertex adjacent to v, then the minimum number of edges in any path $s \rightsquigarrow u$ is given by $d[v] + 1$. Hence, the marking of a vertex on line 9 also serves the purpose of calculating the minimum number of edges in any path from s. Before confirming this fact, let us analyze the running time of BFS().

After the initialization on line 2, no vertex can have its entry in the d array changed back to ∞. Therefore, the test on line 8 and subsequent marking on line 9 ensure that each vertex is enqueued at most once, and therefore will be dequeued at most once. Since the *Enqueue* and *Dequeue* operations are both implementable in $\Theta(1)$ time, the total number of queue operations is $O(V)$ (or $\Theta(V)$ if all vertices are reachable from s). Finally, if we assume the input graph is represented using an adjacency list, then the total time spent accessing the input graph is $O(V + E)$. Specifically, unmarking the vertices on lines 1 and 2 takes $\Theta(V)$ time, and the scanning for adjacent vertices on line 7 takes $O(E)$ time since the sum of the lengths of all adjacency lists is $\Theta(E)$. Therefore the running time of this algorithm is $O(V + E)$, i.e., linear in the size of its input.

In order to verify that BFS() works as advertised, we must show that after applying it to any graph, the value of $d[v]$ for each vertex v reachable from the source s contains the minimum number of edges in any path $s \rightsquigarrow v$, and that a

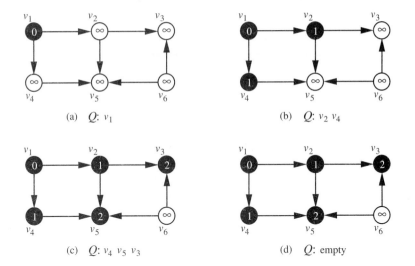

FIGURE 14.6

An example run of BFS() on a directed graph with source vertex v_1. At each step of the algorithm the currently unmarked vertices are white, and the marked ones are black. Inside each marked vertex, as calculated on line 9 of BFS(), is the minimum number of edges in any one path from the source. **(a)** Initially only the source vertex is marked, and the queue is storing v_1. **(b)** The result of processing vertex v_1. Vertices v_2 and v_4 are marked and inserted in the queue. **(c)** The result of processing vertex v_2. Vertices v_5 and v_3 are marked and inserted in the queue. **(d)** The final result, after processing vertices v_4, v_5, and v_3. This processing does not cause any additional vertices to be marked. Note that v_6 is not reachable from v_1, and that it is not marked by the algorithm.

vertex that is not reachable from s will store ∞ in its corresponding entry in the d array. We will demonstrate this fact using induction.

Let us refer to the minimum number of edges in any path $s \rightsquigarrow v$ as the ***distance*** from s to v. For the base case consider the source vertex s, which is at a distance 0 from itself. On line 3, s is correctly marked by setting $d[s] = 0$. Now consider an arbitrary vertex v at a distance k from s (i.e., $d[v] = k$), and assume v has just been dequeued on line 6. Our induction hypothesis is that all vertices at distances of between 0 and k from s are already marked (we have already discussed this), and that the corresponding d entry for each is correct (this implies that no vertex unreachable from s has been marked). On line 9, only those unmarked vertices adjacent to v will be marked. According to the induction hypothesis, if such a vertex u has not been marked at this point, its distance from the source will be at least $k + 1$. But by appending the edge (v, u) to the path $s \rightsquigarrow v$ we can construct a path $s \rightsquigarrow u$ whose length is exactly $k + 1$. Thus, $k + 1$ must be the shortest distance from s to u, and line 9 of the algorithm correctly sets $d[u] = k + 1$. Furthermore, given (by the induction hypothesis) that we have a path $s \rightsquigarrow v$, and only vertices adjacent to v are considered, a vertex unreachable from s cannot be marked during this step of the algorithm. Such a vertex will continue to store the value ∞ in this case.

14.3.2 Depth-First Search

We previously mentioned that by using a stack to store and later retrieve the marked vertices of a graph, a depth-first search of the graph can be performed. In the algorithm given next, rather than explicitly employing a stack, recursion is used to ensure that marked vertices are considered in LIFO order. Once again, we use an array $d[1..|V|]$ to keep track of marked vertices. However, we will now consider a vertex v unmarked if $d[v] = 0$, and marked if this entry is storing any other value. The actual value eventually stored in $d[v]$ will be given by the time at which vertex v is discovered during the search. Thus, a global variable called *time* must be used to keep track of time. In addition to keeping track of the discovery times of vertices using the d array, we will also find it useful to keep track of the time at which the processing from a vertex is completed. The following algorithm uses an array $f[1..|V|]$ to store these finishing times.

Because this is a depth-first search, once a source vertex s is selected, the algorithm will continually search deeper into the graph (from s) until it can no longer find an unmarked vertex. At this point, if there are any remaining unmarked vertices, one of them is selected as the new source for further searching. The DFS() algorithm given next is responsible for initially unmarking all vertices, and picking source vertices. It actually calls the DFS-Visit() algorithm to perform the depth-first search from each source. The recursive calls are made from within DFS-Visit() on line 4, with control returning to DFS() only after all unmarked vertices reachable from a source s have been marked.

DFS(GRAPH $G = (V, E)$)
1   **for each** $v \in V$ **do**
2       $d[v] \leftarrow 0$ ▷ every vertex is undiscovered (i.e., unmarked)
3   *time* $\leftarrow 0$ ▷ *time* is a global variable
4   **for each** $s \in V$ **do**
5   **if** $d[s] = 0$ **then** ▷ is vertex s unmarked?
6   DFS-Visit(G, s)

DFS-Visit(GRAPH $G = (V, E)$, vertex s) ▷ s is the source
1   $d[s] \leftarrow$ *time* $\leftarrow$ *time* $+ 1$ ▷ vertex s is discovered and marked
2   **for each** $u \in adjacent[s]$ **do**
3   **if** $d[u] = 0$ **then** ▷ is vertex u unmarked?
4   DFS-Visit(G, u)
5   $f[s] \leftarrow$ *time* $\leftarrow$ *time* $+ 1$ ▷ finished with vertex s

Notice how the *time* variable is initialized on line 3 of DFS(), and that it is first incremented before assigning it to either $d[s]$ or $f[s]$ on lines 1 and 5 of DFS-Visit(). The reader should also notice that the loop over lines 4–6 of DFS() guarantees that every vertex in the graph will eventually get marked—even if the graph is not connected. A demonstration of DFS() running on an example graph is given in Figure 14.7. This algorithm may also be applied to undirected as well as weighted graphs.

It is easy to see that the running time of DFS() is $\Theta(V + E)$. For each vertex $v \in V$, DFS-Visit() is called exactly once; and on each of these calls, the loop over

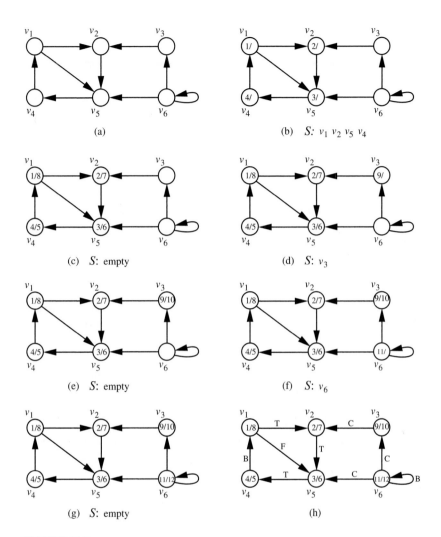

FIGURE 14.7

An example run of DFS() on a directed graph. The processing of vertices starts at v_1 (it could have also been started from any other vertex in the graph). The discovery and finish time for each vertex v is shown inside of it using the format $d[v]/f[v]$. If the inside of vertex v is blank, then it is an undiscovered vertex. If it only contains $d[v]/$, then it is a discovered (but unfinished) vertex; and if it contains $d[v]/f[v]$, then it is a finished vertex. The set S will be used to denote the collection of marked vertices currently being maintained on the run-time stack. **(a)** The input graph. **(b)** The status after the first four vertices have been discovered. Starting from the source v_1, no additional unmarked vertices can be discovered. **(c)** The status after the processing of the first four discovered vertices is completed. **(d)** The search continues from the next source vertex v_3. **(e)** All vertices adjacent to v_3 have already been discovered; thus its processing is completed at the next time step. **(f)** The search from the last source vertex v_6 starts at the 11th time interval. **(g)** The status after all vertices have been processed. **(h)** The classification of edges provided by DFS() (see the discussion in the text), where T is a tree edge, B is a back edge, F is a forward edge, and C is a cross edge.

lines 2–4 in DFS-Visit() considers each vertex adjacent to v. Since the size of all adjacency lists is $\Theta(E)$, we obtain the linear running time $\Theta(V + E)$.

CLASSIFYING EDGES. The main reason that DFS() keeps track of the discovery and finish times for the vertices is that these values can be used to classify the edges in a graph—in fact, this is often the sole reason for using the algorithm. This information can prove quite useful in determining specific properties of a graph.

We can think of the DFS() algorithm as forming a forest of trees on an input graph as it processes it. Specifically, whenever DFS() chooses a new source vertex, a new root is formed. Every vertex discovered in the subsequent calls to DFS-Visit() is a descendent of this root vertex, via the edge used to discover the vertex. Since a call to DFS() eventually causes every vertex to be marked, every vertex in the input graph will be a member of some tree at the completion of the algorithm. Next we consider a classification scheme that can be used to label every edge in a graph according to its relationship to this forest of trees, and then we will demonstrate how DFS() can be used to perform this labeling. Our classification considers four types of edges:

- *Tree edges*—These consist of *any* collection of edges in a graph that form a forest. Every vertex in the graph is either a single-vertex tree with respect to such a collection, or is part of some larger tree through its connection to another vertex via a tree edge. Note that this collection is not unique.
- *Back edges*—Given a collection of tree edges, the back edges in a graph are those edges that connect some descendent vertex in a tree to an ancestor vertex in the same tree.
- *Forward edges*—Given a collection of tree edges, the forward edges are those that are incident from an ancestor in a tree, and incident to a descendent in the same tree.
- *Cross edges*—Given a collection of tree edges, the cross edges are those edges that are adjacent between vertices in two different trees, or between vertices in two different subtrees in the same tree.

It is not difficult to modify DFS() so that it produces a classification of the edges in a graph based on these definitions. Specifically, we can prove (see Exercise 14.5) that the following rules can be used to classify the edges of a graph using DFS():

- Whenever a discovered vertex encounters an undiscovered vertex, label the edge between them a tree edge.
- Whenever a discovered vertex encounters another discovered but unfinished vertex, label the edge between them a back edge.
- Whenever a discovered vertex u encounters a finished vertex v, and $d[u] < d[v]$, label the edge between them a forward edge.
- Whenever a discovered vertex u encounters a finished vertex v, and $d[u] > d[v]$, label the edge between them a cross edge.

In Figure 14.7 (h) we show the labeling these rules produce on the previously considered example graph.

Now that we have gone to the trouble of producing a classification for the edges in a graph, let us investigate what we can do with it. First of all we can show that on an undirected graph, a depth-first search will only produce tree and back edges (i.e., only directed graphs have forward and cross edges). To see why, consider an arbitrary edge (u, v) in an undirected graph, and assume that when DFS() is applied to this graph, u is discovered before v. Since v is adjacent to u, and $d[u] < d[v]$, v must be finished before u. Thus if the edge (u, v) is explored from u, it will be labeled a tree edge; and if it is explored from v, it will be labeled a back edge.

More importantly, by using DFS() to classify edges, we can determine whether or not a graph is acyclic. A necessary and sufficient condition for determining if an undirected graph is acyclic is that when running DFS() on it, no back edges are encountered. The "necessary" portion of this claim is trivial to establish: By definition, a back edge connects a descendent vertex to an ancestor vertex, which obviously forms a cycle. To establish the "sufficient" portion of the claim, we must show that if no back edges are encountered, then the input graph cannot contain a cycle. If DFS() does not encounter any back edges, then since this is an undirected graph, it must contain only tree edges. Therefore the graph must be a forest, which by definition means that it does not have any cycles. In Exercise 14.6 you are asked to show that this claim also holds for directed graphs.

Next we demonstrate how DFS() can be used to solve the topological sorting problem. Consider the following algorithm:

TopologicalSort(DIRECTED ACYCLIC GRAPH $G = (V, E)$)
1   perform DFS(G) inserting vertices at the head of list L as they are finished
2   **return** L

While performing step 1 of this algorithm, DFS() can also be used to check that the input graph is actually acyclic. In order to prove that TopologicalSort() outputs a topological sort of any directed acyclic graph $G = (V, E)$, assume that DFS() has been run on G producing the array $f[1..|V|]$ as discussed previously. We must show that for any two vertices $u, v \in V$, if $(u, v) \in E$, then $f[v] < f[u]$. If this condition holds, then u will be inserted at the head of list L *after* vertex v has been inserted; thus, reading the list returned by TopologicalSort() from head to tail will yield a viable schedule. To establish the necessary condition recall that when edge (u, v) is considered by DFS(), vertex u has been discovered (since the graph is directed and acyclic), and there are three possibilities for vertex v:

1. Vertex v has been discovered. In this case (u, v) is a back edge, and according to Exercise 14.6, G has a cycle. This cannot occur since it contradicts the fact that G is acyclic.

2. Vertex v is undiscovered. This implies that (u, v) is a tree descendent of u, which means that v will be finished before u (i.e., $f[v] < f[u]$).

3. Vertex v is finished. This immediately implies that $f[v] < f[u]$.

This proves that TopologicalSort() outputs a topological sort when supplied with any directed acyclic graph as input.

14.4   MINIMUM SPANNING TREES

Fortunately, the structure of the minimum spanning tree problem lends itself quite naturally to efficient algorithms based on the greedy strategy. To see why, consider the following generic algorithm that grows a minimum spanning tree T of a graph one edge at a time. This is done by maintaining a partitioning of the graph vertices as T is being built: one partition that contains those vertices currently linked by edges in T, and the other, which does not. The algorithm proceeds by continually adding an edge to T that has one endpoint in each of these partitions. In this section we denote the vertices that are currently linked by edges in T, as it is being built, using V_T.

MST-Generic(UNDIRECTED WEIGHTED GRAPH $G = (V, E)$)
1   $T \leftarrow \{(a, b)\}$ ▷ $\{(a, b)\}$ is the lightest weight edge in E
2   $V_T \leftarrow \{a, b\}$
3   **while** $V_T \neq V$ **do**
4   find the lightest edge (u, v) that connects $u \in V_T$ and $v \in V - V_T$
5        $T \leftarrow T \cup \{(u, v)\}$ ▷ add edge $\{u, v\}$ to T
6        $V_T \leftarrow V_T \cup \{v\}$ ▷ add vertices u and v to V_T
7   **return** T ▷ T is a minimum spanning tree

In MST-Generic(), T initially contains the lightest weight edge in E (line 1), and at each step of the algorithm an edge is added that connects one more vertex to the tree. Therefore the test on line 3 guarantees that at the completion of the algorithm, T must be a spanning tree of G. Notice that the most important step of MST-Generic(), line 4, is rather vague; methods for implementing it will be discussed after we have shown that the greedy strategy it employs will cause T to not only be a spanning tree, but a minimum spanning tree. The strategy used in line 4 is greedy because it is based on making locally optimal choices: Only the subset of edges in E that have one endpoint in V_T and the other in $V - V_T$ are considered at each step, and only the lightest one of these edges is selected.

To show that this greedy approach will always produce a globally optimal solution (i.e., a minimum spanning tree), let T be a spanning tree returned by MST-Generic() and assume $T' \neq T$ is a minimum spanning tree for the same graph. We will show that in this case $w(T)$ must equal $w(T')$, which implies that T must also be a minimum spanning tree. The technique we will use involves turning T' into T via a sequence of transformations

$$T' \rightarrow T'' \rightarrow \cdots \rightarrow T^{(i)} \rightarrow \cdots \rightarrow T$$

Starting from any tree $T^{(i)}$ in this sequence, each transformation produces a new tree $T^{(i+1)}$ by removing one edge from $T^{(i)}$ that is in the set $T^{(i)} - T$, and adding one edge to $T^{(i)}$ from the set $T - T^{(i)}$. Thus each transformation brings $T^{(i)}$ closer to T. The key point is that we must also show $w(T') = w(T'') = \cdots = w(T^{(i)}) = \cdots = w(T)$.

To show that all trees in the transformation sequence have the same weight, we make the following inductive argument: For the i-th transformation step, we assume

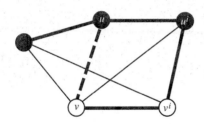

FIGURE 14.8
A portion of a graph used to prove that MST-Generic()
produces a minimum spanning tree. The vertices in V_1 are
black, and the ones in V_2 are white. The edges belonging
to the tree $T^{(i)}$ are shown darkened, and the dashed edge,
(u, v) belongs to T. Because the vertices in V_1 are all
connected by edges in $T^{(i)}$, as are the vertices in V_2,
including the dashed edge (u, v) in $T^{(i)}$ causes the formation
of a cycle; however, by removing the edge (u^i, v^i) from
$T^{(i)}$ this cycle is broken.

$T^{(i)}$ is a minimum spanning tree. As long as $T^{(i)} \neq T$, there must exist at least
one partition of V into two sets V_1 and V_2 such that only one edge (u^i, v^i) in $T^{(i)}$
joins a vertex in V_1 to one in V_2, and at least one edge (u, v) in T (different from
(u^i, v^i)) joins a vertex in V_1 to one in V_2. Recall that the only way (u, v) can be
added to T in MST-Generic() is if it is the lightest weight edge crossing between V_1
and V_2. Furthermore, if the edge (u, v) is added to $T^{(i)}$ it will form a cycle (adding
any one edge to a spanning tree will always cause a cycle to be formed). However,
due to the construction of V_1 and V_2, the edge (u^i, v^i) must also be in this cycle (see
Figure 14.8). Thus if we remove the edge (u^i, v^i) from $T^{(i)}$ we obtain the spanning
tree

$$T^{(i+1)} = T^{(i)} \cup \{(u, v)\} - \{(u^i, v^i)\}$$

which means

$$w(T^{(i+1)}) = w(T^{(i)}) + w(u, v) - w(u^i, v^i)$$

Since (u, v) is the lightest weight edge crossing between V_1 and V_2 this implies
$w(T^{(i+1)}) \leq w(T^{(i)})$. But $T^{(i)}$ is a minimum spanning tree, which means $w(T^{(i+1)}) \geq$
$w(T^{(i)})$. Therefore $w(T^{(i+1)})$ must equal $w(T^{(i)})$, and $T^{(i+1)}$ must also be a minimum
spanning tree.

Let us now consider two efficient means of implementing the vaguely specified
portion of MST-Generic(), namely how to find the lightest weight edge crossing
between V_T and $V - V_T$. The first approach, known as Prim's algorithm, uses the
MELDABLE PRIORITY QUEUE ADT to find this edge; while the second approach, known
as Kruskal's algorithm, uses the DISJOINT SET ADT.

14.4.1 Prim's Algorithm

In Prim's algorithm the edges in T, as it is being grown, always form a single tree.
This algorithm assigns key values to the vertices of the input graph. As T is being
constructed, a meldable priority queue is used to keep track of which vertices are
in V_T, and which are in $V - V_T$. Specifically, throughout the algorithm, the vertices
stored in the priority queue are members of $V - V_T$, and all other vertices are in V_T.
Initially all vertices are placed in the priority queue with a key value of ∞, except for
an arbitrary vertex r, which is assigned a key value of 0. The first vertex removed by
a *DeleteMin*, and therefore placed in V_T, will be r. Next, the *DecreaseKey* operation

is used to decrease the key values of all vertices adjacent to r. This is done in such a way that the next *DeleteMin* operation will return a vertex in $V - \{r\}$ that is connected to r by the lightest weight edge. This edge is the first one added to T. The algorithm proceeds by continually adding edges in this fashion until T connects all vertices.

```
Prim(UNDIRECTED WEIGHTED GRAPH G = (V, E))
1   T ← ∅   ▷ start with an empty tree
2   for each v ∈ V do
3       key[v] ← ∞
4   key[r] ← 0   ▷ r ∈ V is an arbitrary root vertex
5   MakePriorityQueue(P, V)   ▷ initialize P to contain the elements of V
6   while Empty(P) = false do
7       u ← DeleteMin(P)
8       min_wt ← ∞   ▷ reinitialize min_wt
9       for each v ∈ adjacent[u] do   ▷ determine which edge to add to T
10          if w(u, v) < key[v] then
11              DecreaseKey(P, v, w(u, v))
12          if w(u, v) < min_wt then
13              min_wt ← w(u, v)
14              v_min ← v
15      T ← T ∪ {(u, v_min)}   ▷ add edge (u, v_min) to T
16  return T   ▷ T is a minimum spanning tree
```

Lines 1–4 of Prim() initialize the key values of the vertices in the input graph, and all vertices are stored in the meldable priority queue P on line 5. The loop over lines 6–15 serves the purpose of continually finding the lightest weight edge crossing between vertices in V_T and $V - V_T$. On each iteration of this loop, another vertex u is removed from P on line 7. Prior to placing u in the set V_T, the lightest weight edge connecting u to the current members of V_T must be found. This is the purpose of the loop over lines 9–14, which considers each vertex v adjacent to u. If the current weight of the edge (u, v) is less than the key value of v, then v's key value is reduced to $w(u, v)$ on line 11. At the completion of this loop, v_{min} will store the vertex in $V - V_T$ that is connected to u by the lightest weight edge. The edge (u, v_{min}) is then added to T on line 15. Figure 14.9 gives an example of this algorithm processing the graph from Figure 14.3.

The running time of Prim's algorithm depends on the type of data structure used to implement the meldable priority queue P. The initialization phase, lines 1–5, takes $\Theta(V)$ time if a binary heap is used. The loop over lines 6–14 executes $\Theta(V)$ times. On each iteration, one *DeleteMin* requiring $O(\log V)$ time is performed; so the total time taken by *DeleteMin* operations is $O(V \log V)$. The number of iterations performed by the loop over lines 9–14 is bounded by the number of edges in all adjacency lists, which is $2|E|$. On each of these iterations, at most one *DecreaseKey* operation will be performed. Since the *DecreaseKey* operation can be implemented in $O(\log V)$ in a binary heap, the time taken by these operations is $O(E \log V)$. The total running time of Prim's algorithm implemented in this manner is therefore $O(V \log V + E \log V)$, which is $O(E \log V)$ since we are assuming the input graph is connected (i.e., $|E| \geq |V| - 1$).

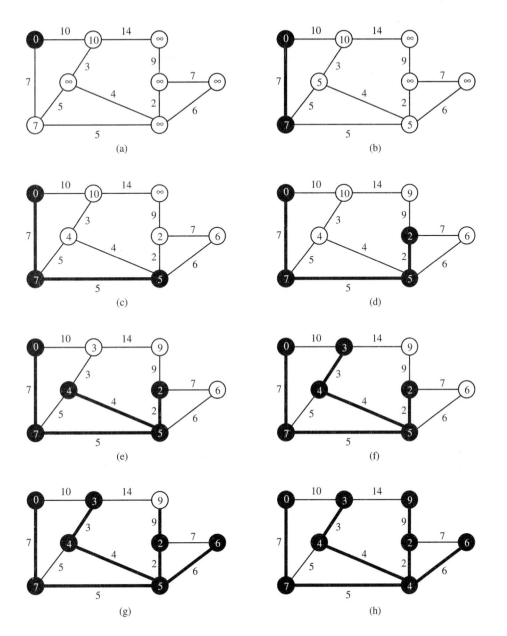

FIGURE 14.9

The execution of Prim's algorithm on the graph from Figure 14.3. At each step of the algorithm, the key value associated with each vertex is shown inside of it, and the black vertices are in V_T. The vertex labeled a in Figure 14.3 is the one whose key is initially set to 0. **(a)** After one iteration of the loop over lines 6–15. The vertex with key 0 has been removed from P, and is now in V_T. Furthermore, the key values of the vertices adjacent to this vertex have been decreased. **(b)–(g)** At each step of the algorithm, the darkened edges belonging to T always form a single tree. **(h)** The final minimum spanning tree.

The asymptotic running time of Prim's algorithm can be improved by using the Fibonacci heap data structure discussed in Section 12.3.3 to implement the meldable priority queue. With this data structure, the heap itself can still be constructed in $\Theta(V)$ time, while the *DeleteMin* and *DecreaseKey* operations can be implemented in $O(\log V)$ and $\Theta(1)$ amortized time, respectively. The fact that both *DeleteMin* and *DecreaseKey* will be executed numerous (i.e., at least V) times in Prim's algorithm means that these amortized bounds are actually worst-case bounds. Thus, by using a Fibonacci heap, we can improve the running time of Prim's algorithm to $O(E + V \log V)$.

14.4.2 Kruskal's Algorithm

In Kruskal's algorithm, the edges in T do not always form a single tree; rather, at certain points during its construction, T may be a forest of trees. This algorithm starts with $|V|$ partitions instead of two, one for each vertex. The DISJOINT SET ADT is used to maintain these partitions. At each step, the lightest weight edge that can join two partitions is found; this edge is then added to the minimum spanning tree being grown, and the number of partitions is reduced by one. The DISJOINT SET ADT discussed in Section 13.3 is used to maintain the partitions required in Kruskal's algorithm.

```
Kruskal(UNDIRECTED WEIGHTED GRAPH G = (V, E))
1   T ← ∅   ▷ start with an empty tree
2   for each v ∈ V[G] do
3       MakeSet(D, v)   ▷ create a collection D of |V| disjoint sets
4   Sort the edges of E by nondecreasing weight
5   for each (u, v) ∈ E in order by nondecreasing weight do
6       if FindSet(D, u) ≠ FindSet(D, v) then   ▷ u and v are in different sets
7           T ← T ∪ {(u, v)}   ▷ add edge (u, v) to T
8           Union(D, u, v)   ▷ unite the sets containing u and v
9   return T   ▷ T is a minimum spanning tree
```

A demonstration of how this algorithm might process the graph shown in Figure 14.3 is given in Figure 14.10.

To determine the running time of Kruskal(), we first note that the sorting of edges on line 4 takes $\Theta(E \log E)$ time in the worst case. However, if G is assumed to be a connected graph we know that

$$|V| - 1 \leq |E| \leq |V^2| - |V|$$

which implies that $|E| = O(V^2)$, and $\lg|E| = O(\log V)$. Therefore, the time required for the sort on line 4 is $O(E \log V)$. The loop over lines 5–8 executes $\Theta(E)$ times, and a constant number of disjoint set operations are performed on each iteration. According to our analysis in Section 13.3.1, if an up-tree data structure is used (along with the union-by-rank and path-compression heuristics), then all of the DISJOINT SET ADT operations in Kruskal's algorithm can be implemented in $O(E \lg^* V)$ time. Once again, since a sequence of operations is being performed, this is a worst-case

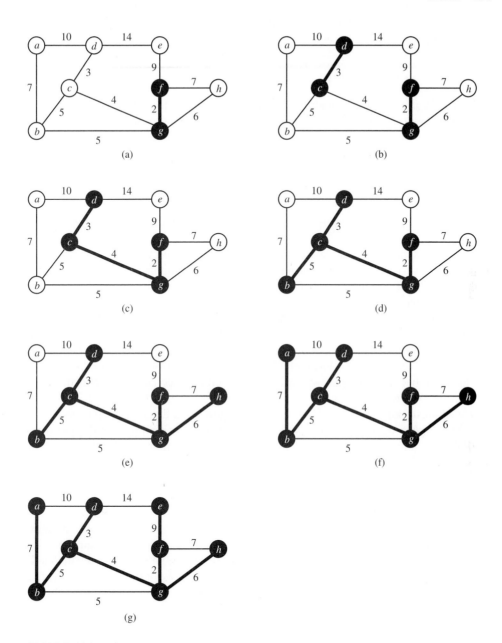

FIGURE 14.10
The execution of Kruskal's algorithm on the graph from Figure 14.3. At each step, the vertices that have been united by a *Union* operation on line 8 are shown black. **(a)** Initially each vertex is a member of a different disjoint set, and a minimum weight edge (f, g) is the first to be added to T. **(b)–(g)** At each step, the smallest weight edge whose endpoints lie in different disjoint sets is added to T. **(h)** The final minimum spanning tree.

bound. Therefore, the running time of Kruskal's algorithm is $O(E \log V + E \lg^* V)$, and since $\lg^* V = O(\log V)$, we obtain a $O(E \log V)$ running time.

14.5   SHORTEST PATHS

We have already seen that breadth-first search can be used to solve the single-source shortest-paths problem for unweighted graphs. For weighted graphs this problem is more difficult. In a weighted graph, a shortest path p from vertex s to vertex d is defined as a path $s \overset{p}{\leadsto} d$ whose total edge weight

$$w(p) = \sum_{(u,v) \in p} w(u, v)$$

is minimal. If d is not reachable from s, then the shortest path from s to d is defined to be ∞.

The presence of negative-weight edges can cause special difficulty when attempting to solve shortest path problems. If a graph contains edges with negative weight, the shortest path from s to d is only defined if there are no negative-weight cycles reachable from s. The problem caused by negative-weight cycles is illustrated in the graph shown in Figure 14.11. The negative-weight cycle in this graph is reachable from any vertex. Thus by continually traversing this cycle, shorter and shorter cycles are produced. Negative-weight edges per se do not cause this problem. For instance, if the edge (v_3, v_4) in Figure 14.11 were changed from -6 to -5, then the shortest path between any pair of vertices in the graph becomes well defined.

In the following section we present Dijkstra's algorithm for solving the single-source shortest-paths problem. This algorithm requires that the input graph contain no negative-weight edges. In Exercise 14.18 we consider the Bellman-Ford algorithm, which allows input graphs to have negative-weight edges, and reports that no solution exists if it finds any negative-weight cycles.

14.5.1   Dijkstra's Algorithm

Given a weighted graph in which all edge weights are nonnegative, the greedy strategy used in Dijkstra's algorithm is similar to the one used in Prim's algorithm. As the shortest paths are being constructed, a partitioning of the graph vertices is maintained. We will refer to these partitions as V_1 and V_2, where V_1 is initially empty, and the first vertex added to V_1 is the source vertex s. At each step, a vertex $v \in V_2$ that is

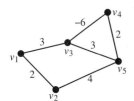

FIGURE 14.11
A weighted graph with a negative-weight cycle. The total edge weight along the cycle v_3, v_4, v_5, v_3 is -1. Since this cycle is reachable from any vertex in the graph, the shortest path between any pair of vertices in this graph is not defined.

closest to V_1 is added to V_1. The algorithm then calculates the shortest paths from the source s to all vertices in the subgraph induced by V_1.[†]

In the following algorithm a meldable priority queue P is used to maintain the partitioning required in Dijkstra's algorithm. The vertices in P are considered to be in partition V_1, and all other vertices are in partition V_2.

```
Dijkstra(GRAPH G = (V, E), vertex s)    ▷ all edges have positive weight
1   for each  v ∈ V  do
2       d[v] ← ∞
3   d[s] ← 0
4   MakePriorityQueue(P, V)
5   while Empty(P) = false do
6       u ← DeleteMin(P)
7       for each v ∈ adjacent[u] do
8           if  d[v] > d[u] + w(u, v)  then
9               d[v] ← d[u] + w(u, v)
10              DecreaseKey(P, v, d[v])
11  return d
```

Figure 14.12 depicts the progress of Dijkstra() on an example directed graph. Since the flow of control in Dijkstra's algorithm is identical to that of Prim's algorithm, a running time of $O(E + V \log V)$ is obtained for Dijkstra's algorithm by using a Fibonacci heap. Furthermore, by running Dijkstra's algorithm $|V|$ times, once from each vertex, we also have a $O(VE + V^2 \log V)$ time algorithm for the all-pairs shortest-paths problem in graphs with nonnegative-weight edges.

To prove the correctness of Dijkstra's algorithm, we will use induction on the size of partition V_1. Our induction hypothesis is that the path lengths computed by Dijkstra(), from s to each vertex in V_1, are the shortest paths in G. It is important to clarify that these shortest paths are the shortest ones not only in the subgraph induced by V_1, but in G as well. For the base case, when V_1 contains only s, the path length is 0, and the induction hypothesis holds trivially. Next assume that the induction hypothesis holds at some point when V_1 has more than one vertex, that the next vertex Dijkstra() chooses to add to V_1 is v_j, and that v_j is closest to $v_i \in V_1$. If p' is the shortest path from s to v_i constructed by Dijkstra(), then this algorithm will construct a path $s \overset{p}{\leadsto} v_j$ by adding edge (v_i, v_j) to p', and line 9 will set $w(p) = d[v_j] = d[v_i] + w(v_i, v_j)$. All we need to show is that p is a shortest path in G from s to v_j—the addition of v_j will not change the lengths of any of the other paths from s to vertices in V_1. Now, suppose there is a shorter path $s \overset{q}{\leadsto} v_j$, i.e., $w(q) < w(p)$, and assume the edge between V_1 and V_2 on path q is (v_a, v_b). We can break the path q into subpaths q_1 and q_2:

$$s \overset{q_1}{\leadsto} v_a \leadsto v_b \overset{q_2}{\leadsto} v_j$$

[†]Given a graph $G = (V, E)$, the **subgraph** induced by $V_1 \subseteq V$ is the graph $G_1 = (V_1, E_1)$ where $E_1 = \{(u, v) \in E \mid u, v \in V_1\}$.

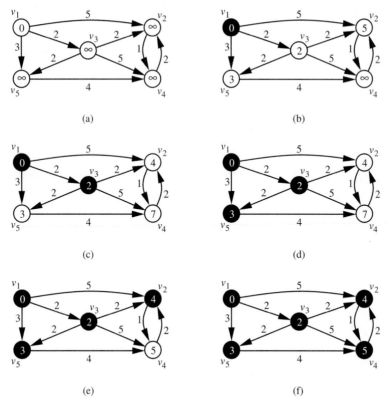

FIGURE 14.12

An example run of Dijkstra() on an example directed graph with source vertex v_1. The vertices in partition V_1 are black, and those in partition V_2 are white. **(a)** Initially all vertices are in partition V_2, and all vertices, except the source, are storing a shortest path length of ∞. **(b)** The first vertex moved to partition V_1 is the source, and the shortest path distance to each adjacent vertex is updated. **(c)–(f)** At each subsequent step, the vertex in partition V_2 that is closest to V_1 is selected, and the shortest path lengths are updated. The values inside of the vertices in part (f) are the shortest path lengths from the source vertex.

as depicted in Figure 14.13. According to the induction hypothesis, when vertex v_a was added to V_1 in Dijkstra(), the shortest path weight from s to v_a was stored in $d[v_a]$. Thus,

$$d[v_a] + w(v_a, v_b) \leq w(q_1) + w(v_a, v_b)$$
$$\leq w(q_1) + w(v_a, v_b) + w(q_2)$$
$$= w(q)$$
$$< d[v_i] + w(v_i, v_j)$$

where the second line follows from the fact that all edge weights are nonnegative, and the last line follows from our assumption that $w(q) < w(p)$. The result we

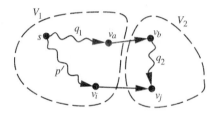

FIGURE 14.13
The construction used to prove the correctness of
Dijkstra's algorithm.

obtain is $d[v_a] + w(v_a, v_b) < d[v_i] + w(v_i, v_j)$, which leads to a contradiction: If this
inequality were true, Dijkstra() should have added v_b to V_1 when it actually added v_j.
Thus our assumption that $w(q) < w(p)$ cannot be true, and the path p constructed
by Dijkstra() must be a shortest path from s to v_j. This verifies the extension step,
and completes the proof that Dijkstra's algorithm correctly computes shortest paths.

14.6   AN EXTENDED EXAMPLE: THE MAKE UTILITY

An important abstraction mechanism offered in all modern programming languages is
separate compilation. By this we mean the ability to develop software subsystems (i.e.,
modules) that may be individually compiled into object code, and linked into a
software system as needed. One advantage offered by this approach is that it allows
different programmers to simultaneously develop or modify the various modules that
comprise a software system. This also allows these modules to be reused in other
systems, which is in complete agreement with the object-oriented design philosophy
discussed in Chapter 4. In addition, if a module is modified, separate compilation
means that only those modules in a software system affected by this change will have
to be recompiled. However, keeping track of which modules affect other modules in
a software system (and therefore require recompilation) is a complicated task which,
if not handled correctly, can lead to bugs that are very difficult to diagnose. For
instance, if we forget to recompile even one of the affected modules, errors may
be introduced that have nothing to do with the current version of the source code a
programmer may be examining.

Fortunately, the UNIX operating system provides a utility called `make` that is
intended to assist programmers in managing the complexity of large programs (containing many files).[†] Instead of entering a large number of compiler commands "by
hand," programmers utilizing `make` can use a single command to automatically rebuild an executable version of a software system after any changes have occurred.
The importance of the `make` utility is that it is able to determine exactly which
modules need to be rebuilt in order to create the executable program. In this section
we will examine the inner workings of `make`, and discuss how it uses some of the
graph algorithms discussed in this chapter.

[†]Most personal computer-based C++ compilers provide a similar project management utility.

In order to understand how `make` works, it is helpful to consider a concrete example. Let us return to the simulation program developed in Section 6.5. The classes developed for this queueing system simulation program were all declared in the file `que_sys.H`, and their corresponding definitions were placed in the `que_sys.C` file. The main program, which actually used these classes to perform a simulation, was placed in the `driver.C` file. Recall (see Figures 6.7 and 6.9) that the classes created for the queueing system simulation made use of a number of previously developed classes—namely a standard queue class, along with a probability distribution function class. These classes were declared in the files `sm_queue.H` (see Figure 6.3) and `pdf.H` (see Exercise 4.13), respectively; hence the `#include` preprocessor directive is used to include these files, as shown in Figure 6.7.

To build an executable version of the simulation program, we need to link all of the object files that were created from these source files; but if any of the source files (or their corresponding header files) have been recently changed, they will need to be recompiled before linking. Thus, the executable program is dependent on the object files, which are in turn dependent on the source files. These relationships can be expressed using a precedence graph. For instance, the dependencies involved in our queueing system simulation program are shown in Figure 14.14.

In order to use `make`, a user must first express the dependencies associated with a program in a *description file*—this is simply a text file that is normally named `makefile`. A `makefile` for the queueing system simulation program is shown in Figure 14.15. Each pair of lines in this figure defines a list of *dependencies*, along with a *rebuilding command*. Consider, for example, the first two lines of Figure 14.15:

```
driver : driver.o que_sys.o sm_queue.o
         CC -o driver driver.o que_sys.o sm_queue.o -lm
```

The name to the left of the colon on the first line is called the *target*, and the file names to the right of the colon are the *dependents* of the target. When `make` encounters this line, it first checks to see if the target exists, and if it does it next checks to see if any of the dependents have been modified since the target was last built. This is easy to do since the operating system stores with each file the time of its last modification. If the target is out of date with respect to its dependents (or if it does not exist),

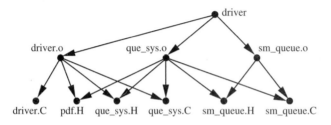

FIGURE 14.14
The precedence graph for the dependencies between files in the queueing system simulation program.

```
driver : driver.o que_sys.o sm_queue.o
        CC -o driver driver.o que_sys.o sm_queue.o -lm

driver.o : driver.C que_sys.H que_sys.C pdf.H
        CC -c driver.C

que_sys.o : que_sys.H que_sys.C sm_queue.H sm_queue.C pdf.H
        CC -c que_sys.C

sm_queue.o : sm_queue.H sm_queue.C
        CC -c sm_queue.C
```

FIGURE 14.15

The makefile for the queueing system simulation program. The C++ compiler is invoked using the command CC. The -c option suppresses linking (i.e., only an object file is created), and the -o option is used to give the final executable file the name driver. The -lm option at the end of the second line causes the math library to be linked with the other object files when the executable file is created.

then make will rebuild the target using the C++ compiler commands on the second line.[†]

Actually, make must do some additional work before the decision to execute a rebuilding command can be reached. Notice in Figure 14.15 that each of the dependents of driver, which is the executable program we are trying to create, are themselves targets on some other line. For instance, this figure shows that driver.C is a dependent of the target driver.o, but driver.o is a dependent of the target driver. Thus, if driver.C was modified after the last time driver was rebuilt, make must first execute the rebuilding command associated with the target driver.o *before* executing the rebuilding command associated with driver. In order to ensure that rebuilding commands are executed in the correct order, make first uses the information contained in the description file to construct a precedence graph for a program. It then traces through the precedence graph to find any files that have been modified since the last build, and issues the appropriate compiler commands to bring these files, and eventually the final executable program, up to date.

Any precedence graph produced by make must be acyclic (i.e., a tree), since all of the vertices in a cycle cannot be simultaneously satisfied. In other words, if there is a cycle, then one of the files would always be out of date with respect to some other file in the cycle. Thus, after make creates a precedence graph, a depth-first search is used to check that the graph is acyclic.

After make determines that the precedence graph is valid, it must determine which targets need to be rebuilt. It is clear from the example given in Figure 14.14 that make needs to process the precedence graph from the bottom up; the executable file driver can be rebuilt only after all of the files on which it depends are up to

---

[†]In the UNIX make utility, the first character of a line containing rebuilding commands must be a tab.

date, but these files can be rebuilt only if their dependents are up to date, and so on. This suggests that the precedence graph should also be processed at this stage using a depth-first search, starting at the root of the tree. Only after this search has reached a leaf can we determine which targets need to be rebuilt. This means that the code for processing the rebuilding commands should be placed *after* the recursive call on line 4 of DFS-Visit(), as shown below:

```
DFS-Visit(GRAPH G = (V, E), vertex s)    ▷ s is the source
1   d[s] ← time ← time + 1    ▷ vertex s is discovered and marked
2   for each  u ∈ adjacent[s]  do
3        if  d[u] = 0  then    ▷ is vertex u unmarked?
4             DFS-Visit(G, u)
5             if  out-of-date[u] = true  then
6                  ▷ execute rebuilding commands for u
```

By placing the code that processes the rebuilding commands within the range of the conditional statement that starts on line 3, we also guarantee that the rebuilding commands associated with a target will be executed at most once—after a vertex is marked it will not be visited again. The only rebuilding commands that may need to be processed after DFS-Visit() is completed are those associated with the root of the tree. The code for handling this should be placed in DFS() after the call to DFS-Visit().

EXERCISES

14.1. The BFS() algorithm given in Section 14.3.1 calculates the value of the shortest path length from the source vertex to every vertex in the graph. It does not, however, keep track of the actual shortest paths. Modify the BFS() algorithm so that it also produces an array $p[1..|V|]$ where $p[v]$ is the predecessor of vertex v in a shortest path from s to v. Discuss how this array can be used to construct a shortest path from s to any reachable vertex in the graph.

14.2. In Exercise 6.8 we considered the problem of traversing a maze. Discuss how a maze can be represented as an undirected graph $G = (V, E)$, and then give a $O(V + E)$-time algorithm that can be used to traverse a maze.

14.3. An undirected graph $G = (V, E)$ is called **bipartite** if V can be partitioned into two disjoint sets V_1 and V_2 such that every edge in E joins a vertex in V_1 with a vertex in V_2. Develop a $O(V + E)$-time algorithm for determining if an undirected graph is bipartite.

14.4. Modify the DFS() algorithm so that it labels each edge of an input graph as a tree, back, forward, or cross edge.

14.5. Prove that the rules proposed in Section 14.3.2 for classifying the edges of a graph using DFS() correctly classify an edge as a tree, back, forward, or cross edge.

14.6. Prove that a directed graph G is acyclic if and only if DFS() does not encounter any back edges when it is run on G.

14.7. Given a tree as an input graph, compare the order in which vertices are visited during a postorder traversal and a depth-first search (starting from the root).

14.8. Given a directed graph $G = (V, E)$, the **transpose** of G, denoted G^T, is obtained by switching the direction of each edge in E. That is, $G^T = (V, E^T)$ where $E^T = \{(u, v) \mid (v, u) \in E\}$. Recall that a directed graph is strongly connected if every pair of vertices in the graph are reachable from each other. The following algorithm uses the transpose of a graph to determine the number of strongly connected components it contains:

> StronglyConnected(DIRECTED WEIGHTED GRAPH $G = (V, E)$)
> 1 DFS(G)   ▷ save the finish time array f
> 2 DFS(G^T)   ▷ on line 4 of DFS(), consider vertices in order of
> ▷ decreasing finish time using the f array from line 1

From within the call to DFS(G^T) on line 2, each call to DFS-Visit() indicates that another strongly connected component has been found.

(*a*) Demonstrate the operation of this algorithm on an example graph.

(*b*) Rigorously prove the correctness of StronglyConnected().

14.9. A connected undirected graph is said to be **biconnected** if no one vertex can be removed from the graph and cause it to become disconnected. If a graph is not biconnected, each vertex whose removal causes the graph to become disconnected is referred to as an **articulation point**. Develop a $O(V + E)$-time algorithm that uses depth-first search to find all articulation points in a connected undirected graph.

14.10. Can the following picture, known as **Mohammed's scimitars**, be drawn using one continuous line without retracing and without lifting pencil from paper?

(Hint: Read the Chapter Notes.)

14.11. A directed graph $G = (V, E)$ is said to be **semiconnected** if for any two vertices $u, v \in V$, $u \rightsquigarrow v$ or $v \rightsquigarrow u$. Develop a $O(V + E)$-time algorithm for determining if a directed graph is semiconnected.

14.12. The n queens problem was presented in Exercise 6.9. Here, you are asked to solve the n queens problem using depth-first search. Specifically, construct a directed graph by including the directed edge (A, B) if and only if the vector A is k-feasible, the vector B is $k + 1$-feasible, and $A[i] = B[i]$ for every $i = 1, 2, \ldots, k$. Describe how a depth-first search can be used to solve the n queens problem using this graph.

14.13. Will Prim's or Kruskal's algorithms work properly if the edges of the input graph can have negative weights?

14.14. Consider the following polynomial-time approximation algorithm for the traveling salesman problem where the collection of cities is represented using the vertices of a completely-connected undirected weighted graph, and the distance between any two cities is given by the weight of the edge between them:

> ApproxTSP2(UNDIRECTED WEIGHTED GRAPH $G = (V, E)$)
> 1 $T \leftarrow$ Prim(G)
> 2 **return** Preorder(root[T])

Step 2 of this algorithm returns the vertices in the minimum spanning tree T in the order they are visited during a preorder traversal. Assuming the triangle inequality holds between any group of three cities:

(a) Demonstrate the operation of this algorithm on an example graph.

(b) Prove that the tour returned by ApproxTSP2() has a ratio bound of 2.

14.15. Find a graph containing negative-weight edges, but no negative-weight cycles, that causes Dijkstra() to produce an erroneous result.

14.16. In the *single-destination shortest-paths problem* one is given a graph $G = (V, E)$, and asked to find the shortest paths from every vertex in V to a destination vertex d. Develop an efficient algorithm for solving this problem.

14.17. Modify Dijkstra() so that if there is more than one shortest path from the source to a destination vertex, it selects the one with the fewest number of edges.

14.18. The *Bellman-Ford algorithm*, given below, solves the single-source shortest-paths problem in the most general case—when the graph is weighted, and the edge weights can be negative. Given a weighted graph and a source vertex s, this algorithm finds the shortest path from s to all vertices if there are no negative-weight cycles in the graph. If there is a negative weight cycle, then this algorithm will indicate that no solution is possible.

```
Bellman-Ford(GRAPH G = (V, E), vertex s)
1   for each  v ∈ V  do
2       d[v] ← ∞   ▷ unmark all vertices
3   d[s] ← 0   ▷ mark the source
4   for  i ← 1 to |V| − 1  do
5       for each  (u, v) ∈ E  do
6           if  d[v] > d[u] + w(u, v)  then
7               d[v] ← d[u] + w(u, v)
8   for each  (u, v) ∈ E  do   ▷ test for negative-weight cycles
9       if  d[v] > d[u] + w(u, v)  then
10          return NULL   ▷ no solution
11  return d   ▷ solution
```

(a) Demonstrate the operation of this algorithm on an example graph.

(b) Prove the correctness of this algorithm.

14.19. Modify Dijkstra() and Bellman-Ford() so that each produces a predecessor array as discussed in Exercise 14.1. Next, develop an algorithm that takes a predecessor array as input, and outputs the vertices in the shortest path to each vertex.

14.20. In Section 14.3.2 we showed how depth-first search can be used to produce a viable schedule for a job from a precedence graph. However, a viable schedule itself is often not enough. For example it may be important to determine the earliest completion time for a job, or if certain tasks can be delayed without affecting the completion time of the job. In order to perform these types of calculations, the time required by each task must be supplied along with the precedence graph. The earliest completion time for a job can then be determined by finding a maximal path (in terms of the time required) from the initial task, to a task with an out-degree of zero.

(a) Develop an algorithm that takes as input a precedence graph, along with the time required by each activity, and outputs the earliest completion time for each task as well as for the entire job. (Hint: Structure the problem as a weighted graph, and modify a shortest-paths algorithm to find longest paths.)

(b) Modify your algorithm from the previous part so that it also computes the latest completion time for each task (i.e., the latest each task can be completed without affecting the earliest completion time).

(*c*) The slack time for each task is the amount of time a task can be delayed without affecting the earliest completion time. Tasks with zero slack time are referred to as *critical tasks*. In every job there is at least one set of tasks (starting from the initial task, and ending with a task having an out-degree of zero in the precedence graph) consisting entirely of critical tasks. These tasks are referred to as a *critical path*. Modify your algorithm from the previous part so that it outputs all critical paths.

CHAPTER NOTES

For references that treat a broader range of graph algorithms, the reader may consult Cormen, Leiserson and Rivest [36], Even [52], or Tarjan [147]. Discovery of the breadth-first search algorithm has been attributed to Moore [103], who used this algorithm to find paths through a maze.

The long and colorful history of the minimum spanning tree problem is the subject of an article by Graham and Hell [68]; the earliest explicit formulation they found for this problem was by Borůvka [22] in 1926. Graham and Hell also point out that although Prim's algorithm is generally attributed to Prim [124], Jarník [78] published the same algorithm in 1930. Kruskal's algorithm originates with Kruskal [88]. Cheriton and Tarjan [31] developed an algorithm that uses ideas from both Prim's and Kruskal's algorithms to solve the minimum spanning tree problem in $O(E \log \log V)$ time. However, Moret and Shapiro [105] showed experimentally (for a number of graph families) that Prim's algorithm runs faster on average than Kruskal's algorithm or Cheriton and Tarjan's algorithm. Furthermore, they obtained the best performance for Prim's algorithm by using a binary heap.

Dijkstra's algorithm [44] was developed in 1959. The Bellman-Ford algorithm was independently developed by Bellman [15] and Ford [57]. In graphs with negative-weight edges, the Bellman-Ford algorithm can be used to solve the all-pairs shortest-paths problem in $O(V^2E)$ time; however, there are a number of dynamic programming solutions to this problem that perform better. These algorithms are treated in Cormen, Leiserson and Rivest [36].

Many authors trace the origins of graph theory to the famous *Königsberg bridge problem* solved by Leonhard Euler in 1736. In the city of Königsberg (now called Kaliningrad in what is now Russia) two islands formed by the Pregel River were connected to each other, as well as to opposite banks, using the arrangement of seven bridges shown below:

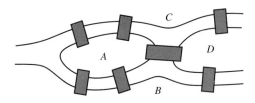

The problem is to devise a route that starts from any of the four land areas (*A*, *B*, *C*, or *D*), crosses each bridge *exactly* once, and returns to the starting point. Euler [51]

elegantly proved that no solution exists for this problem by formulating it as a graph in which the vertices represent the land areas, and the edges represent the bridges. The problem can now be restated as that of finding a closed walk on the graph that visits every edge exactly once (a graph that satisfies this property is duly referred to as a ***Euler graph***). Euler's solution to this problem was in the form of a proof that showed that a connected graph is an Euler graph if and only if all of its vertices have an even degree.

Another famous problem solved using graph-theoretic techniques is notable in that a computer was instrumental in its solution. In the ***four color problem*** we are asked to determine if the countries of any map on the plane (or sphere) can be colored with four or fewer colors such that all countries with common boundaries (not a single point) have different colors. Although cartographers for many centuries appeared to believe that only four colors were necessary to color a map, it took until 1977 to prove this fact. The proof, supplied by Appel et al. [8, 10] (see Appel and Haken [9] for a high-level discussion of this work), treated countries as graph vertices that were connected by an edge if they shared a border. Their proof is combinatorially complicated, requiring the testing of a large number of difficult cases. This testing, which would have been unfathomable "by hand," was completed using 1200 hours of computing time.

The UNIX `make` utility contains a large number of useful options not discussed in Section 14.6; a good reference is provided by Oram and Talbott [113].

APPENDIX
A

MATHEMATICAL
REVIEW:
SUMS AND
RECURRENCES

Much of this book is devoted to the comparison of alternative implementation techniques for various ADTs. This generally involves an analysis of the data structures and algorithms used in specific ADT implementations. This appendix provides some of the mathematical background that is necessary to perform this analysis. A familiarity with college algebra and basic calculus provides a sufficient background for understanding this material.

A.1 ELEMENTARY FUNCTIONS

The functions discussed in this section are often used to characterize the efficiency of algorithms. The ability to specify the efficiency of an algorithm using these functions allows us to compare the performance of different algorithms for solving a given problem.

405

A.1.1 Logarithms, Powers, and Exponentials

Power functions have the form $f(x) = x^r$ where x and r are real numbers. Functions of the form $f(x) = b^x$, where b and x are real numbers, are called ***exponential functions***, and are said to have base b. A ***super exponential function*** is a function whose exponent is either a power function or an exponential function. The functions 2^{x^2} and 2^{2^x} are examples of super exponential functions. Notice that the more rapidly the value of their exponent grows, the more rapidly the value of the super exponential function itself grows.

If b and x are positive real numbers, then the ***logarithm*** to the base b of x, written as $f(x) = \log_b x$, is defined to be the inverse of the exponential function b^x. That is, the solution to $y = \log_b x$ is found by solving $x = b^y$ for y. Some important properties of logarithms are presented below.

For all real $a > 1$, $b > 1$, $x_1 > 1$, $x_2 > 1$, and n,

$$\log_b b^n = n \tag{A.1}$$

$$\log_b x_1 x_2 = log_b x_1 + log_b x_2 \tag{A.2}$$

$$\log_b x_1^n = n \log_b x_1 \tag{A.3}$$

$$\log_b x_1 = \log_b a \cdot \log_a x_1 = \frac{\log_a x_1}{\log_a b} \tag{A.4}$$

$$a^{\log_b n} = n^{\log_b a} \tag{A.5}$$

Properties (A.2) and (A.3) can be used to show that

$$\log_b \left(\frac{x_1}{x_2} \right) = log_b x_1 - log_b x_2 \tag{A.6}$$

In addition, property (A.5) implies that if you have some means of calculating the logarithm base a of a given number x, then you can calculate the logarithm of x to *any* base. Logarithms to the base 2 are used extensively in the analysis of computer algorithms and data structures. For this reason, we use the notation $\lg n$ to denote $\log_2 n$ throughout this book.

An important property of the functions discussed in this section is that they are all monotonically increasing over the intervals that are of interest to us. A real-valued function f defined on an interval I is said to be ***monotonically increasing*** if for any x_1 and x_2 in I, $x_1 > x_2$ implies $f(x_1) > f(x_2)$. The logarithmic function $\log_b x$ is monotonically increasing if I is taken to be the real numbers greater than 0. The same can be said of the power function x^r when $r \geq 1$, and the exponential function b^x when $b > 1$. With these restrictions in mind, it can be shown that as x grows large, any exponential function will dominate any power function, and that any power function will dominate any logarithmic function.[†] You are asked to formally prove this in Exercise A.15.

[†]More formally, we say that a function $g(x)$ dominates a function $f(x)$, written as $f(x) \prec g(x)$, if $\lim_{x \to \infty} (f(x)/g(x)) = 0$.

A.1.2 Floor and Ceiling Functions

The *floor* of a real number x, written as $\lfloor x \rfloor$, is the greatest integer that is less than or equal to x. The *ceiling* of a real number x, written as $\lceil x \rceil$, is the least integer that is greater than or equal to x. For example, $\lfloor 3.2 \rfloor = 3$ and $\lceil 3.2 \rceil = 4$. Also note that $\lfloor -3.2 \rfloor = -4$ since -4 is the greatest integer that is less than -3.2. These floor and ceiling definitions imply that $\lfloor x \rfloor = x = \lceil x \rceil$ if and only if x is an integer.

The floor function can be used to give a useful definition for the *mod operation*—the remainder that results from integer division. Specifically, for integers p and q,

$$p \bmod q = p - q\lfloor p/q \rfloor, \quad \text{for } q \neq 0. \tag{A.7}$$

For example, the remainder that results when 5 is divided by 3 (i.e., 5 mod 3) is $5 - 3\lfloor 5/3 \rfloor = 2$. Note that equation (A.7) can be applied even when p and/or q are negative. Thus, $5 \bmod -3 = 5 - (-3)\lfloor 5/(-3) \rfloor = -1$.

The following properties of the floor and ceiling functions are often useful:

$$\lfloor x \rfloor = n \iff n \leq x < n+1 \tag{A.8}$$

$$\lfloor x \rfloor = n \iff x - 1 < n \leq x \tag{A.9}$$

$$\lceil x \rceil = n \iff n - 1 < x \leq n \tag{A.10}$$

$$\lceil x \rceil = n \iff x \leq n < x + 1 \tag{A.11}$$

For example, property (A.8) can be used to determine how many bits are required to represent an integer number $n > 0$. First note that if $2^{m-1} \leq n < 2^m$, then n can be represented using m bits. Using the fact that $\lg 2^{m-1} = m - 1$, we have that

$$m - 1 \leq \lg n < m \tag{A.12}$$

Adding one to equation (A.12) puts it in the form of equation (A.8):

$$m \leq \lg n + 1 < m + 1$$

Therefore, $m = \lfloor \lg n + 1 \rfloor = \lfloor \lg n \rfloor + 1$ bits are required for the binary representation of an integer number $n > 0$.

A.2 FINITE AND INFINITE SERIES

A *series* is simply a sum of numbers. If the number of terms in the series is finite, then the series is said to be a *finite series*. Conversely, if the number of terms in the series is infinite, then we have an *infinite series*. For example, the sum of the first n integers can be written as the finite series

$$1 + 2 + \cdots + n \tag{A.13}$$

Of course as $n \to \infty$, equation (A.13) becomes an infinite series. In general, we will encounter sums of the form

$$a_1 + a_2 + \cdots + a_n \tag{A.14}$$

where a_i $(i = 1, 2, \ldots, n)$ is said to be the i-th term in the series, and each a_i is a number defined according to a specific rule.

It is often convenient to express a series using the more compact *summation notation*. When equation (A.13) is expressed in summation notation it reads $\sum_{i=1}^{n} i$, and equation (A.14) may be rewritten as $\sum_{i=1}^{n} a_i$.

A.2.1   Arithmetic Series

An *arithmetic series* or arithmetic progression is any series that can be written in the form

$$a_1 + a_2 + \cdots + a_n \tag{A.15}$$

where $a_k = a_{k-1} + c$, and c is a constant. Thus, each term in the series can be derived from the previous term by simply adding the constant value c. Equation (A.13) is an example of an arithmetic series that is encountered quite often. In this series, $a_1 = c = 1$. Furthermore, it can be shown that

$$\sum_{i=1}^{n} i = \frac{n(n+1)}{2} \tag{A.16}$$

This can be proven in the following manner. Let S represent the sum in equation (A.13). Then the product $2S$ is given by

$$
\begin{array}{rcccccccc}
S = & 1 & + & 2 & + \cdots + & n \\
+S = & n & + & n-1 & + \cdots + & 1 \\
\hline
2S = & (n+1) & + & (n+1) & + \cdots + & (n+1)
\end{array}
$$

Dividing the last line by 2 yields the desired result.

For the general case it can be shown that

$$\sum_{i=1}^{n} a_i = \frac{n(a_n + a_1)}{2} \tag{A.17}$$

Notice that equation (A.16) is a special case of equation (A.17) with $a_n = n$ and $a_1 = 1$.

The right hand sides of equations (A.16) and (A.17) are referred to as *closed forms*. By closed form we mean that we can compute the result using a fixed number of operations. That is, the number of operations is independent of n (by operations we mean the number of mathematical operations, not the number of steps a computer algorithm might require to compute these mathematical operations). The same cannot be said for the left hand sides of equations (A.16) and (A.17). We will typically be interested in determining the closed forms of the summations we encounter.

A.2.2   Geometric Series

A *geometric series* or geometric progression is a sum of the form

$$x^m + x^{m+1} + x^{m+2} + \cdots + x^n \tag{A.18}$$

where $0 \le m \le n$. If $m = 0$, equation (A.18) reduces to the sum of the first n powers of x. It is not difficult to show that

$$\sum_{i=0}^{n} x^i = \begin{cases} \frac{x^{n+1}-1}{x-1}, & \text{if } x \ne 1 \\ n+1, & \text{if } x = 1 \end{cases} \qquad (A.19)$$

First, look at the case where $x = 1$. In this case, the sum consists of $n + 1$ terms all of which have the value 1. For the case where $x \ne 1$, we let S represent the sum in equation (A.19), then we subtract the product xS for S obtaining:

$$\begin{array}{rl} xS = & + x + x^2 + \cdots + x^n + x^{n+1} \\ -S = & 1 + x + x^2 + \cdots + x^n \\ \hline (x-1)S = & -1 \qquad\qquad\qquad\qquad\quad + x^{n+1} \end{array}$$

Since we are considering the case where $x \ne 1$, we may divide both sides of the last line by $(x - 1)$ to obtain the desired result.

The summation in equation (A.19) is now used to study infinite geometric series. First let us note that an infinite sum may be restated as the limit of a finite sum, if the limit exists. For example,

$$\sum_{i=0}^{\infty} x^i = \lim_{n \to \infty} \sum_{i=0}^{n} x^i \qquad (A.20)$$

Combining equations (A.19) and (A.20) we have for $-1 < x < 1$,

$$\sum_{i=0}^{\infty} x^i = \frac{1}{1-x} \qquad (A.21)$$

Equation (A.19) also shows that this series diverges to ∞ for $x > 1$, and diverges without limit for $x \le -1$. For the case of $x = 1$, equation (A.19) cannot be used; however, since all terms of the series are 1, the summation $\sum_{i=0}^{\infty} 1^i$ tends to infinity and the series diverges to infinity.

A.3   BOUNDING SUMMATIONS

In Section A.2 we derived the exact closed forms for a number of summations. In many cases, however, all that is necessary in order to perform some analysis is a bound on the value of a particular summation. Typically, we will seek to express such bounds using asymptotic notation. Below we discuss a number of techniques that can be used to bound the value of a summation.

BOUND EACH TERM. An easy way of obtaining an upper bound on a summation is to simply bound each term by the largest term in the summation. This is accomplished by multiplying the number of terms in the summation by the largest term:

$$\sum_{i=1}^{n} a_i \le \sum_{i=1}^{n} \max\{a_i\} = n \cdot \max\{a_i\}$$

For example, the largest term in $\sum_{i=1}^{n} i$ is n. Therefore, $\sum_{i=1}^{n} i \leq \sum_{i=1}^{n} n = n^2$, and from this it follows that $\sum_{i=1}^{n} i = O(n^2)$.

INTEGRAL APPROXIMATION. If a summation can be expressed in the form $\sum_{i=m}^{n} f(i)$, and $f(i)$ is a monotonically increasing function, then upper and lower bounds on the summation can be found by integrating $f(i)$. Specifically,

$$\int_{m-1}^{n} f(x)dx \leq \sum_{i=m}^{n} f(i) \leq \int_{m}^{n+1} f(x)dx \qquad \text{(A.22)}$$

To see why this relation holds, refer to Figure A.1. In Figure A.1 (a), the function $f(x)$ is plotted, and each term in the summation $\sum_{i=m}^{n} f(i)$ is represented by a rectangle of unit width. The total area contained in these rectangles represents the value of the summation. Notice that $f(x)$ passes through the upper right hand corner of each rectangle. Integrating $f(x)$ over the interval $m-1$ to n yields the area of the shaded region shown in Figure A.1 (a)—which obviously represents a lower bound

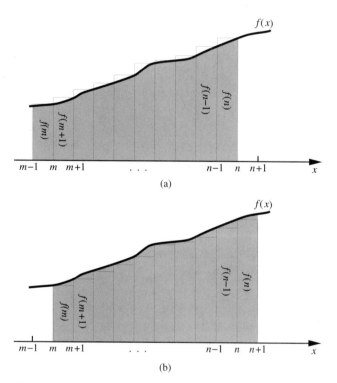

(a)

(b)

FIGURE A.1
Approximation of $\sum_{k=m}^{n} f(k)$ using integrals, where $f(x)$ is a monotonically increasing function. The value of the summation is given by the total area of the rectangles in each graph. **(a)** A lower bound for the summation is obtained from $\int_{m-1}^{n} f(x)dx$, which is represented by the shaded region. **(b)** An upper bound for the summation is obtained from $\int_{m}^{n+1} f(x)dx$, which is represented by the shaded region.

on the summation. Next, shift each rectangle one place to the right, as shown in Figure A.1 (b). Now, if we integrate $f(x)$ over the interval m to $n + 1$, we obtain the area of the shaded region shown in Figure A.1 (b)—which obviously represents an upper bound on the summation. A similar result can be obtained if $f(x)$ is a monotonically decreasing function. In this case we have

$$\int_m^{n+1} f(x)dx \leq \sum_{i=m}^{n} f(i) \leq \int_{m-1}^{n} f(x)dx \tag{A.23}$$

As an example, consider $H(n) = \sum_{i=1}^{n} 1/i$, which is referred to as the n-th **harmonic number**. Since each term in $H(n)$ decreases monotonically with n, equation (A.23) is used:

$$\int_1^{n+1} \frac{1}{x}dx \leq \sum_{i=1}^{n} \frac{1}{i} \leq \int_0^{n} \frac{1}{x}dx$$

Performing the necessary integration for the lower bound yields

$$\sum_{i=1}^{n} \frac{1}{i} \geq \ln(n + 1) \tag{A.24}$$

For the upper bound, there is some trouble with the limits of integration. This is due to the fact that $\ln 0$ is not defined. Therefore we rewrite the sum as

$$\sum_{i=1}^{n} \frac{1}{i} = 1 + \sum_{i=2}^{n} \frac{1}{i}$$

which yields

$$1 + \sum_{i=2}^{n} \frac{1}{i} \leq 1 + \int_1^{n} \frac{1}{x}dx$$

$$= \ln n + 1 \tag{A.25}$$

Taken together, equations (A.24) and (A.25) imply an asymptotically tight bound of $\Theta(\log n)$ for $H(n)$.

A.4   RECURRENCE RELATIONS

Quite often the analysis performed in this text yields recurrence relations that specify some measure of the efficiency of an algorithm. A set of equalities is said to specify a **recurrence relation** if they specify a boundary value for a function, as well as an equation for the value of the function that is based on previous values of the function. The following recurrence relation is shown in Section 1.4.1 to describe the number of moves required by Tower() to solve the Tower of Hanoi puzzle with n disks:

$$T(n) = \begin{cases} 1, & \text{if } n = 1 \\ 2T(n - 1) + 1, & \text{if } n > 1 \end{cases} \tag{A.26}$$

The first equation of this set specifies the boundary value, and the second is a general equation that relates the n-th value of T to previous values of T. In this case, $T(n)$ is obtained by taking the product of $T(n-1)$ and 2, and then adding 1. Given equation (A.26) we can calculate $T(n)$ for any value of n by first calculating $T(1)$ given $T(0)$, and then calculating $T(2)$ from $T(1)$, and so on, until we reach $T(n)$. The problem with this approach is that it may take a long time to compute $T(n)$ when n is large. We will later prove that the following equation yields the same results as equation (A.26):

$$T(n) = 2^n - 1, \quad n \geq 1 \qquad (A.27)$$

Note that equation (A.27) is the closed form of recurrence relation (A.26). Again, by closed form we mean that we can compute the result using a fixed number of operations. The same cannot be said for equation (A.26).

An advantage offered by closed form expressions for recurrence relations is that they give us a better understanding of the behavior of the algorithm that the recurrence relation describes. If a measure of the resources required by a particular algorithm is given by equation (A.26) (where n is the size of the input to the algorithm), and equation (A.27) is the closed form, then we can say that the amount of resources consumed by that algorithm grows exponentially with the size of the input.

Needless to say, whenever we encounter a recurrence relation in our study of data structures and algorithms, we will seek a closed form to represent it. This is not to say that every recurrence relation has a closed form—in fact, many do not.

SOLVING RECURRENCE RELATIONS.   We will say that we have *solved* a recurrence relation if we are able to obtain a closed form representation. Although it may seem unusual at first, one of the most useful methods for solving a recurrence relation is to make an educated guess at the closed form, and then prove that this guess is correct. Typically this involves investigating the recurrence for small values of n, and based on the information obtained, inferring a guess at the closed form. As an example, consider the recurrence relation in equation (A.26). Observing $T(n)$ at small values of n we see that

$$T(1) = 1$$
$$T(2) = 3$$
$$T(3) = 7$$
$$T(4) = 15$$
$$T(5) = 31$$

From this sequence, it appears that $T(n)$ is always one less than a power of 2. More specifically,

$$T(n) = 2^n - 1, \quad n \geq 1 \qquad (A.28)$$

appears to be a good guess at the closed form. We have already shown that equation (A.28) is correct for $0 \leq n \leq 5$, but does this prove that the proposed closed form is correct for all n? No, and it is not feasible to directly test equation (A.28) for all values of n; however, we can effectively do just that by using *induction*.

Mathematical induction is a powerful technique that can be used to prove that some statement involving the integer n is true for all $n \geq n_0$. Assume P is some statement or proposition we wish to prove, and that P involves a parameter n that assumes integer values. The first thing we do is show that P is true when n has its smallest value, n_0; this is called the **basis**. Then we must show that for every $n > n_0$, if P holds for $n - 1$, P also holds for n. The assumption that P is true for all values between n_0 and $n - 1$, inclusive, is called the **induction hypothesis**. In other words, if P is thought of as a list of statements $P_0, P_1, P_2, \ldots$, then the principle of mathematical induction shows that all of these statements are true provided P_0 is true, and that P_n is true whenever P_{n-1} is true.

Let us see how mathematical induction can be used to prove our hypothesis that (A.28) is the closed form of the recurrence relation in (A.26). First, we make the assumption that for all values between 1 and $n - 1$, inclusive, equation (A.28) is true (i.e., the induction hypothesis is that $T(\alpha) = 2^\alpha - 1$ for $1 \leq \alpha \leq n - 1$). Next, we must find a basis. At $n = 1$ we have that $T(1) = 2^1 - 1 = 1$, which agrees with the recurrence relation for the base case. Finally, we must use the induction hypothesis in an extension step. This is accomplished by substituting the induction hypothesis into equation (A.26):

$$
\begin{aligned}
T(n) &= 2T(n - 1) + 1 \\
&= 2(2^{n-1} - 1) + 1 \\
&= 2^n - 1
\end{aligned}
\tag{A.29}
$$

The induction hypothesis was used when $2^{n-1} - 1$ was substituted for $T(n - 1)$ on the second line. We have now proven that equation (A.28) is true for all $n \geq 0$. To understand why, note that from the basis we know that the closed form given in equation (A.28) is correct for $n = 1$. Equation (A.29) can then be used to show that it is also correct for $n = 2$, and this result can be used to prove the validity of equation (A.28) for $n = 3$, and so on.

Recurrence relations are particularly well suited for solution by mathematical induction; however, it requires that we make an appropriate guess. For complicated recurrence relations this can be difficult.

BOUNDING RECURRENCE RELATIONS. When analyzing a recurrence relation that describes the resources used by an algorithm, we are typically only interested in determining the tightest possible asymptotic bound on the closed form. Thus, instead of finding the exact closed form, and then expressing this solution using asymptotic notation, it is often easier to make a guess *directly* at the asymptotic form of the solution, and then verify this guess using induction. This technique is referred to as **constructive induction** because it allows us to fill in the missing specifications necessary to prove some assertion. As an example, consider the recurrence relation

$$
T(n) = \begin{cases} 1, & \text{if } n = 1 \\ T(n - 1) + n, & \text{if } n > 1 \end{cases}
\tag{A.30}
$$

If we wish to prove that $T(n) = O(n^2)$, then according to Definition 1.1, it is sufficient to show that $T(n) \leq cn^2$ for some choice of the positive constant $c > 0$, and for all values of n greater than some positive constant n_0. First, we will assume that $T(\alpha) \leq c\alpha^2$ for $1 \leq \alpha \leq n - 1$. Then we will use this induction hypothesis in an extension step to show that $T(n) \leq cn^2$. This is accomplished by substituting the induction hypothesis into equation (A.30):

$$
\begin{aligned}
T(n) &= T(n-1) + n \\
&\leq c(n-1)^2 + n \\
&= cn^2 - 2cn + c + n \\
&\leq cn^2
\end{aligned}
$$

where the last line holds for all $n \geq 1$ when $c = 1$. This means that n_0 can be any number greater than or equal to 1. To complete the proof, we must show that the induction hypothesis holds for the base case. From equation (A.30) we have that $T(1) = 1$, and from the induction hypothesis $T(1) \leq c(1)^2$. Choosing $c = 1$ will also satisfy this base case, and we have proven that $T(n) = O(n^2)$. A similar proof can be constructed to show that $T(n) = \Omega(n^2)$.

It is important to realize that it is necessary to prove the *exact* form of the induction hypothesis. Not doing so can lead to erroneous results as demonstrated in the following example. Let us attempt to prove that the closed form of recurrence (A.30) is $O(n)$. Thus it is sufficient to show that $T(n) \leq cn$. Our induction hypothesis is that $T(\alpha) \leq c\alpha$ for $1 \leq \alpha \leq n - 1$, and the extension step is:

$$
\begin{aligned}
T(n) &= T(n-1) + n \\
&\leq c(n-1) + n \\
&= cn - c + n \\
&\leq cn
\end{aligned}
$$

Assuming we could find a base case, we might *incorrectly* conclude that $T(n) = O(n)$. The flaw in this proof occurs in the last line of the extension step. In order to satisfy the inequality $cn - c + n \leq cn$, the condition $c \geq n$ must hold. However, according to Definition 1.1, this is impossible since c must be a constant, and n is assumed to grow arbitrarily large.

Sometimes it is necessary to add lower order terms to the induction hypothesis in order to make the math work out properly during the extension step. For example, consider the recurrence relation in equation (A.26). We have already shown that for this recurrence relation $T(n) = O(2^n)$. Let us now verify this using constructive induction. Our induction hypothesis is that $T(\alpha) \leq c2^\alpha$ for $0 \leq \alpha \leq n - 1$, and the extension step proceeds as follows:

$$
\begin{aligned}
T(n) &= 2T(n-1) + 1 \\
&\leq 2c2^{n-1} + 1 \\
&= c2^n + 1
\end{aligned}
$$

From this we see that there is no choice for c that allows us to satisfy $T(n) \leq c2^n$ (i.e., no matter how c is chosen, $c2^n + 1 \leq c2^n$ implies that $1 \leq 0$). The "trick" in these cases, where the inductive hypothesis is off by a lower order term (in this case, the constant 1), is to *subtract* a lower order term from the initial guess. This means that we are actually attempting to prove a stronger result. For instance, let us revise our previous induction hypothesis to include the constant term b. That is, $T(\alpha) \leq c2^\alpha - b$ for $0 \leq \alpha \leq n - 1$. We now obtain

$$
\begin{aligned}
T(n) &= 2T(n-1) + 1 \\
&\leq 2(c2^{n-1} - b) + 1 \\
&= c2^n - 2b + 1 \\
&\leq c2^n - b
\end{aligned}
$$

where the last line holds if $b \geq 1$. All that remains is to choose c so that the base case is satisfied.

EXERCISES

A.1. The series expressions that were discussed in Section A.2 may be expressed as recurrence relations. Rewrite equations (A.13) and (A.19) as recurrence relations.

A.2. Why are the values generated by the sum in (A.13) called the *triangular numbers*?

A.3. Use induction to prove that the sum of the first n natural numbers is $n(n+1)/2$.

A.4. Use induction to prove that equation (A.17) is correct.

A.5. Use induction to prove that for all natural numbers x and n, $x^n - 1$ is divisible by $x - 1$.

A.6. Find a closed form for the following series and prove your result using induction: $\frac{1}{2} + \frac{1}{4} + \frac{1}{8} + \cdots + \frac{1}{2^n}$.

A.7. Show that
  (a) $p \bmod q = (p \bmod q) \bmod q$.
  (b) $\left(\sum_{i=0}^n a_i\right) \bmod q = \left[\sum_{i=0}^n (a_i \bmod q)\right] \bmod q$.

A.8. Use induction to show that $p^i \bmod (p-1) = 1$ for all i.

A.9. What is wrong with the following inductive proof?

> We can prove that all horses are the same color. This is accomplished using induction on the number of horses in a set of size n. If there's just one horse ($n = 1$) then it's the same color as itself, so the basis is trivial. For the induction hypothesis, assume that all sets of horses of size 1 through $n-1$ have the same color. For the extension step, note that if the total number of horses in the world is n, then by the induction hypothesis, horses 1 through $n-1$ are the same color, and similarly horses 2 through n are the same color (these are both sets of size $n - 1$). Furthermore, the middle horses, 2 through $n - 1$, cannot change color based on whom they are grouped with. Therefore, horses 1 and n must be the same color.

A.10. An important arithmetic series is given by $\sum_{k=0}^n (\alpha + \beta k)$. Prove that a closed form for this sum is given by $(\alpha + \frac{1}{2}\beta n)(n+1)$.

A.11. An important geometric series is given by $\sum_{k=0}^n \alpha x^k$. Prove that a closed form for this sum is given by $\frac{\alpha - \alpha x^{n+1}}{1-x}$ for $x \neq 1$. For $x = 1$, it is easily seen that this sum is $\alpha(n+1)$.

A.12. Prove that $\sum_{k=0}^n k2^k = (n-1)2^{n+1} + 2$.

A.13. Show that $H_i \leq \ln i + 1$.

A.14. Use constructive induction to show that the closed form of the recurrence relation in equation (A.30) is $\Omega(n^2)$.

A.15. Prove that any exponential function dominates any power function. (Hint: use L'Hospital's rule from calculus.)

A.16. Derive asymptotically tight bounds for the following sums:

(a) $\displaystyle\sum_{k=1}^{n} k^r$, where $r \geq 0$ is a constant.

(b) $\displaystyle\sum_{k=1}^{n} k \lg k$.

A.17. For each of the following recurrence relations, find the tightest possible asymptotic upper and lower bounds on the closed form. You may assume that $T(n)$ is constant for $n \leq 2$.

(a) $T(n) = T(n-1) + \lg n$
(b) $T(n) = T(n-1) + n^2$
(c) $T(n) = T(\lceil n/2 \rceil) + 1$
(d) $T(n) = 2T(\lfloor n/2 \rfloor) + n$
(e) $T(n) = 2T(\lfloor n/2 \rfloor + 3) + n$
(f) $T(n) = 3T(\lfloor n/2 \rfloor) + n$
(g) $T(n) = 3T(\lfloor n/4 \rfloor) + n$
(h) $T(n) = T(\sqrt{n}) + 1$

APPENDIX NOTES

The excellent text by Graham, Knuth, and Patashnik [69] treats most of the subjects in this appendix in greater depth. In particular, a wide variety of techniques for solving complicated sums and recurrence relations are presented. Other sources for techniques used in the solution of recurrence relations that result from the analysis of algorithms are Brassard and Bratley [23], Greene and Knuth [70], and Lueker [92]. Exercise A.9 is from Pólya [120].

APPENDIX
B

MATHEMATICAL REVIEW: SETS, COUNTING, AND GRAPHS

In this appendix a number of elementary concepts and techniques from discrete mathematics are presented. Discrete mathematics is concerned with the study of discrete objects. Because the manipulation of discrete objects pervades modern computing, discrete mathematics provides another important component of the foundation necessary for the study of data structures and algorithms.

B.1 SETS

The set is a fundamental structure in mathematics that is used to group objects together. The objects in a set are called the *elements* or *members* of the set. These elements are taken from the *universal set* U, which contains all possible set elements. Thus, any given set will consist of elements from the set U. In addition, all the members of a given set are unique; that is, a set may not contain two or more copies of the same element. The number of elements contained in a set S is referred to as the *cardinality* of S, denoted by $|S|$. We will often refer to a set with cardinality n

as an n-set. The members of a set are typically listed between braces. For example, the set of positive prime numbers less than 20 can be expressed as

$$S = \{2, 3, 5, 7, 11, 13, 17, 19\}$$

For this example, $|S| = 8$. The elements of a set are not ordered. Thus, $\{1, 2, 3\}$ and $\{3, 2, 1\}$ represent the same set.

Another way to represent a set is to use ***set builder notation***, which has the form

$$S = \{x \mid \text{properties of } x\}$$

Using this notation, an element is said to be a member of the set S if it has one of the properties associated with x. Thus, another way to represent the set of positive prime numbers less than 20 is:

$$S = \{x \mid x \text{ is a positive prime number } < 20\}$$

which is read as "the set of all x such that x is a positive prime number less than 20." This notation is useful to describe sets for which it is impossible to list all the elements of the set. For example, the set of all prime numbers is given by

$$S = \{x \mid x \text{ is a prime number}\}$$

Set membership is denoted by $a \in A$, which states that a is a member of the set A. Conversely, $a \notin A$ indicates that a is not a member of the set A. The special set that contains no elements is called the ***empty set***, and is denoted by either $\emptyset$ or $\{\}$. Two sets A and B are said to be ***equal***, written as $A = B$, if they contain the same elements. Furthermore, A is said to be a ***subset*** of B, written as $A \subseteq B$, if and only if every element of A is also an element of B. Thus, the set of all positive prime numbers less than 20 is a subset of the set of all positive prime numbers. Note that the empty set is a subset of every set, that is $\emptyset \subseteq S$, for any set S. Finally, A is a ***proper subset*** of B, written as $A \subset B$, if A is a subset of B, but $A \neq B$. For example, if $A = \{a, b, c\}$ and $B = \{a, b, c, d\}$, then $A \subseteq B$ and $A \subset B$, but $B \nsubseteq A$.

There are many different ways to combine the elements of two sets. We introduce three basic operations used to combine set elements next. If A and B are sets, then the ***union*** of A and B, denoted by $A \cup B$, is the set that contains those elements that are either in A or in B, or in both. The ***intersection*** of A and B, denoted by $A \cap B$, is the set that contains those elements that are both in A and in B. Finally, the ***difference*** of A and B, denoted by $A - B$, is the set that contains those elements that are in A but not in B. Therefore, if $A = \{a, b, c, d, e, f\}$ and $B = \{a, c, e, g, i\}$, then $A \cup B = \{a, b, c, d, e, f, g, i\}$, $A \cap B = \{a, c, e\}$, and $A - B = \{b, d, f\}$.

It is often useful to consider set-like structures in which the ordering of the elements is important. We will refer to a collection of n such elements as an ***ordered n-tuple***. Specifically, an ordered n-tuple

$$(a_1, a_2, \ldots, a_n)$$

is a collection of n elements in which a_1 is the first element, a_2 is the second element, and so on.[†] Ordered 2-tuples are referred to as ***ordered pairs***. Thus, ordered pairs (a_1, a_2) and (b_1, b_2) are equal if and only if $a_1 = b_1$ and $a_2 = b_2$.

[†]Parentheses "( )" are used here, and throughout the text, to emphasize that the elements are ordered.

The ***Cartesian product*** of two sets A and B, denoted $A \times B$, is the set of all ordered pairs (a, b) such that $a \in A$ and $b \in B$. That is,

$$A \times B = \{(a, b) \mid a \in A \text{ and } b \in B\}$$

For example, the cartesian product of $\{1, 3\}$ and $\{1, 2, 3\}$ is $\{(1, 1),\ (1, 2),\ (1, 3),\ (3, 1),\ (3, 2),\ (3, 3)\}$. Note that $|A \times B| = |A| \cdot |B|$.

B.2 COUNTING

The analysis we perform in this text often requires that we count the number of steps executed by a given algorithm, or enumerate all possible inputs to an algorithm. The branch of discrete mathematics known as combinatorics is concerned with such matters. Specifically, combinatorics deals with the study of arrangements of objects. The following basic counting rules underlie all of combinatorics.

> **Definition B.1. Sum rule.** The number of ways to choose a single element from one of two disjoint sets is given by the sum of the cardinalities of the sets.

As a demonstration of the sum rule, assume a cafeteria has two lines, one for hot food and one for cold food. There are 5 entrées in the hot line, and 4 entrées in the cold line. How many different ways are there to choose a single entrée? Since there are 5 ways to choose an entrée from the hot line, and 4 ways to choose an entrée from the cold line, it follows from the sum rule that there are $5 + 4 = 9$ ways of choosing a single entrée.

The sum rule is easily extended to more than two sets. Suppose we must choose an element from one of n disjoint sets $S_1, S_2, \ldots, S_n$. The sum rule can be extended to show that the number of ways of choosing this element is $|S_1| + |S_2| + \cdots + |S_n|$.

> **Definition B.2. Product rule.** The number of ways to choose one element from one set and a second element from another set is given by the product of the cardinalities of the two sets.

As a demonstration of the product rule, assume the aforementioned cafeteria also has a dessert line in which the customer is allowed to construct an ice-cream sundae by choosing one flavor of ice cream and one topping. If there are 5 different flavors of ice cream, and 4 different toppings to choose from, then the customer is able to construct $5 \cdot 4 = 20$ different types of sundaes.

The product rule can also be extended to a more general form in which k elements must be selected, and there are n_i ways to choose the i-th element, for $i = 1, 2, \ldots, k$. In this case, the number of ways to choose the k elements is given by $n_1 \cdot n_2 \cdots n_k$. We can use this version of the product rule to determine how many different subsets an n-set has (this collection of subsets is referred to as the ***power set***). For each element in the n-set, we have two choices—either to include or not include that element. Since there are n elements, this means that there are a total of 2^n subsets (this includes the empty set) in the power set. This is equivalent to the number of bit strings we can construct with n bits. In this case, for each bit we have two choices—either 0 or 1.

Expressions for permutations or combinations of set objects can be derived from the product rule. A **permutation** of an n-set is an *ordered* arrangement of all the elements in the set. The number of permutations of an n-set is given by the product rule as

$$n \cdot (n-1) \cdot (n-2) \cdots 1 = n! \tag{B.1}$$

In other words, there are n ways to choose the first element from the n-set, $(n-1)$ ways to choose the second, and so on, and only one way to choose the last element. For example, there are $3! = 6$ permutations of $S = \{a, b, c\}$, namely: (abc), (acb), (bac), (bca), (cab), and (cba).

A k-**permutation** of an n-set is an ordered arrangement of only k elements from the n-set. The number of k-permutations in an n-set is given by

$$P(n, k) = \frac{n!}{(n-k)!} \tag{B.2}$$

This is explained by noting that there are n ways to choose the first element, $(n-1)$ ways to choose the second, and so on, until k elements have been chosen. Thus, by the product rule we have that

$$P(n, k) = n \cdot (n-1) \cdots (n-k+1)$$

Multiplying the right side of this equation by $(n-k)!/(n-k)!$ yields equation (B.2).

A k-**combination** of an n-set is an *unordered* arrangement of k elements from the n-set (i.e., a k-subset of the n-set). The number of k-combinations in an n-set is given by

$$C(n, k) = \frac{n!}{k!(n-k)!} \tag{B.3}$$

The term $C(n, k)$ is often written as $\binom{n}{k}$, and pronounced "n choose k." Equation (B.3) can be derived by noting that the number of different ways to choose k elements from an n-set when the ordering of the elements does not matter is equal to the number of ways to choose k elements when the order does matter, divided by the number of possible orderings (i.e., permutations) for k elements. That is,

$$\binom{n}{k} = \frac{P(n, k)}{P(k, k)} = \frac{n!/(n-k)!}{k!} = \frac{n!}{k!(n-k)!}$$

For example, there are $\binom{3}{2} = 3$ 2-combinations of $S = \{a, b, c\}$, namely: $\{ab\}$, $\{ac\}$, and $\{bc\}$. Note that since order does not matter in k-combinations, $\{ab\}$ and $\{ba\}$ represent the same 2-combination.

The numbers $\binom{n}{k}$ are called **binomial coefficients** because they appear in the following identity known as the **binomial theorem**:

$$(x + y)^n = \sum_{k=0}^{n} \binom{n}{k} x^k y^{n-k} \qquad n > 0$$

where n and k are positive integers, and x and y are arbitrary reals.

B.3   ELEMENTARY PROBABILITY THEORY

In some analyses in this text we are interested in using probability theory to analyze the average behavior of algorithms. The counting techniques discussed in the previous section are often used when performing this type of analysis.

The mathematical theory of probability allows us to calculate the likelihood of specific events if we assume these events are governed by an appropriate set of axioms. First we define the *probability space*, which is the set U whose elements are called *elementary events*. Next we must specify a *probability distribution Pr()* that assigns a probability to each of these elementary events. An *event* is any subset of U. The probability of a specific event $x \subseteq U$ is denoted by $Pr(x)$. For our purposes, the most important probability distribution is the *discrete uniform distribution*. In this distribution any elementary event $x \in U$ is equally likely (i.e., $Pr(x) = 1/|U|$). Any probability distribution is assumed to satisfy the following axioms:

1. $0 \leq Pr(x) \leq 1$, for any event $x \in U$.
2. $Pr(U) = 1$.
3. If $x_1, x_2 \subseteq U$ are mutually exclusive events (i.e., the intersection x_1 and x_2 is empty), then the probability that either of these events occur, denoted as $Pr(x_1 \cup x_2)$, is given by $Pr(x_1) + Pr(x_2)$.

For any countable sequence $x_1, x_2, \ldots$ of pairwise mutually exclusive events, the third axiom may be rewritten as

$$Pr\left\{ \bigcup_i x_i \right\} = \sum_i Pr(x_i)$$

Thus, if the probability space U is discrete (i.e., the possible outcomes of an experiment are countable), the second axiom may be rewritten as

$$Pr(U) = \sum_i Pr(x_i) = 1$$

where $x_1, x_2, \ldots$ in this case are the elementary events (which by definition are mutually exclusive) that make up U. Finally, if some event is composed of *independent* elementary events (i.e., the probability of one elementary event does not depend upon whether some other has occurred), then the probability of the event is given by the product of the elementary events that it includes. We now illustrate these concepts with an example.

Consider a simple experiment that involves flipping a coin. In this case the two elementary events in the probability space correspond to the outcomes of heads (H) or tails (T). Because the outcome of such an experiment is not certain, it is referred to as a *random variable*. More formally, a random variable is a function defined on the events of a probability space. For instance, if our experiment involved flipping a coin three times, then the events of interest include all possible combinations of heads and tails that can occur on three coin tosses, namely $U = \{$HHH, HHT, HTH, HTT, THH, THT, TTH, TTT$\}$. We can define a random variable X to be the number of heads that occur on any given sequence of three such tosses. If the coin is fair (i.e., the probability distribution is uniform), then

$$Pr(X = 0) \ = \ Pr(\text{TTT}) \ = \ \frac{1}{2} \cdot \frac{1}{2} \cdot \frac{1}{2} \ = \ \frac{1}{8}$$

and

$$Pr(X = 1) \ = \ Pr(\text{HTT}) + Pr(\text{THT}) + Pr(\text{TTH})$$
$$= \ \frac{1}{8} + \frac{1}{8} + \frac{1}{8} \ = \ \frac{3}{8}$$

Likewise we can show that $Pr(X = 2) \ = \ 3/8$, and $Pr(X = 3) \ = \ 1/8$.

In a probabilistic analysis of an algorithm, we will be interested in determining its average (i.e., expected) behavior. The most common measure of the average behavior of random variable X is given by its **expected value**, which is defined as

$$\sum_i i \cdot Pr(X = i)$$

where the sum is taken over all possible values that X can assume. For the coin tossing experiment discussed above, the expected number of heads observed on three tosses is 1.5.

B.4   GRAPHS

In many applications we are interested in specifying a relationship among a finite set of elements. Because of their simplicity, graphs are often used to represent such relationships. An **undirected graph** $G = (V, E)$ consists of two finite sets: the **vertex set** $V \ = \ \{v_1, v_2, \ldots\}$, which contains the set of **vertices** in G; and the **edge set** $E = \{e_1, e_2, \ldots\}$, which is a set of unordered pairs of distinct vertices in G. Each element of the edge set $e = (u, v)$ is referred to as an **edge**, and is said to join the vertices u and v. If $e = (u, v)$ is an edge in G, then the vertices u and v are **adjacent**. In addition, e is said to be **incident on** vertices u and v. Since we are dealing with unordered pairs, (u, v) and (v, u) represent the same edge. Furthermore, since the unordered pair must be distinct, **self-loops**—an edge from a vertex to itself—are not possible. The **degree** of a vertex in a undirected graph is given by the number of edges incident on that vertex.

Typically, an undirected graph is represented by means of a diagram, with vertices depicted by circles and edges by line segments. Figure B.1 (a) is a diagram of the undirected graph $G = (V, E)$, with vertex set $V = \{v_1, v_2, v_3, v_4\}$, and edge set $E = \{e_1 = (v_1, v_4), e_2 = (v_1, v_2), e_3 = (v_1, v_3), e_4 = (v_3, v_4)\}$. In this figure, the degree of vertex v_1 is 3, the degree of vertex v_2 is 1, and degree of vertices v_3 and v_4 is 2.

A **directed graph** $G \ = \ (V, E)$ also consists of a vertex set and an edge set. However, in directed graphs, the edge set consists of *ordered* pairs of vertices from V. In other words, the "direction" of the edge is important in directed graphs. Thus, the edge $e = (u, v)$ that joins vertices u and v in the directed graph G is said to be **incident from** vertex u, and **incident to** vertex v. Furthermore, v is said to be **adjacent**

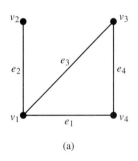

(a)

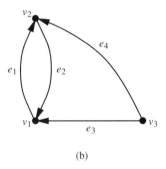

(b)

FIGURE B.1
(a) A undirected graph containing 4 vertices and 4 edges. (b) A directed graph containing 3 vertices and 4 edges.

to u, and u is said to be *adjacent from v*. The *out-degree* of a vertex in a digraph is given by the number of edges that are incident from it; while the *in-degree* is given by the number of edges incident to the vertex. The degree of a vertex in a directed graph is defined as the sum of in-degree and out-degree of the vertex. Like graphs, directed graphs can also be represented by means of a diagram. In this case the edges are drawn with arrows to show the direction of the edge. Figure B.1 (b) is a diagram of the directed graph $G = (V, E)$ with vertex set $V = \{v_1, v_2, v_3\}$ and edge set $E = \{e_1 = (v_1, v_2), e_2 = (v_2, v_1), e_3 = (v_3, v_1), e_4 = (v_3, v_2)\}$. The in-degree of v_1 is 2, of v_2 is 2, and of v_3 is 0; while the out-degree of v_1 is 1, of v_2 is 1, and of v_3 is 2. Thus the degree of v_1 and v_2 is 3, and of v_3 is 2.

When using either directed or undirected graphs to model certain relationships, it is often useful to associate a weight with each edge of a graph. We will use $w(u, v)$ to denote the weight assigned to edge (u, v). A weight assignment to a graph $G = (V, E)$ is given by the mapping $w : \{(u, v) \in E\} \to \mathbb{R}$. We will refer to graphs that have such an assignment as *weighted graphs*.

We now introduce a number of terms that are associated with directed and undirected graphs. Unless specified otherwise, we will use "graph" to refer to both directed and undirected graphs. First, a *walk* in a graph is defined as an alternating sequence of vertices and edges, beginning and ending with vertices, such that each edge is incident with the vertices preceding and following it. For example, in Figure B.1 (a), $v_1, e_3, v_3, e_4, v_4, e_1, v_1, e_2, v_2$ is a valid walk, and in Figure B.1 (b), $v_3, e_3, v_1, e_1, v_2, e_2, v_1$ is a valid walk. A walk that begins and ends at the same vertex is called a *closed walk*. In Figure B.1 (a), $v_1, e_3, v_3, e_4, v_4, e_1, v_1$ is a closed walk. A walk that is not closed is called an *open walk*. A *trail* is a walk in which no edge is repeated, while a *path* is a walk in which no vertex is repeated. If there is a path from vertex u to vertex v, then we say that v is *reachable* from u. This is written as $u \rightsquigarrow v$, or as $u \overset{p}{\rightsquigarrow} v$ if we wish to indicate a specific path p by which v is reachable from u. For example, in Figure B.1 (a) $v_2 \overset{p}{\rightsquigarrow} v_3$ through the path $p = v_2, e_2, v_1, e_3, v_3$. Note that in Figure B.1 (b), $v_1 \not\rightsquigarrow v_3$ and $v_2 \not\rightsquigarrow v_3$; that is, v_3 is not reachable from either v_1 or v_2.

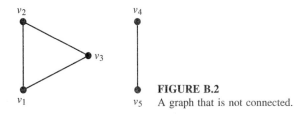

FIGURE B.2
A graph that is not connected.

A closed trail in a graph is referred to as a *circuit*, and a circuit whose vertices are distinct is called a *cycle* (we exclude the last vertex that we must return to in order to form a circuit in this definition of a cycle). A graph or directed graph that does not contain any cycles is said to be *acyclic*. The walk $v_1, e_3, v_3, e_4, v_4, e_1, v_1$ in the graph of Figure B.1 (a) is a circuit. It is also a cycle since no vertex, except the first and last, is repeated in the walk. A graph is said to be **connected** if at least one path exists between every pair of vertices in the graph. The graph in Figure B.1 (a) is connected, while the graph shown in Figure B.2 is not connected. For example, a path does not exist between v_1 and v_4 in the graph of Figure B.2. A directed graph is said to be *strongly connected* if every two vertices in the directed graph are reachable from each other. The digraph in Figure B.1 (b) is not strongly connected since v_3 is not reachable from either v_1 or v_2.

Given the definitions above, we may define a *forest* as an acyclic graph, and a *tree* as a connected acyclic graph. Figure B.3 shows all the possible trees containing four or fewer vertices. Notice that a single vertex is considered a tree, and that trees with more than 3 vertices are not unique. From a computer science perspective, trees are probably the most important type of graph. Trees can be used to impose a hierarchical structure on a problem or a collection of data. For example, the genealogy of a family is typically represented using a tree. The sorting of mail according to ZIP code can also be described using a tree structure as follows. The mail arriving at a post office is first sorted into ten piles according to the most significant digit in the ZIP code. Each of these ten piles is then sorted into ten additional piles according to the next most significant digit, and so on, until the mail is completely sorted. For the case of a 5-digit ZIP code, this would result in at most 10^5 separate piles of mail.

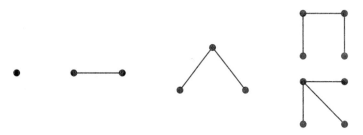

FIGURE B.3
All possible trees with one, two, three, and four vertices.

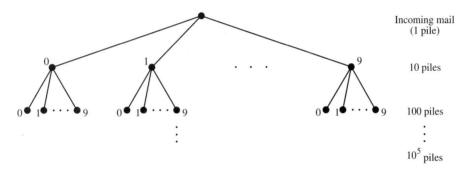

FIGURE B.4
A tree for the mail sorting problem. The mail on the i-th level of this tree is sorted according to the $(i + 1)$-th most significant digit in the ZIP code.

The tree for this problem is shown in Figure B.4. Trees are used extensively in this text as a means of organizing data for efficient search and retrieval of information.

B.4.1 Tree Vocabulary

A tree in which one vertex is distinguished from all the other vertices is called a *rooted tree*. Throughout this book we will assume that a tree is a rooted tree unless it is explicitly stated otherwise. The unique vertex in a rooted tree is referred to as the *root* of the tree. All vertices connected via edges to the root are called *children* of the root, and the root vertex is considered the *parent* of these children. This same relationship holds for the other vertices in a tree. We will refer to all of the children of a given vertex as *siblings*. Typically the root vertex is drawn at the top of the tree. Thus, in Figure B.5, if we choose v_1 to be the root, then v_2, v_3, and v_4 are the children of the root, while v_5 and v_6 are the children of v_2, and v_7 is the child of v_3. In this case, the root vertex is considered unique because it is the one vertex in the tree that does not have a parent. A *leaf* or *external vertex* is any vertex that has no children. A nonleaf vertex is referred to as an *internal vertex*. The leaves in the

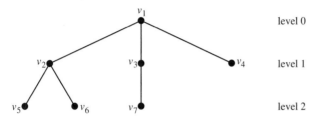

FIGURE B.5
A 7-vertex tree with height 2.

tree of Figure B.5 are v_4, v_5, v_6, and v_7—all other vertices are internal. A vertex v_b is said to be a ***descendent*** of a vertex v_a if it is a child of v_a, a child of one of the children of v_a, and so on. If v_b is a descendent of v_a, then v_a is an ***ancestor*** of v_b. All descendents of a vertex form a ***subtree*** that is said to be rooted at that vertex. For example, in Figure B.5 the subtree rooted at v_2 is comprised of the vertices v_2, v_5, and v_6. The ***height*** of a vertex is defined to be the length of the longest path from that vertex to a leaf that is a descendent of the vertex (where the length of a path equals the number of edges in the path). The height of a tree is given by the height of its root vertex. Thus, the tree in Figure B.5 has height 2. Quite often it is convenient to refer to the ***depth*** of a vertex in a tree. This is simply the length of the path from the root to the vertex of interest. All vertices at a depth i in a tree are said to be on the i-th ***level*** of the tree. Notice that sibling vertices all have the same depth, but not necessarily the same height. Quite often we will assign a data value, or ***label***, to the vertices in a tree. Such a tree is referred to as a ***labeled tree***.

TRAVERSAL ORDERS. An operation that is commonly performed on trees involves traversing all of the vertices in a tree, while executing a specific operation at each vertex. This requires that we impose some ordering on the vertices in the tree, and leads to the definition of ordered trees. In an ***ordered tree***, the children of a vertex have a specific linear ordering. Thus, we may refer unambiguously to the children of a vertex in an ordered tree as the first child, second child, and so on. A tree in which such ordering is not considered is called an ***unordered tree***. When considering ordered trees, we will follow the convention that the children of a vertex are ordered from left to right. This ordering can be extended to the subtrees appearing in a given tree. Specifically, if we say that subtree T_a is to the left of subtree T_b, then every vertex in T_a is to the left of every vertex in T_b. For example, in Figure B.5, the subtree rooted at v_2 is to the left of the subtrees rooted at v_3 and v_4.

We may now define the following traversal orders. In each, we abstractly define the operation that is performed on each vertex during the traversal as a ***visit***. It is assumed that the tree consists of at least a root vertex, and possibly additional vertices that are descendents of the root. These descendents comprise the subtrees of the root. If we assume there are k subtrees, with the leftmost subtree designated by T_1 and the rightmost subtree designated by T_k as shown in Figure B.6, then:

1. A ***preorder traversal*** of a tree involves first visiting the root vertex of the tree, followed by a preorder traversal of the subtrees of the root in the order $T_1, T_2, \ldots, T_k$.

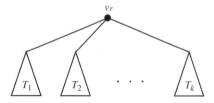

FIGURE B.6
A tree represented as root vertex v_r, with k subtrees labeled $T_1, T_2, \ldots, T_k$.

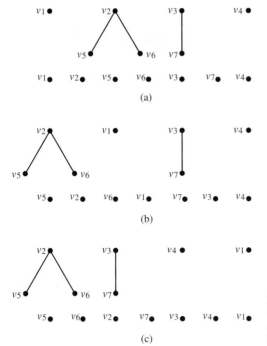

FIGURE B.7

Steps taken during the **(a)** preorder, **(b)** inorder, and **(c)** postorder traversals of the tree in Figure B.5.

2. An *inorder traversal* of a tree involves first visiting the vertices of T_1 using an inorder traversal, followed by a visit to the root, and then inorder traversals of the remaining subtrees in the order $T_2, T_3, \ldots, T_k$.

3. A *postorder traversal* of a tree involves the postorder traversal of the subtrees of the root vertex in the order $T_1, T_2, \ldots T_k$, followed by a visit to the root.

Figure B.7 shows the steps taken when each of these traversal orders is applied to the tree in Figure B.5. In this figure, vertices (subtrees) are drawn in the order they are visited, with the vertices (subtrees) on the left side of the figure being visited before vertices (subtrees) on the right side of the figure. The top portion of Figure B.7 (a) shows the first step in a preorder traversal. In this step, the root vertex v_1 is visited first, then each of the subtrees of the root are visited from left to right. Thus, vertex v_1 is drawn first, the subtree rooted at v_2 (the leftmost subtree of the root) is drawn next, followed by the subtrees rooted at v_3 and v_4, respectively. In the next step of Figure B.7 (a), the subtrees drawn in the previous step are visited using a preorder traversal. For instance, the subtree rooted at v_2 is visited in the order v_2, v_5, v_6. Since the height of the tree in Figure B.5 is only 2, this is the last step in the preorder traversal process.

Notice that each of the traversal orders given above is defined in terms of itself. This suggests that recursive algorithms can be constructed to perform these traversals. For example, an algorithm that visits the vertices of a tree using an inorder traversal

activation record	*line*	
		Inorder(v_1)
1	4	Inorder(v_2)
2	4	Inorder(v_5)
3	2	visit v_5
2	5	visit v_2
2	7	Inorder(v_6)
4	2	visit v_6
1	5	visit v_1
1	7	Inorder(v_3)
5	4	Inorder(v_7)
6	2	visit v_7
5	5	visit v_3
1	7	Inorder(v_4)
7	2	visit v_4

FIGURE B.8

The recursive procedure calls that result when Inorder() is executed on the root vertex of the tree in Figure B.5.

is shown below:

```
Inorder(vertex v)
1    if  v is a leaf then
2         visit  v
3    else
4         Inorder(root of v's subtree T₁)
5         visit v
6         for i ← 2 to k do
7              Inorder(root of v's subtree Tᵢ)
```

Applying this algorithm to the tree in Figure B.5 yields the sequence of steps shown in Figure B.8, and results in the vertices being visited in the order v_5, v_2, v_6, v_1, v_7, v_3, v_4. This agrees with the order given in Figure B.7 (b).

B.4.2 Binary Trees

Binary trees are a special type of tree frequently used in computer applications. A *binary tree* is an ordered tree in which each vertex in the tree has either no children, one child, or two children. If a vertex has two children, the first child is referred to as the *left child*, and the second child is referred to as the *right child*. If a vertex has only a single child, then that child may be positioned as either a left child or a right child. If we allow the empty binary tree (i.e., a tree with no vertices), then a binary tree is often defined recursively as a tree that is either empty, or is a vertex with left and right subtrees that are also binary trees.

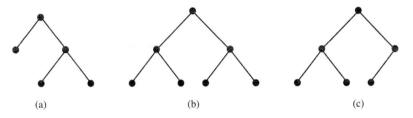

FIGURE B.9
(a) A 5-vertex full binary tree. (b) A 7-vertex perfect binary tree. (c) A 6-vertex complete binary tree formed by removing the rightmost leaf from the tree in part (b).

A binary tree is said to be *full* if every vertex in the tree either has two children or it is a leaf. That is, there are no vertices with only one child. The number of leaves in a full binary tree is always one more than the number of internal vertices in the tree. A *perfect* binary tree is a full binary tree in which all leaves have the same depth. It is easy to show that the number of vertices in a perfect binary tree is always one less than a power of two. We also define a *complete* binary tree as follows. A complete n vertex binary tree is formed from a perfect $n + q$ vertex binary tree by removing the q rightmost leaves from the perfect binary tree. Thus, if n is one less than some power of 2, then q must equal 0, and the complete binary tree is also a perfect binary tree. An example of each of these types of binary trees is given in Figure B.9.

These concepts can be extended to k-ary trees, where k represents the maximum number of children at each vertex (i.e., a binary tree can also be called a 2-ary tree). How many vertices does a perfect k-ary tree of height h have? The root of such a tree has k children at depth 1, each of which has k children at depth 2, for a total of k^2 vertices at depth 2. Continuing in this fashion, the number of leaves at depth h must equal k^h. Letting n represent the number of vertices in the perfect k-ary tree, we have

$$n = 1 + k + k^2 + \cdots + k^h = \sum_{i=0}^{h} k^i$$

Using equation (A.19), this can be rewritten as $n = \frac{k^{h+1}-1}{k-1}$. We can use this result to show that a perfect binary tree of height h has $2^{h+1} - 1$ vertices. Furthermore, since a perfect binary tree is also a full binary tree, 2^h of these vertices are leaves, and the other $2^h - 1$ vertices are internal vertices.

EXERCISES

B.1. Given the sets $A = \{0, 3, 6, 9, 12\}$ and $B = \{x \mid x$ is a real number less than 10$\}$, list the members of the following sets:
    (*a*) $A \cup B$
    (*b*) $A \cap B$
    (*c*) $B - A$
    (*d*) $A - B$

B.2. How many bit strings are there
   (*a*) of length eight?
   (*b*) of length eight that begin with a 1?
   (*c*) of length eight or less?

B.3. A *palindrome* is a string that reads the same backwards or forwards. How many different palindromes can be constructed from length-n bit strings?

B.4. How many different identifiers for variable names are possible in a programming language that restricts identifiers to 16 alphabetic characters?

B.5. Make a table in which the rows are the integer numbers $n = 0, 1, \ldots, 10$, and the columns are the binomial coefficients $\binom{n}{0}$, $\binom{n}{1}$, ..., $\binom{n}{10}$. Fill in each entry in this table with the appropriate value. For example, the entry in row 6, column 3 would be $\binom{5}{2} = 10$. (Note that $\binom{n}{k} = 0$ for $k > n$.) This table is known as *Pascal's triangle*.

B.6. Write a recursive pseudocode algorithm that generates the permutations of the n-set $\{1, 2, \ldots, n\}$.

B.7. Prove the following identities:
   (*a*) $\binom{n}{k} = \binom{n}{n-k}$.
   (*b*) $k\binom{n}{k} = n\binom{n-1}{k-1}$.

B.8. The *Catalan numbers* are given by the recurrence relation

$$C(n) = \sum_{i=0}^{n-1} C(i)C(n - 1 - i)$$

with $C(0) = 1$.
   (*a*) Show that $C(n) = \binom{2n}{n}/(n + 1)$. (Hint: for any real number n and integer k, we can write $\binom{n}{k} = n(n - 1) \cdots (n - k + 1)/k!$ if $k \geq 0$, and 0 otherwise.)
   (*b*) Show that $C(n) = \frac{4^n}{\sqrt{\pi n^{3/2}}}(1 + O(1/n)) = \Omega(4^n/n^{3/2})$.

B.9. Find a closed form for

$$\sum_{i=1}^{k} i\binom{k}{i}(n - 1)^i$$

by replacing the first term in the summation (i.e., i) with an equivalent term $[\frac{\partial e^{ix}}{\partial x}]_{x=0}$, and then manipulating the resulting summation so that the binomial theorem can be used.

B.10. Given a biased coin in which $Pr(H) = 1/4$ and $Pr(T) = 3/4$, what is the expected number heads in an experiment involving three coin tosses?

B.11. Given two fair dice, define the random variable X to be the sum of the numbers showing on the top face of the die after they have been rolled. Calculate the probability that $X = 1, 2, \ldots, 12$, and then calculate the expected value of this random variable.

B.12. In a typical lottery, a person wins a large amount of money if he or she can correctly pick the six integer numbers, between 1 and 49, that will be drawn (according to a uniform distribution) at some later date. If we assume that each number must be unique, what is the probability of correctly picking the winning numbers?

B.13. Write pseudocode algorithms for the preorder and postorder tree traversal algorithms.

B.14. Given the following tree, write the order in which vertices would be visited during preorder, inorder, and postorder traversals:

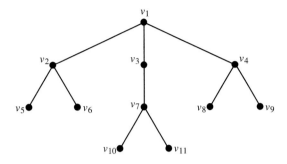

B.15. What is the height of a perfect k-ary tree containing n vertices?

B.16. The file-system organization of many operating systems (e.g., MS-DOS and UNIX) is based on a tree structure, where each vertex is a directory that may contain an arbitrary number of files, and the children of any directory are referred to as subdirectories. For example, in the UNIX operating system, the root directory is denoted by /, and typical subdirectories of the root include /user, /lib, and /bin. Given a tree that represents a file system, and assuming that any directory may contain an arbitrary number of subdirectories, write a pseudocode algorithm that prints a listing of all files in the file system, along with the directory to which each belongs. The files that appear at depth d in a directory tree should appear indented d spaces in the listing.

B.17. Write a pseudocode algorithm to compute the height of a binary tree. What is the running time of your algorithm?

B.18. Write a linear-time pseudocode algorithm that visits the vertices of a binary tree in *level-order*. That is, the root is visited first, followed by the vertices at depth 1, followed by the vertices at depth 2, and so on.

B.19. Two binary trees are said to be *similar* if both are either empty or nonempty, and have similar left and right subtrees. Write and analyze the running time of an algorithm that can determine if two binary trees are similar.

B.20. The *internal path length* of a rooted tree is the sum of the depths of all internal vertices in the tree, while the *external path length* is the sum of the depths of all external vertices. Let $I(n_i)$ and $E(n_i)$ denote the internal and external path length, respectively, of a binary tree containing n_i internal vertices. Using induction, show that for a full binary tree $E(n_i) = I(n_i) + 2n_i$; then argue that $E(n_i) \leq I(n_i) + 2n_i$ for any binary tree.

APPENDIX NOTES

Most books dealing with discrete mathematics treat this appendix material in more detail. Some references include Rosen [131], and Finkbeiner and Lindstrom [54]. An excellent introduction to combinatorics and graph theory is given in Roberts [129]. Other references for elementary combinatorics and graph theory include Knuth [84] and Liu [95]. Books that deal specifically with graph theory include Deo [40] (the mail sorting example is from this book), and Chartrand and Lesniak [29]. The values produced by the recurrence relation in exercise B.8 are named after Eugène Catalan, who wrote about them in 1838 [28].

BIBLIOGRAPHY

[1] N. Abramson. *Information Theory and Coding*. McGraw-Hill, New York, 1983.

[2] W. Ackermann. Zum Hilbertschen aufbau der reellen zahlen. *Mathematische Annalen*, 99:118–133, 1928.

[3] G. M. Adel'son-Vel'skiı and E. M. Landis. An algorithm for the organization of information. *Soviet Mathematics Doklady*, 3(4):1259–1263, 1962.

[4] A. V. Aho, J. E. Hopcroft, and J. D. Ullman. *The Design and Analysis of Computer Algorithms*. Addison-Wesley, Reading, MA, 1974.

[5] A. V. Aho, R. Sethi, and J. D. Ullman. *Compilers, Principles, Techniques, and Tools*. Addison-Wesley, Reading, MA, 1986.

[6] B. Allen and I. Munro. Self-organizing search trees. *Journal of the ACM*, 25(4):526–535, 1978.

[7] *American National Standard for Information Systems—Programming Language C, X3.159-1989*. American National Standards Institute, New York. 1989.

[8] K. Appel and W. Haken. Every planar map is four colorable. Part I: Discharging. *Illinois Journal of Mathematics*, 21(3):429–490, 1977.

[9] K. Appel and W. Haken. The solution of the four-color map problem. *Scientific American*, 237(4):108–121, 1977.

[10] K. Appel, W. Haken, and J. Koch. Every planar map is four colorable. Part II: Reducibility. *Illinois Journal of Mathematics*, 21(3):491–567, 1977.

[11] S. Baase. *Computer Algorithms: Introduction to Design and Analysis*. Addison-Wesley, Reading, MA, 2nd edition, 1988.

[12] D. W. Barron. *Recursive Techniques in Programming*. McDonald, London, 1968.

[13] R. Bayer. Symmetric binary B-trees: Data structure and maintenance algorithms. *Acta Informatica*, 1(4):290–306, 1972.

[14] R. Bayer and E. M. McCreight. Organization and maintenance of large ordered indexes. *Acta Informatica*, 1(3):173–189, 1972.

[15] R. Bellman. On a routing problem. *Quarterly of Applied Mathematics*, 16(1):87–90, 1958.

[16] J. L. Bentley. Multidimensional binary search trees used for associative searching. *Communications of the ACM*, 18(9):509–517, 1975.

[17] J. L. Bentley and J. H. Friedman. Data structures for range searching. *ACM Computing Surveys*, 11(4):397–409, 1979.

[18] J. L. Bentley and C. C. McGeoch. Amortized analysis of self-organizing sequential search heuristics. *Communications of the ACM*, 28(4):404–411, 1985.

[19] G. M. Birtwistle, O.-J. Dahl, B. Myhrhaug, and K. Nygaard. *SIMULA Begin*. Auerbach Press, Philadelphia, 1973.

[20] J. R. Bitner. Heuristics that dynamically organize data structures. *SIAM Journal on Computing*, 8(1):82–110, 1979.

[21] G. Booch. *Object-Oriented Design: With Applications*. Benjamin/Cummings, Redwood City, CA, 1991.

[22] O. Borůvka. O jistém problému minimálním. *Práce Moravské Přírodovědecké Společnosti v Brně (Papers of the Moravian Science Society in Brno)*, 3:37–58, 1926.

[23] G. Brassard and P. Bratley. *Algorithmics: Theory and Practice*. Prentice Hall, Englewood Cliffs, NJ, 1988.

[24] P. Bratley, B. L. Fox, and L. E. Schrage. *A Guide to Simulation*. Springer-Verlag, New York, 2nd edition, 1987.

[25] T. Budd. *An Introduction to Object-Oriented Programming*. Addison-Wesley, Reading, MA, 1991.

[26] W. H. Burge. *Recursive Programming Techniques*. Addison-Wesley, Reading, MA, 1975.

[27] J. L. Carter and M. N. Wegman. Universal classes of hash functions. *Journal of Computer and System Sciences*, 18(2):143–154, 1979.

[28] E. Catalan. Note sur une équation aux différences finies. *Journal de Mathématiques pures et appliquées*, 3:508–516, 1838.

[29] G. Chartrand and L. Lesniak. *Graphs & Digraphs*. Wadsworth & Brooks/Cole, Pacific Grove, CA, 2nd edition, 1986.

[30] W. Cheney and D. Kincaid. *Numerical Methods and Computing*. Brooks/Cole, Monterey, CA, 1985.

[31] D. Cheriton and R. E. Tarjan. Finding minimum spanning trees. *SIAM Journal on Computing*, 5(4):724–742, 1976.

[32] J. Cohen and M. Roth. On the implementation of Strassen's fast multiplication algorithm. *Acta Informatica*, 6(4):341–355, 1976.

[33] R. Cole and A. Siegel. River routing every which way, but loose. In *Proceedings of the 25th Annual IEEE Symposium on Foundations of Computer Science*, pages 65–73, 1984.

[34] J. W. Cooley and J. W. Tukey. An algorithm for the machine computation of complex Fourier series. *Mathematics of Computation*, 19(90):297–301, 1965.

[35] J. O. Coplien. *Advanced C++ Programming Styles and Idioms*. Addison-Wesley, Reading, MA, 1992.

[36] T. H. Cormen, C. E. Leiserson, and R. L. Rivest. *Introduction to Algorithms*. McGraw-Hill, New York, 1990.

[37] B. J. Cox. *Object-Oriented Programming: An Evolutionary Approach*. Addison-Wesley, Reading, MA, 1986.

[38] C. A. Crane. Linear lists and priority queues as balanced binary trees. Technical Report STAN-CS-72-259, Stanford University, Stanford, CA, 1972.

[39] J. Culberson. The effect of updates in binary search trees. In *Proceedings of the 17th Annual ACM Symposium on the Theory of Computing*, pages 205–212, 1985.

[40] N. Deo. *Graph Theory with Applications to Engineering and Computer Science*. Prentice Hall, Englewood Cliffs, NJ, 1974.

[41] L. Devroye. *Non-Uniform Random Variate Generation*. Springer-Verlag, New York, 1986.

[42] G. Diehr and B. Faaland. Optimal pagination of B-trees. *Communications of the ACM*, 27(3):241–247, 1984.

[43] W. Diffie and M. E. Hellman. New directions in cryptography. *IEEE Transactions on Information Theory*, IT-22(6):644–654, 1976.

[44] E. W. Dijkstra. A note on two problems in connexion with graphs. *Numerische Mathematik*, 1:269–271, 1959.

[45] E. W. Dijkstra. *Structured Programming*. Academic Press, New York, 1972.

[46] J. R. Driscoll, H. N. Gabow, R. Shrairman, and R. E. Tarjan. Relaxed heaps: An alternative to fibonacci heaps with applications to parallel computation. *Communications of the ACM*, 31(11):1343–1354, 1988.

[47] J. R. Driscoll, N. Sarnak, D. D. Sleator, and R. E. Tarjan. Making data structures persistent. In *Proceedings of the 18th Annual ACM Symposium on the Theory of Computing*, pages 109–121, 1986.

[48] H. Edelsbrunner. *Algorithms in Combinatorial Geometry*. Springer-Verlag, New York, 1987.

[49] Édouard Lucas. *Récréations Mathématiques*, volume 3. Reprinted by Albert Blanchard, Paris, 1960.

[50] J. L. Eppinger. An empirical study of insertion and deletion in binary search trees. *Communications of the ACM*, 26(9):663–669, 1983.

[51] L. Euler. Solutio problematis ad geometriam situs pertinantis. *Academimae Petropolitanae* (St. Petersburg Academy), 8:128–140, 1736. English Translation in *Scientific American*, pages 66–70, July, 1953.

[52] S. Even. *Graph Algorithms*. Computer Science Press, Potomac, MD, 1979.

[53] R. E. Fairley. *Software Engineering Concepts*. McGraw-Hill, New York, 1985.

[54] D. T. Finkbeiner II and W. D. Lendstrom. *A Primer of Discrete Mathematics*. W. H. Freeman, New York, 1987.

[55] R. A. Finkel and J. L. Bentley. Quad trees: A data structure for retrieval on composite keys. *Acta Informatica*, 4(1):1–9, 1974.

[56] R. W. Floyd. Algorithm 245: Treesort 3. *Communications of the ACM*, 7(12):701, 1964.

[57] L. R. Ford, Jr. and D. R. Fulkerson. *Flows in Networks*. Princeton University Press, Princeton, NJ, 1962.

[58] M. L. Fredman and J. Komlós. On the size of separating systems and families of perfect hash functions. *SIAM Journal on Algebraic and Discrete Methods*, 5(1):61–68, 1984.

[59] M. L. Fredman and R. E. Tarjan. Fibonacci heaps and their use in improved network optimization algorithms. *Journal of the ACM*, 34(3):596–615, 1987.

[60] Z. Galil and G. F. Italiano. Data structures and algorithms for disjoint set union problems. *ACM Computing Surveys*, 23(3):319–344, 1991.

[61] B. A. Galler and M. J. Fischer. An improved equivalence algorithm. *Communications of the ACM*, 7(5):301–303, 1964.

[62] M. Gardner. About phi, an irrational number that has some remarkable geometrical expressions. *Scientific American*, 201(2):128–134, 1959.

[63] M. R. Garey and D. S. Johnson. *Computers and Intractability: A Guide to the Theory of NP-Completeness*. W. H. Freeman, New York, 1979.

[64] J. A. Goguen, J. W. Thatcher, and E. G. Wagner. An initial algebra approach to the specification, correctness and implementation of abstract data types. In R. T. Yeh, editor, *Current Trends in Programming Methodology*, volume 4, Data Structuring. Prentice-Hall, Englewood Cliffs, NJ, 1977.

[65] G. H. Gonnet. *Handbook of Algorithms and Data Structures*. Addison-Wesley, Reading, MA, 1984.

[66] G. H. Gonnet, L. D. Rogers, and J. A. George. An algorithmic and complexity analysis of interpolation search. *Acta Informatica*, 13(1):39–52, 1980.

[67] R. L. Graham. An efficient algorithm for determining the convex hull of a finite planar set. *Information Processing Letters*, 1(4):132–133, 1972.

[68] R. L. Graham and P. Hell. On the history of the minimum spanning tree problem. *Annals of the History of Computing*, 7(1):43–57, 1985.

[69] R. L. Graham, D. E. Knuth, and O. Patashnik. *Concrete Mathematics: A Foundation for Computer Science*. Addison-Wesley, Reading, MA, 1989.

[70] D. H. Greene and D. E. Knuth. *Mathematics for the Analysis of Algorithms*. Birkhauser, Boston, 1982.

[71] L. J. Guibas and R. Sedgewick. A diochromatic framework for balanced trees. In *Proceedings of the 19th Annual IEEE Symposium on Foundations of Computer Science*, pages 8–21, 1978.

[72] J. Guttag. Abstract data types and the development of data structures. *Communications of the ACM*, 20(6):396–404, 1977.

[73] D. Harel. *Algorithmics: The Spirit of Computing*. Addison-Wesley, Reading, MA, 1987.

[74] C. Hoare. Quicksort. *Computer Journal*, 5(1):10–15, 1962.

[75] J. E. Hopcroft and J. D. Ullman. Set-merging algorithms. *SIAM Journal on Computing*, 2(4):294–303, 1973.

[76] E. Horowitz and S. Sahni. *Fundamentals of Computer Algorithms*. Computer Science Press, Rockville, MD, 1978.

[77] D. A. Huffman. A method for the construction of minimum-redundancy codes. *Proceedings of the Institute of Radio Engineers*, 40:1098–1101, 1952.

[78] V. Jarník. O jistém problému minimálním. *Práce Moravské Přírodovědecké Společnosti v Brně (Papers of the Moravian Science Society in Brno)*, 6:57–63, 1930.

[79] R. A. Jarvis. On the identification of the convex hull of a finite set of points in the plane. *Information Processing Letters*, 2(1):18–21, 1973.

[80] A. T. Jonassen and D. E. Knuth. A trivial algorithm whose analysis isn't. *Journal of Computer and System Sciences*, 16(3):301–322, 1978.

[81] D. W. Jones. An empirical comparison of priority-queue and event-set implementations. *Communications of the ACM*, 29(4):300–311, 1986.

[82] A. Kelley and I. Pohl. *A Book on C: Programming in C*. Benjamin/Cummings, Redwood City, CA, 2nd edition, 1991.

[83] B. W. Kernighan and D. M. Ritchie. *The C Programming Language*. Prentice Hall, Englewood Cliffs, NJ, 2nd edition, 1988.

[84] D. E. Knuth. *The Art of Computer Programming*, volume 1, *Fundamental Algorithms*. Addison-Wesley, Reading, MA, 1973.

[85] D. E. Knuth. *The Art of Computer Programming*, volume 3, *Searching and Sorting*. Addison-Wesley, Reading, MA, 1973.

[86] D. E. Knuth. Big omicron and big omega and big theta. *SIGACT News*, 8(2):18–24, 1976.

[87] D. E. Knuth. *The Art of Computer Programming*, volume 2, *Seminumerical Algorithms*. Addison-Wesley, Reading, MA, 2nd edition, 1981.

[88] J. B. Kruskal. On the shortest spanning subtree of a graph and the traveling salesman problem. *Proceedings of the American Mathematical Society*, 7(1):48–50, 1956.

[89] P.-A. Larson. Linear hashing with separators—A dynamic hashing scheme achieving one-access retrieval. *ACM Transactions on Database Systems*, 13(3):366–388, 1988.

[90] E. L. Lawler. *Combinatorial Optimization: Networks and Matroids*. Holt, Rinehart and Winston, New York, 1976.

[91] D. A. Lelewer and D. S. Hirschberg. Data compression. *ACM Computing Surveys*, 19(3):261–296, 1987.

[92] G. S. Leuker. Some techniques for solving recurrences. *Computing Surveys*, 12(4):419–436, 1980.

[93] S. B. Lippman. *C++ Primer*. Addison-Wesley, Reading, MA, 2nd edition, 1991.

[94] W. Litwin. Linear hashing: A new tool for file and table addressing. In *Proceedings of the Sixth VLDB Conference*, pages 212–223, Montreal, 1980.

[95] C. L. Liu. *Introduction to Combinatorial Mathematics*. McGraw-Hill, New York, 1968.

[96] V. Y. Lum, P. S. Yuen, and M. Dodd. Key-to-address transform techniques: A fundamental performance study on large existing formatted files. *Communications of the ACM*, 14(4):228–239, 1971.

[97] H. Mannila and E. Ukkonen. The set union problem with backtracking. In *Proceedings of the 13th International Colloquium on Automata, Languages and Programming*, volume 226, *Lecture Notes in Computer Science*, Springer-Verlag, Berlin, pages 236–243, 1986.

[98] J. J. Martin. *Data Types and Data Structures*. Prentice Hall, Englewood Cliffs, NJ, 1986.

[99] J. H. Mathews. *Numerical Methods for Computer Science, Engineering, and Mathematics*. Prentice Hall, Englewood Cliffs, NJ, 1987.

[100] J. Matoušek. Geometric range searching. *ACM Computing Surveys*, 26(4):421–461, 1994.

[101] B. Meyer. *Object-Oriented Software Construction*. Prentice Hall, Englewood Cliffs, NJ, 1988.

[102] S. Meyers. *Effective C++: 50 Specific Ways to Improve Your Programs and Designs*. Addison-Wesley, Reading, MA, 1992.

[103] E. F. Moore. The shortest path through a maze. In *Proceedings of the International Symposium on the Theory of Switching*, pages 285–292, Harvard University Press, 1959.

[104] B. M. E. Moret, P. Helman, and H. D. Shapiro. An exact characterization of greedy structures. *SIAM Journal of Discrete Mathematics*, 6(2):274–283, 1993.

[105] B. M. E. Moret and H. D. Shapiro. *Algorithms from P to NP*, volume 1, *Design and Efficiency–P*. Benjamin/Cummings, Redwood City, CA, 1991.

[106] R. Morris. Scatter storage techniques. *Communications of the ACM*, 11(1):38–44, 1968.

[107] D. R. Morrison. PATRICIA—Practical algorithm to retrieve information coded in alphanumeric. *Journal of the ACM*, 15(4):514–534, 1968.

[108] R. Motwani and P. Raghavan. *Randomized Algorithms*. Cambridge University Press, Cambridge, 1995.

[109] J. I. Munro, T. H. Papadakis, and R. Sedgewick. Deterministic skip lists. In *Proceedings of the Third Annual ACM-SIAM Symposium on Discrete Algorithms*, pages 367–375, 1992.

[110] J. Nievergelt, H. Hinterberger, and K. C. Sevcik. The grid file: An adaptable symmetric multikey file structure. *ACM Transactions on Database Systems*, 9(1):38–71, 1984.

[111] I. Niven and H. S. Zuckerman. *An Introduction to the Theory of Numbers*. John Wiley and Sons, New York, 4th edition, 1980.

[112] A. V. Oppenheim, A. S. Willsky, and I. T. Young. *Signals and Systems*. Prentice Hall, Englewood Cliffs, NJ, 1983.

[113] A. Oram and S. Talbott. *Managing Projects with make*. O'Reilly & Associates, Sebastopol, CA, 1991.

[114] M. H. Overmars. *The Design of Dynamic Data Structures*, volume 156, *Lecture Notes in Computer Science*. Springer-Verlag, Berlin, 1983.

[115] C. H. Papadimitriou. *Computational Complexity*. Addison-Wesley, Reading, MA, 1994.

[116] C. H. Papadimitriou and K. Steiglitz. *Combinatorial Optimization: Algorithms and Complexity*. Prentice Hall, Englewood Cliffs, NJ, 1982.

[117] Y. Perl and E. M. Reingold. Understanding the complexity of interpolation search. *Information Processing Letters*, 6(6):219–222, 1977.

[118] G. E. Peterson, editor. *Tutorial: Object-Oriented Computing*, volume 1, *Concepts*. IEEE Computer Society Press, Washington, DC, 1987.

[119] W. W. Peterson. Addressing for random access storage. *IBM Journal of Research and Development*, 1(2):130–146, 1957.

[120] G. Pólya. *Induction and Analogy in Mathematics*. Princeton University Press, Princeton, NJ, 1954.

[121] T. W. Pratt. *Programming Languages: Design and Implementation*. Prentice-Hall, Englewood Cliffs, NJ, 2nd edition, 1984.

[122] F. P. Preparata and M. I. Shamos. *Computational Geometry: An Introduction*. Springer-Verlag, New York, 1985.

[123] W. H. Press, B. P. Flannery, S. A. Teulolsky, and W. T. Vetterling. *Numerical Recipes in C: The Art of Scientific Computing*. Cambridge University Press, Cambridge, 1988.

[124] R. C. Prim. Shortest connection networks and some generalizations. *Bell System Technical Journal*, 36(6):1389–1401, 1957.

[125] W. Pugh. Skip lists: A probabilistic alternative to balanced trees. *Communications of the ACM*, 33(6):668–676, 1990.

[126] E. M. Reingold, J. Nievergelt, and N. Deo. *Combinatorial Algorithms: Theory and Practice*. Prentice Hall, Englewood Cliffs, NJ, 1977.

[127] R. L. Rivest. On self-organizing sequential search heuristics. *Communications of the ACM*, 19(2):63–67, 1976.

[128] R. L. Rivest, A. Shamir, and L. M. Adleman. A method for obtaining digital signatures and public-key cryptosystems. *Communications of the ACM*, 21(2):120–126, 1978.

[129] F. S. Roberts. *Applied Combinatorics*. Prentice Hall, Englewood Cliffs, NJ, 1984.

[130] J. S. Rohl. *Recursion via Pascal*. Cambridge University Press, Cambridge, 1984.

[131] K. H. Rosen. *Discrete Mathematics and its Applications*. Random House, New York, 1988.

[132] D. J. Rosenkrantz, R. E. Stearns, and P. M. Lewis. An analysis of several heuristics for the traveling salesman problem. *SIAM Journal on Computing*, 6(3):563–581, 1976.

[133] H. Samet. *Applications of Spatial Data Structures: Computer Graphics, Image Processing, and GIS*. Addison-Wesley, Reading, MA, 1989.

[134] H. Samet. *The Design and Analysis of Spatial Data Structures*. Addison-Wesley, Reading, MA, 1989.

[135] R. Sedgewick. *Algorithms*. Addison-Wesley, Reading, MA, 2nd edition, 1988.

[136] A. Silberschatz and J. L. Peterson. *Operating System Concepts*. Addison-Wesley, Reading, MA, 1988.

[137] G. J. Simmons, editor. *Contemporary Cryptology: The Science of Information Integrity*. IEEE Press, New York, NY, 1992.

[138] D. D. Sleator and R. E. Tarjan. Amortized efficiency of list update and paging rules. *Communications of the ACM*, 28(2):202–208, 1985.

[139] D. D. Sleator and R. E. Tarjan. Self-adjusting binary search trees. *Journal of the ACM*, 32(3):652–686, 1985.

[140] D. D. Sleator and R. E. Tarjan. Self-adjusting heaps. *SIAM Journal on Computing*, 15(1):52–69, 1986.

[141] R. Sprugnoli. Perfect hashing functions: A single probe retrieving method for static sets. *Communications of the ACM*, 21(11):606–611, 1979.

[142] V. Strassen. Gaussian elimination is not optimal. *Numerische Mathematik*, 13:354–356, 1969.

[143] B. Stroustrup. *The C++ Programming Language*. Addison-Wesley, Reading, MA, 1986.

[144] B. Stroustrup. *The C++ Programming Language*. Addison-Wesley, Reading, MA, 2nd edition, 1991.

[145] E. H. Sussenguth Jr. Use of tree structures for processing files. *Communications of the ACM*, 6(5):272–279, 1963.

[146] R. E. Tarjan. Efficiency of a good but not linear set union algorithm. *Journal of the ACM*, 22(2):215–225, 1975.

[147] R. E. Tarjan. *Data Structures and Network Algorithms*. CBMS Regional Conference Series in Applied Mathematics 44. Society for Industrial and Applied Mathematics, Philadelphia, 1983.

[148] R. E. Tarjan. Amortized computational complexity. *SIAM Journal on Algebraic and Discrete Methods*, 6(2):306–318, 1985.

[149] R. E. Tarjan and J. van Leeuwen. Worst-case analysis of set union algorithms. *Journal of the ACM*, 31(2):245–281, 1984.

[150] R. D. Tennent. *Principles of Programming Languages*. Prentice Hall, Englewood Cliffs, NJ, 1981.

[151] A. Turing. On computable numbers with an application to the entscheidungsproblem. *Proceedings of the London Mathematical Society*, 42:230–265, 1936.

[152] J. van Leeuwen and T. van der Weide. Alternative path compression techniques. Technical Report RUU-CS-77-3, Dept. of Computer Science, University of Utrecht, Utrecht, The Netherlands, 1977.

[153] J. S. Vitter and W.-C. Chen. *Design and Analysis of Coalesced Hashing*. Oxford, New York, 1987.

[154] J. Vuillemin. A data structure for manipulating priority queues. *Communications of the ACM*, 21(4):309–315, 1978.

[155] J. Westbrook and R. E. Tarjan. Amortized analysis of algorithms for set union with backtracking. *SIAM Journal on Computing*, 18(1):1–11, 1989.

[156] J. W. Williams. Algorithm 232: Heapsort. *Communications of the ACM*, 7(6):347–348, 1964.

[157] A. C. Yao and F. F. Yao. The complexity of searching an ordered random table. In *Proceedings of the 17th Annual IEEE Symposium on Foundations of Computer Science*, pages 173–176, 1976.

INDEX